P9-DVZ-346

The Bibliographic Instruction-Course Handbook

a skills and concepts approach to the undergraduate, research methodology, credit course—for college and university personnel

by

HELEN RIPPIER WHEELER

THE SCARECROW PRESS, INC.
Metuchen, N.J., & London 1988

Acknowledgments

We are grateful to The H. W. Wilson Company (Bronx, New York) for permission to reproduce sample entries from their Indexes:

Applied Science & Technology Index, Copyright © 1972, 1973, 1979, 1980, 1985, 1986

Bibliographic Index, Copyright © 1985, 1986

Biography Index, Copyright © 1981, 1982, 1983, 1984

Book Review Digest, Copyright © 1985, 1986

Education Index, Copyright © 1984, 1986

Essay and General Literature Index, Copyright © 1970, 1971, 1972, 1973, 1974, 1975, 1976, 1977, 1978, 1979, 1980

Humanities Index, Copyright © 1976, 1977, 1978, 1985, 1986

Readers' Guide to Periodical Literature, Copyright © 1976, 1977, 1984, 1985

Social Sciences Index, Copyright © 1976, 1977, 1978, 1979, 1985, 1986

All excerpts reproduced by permission of the publisher.

The cartoon on page 116 reproduced by permission of Scott McCullar, Texas A&M University Library, College Station, Texas 77843, and by American Libraries.

British Library Cataloguing-in-Publication data available

Library of Congress Cataloging-in-Publication Data

Wheeler, Helen Rippier.
    The bibliographic instruction-course handbook : a skills and
concepts approach to the undergraduate, research methodology, credit
course : for college and university personnel / by Helen Rippier
Wheeler.
        p.   cm.
    Includes index.
    ISBN 0-8108-2131-1
    1. Bibliography--Methodology--Study and teaching (Higher)
2. Research--Methodology--Study and teaching (Higher) 3. College
students--Library orientation. 4. Libraries and students.
I. Title.
Z711.2..W48   1988
010'.7'11--dc19   88-14003

Copyright © 1988 by Helen Rippier Wheeler
Manufactured in the United States of America

Contents

Foreword

Something seems to have gone terribly wrong with education in this country. Time was when the United States could take pride in its literacy rate, its rising number of high school and college graduates, its lively regional cultures. I'm not talking about eminent scientists, Nobel Prize winners, scholars in academe. Just plain people who read because they enjoyed learning about new ideas, discoveries, controversies and who explored with zest what books and theaters and newspapers and films and pamphlets had to tell them. Today, Jonathan Kozol, author of Illiterate America, tells us 25 million Americans can't read well enough to understand the antidote instructions on a can of Drāno. And among the college and university students who can read with comprehension more and more do not learn how to find their way to an education through a glut of information.

This book contains a thoughtful, well-conceived proposal which administrators, faculty, and librarians on college and university campuses should read, digest, and implement. Helen Wheeler wants colleges to provide education to all their undergraduates, and she defines education as the ability to conceive an idea, to find relevant resources related to that idea, to organize the information available from those resources and to draw rational, supportable conclusions. She regards all college and university teachers and librarians as the people who can guide undergraduates to an education, and this book is a guide for the guides. Read it as a treasure-house of practical ways with which to implement an idealistic concept.

Helen Wheeler's own rich background in education ensures her competence and ability in this field. She has been teacher, administrator, innovator, supervisor, scholar, and inspirer. She has taught university courses in bibliographic instruction which led her to the much expanded concept described in this volume. She has had diverse experience in higher education in New York, Illinois, California, Hawaii, Louisiana, and Japan and incorporates what she has observed and learned in her current work. I have used and recommended some of her publications in my own teaching and look to her for guidance and help in the fields of women's studies, communications, and mass media. Most of all I respect her continuous dedication to the need for education and to the search for the ways in which we can teach and learn effectively.

Fay M. Blake, Ph.D., Senior Lecturer
Emerita
University of California--Berkeley

v

Introduction

"...only that education deserves emphatically to be termed cultivation of mind which teaches young people how to begin to think."

Mary Wollstonecraft (1759-1797).
On National Education.

Originally my working title and perspective were The Bibliographic Instruction Handbook. As work progressed, I realized that library bibliographic instruction is too limited, perhaps even restrictive, for what is needed. It became a point of departure for the concept and course presented here. The Bibliographic Instruction-Course Handbook: A Skills and Concepts Approach to the Undergraduate, Research Methodology, Credit Course--For College and University Personnel should be useful to librarians and to that related but separate group, library educators. It is, in fact, intended for all campus academic personnel-- administrators, teachers, and librarians, who are frequently said to share "equivalent faculty status." College and university administrators and teachers in the disciplines and interdisciplinary programs, librarians and library educators, and counselors too will benefit from it, for only through the concerned, united actions of all such persons can this type of course be introduced and sustained in the campus community.

Like motherhood and apple pie, libraries are respectable, accreditable fixtures of our American way of life, endorsed by all segments of campus society. Where their status may have been diminished, their original goodness continues to be acknowledged in some mutant form--the "LRC," or learning resources center, for example. Not much has really changed in and around libraryland. Automation, online catalogs, and operations research notwithstanding, undergraduates continue to bring with them challenges to all aspects of the college and university structure, including the library. College orientation has generally come to include library orientation, supplemented with library instruction referred to by librarians as bibliographic instruction, or BI in jargonese. On some university campuses, there are undergraduate BI courses, typically a "free elective" fulfilling no degree requirements and perhaps providing one credit or unit. Notably, eight of the fifty-seven American universities boasting graduate-level, professionally-accredited programs of library-information science education report involvement of some sort with an undergraduate, BI credit course in some way. [1]

During the eight years I taught an undergraduate BI credit course, I developed a commitment to its value and to what it could be. I attribute my enthusiasm and professional appreciation to an Ivy League liberal arts undergraduate preparation, an accredited M.S. degree in library science, a doctorate in education, experience as a professional librarian as well as faculty member of programs of graduate education, and to the development and publication of commercial media kits for teaching library use.

1

The relatively few undergraduate BI credit-courses are, for a variety of in- and out-of-the-library reasons, generally under-attended. Most library administrators are unwilling, and thus unable, to consider seriously the lower division course as an aspect of library BI. Many college and university administrations and the general "classroom faculty" are light years away from recognition of college students' varied needs with regard to using information, publications, and libraries in relationship to their deficiencies and strengths, and the possibilities for their futures. I soon came to realize that, while almost any undergraduate BI course is better than mere library orientation, what relates to the condition of collegiate education is not merely a pleasant, busy-work experience in use of one library, but a respectable, academic, credit course that provides instruction in use of subject-information, all media forms of publication, and libraries, on both local and principles bases, for research, albeit undergraduate "research."

This is not a reference book. The intent is serious reading with a view for change and consideration of the status of college-level BI by college and university campus academic personnel including professional librarians. Chapters One and Two are particularly addressed to non-librarians and practitioners. The Course as advocated in Chapter Three may well elicit a knee-jerk "pie in the sky" indictment from some professional librarians. "I never heard of a librarian who seriously rocked the boat...," as Florynce Kennedy put it. [2] Questionnaires elicited adjustment throughout the United States to the status quo, while private conversations revealed some willing librarians who are stymied by their administrations. In point of fact, such a course of action ultimately could be cost effective, with spinoff benefits effecting for the better such things as graduate level work, traditional librarianship (librarians), and education for professional librarianship, or whatever it is called on your campus by the time you read this. Ultimately, a full-blown, course program integrated in and recognized as part of the campus structure can enhance overall curricular standards, innovation and accreditations. Several major reports have emanated from government and private agencies in recent years which relate to collegiate education's deficiencies and provide recommendations. The course program advanced herein relates to some of their indictments and to their recommendations.

An explanation of related nomenclature employed and a survey of the literature are in order. As background, the results of two questionnaires may be of interest: one surveyed one hundred randomly-selected faculty at a university which has offered a BI course; the other polled university libraries and library schools throughout the United States. Librarians who have taught BI courses and personnel who aspire to do so may profit from Chapter Two, an attempt to address the often-raised questions and problems typically cited by them. Librarians and others who wish to introduce a course into the campus curricular and political structures have particular questions, and they may face blocks too easily accepted as insurmountable. Identification of some of the standard unspoken BI course-related problems encountered and sometimes not acknowledged by instructors (coordinators, managers, and librarians) may also be helpful. Three examples are excessive wear and tear on expensive library reference tools which presumably might not take place were there not "those students from that course using them," how to attract students to an elective version or to provide for the large number in a required version, and plagiarism. Yes, there are ways at least to approach all of these.

Information about initiating a collegiate level BI course--whether in the college or university setting--and doing the course itself, the hands-on mechanics are sought. I receive three levels of inquiry: 1) how to start up: public relations, budget, integration into the campus structure, staffing, etc.; 2) how to continue to manage once the program is underway; and 3) how to teach it. The literature of BI relates to all types of structures and consists of some symposia "ADDRESSES, ESSAYS AND LECTURES" compilations, association publications, and Educational Research Information Center (ERIC) reports, but relatively little focusing on the BI course. What are needed are the day-to-day, week-to-week term plans and proven materials, at the level of applicability to any college and including keyed problems, together with their application. Many BI instructors are recent library school graduates, professional librarians, and/or inexperienced teachers. In teaching BI concepts and skills, I have consciously evolved examples, demonstrations, and problem sets built around the study of varied, representative people, conditions, and subject fields as well as contemporary and ongoing undergraduate courses' concerns. I introduced the phrase "skills and concepts" (since utilized by several libraryland residents) some years ago in my media production. [3] Although this book is intended for use by educators, faculty including librarians, planners, etc., rather than as a text for students, it does focus on BI as a base for a formal, academic credit course, as opposed to library orientation, informal lectures or other library BI provisions. Section II provides such a course in a basic form designed as a lower division library instruction course "plus." The Course is provided with keyed problems and instructional materials usable with few or no local adaptations. [4] It is geared to collegiate level courses, subject matters, and interdisciplinary programs. Because it has potential relevance to all four college levels (freshman through senior), it has potential for departmental and senior seminars, and by further extension, Master's degree level work, as well as advanced placement high school and re-entry students in the campus milieu. The main emphasis is on inspiring a recognition of need for campuswide support for a course required of all new students. Chapter Four narrates one state's multicampus university system's varied and various provisions for BI courses.

Section III: Resources extends the possibility of implementation of such courses, particularly the lower division, basic course-program, by provision of additional materials, keyed problems, etc. Bibliographic support for the course concept is also part of Section III, which includes lists of clearinghouses, audiovisuals, and text-materials.

Part of the intent of this book has been a greatly needed exposure of the crisis condition of undergraduate education to concern by the campuswide community. Libraries, library schools, and librarians, for a variety of reasons, are often unable to provide this greatly needed course structure and perspective. They cannot and should not be expected to do so singlehandedly, although they should be involved, and if they wish to, participate in it. During 1986 I attempted to communicate concerning this book with higher education personnel, including professional librarians, by means of attendance at professional meetings and publication of notices in professional media. Only the National Women's Studies Association NWSA Perspectives and Librarians' Task Force Newsletter and the Chronicle of Higher Education, to my knowledge, published my invitation for input from those who are concerned in any way with for-credit, undergraduate, BI programs or courses. From the Library of Congress, however, came a wish for "...speedy progress with your book. Since bibliographic instruction is one of the most important topics to be taught to undergraduates, the need ... is critical."

Notes

1. The administrators of the fifty-nine graduate-level American Library Association-accredited, professional schools of library-information science education in the United States were contacted. Twenty-eight responses were received; two schools were reported no longer in existence. This survey is considered in Chapter Two.

2. American Libraries 17 (July-August 1986): 547. Addressing the American Library Association, Flo Kennedy declared that "Librarians are too comfortable and well-behaved." She advised them to "...get out of the rut you're in."

3. Learning the Library; A Skills & Concepts Series. Freeport, New York: Educational Activities, Inc., 1975.

4. The author and publisher hereby grant permission to reproduce keyed problems, instructional materials, and other student handout sheets that are printed on pages without running heads.

SECTION I

Chapter 1

Books, Band-Aids, and Bibliographic Instruction

> "The colleges, whilst they provide us with libraries,
> furnish no professor of books; and I think no chair is
> so much wanted."
> Ralph Waldo Emerson (1803-1882).
> Society and Solitude: Books.

It can be demonstrated that college instructors do not always assign students work which is covered by the textbook, assume students are able (which includes willing, which includes motivated) to utilize the college library for assignments, and do not perceive responsibility for initiating course-integrated library instruction. Likewise, the corollary exists that academic librarians do not always recognize and take responsibility to deal aggressively with this gap.

These deficiencies have been demonstrable for me for more than a decade, during which I have served as a volunteer, responding to requests for help from people in academe. A significant portion emanates from college students throughout the United States, who request course-related information, publications, and guidance. A typical request begins with a firm declaration that the question cannot be answered or the information found at their college library; or a plaintive plea may be conveyed with an assumption that this is the case. They resort to expending time, effort, and money writing around, as I refer to it, in vicious circles to organizations which they chance upon or which a teacher or librarian suggests. If they use computer-generated directories, they are likely to pick up organizations such as the Women's History Research Center, Inc. (a distributor of microfilms) based on keyword inputs. They aim to receive a document containing concise information, but short of that, a reference to it. Some students in women's studies, history, research, and any course in any discipline with a unit concerned with such things as gender, sex, pay equity, the United States Constitution, sociolinguistics, roles, careers, parenting, education, incest, etc. may attempt to cope. Others, required to do nothing, do nothing.

There may be a specific question which could be answered by use of standard "ready reference" tools and/or with the assistance of a professional librarian. I respond to all of these queries mainly by referring each writer to relevant basic tools which my experience leads me to believe are in the collections of libraries of regionally-accredited colleges and by providing pathfinder suggestions. These requests continue to come from college-level students enrolled in educational institutions of varied types and sizes throughout the United States, including the county in which the Center is located, and related to various subject matters. Moreover, there has been at least one such query from someone at each of the graduate level, professionally-accredited, influential schools of education for professional librarianship and information science, as well as from the member institutions of the Holmes Group of research institutions committed to teacher-education reforms. [1]

The intent of this chapter is communication with all campus academic personnel, particularly classroom teachers in the academic and other less-respectable disciplines, fields, and interdisciplinary programs, as well as administrators, counselors, and librarians. It will be beneficial reading for library education faculty and administrators, inasmuch as bibliographic instruction, to use their term, is not generally included in their curricula, while one of the criticisms of functioning professional librarians out in the field has long been their failure to stay in touch. The Education for Bibliographic Instruction Committee of the Association of College and Research Libraries' survey of library schools in June 1984 found less than half offer a course on this subject matter. [2] Dyer had reported much the same in 1978. [3] The library school dean who commented freely at a meeting that "any faculty member who wants to teach a BI undergraduate course should see a psychiatrist" did not respond, an indication of the interest of persons with influence.

The non-librarian should note that bibliographic instruction, or BI, is distinct from such terms as Social Sciences [Humanities, Women's Studies, Latin American, etc.] Bibliographer or bibliographic control. BI is generally considered in the domain of the reference librarian--a quick-fix, skill-producing, finite library activity. Advertisements for college and university BI-related positions typically also involve reference desk and collections responsibilities, library tours and lectures, and online searching capability.

Some foundation in the related terminology generally used in academe and herein is in order. The concept of a library as more than an archive, and thus a librarian's role more than an archivist, is not new. Nor is the idea of the professional librarian instructing the patron in library use as an aspect of library programming. Bibliographic instruction has entered the realm of professional jargon--"BI." Position descriptions now refer to BI responsibilities, and occasionally to a BI librarian. Several such positions evident during 1986 in recruitment of professional librarians appear to be representative. The Affirmative Action Register is a commercial subscription periodical consisting of advertisements for a variety of college, university, and government jobs. The Chronicle of Higher Education is a subscription newspaper with classified advertisements focusing on professional employment in higher education. American Libraries, the journal of the American Library Association, advertises professional positions in all types of libraries; College & Research Libraries News of the Association of College and Research Libraries (ACRL), a part of the American Library Association, focuses on these types of employers. There is also a gratis professional placement center at the semiannual conferences of the American Library Association. Most of the known positions having some BI-related responsibilities were on the library staffs of public universities, occasionally independent colleges. Frequently they were extended or reopened searches, symptomatic of at least one previous search process, which may have failed to generate a pool of applicants sufficient to document an affirmative process and/or an acceptable applicant who was considered qualified. Most postings stated commitment to both affirmative action and equal opportunity. Several practiced search techniques which have been shown to be potentially discriminatory, and thus poor management (e.g. stipulation of costly and time-consuming transcripts and letters of recommendation in the initial paper-screening stage), inadequate time between delivery of the periodical and closing date for applications, and failure to identify the closing date. None of these position descriptions involved responsibility for a BI course, although one referred to teaching duties in the institution's continuing education program; all included responsibilities and expertise other than BI.

Bibliographic instruction is the means by which college and university librarians assist library users in locating information in their collections. Many librarians consider BI important because they expect continued reductions in library resources will include staff, making greater demands on librarians for activities of greater value. [4] Another definition, derived from a 1980 glossary of BI terms, does not restrict it to any type of library and considers that BI encompasses all activities designed to teach the user about library resources and research techniques. [5] ACRL is the American Library Association division within which much of the professional concern for BI is concentrated. An ACRL 1979 publication perceived bibliographic and library instruction as synonymous, used to refer to activities other than the reference interview, designed to teach the library user to locate information efficiently; the essential goals are understanding of the library's system of organization and ability to use selected reference materials. In addition, instruction may cover the structure of the literature and research methodology appropriate for a discipline. [6] A move away from library bibliographic skills to understanding of strategies and methods of library research can be seen.

The variety of activities which librarians may undertake as part of a BI, library instruction, or user education program necessitates clarification of several related items. Course-related instruction usually involves a single lecture by the librarian and centering on specific needs of students at a particular point in a particular course. The ACRL refers to "any library or bibliographic instruction that provides students in a given course with library and literature skills necessary to meet the objectives of the course." It may provide them with an understanding of the subject's literature, its structure and effective methods of accessing it, and it takes place during class and with the cooperation of the instructor. Assignment-related instruction differs in that instruction is provided for a specific course-related assignment, but usually outside of regular class time and not necessarily with faculty cooperation. [7]

Course-integrated instruction is distinct from course-related instruction. Renford and Hendrickson believe that "the objectives of a non-library course include library instruction as an essential part of the course. Its importance is often demonstrated by its inclusion in the course of study for the class." [8] "Any library or bibliographic instruction which is part of a course's objectives" is considered by the ACRL to be course-integrated instruction. That "integration is usually achieved by discussion between faculty and librarians at the time the course is designed," [9] however, still appears to many librarians and educators to be the goal rather than actual practice!

Point-of-use instruction is likely to be the non-librarian's view of what constitutes both the status quo and expectation of bibliographic or library instruction and of librarians. Renford and Hendrickson refer to "a detailed explanation of how to use a specific research tool," which might consist of print or non-print information located near the tool being explained. A slide-tape program of Psychological Abstracts, or a printed handout on The American Statistics Index are illustrations. [10] In addition to signs, personal directions, tape-slide explanations, a class lecture, etc., BI particularly in undergraduate libraries may take the form of term paper consultation, orientation tours, self-paced cassette tours with related exercises, handouts, and pathfinders. A pathfinder consists of printed material that arranges in search strategy order the basic tools for doing research on a particular subject. A pathfinder is not synonymous with bibliographic guide. Pathfinders, as copyrighted by Addison-Wesley, referred to a commercially-produced series of topical guides. In practice, one-page, formula pathfinders are sometimes available in quantity in the library and reflecting the topics currently mentioned by undergraduate students at the reference desk and course needs. [11]

And finally, approaching the concerns of this book, there is the formal bibliographic, library, or user education instruction course. Renford and Hendrickson mention "formal courses on library resources, research methodology and information retrieval ... recognized as a course by the college or university ... offered for one, two or three credits." [12] The ACRL refers to a formal course "...approved through the institution's regular curriculum review procedures ... non-credit or for credit." [13] Three important considerations have been introduced: the research perspective, regularization within the institution's course offerings, and credit including the amount of credit associated with successful completion of such a course.

A term related because it is sometimes equated with library instruction is library orientation. This writer agrees with Renford and Hendrickson that library orientation consists of "activities that introduce patrons to the facilities, services, and policies of the library. Guided and self-guided tours are common examples of orientation activities." [14] If one regards a college or university library as a repository, or assumes that today's college students arrive having already learned how to use such a collection, or believes that it is possible to acquire library research skills, methods, and attitudes independently and spontaneously, then orientation may suffice, and course-work may be superfluous. Orientation to anything carries a built-in assumption of prior experience with and even mastery of other things of the same ilk. Student guides may perk up freshman orientation by pointing out the library's terminals, lounge with vending machines, course reserves, and exams files. When college freshmen tour the campus, there may be a blasé collective assumption that everyone has used a library, that they are similar, and one need learn only where the library, catalog, and Readers' Guide are located. Orientation generally assumes knowledge of how to use what basically is merely a new example: "Here's the cafeteria" implies that Student knows how to eat, perhaps even how to budget a balanced meal from today's menu.

• • •

"We must stop applying Band-Aids to festering sores... [Students] have bits of information, but they haven't learned the business of logical inqiry."
Shirley Chisholm ... At the American Dreams: The National Debate About the Future of Education symposium, Indiana University of Pennsylvania, 1986. [15]

Whether college presidents believe libraries are central to their institutions and act on that belief and whether professional standards of library programing are implemented can be synergistic. Standards developed by the ACRL for college libraries were revised in 1986. (This set of standards is not designed for use in two-year colleges, large universities, or independent professional schools.) "There is a glaring discrepancy between theory and practice" declared one college president at the meeting to discuss approval of the new college library standards. Another objection voiced was the perception of emphasis on quantitative measures, a criticism which had been heard less as standards became more qualitative and as some librarians consider, less functional. "If the library does not relate to the educational program of an institution and its collections are not used, its size is meaningless" is a truism cited by the executive director of the Middle States Commission on Higher Education accrediting body at the meeting. Institutional administrators have tended to associate the library's collection size with volume-count figures, but staff and services are concomitants requiring guaranteed minimum support. The same administrator referred to the new standards as "so passive that there is little emphasis on the library participating in the teaching and learning on campus." [16]

The previous (1975) Standards consisted of eight sections, which have been retained: objectives, collections, organization of materials, staff, services, facilities, administration, and budget. Standard Number Five: Service, subsection 1, states, "The Library shall provide information and instruction to the user through a variety of techniques to meet differing needs. These shall include, but not be limited to, a variety of professional reference services, and bibliographic instruction programs designed to teach users how to take full advantage of the resources available to them." The discussion of this states that "A fundamental responsibility of a college library is to provide instruction in the most effective and efficient use of its materials. Bibliographic instruction and orientation may be given at many levels of sophistication and may use a variety of methods and materials, including course-related instruction, separate courses (with or without credit), and group or individualized instruction." [17] The ACRL Bibliographic Instruction Task Force developed a one-page Guidelines for Bibliographic Instruction in Academic Libraries, which has been available since 1977. This document refers to "various methods of instruction for all segments of the academic community who have need to use library resources and services," but does not include a course among them. [18]

The relatively recent emergence of emphasis on bibliographic library instruction and the numerous and varied ways it is perceived have been touched upon. Even when focusing on academic (not public or special) libraries or on higher education (not elementary or secondary schools), the body of related literature is considerable, if uneven. The literature of bibliographic instruction consists largely of accounts of individual persons' and institutions' library experiences; group and association publications including articles and issues, newsletters and accounts of meetings; and some sponsored and trade publications. A computer-assisted search of such data bases as Dissertation Abstracts Online (1961-), ERIC (1966-), LISA (Library and Information Science Abstracts (1969-), and Social SciSearch (1972-), or a hand search of such printed tools as Comprehensive Dissertation Index (1861-), Current Index to Journals in Education (1969-), Library Literature (1921-), Resources in Education (1966-), and Social Sciences Citation Index (1972-) is a useful starting point in a literature search. Abstracts are available for all except Library Literature, Social Sciences

Citation Index, and Social SciSearch. In addition to trade publishers, sources include clearinghouses, professional associations, and organizations. One's college or university must be a member of a clearinghouse such as LOEX (Library Orientation-Instruction Exchange). [19] Membership in the California Clearinghouse on Library Instruction, for example, can be personal or institutional, as part of California Library Association membership, or independently. Clearinghouse information is included in Section III: Resources, which also includes a BI course-related bibliography.

At least sixty publications have included the keyword "course[s]" in their titles or have related in some specific way to provision of this type of structured learning since 1965. Approximately half have appeared since 1980. Of this core, few conceive of an undergraduate, credit course which is research methodology-related and which could be considered academic.

Many BI courses provide opportunity for students to apply their acquired library skills to a personal topic--this is the current thinking, the state of the art. But it lends itself too easily to some librarians' justification of provision for BI only or mainly in dabs here and there, for classes and subjects where the instructor requests it--the one- or two-hour "stand." The biology student who hears about and perhaps sees a volume of XYZ Reference Book brought by the librarian to the classroom but who has no idea of how to discover and to manipulate efficiently such a tool, let alone relate it to others, is frustrated, forced further into the corner of defensive, derisive scorn or apathy for systematic use of information, publications, and libraries.

Research involves systematic scholarly or scientific investigation or inquiry. To seek out and to search again are the dictionary elements applicable to undergraduate students and unpopular with them because they signify not merely work, but endeavors in which students have not been encouraged: reading, abstract thinking, positive criticism, comparison, systematic examination, processing, inquiry. Beaubien's 1982 overview of pros and cons of library courses advocates the supremacy of the BI course of whatever length over any other mode of instruction. [20] Breivik's Planning the Library...., also published in 1982, discusses difficulties associated with formal courses as opposed to other types of BI, and contends that course integration, team teaching, and required instruction offer solutions. [21] A recent publication is Adams and Morris' 1985 Teaching Library Skills for Academic Credit. Although their title includes reference to academic credit, some of their case studies apparently do not refer to credit-generating activities, and some are not, strictly speaking, courses. They refer to BI as "the teaching of students to use a library effectively." [22] Others perceive it as much more--to paraphrase, putting it all together for creditable, academic research-strategy coursework.

• • •

"Books and ideas are the most effective weapons against intolerance and ignorance."
> Lyndon Baines Johnson (1908-1973). Comment as he signed into law a Bill providing increased federal aid for library service, February 11, 1964.

Authorities cite many values of reading. Personal satisfaction, self-improvement, and vicarious experience are often mentioned. Some of these occasionally also apply to other types of media, but print media and reading are particularly relevant to the needs of college students. Reading requires personal endeavor and participation. Reading is an individual or a group undertaking. It often explains the why and value of things. It does not deal merely in the two-dimensional world of pictures and sounds, although it does encourage reflection, introspection, and development of perception. Reading paces itself and allows for the individual's own rate of growth, while providing experiences and understandings at more than one level at a time. Reading is, of course, a personal and internalized thing. Each person interprets words and ideas on the bases of past experiences, making each interpretation unique and only in part influenced by outside stimuli. Therefore, the reading experience belongs to the individual in a more total way than does any other learning experience medium.

Compared to audiovisual media, books are extremely portable and inexpensive to acquire and maintain. Individual reading can provide for and stimulate individual interests to almost any desired depth and breadth. Reading allows for individual differences in ability and progress. Reading permits interruption, resumption, and backtracking to a degree impossible with motion pictures, for example. Machines and mediated instructional materials do not require the viewer-listener to use her/his imagination--that power with which human beings alone can create and think. And books provide the only complete record of mankind's culture and achievements.

The enormous accessibility of books as compared with other media (and their supporting machinery) throughout a college career as well as their accommodation to the student's schedule, could serve as sufficient reason for placing the highest value on broad reading and the provision of a college library instruction program. Films and other audiovisual nonprint learning resources are often misunderstood by teachers and administrators to cost less than library books and periodicals on a per student basis. A book collection provides infinite selectivity, and is not limited to what is available in canned and prepackaged forms. Though nonprint media and programed instruction can facilitate students to gain knowledge and can make learning easier for some students who are not required or not yet able to grapple with abstract ideas, and although they allegedly require less professional staffing, there are limitations to their use. The materials must--or should--be prepared for use in this situation. Only materials which are available for feeding the machine or which exist in audiovisual form can be used. Contrasted to this, the number of book titles available potentially to the reader-student is limitless. In the modern library it is possible to find books and periodicals on any subject of interest, or in any direction the teacher encourages. The college teacher is able to count on breadth and depth in the scope of what otherwise might be limited subject matter and resources for her/his students.

Nonprint media and audiovisual aids contribute to the learning process and reinforcement of concepts. But to develop a lifetime of learning, perception, and powers of evaluation, only reading and mastery of research strategy skills suffice.

Reform on Campus, the 1972 report of the Carnegie Commission on Higher Education, stressed the objective of imparting skills for the continuing self-education of the student, bringing the library into the role of a more active participant in the instructional process, particularly in indepth study and through

13

the library. [23] The 1980's decade has produced several documents criticizing education in the United States and making recommendations related to post-high school education in particular. Involvement In Learning; Realizing the Potential of American Higher Education, the final report of the Study Group on the Conditions of Excellence in American Higher Education, was sponsored by the National Institute of Education and published in 1984. Whereas recent reports had focused on elementary and secondary schools, its concern was post-secondary, including community college, education. Several warning signals were cited. Only half of the students entering college with the intention of receiving a bachelor's degree eventually did so. Mean scores had declined on most of the tests taken by college graduates. Both colleges and students had become too vocational in their orientation, while the idea of "breadth" in undergraduate education had been lost. College curricula had become fragmented, and the idea of interaction of knowledge diminished. Colleges had become more bureaucratic and impersonal, with fewer opportunities for students to become intensely involved with academic life. Student learning had suffered as a result of deterioration of physical plants and equipment. And few colleges examined the learning and growth of the graduating students.

The Study Group declared that reform in the freshman year was needed. Their recommendations included the "front loading" strategy, in which college administrators reallocate faculty and other resources towards increased service to lower division students. Faculty making greater use of active modes of teaching and requiring students to take greater responsibility for their learning were recommended. Academic administrators were urged to consolidate as many part-time teaching lines into full-time positions as possible. Faculty members and the chief academic officer of each institution should agree upon and disseminate a statement of the knowledge, capacities and skills their students must develop in order to graduate. All bachelor's degree recipients should have at least two full years of liberal education. Liberal education requirements should be expanded and reinvigorated to insure that 1) curricular content is directly addressed in regard to subject matter, as well as development of capacities of analysis, problem solving, communication and synthesis, and 2) students and faculty integrate knowledge from various disciplines. Institutions should offer remedial courses and programs when necessary but should set standards and employ instructional techniques in those programs to enable students to perform well subsequently in college-level courses. Students were advised to take at least one independent study course and one internship during college, and to make certain these experiences involved research and the opportunity to apply theory to problems in the world beyond the campus. [24]

The same year, 1984, William J. Bennett (later, Secretary of Education) called for a restoration of coherence and vitality to undergraduate programs in the humanities in his To Reclaim a Legacy report. [25]

Also issued in 1984 was the Association of American College's report based on its Project on Redefining Meaning and Purpose of Baccalaureate Degrees. The committee of eighteen prominent educators responsible for the conclusions expressed in Integrity in the College Curriculum contended that universities have relaxed their course requirements for undergraduate degrees so much that "almost anything goes. We have reached a point at which we are more confident about the length of a college education than its content and purpose" with regard to what passes for a college curriculum. Much of the blame for what was described as the "decline and devaluation" of undergraduate education was placed on faculty members. In calling for a return to coherence in the curriculum, the Committee did not advocate solving the curricular problems of higher education by simply strengthening distribution requirements or adding multidisciplinary general education courses. Minimum requirements for the baccalaureate degree program should provide for inquiry, literacy, understanding of numerical data, historical consciousness, science, values, art, intellectual and multicultural experiences, and study in depth. [26]

The first requirement--inquiry, abstract logical thinking, critical analysis--surely relates to all undergraduate students and suggests a required, creditable and credit-generating research methodology core course early in the college program. As the writers of Integrity in the College Curriculum expressed it,

> ...thinking can be lazy. It can be sloppy. It can be reactive rather than active. It can be inert. It can be fooled, misled, bullied. In colleges and universities it is all of these things.... Students possess great untrained and untapped capacities for logical thinking, critical analysis, and inquiry, but these are capacities that are not spontaneous; they grow out of wise instruction, experience, encouragement, correction, and constant use. [27]

Study in depth relates particularly to ability and willingness to utilize information, publications, and libraries on both local and principles bases for research. This report referred to "the year-long essay, the senior thesis, the artistic discipline undertaken after a sound grasp of the fundamentals of the discipline or art has been established, [and] ... the thrill of moving forward in a formal body of knowledge [such as the student's major] and gaining some effective control...." [28]

The American Council on Education's 1985-1986 trends-survey reported that calls for undergraduate education reform have influenced faculty members at most colleges at least to discuss them, and that changes in academic programs have begun at more than a third. The problem seems to be agreement on the manner of assessment of student learning. There is divergence between what colleges believe are the appropriate ways to assess students and what they actually do about it. Ten percent of the chief academic officers surveyed agreed that a potential obstacle to student assessment was that students would be unhappy about it; 41 percent considered this a potential obstacle! [29]

In mid-1986 the nongovernmental Education Commission of the States called on state government officials to become more involved in college reform. The Commission report, Transforming the State Role in Undergraduate Education, drew on the Involvement in Learning, To Reclaim a Legacy, Integrity in the College Curriculum, and Higher Education and the American Resurgence studies. Several of its twenty-two recommendations to state leaders relate to the concerns of this book and this writer, including working with high schools to raise the quality of entering freshmen and encouraging college students to avoid specialization too early.

Three of the challenges deriving "...from an overall mismatch between the educational needs of the nation and current practice in undergraduate education" are particularly apt here: the challenges to prepare students for the wide range of opportunities offered by a changing work force and society, to improve overall rates of college participation and completion, and to meet the educational needs of an increasingly diverse student population. Recommendations to state leaders include ascertaining what former students think about their undergraduate experiences; matching requirements for remediation with support for it; establishing "early assessment" programs; strengthening programs for assessing the educational needs of new and returning students; delegating responsibility to institutional leaders, enabling them to improve undergraduate education, and encouraging creativity and risk-taking; and providing incentives to institutions to encourage faculty to improve undergraduate education. [30]

These reports convey other observations and recommendations having implications for bibliographic instruction coursework and for a fully developed, required, research strategy course-program in particular. One can readily infer significant need for a required, undergraduate course which integrates information, media, and libraries with research methodology and which is much more than how-to-use-the-library. Yet none of these documents directs specific recommendations to this area of academic instruction. In their failure to focus upon the role and status of the college library program, as one element in this, the eminent representatives of American academe and government exert great influence.

The National Institute of Education's Involvement in Learning study declared reform in the freshman year is needed, and that 47 percent of American colleges are giving special attention to the freshman year. In 1982 the national Conference on the Freshman Year Experience began a series, said to attract thousands of educators annually, dedicated to helping ease the transition for students from high school to college and enhancing the quality of their first year of college. The originator and one of the host institutions--the University of South Carolina--is a Holmes Group member and boasts a professionally accredited school of education for library-information science. Conference topics are solicited in such categories as teaching and understanding freshmen, freshman seminar courses, easing the student's transition, research, and cross cultural programs.

Finally, in this round-up at least, is the Carnegie Foundation's 1986 report-- College: The Undergraduate Experience in America, based on studies of colleges and universities and surveys of faculty, college students, and college-bound high school students. Colleges are found to be torn by divisions and confused over roles that prevent them from providing coherent educational experiences for their students. The heart of higher learning, the undergraduate college, is described as a troubled institution which is, however, ready for renewal. [31]

Most of the major recommendations for improvement of the undergraduate experience relate in some way to the advocacy of The Bibliographic Instruction-Course Handbook; several relate directly to it. These recommendations are concerned with:

1. Transition from school to college.
2. Goals.
3. Orientation.
4. Proficiency in the written and spoken word.
5. General education.
6. The enriched major.
7. Faculty priorities.

8. Creativity in the classroom.
9. Resources for learning.
10. The quality of campus life.

An integrated vertical core approach to general education extending from fresh-man to senior year is recommended around a framework of language, art, society, nature, ecology, work, and identity. General education has usually consisted of required courses in such learning skills as English and mathematics, using some library resources, and sampling the major systems of human thought--the social sciences and humanities. Many of the undergraduate students in my classes since 1978 have been unable to distinguish between these two areas, rarely among the disciplines comprising them. It is not unusual for upper division BI course students to report a new, expanded perception of their major field of interest. At another extreme is the need to cope with basics of spelling, grammar, and punctuation. In addition to courses, a thesis that relates some aspect of the student's major to historical, social, or ethical concerns is recommended by the writers of College: The Undergraduate Experience in America. Participation in a senior seminar in which the student presents the report orally to colleagues and also critiques the papers of fellow students is recommended. The value of teaching teachers, as opposed to published researchers, is stressed, and the Scholar-Teacher is proposed--people in the forefront of their profession who know the literature of their fields and skillfully communicate this information to their students. A balance between full and part-time faculty is recommended, with a maximum of 20 percent part-time undergraduate faculty. Top priority is to be given to classes for lower division students, i.e. freshmen and sophomores. The report refers to investigations that have disclosed that one out of every four undergraduates spends no time in the library during a typical week, and that 65 percent use the library four hours or less each week. (Had the report-makers consulted librarians or engaged in action research, they might have concluded that the 65 percent are present in the library four hours or less each week.) The gap between the classroom and the library, reported on almost a half cen-tury ago, still exists today. Students are cranking out photocopies of library reference books, stealing pages or volumes of reference books, and "reading" (skimming) textbooks with felt-tip colored markers. "All undergraduates should be introduced carefully to the full range of resources for learning on a campus. They should be given bibliographic instruction and be encouraged to spend at least as much time in the library--using its wide range of resources--as ... in classes." This in essence legitimizes the library BI programing activities for which many academic librarians are endeavoring to obtain support from college administrators, including administrative librarians, as well as cooperation from their classroom teacher-colleagues.

Teachers generally not considering librarians as teachers (and indeed, some librarians are not) and too many classroom teachers equating "library use" with sending undergraduate students to the library are old problems which have not even been acknowledged, and thus not addressed, in any of these reports. The cycle needs to be broken.

• • •

"I don't believe that the kind of student I respect needs any formal training in library use; the interest should come from a need to use the library to find out stuff."

"Using the library is equivalent to using a sliderule, and we don't give credit for instruction in its use."

Faculty members of two universities, 1985, 1986.

In spring and summer 1986 one hundred randomly-selected, university faculty who teach undergraduate students were contacted to ascertain their perceptions of the undergraduate BI course concept and their university's elective BI credit course in prticular. They spanned the traditional disciplines as well as innovative programs and fields, and consisted largely of males, due to my having queried "regular faculty," a euphemism signifying Academic Senate Faculty members, who are generally tenured or tenure track faculty other than librarians. Respondents were anonymous; the very brief questionnaire was not coded. Twenty-five responses were received.

With regard to the concept of an undergraduate BI course, most agreed strongly that library instruction and research methodology are interrelated, and that all new undergraduate students including transfers should be required to take such a course during their first term on campus or as soon thereafter as they can schedule it. However, they were unwilling to go so far as to agree with the possibility that "In today's library-information science environment, 'library skills' is an outdated term which should be replaced by a research methodology concept." This flip-flop of support for the au courant in tandem with realism which touches their domain was characteristic throughout their responses.

These faculty agreed that all sections of such a course-program must be coordinated so that the same things are emphasized for the same credit and have the same course grade components, regardless of who the instructor is. They considered that regular classroom instructional faculty affiliated with academic disciplines (departments, divisions, schools) as well as professional librarians should be able to teach a BI course which will provide students with academic credit. They were unaware that at their university it is necessary to offer (administrate) any credit course through a department if it is to provide the student with credit, and that their library is not considered a department.

With regard to their own undergraduate, elective, credit, BI course-program, most faculty respondents agreed that most undergraduates have not acquired library research skills by the time they arrive at the campus. They disagreed with the suggestion that "most lower division students are not required to use university libraries in connection with their coursework," with which even the students agree and which they frequently volunteer! However, they also disagreed with the suggestion that "library needs of most undergraduates are met by the Undergraduate Library." And they disagreed with the proposition that professional librarians at most American universities have faculty status.

A list of categories of students was presented, from which they were asked to indicate those for which it "is a good course":

Athletes
Advanced placement high school students

Disabled students
Ethnic minority students
Freshmen
Freshmen and other new students
Honors students
Re-entry women students
Re-entry men students
Students from abroad
Students in majors requiring a senior thesis
Students on probation

The majority indicated "all" groups.

Despite agreement with the principle that such a course must be coordinated so that the same things are emphasized in all sections and course grade components are uniform, faculty respondents were ambivalent regarding requiring a final examination on which all sections and instructors' students must achieve at the same level. There was unanimous agreement that their university's BI course is distinct from the typical collegiate library use course. These faculty as a group evidenced chauvinism and support for the worthy cause principle. But in terms of actual application and thus possibly their active support, their responses were uninformed and contradictory, although many demonstrated serious application of time and attention to the questionnaire. The one exception is notable here. His attitude is characterized by his declaration across the bottom of the form: "I don't believe that the kind of student I respect needs any formal training in library use; the interest should come from a need to use the library to find out stuff." Across the posit that in today's library-information science environment, "library skills" might be an outdated term which should be replaced by a research methodology concept, and that library instruction and research methodology are interrelated, he scrawled, "Who cares??!!" This lack of facts-of-life information and concern about the educational status quo, in association with a faculty member's relative security and influence (power) must also be addressed.

· · ·

Bibliographic instruction sounds bookish, and many college and university personnel associate it with books and bibliographers. Similarly, library instruction may connect with libraries and librarians. Some academic community members assume that BI is, or should be, a major concern within the field (rarely do they say "discipline") of education for professional librarianship, referring to the professionally-accredited, graduate level degree(s) programs which are part of approximately fifty-seven public and independent institutions of higher education in the United States. Few associate it with the field of professional education. However, the subject of bibliographic instruction for librarians does not receive significant consideration in the curricula leading to the basic Master's degree in library-information science. A survey of administrators of accredited library schools on the status of bibliographic instruction within their curricula reported in 1978 found that "this subject is frequently integrated within appropriate courses, e.g. school media, or presented in workshops and conferences; formal courses devoted entirely to library instruction are virtually nonexistent." [32] Examination of current reading lists and outlines of academic librarianship courses, offered by most but not all library schools, reveals little consideration for BI as an area and less for the BI course concept. Library school catalog annotations and announcements describing college and university librarianship courses confirm this. Furthermore, librarianship courses are not always part of the library-information science core, may be elective, and are often taught by off-campus adjuncts.

The Education for Bibliographic Instruction Committee of the Association of College & Research Libraries (ACRL) has been involved in a project to continue the effort to identify library schools incorporating the teaching of BI in the library-information science education curriculum. They report a great deal of interest and growing support, but it appears from survey responses that approximately one sixth (nine) of United States library schools report in their curricula a course on the subject of BI for librarians employed in all types of libraries. [33] Brundin in his 1985 paper reports that education for BI in libraries has been given little attention in library schools' curricula, and refers to recent studies having shown that many North American library schools are reluctant to incorporate education for BI librarians into them. His summary of major reasons for BI having been neglected in library school curricula includes library educators' reluctance to become involved with the field of professional education and their advocacy of the reference librarian's conventional noneducational role; their perception of library education's responsibilities as theory and research; their contention that an insignificant number of library science students are interested; library science students' lack of "education" background; and basic reference courses leaving insufficient time for BI coursework. [34]

The possibility that a library school could or should sponsor, in addition to, but administrated separately from its graduate professional degree program, a campuswide, multisection undergraduate BI course may be viewed form two perspectives. What, if any, educational responsibility for provision of such a learning experience locally does a library school have? What might be in it for the library school? Somewhere between these two considerations is the related fact of life that, on many campuses, because the library is not perceived as an academic department, no credit can accompany a course it sponsors. Although library schools and libraries are usually two separate entities, library schools exist on such campuses, and "logic" has it that courses taught by library librarians (as opposed to library school faculty members, some of whom have library degrees and employment experience as professional librarians) can sometimes generate credit if administered through the library school. In the University of California system, for example, on three campuses that have no library schools (Davis, Irvine, and San Diego), undergraduate credit BI courses are taught by library librarians and administered through English, Interdisciplinary, and Contemporary Issues departments. The undergraduate credit BI courses on the Berkeley and Los Angeles campuses are administered through their graduate professional schools of library-information science. Reliance on teaching assistants and library school students becomes a consideration. Ultimately the need to rely on part-time, non-library librarians to cover all sections of an undergraduate course-program can become exploitative. It would seem that a graduate library-information science, professional degrees program has at least an indirect role in the possibility for and success of an undergraduate BI course in a university campus community today. Some contend it has a direct leadership role, even responsibility, at campus and national levels for introduction of the concept of a quality academic, credit course which includes provision of bibliographic instruction. They point to the related facts that libraries of the same institutions of higher education tend to employ their alumni and to be influenced by relationships with them, a library school library is normally part of the libraries system, many of these libraries systems are members of the influential Association of Research Libraries, and approximately one third of the library schools offer one or more doctoral programs and post-Master's certificates in addition to Master's degrees, all of which generate a population seeking both income and experience.

But the undergraduate BI courses with which some library schools have associated themselves are not particularly academic. Indeed, there has been resistance to acknowledging responsibility or need for a course providing undergraduate students with concepts and mastery of research skills related to information, media and libraries on both local and principles bases. Where library school involvement with an undergraduate course exists, it tends to relate to internship, "teaching associate," and practice-teaching spinoff benefits for library science graduate students ipso facto the library school.

• • •

The chief administrative officers of the library school and of the library systems of institutions of higher education located in the United States which have accredited library schools were surveyed in summer 1986. For uniformity, the term "library school" is used to refer to the Master's degree and higher-level programs of education for professional librarianship-information science. (Few undergraduate library science majors survive today.) Twenty four of the library schools contacted also have one or more doctoral programs. "Dean" is used here to refer to the chief administrative officer of such a program, although they are variously titled dean, director, chairman, chair, etc. The chief administrative officer of the library or library system is referred to here as "library director."

In a very brief questionnaire, library school deans and library directors were asked whether an undergraduate, for-credit, BI course is offered on their campus, and when this was the case, information was requested about its administration and whether it satisfies any undergraduate requirements. Because many of the inquiries I have received about BI coursework have related to their establishment, maintenance, staffing, intracampus relationships, publicity, etc., concern for problems as well as activist solutions was included in the questionnaire. Their responses provide a picture of the status of for-credit undergraduate BI courses at influential institutions of higher education throughout the United States. These institutions influence the education of undergraduate students as well as preparation of professional librarians. Students observe role models in classrooms, libraries, and administrative offices. The university itself employs all types of workers in substantial numbers--clerical, instructional, technical, and professional, and including the gender-role specific jobs associated with libraries and administration. Young professionals acquire their basic standards, perspectives, ethics, and initial placements in their preparation phase. Academe is the place of numerous continuing education experiences and contacts. National and regional as well as professional associations are involved in this leadership by means of such things as their accreditation of programs, publishing activities and recruitment. Future professionals including librarians, teachers and managers are indoctrinated during their college and university years. Certification and licensing procedures are closely allied to state colleges and universities.

Of the 59 institutions queried, 37 library directors and 28 library school deans responded or arranged for a response. (Two library schools were closed.) 18 directors reported a course on their campus involving the library in some way;

11 deans reported an undergraduate BI for-credit course presently associated with the library school in some way. Both the library director and library school dean of 21 universities responded. Seven pairs reporting a course also provided narrative comments, which are enlightening in tandem. (Terminology has been standardized somewhat.)

<u>Library Director #1</u>: "Because of staff reduction the course will be dropped next year. It is administrated through and by the library school but taught by library staff."

<u>Library School Dean #1</u>: "Course is a library school course but it is taught by staff of the University Library. The faculty has felt some concern about this since the course is part of the library science curriculum yet we do not have control over the content or the selection of the instructors."

<u>Library Director #2</u>: "It is listed as a library school class and an Arts & Sciences class, but administered by the Library. [Problems:] Very time-consuming to teach such a small percentage of students. Teacher (librarians) overload. Lack of relevance to students' real academic life outside. Often taken as an easy A or 'need 1 credit to graduate.' Other library missions suffer because of demands of this course on librarians' time. Very time consuming to administer as well. The advantage of teaching this credit course is the personal satisfaction reported by the teachers--a reward they seldom enjoy. Lectures/presentations at the request of teaching faculty (someone else's class) seldom offer that opportunity ... knowing you've gotten through to a student!"

<u>Library School Dean #2</u>: "The course serves as a free elective for just about any undergraduate degree ... is taught as a 1 credit hour elective course by the Reference staff of the University Library, and they have responsibility for developing the curriculum. However, since the Library is not an academic unit that can offer courses for credit, students can sign up either under the College of Arts & Sciences or the library school. Neither group has any real influence on the program, and at this point what we want and get are the credit hours. As such, there are no real problems, and certainly none that affect the library education program. The Library perceives this as a valuable service, and protects its control over the course. What problem there is results from how few undergraduate students we reach. I would estimate this as about one percent and it is the library's argument that this is all they can teach given their staffing levels. Were the library school to achieve control over this course, I would expand its impact by offering more sections and larger class sections, and at least introducing the question of whether the course should be required in some undergraduate disciplines. I would use regular librarians as well as our own doctoral students as instructors, and I would pay them extra compensation as overload salaries to help spur on their enthusiasm. The present approach really causes no problems for this school and probably none for the librarians except that they complain that they are already overburdened and receive no recognition for this. At the same time, if bibliographic instruction is useful (and I would think that a minimum orientation should be required for freshmen or sophomores), then our present approach really doesn't reach very many of these students. At the present or even the proposed level of content, the course has no impact on graduate library school curriculum, particularly as long as we don't use regular faculty to teach this material. I know of no library school with enough faculty to be able to afford to do this."

Library Director #3: "Convincing university administration of the merit of such a course [is a problem]. If one were approved, faculty librarians would have to be 'drafted' to prepare and teach the various units. Our formal program of library instruction is only one year old and we are not yet ready to initiate a course."

Library School Dean #3: "This program is not offered. Our program addresses particular needs for particular classes. Nothing is offered on a 'for credit' basis."

Library Director #4: "It qualifies for 'General Distribution Course.' [Problems:] Unable to teach as many sections as we would like (currently teach five per semester). It is fairly labor intensive as we teach it--individual worksheets for each student each week, wear and tear on some reference books as well as dominating them, making 'noncourse' students wait to use them. Library instruction is an important part of the library program, but as more is added to job assignments, value of time used for course is questioned, especially by nonteaching library staff."

Library School Dean #4: "No problems [for library school]. Normally all sections are taken; it would be advisable to open more sections in the future."

Library Director #5: "As an undergraduate librarian, I worked with a library school faculty member to develop the course. We had complete support from the library school. The library has provided instructors on an extra-service basis from the reference staff. Teaching the course is very time consuming. Librarians have a real advantage by working at the library and teaching the course simultaneously because they know where sources are, new library developments and have 'connections' in general. We have sought to personalize assignments which is proving too time-consuming as the course grows. Also, the teacher has had to help with publicizing the course. I believe the course enhances rather than impinges on the library program."

Library School Dean #5: "Taught mostly by library faculty. Course per se is perceived as excellent by students, but it has taken over a year to get sufficient visibility for the course through various marketing strategies. This is because the library school here is a small independent unit and therefore relatively invisible in a campus of 30,000+. Problems involved: finding the right library faculty members to teach undergraduates--many can do a one hour BI presentation in, say, an English class but cannot sustain their efforts for thirty contact hours, plus grading, etc. As a group, the public service library faculty see this course as an opportunity for greater campus visibility, a greater role in the university's teaching learning process, and to get more 'points' for tenure and promotion--though not as many points as published research. There is a good feeling about the course between the school and the librarians who've taught it. Course was designed by [library school] faculty member (myself) and the head of reference in our undergraduate library and then team-taught twice by us. It's got more intellectual content to it than most I've seen--it's not just a 'library mechanics' course. Problem [is] we can pay only $1,500 per course at our piecemeal rate for adjunct faculty. This gives the library school a greater service visibility on campus, and several students who've taken it have entered our MLS program later. It has only one section so far ... and doesn't bring in enough money yet to help underwrite other areas of our program as does Berkeley's course."

Library Director #6: "[Problems are] extensive staff time required to teach a small number of students. Lack of relatedness with students' other academic work."

Library School Dean #6: "We have been considering such a course for some time, and will probably offer it within the next three years on a trial basis. We expect to team-teach it with responsibility shared with practitioners in the university's library system."

Library Director #7: "We have tried offering the course through the library school. Students do not often want to take courses that do not count on their degree programs. We found it complementary to our library program."

Library School Dean #7: "We offered a one hour course for freshmen (or sophomores) but recently the coordinating board [in our state] ruled that all such courses are 'remedial,' and therefore not eligible for formula funding."

Comments of librarians at universities with accredited library schools but who report no undergraduate BI courses are of interest.

Librarian #1: "While I feel that the most effective means of instruction in library use is to have the instructor and the librarian work out an assignment which fulfills the objectives of both, I realize that course-integrated BI is not always possible. I have come to believe that a separate course in BI even though the assignments sometimes may be considered 'busy work' by the students enrolled can be an effective though perhaps not ideal way of teaching the research process. Last year the College of Continuing Studies asked for suggestions to help both graduate and undergraduate students enrolled in their program update their knowledge of the library. This inquiry offered an opportunity to design a 10-hour non-credit course entitled 'Introduction to the library' ... constructed in 6 sessions and was to be taught by Library staff. Unfortunately ... there was little interest then. It is to be offered again ... limited to 20-25 students. If the reception is good, this could be the first stepping stone to a more formal, for-credit BI course. BI which undergraduates receive comes through requests by the instructor either for an instructional class on a particular subject or for a tour of the facilities. BI participates in the Freshman English Program by offering a one-class session of approximately 50 minutes to all sections. In this class session, taught by teaching assistants [from the library school], students are shown in a 20-minute slide presentation how to locate both books and serials on their particular topics; then they are taken on a brief tour of the library. This instruction precedes the assignment of a research paper. There are an infinite number of variables to be considered in speculating about the problems which might arise in offering such a course. I believe that student enthusiasm is essential for success. Follow-up questionnaires completed by students who took the course would be helpful in evaluating the students' ability to apply the information processes which they have been taught. Here at the ... Libraries release time for the instructor would have to be considered; obviously the instructor would need time for preparation and grading. The library school offered a reference course, which is not open to undergraduates. It offers no BI course at all. I do not foresee a conflict should the university

24

libraries decide to offer an elective course for undergraduates in BI.
A well-taught, for-credit course in BI would strengthen the library's image
across campus." [The Library school dean did not respond.]

Librarian #2: "We do not offer such a course due to a variety of practical and
theoretical reasons. The undergraduate library ... has developed and implemented an award-winning course-integrated BI program over the last ten
years. Given the size of the student body (25,000 undergraduates), our
philosophy of offering information at the student's time of need (as opposed
to course-related), and our desire to reach all incoming students, we have
not pursued for credit BI courses. I have serious reservations about such
courses; my experience has been that BI integrated into the courses which
have library or information based assignments is more appropriate and effective than stand alone courses."

Librarian #3: [Problems with such a course:] Maintaining enrollment. Our
course was required for all entering freshmen for 20 years or longer.
Some 7 or 8 years ago, it was dropped as an overall requirement. It currently is required only for the following degrees: criminal justice, international agriculture, horticultural science, entomology, industrial arts education, and industrial technology. For the past few years, we have taught
several sections each semester, but that number is diminishing. This summer for the first time, no summer sections will be taught. Another problem
or conflict with the credit course is the lack of coordination between that
course and other BI lectures ... some changes in the future relative to
improving this lack of organization, the course content, and in other areas,
but I have no plans for any immediate action in BI." [The library school
dean did not respond.]

Librarian #4: "As BI Coordinator for the Undergraduate Library, I have always
felt that a credit course was too great a drain on library resources for the
number of undergraduates that you could reach. If we were to attempt to
reach any significant portion of the undergraduate population, it would take
far more staff than we have available. To reach a very few students with
an intensive course in library skills seems to me not to be a good use of
our staff." [The library school dean did not respond.]

Librarian #5: "Our main problem would be staffing. I like the idea of a course
for undergraduates and would like to teach one, but because our library
has only two professionals, it would be a real problem."

Librarian #6: "[This] is a professional school. Although 25 percent of the curriculum is devoted to liberal arts courses, neither the Liberal Arts nor the
other professional schools are willing to give up credit bearing courses for
BI. The library offers subject oriented bibliographic lectures at the beginning of each semester."

Librarian #7: "[The University] gave up a BI course in the 50's and has offered
a program of team-teaching, subject-related credit courses, and lectures to
individual classes (some multisession, with exercises). We have been considering reinstituting a course under the General Education grouping, but
have difficulty convincing the curriculum committees of its need. One possibility of having incoming freshmen take a placement test as they do in
math and languages is under consideration."

Librarian #8: "Yes [the institution offers a BI course], but it has not been offered for several years. Students have too many other units to fit in any
extras. The libraries' 'one hour stand' in freshmen and junior writing
courses is now our major focus. Few students want to know that much
about the library, i.e. as much as a course would provide."

Librarian #9: "We tried to set up a course through the library school. They
were very enthusiastic, but the librarians here didn't want to give up
control over the course content ... there were some other basic skills
courses we thought we might work with to integrate a library module into,
but since we are all committee volunteers (there is no official BI coordinator
here), we were always too busy to pursue."

Comments by librarians on campuses which do have undergraduate BI
courses for which they are responsible provide another perspective.

Librarian #1: "Library program is tied to Freshman English and course-related
instruction as requested by faculty. Course is broader and deeper,
focuses on information sources, resources and research skills. Course is
structured for the most part as independent learning to meet individual
needs à la Library-College concept. Greatest problem is in convincing
advisers to direct students to the course. No conflicts with library program seen. Course is taught by one university librarian as adjunct library science faculty member."

Librarian #2: "Many of the library school personnel do not like or want to teach
the course. There are usually three sections of the course of at least
thirty students each. The classes must be limited to freshmen and sophomores only because of the demand for the class. There are usually many
academically deficient students in the classes, also. There, many of the
problems (besides lack of enthusiasm for teaching it on the part of library
school personnel) include: large class size, diverse majors among the
students, and diverse academic backgrounds." [The library school dean
did not respond.]

Librarian #3: "[Problems seen:] 1. low enrollments: 15 average in fall,
8 average in spring. We want to offer students this opportunity to learn
about the library/information world, but the time spent is considerable for
the number reached. 2. Students typically evaluate the course highly
and suggest the need for all students to have such a background early in
college--we hesitate to pursue 'required' status for the course because of
the staffing required to teach 50-75 sections each term. Administrated by
Honors Program." [The library school dean did not respond.]

Librarian #4: "We have a typical program supporting our Writing Program pri-
marily, although recently we've turned over much of the actual instruction
to the Writing instructors themselves, in part so that we might concentrate
more on upper division classes. We did propose an undergraduate, for
credit BI course last year: our undergraduate council felt, even on an experimental basis, that the class was not worthwhile, and especially not de-
serving of credit. (One member suggested using the library was equivalent
to using a sliderule, and we don't give credit for instruction in its use.)
We will likely resubmit our proposal at a later date."

Librarian #5: "The course is offered twice a year through a College, not a department. It is listed as part of their offerings and they handle registration, grades, etc. The biggest problem, to date, has been making sure the paper work is sent to the correct instructor." [The library school dean did not respond.]

Librarian #6: "Yes in various colleges it does satisfy undergraduate requirements. We have offered the Library Skills course since 1979 and approximately 500 students enroll in the course each semester. We have faced no serious problems offering the course in the library and have it administered through the Library School. In fact it serves as a good public relations tool for the library. Not being a teaching department, the library had to house the course in a teaching department. Moreover we use library school graduates as teaching assistants for this course and a reference librarian serves as the coordinator of the course." [The library school dean did not respond.]

Librarian #7: "We have offered the course several times. Usually it is offered 1 semester per year. Our greatest problem is staffing. Assignment of the course to a member of the Library faculty reduces desk coverage. This coming semester, we will be assigning it to a member of our faculty on an overtime basis, i.e. he will be paid to teach the course on an adjunct basis. The [institution] as a whole has been very supportive and appreciative of our efforts in BI. Our work has greatly strengthened our relationships with the English Department, with English as a Second Language office, and other departments as well. If staffing were available, I am convinced we could attract upwards of 50 students per semester and offer 2 sections." [The library school dean did not respond.]

Librarian #8: "It is an elective course taken by a student in any major plus library science students. The worst problem is the students' attitudes towards the work required in the course. The type of student taking this course wants a certain A with no concomitant work effort on his or her part. The course instruction is wide-ranging and varied; students learn about the usual departments of a library. They learn how to cite an article accurately and they know how to prepare a bibliography. Most of the instructors arrange to have the students go to a bibliographic instruction class presented by a librarian." [The library school dean did not respond.]

Librarian #9: "Faculty advisors do not encourage students to take the course. For the size of our student body (13,000) we have very poor response (approximately 40 a year). The reference staff share the teaching load and are given no release time for preparation, grading papers, etc. The ends simply do not justify the means." [The library school dean did not respond.]

Librarian #10: "Required for graduation. New course to be introduced Fall 1987." [The library school dean did not respond.]

Comments of some other library school deans and their representatives are of interest.

#1: "Very well received course. The only problem has been funding, since it has to be paid for by the library school part-time faculty line, and this has been reduced."

#2: "A course that examines bibliographic resources as a link in the information transfer process within disciplines would be of immense value to all levels of the academic community. I believe it is the proper role for reference librarians to conduct these courses as a reflection of faculty status. One of the main problems with the library offering for-credit courses is its lack of status as an academic department. On this campus only academic departments may offer courses for academic credit for use toward a degree."

#3: "It is taught by TAs or librarians." [The library director did not respond.]

#4: "Major problem with the library school attempting such a course would be perceived as threatening by library staff." [The library director did not respond.]

#5: "It belongs in the library administered by the library! We do offer a course in bibliographic instruction ... and I'd be interested in finding out about courses offered at other library schools."

#6: "Lack of staff and faculty." [The library director did not respond.]

Responses from library and library school administrators throughout the United States indicate that most consider that they lack funds, for staff mainly, and enthusiasm for support of an undergraduate bibliographic instruction course. And frontline staff librarians who tend to support in principle a library-based BI course usually find that in practice it represents overload, stress, and little or no contribution to documentation necessary for their professional advancement.

Notes

1. "90 Research Institutions Join Teacher-Education Reform Group; 25 Reject Offer." Chronicle of Higher Education 33 (November 26, 1986): 15. The Holmes Group received a Ford Foundation grant to establish a national office at Michigan State University. Judith E. Lanier, dean of the MSU College of Education, is "chairman" of the Group. Tomorrow's Teachers, a 97-page report, details the Group's "reform package," calling for prospective teachers to major in a liberal arts discipline instead of education, for a three-tier approach to licensing teachers that would require "professional" teachers to complete graduate work, for new ways to evaluate prospective teachers, and for closer ties between universities and the schools. The Group plans one national conference each year that will focus on one of its goals. Its first major meeting focused on improving the undergraduate liberal arts curriculum.

2. Larson, Mary Ellen and Ellen Meltzer. "Education for Bibliographic Instruction." Unpublished paper in preparation. See also Journal of Education for Library and Information Science 28 (Summer 1987): 9-16.

3. Dyer, Esther. "The Visible College." Journal of Education for Librarianship 18 (Spring 1978): 359-361. Robert E. Brundin's "Education for Instructional

Librarians; Development and Overview" is an update and summary: Journal of Education for Library and Information Science (the Journal of Education for Librarianship's current title) 25 (Winter 1985): 177-189. Sue Galloway's "Nobody is Teaching the Teachers" is also notable: Booklegger 3 (1976): 29-31.

4. Smith, Barbara J. "The State of Library User Instruction in College and Universities in the United States." Peabody Journal of Education 58 (October 1980): 15-21.

5. Renford, Beverly and Linnea Hendrickson. Bibliographic Instruction: A Handbook. New York: Neal-Schuman, 1980. A "Glossary of Bibliographic Instruction Terms" is provided on pages 184-185.

6. Association of College and Research Libraries. Bibliographic Instruction Handbook. Chicago, Illinois: American Library Assoc., 1979. A "Glossary of Bibliographic Instruction Terms" is provided on pages 57-60. (This is also available from ERIC. ED188-623, 70 pages.)

7. Ibid. p. 58, p. 57.

8. Renford. p. 184.

9. Association of College and Research Libraries. p. 58.

10. Renford. p. 185.

11. Some "pros and cons" of various modes of bibliographic instruction are summarized on pages 46-55 of the Association of College and Research Libraries' Handbook.

12. Renford. p. 185.

13. Association of College and Research Libraries. p. 58.

14. Renford. p. 185.

15. Chisholm, Shirley. "From Oxford and Heidelberg, I Came Home Angry and Upset." Chronicle of Higher Education 33 (November 5, 1986): 49.

16. "College Library Standards Get Mixed Reception." American Libraries 17 (July-August 1986): 542-543.

17. "Standards for College Libraries, 1986." C&RL News 47 (March 1986): 189-200. [Emphasis is mine.]

18. "Guidelines for Bibliographic Instruction in Academic Libraries." C&RL News 38 (April 1977): 92.

19. LOEX (Library Orientation-Instruction Exchange.) Center for Educational Resources. Eastern Michigan University, Ypsilanti, Michigan 48107. LOEX News newsletter, 1974- .

20. Beaubien, Anne K., et al. Learning the Library; Concepts and

Methods for Effective Bibliographic Instruction. New York: R. R. Bowker Co., 1982.

21. Breivik, Patricia Senn. Planning the Library Instruction Program. Chicago, Illinois: American Library Association, 1982.

22. Adams, Mignon S. and Jacquelyn M. Morris. Teaching Library Skills for Academic Credit. Phoenix, Arizona: Oryx Press, 1985.

23. Carnegie Commission on Higher Education. Reform on Campus; Report and Recommendations of the Commission. New York: McGraw-Hill, 1972. This objective was stressed in Chapter 4, "Forces for Change." "A problem thus arises over what an educated person can and should know about society and self, and how best to make this knowledge available. The teaching of existing knowledge becomes comparatively less essential to the task of higher education, and the imparting of skills for continuing self-education comparatively more, particularly in independent study and through the library." pp. 23-24.

24. Involvement in Learning: Realizing the Potential of American Higher Education; Final Report of the Study Group on the Conditions of Excellence in American Higher Education. Sponsored by the National Institute of Education; Panel "Chairman," Kenneth P. Mortimer. October 1984. The text of the Report was published in the Chronicle of Higher Education 29 (October 24, 1984): 35-49.

25. Bennett, William J. To Reclaim a Legacy, November 1984.

26. Association of American Colleges. Integrity in the College Curriculum; A Report to the Academic Community. [Based on the Project on Redefining Meaning and Purpose of Baccalaureate Degrees.] Washington, D.C.: The Association, 1985. The text of the Report was published in the Chronicle of Higher Education 29 (February 13, 1985): 12-30, and is cited below.

27. Ibid. p. 18.

28. Ibid. p. 22.

29. American Council on Education. Campus Trends, 1986. Washington, D.C.: The Council, 1986. [Emphasis is mine.]

30. Education Commission of the States. Transforming the State Role in Undergraduate Education: Time for a Different View [Report of a Committee]. Denver, Colorado: The Commission, 1986. The text of the report was published in the Chronicle of Higher Education 32 (July 30, 1986): 13-18.

31. Carnegie Foundation for the Advancement of Teaching. "College: The Undergraduate Experience in America." [Prologue and Major Recommendations] Chronicle of Higher Education 33 (November 5, 1986): 16-22.

32. Dyer.

33. Larson.

34. Brundin, Robert E. "Education for Instructional Librarians;

Development and Overview." Journal of Education for Library and Information Science 25 (Winter 1985): 177-189.

Chapter 2

Instruction Becomes Education: A Proposal

It is proposed that undergraduate students be provided with a course of instruction in locating and relating information and media available in libraries for research on both local and principles bases. The minimum goal should be access to and use of subject matter published in various formats, with emphasis on their college library. Such a course is an important element in meeting their needs as well as implementing recommendations associated with the reports and surveys described in Chapter One. Most new college students are freshmen, part of the lower division. There are also significant numbers of new-to-the-college re-entry and transfer students who are part of the upper division of four-year, or senior, colleges. The Course advocated is designed for this large population for which there is particular concern. What is needed is a credit-generating academic course which includes bibliographic instruction but is not library use per se.

A number of considerations relating to introduction and maintenance of The Course proposed loom. Some of these have been pitfalls associated with remediation, library bibliographic instruction, and some other lower division undergraduate courses. This chapter considers some of the recurring concerns and potential problem areas and will offer some recommendations for planners, managers and teachers of The Course which is detailed in Chapter Three. There are numerous texts on course development, and there have even been some contributions to bibliographic instruction pedagogy.

MANAGING

"You must do the thing you think you cannot do."
Anna Eleanor Roosevelt, 1884-1962

Given the process for introduction of a course into many campus offerings, it is of necessity often an elective course. To attract enrollment and to build a reputation as well as a base during the phase-in period, all undergraduates should be able to elect The Course, and it should serve to fulfill an undergraduate requirement such as distribution, breadth, general education, etc. [1] Effort should be invested in reaching students during their first two terms and counseling them to enroll while they are in the lower division. As soon as it becomes a well-known, popular program and increased demand for places in The Course necessitates pre-enrollment, it should be restricted to lower division and other new students; later, to freshmen and other new students. All told, this might constitute a five-year plan. The Course program should be part of an established interdisciplinary department, e.g. Interdisciplinary Studies or Communications, whose offerings include an undergraduate major of which The Course is not a component.

Ultimately, phasing The Course into a requirement for all undergraduates and part of the curricular core should be considered, the requirement to be met during the first academic year on campus. If, for some reason, it cannot be scheduled then by the student, before junior class status would be an alternative. Students transferring or returning to upper division status, who are encouraged to enroll in The Course, may offer some similar sounding course for three transfer credits; they might be provided with a testing out option. There are of course some disadvantages to requiring any course of all students.

• • •

The Course program staff must be conscious of special need to establish and sustain a strong positive academic reputation. Excessive numbers of grade changes and Incompletes and inordinate numbers of A's not possible in normal grade spans contribute to a reputation as a remedial or "snap course." The granting of an Incomplete is intended to serve justifiable crises needs and should be used only for that purpose. Instructors who are unfamiliar with the criteria for its issuance and those who regularly grant Incompletes should be identified by the program administrator and the situation dealt with. A course which is known to be a good one to take for Pass/Not Pass usually is also known to be "a snap." If possible, the Pass/Not Pass option should not apply to The Course. The presence of relatively large numbers of freshmen and seniors in classes together also has the potential for some of the students' [under]achieving at disparate rates of work and learning. Most colleges and universities today have a formula which declares that one unit represents three hours of work per week by the student, including both class attendance and preparation. Students should be introduced to or reminded of this level of expectation during the first meeting of The Course. More importantly, it should immediately become a fact of life. [See Also: Chapter Three-- Course Information.]

• • •

To merit a place in the curriculum and three credits (or units), a collegiate course must be able to achieve academic respectability with the college or university Faculty and their disciplines. Many faculty members have come up in traditional library environments and have had no professional education training, have experienced and are established within the status quo, which tends to perpetuate itself in the culture of the academy as in other areas of life. Younger faculty (professionally) and doctoral candidates waiting in the wings are indoctrinated by and subject to the older ones and so on and on. While the words "bibliography" and "library" may have some status-related effect and may be conducive to attracting some elitest faculty and students, they can also bring with them a semantics problem.

Librarians' wish to utilize bibliographic instruction as an umbrella term to encompass library activities which relate to guiding patrons is logical. Most library schools have "bibliography" somewhere in one or more course titles. But for The Course, "bibliography" can both mislead and inhibit students who might elect it; if required to take it, they may be misled in what they expect from it and how much effort to put into it. They may be the college freshmen who think a "report" consists of going to the library and finding "the article" on "the topic" [and copying it]. Some undergraduates assume that a course with "bibliography" in the title will consist mainly of orientation tours of the college library and turning in a bibliography, which they consider they already know how to do, ipso facto easy credits for some attendance. Such courses, with or without euphemistic titles, do not merit academic credit. Others have commented that course titles which include variations of the term bibliographic instruction are counter productive--"a turn off."

A course which will require three credits work should provide for the skills-building implied above as well as accessing and using information, media and libraries in a research mode. To attract support in the introductory phase as well as to maintain enrollment, an attractive, communicative and reliable course title is essential. Some library-related course planners have apparently recognized this and have introduced such course titles as Information and Academic Libraries, Library Research Strategies, Information Resources and Libraries, and Library Research, etc. which avoid bibliography-truncated words. Both of these words--"library" and "bibliography"--should be excluded from The Course's title, although they may appear in the catalog description. For a lower division course, I suggest "Introduction to...."

● ● ●

It is not surprising, even fairly logical, that library BI courses often plod through various types of tools, following approximately the same menu librarians experience in some library school reference-bibliography classes: dictionaries, encyclopedias, directories, etc. College library self-paced BI courses are often arranged thusly. These topics may need to be covered or caught up, but what is typically lacking is an integrated, research, conceptual approach accompanied by skills acquisition and practice course.

The Course planners should think through and describe in detail and as a precondition to both teaching and test preparation, particular student behaviors that will indicate student competence. Without this approach, course objectives become by default whatever results turn up on the examination. In determining objectives, it is useful to begin by developing a series of general goal statements covering the major aspects of The Course. For The Course, think in terms of knowledge, comprehension, and application of associated skills. [2] These students learn from small lesson units with immediate reinforcement. They are likely to be accustomed to textbook introductions to subjects which go from simple to complex, familiar to unfamiliar, concrete to abstract. New terms should be defined when introduced, and concepts developed by use of different contexts. Keep assumptions relating to previous knowledge to a minimum. The goal is to enable as many students as possible to proceed as independently as possible by providing the basic facts, concepts and generalizations required for further study and ultimate independence.

The educational objectives include factual, conceptual, and principles learning as well as problem solving, which can result in:

● recognition of a systems approach to locating information and materials;

● achievement of independence in use of some standard research-related reference tools and methodology;

- mastery of the subject approach to information and media--print and nonprint--by means of library catalogs; Readers' Guide as a basic locator example of periodical information; and several types of reference works: dictionary, encyclopedia, annual, handbook, biographical and geographical tools, with illustrations of each basic type;

- acquisition of techniques applicable to all;

- application of this methodology for locating specialized information and publications related to an interdisciplinary multifaceted topic for research to document acquisition of attitude and skills methodology for "putting it all together" in a systematic search for information related to a purpose.

Collective objectives to present to and share with the students include the need "to:

- gain working knowledge of the campus libraries;

- become skilled in research techniques which will enable you to use any library more effectively;

- develop a systematic method of research which you can then apply to writing term papers and reports in your field."

Critical thinking is often associated with a truly "academic" course. The use of thoughtful questions by instructors of The Course can help develop such skills as the following:

Seeking Evidence. Example: If this were your proposition, how would you go about testing it, and where would you look for information to support it?

Identifying Assumptions. Example: What can be assumed in the statement, "This must be a good topic to research and report on because there are lots of articles about it in magazines now."

Testing For Inferences. Example: Since there are currently many books being published on this subject, what does that tell you about need for information about it?

Analyzing Arguments. Examples: What is the major issue raised in this editorial? How is it possible for two reviewers reviewing the same book to disagree strongly?

Formulating Conclusions. Examples: "There are so many other publications on this subject that I don't need to bother with these six books which were on the Banned Books list anyway." "Classification has relatively little space for classifying communism, AIDS, the U.S.S.R., etc. because it is a classification scheme formulated by the United States Library of Congress." "There is relatively little in the library about women in the U.S. military service during World War II and about Blacks in the Civil War, which means that there was nothing to write about, there was nothing written, or there was no interest in reading about these topics."

[See Also: Chapter Three--Course Information.]

•   •   •

The Course which is proposed provides lower division students with opportunity to earn three credits a semester. Classes of no more than twenty-five students are important for its success. To be at all effective such a course must relate the instructional material to disciplines with which each student normally is concerned. The instructor must be prepared to give literature search guidance on diverse topics. It simply is not possible to do this for many more than twenty-five students in the time allotted. Undergraduate bibliographic instruction is inherently rather indistinct; there is structure, but not in a purely mechanical, reliable way. A good deal of student-teacher interaction is necessary. Mass instruction solely by means of audiovisual or programmed materials is not possible.

An approximate ratio of three classroom meetings to one library class is recommended. Because The Course involves some classes outside the classroom, there is need for a master schedule posted on a bulletin board accessible at all times, under glass if necessary, the location of which is stressed at the first class meeting and if possible, pointed out during the first library class meeting.

•   •   •

Recruiting students for an elective course relates to their knowing about it and being attracted by it. The appeal can be based on its reputation, its fitting into their scheduling needs and preferences (Monday morning and Friday afternoon are "bad times," whereas Tuesday/Thursday 11-12:30 classes usually appeal), the number of credits they need and it provides, and the possibility of fulfilling any requirements or prerequisites for other courses or programs. The most potentially productive recruitment methodologies for The Course when it is a new, lower division, elective offering include advertising in the campus newspaper during the preenrollment period or first week of the term before classes start; managing to have it mentioned during freshman and new student orientations; building a support network among counselors, librarians, advisors, former students of The Course, high school teachers and counselors, and personnel associated with socalled special interest groups, e.g. physically disabled, advanced placement high school, and re-entry students programs. Build a reputation for The Course itself as very useful for majors in whatever discipline as well as graduate school admissions and achievement. It can honestly be said that there are no students for whom this course does not have the potential to make a real difference in their academic and subsequent life.

For merely the cost of an 8½" x 11" handout, dark ink on cheap one-color throwaway paper, plus some staff effort, the most directly potential market--lower division students in a captive audience situation--can be systematically reached at the very moment when they are considering electives in their plans for the following term. It is not difficult to identify lower division undergraduate courses with large enrollments. They often fulfill degree requirements or are prerequisites for entrance into majors. They are associated with the large lecture halls and auditoria where The Professor lectures and a TA population, possibly with undergraduate library reserves. They may include first courses in anthropology, biology, economics, geography, physics and sociology, as well as a remediation course for students not able to enter the basic freshman year English course directly. A few weeks into the second half of the term, a call from The Course administrator to The Professor during office hours to request permission to distribute a flier to each student generally results in prompt consent. Ascertain the number of students and schedule a class at which the fliers can be distributed by one or two instructors of The Course, who arrive five minutes before class to catch and remind The Professor. That these professors may initially focus on the goodness of knowing how to find a book in the library, evidence no real idea of what The Course provides, and not connect it with a report or requirement in their class is not the point if, while the fliers are rapidly distributed, they identify what their students are receiving and bless The Course. They will come to know it by reputation and due to other systematic ways which The Course program can develop. The Course administrator should also arrange for distribution of the fliers to students' campus and dormitory mail boxes.

Also important are word-of-mouth among former students, who typically will be declaring that it should be required, and signs in such undergraduate hangouts as the library, lounge, counseling center, gym, women's center, learning center, and bookstore. Counselors and advisors of transfers, freshmen, minority persons, females, re-entry students, and others should systematically be communicated with by means of mailings for which The Course administrator will develop with staff assistance a packet, "open house" sharing of course materials, etc. Getting The Course on the list approved for fulfilling various requirements unrelated to students' majors is exceedingly productive. Structure The Course so that it clearly supports and is conducive to success in senior honors or thesis-related coursework.

Spinoff or bonus benefits are psychologically useful. Students who achieve A- or better (in the normal course of events there is likely to be an A+ course achiever in each class) in The Course might automatically receive a pass to any stacks from which undergraduates are normally excluded, good for the balance of their undergraduate career. Infusions of such experiences as computer-assisted literature searching demonstrations and a brief search for each student in the field of her/his project are popular and justified. A brochure listing titles of representative and appealing projects will be useful for communicating with other faculty and counselors as well as responding to inquiries about The Course as it becomes well known; format it so that it can be converted into a poster. Distribute statistics regarding enrollment, retention, etc. in defending and expanding the program; include alumni comments. Releases to various types of news media should be considered.

Accessibility to and visibility of instructors of The Course is essential. Appointment of an administrator with time and ability to coordinate all of these programatic elements should be recognized. They should be active in professional associations at all levels and make presentations and participate in conferences. Communication among all staff members is essential. Regular "required" staff meetings and regular, numbered administrative memoranda to summarize meetings and developments until the next meeting will contribute to it. The copies of the Projects on reserve in the library should be inscribed with an inviting "for further information about this course, contact...."

•   •   •

The Course requires no purchases other than a notebook binder, nor preparation at this time by the program staff of a course handbook. A required-purchase, locally-produced handbook can provide up-to-date information about the college library or the university library system, which typically will continue to change for some time. It is also useful for providing a syllabus which instructors should cover. But once introduced, it rapidly becomes outdated for the same reason that it is needed. While providing "publications" credits or infusions of income, cut-and-paste revisions by one or two persons deteriorate into patchwork and are not justifiable. The handbook needs systematic management and budget provision for planned updating coordinated by The Course program administrator and to be part of all instructors' faculty responsibilities.

The Course as presented in Chapter Three does not yet depend upon such a handbook. Assignments 1-7 consist of content information (required reading) as well as activities (homework), and there are also handouts. In the early stage of The Course, students should be required to maintain all of these materials in sequence in a notebook which they bring to class regularly and regard as a reference-text. All materials should therefore be duplicated with three holes punched.

Ultimately a local handbook should be budgeted, produced, and regularly revised. It should be a required purchase through the Bookstore, and of such caliber and significance in the student's life that s/he will be unwilling to sell it, thus avoiding the problem of outdated copies flooding nearby used-book stores. It can be a paperback with three holes punched. Input the handbook in the ERIC database and refer off-campus inquiries about it to its ERIC "ED number" and to the campus Bookstore by use of a form response postal card.

Some of the trade textbooks on the market are identified in Section III: Resources. It is unlikely that most lower division students are willing and able to read these in connection with such a course, but for those who are and for supplementary reading and reference, several titles should be maintained on reserve in the college library collection for The Course. A copy of each should also be in The Course office collection. [See Also: Chapter Three--Library Basics, More Library Basics, Assignments 1-7.]

•　　•　　•

State-of-the-art information tells us clearly that undergraduate students are most motivated by a learning experience culminating in opportunity to integrate and apply new acquired concepts and skills. A bibliographic research project should be required of all students enrolled in The Course. It should be graded and contribute to The Course grade; 25 percent is recommended. It should be clear in all sections that students opting for a Pass/No Pass "grade" must complete all requirements, including the project; likewise students who are satisfied with a lower course grade than they would have achieved had they not turned in a project. A span of representative projects in the humanities, social sciences, and sciences-technologies should be available on noncirculating library reserve for examination in the library. A duplicate set of these projects should be available in The Course office for consultation and discussion with and among the instructors.

The college should encourage subject departments to enable students achieving grades of B- (for instance) or better in both The Course and project to utilize

The Course to fulfill part of any breadth, general education, etc. requirements in science, social sciences, or humanities. In such a case the project would be clearly within this area or discipline and meet criteria. Departmental representatives might be involved as consultants in developing the criteria, which during the phasing in of The Course program also has potential for public relations and communications. All project topics should be proposed by students and approved by The Course instructor(s) before the midpoint of the term, at which time this option would be contracted for by the student.

The Project work should be pursued within the campus library system, i.e. all sources and titles discovered by use of these sources will be located in the libraries' collections. However, the students might be expected to identify and report in the introductory essay two types of off-campus libraries or collections specializing in the project area--a noncirculating research library, and one for which union lists would be utilized in connection with an interlibrary loan. Students' individual project topics and work should not be part of examinations, which should be over The Course itself and be returned to the students to keep.

An introductory essay communicating an awareness of the project topic, placing it in the context of a real course, which might be in one's major, and demonstrating some awareness of the organization of the literature should be accompanied by the outline of a potential or actual term paper to be prepared based on this repertoire of twenty-five selected, locally-available titles. A separate discussion of the research strategy employed should note serendipitous discoveries along the way. Each of the twenty-five units in the selected, annotated bibliography should be displayed in such a way that the sequence of exact source location which led to the library's holdings record and ultimately to the publication is documented. A bibliographic citation based on a style manual should be annotated to describe how the particular publication would fit into the term paper and its outline ... why it was selected and was competitive compared with similar publications in the library's collection which were not selected.

Two copies of the project and all bibliography cards, not just those for the twenty-five selectees, should be turned in. Construction of an accurate and revelatory title which includes key words should be a requirement. A keyword index based on project titles and maintained cumulatively and copies of all projects for the last five years should be stored in The Course office for staff use only.

It is counterproductive to declare a minimum number of pages or words for the length of the essay, strategy account, annotations, or project overall. The sample projects will provide insights for trepid students. You will be available to consult and reassure during office hours. If necessary, respond to the "how many pages does it have to be?" with a serious "as many as you need--feel free" and a reminder of the sample projects "on our library reserve."

Plagiarism and cheating can be problems throughout The Course because of the nature of the work and because it is not part of a major. A required course with numerous sections is more subject to this problem than others. The student who during office hours or after class the first week of the term seeks guaranteed acceptability of a potential project topic may simply be keenly interested and perhaps know of a concurrent course requiring a paper. But if there is a xeroxed project from a previous term or a DIALOG search printed offline sticking out of a notebook, you need to proceed carefully. Sophisticated students will change titles, of course. At the point when project topics are proposed and approved, those which have been previously done should be headed off at the pass--never refused or rejected, but, rather, discussed and cautioned and a revised proposal required in such a way that they are clearly doing their own unique thing. This is not easy when hundreds of freshmen are enrolled in the same basic courses, some of which may require one report on the same topic, e.g. the psychological effect of advertising. The provision of project guidelines which are discussed well in advance, pathfinder assignments, and enforcement of these standards can provide a learning experience, however. Ultimately, the reputation of the program and The Course should limit these problems. Avoid prolonged discussions among staff members regarding the possibility of a student's having borrowed a portion of a project in terms of whether or not this could possibly be plagiarized--his niceness or her good qualities, etc.--it is generally a yes or no matter requiring prompt and decisive action.

Devote a class during the first half of the term to discussion of the Project Guidelines and the project. Mention the presence of the projects file in The Course office (the reason they must turn in two copies, one of which will be returned), which is accessible only to instructors. During the latter part of the term after Assignment 7 has been turned in, there should be no outside-of-class work required other than completion of the project. [See Also: Chapter Three-- Project Guidelines; Pathfinder Assignments 5 and 6; Bibliography Cards & Style Manuals.]

TEACHING

> "How shall I ever find the grains of truth embedded in all this mass of paper."
> Virginia Woolf (1882-1941) A Room of One's Own. Chapter 2. 1929.

One hopes that instructors of most undergraduate courses recognize the need to relate to the college library in a way which goes beyond assumptions. Any course which involves bibliographic instruction and/or requires undergraduates to use library reference tools and services is particularly subject to a unique relationship with the campus library system. Some of the related considerations have to do with basic standards and professionalism. The appointment by a library administrator of a librarian who is a member of the reference department or undergraduate library staffs to liaison with The Course program is desirable. S/he should be invited to attend The Course faculty meetings and encouraged by The Course program (and the library administration) to teach a section occasionally.

Teachers of The Course should provide the library staff via the library liaison, or if there is none, The Course administrator, with advance copies of assignments for which the library is the students' laboratory. It is not necessary to provide a copy of the answer key because the goal is to alert librarians to locational questions rather than instruct students, who may view them as potential short cuts. Some students will attempt to get the librarian on duty to write a message vindicating their attempt or documenting the impossibility of a question on their assignment. One of the most important things undergraduate students can learn about the library is how to ask the reference librarian for help. But in this instance, arrange via the library liaison to have reference librarians report unproductive assignment questions of which they become aware. They may well be reluctant to point, however. On the other hand, be prepared for the student whose excuses for not having the assignment ready include "even the librarian couldn't do this." Her/his repertoire of attempted snow jobs which have apparently worked is likely also to include such irrefutables (except that you have distributed the assignment well ahead and they have had ample time) as power failure, dental appointment, the coach assigned extra practice, the book was missing. Teachers should teach in such a way that students will come to them with their questions. Sufficient office hours in or near the library and accessibility are important. Librarians who teach should hold separate office hours. Coordinate class sessions with instructors of other sections in the program which meet at the same time so that only one class meets in the library at any given time. One such class should be scheduled for every section early in the term, to be devoted to the layout of the reference collections and their catalog access, with individual practice in independently accessing them. While in a library, spend approximately half the time in instruction, and the balance with students working on individual worksheets reinforcing what was taught, while you actively roam among them.

Instructors introduce the students to the campus library system by use of a laboratory approach: the libraries are teaching laboratories. Class assignments should expose students to the wide variety of libraries and resources--books, periodicals, reference works, government publications, microforms, computer, catalogs, reference services, etc. Instructors do not expect librarians to teach nor to verify the students' assignment answers. Provide students with guidelines as to when in this course they should (may) seek help from a professional librarian, and when to delay in order to discuss with you, the instructor, any problems they encounter in doing assignments. They should also learn what they can expect generally from a reference librarian, and be introduced to the interaction and variables that affect levels of reference service. Make clear to them that not all library employees are professional librarians. What constitutes a professional librarian is useful information, although it is well to avoid reference to "faculty status," inasmuch as it genuinely rarely exists. Make clear to all students what is considered an acceptable response on assignments should they run into difficulty in this course: a description of how s/he attempted to cope, in lieu of no answer.

A master schedule for the term should be distributed during the first week of classes in each section. Distribute assignments well in advance. Where several responses are possible, make this clear in wording questions. Stress practice experience with basic concepts rather than trick questions. Collect assignments at the beginning of the class on the date due, check them all, and return them promptly. Introduce the tradition of assignments turned in as they enter the classroom on the due date. Demonstrate that you have indeed examined every assignment, but eschew marks which communicate merely that its presence was checked. Check assignments in terms of library changes before you reuse them, four years later or perhaps variations of them in the interim. Problems with inaccurate call numbers, main entries, library locations, etc. cause unnecessary frustration for students and inhibit the learning process. Keep in mind that in the modern academic library, catalogs and thus shelving locations are experiencing radical changes rather than mere ongoing change. Provide all reference tools mentioned in assignments with library call numbers and unique locational information.

Insofar as possible, it is wise to avoid in-library class activities which involve using copies of reference works kept at "the desk" or which need to be checked out. Be aware that not blocking public access to material or files any longer than necessary is important for The Course's campus image. Longer instructional comments are less disruptive if made in out-of-the-way areas within the library. The Course administrator should coordinate every term with the library liaison so that faculty members and reference librarians are at least introduced to each other.

Require students to use pencil for all work other than the project, which is typed, and that they reshelve all reference works used, whether or not they were found in their "right place." If necessary, remain after class and visibly do this chore.

Make sure your students know your name. If you expect them to regard you as Ms or Mr XYZ while addressing them by their first names, be aware that you are regarding them as children. Yes, this can be a no-win situation because one of the alternatives involves having them address you by your first name, which can offend traditional people whether they are freshmen or seniors, young or old, male or female.

The Course administrator should be an experienced instructor of The Course and thus a person with whom new instructors especially can discuss their work. Instructors will cover the same material, implement the same course requirements, particularly for the project, and utilize a course grade formula. The same final examination should be administered to all students as part of Examination Week. The extremes and potential disparate experiences which can come about among multiple sections will thusly be minimized.

Space has been provided in Chapter Three throughout The Course materials to insert library locations and call numbers, which is especially important in view of the premise that use of an atypical "laboratory collection" for The Course is unproductive. "Dry labs," dummy collections, segregated small batches of superseded cast-off reference books, and book trucks are variations on the same theme. [See Also: Chapter Three--Introduction to Assignments 1-7.]

•   •   •

"...one of the greatest improvements in education is that teachers are now fitted for their duties by being taught the art of teaching."
Mary Somerville (1780-1872). God and His Works: "Benevolence"

Effective teaching needs to be accompanied by a spirit of excitement--about acquisition of valuable tools which will help all students throughout all of their lives, with part of the big payoff immediately in the case of The Course. It is not easy to teach a course which is unassociated with status, a major, or requirement. Rote learning is boring and discouraging, but there are things to be learned here, even memorized, and it is going to mean a little work which includes memorizing, practicing, following instructions, and striking out on one's own.

"Affirmative action" is a good philosophical as well as managerial point of departure in considering qualifications needed by people to do this job and their recruitment, retention, advancement, and termination. Personnel action which is affirmative, as opposed to mere passive equal opportunity, is nothing more nor less than good management. The qualifications of an instructor able to teach The Course well should be clearly identified and detailed in terms of minimum and desirable. During the phase-in period of The Course, while it is offered in a limited number of sections and is probably elective, there should be a core staff of regular career status faculty teaching full-time. As sections are added and The Course expands, there may be need and justification for occasional part-time personnel to teach a section. Staff members should be fully involved in the program, i.e. not merely present for class meetings of one section, come and go. Committee work, professional and curriculum development, recruitment, etc. are necessary aspects of the work of a faculty member.

A developing young program can become saddled with the assumption that part-time and thus transient personnel must be utilized. To evolve a professional accreditable course and program a core of full-time committed regular faculty is essential. As the number of sections and specializations evolve, the possibility of qualified persons being employed to teach a section may be worth consideration, if they meet the same qualifications and are willing and able to maintain the same standards of teaching, if not professional activities and contributions. According to the National Center for Education Statistics, part-time faculty represent 32 percent of the total teaching force in higher education. (This figure does not include graduate assistants.) [3] It is difficult to obtain statistics on the percent of teaching done by part-time temporary lecturers at most universities, largely because these positions are constantly being shifted and replaced. [4]

The Course instructors' qualifications should meet those of regular teaching faculty. Qualifications should include some so-called education training as well as a professionally accredited Master's degree in library science. A major consideration is recognition of need for the administrator to have taught The Course and who has full time for coordinative management of multi-sections and instructors as well as more than the usual amount of intra-campus relationships experienced by an academic department. S/he should teach the course periodically. Librarians whose professional experiences already include teaching undergraduate courses should be considered in the pool of instructors of The Course.

At a time of calls for excellence and more rigorous standards in higher education, the abuse of non-tenure track appointments can undermine academic standards and lead to the erosion of the quality of undergraduate education. Given all the other ways in which colleges and universities are gradually losing their ability to compete for current and future faculty talent, the continuing proliferation of these temporary positions, filled by underpaid instructors, full and part-time, with low status and no job security, seems shortsighted and counterproductive. [5] Women are better represented in the academic underclass than in the traditional tenure-track group. The Course, while not a library course, is related by parsimony and tradition. It is "feminine" and it attracts female staff. [6] In 1984 an American Association of University Professors survey indicated that 40-50 percent of nontenure track posts were held by women--a striking statistic when one considers that women held only 25 percent of the total number of full-time faculty positions covered in the survey. The role of temporary faculty on their campuses in some respects does not differ from that of teaching assistants. Senior professorial faculty are largely responsible because they have acquiesced. With the start of a new program, the opportunity to work a fresh slate is provided. [7]

The possibility of subject-specialized or discipline specialized sections as The Course program grows and expands as well as an upper division course related to senior theses seminars and honors work should be considered in planning for future faculty needs. Subject-specialists will be needed for these. Opportunities for practice-teaching under skilled master teachers should ultimately be created by The Course. Future teachers of undergraduates and of library-information science and education should learn from a structured experience under such tutelage. The mature program will also be able to sustain an intern.

• • •

Long-term evaluation of bibliographic instruction has been almost nonexistent. It is generally recognized that evaluation of faculty involves a spectrum of approaches including student feedback of teaching (sometimes titled Course Evaluation), self-assessment, evaluations by colleagues (sometimes called peer evaluation), measurements of student learning, and assessment of research, advising, and public service. Any instructor who does not recognize the potential for improvement of her/his teaching, as well as that of the course, via eliciting feedback in a structured situation is not an educator. Over-reliance on the peer review reflects need for built-in assurance of security on the part of administrators, pseudo-peers, journal editors, and referees. James Lloyd has referred to "...subtle and powerful constraints and pressures that promote silent submission to the system." [8]

For personnel decisions, rating of a teacher across courses should be considered, the minimum number of courses depending on the number of student raters in each course. In general, five or more courses of at least fifteen students are needed for a dependable assessment. Overuse of student ratings results in the students' getting bored and responding haphazardly or not at all. It has been recommended that tenured staff collect ratings in one course each year and in new courses, and that nontenured staff collect ratings in their various courses but not in every section. Limitations of student ratings include their eliciting numerical responses that can be scored and quantified, resulting in a too easy tendency to assign them precision that they do not possess. The manipulations of ratings by teachers must be considered when ratings are used for personnel decisions. Over-interpretation of small variations and between and among instructors may tempt an administrator; there is little practical difference between a teacher whose mean rating is at the 60th percentile and another who is at the 65th percentile. [9] Too much weight in relation to other criteria is a problem. Students' ratings may mislead the instructor into thinking there is nothing more needed in order to upgrade her/his teaching. The law is clear that colleges must use job-related and nondiscriminatory practices in making personnel decisions, and that they observe the principles of due process. (Enforcement of the law is admittedly another matter.)

Student learning is among the fairest and most objective methods to assess teachers' effectiveness. Information on what and how much students have learned in a course undoubtedly is critical for course and instructional improvement, but there are too many factors other than teacher competence which can affect examination results. Testing students at the beginning of the term as well as at the end of The Course is important. The recommended situation is one in which faculty members teach different sections of The Course with a common syllabus and a common final examination. Ratings of teachers by their students should be used wisely or not at all. [10]

On some campuses, student organizations distribute summaries of some teachers' past ratings. Students have been known to hatch plans to "get" an unpopular teacher by giving unfavorable ratings, or to boost ratings of a popular faculty member. Some faculty have used "research" results to try to demonstrate the lack of reliability and validity of these evaluations and thus to discredit the system. Discrediting the system is not the answer. Students can and should have something to say about their education. Reliability does not seem to be the issue. Validity is a question. "Student ratings are affected by a number of factors--class size, sex of the teacher and the student evaluator, whether the course is required or elective--that are beyond the teachers' control." [11] The method of administering the evaluations also influences the results. In their 1982 investigation of the legal aspects of teacher-performance appraisals, Dolts and Holtfreter stated that federal standards "probably are not being met by college and secondary education administrators ... [when evaluations] are, at least in part, based on student ratings or instructors." [12]

The right to evaluate should carry with it the obligation to be responsible for one's actions. Anonymity is said to encourage frankness, and to be uncritical, frankness implies honesty. [13] Anonymity also fosters irresponsibility. Only in investigative police work is anonymous information officially acted upon, and verification is sought. In law it has no standing whatsoever. "[A]nonymity encourages irresponsibility in students who should be learning to be responsible; anonymous and hence unchallengeable evaluations are inherently unfair to faculty members whose evaluations of students are subject to challenge. Anonymity renders impossible most meaningful research on the reliability of student evaluations." [14]

•   •   •

A sequence of handouts, activities, and potential related problem situations is provided in Chapter Three and Section III: Resources.

The distinctive disciplinary contexts and research processes and their modes of access in the humanities, sciences-technologies, and social sciences can be the framework for another model, an elective upper division course which might also provide for senior seminars in majors offering theses or the structure for honors work. The Integrity In the College Curriculum report refers to "the year long essay, the senior thesis, the artistic discipline undertaken after a sound grasp of the fundamentals of the discipline or art has been established, [and] ... the thrill of moving forward in a formal body of knowledge [such as the student's major] and gaining some effective control...." [15] An upper division, credit course based ideally on the student's having completed the basic, lower division model of The Course should be considered, but the primary need is to innovate the lower division, credit course. College: The Undergraduate Experience in America refers to the "the enriched major" which, in addition to courses, provides for a thesis that relates some aspect of the major to historical, social, or ethical concerns and participation in a seminar in which the student presents the report orally to colleagues and also critiques those of her/his peers. [16]

The final handout appended to The Course sequence of materials provided as Chapter Three is one focal point for discussion which would be associated with a research seminar, a term-length course which would involve the faculty who have provided campuswide support for The Course requirement. Women's studies provides an ideal setting for discussion of such a course. It is interdisciplinary, its courses' contents are relevant to all students, and they are offered on an ever increasing number of campuses [17]. Women's studies content generates a great variety of not "overdone" topics, thereby limiting the potential for staleness, apathy, and plagiarism problems.

Notes

1. An integrated core approach to general education extending from freshman to senior year has been recommended by the Carnegie Foundation for the Advancement of Teaching. See College: The Undergraduate Experience in America. The Prologue and major recommendations appear in the Chronicle of Higher Education 33 (November 5, 1986): 16-22.

2. Centra, John A. Determining Faculty Effectiveness. San Francisco, California: Jossey-Bass, 1979.

3. "The Status of Part Time Faculty." Academe 67 (February-March 1981): 30.

4. What has the library science profession done to improve the situation for part-time librarians? In 1976 the American Library Association issued what is still a little-known resolution. It seems clear that the Association was aware that attitudes toward part-time work had been discriminatory, and that its goal at that time was upgrading of permanent part-time jobs for librarians. The solution called for prorated pay, fringe benefits, and opportunities for advancement and tenure for the part-time in all libraries. But only in 1984 did the Association's executive board vote to provide prorated benefits for its own employees! See: Braudy, Judith and Susan Tuckerman. "The Part-Time Academic Librarian: Current Status, Future Directions." Library Journal 8 (April 1, 1986): 38-41.

5. Heller, Scott. "Extensive Use of Temporary Teachers is Crippling Academe, AAUP Charges." Chronicle of Higher Education 32 (July 30, 1986): 23, 26. The 1986 Report on Full-Time Non-Tenure Track Appointments was published in the July-August 1986 Academe, the magazine of the American Association of University Professors.

6. "The Reference Librarian Who Teaches: The Confessions of a Mother Hen," by John C. Swan is part of a special issue of the Reference Librarian devoted to library instruction in the context of reference services. (Volume 10, Spring/Summer 1984.)

7. See Campbell, Patricia B. "Racism and Sexism In Research." In Encyclopedia of Educational Research, 5th edition, 3:1515-20. New York: Macmillan, 1982. Women are better represented in the academic underclass than they are in the traditional tenure-track group. Data in a 1984 AAUP survey showed 40-45 percent of non-tenure track posts held by women--a striking statistic in view of the fact that women held only 25 percent of the full-time faculty positions covered in the survey. The role of temporary teachers on their campuses "in some respects does not differ from that of teaching assistants.... Ultimately the two-tier system brings with it a class consciousness that affects the faculty's perception of themselves, the students' perception of the faculty,

and the outside world's perception of academe." Chronicle of Higher Education 32 (July 30, 1986): 23, 26.

8. Chronicle of Higher Education 30 (June 26, 1985): 64.

9. Centra, John A. Determining Faculty Effectiveness. San Francisco, California: Jossey-Bass, 1979. 44.

10. Ellis, Randi S. "Ratings of Teachers by Their Students Should Be Used Wisely--Or Not at All." Chronicle of Higher Education 31 (November 20, 1985): 88.

11. Ellis.

12. Uniform Guidelines on Employee Selection Procedures.

13. McBrearty, Paul. "We Should Abolish Anonymous Evaluations of Teachers by Their Students." Chronicle of Higher Education 24 (July 7, 1982): 48.

14. "Fact File." Chronicle of Higher Education 33 (January 14, 1987): 40.

15. Association of American Colleges. Integrity in the College Curriculum; A Report to the Academic Community. [Based on the Project on Redefining Meaning and Purpose of Baccalaureate Degrees.] Washington, D.C.: The Association, 1985.

16. Carnegie Foundation for the Advancement of Teaching. "College: The Undergraduate Experience in America." [Prologue and Major Recommendations] Chronicle of Higher Education 33 (November 5, 1986): 16-22.

17. More than 507 programs in 1986. Directory of Women's Studies Programs, 1986 edition. College Park, Maryland: National Women's Studies Association.

Some Useful References

Bloom, Benjamin. Taxonomy of Educational Objectives. Volume I: The Cognitive Domain. New York: David McKay, 1956.

Davis, James R. Teaching Strategies for the College Classroom. Boulder, Colorado: Westview Press, 1976.

Hopkins, Frances L. "A Century of Bibliographic Instruction: The Historical Claim to Professional and Academic Legitimacy." College & Research Libraries 43 (May 1982): 192-198.

Kobelski, Pamela and Mary Reichel. "Conceptual Frameworks for Bibliographic Instruction." Journal of Academic Librarianship 7 (May 1981): 73-77.

Meyers, Chet. Teaching Students to Think Critically; A Guide for Faculty in All Disciplines. San Francisco, California: Jossey-Bass, 1986.

Oberman, Cerise. Petals Around a Rose: Abstract Reasoning and Bibliographic Instruction. Chicago, Illinois: Association of College & Research Libraries, 1981. Also ERIC ED 229013, 1980, 25 pages.

Smalley, Topsy N. "Bibliographic Instruction in Academic Libraries: Questioning Some Assumptions." Journal of Academic Librarianship 3 (November 1977): 280-283.

Wilson, Pauline. "Librarians As Teachers; The Study of an Organization Fiction." Library Quarterly 49 (April 1979): 146-152.

Working With Teaching Assistants (pamphlet). Division of Instructional Development, University of Illinois, 307 Engineering Hall, 1308 West Green Street, Urbana, Illinois 61801. 1987.

SECTION II

Chapter 3

The Course

<u>To the Teacher</u>

The materials which follow consist of assignments, in-library exercises, in-class practice, instructional handouts, and testing for the lower division course which is advocated. This is not a reproduction of an existing course, although the components and methods have been used, modified, and taught successfully. Related suggestions, instructions, and guidelines for the teacher are interspersed in sequence. The Course and these materials have some potential for inexperienced as well as experienced educators. An effort has been made to present them in a way which should enable many professional bibliographic instruction (BI) librarians who are not trained and experienced teachers. A key follows each structured situation requiring exercises or response to testing. By reference to Section III, these materials and forms can be reused and varied while departmental and personal files are being built.

The range of quantitative and qualitative variables found in college or university library programs is great. The Course itself is suitable in any setting from a multisection, departmental course-program, part of the curriculum of a university with a library system, for example, to the college with an LRC.

<u>All materials must be adapted to the local library organization.</u> Be alert to need for you to adjust the phrasing of the instructions to students in terms of the local campus system of libraries or "the" college library. Reference tools need to be accompanied by library locations and call numbers. Space has been provided in the materials to insert this information, which is especially important in view of the premise that use of the atypical "laboratory collection" for such a course is unproductive.

The main local variable for which you must provide is the extent to which bibliographic access to the local library collection(s) has progressed, i.e. how much of the work on computerizing storage and retrieval capability of data accessing the library collection(s) has been completed, so that the information is in a form readily available at all times by everyone. Some modifications of these materials will have to be made, and distinctive local routines taught. Many campuses presently have both a conventional card catalog and terminals providing some degree of online access for recent book acquisitions. Most have a serials file or record, whether online, in printed or fiche format, or both. The conceptual and methodological overlaps as well as transitional aspects will continue for sometime, requiring teaching of associated skills and attitudes. These materials have been planned so that they can be related to this norm.

Less problematic are such variables as the presence of divided or dictionary catalogs or both, union catalogs, costly abstracting tools and citation indexes, etc. If the college library does not have any citation indexes, for example, it becomes less important for citation indexing, keyword, and permuted indexing concepts to be introduced at this time. More than enough materials have been provided for a term course. And some users of The Course may consider citation indexes and some abstracts suitable for an elective, upper division course.

"XYZ College" has been used where the sense of the presentation required some verbalization. Your course title and name should be provided throughout. "The catalog" has been used to refer to card catalog(s), microfiche files, online catalogs with terminals, and the combination providing bibliographic access to records of the holdings of "the library."

Recommendations discussed in Chapter Two have been implemented here. For example, The Course envisions no required purchases other than a notebook binder by the student, nor preparation at this time by the institution of a course handbook. Three-hole punched handouts should be provided the students, some perhaps duplicated on paper colored to correspond with any local color codes (e.g. Assignments 3 and 4, which relate to serials).

A variable affecting how these methods and materials might be utilized is class size. A section of twenty-five students requires more preparation in the classroom preceding a class in the library's government documents department, for example, than does a smaller section. In my experience, fewer than fifteen students may not provide sufficient interaction and energy, however. Students should have individual problems for in-library work. The smaller the class, the more feasible provision of an exercise in the abstracting tool related to the student's Project field, for example. But, as the departmental and instructor's files are built, this difficulty diminishes considerably. While developing a course, a compromise is the use of one problem for several students, of course. With a large section, it is well to distribute several forms, i.e. sets of assignments 1-7. Section III: Resources provides additional problems and exercise variations.

The materials can be rearranged. The sequence presented here is designed to span a term of fifteen weeks, with two one-and-a-half-hour (eighty net minutes), weekly class-meetings.

Course   Syllabus: <u>Course Information</u>
Institution   3 Credits
Instructor   Building, room. Days, time.

OFFICE HOURS: Unless otherwise announced or posted, office hours are held
in the library,   , and by appointment.

COURSE DESCRIPTION, from the Schedule of Classes:

OBJECTIVES: While in college, you should take the opportunity to learn how
to investigate almost anything. You should become able to know where and
how to find what you want efficiently. Learn to use libraries on principles as well as local bases (to use the college library as well as
to walk into any other library anywhere, able to cope fairly well). It
means putting it all together too: information + documents + libraries.
Writing grows out of effort to find information, reclaim and inter-
relate it, and to use it for your own special purposes. The research
paper (sometimes called the reference, library, term, or source paper)
has a place in many college courses, and it is not limited to the social
sciences or humanities or sciences or technologies. A merely satis-
factory <u>or</u> an honors paper calls for knowledge and skills in exploiting
libraries and other resources, critical judgment in transforming data
and information into cogent support of an argument (thesis or hypothesis),
and skill in organizing and putting it all together.

Specific objectives:
        - to gain a working knowledge of the campus libraries;
        - to become skilled in research techniques which will enable you
          to use any library more effectively; and
        - to develop a systematic method of research which you can then
          apply to writing term papers, reports, etc. in your field.

Classes held in classroom and library consist of informal lectures introducing new material, computer demonstrations, an individual conference
to discuss your Project, in-class assignments, and seven "outside" assignments designed to provide you with practical experience.

REQUIREMENTS include regular attendance, two exams, demonstrated acquisition of skills using library tools through guided practice and the
assignments. The University considers that a 3 credit course requires 9
hours (including classes) weekly of a student's time. Therefore, you will
need to plan 6 hours each week for work which will for the most part take
place in the library. Be sure to notify your instructor promptly if you
need more hours a week outside of class. Mainly for your own learning
experience, you are required to work independently. The nature of this
course is cumulative, meaning that it is not possible to have a catch-up
orgy no matter how much time and effort you ultimately apply to it and
that all assignments are due at the beginning of class on the dates
listed on your schedule (the other part of this syllabus.) You have at
least a week to work on each assignment, usually longer.

Page 1 of 4

The two exams consist of objective-type questions. One is scheduled during Examination Week after instruction ends. They cover the course, the written assignments and their associated handouts, as well as in-library work. In fairness to all, they should be given once; please be present on scheduled dates. There will be no make up for other than unavoidable, documented crises. Since you receive a schedule of all dates today, you can plan accordingly. Completion of the course involves all of the following, with the course grade based on 20% each: two exams, a bibliographic Project, active participation, and the written assignments.

COMMUNICATION is possible by means of the instructor's 2 boxes, one located inside the departmental office, and one located outside the department office and accessible at all times. The outside box: Assignments will be returned promptly. If you are not present in class when they are returned, they will be placed in the outside box within 24 hours for you to retrieve. Also check the box after being absent, before returning to class for any handouts, assignments, etc. distributed and for inclass or inlibrary work missed during your absence. It is your responsibility to assure having received all assignments and completed all requirements. The outside box is the place for me to leave things for you; do not leave messages or other things there. The inside box: If necessary to contact me, leave a note in the inside box, within the departmental office. If you are absent and do not communicate, it can only be assumed after a week that you are no longer part of the class. You can also leave telephone messages at   /   -   ; allow for 24 hours relay. The bulletin board outside the department office has a master schedule with last minute information for our class.

Emphases in this course are on learning techniques and practicing skills. You are not required to purchase any books. You are required to maintain everything you receive in order, in a notebook (not a folder), and to bring it to class regularly. Insofar as possible, all handouts will be 3-hole punched.

Most of the publications referred to in this course are in several campus libraries, including the undergraduate and main reference libraries. In your coursework, utilize the catalogs and collections of all campus libraries. If you can't locate a library publication, consult a library staff member who is a professional librarian and only after you have tried the catalogs in and for that library and looked on the shelves. Several supplementary titles are available in the library or bookstore; use the latest edition of:

- Dwight, John A. & Dana C. Speer. How To Write A Research Paper.
- Gates, Jean K. Guide to the Use of Library and Information Sources.
- Turabian, Kate L. A Manual for Writers of Term Papers, Theses, and Dissertations. Or 5th edition (1987) by Bonnie Honigsblum.

All assignments except the Project and all in-library work should be done in pencil. The Project should be typed. Project Guidelines will be distributed early in the course. In brief, the Project is not a term paper; it consists of a selective, annotated bibliography of publications in our library which would enable you to write a term paper on a research topic such as you would have in a college course; an introductory essay is part of the Project.

<u>When</u>	<u>Where</u>	<u>For Today</u>
Week #1		Classes will start promptly, whether in the classroom or the library. Consult your Schedule and allow time to reach the
Day-Date	CLASSROOM	particular location within the building.
Day-Date	CLASSROOM	Read <u>Syllabus</u>; bring questions. Study <u>Library Basics</u>, pp. 1-4.
Week #2		
Day-Date	Meet in the lobby of the Main Library.	
Day-Date	CLASSROOM	Study <u>Library Basics</u>.
Week #3		
Day-Date	CLASSROOM	Assignment #1 due at beginning of class.
Day-Date	CLASSROOM	
Week #4		
Day-Date	Meet by the A's of the Card Catalog, Main Library	
Day-Date	CLASSROOM	Assignment #2 due
Week #5		
Day-Date	CLASSROOM	Possibility of quiz.
Day-Date	CLASSROOM	Study <u>Project Guidelines</u>; bring questions.
Week #6		
Day-Date	Meet in the foyer outside Periodicals Department, Main Library.	Assignment #3 due; study <u>More Library Basics</u>
Day-Date	CLASSROOM	Project <u>Proposal</u> due
Week #7		
Day-Date	Main Library lobby.	
Day-Date	CLASSROOM	Assignment #4 due.

When   Where   For Today

Week #8
  Day-Date CLASSROOM   Exam (50 minutes): everything to date
                                        other than your Project work.
  Day-Date CLASSROOM

Week #9
  Day-Date Main Library   Assignment #5 due.

  Day-Date CLASSROOM   Read Government Publications

Week #10
  Day-Date GOVERNMENT DOCUMENTS
           LIBRARY Department
  Day-Date CLASSROOM   Assignment #6 due

Week #11
  Day-Date

  Day-Date

Week #12
  Day-Date CLASSROOM   Assignment #7 due. Study Reference
                                        handouts.
  Day-Date Meet in foyer outside
           Reference Department.

Week #13
  Day-Date CLASSROOM   Study Biography handouts.

  Day-Date Meet in foyer outside
           Reference Department

Week #14
  Day-Date

  Day-Date

Week #15
  Day-Date CLASSROOM   Project due. Study Citation Indexes

  Day-Date CLASSROOM   Review and Feedback.

INVENTORY

Question IV can be derived from the Chronicle of Higher Education, which publishes "What They're Reading on College Campuses" each month, a list of the ten best-selling books compiled from information supplied by stores serving universities throughout the United States. (The list from which these five titles were derived appeared on page 2 of the October 8, 1986, volume 33 issue; reports covered sales of hardcover and paperback trade books in August 1986.) Question IV and part of I might be replaced with questions eliciting knowledge of accessing the local library collections, particularly if the Inventory is used in connection with "testing out" of a required course. Topics for Question VIII are provided in III: Resources: Multiple-Subject Topics With Developed Literature Searches.

This is not a test. If you want to know and to discuss the answers, come to office hours.

I. Use the "catalog card" to answer these questions:

1. This card would be filed in the M's or the S's or the W's?_____
2. How many pages in this book? 25, 412, 431 or 448?_____
3. What is its complete "call number"?_____
_____
4. You can tell by looking at this card that the library classifies most of its books using what classification system? The Dewey Decimal, or MARC, or Library of Congress, or ISBN?

WOMEN IN SOVIET CENTRAL ASIA

HQ1774
.C45
M33
1974

Massell, Gregory J   1925–
    The surrogate proletariat: Moslem women and revolutionary strategies in Soviet Central Asia, 1919–1929 [by] Gregory J. Massell. Princeton, N. J., Princeton University Press [1974]

    xxxvi, 448 p. map. 25 cm.

    Bibliography: p. 412–431.

    1. Women, Muslim. 2. Women in Soviet Central Asia. 3. Communism and Islam. 4. Soviet Central Asia—Politics and government. I. Title.

HQ1774.C45M33   301.41′2′09584   73–16047
ISBN 0–691–07562–X   MARC
Library of Congress   74 [4]

---

5. If this book turned out to be exactly the information you needed and so you wanted another book on exactly the same subject-matter, you could consult the catalog by looking under the wording_____
6. There would be a total of how many access points (cards) for this book in a card catalog?_____

II 7. You're in the library looking at this page in the Social Sciences Index, which works much like Readers' Guide. You need to read the article with the arrow. Your next step is to consult (check the one best answer):
    the card catalog, where you'd check in the W's, for Warren
    the serials record, where you'd check in the L's, for Law
    the online catalog, where you'd check in the I's, for Involuntary

8. The article with the arrow is one of 10 articles cited in this indexing which are about_____

9. If you needed periodical articles on the subject of mental health knowledge, you'd look in this Index under the wording_____

Mental health knowledge. See Health knowledge
Mental health laws
   Avenues to legislative success. H. Dörken. Am Psychol 32:-738-45 S '77
   Collaboration between Ohio psychiatrists and the legislature to update commitment laws. V. M. Victoroff. Am J Psych 134:752-5 Jl '77
   Informed consent and confidentiality: proposed new approaches in Illinois. R. Shlensky. Am J Psych 134:1416-18 D '77
   Involuntary commitment for mental disorder: the application of California's Lanterman-Petris-Short act. C. A. B. Warren. bibl Law & Soc R 11:629-49 Spr '77
   Put away [Great Britain]. D. Gould. New Statesm 94:239 Ag 19 '77
   Reformed commitment procedures: an empirical study in the courtroom. V. A. Hiday. bibl Law & Soc R 11:651-66 Spr '77
   Regulating psychiatric practice. P. R. Fleischman. bibl Am J Psych 134:296-8 Mr '77
   Social discrediting of psychiatry: the protasis of legal disfranchisement. P. E. Dietz. Am J Psych 134:1356-60 D '77
   Society's outcasts. H. Hills. il Center Mag 10:2-14 Jl '77
   Some current legal issues [symposium]. Am J Psych 134:273-95 Mr '77
    See also
Mentally ill—Civil rights

---

10. "Society's outcasts" was written by H. Hills, published in the Illinois Center Magazine issue dated October 2, starting on page 14. TRUE   FALSE

III. Arrange the following ten subject headings in alphabetical order, using 1, 2, 3, etc.

Nevada_____   Newark-- Bibliography_____

New England_____   Newlyweds_____   Newspapers_____

New Zealand_____   Newts_____   Newsmakers_____

News_____   Newark_____

IV. What do the following books currently have in common? LAKE WOBEGON DAYS
     by Garrison Keillor; FATHERHOOD by Bill Cosby; WOMEN WHO LOVE TOO MUCH by
     Robin Norwood; IACOCCA: AN AUTOBIOGRAPHY by Lee Iacocca with William
     Novak; and YOU'RE ONLY OLD ONCE by Dr. Seuss.

They are all_____

V.   Arrange these 7 call numbers in order as they would appear on the
     library shelves, using 1, 2, 3, etc.

H41	E188	E188	E188	HQ9	HB9	HQ9
D9	S5	.S6	S58	S741	D82	S741
						1983

VI. There was an illustrated magazine article on the New York ferry boats
    sometime during the past thirty years. You need to locate it. You'd first

        look in the library card catalog
        check the NEW YORK TIMES Index
        consult Readers' Guide To Periodical Literature

VII. Which two of these persons would you not expect to find in the current
        edition of Who's Who In America?
        Goldie Hawn   Gloria Steinem
        Herbert Hoover   Margaret Thatcher
        Ronald Reagan

                                   Why?_____

VIII. You're starting to do library research for a major paper on the follow-
     ing topic: the social consequences of the "Black Death" (plague)
     in Europe, especially Medieval Britain.

     Very briefly, list the first 5 steps you'd take. You can list 5 library
     tools you'd use early in a systematic "literature search", if you prefer
     to think of it that way.

     1. _____
     2. _____
     3. _____
     4. _____
     5. _____

This is not a test. If you want to know and to discuss the answers, come
to office hours.

I. Use the "catalog card"
   to answer these questions:
   1. This card would be
      filed in the M's or the
      S's or the W's? W's
   2. How many pages in this
      book? 25, 412, 431 or
      448? 448 [+ 36 prelim.)
   3. What is its complete
      "call number"? HQ1774.C
      45M33/1974
   4. You can tell by looking
      at this card that the
      library classifies most
      of its books using what
      classification system?
      The Dewey Decimal, or
      MARC, or Library of Con-
      gress, or ISBN?   Library of Congress

WOMEN IN SOVIET CENTRAL ASIA

HQ1774
.C45
M33
1974

Massell, Gregory J   1925–
   The surrogate proletariat: Moslem women and revolu-
tionary strategies in Soviet Central Asia, 1919–1929 [by]
Gregory J. Massell. Princeton, N. J., Princeton University
Press [1974]

   xxxvi, 448 p. map. 25 cm.

   Bibliography: p. 412–431.

   1. Women, Muslim. 2. Women in Soviet Central Asia. 3. Communism and Islam. 4. Soviet Central Asia—Politics and government.
I. Title.

HQ1774.C45M33   301.41′2′09584   73–16047
ISBN 0-691-07562-X   MARC

Library of Congress   74 [4]

5. If this book turned out to be exactly the information you needed and
   so you wanted another book on exactly the same subject-matter, you could
   consult the catalog by looking under the wording WOMEN, MUSLIM (and other subjects)
6. There would be a total of how many access points (cards) for this book
   in a card catalog? 6 (4 subjects+ 1 main entry(author) + 1 added entry, the title.)

II 7. You're in the library looking at this page
   in the Social Sciences Index, which works
   much like Readers' Guide. You need to read
   the article with the arrow. Your next step is
   to consult (check the one best answer):
      the card catalog, where you'd check in the
         W's, for Warren
   X the serials record, where you'd check in
         the L's, for Law
      the online catalog, where you'd check in
         the I's, for Involuntary
   8. The article with the arrow is one of 10
   articles cited in this indexing which are
   about MENTAL HEALTH LAWS
   9. If you needed periodical articles on the
   subject of mental health knowledge, you'd look in this Index under the wording   HEALTH KNOWLEDGE

Mental health knowledge. See Health knowledge
Mental health laws
  Avenues to legislative success. H. Dörken. Am Psychol 32:-
   738-45 S '77
  Collaboration between Ohio psychiatrists and the legislature
   to update commitment laws. V. M. Victoroff. Am J Psych
   134:752-5 Jl '77
  Informed consent and confidentiality: proposed new approaches in Illinois. R. Shlensky. Am J Psych 134:1416-18 D
   '77
  Involuntary commitment for mental disorder: the application
   of California's Lanterman-Petris-Short act. C. A. B. Warren.
   bibl Law & Soc R 11:629-49 Spr '77
  Put away [Great Britain]. D. Gould. New Statesm 94:239 Ag
   19 '77
  Reformed commitment procedures: an empirical study in the
   courtroom. V. A. Hiday. bibl Law & Soc R 11:651-66 Spr '77
  Regulating psychiatric practice. P. R. Fleischman. bibl Am J
   Psych 134:296-8 Mr '77
  Social discrediting of psychiatry: the protasis of legal disfran-
   chisement. P. E. Dietz. Am J Psych 134:1356-60 D '77
  Society's outcasts. H. Hills. il Center Mag 10:2-14 Jl '77
  Some current legal issues [symposium]. Am J Psych 134:273-
   95 Mr '77
   See also
Mentally ill—Civil rights

10. "Society's outcasts" was written by H. Hills, published in the Illinois
    Center Magazine issue dated October 2, starting on page 14. TRUE X FALSE ... in
    Center Magazine issue dated July 1977, starting on page 2. (Volume 10.)
III. Arrange the following ten subject headings in alphabetical order,
    using 1, 2, 3, etc.

Nevada __1__   Newark-- Bibliography __5__

New England __2__   Newlyweds __6__   Newspapers __9__

New Zealand __3__   Newts __10__   Newsmakers __8__

News __7__   Newark __4__

IV. What do the following books currently have in common? LAKE WOBEGON DAYS by Garrison Keillor; FATHERHOOD by Bill Cosby; WOMEN WHO LOVE TOO MUCH by Robin Norwood; IACOCCA: AN AUTOBIOGRAPHY by Lee Iacocca with William Novak; and YOU'RE ONLY OLD ONCE by Dr. Seuss.

They are all___current best-sellers in college bookstores_____

V. Arrange these 7 call numbers in order as they would appear on the library shelves, using 1, 2, 3, etc.

H41	E188	E188	E188	HQ9	HB9	HQ9
D9	S5	.S6	S58	S741	D82	.S741
						1983
4	1	3	2	6	5	7

VI. There was an illustrated magazine article on the New York ferry boats sometime during the past thirty years. You need to locate it. You'd first

      look in the library card catalog
      check the NEW YORK TIMES Index
 X consult Readers' Guide To Periodical Literature

VII. Which two of these persons would you not expect to find in the current edition of Who's Who In America?
    Goldie Hawn   Gloria Steinem
 X Herbert Hoover   X Margaret Thatcher
    Ronald Reagan

                  Why? Hoover is deceased; Thatcher is not American.

VIII. You're starting to do library research for a major paper on the following topic: the social consequences of the "Black Death" (plague) in Europe, especially Medieval Britain.

Very briefly, list the first 5 steps you'd take. You can list 5 library tools you'd use early in a systematic "literature search", if you prefer to think of it that way.

1. consult the subject-entries in the card (or other) catalog (Use established subject headings)
2. have a conference with a librarian who specializes in history
3. consult some periodical indexes for articles on this topic
4. try to find a good selective bibliography on this topic (to save work!)
5. take a dry-run in the stacks for the articles and books I've accumulated before proceeding

Course

Date

_____

Please provide the following information. I need it in order to meet your needs and interests in this course. I will keep it all confidential.

Campus (local) address_____

_____Zip code:_____

    Local telephone number: ____ / ____ - _____

Permanent (home) address_____

_____Zip code:_____

    Telephone number: Area code_____ / ____ - _____

Year in college (circle):   Freshman   Sophomore   Junior Senior

    Other_____

Where else have you attended college?_____

Is this your first term at XYZ College?_____ Your first year?_____

What languages other than English have you studied or do you know?_____

_____

Who recommended this course to you?_____

Have you ever been enrolled in this course before?_____

How many units are you carrying this term?_____

What is your major or probable major?_____

What are your career plans or tentative career plans?_____

_____

What are your personal concerns and interests?_____

_____

What books have you read in the last three months?_____

_____

_____

What newspapers do you read more or less regularly?_____

_____

Describe your library experience-- how much, what libraries, where, why?

_____

What is your main reason for taking this course? What are your specific goals?_____

_____

If you have a topic which you are interested in developing and proposing for your Project, you can mention it now. It's not a commitment._____

_____

_____

Please leave the other side blank.

THE CATALOG CARD
The first step in learning to use any library is understanding the information provided in bibliographic records which describe the library's
collection. Regardless of the type of catalog, the principles described
here are basic. The card below is a typical main entry (See Glossary)
and illustrates the following discussion.

Call Number:
 LC Classification
 Book Number

 Title   Author (Main Entry)

                                                        Imprint: Place
                                                        of publication.
                                                        Publisher.
BF173.   Lerman, Hannah   Date of publi-
F85   A mote in Freud's eye; from psychoanalysis   cation.
L38   to the psychology of women.   New York:
1986   Springer, 1986.   Collation
             228p   (Springer series, Focus on Women: v.9) Series Note
         Includes Index and References pp 195-219.

                                                        Tracings:
                                                        Subjects.
1.Freud,Sigmund,1856-1939 Relations with women.   Added Entries.
2.Psychoanalysis. 3.Women--Psychology.   I.Title.
II.Series

CALL NUMBER   The call number is not just a number. Here, it's BF173.F85
L38/1986. It consists of a series of capital letters, numbers, letters
and numbers... everything in the upper left corner. A call number has
several components:

CLASSIFICATION The Library of Congress Classification (See pages 7-9)
is used to communicate the subject area. In this call number the LC
Classification portion is BF173.F85. Books in this LC class will thus
be shelved with other books on the same subject.
BOOK NUMBER   Not really a number, it is the second set of data, and
usually determined by the author's surname (Lerman). L38 is read as a
decimal "number": .L38, whether or not the decimal point is indicated.
Failure to remember that the book number is read as a decimal number
often leads to confusion when looking for a book on the shelves.
YEAR OF PUBLICATION on a separate line in this location is used by many
libraries for some or all of their books.
LOCATIONAL CODE is often used in a library system as the final element
of the call number, e.g. BIOL for a book in the Biology Library.

In the following example, the classification numbers are read as <u>whole</u> numbers: BF161 before BF173. The book numbers are used <u>decimally</u> despite the absence of any decimal point. Thus, S25 is read <u>.S25</u> and is shelved before S3. The year a book was published is often used as the final element of a call number, on a separate line.

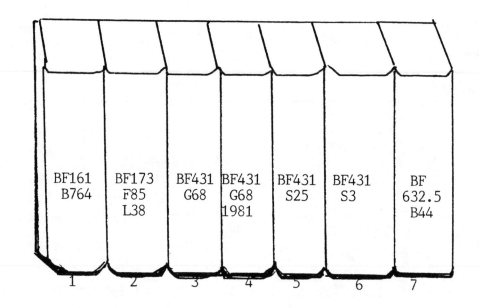

-The Lerman book analyzed on the previous page is the second book on the shelf.
-The third and fourth volumes are likely to be the same title by the same author (Gould). They would differ in that the fourth book was published in 1981, and the third book on the shelf is an earlier edition.
-The fifth and sixth are two different books classified in the same subject area, BF431. They are by two different authors whose surnames appear to begin with S. If the fifth volume's book number -- .S25 -- refers to an author named Smith, then .S3 will <u>not</u> refer to Sanchez. It is more likely that the sixth book's book number --.S3 -- refers to Snyder, South, or Suehiro.

The six points of access (cards) which are detailed on the following page are derived from the one main entry card (a main entry by a personal author named Hannah Lerman) begun on page 1. How would these six cards file alphabetically in a dictionary catalog (see page 11.) Use the six blank cards provided on page 6 to work this out. Just the information on the first two or three lines of each card will do it. Keep in **mind that all cards for a book** are initially the main entry (author) card, to which is added above the author a line of information such as the title or a subject-heading, etc.

FREUD, SIGMUND, 1856-1939-- RELATIONS WITH
WOMEN
Lerman, Hannah
A mote in Freud's eye; from psychoanalysis
to the psychology of women
Springer, 1986.
228p (Springer series, Focus on Women; volume 9)
Includes Index and Refer...
BF173.
F85
L38
1986

WOMEN-- PSYCHOLOGY
BF173. Lerman, Hannah
F85 A mote in Freud's eye; from psychoanalysis
L38 to the psychology of women. New York:
1986 Springer, 1986.
228p (Springer series, Focus on Women; v.9)
Includes Index and Refer...

PSYCHOANALYSIS
BF173. Lerman, Hannah
F85 A mote in Freud's eye; from psychoanalysis
L38 to the psychology of women. New York:
1986

A mote in Freud's eye
BF173. Lerman, Hannah
F85 A mote in Freud's eye; from psychoanalysis
L38 to the psychology of women. New York:
1986 Springer, 1986.
228p (Springer series, Focus on Women; v.9)
Inclu...
1.Freud,Sigmund
2.Psychoanalysi
II.Series

BF173. Lerman, Hannah
F85 A mote in Freud's eye; from psychoanalysis
L38 to the psychology of women. New York:
1986 Springer, 1986.
228p (Springer series, Focus on Women; v.9)
Includes Index and References pp 195-219.

1.Freud,Sigmund,1856-1939--Relations with women.
2.Psychoanalysis. 3.Women--Psychology. I.Title.
II.Series

AUTHOR, OR MAIN ENTRY. All the books in the library by a particular author are listed under the author's name in the catalog. The author may be a PERSON, e.g. Adrienne Rich, Ernest J. Gaines, Lady Murasaki. Or the main entry (author) may be a CORPORATE BODY such as the United States Department of State, International Business Machines Corp., the American Red Cross, or a university. In a few cases when the individual person (author) cannot be determined, the TITLE will be used for the main entry; this is often the case for books such as the Encyclopaedia Britannica or The World Almanac or a book of quotations, where numerous faceless or unidentified persons are responsible. Title main entries are often used for magazines.

Main entry under CORPORATE AUTHOR

R725.
A55
1981

American Medical Association. Judicial Council.
    Current opinions of the Judicial Council of the American Medical Association : including the principles of medical ethics and rules of the Judicial Council / prepared and approved by the Judicial Council. — Chicago, Ill. (535 N. Dearborn St., Chicago 60610) : The Association, 1981.
    ix, 11 p. ; 26 cm.

Main entry under TITLE

PS508.
J36Y64
1983

Yoisho! : an anthology of the Japantown Art and Media Workshop.
    — San Francisco, CA : JAM Writers' Workshop, c1983.
    70 p. : ill. ; 22 cm.
    ISBN 0-9606410-0-9 (pbk.) : $3.00

—Disci-
le.

187332
MARC

    1. American literature—Japanese American authors. 2. American literature —California—San Francisco. 3. American literature—20th century. 4. Japanese Americans—Literary collections.   I. Japantown Art and Media Writers' Workshop (San Francisco, Calif.)

    PS508.J36Y64   1983   81-82233
                        810'.8'08956073—dc19
                                          AACR 2   MARC

Main entry under PERSONAL AUTHOR

LB2332.
3.T44
1985

Theodore, Athena
    The campus troublemakers: academic women in protest.   Houston, Texas: Cap and Gown Press, c1986.
    293p Bibliography. Includes index.

1.Women,college teachers--U.S. 2.Women college graduates--Employment--U.S. 3.Sex discrimination in education--U.S. 4.Sex discrimination against women--U.S. I.Title

FILING Here are some basic rules common to most library card catalogs. These sometimes apply to other types of catalogs (e.g. fiche, online, which usually have additional rules.)

1. THIS WAY: NOT THIS WAY:

New Bern	Newark
New England	New Bern
New York	Newborough
New Zealand	New England
Newark	Newmarket
Newborough	Newport
Newmarket	New York
Newport	New Zealand

Filing is WORD-BY-WORD, not letter-by-letter; that is, shorter words are filed before longer words beginning with the same letters.

2. ARTICLES in all languages at the beginning of titles are ignored. A, an, the, la and el, las and los, etc. For example:
"An American Dilemma..." is filed in the A's for American (not A for An)
"A Century of Struggle" is filed in the C's for Century (not A)
"The Right to Be People" is filed in the R's for Right (not T for The)

3. NAMES WITH A PREFIX may be filed either under the prefix, with the remainder of the surname as one word (example #1) OR right under the name (example #2):

> #1: DeCrow, Karen   #2: Casas, Bartolomé de las
>   LaFontaine, Jean de   Gogh, Vincent van

It depends on the language used and the nature of the prefix. The main thing is to be aware of the possibility and of the cross references provided in catalogs. For example, if you look in the D's for books by Simone De Beauvoir, you'll likely find a SEE cross-reference leading you from De Beauvoir to (go and "see") Beauvoir, Simone de, in the B's.

4. MAC and MC are INTERFILED as if both were "Mac". As in this catalog "tray":

McCarthy, Abigail	Mace, Vera	Mackenzie, Midge
McCarthy, Mary	McGinnis, Patricia	McPhee, Carol
Maccoby, Eleanor	"The Machismo Ethic"	MACY, EDITH DOWNING
McCullers, Carson	Mack, G.E.	"Madam Prime Minister"

5. ABBREVIATIONS and NUMERALS IN TITLES are filed as though spelled out. Some examples:

Dr. = Doctor	100 = one hundred
Mr. = Mister	"Henry VIII and the Lutherans" is
Mrs. = Mistress (sometimes as Missus)	filed as if spelled Henry the
St. = Saint, Street	Eighth
U.S. = United States	"8 Charing Cross Road" = "Eight...

6. Books about a person (the person is the subject) are filed directly after the books by that person (the person is the author):

> McCarthy, Mary Therese, 1912-   . "The Group".   [the novel]
> MCCARTHY, MARY THERESE, 1912-   . "Memories of a Catholic
>   Girlhood"   [autobiographical]

CLASSIFICATION

There are numerous classifications--or classification systems-- in life. For example, the systematic grouping of organisms into categories based on shared characteristics or traits, in biology. Materials in library or other collections may be classified in terms of such things as their format, or more usually-- by subject-matter. The main goal is organization to facilitate retrieval. The two major classification schemes for the organization of library materials by subject-matter information are the Dewey Decimal system and the U.S. Library of Congress system. Classifications have problems! The organization of knowledge, overlap of subjects, perception of information, developments and changes, etc. all make it difficult to place a subject in one exact location within the hierarchy of a classification. A book is classified in one location in a classification, but fortunately can receive several relevant subject-headings.

Most college and university libraries in the United States are classified by "LC". (The Library of Congress Subject Headings are a separate matter. Some libraries use the LC classification and another subject-heading thesaurus, and vice versa.) Within the twenty-one main "classes" of the "LC", it is possible to expand each to provide for more specific subject-matter within them. If you are accustomed to the Dewey Decimal Classification, note especially that the LC begins each book's classification with two (sometimes one) capital letters. Expansion is possible by the addition of numbers, and then additional letters and numbers. For example, see page 9.

Remember, an LC Classification is not merely a capital letter or two. Listed here are only the twenty-one main classes and parts of some of the four hundred ninety summaries. Library books are shelved alpha-numerically, according to the LC classification. When a book treats more than one topic it is not given several classifications, nor is it shelved in several locations in the collection. A book is assigned only one classification, and therefore can be shelved in only one place in the library stacks.

It is useful to keep in mind, however, that when books first arrive in a library's processing office, they may be assigned random accession or acquisition numbers which are referred to temporarilly; these might result in recently arrived books (regardless of when published) being organized by authors, titles, date of arrival, or even their size! Occasionally libraries use a small "f" (not a capital F) at the beginning of a call number. This usually designates an oversized book exceeding 12" x 19", and it communicates that these folios are shelved together and not in sequence with the regular sized books in that classification. (Usually they're nearby; if you don't see the book you want, ask.)

Keep in mind that a call number consists of the LC classification + the "book number" (see pages 1,2). And it can, additionally, consist of the year of publication (on a separate line) and a helpful mnemonic library-location code.

A. General Works
  AC Collections
  AE Encyclopedias
  AI Indexes
  AN Newspapers
  AP Periodicals
  AZ History of Knowledge

B. Philosophy, Psychology,
  Religion
  B   Collections, History,
  BC Logic
  BD Metaphysics
  BF Psychology
      BF173-BF175 Psychoanalysis
      BF511-BF593 Emotion
        (See page 9 for further
        expansion of BF)
  BH Esthetics
  BJ Ethics
  BL Religions, Mythology
  BM Judaism
  BR Christianity
  BS Bible

C. History and "Auxiliary
  Sciences"
  CB History of Civilization
  CS Genealogy
  CT Some Biography

D. History (Except America)
  D   General History
  DA Great Britain
  DC France
  DD Germany
    etc.

E and F. History and Geography
  of The Americas
  E31-E50 North America (general)
  E151-E770   U.S.A.
  F1-F970   U.S.A. (local)
  F1201-F3899 Latin America

G. Geography, Anthropology, etc.
  G   Geography, Voyages, Atlases
  GA Geography, Mathematical and
      Astronomical
  GB Geography, Physical
  GN Anthropology, Ethnology,
      Ethnography

GR Folklore
GV Sports, Dance, Recreation

H. Social Sciences
  H   Social Sciences (general)
  HA Statistics
  HB Economics
  HD Labor
  HE Transportation, Communication
  HF Commerce
  HG Finance
  HJ Public Finance
  HM Sociology, General & Theoretical
  HN Social history and Reform
  HQ Family, Marriage, Home
  HT Communities, Classes
  HV Social Pathology and Corrections
  HX Communism, Socialism,
      Anarchism

J. Political Science
  J   Documents
  JA General Works
  JC Theory of the State
  JF-JX Constitutional History
    JK U.S.A.
    JQ Asia, Africa, Australia, etc.

K. Law

L. Education
  LA History of Education
  LB Theory & Practice, Educational
      Psychology, Teaching
  LD-LT Universities and colleges,
      by country.

M. Music
  ML Literature of Music
  MT Musical Instruction

N. Fine Arts
  NA Architecture
  NB Sculpture
  NC Graphic Arts, Design, Drawing
  ND Painting
  NK Applied Art

P. Language & Literature
  P   Philology, Linguistics
  PA Greek and Latin Philology and
      Literature

P. Language & Literature, contd.
  PB Modern European Languages
  PC Modern Romance Languages
  PE English language
  PF German
  PG Slavic
  PM Artificial Language, American
      Indian
  PQ Romance Literatures
      PQ1-PQ3981 French literature
  PR English literature
  PS American Literature

Q. Science
  QA Mathematics
  QB Astronomy
  QC Physics
  QD Chemistry
  QE Geology
  QH Natural History
  QK Botany
  QL Zoology
  QM Human Anatomy
  QR Bacteriology

R. Medicine

S. Agriculture, Plant and
   Animal Industry
  SD   Forestry
  SF   Veterinary Medicine

T. Technology
  TK   Electrical Engineering
  TR   Photography

U. Military Science

V. Naval Science

Z. Bibliography & Library
   Science
   Z116-Z550 Book Industry
   Z665-Z997 Libraries, Library
              Science

An Expansion of BF (Psychology) would look like this (Ethnic psychology is in GN; social psych is in HM):

BF173-BF175	Psychoanalysis
BF180-BF210	Experimental psychology
BF231-BF299	Sensation
311-499	Cognition. Perception. Intelligence
511-593	Emotion
608-635	Will
636-637	Applied psychology
660-687	Comparative psychology
683	Motivation
698	Personality
699-711	Genetic psychology
712-724	Developmental psychology
721-723	Child psychology
795-839	Temperament. Character.
840-861	Physiognomy
866-885	Phrenology
889-905	Graphology
908-940	The hand. Palmistry
1101-1389	Parapsychology
1405-1999	Occult sciences

GLOSSARY

ADDED ENTRY: The heading above the author line on a catalog card; the
   card is filed by this entry. A catalog entry other than the main
   or subject entry by which an item is represented in a catalog file.
   There may be added entries for titles, series, translators, illus-
   trators, authors of an introduction, joint authors, etc. They are
   identified in the Roman numeraled (I, II, III, etc.) items in the
   tracings at the bottom of the card or other file entry.

BOOK CATALOG: A catalog in book-form, created by photocopying catalog
   cards or by computer print-out. (The catalog of the Library of
   Congress is available in book form.)

CATALOG: A catalog is an arrangement of bibliographic records accessible
   by author, title, subject, etc. Catalog formats include cards,
   microfiche, online, and book catalogs.

CITATION: The listing of a publication in a bibliography, footnote, or
   index. It should have enough information to enable someone else
   to locate the same publication without much effort.

COPYRIGHT DATE: The year in which the author's application to the Library
   of Congress for copyright on a book is granted. Like a patent, it
   insures the author against intellectual theft. It usually appears
   on the verso of the title page; a "copyright date" is preferable
   to another.

CORPORATE AUTHOR: A body, such as a government, society or institution,
   which authorizes publication of materials which are published with
   that body as the author. (One or more persons involved with its
   creation may be identified by means of the added entries.)See page 4.

CROSS REFERENCE: A direction from one heading (a subject or a person per-

haps) is a SEE type cross reference; a direction to an additional
source of information (usually a subject) is a SEE ALSO.

DICTIONARY CATALOG: A catalog in which author, title and other types of
added entries are all interfiled together alphabetically in one
sequence. Contrast this with a divided catalog.

DIVIDED CATALOG: A catalog which is divided, usually into two separate
but nearby catalogs or files. One contains only the subject entries
(all the subject cards,whose first lines consist of subject-headings),
and that part is referred to as the Subject Catalog. The other
is the Author-Title Catalog-- a slight misnomer inasmuch as all
the entries (cards) other than subjects are filed there, i.e. there
would be author (main entry), title, and other types. (See Added
Entry.)

IMPRINT: A collective term which refers to a book's place of publication,
publisher, and date of publication ; they usually appear in that
order in a catalog.   See page 1.

MAIN ENTRY: The basic --or main-- entry in a catalog from which all other
entries are made. The main entry can be a personal author, or a
corporate author, or by the title. In some library catalogs, the
main entry may be the only source of complete bibliographic and
holdings information.

ONLINE CATALOG: One in which entries are stored in a computer by a numbered system and are accessible through local terminals by many
"fields" of information, e.g. author, title, subject, series,etc.

PERSONAL AUTHOR: The person chiefly responsible for the intellectual or
artistic content of a work under whose name that work appears in

a catalog or index. A personal author should be distinguished from corporate author, another type of main entry. See page 4.

PUBLICATION DATE: The year a book or other publication comes off the press and goes on the market. For a book, it is usually the same as the copyright date. Date of publication is usually the third part of the imprint.

PUBLISHER: The company or agency responsible for issuing a publication. Governments are publishers too. The publisher is usually the second part of the imprint.

SEE ALSO: A type of cross reference; the other type is a See. A direction from a term or name under which entries are listed to another term(s) or name under which additional information can be found.

SEE: A type of cross reference; the other type is a See Also. A direction from a term or name under which no entries are listed to a term or name under which entries are listed.

SERIES: A number of separate works, usually related to one another and usually numbered, issued in succession, normally by the same publisher, with a uniform style. Each part of the series usually has something in common with the others, but has its own individual title. There is also a collective series title. See page 1.

SHELF LIST: A catalog of publications in a library arranged in call number order, i.e. in the same way they are on the shelf (shelves). There is usually one entry (a main entry card) for each publication.

SUBJECT ENTRY: An entry in a catalog or bibliography under a heading that indicates the subject.

SUBTITLE: A secondary title which follows the main title and often a semi-colon, colon or dash. The subtitle is usually explanatory, especially

with nonfiction works. For example, in The Lowell Offering: Writings
by New England Mill Women, 1840-1845, "Writings by New England Mill
Women, 1840-1845" is the subtitle.

TITLE ENTRY: The record of a work in a catalog or a bibliography under
the title. A title entry may be a main entry (one of the three
types) or an added entry.   See page 4.

TRACINGS: A list, located at the end of a catalog entry (at the bottom of
a card) tracing all the subject (Arabic numeraled) and then all the
added (Roman numeraled) entries for that particular book in that
catalog.

UNION CATALOG: A catalog or list of all of the holdings of a specific
group (or "union") of libraries. Usually, the holdings are entered
under the main entry only. The National Union Catalog is an example.

VERSO: The left-hand page of a book or the reverse side of a leaf. We
speak of a book's title-page verso.

Library research on a particular topic generally follows a logical sequence. All of the assignments in this sequence contain work which can relate to developing your Project. However, they concentrate on acquisition of the general knowledge and skills needed to research any topic effectively:

Assignment 1: Catalogs and Related Tools (Mostly Books)
Assignment 2: Catalogs and Related Tools, continued.
Assignment 3: Locating Periodical Information & Articles (Mostly Serials)
Assignment 4: Locating Periodical Information & Articles, continued.
Assignment 5: Working Through a Topic: a Pathfinder for Your Project.
Assignment 6: Working Through a Topic: Project Pathfinder, contd.
Assignment 7: Identifying and Using Some Specialized Sources.

It is strongly advised that you begin work on each assignment as soon as you receive it, and work on it in relatively brief periods of time ongoingly, rather than delaying and counting on a last minute or last day orgy. Ample time has been provided for completion of each activity-- in most cases, ten days. The final assignment (#7) is due well before the end of the term, leaving plenty of time during which there will be no assignments other than completion of your Project, which you can begin with "pathfinder" assignments 5 and 6.

First, read the entire assignment. Then begin at the beginning and proceed systematically. The catalog "cards" which appear in some may not all be identical reproductions of those in the library's files; the contents of any catalog, fiche or online files may vary from time to time. The work can be done in the Reference Department, and it is recommended that you do some of it during office hours. The assignments and the questions within each are planned so that concepts presented evolve and so that you have opportunity to practice the skills related to them. However, it is unproductive and a waste of your time to dwell on a problem if you don't understand what you're doing. When you've done all that you can on your own, ask for my help, and in the meantime possibly go on to the next question. The main goal of these activities is not for you to get something down on the page by the time it's due... The main goal is to learn, understand, and practice, and to get something of your own down on the page by the time it's due!

Pencil is required; do not use ink. Return all reference books to their shelved-locations. Work independently. Do not impose upon the library staff to answer or even interpret the assignment. Instead, check with me during office hours with any questions, or if necessary, make an appointment. Assignments are due at the beginning of class on the date indicated on your schedule. They will be returned promptly with a letter grade. These activities should not be regarded as "work sheets"; taken together, they constitute a partial handbook for the course. Be sure you understand everything covered in written activities and in class; if in doubt, ask. There will be exam questions related to these assignments.   When referring to libraries, periodical titles, etc., do not abbreviate.
When referring to SUBJECT HEADINGS, include the complete subject heading, with all the commas, dashes, etc. exactly as they are worded and used. Do not skip any questions; if you're unable to find the information, describe how you attempted to cope. The answers will be available in an annotated key during office hours.

Your Name _____
Assignment 1: Catalogs and Related Tools
(Mostly Books). Due: In class on date
on your schedule.

Required reading: "Library Basics".
First, read the Introduction to Assignments 1-7. You should be able to do
questions 1-4 based on class discussion and handouts without going to the
library or consulting anyone. Test yourself.
----

1. Circle the complete call number on the catalog card below.
    Copy its classification here: _____
    For what word does the letter ___M___ in the call number stand,
    specifically?_____ What does ___HD___ in the
    call number communicate?_____
    From the cataloging information, would you judge that the book contains
    a bibliography or some form of bibliographic support?_____ Why?____
    _____ Is this card an author entry, or a subject
    entry, or a title entry? (Consider the first line information)_____
    Examine the book's "imprint", and write here the name of the publisher:
    _____ How can you tell from the cataloging
    information that the book is part of a series?_____
    _____
    What is the title of that series?"_____
    _____"
    Under what letter of the alphabet will the title card for this book
    file?_____ Under what subject heading(s) would this book be found?
    Be specific; use the exact wording(s):

    _____

    _____

    _____

    In addition to subject access, there are "added entries" (not subject-
    headings) which would appear in a catalog for this book. These are
    the Roman-numeraled clues in the tracings. Be specific; use exact words
    for the first (I) one:_____
    A total of how many entries for this book would file in a library
    catalog?____
    Adjust the card right here so that it becomes the first (1.) subject card referred to in the subject-tracings.

HD5365.	**McCord, Norman.**
A6M32	Strikes / Norman McCord. — New York : St. Martin's Press,
1980	1980.

    136 p. ; 23 cm. — (Comparative studies in social and economic history ; 2)

    Bibliography: p. [129]-134.
    Includes index.
    ISBN 0-312-76640-8 : $20.00

    1. Strikes and lockouts—Great Britain—History.   2. Strikes and lockouts—
    United States—History.   I. Title.   II. Series.

    HD5365.A6M32   1980   331.89'29—dc19   80-52362
                                                      MARC

    Library of Congress

2. What type of <u>main entry</u> has been assigned to this book's cataloging? (Consult the <u>card below</u>) _____

What type of catalog card is it? _____

PRISONERS--ENGLAND

HV9647
C54
1978

Church of England. Board for Social Responsibility.
   Prisons and prisoners in England today : a report of the Board for Social Responsibility. — London : CIO Publishing for the General Synod Board for Social Responsibility, 1978.

   vii, 73 p. ; 22 cm.   GB78-08060

   Bibliography: p. 73.
   ISBN 0-7151-6552-6 : £1.50

   1. Prisons—England. 2. Prisoners—England. 3. Imprisonment—England.
   I. Title.

   HV9647.C54   1978   365'.941   78-323979
                                                                 MARC

   Library of Congress   79

A total of how many entries for this book would be filed in a library catalog? _____
For what does the C in the call # stand, specifically? _____

3. What type of main entry has been assigned to this book's cataloging (not the type of card or entry)? _____

When was the book published? _____

According to the first subject heading, what is it about? _____

According to this information, the book is in the collection of which library? _____

QP801.
A3M43
BIOL

Wright, John William
Metabolic effects of alcohol / Vincent Marks, John Wright, guest editors. — London ; Philadelphia : W. B. Saunders Co., 1978.

   vii, 466 p. : ill. ; 24 cm. — (Clinics in endocrinology and metabolism ; v. 7, no. 2)   GB•••

   Includes bibliographies and index.

   1. Alcohol —Physiological effect. 2. Alcohol Metabolism. 3. Alcoholism.
   I. Marks, Vincent. II. Wright, John William. III. Series.

   QP801.A3M43   612'.39   79-308053
                                                                 MARC

   Library of Congress   79

Now adjust the card so that it becomes the card which could be filed in that library's shelf list for this book. Remember: The shelf list card for any book looks the same as its main entry (or author) card.

4. In the space provided on the following page, "interfile" all of the SUBJECT CARDS alphabetically. Copy the complete subject-heading in each case, but put all of the subject entries for the three books appearing in questions 1, 2 and 3 in the right sequence. Suggestion: Get into the habit now of recording subject headings in ALL CAPS.

4. contd.

   1st_____
   2nd_____
   3rd_____
   etc._____
       _____
       _____
       _____
       _____
       _____

5. Go to the Undergraduate Library. Using the regular card catalog,
    answer the following questions about:

    "The Woman Within, 1st ed." by Ellen Glasgow, published in
    1954 by Harcourt.

    Tray #(s) for main entry (author) cards for books by this author_____

    Tray #(s) for subject cards for books about this author _____

    According to the Library of Congress Classification for this book,
    with what nation is this author's writing associated?_____

Your Name _____
Assignment 1: Catalogs and Related Tools
(Mostly Books). Due: In class on date
on your schedule.

Required reading: "Library Basics".
First, read the Introduction to Assignments 1-7. You should be able to do
questions 1-4 based on class discussion and handouts without going to the
library or consulting anyone. Test yourself.
----

1. Circle the complete call number on the catalog card below.
    Copy its classification here: HD5365.A6 _____
    For what word does the letter __M__ in the call number stand,
    specifically? _McCord_____ What does __HD__ in the
    call number communicate? Economic history_____
    From the cataloging information, would you judge that the book contains
    a bibliography or some form of bibliographic support? Yes Why? Follow-
    ing the collation line page#s Is this card an author entry, or a subject
    entry, or a title entry? (Consider the first line information) author
    Examine the book's "imprint", and write here the name of the publisher:
    St. Martin's Press _____ How can you tell from the cataloging
    information that the book is part of a series? "Comparative studies in ...
    ; 2" in parentheses on the collation line; also the II in tracings
    What is the title of that series?"Comparative Studies in Social and
    Economic History
    Under what letter of the alphabet will the title card for this book
    file? _S___ Under what subject heading(s) would this book be found?
    Be specific; use the exact wording(s):
    STRIKES AND LOCKOUTS-- GREAT BRITAIN-- HISTORY / STRIKES AND LOCKOUTS--

    UNITED STATES-- HISTORY.

    In addition to subject access, there are "added entries" (not subject-
    headings) which would appear in a catalog for this book. These are
    the Roman-numeraled clues in the tracings. Be specific; use exact words
    for the first (I) one: _Strikes_____
    A total of how many entries for this book would file in a library
    catalog? 5
    Adjust the card
    right here so
    that it becomes
    the first (1.)
    subject card
    referred to in
    the subject-
    tracings.

STRIKES AND LOCKOUTS -GREAT
BRITAIN— HISTORY

HD5365.
A6M32
1980

McCord, Norman.
    Strikes / Norman McCord. — New York : St. Martin's Press,
1980.

    136 p. ; 23 cm. — (Comparative studies in social and economic history ; 2)

    Bibliography: p. [129]-134.
    Includes index.
    ISBN 0-312-76640-8 : $20.00

    1. Strikes and lockouts—Great Britain—History. 2. Strikes and lockouts—
United States—History.   I. Title. II. Series.

HD5365.A6M32 1980   331.89'29—dc19   80-52362
                                                 MARC

Library of Congress

2. What type of <u>main entry</u> has been assigned to this book's cataloging? (Consult the <u>card below</u>) <u>Corporate   main entry</u>

<u>What type of catalog card is it? SUBJECT</u>

```
          PRISONERS--ENGLAND

HV9647   Church of England.  Board for Social Responsibility.
C54         Prisons and prisoners in England today : a report of the Board
1978      for Social Responsibility. — London : CIO Publishing for the
          General Synod Board for Social Responsibility, 1978.
              vii, 73 p. ; 22 cm.                          GB78-08060
              Bibliography: p. 73.
              ISBN 0-7151-6552-6 : £1.50



          1. Prisons—England.  2. Prisoners—England.  3. Imprisonment—England.
       I. Title.
          HV9647.C54   1978          365'.941           78-323979
                                                            MARC

          Library of Congress        79
```

A total of how many entries for this book would be filed in a library catalog? <u>5</u>
For what does the <u>C</u> in the call # stand, specifically?

<u>Church</u>

3. What type of main entry has been assigned to this book's cataloging (not the type of card or entry)?   <u>Title main entry</u>

When was the book published? <u>1978</u>

According to the first subject heading, what is it about? <u>physiological effect of alcohol</u>

According to this information, the book is in the collection of which library? <u>Biology Library</u>

```
QP801.   ~~Wright, John William~~
A3M43    Metabolic effects of alcohol / Vincent Marks, John Wright, guest
BIOL       editors. — London ; Philadelphia : W. B. Saunders Co., 1978.
              vii, 466 p. : ill. ; 24 cm. — (Clinics in endocrinology and metabolism ; v. 7,
           no. 2)                                                    GB•••
              Includes bibliographies and index.



           1. Alcohol —Physiological effect.  2. Alcohol  Metabolism.  3. Alcoholism.
        I. Marks, Vincent.  II. Wright, John William.  III. Series.
           QP801.A3M43               612'.39             79-308053
                                                             MARC

           Library of Congress        79
```

Now adjust the card so that it becomes the card which could be filed in that library's shelf list for this book. Remember: The shelf list card for any book looks the same as its main entry (or author) card.

4. In the space provided on the following page, "interfile" all of the SUBJECT CARDS alphabetically. Copy the complete subject-heading in each case, but put all of the subject entries for the three books appearing in questions 1, 2 and 3 in the right sequence. Suggestion: Get into the habit now of recording subject headings in ALL CAPS.

4. contd.

1st ALCOHOL-- METABOLISM

2nd ALCOHOL-- PHYSIOLOGICAL EFFECT

3rd ALCOHOLISM

etc. 4 IMPRISONMENT-- ENGLAND

   5 PRISONERS-- ENGLAND

   6 PRISONS-- ENGLAND

   7 STRIKES AND LOCKOUTS-- GREAT BRITAIN-- HISTORY

   8 STRIKES AND LOCKOUTS-- UNITED STATES-- HISTORY

5. Go to the Undergraduate Library. Using the regular card catalog, answer the following questions about:

"The Woman Within, 1st ed." by Ellen Glasgow, published in 1954 by Harcourt.

Tray #(s) for main entry (author) cards for books by this author _____

Tray #(s) for subject cards for books about this author _____

According to the Library of Congress Classification for this book, with what nation is this author's writing associated?   U.S.A.

The United States. "PS" at the beginning of the classification (which is at the beginning of the call number) refers to the literature of this nation. See page 9 of the Library Basics handout.

Required Reading: "Library Basics" and "Using A Thesaurus".

1. SUBJECT ACCESS AND SUBJECT FILES:
    ∗ Use main entry cards (and entries) and title cards (and entries)
      mainly to know more about a particular book, a specific author-title
      combination, to "identify."
    ∗ Use subject-headings, subject cards and subject files mainly to know
      about everything a library has on a particular subject. To "inventory"
      something you are interested in, you take the specific subject-
      approach.
    ∗ Never jump into a subject catalog or subject file. Always first
      consult the U.S. Library of Congress Subject Headings (LCSH) lo-
      cated near the catalog. Notice the LCSH "scope notes", which help
      you understand what is and is not included in a subject heading's
      coverage.

Does the LCSH provide Library of Congress classifications for every subject
heading?_____ How does the LCSH indicate "SEE ALSO's"?_____

You need information on the following topic. According to the LCSH, how
is the subject heading worded? In what tray(s) of the library catalog
are there cards for that subject heading?

| For... | See... | In . . . |
Topic (not subject-heading)	LC Subject Heading Wording (Get this from the LCSH)	Tray Number(s)
Anthracosis	_____	_____
Chicanos	_____	_____
Kaapor Indians	_____	_____
Sex determinant antigen	_____	_____

The LCSH and the library catalogs are both arranged alphabetically. But
keep in mind the exception occurs in the sub-division breakdown by period
(chronologically) for HISTORY. For example, United States dash HISTORY
dash various periods of time. The library catalog tray # for the history
of ___Mexico during the Conquest_____ is _____.
If you didn't already know the dates for this historical subject, you
could get them from the LCSH itself, in volume #____ on page #_____.

2. On catalog cards, the Arabic-numbered tracings represent the subject-
    headings assigned to a book-- what the book is about. But the subject
    headings, by means of standard SUBDIVISIONS, are very functional in
    additional ways. They can communicate the publication's format, or
    form, for example. Learn to utilize these possibilities in your
    work. Does the subject card on the next page indicate that this book
    is about: Yes or No:
-- the subject of   George Sand?   _____
-- the subject of bibliography?   _____

```
         SAND, GEORGE, PSEUD. OF MME. DUDEVANT, 1804-
         1876-- BIBLIOGRAPHY
PQ2412  Sand, George, pseud. of Mme. Dudevant, 1804-1876.
A2E5        My life / by George Sand ; translated from the French and
1979     adapted by Dan Hofstadter. — 1st ed. — New York : Harper &
         Row, c1979.

         viii, 246 p. ; 25 cm.

         Translation of Histoire de ma vie.
         Includes index.
         ISBN 0-06-013767-3 : $12.95


         1. Sand, George, pseud. of Mme. Dudevant, 1804-1876—Bibliography.  2.
         Novelists, French—19th century—Biography.   I. Hofstadter, Dan.  II. Title.
         PQ2412.A2E5  1979          843'.7                     77-3770
                                    [B]                        MARC

         Library of Congress              78
```

3. Here's a topic much like one you might have to write a term paper on.
    You would need to find publications as well as to "perfect" the topic
    and a title. Imagine you are starting now on a library literature
    search while at the same time developing or focusing the topic itself.
    One of the first steps is to inventory the library holdings by means
    of the subject approach.   The topic is:

    For a public health, sociology or other course, you need information
    about care of people with chronic diseases in the United States,
    including information about the Hospice Movement.

Consult the LCSH to find subject headings on this topic. List at least
8 possible subject headings which you predict may lead to books (or parts
of books) having any potential relevance. Remember the possibilites for
geographical and other types of subdivisions discussed in class. Avoid comprehensive "big" subject headings; favor specific ones. Check out all the
SEE ALSO's. The "sa" is not repeated; it applies to all terms listed --
indented -- under the first such heading. For example, there are 3 separate
and distinct subject headings listed to "see also" related to TEXTILE DE-
SIGN. RESIST-DYED TEXTILES is the first; TEXTILE PAINTING is the third.
Subdivisons are the part after the dash.   Start your search with the words
in your topic.

Established SUBJECT HEADINGS	LCSH Vol.#	LCSH Page #	LC Classification, If LCSH Provides One

4. Which one of the subject headings you've just listed now appears to
   be the best, the closest?_____
Now check the library catalog under that subject heading. Does the catalog
   have it in exactly the same wording as the LCSH?_____ If may well
   have it in a variation by means of time periods, forms, and other useful
   subdivisions which can often lead to even more specific information!
   Tray #_____.   If, however, this subject heading is NOT at all
   represented in the catalog, then you might tentatively conclude it's
   not such a great subject heading for this term paper topic after all.
   And if there are trays and trays of cards with this subject heading,
   it would appear to be too broad, not specific enough to help researching.
List one publication assigned this subject heading:
   Complete main entry_____
   Complete title "_____
   _____".
   Call #_____ Library_____
If "no", try each of your other 7 subject headings.

Why is it often wise to begin a literature search by taking the "subject
approach" in the library's catalog? Because there you'll probably be able to
   1. Develop further usable subject headings and to locate other clues
      by means of the tracings and all the other information on the card
      (or other type of display).
   2. Get an idea of HOW MUCH information (how many books) is available
      on campus in "your library" AND where it is. And to a certain ex-
      tent, you can also get a view of the relative number of books,
      periodicals, bibliographies, proceedings, "reference books," etc.
      available to you in the library.
   3. Identify the relevant class(es) too. (Remember: Classification is
      different from subject heading.)
   4. Latch onto other good subject headings via the subject tracings and
      the subject headings in the vicinity of "your" card or other access
      point.
   5. Identify some authorities and "landmarks' on your subject.
   6. Identify so-called GUIDES-to-the-LITERATURE of your subject. More
      on this later in pathfinder assignment 6; for now, a guide-to-the-
      literature is like, but better than, a bibliography!

5. The KEYWORD concept is very important for all types of library research.
   Keywords are not the same as subject headings. Some library catalogs
   and reference books today have KEYWORD INDEXES. For example, a book
   titled "Sign Language for the Deaf" would be listed alphabetically 3
   times, under DEAF, under LANGUAGE, and under SIGN. This makes it important for an author to title her/his book fully and specifically!

   Suppose you were using a keyword file based on one keyword derived
   from the title of the book which appeared at the top of page 2.
   Which one word would you select as most specific if you were the
   cataloger?_____

Course, Date
Instructor   KEY
  Page 1 (of 3)

Your Name _____
Assignment 2: Catalogs and Related Tools,
contd. Due: In class on date on your
        schedule.

Required Reading: "Library Basics" and "Using A Thesaurus".
1. SUBJECT ACCESS AND SUBJECT FILES:
    * Use main entry cards (and entries) and title cards (and entries)
      mainly to know more about a particular book, a specific author-title
      combination, to "identify."
    * Use subject-headings, subject cards and subject files mainly to know
      about everything a library has on a particular subject. To "inventory"
      something you are interested in, you take the specific subject-
      approach.
    * Never jump into a subject catalog or subject file. Always first
      consult the U.S. Library of Congress Subject Headings (LCSH) lo-
      cated near the catalog. Notice the LCSH "scope notes", which help
      you understand what is and is not included in a subject heading's
      coverage.

Does the LCSH provide Library of Congress classifications for every subject
heading? No How does the LCSH indicate "SEE ALSO's"? By use of "sa" preceding the first term to See Also.
You need information on the following topic. According to the LCSH, how
is the subject heading worded? In what tray(s) of the library catalog
are there cards for that subject heading?

For...	See...	In . . .
Topic (not subject-heading)	LC Subject Heading Wording (Get this from the LCSH)	Tray Number(s)
Anthracosis	LUNGS-- DUST DISEASES	_____
Chicanos	MEXICAN AMERICANS	_____
Kaapor Indians	URUBU INDIANS	_____
Sex determinant antigen	H-Y ANTIGEN	_____

The LCSH and the library catalogs are both arranged alphabetically. But
keep in mind the exception occurs in the sub-division breakdown by period
(chronologically) for HISTORY. For example, United States dash HISTORY
dash various periods of time. The library catalog tray # for the history
of __Mexico during the Conquest_____ is _____.
If you didn't already know the dates for this historical subject, you
could get them from the LCSH itself, in volume # 2 on page # 1472 .
(9th edition)
2. On catalog cards, the Arabic-numbered tracings represent the subject-
    headings assigned to a book-- what the book is about. But the subject
    headings, by means of standard SUBDIVISIONS, are very functional in
    additional ways. They can communicate the publication's format, or
    form, for example. Learn to utilize these possibilities in your
    work. Does the subject card on the next page indicate that this book
    is about: Yes or No:
-- the subject of   George Sand?   Yes
-- the subject of bibliography?   No

SAND, GEORGE, PSEUD. OF MME. DUDEVANT, 1804-
1876-- BIBLIOGRAPHY

PQ2412   Sand, George, pseud. of Mme. Dudevant, 1804-1876.
A2E5   My life / by George Sand ; translated from the French and
1979   adapted by Dan Hofstadter. — 1st ed. — New York : Harper &
         Row, c1979.

         viii, 246 p. ; 25 cm.

         Translation of Histoire de ma vie.
         Includes index.
         ISBN 0-06-013767-3 : $12.95

         1. Sand, George, pseud. of Mme. Dudevant, 1804-1876—Bibliography. 2.
         Novelists, French—19th century—Biography.   I. Hofstadter, Dan.   II. Title.

         PQ2412.A2E5   1979   843'.7   77-3770
                                       [B]   MARC

         Library of Congress   78

3.   Here's a topic much like one you might have to write a term paper on.
     You would need to find publications as well as to "perfect" the topic
     and a title. Imagine you are starting now on a library literature
     search while at the same time developing or focusing the topic itself.
     One of the first steps is to inventory the library holdings by means
     of the subject approach.   The topic is:

         For a public health, sociology or other course, you need information
         about care of people with chronic diseases in the United States,
         including information about the Hospice Movement.

Consult the LCSH to find subject headings on this topic. List at least
8 possible subject headings which you predict may lead to books (or parts
of books) having any potential relevance. Remember the possibilites for
geographical and other types of subdivisions discussed in class. Avoid comprehensive "big" subject headings; favor specific ones. Check out all the
SEE ALSO's. The "sa" is not repeated; it applies to all terms listed --
indented -- under the first such heading. For example, there are 3 separate
and distinct subject headings listed to "see also" related to TEXTILE DE-
SIGN. RESIST-DYED TEXTILES is the first; TEXTILE PAINTING is the third.
Subdivisons are the part after the dash.   Start your search with the words
in your topic.

Established SUBJECT HEADINGS	LCSH Vol.#	LCSH Page #	LC Classification, If LCSH Provides One
TERMINAL CARE FACILITIES	2	2326	-
CHRONICALLY ILL-- CARE AND TREATMENT	1	430	-
CHRONICALLY ILL-- INSTITUTIONAL CARE	1	430	-
RIGHT TO DIE	2		
DEATH--PSYCHOLOGICAL ASPECTS	1	622	BF789.D4
CHRONICALLY ILL CHILDREN-- HOME CARE	1	334	-
TERMINALLY ILL CHILDREN	2		
CHRONIC DISEASES	1	430	RA642.2-.5; RB156
CANCER PATIENTS	1	334	-
CHILDREN AND DEATH	1	403	-

4. Which one of the subject headings you've just listed now appears to
be the best, the closest?_____
Now check the library catalog under that subject heading. Does the catalog
    have it in exactly the same wording as the LCSH?_____ If may well
    have it in a variation by means of time periods, forms, and other useful
    subdivisions which can often lead to even more specific information!
    Tray #_____ .   If, however, this subject heading is NOT at all
    represented in the catalog, then you might tentatively conclude it's
    not such a great subject heading for this term paper topic after all.
    And if there are trays and trays of cards with this subject heading,
    it would appear to be too broad, not specific enough to help researching.
List one publication assigned this subject heading:
    Complete main entry_____
    Complete title "_____

_____ " .
    Call #_____ Library_____
If "no", try each of your other 7 subject headings.

Why is it often wise to begin a literature search by taking the "subject
approach" in the library's catalog? Because there you'll probably be able to
    1. Develop further usable subject headings and to locate other clues
       by means of the tracings and all the other information on the card
       (or other type of display).
    2. Get an idea of HOW MUCH information (how many books) is available
       on campus in "your library" AND where it is. And to a certain ex-
       tent, you can also get a view of the relative number of books,
       periodicals, bibliographies, proceedings, "reference books," etc.
       available to you in the library.
    3. Identify the relevant class(es) too. (Remember: Classification is
       different from subject heading.)
    4. Latch onto other good subject headings via the subject tracings and
       the subject headings in the vicinity of "your" card or other access
       point.
    5. Identify some authorities and "landmarks" on your subject.
    6. Identify so-called GUIDES-to-the-LITERATURE of your subject. More
       on this later in pathfinder assignment 6; for now, a guide-to-the-
       literature is like, but better than, a bibliography!

5. The KEYWORD concept is very important for all types of library research.
   Keywords are not the same as subject headings. Some library catalogs
   and reference books today have KEYWORD INDEXES. For example, a book
   titled "Sign Language for the Deaf" would be listed alphabetically 3
   times, under DEAF, under LANGUAGE, and under SIGN. This makes it important for an author to title her/his book fully and specifically!

   Suppose you were using a keyword file based on one keyword derived
   from the title of the book which appeared at the top of page 2.
   Which one word would you select as most specific if you were the
   cataloger?_____

FILING   Part 1

Assign the very brief introduction to filing basics (pages 5 and 6) provided in the "Library Basics" handout.

   Distribute the "Surnames Filing Rule--An Exception" pages 1 and 2. PURPOSE: To teach and provide guided-practice in class dealing with the so-called "Surnames" filing rule applicable in most large files such as found in college and university card catalogs. It is also referred to by some as the "exception" rule. Understanding of it is crucial to efficient use of an author-title catalog; this is the type of catalog which often functions as a union catalog for campus holdings. At the same time, it is a totally new concept for most undergraduates and some graduate students. Possible secondary functions of this instruction may include: introduction of compound surnames; reinforcement of the "see" cross reference; articles disregarded as first word in filing; and corporate main-entry, and distinction among types of main-entries generally.

   Mastery of this filing rule is facilitated by students being able to recognize and distinguish among various types of main entries, but they are typically acquiring this informational skill simultaneously. They should have visited the library and have awareness of where and what the catalogs are.

   Explain it to them on the basis of its looking straightforward enough but ... there are actually "two separate alphabets here." In this situation: first file all of the single surnames, then file all the rest--all the "leftover cards." Ask the class to "file these Green cards." Give them five minutes, and wander among them helping and noting who thrives and who is lost. Now distribute the display with the correct alphabetization, which is page 3 of this handout; re-iterate that all the single surnames are filed first, which results in the second alphabet consisting of title entries, compound-surnames, and corporate main entries. Conclude by reminding them of office hours and "the next time you're in the library, check this out in the [applicable] catalog ... try 'Brown' or 'King' trays."

   Incorporate in the next test; additional demonstrations are provided in Section III: Resources.

Single surnames such as Honda comma, Green comma, Sadat comma, are filed
together in one "alphabet", or series, followed immediately by another
"alphabet", or series consisting of a mixture of <u>titles</u>, <u>compound names</u>
(such as Jones-Smythe, Newton John, Delgado Espinosa, etc.), <u>corporate</u>
names (such as Sears Roebuck, Smith Construction Company, etc.), and
names of kings. To put it another way: single surnames are filed together
first, and then all the other types of cards.

This is an exception crucial to your understanding in order not to miss
out on anything. It applies to our catalog and to most such very-large
card catalogs.

Consider the first word(s) of the first line of each of the several types
of "cards" below - each could be interfiled in the Author-Title catalog.
They are listed below in a "straight" alphabetical order, which is NOT the
way you'd find them in a very large file such as the Author-Title catalog.
See if you can apply the rule described above: SINGLE SURNAMES PRECEDE ALL
OTHER ENTRIES BEGINNING WITH THE SAME WORD (Green).   Rearrange them.

        Green Light
Douglas, Lloyd Cassel
        Green Light

Green Laboratories, Brooklyn, New York
    Definitive Explosives Manual.

Green-Jones, Mary Jane
        How to Litigate Your Own Divorce.

Green, Graham, 1904-
   SEE
Greene, Graham. 1904-

Green, Douglas B.
        Country Roots.

Green, Douglas B.
        Country Music.

    Green Dolphin Country
Goudge, Elizabeth
        Green Dolphin Country

        The Green Thumb Cookbook
Moyers, Anne, ed.
        The Green Thumb Cookbook

Green, Stanley
        The world of musical comedy

        Green-Sky Triology
Snyder, Zilpha
        Green-Sky Triology

Green, Phyllis
        Mildred Murphy, How Does Your
Garden Grow?

The Green Olive Trade Association
        Seasonal Changes and Growth Rates.

        Green, Maury, jt. author
Franklin, Lynn
        Sawed-off justice.

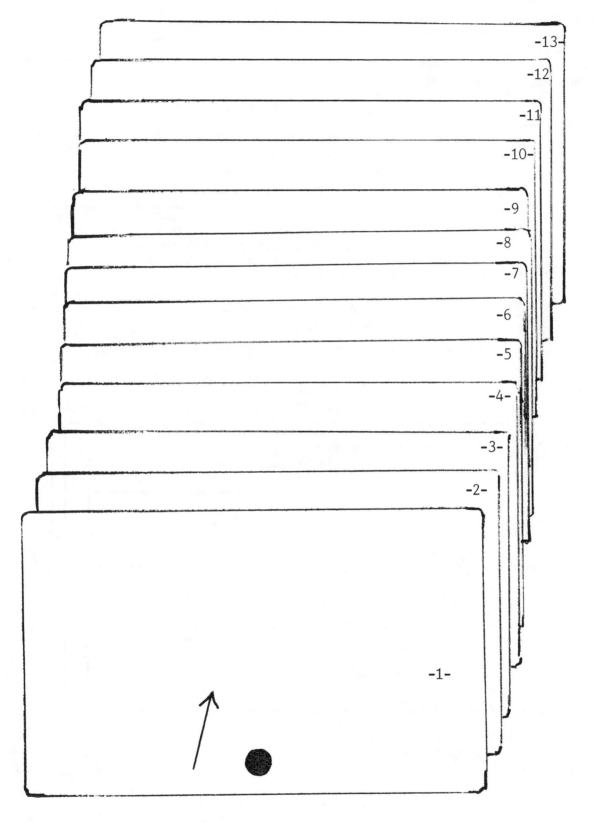

The Green Thumb Cookbook
Moyers, Anne, ed.
The Green Thumb Cookbook

Green-Sky Triology
Snyder, Zilpha
Green-Sky Triology

The Green Olive Trade Association
Seasonal Changes and Growth Rates.

Green Light
Douglas, Lloyd Cassel
Green Light

Green Laboratories, Brooklyn, New York
Definitive Explosives Manual.

Green-Jones, Mary Jane
How to Litigate Your Own Divorce.

Green Dolphin Country
Goudge, Elizabeth
Green Dolphin Country

Green, Stanley
The world of musical comedy.

Green, Phyllis
Mildred Murphy, How Does Your
Garden Grow?

Green, Maury, jt. author
Franklin, Lynn
Sawed-off justice.

Green, Graham, 1904-
SEE
Greene, Graham, 1904-

Green, Douglas B.
Country Roots.

Green, Douglas B.
Country Music.

To understand is to recognize that the 7th card begins a "second Green series", and that, if this exception did NOT apply, the 7th card would file first!

FILING   Part 2

Purpose: To teach and provide guided-practice in class dealing with the major
difference between filing in a dictionary catalog and a divided file: the problem
of "one alphabet" filing's provision for subject cards or entries, as well as for
the other types.   Undergraduates generally see this as "What happens when the
author is the subject?"   Possible secondary functions include: clarification of the
difference between biography and autobiography; how a book in a university library can be "biographical but not a biography book"; reinforcement of the main
entry concept; recognition of the structure of information requiring consideration
whether in conventional card or online files.

Begin by assigning again the very brief introduction to filing basics (pages
5 and 6) provided in the "Library Basics" handout.   Previous in-library work
should have provided clear understanding of which file is a dictionary catalog
(possibly the undergraduate library) and which a divided, as well as the author-
title and subject portions within the divided catalog.   Distribute the "Filing in
Dictionary and Divided Files" one-page handout: Lady Sings the Blues.   Start
by working it out at the board, talking it along with them.   Stress their reading
the instructions, however brief, carefully.   Try to get them to recognize and to
point out that all three cards start off basically the same.   Quickly make three
identical, main entry cards.   Then get to the matter at hand:

What goes on the first lines ... what are these three points of access ...
what words ... where do you get this information from?   Point out the mnemonic
A (for author) coming alphabetically before S (for subject).   Downplay the finer
points of imprint, pagination, etc.   If your library locates the first line of the
call number on the same line as the main entry, this should be incorporated, however, as part of this process.   It is not necessary to distribute copies of The
Answer; instead, it goes on the board.   Additional examples are provided in
III: Resources.   This concept can be used as a test question.

Depending on the time available, and for an upper division class, it would
be well to continue by distributing Cottage Life in a Hertfordshire Village, with
the expectation that everyone should now be able to cope with it in a few minutes.

There are 5 access points in a one-alphabet DICTIONARY catalog (such as
that in the   Library) for this book. Record the first
two lines for each of them, in order, here.

Grey, Edwin.
  Cottage life in a Hertfordshire village / [by] Edwin Grey. —
[1st ed. reprinted] ; with an introduction by F. M. L. Thompson.
— Harpenden : Harpenden and District Local History Society,
1977.

  253 p., [4] p. of plates : ill., ports. ; 19 cm.   GB78-05664

  Reprint of the 1935 ed. published by Fisher, Knight & Co., St. Albans.
  ISBN 0-9505941-0-5. : £3.50

  1. Harpenden, Eng.—Social life and customs. 2. Agricultural laborers—
England—Harpenden. 3. Grey, Edwin.   I. Title.

DA690.H3G7 1977   942.5'85   79-307651
                                                              MARC

Library of Congress   79

There are 5 access points in a one-alphabet DICTIONARY catalog (such as
that in the   Library) for this book. Record the first
two lines for each of them, in order, here.

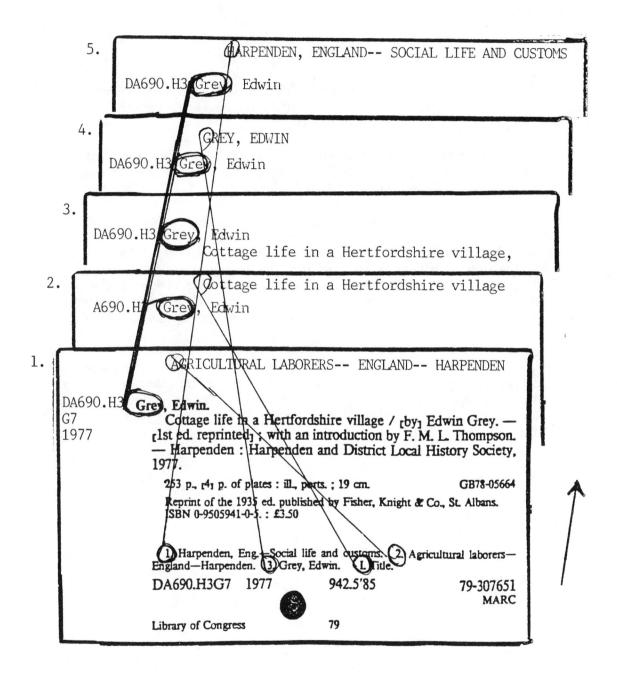

5.   HARPENDEN, ENGLAND-- SOCIAL LIFE AND CUSTOMS

DA690.H3 Grey, Edwin

4.   GREY, EDWIN

DA690.H3 Grey, Edwin

3.

DA690.H3 Grey, Edwin
              Cottage life in a Hertfordshire village,

2.   Cottage life in a Hertfordshire village

A690.H Grey, Edwin

1.

DA690.H3   Grey, Edwin.
G7   Cottage life in a Hertfordshire village / [by] Edwin Grey. —
1977   [1st ed. reprinted] ; with an introduction by F. M. L. Thompson.
                  — Harpenden : Harpenden and District Local History Society,
                  1977.

      253 p., [4] p. of plates : ill., ports. ; 19 cm.   GB78-05664

      Reprint of the 1935 ed. published by Fisher, Knight & Co., St. Albans.
      ISBN 0-9505941-0-5. : £3.50

      1. Harpenden, Eng.—Social life and customs. 2. Agricultural laborers—
      England—Harpenden. 3. Grey, Edwin. I. Title.

      DA690.H3G7   1977   942.5'85   79-307651
                                    MARC

      Library of Congress   79

FILING   Part 3

<u>Purpose</u>: To review or test several basic filing rules. Possible secondary func-
tions include: recognition and application of "See" cross reference; filing several
things with the same "first line" information.

Discuss any questions about filing and catalogs. Distribute "Filing Practice" three-page handout (instructions and two pages of numbered, blank cards).
In this demonstration, there are 16 "cards" (including a "See" cross reference
card) to be filed.

Go over it with them. Together circle the first letter of the first word to
be regarded before putting them on their own to file. Allow fifteen minutes for
this work, as well as fifteen to go over the results together. This is not a good
exercise for students to work on in small groups. Wander around while they fill
in the blank cards in order to help and to get an idea of who may be lagging.
A key should be available during office hours for reflection and discussion.

Ask a volunteer to start.... When s/he gets off the track, ask whoever
recognizes the mistake to carry on, and so forth. Then, after everyone clearly
has adjusted their work, answer questions and focus on the "hot spots." Although this requires more time and topical focus than the ideal test question, it
can be used for testing. Additional sets appear in <u>III: Resources</u>.

Cards for these books are filed, together with one cross-reference card, alphabetically, in a library catalog comparable to our   .
The 16 cards' first-line information has been randomly presented below.

Arrange the 16 "cards" by recording the first lines and, where relevant, the second lines on the blank cards. There are no subject-cards here.

Suggestion:
Go through the list below and circle the first letter of the first word you're "regarding" (filing by) before you begin.

----

(1)   "10 Brazilian Artists"   by   (2) the Ontario Art Institute

(3)   "Mrs. Balfame"   by   (4) Gertrude Atherton

(5)   "A Low Blood Sugar Gourmet

       Cookbook"   by   (6) Maureen McCabe

(7)   "Bay Area Ecology"   by   (8) Ivison Macadam

(9)   "Stride Toward Freedom"   by   (10) Martin Luther King

(11)   "King Edward In His True

       Colours"

(12)   is a SEE card from DeBeauvoir

       to Beauvoir

(13)   "Les Belles Images"   by (14) Simone de Beauvoir

(15)   "The Lower Depths"   by (16) Gertrude Atherton

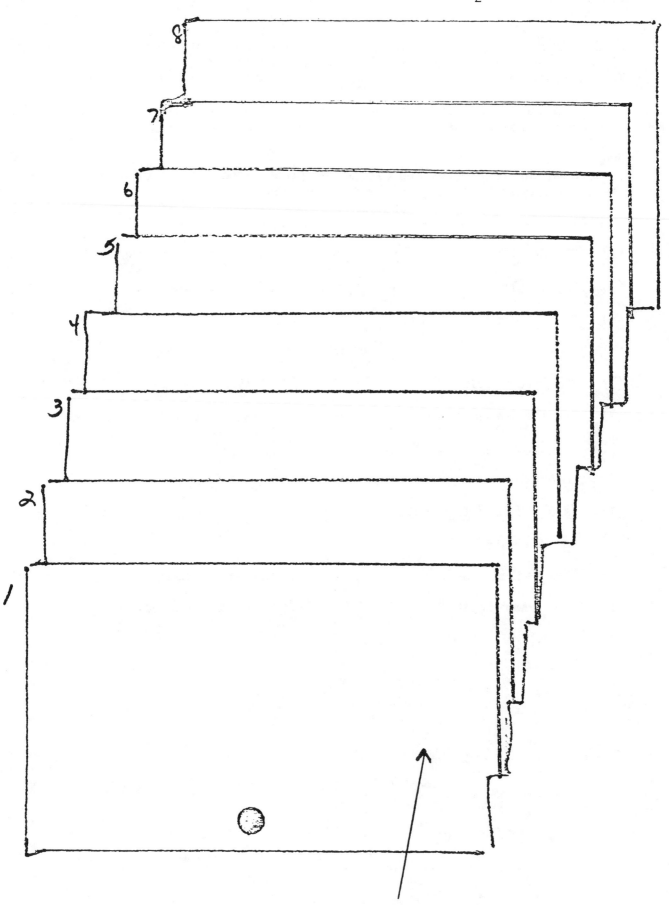

98

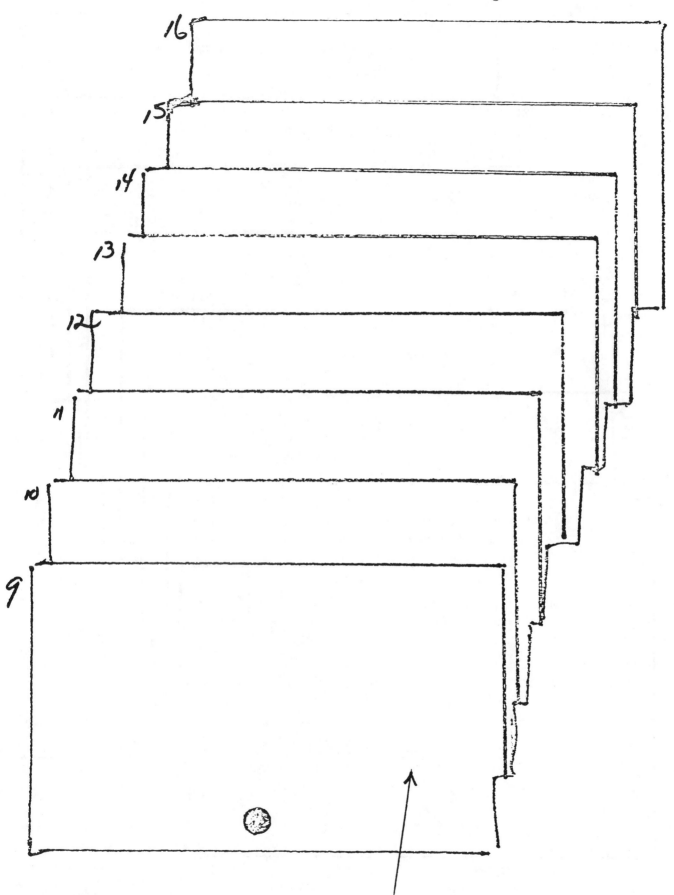

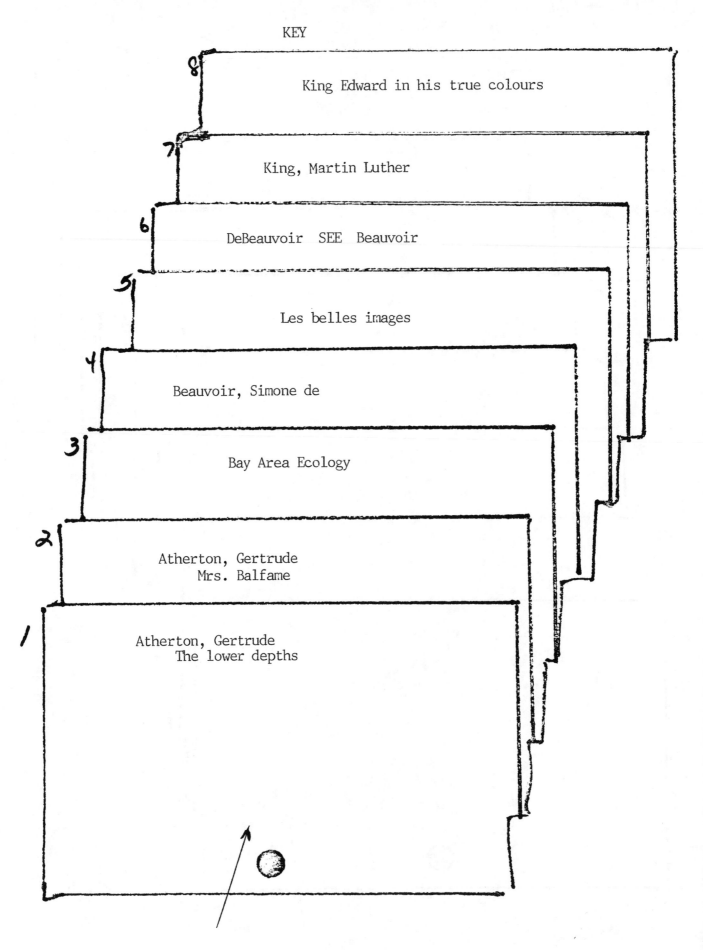

KEY

8 King Edward in his true colours

7 King, Martin Luther

6 DeBeauvoir SEE Beauvoir

5 Les belles images

4 Beauvoir, Simone de

3 Bay Area Ecology

2 Atherton, Gertrude
Mrs. Balfame

1 Atherton, Gertrude
The lower depths

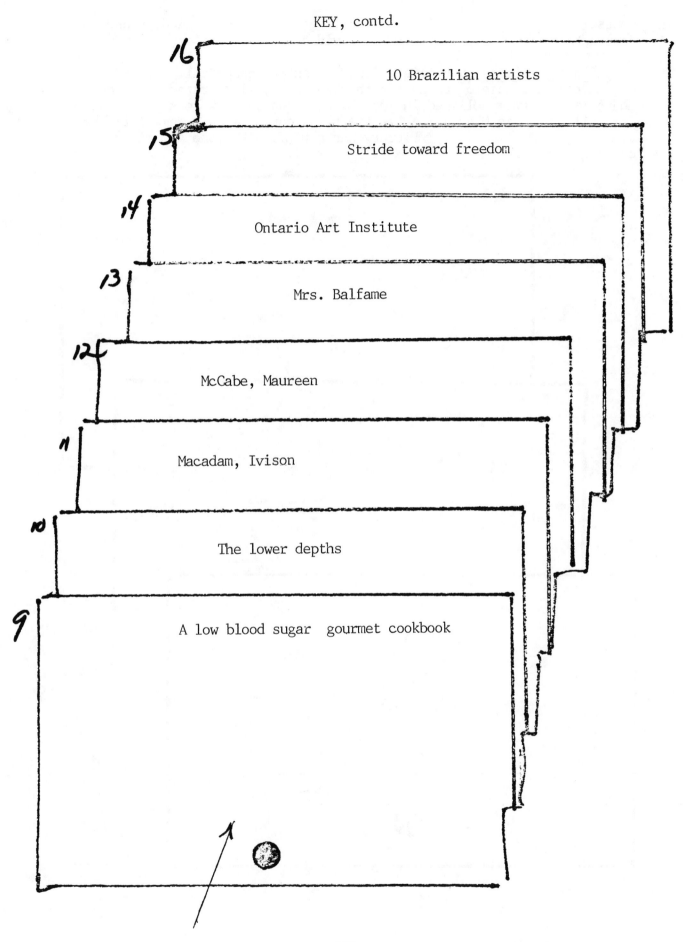

16

10 Brazilian artists

15

Stride toward freedom

,14

Ontario Art Institute

13

Mrs. Balfame

12

McCabe, Maureen

11

Macadam, Ivison

10

The lower depths

9

A low blood sugar gourmet cookbook

1

Lady Sings the Blues by Billie Holiday is autobiographical. How would
the Library's 3 catalog cards for this 236-page, illustrated book look
and file? It was published in 1956 by Doubleday, a New York publisher.
Its call number is ML420H58. Use the blank cards below. Remember: the
                        Library has a DICTIONARY (one alphabet)
catalog.

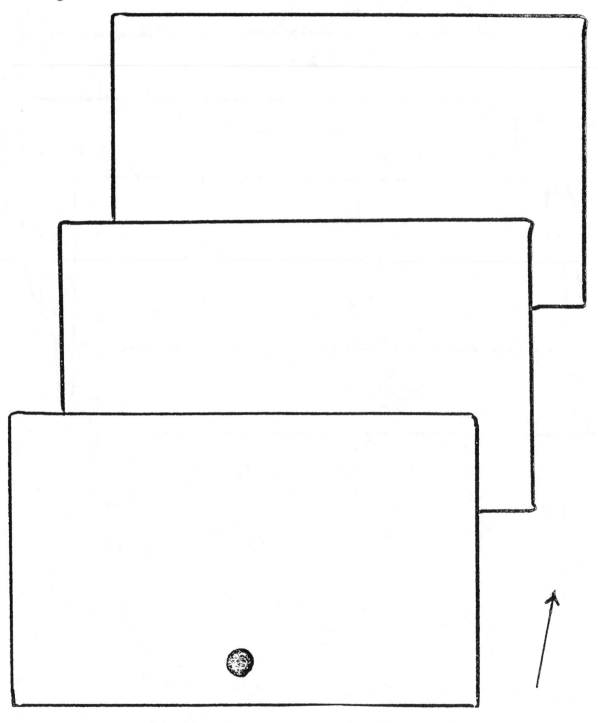

```
                    Lady sings the blues
        ML420 Holiday, Billie
        H58       Lady sings the blues.     New York, Doubleday,
             1956.
                    236p  il
```

```
                   HOLIDAY, BILLIE
        ML420  Holiday, Billie
        H58       Lady sings the blues.     New York, Doubleday,
             1956.
                    236p  il
```

```
        ML420  Holiday, Billie
        H58        Lady sings the blues.     New York, Doubleday,
             1956.
                    236p     il




        1. Holiday, Billie     I. Title
```

CLASSIFICATION

Instructor's CLASSIFICATION-Related Discussion (Classroom)

Ask the class to refer to pages 7-9 of the Library Basics handout. Discuss the points made on page 7. Some highlights related to the summary include:

A.   General Works.
      These are not necessarily "reference books," but because they are
      general, in a sense, about everything, they are often found in the
      reference collection rather than circulating books to be read from
      cover to cover and therefore shelved in the library stacks. An AE
      general encyclopedia might be the Encyclopaedia Britannica; AI,
      Readers' Guide indexes general, popular magazines.

HQ.   Provide an opportunity to demonstrate the point about organization
      of information depending on perceptions and changing perceptions:
      HQ is frequently considered "the place" for "Family, marriage, and
      women."

M.   Music (and T Technology)
      Provide examples of "mnemonic."

P.   Language & Literature
      Discuss that P is a large class encompassing two sometimes-
      separate things, e.g., PE = English language, PR = English liter-
      ature. Provide examples, e.g. dictionary, Jane Austen. They may
      be acquainted with libraries wherein fiction (which they may con-
      sider "literature") is segregated, alphabetically arranged by
      novelists' surnames. Point out that from the scholar's point of view,
      it is often most useful to have publications by and related to a
      writer such as Virginia Woolf together: novels, nonfiction, bio-
      graphical material, bibliographies, commentary, etc.

R.   Medicine
      Ask, "Where would psychiatry and psychoanalysis be classified in
      the LC Classification?"

Move into questions. "According to just this brief information from the LC Classification, where would the following publications be classified ... in which classes?"

The Encyclopedia of PHILOSOPHY.   [B]
The Oxford Companion to AMERICAN LITERATURE.   [PS]
The Encyclopedia of PHYSICS.   [QC]
Pamphlet on the Four Basic Dialects of Pig Latin, by William Cheney.
      Yes this is a real book.   [PM]

Festivals of the JEWISH Years; A Modern Interpretation.	[BM]
Applied Linear ALGEBRA.	[QA]
The Odd Couple, by Neil Simon. Play it by ear; if there is little response, add "...Simon, the American playwright."	[PS]
Understanding The OLD TESTAMENT.	[BS]
Selected Poems, by Gwendolyn Brooks. [...the American poet.]	[PS]
Hysteria; The History of a DISEASE.	[R]
Webster's New International Dictionary [of WORDS].	[PE]
The Sonnets of William Shakespeare.	[PR]
The Background to Shakespeare's Sonnets.	[PR]
The Faulkner Reader, an anthology by William Faulkner.	[PS]
Faulkner's Women; Characterization and Meaning, by Sally Page.	[PS]
American Sign Language.	[PM]
The New International Encyclopedia of the Social Sciences.	[H]

If your campus has several libraries which are subject-collections, some form of the following is useful. Ask them to predict "right now at the beginning of the term, which of the LC classes will mostly constitute the collections of these campus libraries?"

Anthropology Library	G, GN's
Chemistry Library	QD
Earth Sciences Library	QE
Education-Psychology Library	L and BF
Engineering Library	TA
Environmental Design Library	NA
Library School Library	L and Z
Music Library	M
Physics Library	QC
Social Science Library	H's

Wind up with a reminder that although a book will be classified in a library collection in one class, it may contain information which is useful for several purposes, from several perspectives. For example, Women in Judaism (by Leonard Swidler, classified in BM) from religion and women studies perspectives. "How would you be able to know about all of this seemingly buried information?" By utilizing subject-headings! (In this case WOMEN IN JUDAISM.) Other examples can be generated by using interdisciplinary studies as a point of departure.

USING A THESAURUS

Instructor's <u>LCSH</u> Script

Organization of information and documents in libraries will likely continue for some time to involve use of thesauri. Thesauri may concern libraries and their patrons because they relate to subject-matter fields and disciplines and to online computer-assisted retrieval of information stored in specialized data bases, e.g. <u>The ERIC Thesaurus of Descriptors</u>. Access to information contained in the collections of most American college and university libraries is based on the United States <u>Library of Congress' Subject Headings</u> (hereafter "LCSH"). The 9th edition was published in 1980 and covered through 1978; the 10th edition was published in 1986. Between editions interim supplements are issued, and the whole is available in cumulated microform. The classroom-teaching LCSH handout which follows is built on the 10th edition. If your library does not have the 10th edition, most of the subject headings generated by the handout model can also be established by reference to the 9th edition. <u>Section III: Resources</u> provides exercises related to both editions.

The following material relates to the LCSH volumes and provides a basis for two classroom sessions of lecture-practice based on a handout which could stand alone or supplement pages in a locally-produced handbook. If only a handbook is used, it should include pages of the LCSH, which is in the public domain, selected to provide examples of as many as possible of the contingencies discussed in this material. Neither a handbook nor library worksheet, however, can provide the essential demonstration of the process of systematically proceeding through a branching, topic-related search, for which at least five steps are recommended.

The "We're not training librarians" snappy retort is a cop-out. There continue to be academic libraries whose users are not expected to understand this concept and use of the LCSH because they have access to a catalog with some cross references filed in it. Such a contention sometimes emanates from small colleges relying on card catalogs. It involves several assumptions including that all filing, including cross references, are up-to-date. It usually relates to libraries which do not make the LCSH available to their patrons.

The main objectives of this work are introduction of the thesaurus concept, and practice of efficient use of the LCSH in order to:

- locate functional subject headings related to a complex topic

- acquire skills in focusing or broadening a research topic, as well as to understand the application of these concepts and of information to such formats as card catalogs, fiche files, and online data bases.

Related to these main objectives are:

- occasional use of a thesaurus to identify relevant parts of the Library of Congress Classification

- need for several subject headings to describe each book

- need for a list of several subject headings for a literature search to support a quality term paper

- potential of subject tracings on (cards and fiche) file entries sometimes to generate additional functional subject headings and thus lead to books and other types of publications on the same subject in the library's collections.

Preparation

This instruction should take place early in the course but after the subject approach, cards/entries and catalog as well as cross references have been pointed out and experienced. Before teaching these classes the first time, check the library's catalog for local subject headings. Also recognize that this material should be adjusted to whether the main local bibliographic records include or consist of a divided or dictionary catalog, card or other types of catalogs, e.g. fiche files and online acronym-titled catalogs, etc.

At the conclusion of the previous class meeting, encourage or require students to examine the LCSH set in the library before the next (this) class meeting.

"Try to use it. Spend five minutes making a list of all the subject headings you can find which you could take to our catalog to locate books for a paper about domestic violence in the United States today. Don't consult the card catalog. Bring your list to class next time."

The assignment need not be listed on the schedule you distribute at the beginning of the course. Include reference to the handbook, if any. Or, omit this if there does not appear to be need. Someone may ask whether you're going to collect them, and how many subject headings is a list. If the previous class meets in the library, and one or two students finish their work a few minutes before the end of the class time, take this opportunity to direct them to the LCSH, especially in libraries where there is only one set available to the public. (And it is unwise to encourage rushing through in-library individual work with the expectation of departing early!) The LCSH handout can be duplicated on paper colored to correspond with a local color code associated with SUBJECTS.

Part I

On The Board: Related Terminology

to broaden	See Also cross reference type *
classification	subject card/subject entry
cross references *	sub-subject heading
descriptor	subdivision
dictionary catalog *	term

divided catalog *	thesaurus
to focus	tracings *
See cross reference type *	working title

Students should come to this activity with some knowledge of *'d terms. A glossary of terms related to the course should be part of a local handbook, but it is recommended that these related terms be listed on the board at the start of this class. Some will already have been encountered in the course, but they are all interrelated.

Before really beginning, as it were, inquire briefly about their success using the LCSH to generate the list of subject headings which could be used in libraries for a paper about domestic violence in the United States today. LCSH sample search results:

> Domestic violence: see FAMILY VIOLENCE (10th ed.); See CONJUGAL VIOLENCE (9th ed.).

> CONJUGAL VIOLENCE; FAMILY VIOLENCE; CHILD ABUSE; HUSBAND AND WIFE; BATTERED CHILD SYNDROME; WIFE ABUSE; ABUSED WIVES; WOMEN--CRIMES AGAINST.

Additional Sample Searches are included in Section III: Resources.

Distribute the LCSH handout. Build a brief discussion around:

- What is a thesaurus? The edition of Roget's thesaurus in the bookstore may not be a real thesaurus. Thesaurus is distinct from a dictionary in that it interrelates terms, back and forth. They may not be synonyms but they will be related.

- Not all of the subject headings in the LCSH are going to appear in our catalog. Why?

- There will be some subject headings which are in use in our catalog, but which aren't in the LCSH. How come?

- A single word may sometimes constitute a subject heading, but usually a subject heading consists of more than one word. The most specific subject headings are the ones with the subdivisions. Go for, prefer complex, multiple-worded subject headings because they are more likely to lead you to books which are most useful. Why? The LCSH handout contains examples of all contingencies mentioned throughout this script.

- You may hear about or see LCSH supplements, published after the last edition to communicate new subject headings and changes in the old ones. But you will not need to use the supplements for your work in this course.

For an upper division course, you might explain that there is always some lag between practice and thesaurus. Discuss examples from the past of evolution and additions, e.g. NEGROES/AFRO AMERICANS/BLACKS; AIDS is not provided for in the 9th edition; some terms are not yet provided with acceptable leads, e.g.

Comparable Worth, which is provided with only a See EQUAL PAY FOR EQUAL
WORK, but which is in the 10th edition, etc. When relevant, point out that the
library has a cumulated, up-to-date LCSH in microform. The senior seminar or
honors student might want and/or need to know of changes and additions.

Begin demonstrating the search described in the handout by proposing that

> "Someone has to do a paper for a political science or an American history
> or a journalism course but has some leeway and responsibility for evolving
> the topic from the very general one which the instructor announces, The
> Watergate Scandal. During the course, the student has become interested
> in the involvement of the press, as well as the idea of 'official secrets.'"

This assignment or just the key words can go on the board. Note that it is the
type of situation useful for the final question of the pretest inventory.

> "In this situation, always start with what you have--the actual key words:
> Watergate Scandal, the press, and official secrets. Whenever you are
> looking for subject information, rather than a specific author-and-title
> combination, start with the words you have. Don't broaden, which may
> be the temptation. If you're looking for information and publications
> about the Watergate scandal, don't begin by looking under political
> science, or American history, or scandals or the presidency. Start by
> checking the LCSH in the W's under Watergate. The LCSH is a two
> volume, alphabetically arranged A-to-Z thesaurus. Would you start by
> consulting volume one or volume two?"

Move to the first step of the handout, and develop the search strategy
branching-out process.

> "There is no established subject heading consisting of the word Watergate.
> Start with the words you have: Watergate scandal. On page 3442 in the
> second volume of the LCSH, we find, in light print, Watergate Scandal,
> 1972-1974, followed by See Watergate Affair, 1972-1974. This is a See
> reference--one of the two types of cross references we've already had
> [in use of the library's catalog or other files.] The thesaurus is saying,
> 'There is no established subject heading Watergate Scandal, but there is
> one related to this which consists of the words WATERGATE AFFAIR,
> 1972-1974. Go and See it.' It begins on page 3441. Dark print is used
> for established subject headings you can use. These are the ones which
> may be in use in the library's card catalog to describe our publications
> on this subject."

Contrast light print used for terms which are not established subject headings,
e.g. Waterfront workers and Waterfront workers' writings, just above.

> "The message is that WATERGATE AFFAIR, 1972-1974 is an established
> subject heading. On the same line as a subject heading, in parentheses
> and italics, sometimes is provided the Library of Congress Classification
> location for that subject. E860 refers to a classification, not to a particu-
> lar book. Not all established subject headings in the LCSH are provided
> with this bonus information of the relevant classification. Get it down in
> your notes. You could use it later--in the stacks perhaps. A book is

classified in one part of a classification so that it will always be shelved in one particular part of the collection, but the same book might have several subject headings assigned to it. Why?"

Illustrations of multiple subject tracings assigned to a book are included in the handout, pages 7, 8, and 9. An upper division course could include here reference to shelf list, as well as to several LC classifications for aspects of a subject heading, e.g. WATERMELONS in the LCSH handout.

"The next line communicates that there is one established Watergate Affair-related subject heading: indented, 'sa WATERGATE TRIAL, WASHINGTON, D.C., 1973,' to See Also, the other type of cross reference. The LCSH uses shorthand you must understand and apply yourself.

"So, if you look in the LCSH under the words you have, you can usually count on help with exactly what wording to use. Notice all the See references? One of the two types of cross references. Waterfront workers, in light print eight lines above, is not an established subject heading. If you'd started a search under those words, waterfront workers, the next step would have been to See the full display, or analysis. Where? In this same volume: In the S's under STEVEDORES. But never rearrange the words yourself. Follow only the instructions the LCSH gives. And always follow through on all the sa's indented underneath an established subject heading. Sa for See Also. So far we've identified two established subject headings related to our report."
[Start a list in ALL CAPS on the board]:

    WATERGATE AFFAIR, 1972-1974
    WATERGATE TRIAL, WASHINGTON, D.C., 1973

"You need at least five or six for a library literature search. A goal of five subject headings for starters is a good habit to get into. What about the official secrets aspect? [Proceed in the handout.] OFFICIAL SECRETS in dark print is an established subject heading. Indented underneath is the full analysis of OFFICIAL SECRETS, all the information you need in order to use this subject heading and possibly to find additional ones. This time there are three additional, established subject headings in use in the LCSH thesaurus which you should See Also. The sa, for See Also, is not repeated for the second and third. It appears only in front of the first of the three, related, alphabetically listed subject headings to See Also. The first one is DEFENSE INFORMATION, CLASSIFIED; the second is EXECUTIVE PRIVILEGE (GOVERNMENT INFORMATION); and the third is SECURITY CLASSIFICATION (GOVERNMENT DOCUMENTS). You'd look in the D's, the E's, and the S's for the full display for each. And OFFICIAL SECRETS would probably be listed as a See Also under each of them, back and forth. So now we have four more possible subject headings which may be useful for a term paper related to the Watergate Affair. It's a good idea to get into the habit of recording subject headings in ALL CAPS." [Add to the list on the board]:

    OFFICIAL SECRETS
    DEFENSE INFORMATION, CLASSIFIED
    EXECUTIVE PRIVILEGE (GOVERNMENT INFORMATION)
    SECURITY CLASSIFICATION (GOVERNMENT DOCUMENTS)

"Is OFFICES an established subject heading?" [Yes]

"How many related subject headings are suggested to See Also?" [15]

"Is OFFICES dash Decoration an established subject heading?" (No, it's a See reference]

"What subject heading would you use for information about decorating offices?" [OFFICE DECORATION]

Return to OFFICIAL SECRETS, explain single x's and double xx's, concluding,

"In general, don't consider the xx terms unless you're desperate for leads, because they are broader than your specific topic. Like algebra is part of math: math is bigger, broader than algebra. Here, GOVERN-MENT INFORMATION, the fourth xx, is broader than OFFICIAL SECRETS. OFFICIAL SECRETS is narrower than just SECRECY, the sixth xx. Again, the LCSH does not repeat after the first single x and after the first double xx. But GOVERNMENT AND THE PRESS, the third xx under OFFICIAL SECRETS, does contain our keyword, press. So let's get it down in our notes, and see what develops." [Add GOVERNMENT AND THE PRESS to the list on the board.]

"A total of how many established subject headings are related to, but broader than, OFFICIAL SECRETS?" [6]

"What next? Let's follow through on one of the sa's suggested under OFFICIAL SECRETS. The second one is EXECUTIVE PRIVILEGE (GOV-ERNMENT INFORMATION). We expect to find it alphabetically in the E pages in dark print. It would be on page 1107 of the first volume of the LCSH. Does the display provide the Library of Congress classification for this subject heading?" [No.]

"How many See Also's are provided for EXECUTIVE PRIVILEGE (GOV-ERNMENT INFORMATION)?" [One: GOVERNMENT AND THE PRESS.]

"You could check that one out in the G's."

"Where would information about EXECUTIVES dash CONDUCT OF LIFE be classified according to the Library of Congress Classification?" [HF5000.2]

"Sometimes as you proceed you'll notice references to established sub-ject headings that sound relevant, like EXECUTIVE POWER, although it's broader than EXECUTIVE PRIVILEGE (GOVERNMENT INFORMATION)." [Add to list.]

"For now let's follow through on that interest in the press' involve-ment. Is there anything under that word press? There may be but we can't tell from the excerpt because press would come alphabetically before this. Notice how the LCSH alphabetizes?"

PRESS nothing
PRESS dash EMPLOYEES ... subject dash subdivision
PRESS comma BAPTIST ... subject comma modifier
PRESS AGENTS ... subject heading which starts with this word

"This arrangement results in PRESS dash EMPLOYEES preceding PRESS comma COMMUNIST. And PRESS comma SOCIALIST comes before PRESS AGENTS! For our purposes, PRESS AND POLITICS would be more focused, more specific, than just PRESS. Look at the PRESS AND POLITICS display. Which of the following are true and which false? PRESS AND POLITICS is:

- an established subject heading, [True]
- with four additional subject headings to See Also. [True]
- Three other subject headings are related, but they are all broader than PRESS AND POLITICS. [True]
- One term, politics and the press, has a single x preceding it to indicate that it is not the wording for any LCSH subject heading." [True]

"If you'd looked under Politics and the press, what would you have found? [See PRESS AND POLITICS.] Any questions?" [Add PRESS AND POLITICS to the list on the board.]

"Sometimes there will be a term paper topic for which it isn't so easy to develop several different subject headings to take to the library's catalog. Sometimes you must push yourself further, struggle to think of ideas, and to put them into words related to your research topic, especially when you come up with a subject heading with no related terms to See Also. If we thought about it and had time today, we could think of some additional approaches for even the Watergate Affair topic. The Cabinet, for example. And there are usually people associated with an event or topic. Who are some personalities associated historically with Watergate?" [H. R. Haldeman, John Dean, G. Gordon Liddy, John Mitchell, Richard Nixon, John Sirica, Maurice Stans, Carl Bernstein and Bob Woodward....]

"How about some women?" [Maureen Dean, Martha Mitchell, Rose Mary Woods. It is possible that someone will contribute Mrs. Haldeman, Mrs. Dean, Mrs. Liddy, etc. There are ways to convert this type of response to part of the learning experience, e.g. "What are their names?" Or a nod of acknowledgment and proceed.]

"Of course it's not possible for the LCSH to list the names of all of the individual persons about whom books and parts of books have been written, but they will appear as subject headings in the catalog if the library has books about them.

"So we have at least ten established subject headings we could potentially take to any library's catalog to find books and other types of publications about the Watergate Affair, involvement of the press, and official secrets. At this point, it's time to decide on a working title for the actual topic on which the student is going to report. The sooner you can produce a working title and an outline, the easier and better your work will be. You can improve them as you go along. For future reference, it's usually difficult and always unwise to attempt a term paper on the basis of one subject heading. This will definitely apply to your Project required for this course."

You might include a second list, of the See or x terms in an upper division course LCSH handout, at which point you would explain its potential when help in verbalizing subject heading wordings is needed, especially when using such searching tools as specialized periodical indexes, which are not structured on the basis of the LCSH.

Remind them to bring this handout to the next class. At the beginning of the semester, instruct the class to bring all handouts, which should be 3-hole punched when distributed, to all class meetings and to maintain them, in order, for ready reference. (This is in lieu of a handbook.) Assign for next time making a list of six LCSH subject headings which would probably be useful for a paper about current concerns about sexually-transmissible diseases in the U.S.A. Point out that they do not have to use the library catalog for this, 5 minutes and the LCSH, and they will be collected. LCSH sample search results:

Sexually transmitted diseases. See VENEREAL DISEASES.

VENEREAL DISEASES; GONORRHEA; GRANULOMA; VENEREUM; HYGIENE, SEXUAL; LYMPHOGRANULOMA VENEREUM; SPERMATORRHEA; SYCOSIS (HOMEO-PATHY); SYPHYLLIS. Some of the other possibilities include SEX INSTRUCTION and CONDOMS. AIDS will probably come to mind first. (It is a See to ACQUIRED IMMUNE DEFICIENCY SYNDROME in the LCSH 10th ed.) The methodology involves checking first "the words you have," however.

Part II

Before class on board: Watergate list; the United States history list, and the form sub-divisions list, both in this section.

Collect the Sexually-transmitted diseases in the U.S.A. searches.

Return the basic Watergate list to the board before the class begins, and remind them of it by picking up at that point in the LCSH handout. Then turn to pages 7 and 8 (and 9), "examples which demonstrate how subject tracings can sometimes be an additional source of Library of Congress established subject headings. They could be useful if you have already located a great library book for your purposes, and want others much like it. They'd likely have the same subject heading assigned to them. These books are all classified in different parts of the LC Classification, so the books themselves would be spread around in separate locations throughout the library collection. But, when you can use the LCSH efficiently, the subject headings bring related information together. What additional established subject heading exists which may help with our Water-gate topic?" [Republican Party]

"Another source of subject tracings which have been assigned to a book on a subject of interest can be a book itself. At the left (page 10) is a book's title page; at the right is the verso of that title page."

Explain Cataloging in Publication.

"If you'd read The Mind of Watergate and then wanted more books like it, what subject heading could you add to your list? [CORRUPTION (IN POLITICS)--UNITED STATES. PSYCHOANALYSIS. Discuss standard subdivisions.]
"Subdivisions of subject headings provide another way to give your research focus. The LCSH uses a dash to lead to a subdivision, and two dashes to indicate a subdivision of a subject heading that is already subdivided, and so on! A dash in your typed assignments and handouts consists of two hyphens, however. CABBAGE is an established subject heading. Page 5 of the LCSH handout. CABBAGE dash DISEASE AND PEST RESISTANCE is another subject heading, created by adding to the basic subject a dash and the subdivision DISEASE AND PEST RESISTANCE. Turn back to the beginning of the LCSH entry for WATERGATE AFFAIR, 1972-1974, page 2, the right hand box. The second double xx, UNITED

STATES dash POLITICS AND GOVERNMENT dash 1969 hyphen, for 'to,' 1974, consists of the basic UNITED STATES subdivided by a dash POLITICS AND GOVERNMENT. It refers to political and governmental aspects of the United States. And finally, it's sub subdivided to a particular period of time: from 1969 through 1974. How many separate subject headings are based on CABBAGE by means of the dash and subdivisions?

CABBAGE
CABBAGE--DISEASE AND PEST RESISTANCE
CABBAGE--MARKETING
CABBAGE--VARIETIES? [Four, including CABBAGE.]

"How many separate subject headings are based on OFFICES by means of the dash and subdivisions?

OFFICES
OFFICES--LOCATION?" [Two, including OFFICES]

"Some subdivisions can be added to any basic subject heading stem. These are standard subdivisions. They can be used to subdivide any topic geographically, chronologically, or in terms of whatever physical form the publication takes. They are not always spelled out in the LCSH.

"Geographical location subdivisions are the names of a country or other political entity, region or geographic feature. A geographic subdivision can be added to any subject heading where it is needed to describe a publication's contents. For example, on page nine of the LCSH handout, David Halberstan's The Powers That Be and four other titles are about PRESS AND POLITICS in the UNITED STATES specifically--thus the subject heading PRESS AND POLITICS--UNITED STATES has been assigned to them. And on page eight, the subject tracings for the second book (the one by and about Maurice H. Stans) include CABINET OFFICERS--UNITED STATES--BIOGRAPHY, the third subject heading assigned to this book.

"Chronological, time period subdivisions are often found after countries or nations to subdivide their history or literature, for example:

U.S. dash HISTORY
U.S. dash HISTORY dash QUEEN ANNE'S WAR, 1702-1713
U.S.--HISTORY--KING GEORGE'S WAR, 1744-1748
U.S.--HISTORY--FRENCH AND INDIAN WAR, 1755-1763
U.S.--HISTORY--REVOLUTION."

If previous classes have considered filing in both card catalog and computer-generated files, this sequence should appear alphabetically-arranged as in a card catalog. In a computer-based file, they might be U.S.--HISTORY--FRENCH ..., KING..., QUEEN..., REVOLUTION.

"Form subdivisions are provided to identify the particular format in which the publication exists. They can be added as the last part of any heading, the final subdivision. They do not describe what the book is about, but, rather, of what it consists. The subdivisions by form which will be most useful in your research are:

SUBJECT dash BIBLIOGRAPHY

SUBJECT dash DICTIONARIES AND ENCYCLOPEDIAS (For example, the Encyclopaedia Britannica)
SUBJECT--DIRECTORIES
SUBJECT--HANDBOOKS, MANUALS, ETC. (For example, 'how to' books)
SUBJECT--INDEXES
SUBJECT--PERIODICALS (For example, Scientific American)
SUBJECT--PERIODICALS--INDEXES (For example, Art Index)
SUBJECT--YEARBOOKS

But there's a rule connected with this: This form type of sub subject heading must appear last, as the final subdivision. Strictly-speaking, are they subjects? Is the book on page seven by Myron J. Smith about the Watergate Affair? [Yes] Is it about bibliography? No, it is a bibliography on the subject of Watergate. It consists of sources published in English from 1972 to 1982."

Communicate them as additional possible write-ins authorized by the LCSH. Turn to the basic list of Watergate subject headings, on the board or page six in the handout.

"So we could expect the possibility of publications with these established subject headings, for example, to be listed in the library's catalog with geographic subdivisions. And especially at the beginning of a literature search we hope for some selective bibliographies. Why?"

Page nine provides examples of fiche subject entries which can be utilized for these various considerations if relevant locally.

"Turn to the LCSH entry for OFFICIAL SECRETS, page three. Suppose you were doing a term paper specifically on official secrets in California. Although the LCSH doesn't spell it out, you'd know you're authorized to expect the possibility of a book containing this information to be described with this geographic subdivision. [Add dash UNITED STATES dash CALIFORNIA to OFFICIAL SECRETS.] The (Indirect) in italics in parentheses instructs the cataloger to use this particular indirect form." [(Direct) is no longer used and does not appear in the LCSH 10th edition].

Distribute to each student one of several versions of the worksheet titled Practice Using the LCSH which are provided in the concluding Section III: Resources. Use 9th or 10th edition forms as local needs require. Give them twenty minutes to complete it, and then collect them. Return them at the end of the next class meeting; suggest that anyone not achieving nine should see you during office hours to catch up.

USING A THESAURUS...

- To locate functional subject-headings
- To help focus on a research topic
- To focus and specify information
- To broaden information
- Sometimes to identify relevant parts of a classification
-

USING SUBJECT TRACINGS from Catalog Cards and Fiche Entries...

- To discover additional functional subject-headings
- To identify books on the same subject which are in the library
-

A thesaurus is distinct from a dictionary in that it interrelates words and terms, back and forth.

THESAURUS: An authority file or list of subject-headings or descriptors, usually with cross-references, used in indexing a collection of documents. A related term is CONTROLLED VOCABULARY. The American Heritage Dictionary, New College edition defines thesaurus: A book of selected words or concepts, as a specialized vocabulary for music, medicine or the like. A book of synonyms and antonyms. Latin derivation from treasure.

The United States Library of Congress Subject Headings, 10th edition (1986) (the two red volumes in most libraries) is the thesaurus you will use most. Brief Key to the LCSH:

Bold-faced dark print = An established subject-heading which you can use.

sa   = You may also wish to use this heading; "sa" stands for see also.

xx   = Refers to established subject-headings which are related but which are broader in scope.

x   = Do not use this wording. It is not an established subject-heading in the LCSH thesaurus.

Reprinted by Permission: Scott McCullar Texas A & M University Library, College Station Texas 77843 & American Libraries

I GIVE UP! WHAT IS ANOTHER WORD FOR SYNONYM?

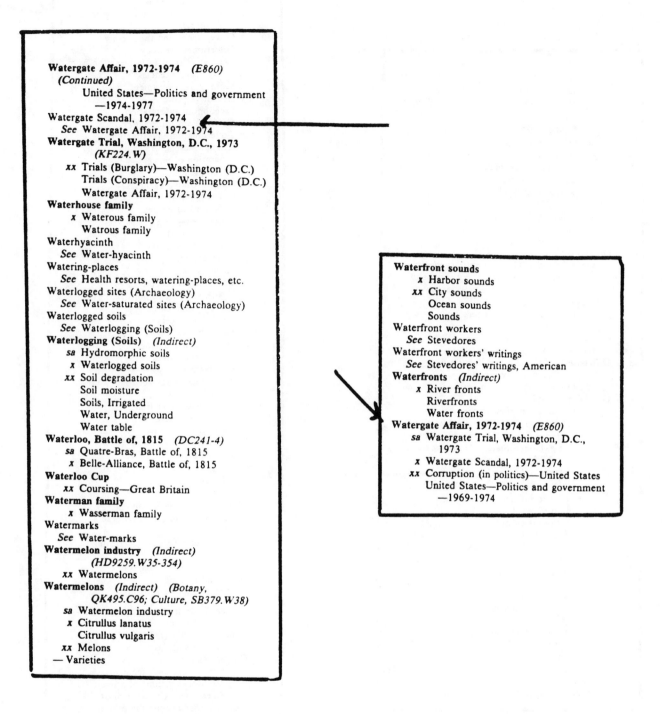

Watergate Affair, 1972-1974 *(E860)*
  (Continued)
         United States—Politics and government
              —1974-1977
Watergate Scandal, 1972-1974
  See Watergate Affair, 1972-1974
Watergate Trial, Washington, D.C., 1973
         (KF224.W)
    xx Trials (Burglary)—Washington (D.C.)
         Trials (Conspiracy)—Washington (D.C.)
         Watergate Affair, 1972-1974
Waterhouse family
    x Waterous family
       Watrous family
Waterhyacinth
  See Water-hyacinth
Watering-places
  See Health resorts, watering-places, etc.
Waterlogged sites (Archaeology)
  See Water-saturated sites (Archaeology)
Waterlogged soils
  See Waterlogging (Soils)
Waterlogging (Soils) *(Indirect)*
    sa Hydromorphic soils
    x Waterlogged soils
    xx Soil degradation
       Soil moisture
       Soils, Irrigated
       Water, Underground
       Water table
Waterloo, Battle of, 1815 *(DC241-4)*
    sa Quatre-Bras, Battle of, 1815
    x Belle-Alliance, Battle of, 1815
Waterloo Cup
    xx Coursing—Great Britain
Waterman family
    x Wasserman family
Watermarks
  See Water-marks
Watermelon industry *(Indirect)*
         (HD9259.W35-354)
    xx Watermelons
Watermelons *(Indirect) (Botany,*
         QK495.C96; Culture, SB379.W38)
    sa Watermelon industry
    x Citrullus lanatus
       Citrullus vulgaris
    xx Melons
  — Varieties

Waterfront sounds
    x Harbor sounds
    xx City sounds
       Ocean sounds
       Sounds
Waterfront workers
  See Stevedores
Waterfront workers' writings
  See Stevedores' writings, American
Waterfronts *(Indirect)*
    x River fronts
       Riverfronts
       Water fronts
Watergate Affair, 1972-1974 *(E860)*
    sa Watergate Trial, Washington, D.C.,
         1973
    x Watergate Scandal, 1972-1974
    xx Corruption (in politics)—United States
       United States—Politics and government
         —1969-1974

LCSH, 10th edition
Volume 2, Page 3442

LCSH 2:3441

Offices
    sa Dental offices
       Law offices
       Medical offices
       Office decoration
       Office leases
    xx Office buildings
    — Decoration
          See Office decoration
    — Location   (Indirect)
          x Location of offices
Offices, Sale of
    See Sale of public office
Official gazettes
    See Gazettes
Official jargon
    See subdivision Government jargon under
           names of languages, e.g. English
           language—Government jargon
Official libraries
    See Libraries, Governmental,
           administrative, etc.
Official misconduct
    See Misconduct in office
Official Production System Version 5
       (Computer system)
    See OPS5 (Computer system)
Official publications
    See Government publications
       subdivision Government publications
           under names of countries, cities, etc.,
           e.g. United States—Government
           publications
Official secrets   (Indirect)
    sa Defense information, Classified
       Executive privilege (Government
           information)
       Security classification (Government
           documents)
    x Disclosing official secrets
       Government secrecy
       Secrecy in government
       Secrets, Official
       Secrets of state
    xx Confidential communications
       Criminal law
       Government and the press
       Government information
       Ministerial responsibility
       Secrecy
Officialese
    See English language—Government jargon

LCSH 2:2269

Executive power (Canon law)
Executive privilege (Government information)
       (Indirect)
    sa Government and the press
    x Government secrecy
       Legislative right to information from
           executive agencies
       Secrecy in government
    xx Executive power
       Freedom of information
       Government information
       Governmental investigations
       Official secrets
       Separation of powers
Executive reorganization
    See Administrative agencies—
           Reorganization
Executive victims of crimes
    See Executives—Crimes against
Executives   (Indirect)
    sa Arts administrators
       Cemetery managers
       Executive ability
       Government executives
       Health services administrators
       Library administrators
       Middle managers
       Minority executives
       Personnel management
       Retired executives
       Risk managers
       Sound recording executives and
           producers
       Supervisors, Industrial
       Women executives
    x Business executives
       Corporation executives
       Managers
    xx Business
       Industrial management
       Management
       Personnel management
Example under White collar workers
    Ability testing
          See Executive ability—Testing
    Attitudes
       xx Attitude (Psychology)
    Books and reading
    Collective labor agreements

          See Collective labor agreements—
               Executives
    — Conduct of life   (HF5500.2)
       xx Business ethics
    — Crimes against
          x Crimes against executives
             Executive victims of crimes
             Executives, Crimes against
          xx Offenses against the person
             Victims of crimes

LCSH 1 :1107

Liquor problem in the press
Local government and the press
Minorities in the press
News agencies
Newspapers
Nuclear industry in the press
Periodicals
Petroleum industry and trade in the
   press
Police and the press
Press agents
Press and propaganda
Press law
Public opinion
Race relations and the press
Street literature
Syndicates (Journalism)
Underground press
Women in the press
  xx Journalism
    Newspapers
    Periodicals
    Propaganda
    Public opinion
    Publicity
— Baptists
    See Press, Baptist
— Catholic Church
    See Press, Catholic
— Censorship
    See Freedom of the press
       Press law
       Prohibited books
— Confidential communications
    See Confidential communications—
       Press
— Employees
    sa Trade-unions—Press employees
— Lutheran Church
    See Press, Lutheran
— Social aspects
    See Journalism—Social aspects
— Societies, etc.
    See Journalism—Societies, etc.
Press, Afro-American
  See Afro-American press
Press, Baptist (Indirect)
  x Baptist journalism
    Baptist press
    Press—Baptists
  xx Journalism, Religious
    Press, Protestant
    Religious newspapers and periodicals
Press, Catholic (Indirect)
    Here are entered works dealing with
       Catholic opinion, literary production,
       and propaganda as expressed in Cath-
       olic journals, newspapers, and periodi-
       cals.
  sa Journalism, Religious
  x Catholic journalism
    Catholic press
    Press—Catholic Church
  xx Catholic Church—Apologetic works
    Catholic Church—Periodicals
    Catholic literature
    Journalism, Religious
    Religious newspapers and periodicals
Press, Communist (Indirect)
  x Communist press
  xx Journalism, Communist
Press, Islamic (Indirect)
  x Islamic press
    Muslim press
    Press, Muslim
  xx Religious newspapers and periodicals
Press, Juvenile (Indirect)
  sa Children's periodicals
  x Children's press
    Juvenile press

Press, Labor (Indirect)
  sa Labor literature
  x Labor press
  xx Journalism, Labor
Press, Lutheran (Indirect)
  x Lutheran journalism
    Lutheran press
    Press—Lutheran Church
  xx Journalism, Religious
    Press, Protestant
    Religious newspapers and periodicals
Press, Muslim
  See Press, Islamic
Press, Political party (Indirect)
  x Party press
    Political party press
  xx Political parties
    Press and politics
Press, Protestant (Indirect)
  sa Press, Baptist
    Press, Lutheran
  x Protestant press
  xx Journalism, Religious
    Protestantism
    Religious newspapers and periodicals
Press, Socialist (Indirect)
  x Socialist press
  xx Journalism, Socialist
Press agents (Indirect)
  xx Press
    Public relations
    Publicity
Press and city planning
  See City planning and the press
Press and crime
  See Crime and the press
Press and government
  See Government and the press
Press and journalism in literature
  x Journalism in literature
    Press in literature
Press and politics (Indirect)
  sa Advertising, Political
    Government and the press
    Journalism—Political aspects
    Press, Political party
  x Politics and the press
  xx Advertising, Political
    Government and the press
    Journalism—Political aspects

LCSH 2:2547

Cabbage *(Indirect) (SB331)*
   sa Broccoli
      Brussels sprouts
      Cauliflower
      Chinese cabbage
      Cookery (Cabbage)
      Kale
      Sauerkraut
  — Disease and pest resistance
  — Diseases and pests *(SB608.C14)*
     sa Cabbage aphid
        Cabbage looper
        Cabbage maggot
        Cabbage web-worm
        Cabbage yellows
        Clubroot
  — Marketing
     Example under Vegetables—Marketing
  — Varieties
Cabbage angelintree
  See Andira inermis
Cabbage aphid
   x Brevicoryne brassicae
  xx Cabbage—Diseases and pests
Cabbage bark
  See Andira inermis
Cabbage black ring spot
  See Turnip mosaic virus
Cabbage family
Cabbage fly
  See Cabbage maggot
Cabbage industry *(Indirect)*
      (HD9235.C3-32)
Cabbage looper *(SB945.C)*
  xx Cabbage—Diseases and pests
Cabbage maggot *(SB608.C14)*
   x Cabbage fly
      Cabbage root fly
      Cabbage-root maggot
      Erioischia brassicae
      Hylemya brassicae
      Hylemyia brassicae
      Pegomyia brassicae
      Phorbia brassicae
  xx Cabbage—Diseases and pests
Cabbage Patch dolls
  See Cabbage Patch Kids dolls
Cabbage Patch Kids dolls
   x Cabbage Patch dolls
  xx Dolls—United States
      Soft toys—United States
Cabbage root fly
  See Cabbage maggot
Cabbage-root maggot
  See Cabbage maggot
Cabbage tree
  See Andira inermis
Cabbage web-worm
  xx Cabbage—Diseases and pests
Cabbage yellows
  xx Cabbage—Diseases and pests

Cabbala
  See Cabala
Cabdriver robberies *(Indirect)*
  xx Robbery
      Taxicabs
Cabe family
  See McCabe family
Cabernet (Wine)
  xx Wine and wine making
Cabeza, Virgen de la *(BT660.C)*
   x Virgen de la Cabeza
  xx Mary, Blessed Virgin, Saint—Cult—
      Spain
Cabin atmospheres (Space environment)
  See Space cabin atmospheres
Cabin Creek, 2d Battle, 1864
  xx United States—History—Civil War,
      1861-1865—Campaigns
Cabin cruisers
  See Motorboats
Cabin John Creek (Montgomery County, Md.)
  xx Rivers—Maryland
Cabinet government
  See Cabinet system
Cabinet hardware *(TS885)*
   x Furniture fittings
      Furniture hardware
      Hardware, Cabinet
  xx Cabinet-work
      Hardware
      Locks and keys
Cabinet makers
  See Cabinet-workers
Cabinet officers *(Indirect) (United States,*
     JK610-616)
   sa Ministerial responsibility
      Prime ministers
   x Ministers of State
      Secretaries of State
Cabinet organ
  See Reed-organ
Cabinet system *(Indirect) (JF331-341)*
   sa Coalition governments
      Confidence voting
      Ministerial responsibility
   x Cabinet government
      Parliamentary government
  xx Political science
      Representative government and
        representation
Cabinet-work *(Indirect) (TT197)*
   sa Cabinet hardware
      Furniture making
      Gluing
      Kitchen cabinets
      Loud-speaker cabinets
      Marquetry
      Veneers and veneering
      Woodwork
  xx Carpentry
      Furniture making
      Joinery
      Woodwork

LCSH 1:444

Summary of Subject Headings, Key Words and Terms, Classifications, and Other
Useful Information Gathered:

Established LC Subject Headings:

WATERGATE AFFAIR, 1972-1974

WATERGATE TRIAL, WASHINGTON, D.C., 1973

OFFICIAL SECRETS

DEFENSE INFORMATION, CLASSIFIED

EXECUTIVE PRIVILEGE (GOVERNMENT INFORMATION)

SECURITY CLASSIFICATION (GOVERNMENT DOCUMENTS)

GOVERNMENT AND THE PRESS

EXECUTIVE POWER

PRESS AND POLITICS

CABINET OFFICERS

LC Classifications In Shelf List Order:

E860

JK610-JK616

x:

Disclosing official secrets

Government secrecy

Legislative right to information from executive agencies

Politics and the press

Secrets of state

Secrets, Official

Secrecy in government

Watergate Scandal, 1972-1974

Using Subject Tracings From Catalog Entries

                        PRESIDENTS-- U.S.-- ELECTION-- 1972-
JK   Ripon Society
2357   Jaws of victory; the game-plan of politics
R482   of 1972.   Boston, Mass.: Little, Brown,
1974   1974.

1. Republican Party. 2.Presidents-- U.S.-- Election--
1972. 3.Watergate Affair,1972-1974. I.Brown, Clifford
Waters, 1942-   II. Ti+l

                    WATERGATE AFFAIR, 1972-1974-- BIBLIOGRAPHY
Z1245 Smith, Myron J.
S64   Watergate: an annotated book of sources in
1983   English, 1972-1982.   Metuchen, New Jersey:
       Scarecrow Press, 1983.
           xiii, 329p.
           Includes index

                                        Bibl.   I.Title

1. Waterga   NIXON, RICAHRD MILHOUS, 1913-   --DRAMA
PS   Myers, Robert John
3563   The tragedie of King Richard, the Second;
M9953t the life and times of Richard II (1367-1400)
       King of England (1377-1399) compared to those
       of Richard of America in his second administra-
       tion.   Washington, D.C.: Acropolis,
       1973.

       1.Nixon, Richard Milhous, 1913-   --Drama. 2.
       Shakespeare, William, 1564-1616. King Richard II--
       Parodies, travesties, etc.   3.Watergate Affair, 1972-
       1974-- Anecdotes, facetiae, satire, etc.   I.Title

                    WATERGATE AFFAIR, 1972-1974
KF4570 Friedman, Leon, comp.
A7F741   United States v. Nixon; the President
       before the Supreme Court. Edited by Leon
       Friedman.   New York, Chelsea House Pub-
       lishers, 1974.
           xxi, 619p.   25cm.
           Includes bibliographic references

1.Executive privilege (Government information)-- United
States-- Cases. 2.Nixon, Richard Milhous, 1913-
3. Watergate Affair, 1972-1974. I.Title

Using Subject Tracings From Catalog Entries

E859   Watergate: the full inside story by Lewis
W3771   Chester and others.   New York:
          Ballantine Books, 1973.
          vii, 280p illus

1. Watergate Affair, 1972-1974   I. Chester, Lewis

STANS, MAURICE H., 1908-
E860   Stans, Maurice H   1908-
S8   The terrors of justice : the untold side of Watergate / Maurice
        H. Stans. — 1st ed. — New York : Everest House, c1978.

        xii, 478 p. ; 24 cm.

        Includes bibliographical references and index.
        ISBN 0-89696-020-X : $10.95

        1. Watergate Affair, 1972-   —Personal narratives. 2. Stans, Maurice
        H., 1908-   3. Cabinet officers—United States—Biography.   I. Title.
E860.S8

Library of C

                    WATERGATE AFFAIR, 1972-1974
          E860   United States. Watergate Special Prosecution
          1977   Force
          DOCS   Final Report.   Washington: Supt. of
                  Documents, U.S. Government Printing Office,
                  1977.
                       76p.; 27 cm.

1. Watergate Affair, 1972-1974

GREAT BRITAIN-- POLITICS AND GOVERNMENT--
          1945-1964
DA591.   Marsh, Richard, Sir, 1928-
M37A36   Off the rails : an autobiography / by Richard Marsh. — Lon-
1978   don : Weidenfeld and Nicolson, 1978.

          214 p., [4] leaves of plates : ill. ; 23 cm.   GB•••

          Includes index.
          ISBN (invalid) 9297773879 : £6.95

          1. Marsh, Richard, Sir, 1928-   2. Great Britain—Politics and govern-
        ment—1945-1964. 3. Great Britain—Politics and government—1964-
        4. Statesmen—Great Britain—Biography.   I. Title.
        DA591.M37A36   385'.092'4   79-305075
                              [B]   MARC

        Library of Congress   79

```
                                        K 16
WATERGATE AFFAIR, 1972--- PERSONAL NARRA        CATALOG 2: SUBJECTS              MAY 14, 1983         Page 57106

=====> WATERGATE AFFAIR, 1972--- PERSONAL NARRATIVES.
E860.L53        MAIN Liddy, G. Gordon.        Will : the autobiography of G. Gordon Liddy.    New York : St. Martin's Press,
                          c1980.                                                                                        374
                          p.  [4] leaves of plates : ill. ; 24 cm.    SUBJECT: Liddy, G. Gordon.    SUBJECT*: Watergate Affair,
                          1972- ---Personal narratives.
                          RLIN: CUBG18879969-8.
                                                                                                                    63358477
E860.L53        UNDE Liddy, G. Gordon.        Will : the autobiography of G. Gordon Liddy.    New York : St. Martin's Press,
                          c1980.                                                                                        374
                          p.  [4] leaves of plates : ill. ; 24 cm.    SUBJECT: Liddy, G. Gordon.    SUBJECT*: Watergate Affair,
                          1972- ---Personal narratives.
                          RLIN: CUBG18879969-8.
                                                                                                                    65123505

=====> WATERGATE AFFAIR, 1972--- PUBLIC OPINION.
E860.T74 1979   MAIN Trezise, James.        Watergate, a crisis for the world : a survey of British and French press reaction
                          toward an American political crisis / by James Trezise, James Glen Stovall, and Hamid Rowlana.
                          1st ed.   Oxford ; New York : Pergamon Press, 1980.
                          xi, 260 p. ; 22 cm.    NOTE: Bibliography: p. 247-251.    SUBJECT: Public opinion--Great Britain.
                          SUBJECT: Public opinion--France.    SUBJECT: Press--Great Britain.    SUBJECT: Press--France.
                          SUBJECT*: Watergate Affair, 1972- --Public opinion.
                          RLIN: 20888945.
                                                                                                                    6321538X

=====> WATERGATE AFFAIR, 1972--- SOURCES.
J61.J9 93rd v.26 DOCS Nixon, Richard M.        Transcripts of eight recorded Presidential conversations.    Washington..
                          v, 218 p.    SUBJECT*: Watergate Affair, 1972- --Sources.
                          OCLC: ocm01285106.
                                                                                                                    69094214

=====> WATERGATE TRIAL, WASHINGTON, D.C., 1973.
KF224.W33.S57   MAIN Sirica, John J.        To set the record straight : the break-in, the tapes, the conspirators, the
                          pardon / John J. Sirica.    1st ed.    New York : Norton, c1979.
                          394 p. : ill. ; ports ; 24 cm.    NOTE: Includes bibliographical references and index.    SUBJECT:
                          Nixon, Richard Milhous, 1913- --Pardon.    SUBJECT: Sirica, John J.    SUBJECT: Watergate Affair,
                          1972-.    SUBJECT*: Watergate Trial, Washington, D.C., 1973.
                          RLIN: 13318780.
                                                                                                                    60873430
KF224.W33.S57   UNDE Sirica, John J.        To set the record straight : the break-in, the tapes, the conspirators, the
                          pardon / John J. Sirica.    1st ed.    New York : Norton, c1979.
                          394 p. : ill. ; ports ; 24 cm.    NOTE: Includes bibliographical references and index.    SUBJECT:
                          Nixon, Richard Milhous, 1913- --Pardon.    SUBJECT: Sirica, John J.    SUBJECT: Watergate Affair,
                          1972-.    SUBJECT*: Watergate Trial, Washington, D.C., 1973.
                          RLIN: 13318780.
                                                                                                                    6283762X
```

```
                                        F 9
OFFICIAL SECRETS--UNITED STATES.                CATALOG 2: SUBJECTS              MAY 14, 1983         Page 38039

                          Official secrets United States. United States. Congress. S...(continued)
                          vi, 908 p. : ill. ; 24 cm.    NOTE: Includes bibliographical references.    SUBJECT: Security
                          classification (Government documents)--United States.    SUBJECT: Executive privilege (Government
                          information)--United States.    SUBJECT*: Official secrets--United States.
                          RLIN: CUBG82-B19258.
                                                                                                                    69112629

=====> OFFICIAL SECRETS--UNITED STATES--HISTORY.
KF4570.H63      MAIN Hoffman, Daniel N., 1942-.        Governmental secrecy and the founding fathers : a study in
                          constitution controls / Daniel N. Hoffman.    Westport, Conn. : Greenwood Press, 1981.
                          ix, 339 p. ; 22 cm.    (Contributions in legal studies ; 17)    NOTE: Bibliography: p. [317]-324.
                          SUBJECT: Executive privilege (Government information)--United States--History.    SUBJECT: Government
                          information--United States--History.    SUBJECT*: Official secrets--United States--History.
                          RLIN: CUBG82-B20818.
                                                                                                                    63947961
```

```
                                        L 7
PRESS AND POLITICS--UNITED STATES.              CATALOG 2: SUBJECTS              MAY 14, 1983         Page 42197

=====> PRESS AND POLITICS--UNITED STATES.   (CONTINUED)
PN4888.P6.H3    MAIN Halberstam, David.        The powers that be / David Halberstam.    New York : Knopf, 1979.
                          771 p. ; 25 cm.    NOTE: Bibliography: p. 743-771.    SUBJECT*: Press and politics--United States.
                          RLIN: 10687823.
                                                                                                                    61661624
PN4888.P6.H3    SOCS Halberstam, David.        The powers that be / David Halberstam.    New York : Knopf, 1979.
                          771 p. ; 25 cm.    NOTE: Bibliography: p. 743-771.    SUBJECT*: Press and politics--United States.
                          RLIN: 10687823.
                                                                                                                    62381519
PN4888.P6.H3    UNDE Halberstam, David.        The powers that be / David Halberstam.    New York : Knopf, 1979.
                          771 p. ; 25 cm.    NOTE: Bibliography: p. 743-771.    SUBJECT*: Press and politics--United States.
                          RLIN: 10687823.
                                                                                                                    65145653
E868.M42        MAIN Media agenda-setting in a Presidential election : issues, images, and interest / David H. Weaver ... [et
                          al.    New York, N.Y. : Praeger, 1981.
                          227 p. : ill. ; 24 cm.    NOTE: Bibliography: p. 213-220.    SUBJECT: Presidents--United
                          States--Election--1976.    SUBJECT*: Press and politics--United States.
                          RLIN: 24665240.
                                                                                                                    64788659
JK468.I6.P468   MAIN Petrusenko, Vitalii Vasilevici.        A dangerous game : CIA and the mass media / Vitaly Petrusenko ;
                          translated from the Russian by Nicolai Kozelsky and Vladimir Leonov.    Prague : Interpress, 1977.
                          190 p. ; 24 cm.    NOTE: Includes bibliographical references.    SUBJECT: United States. Central
                          Intelligence Agency.    SUBJECT: Journalism--United States--Political aspects.    SUBJECT*: Press and
                          politics--United States.
                          RLIN: 18821367.
                                                                                                                    60853736
JK518.P748 1982 MAIN The President & the public /.    Philadelphia :.
                          x, 310 p. :.    NOTE: Bibliography: p. 287-300.    SUBJECT: Presidents--United States--Public opinion.
                          SUBJECT: Public opinion--United States.    SUBJECT: Government and the press--United States.
                          SUBJECT*: Press and politics--United States.
                          OCLC: ocm08306583.
                                                                                                                    66554640
E839.5.R82 1981 MAIN Rubin, Richard L.        Press, party, and presidency /.    1st ed.    New York :.
                          246 p. :.    SUBJECT: Presidents--United States--Election.    SUBJECT: United States--Politics and
                          government--1945-.    SUBJECT*: Press and politics--United States.
                          RLIN: CUBG82-B5669.
                                                                                                                    65459635
E839.5.R82 1981 UNDE Rubin, Richard L.        Press, party, and presidency /.    1st ed.    New York :.
                          246 p. :.    SUBJECT: Presidents--United States--Election.    SUBJECT: United States--Politics and
                          government--1945-.    SUBJECT*: Press and politics--United States.
                          RLIN: CUBG82-B5669.
                                                                                                                    65641723

=====> PRESS AND POLITICS--UNITED STATES--HISTORY--20TH CENTURY.
E743.J83        UNDE Juergens, George.        News from the White House :.    Chicago :.
                          x, 348 p., [12] p. of plates :.    NOTE: Bibliography: p. 309-324.    SUBJECT: Progressivism (United
                          States politics).    SUBJECT: United States--Politics and government--1901-1909.    SUBJECT: United
                          States--Politics and government--1909-1913.    SUBJECT: United States--Politics and
                          government--1913-1921.    SUBJECT*: Press and politics--United States--History--20th century.
                          RLIN: CUBG82-B2358A.
                                                                                                                    65314827
```

The Mind of Watergate

of Watergate

An Exploration of the

Compromise of Integrity

LEO RANGELL, M.D.

W · W · NORTON & COMPANY · NEW YORK · LONDON

125

Copyright © 1980 by Leo Rangell

Published simultaneously in Canada by George J. McLeod Limited, Toronto. Printed in the United States of America.
All Rights Reserved
First Edition

Excerpts from the following columns by Art Buchwald are reprinted with his kind permission. Copyright © 1974 by Art Buchwald.

"Taking the Watergate Trivia Test," March 31, 1974; "Tape Offer Receives Poor Reception," April 8, 1974; "Alice's Adventure in Briefingland," May 16, 1974; "Touching All the Bases for Gerry," June 2, 1974; "A Very Good Year at Watergate Industries," June 9, 1974; "To Dick and Pat, From the Cat in the Hat...," July 30, 1974; "An Old Hand at Putting Words in Mouth," August 1, 1974; "Nude Deal Coverup in Cloak of Secrecy," August 4, 1974; "Sad Chat With the Late Mr. Checkers," August 9, 1974; "Button, Button, Who's Got the Button?" August 11, 1974; "Just Like Any Other Tom, Dick or Gerry," September 12, 1974.

Library of Congress Cataloging in Publication Data

Rangell, Leo, M.D.
    The Mind of Watergate.

    Bibliography: p.
    Includes index.
    1. Watergate Affair, 1972-2. Corruption (in politics)—United States. Psychoanalysis. I. Title.
E860.R36 1980   364.1′32′0973   79-22408
ISBN 0-393-01308-1

1 2 3 4 5 6 7 8 9 0

These questions relate to this excerpt from
the Library of Congress Subject Headings(LCSH)

Aid to underdeveloped areas
   See Economic assistance
      Technical assistance
AIDS (Disease)
   See Acquired immune deficiency syndrome
Aids (Horsemanship)
   See Riding aids
Aids to air navigation *(Indirect)*
   sa Aeronautical charts
      Airways
      Electronics in aeronautics
      Meteorology in aeronautics
      Radar in aeronautics
      Radio in aeronautics
      *names of specific equipment and
        systems, e.g.* Runway localizing
        beacons; Instrument landing systems
   x Air navigation aids
      Navigational aids (Aeronautics)
   xx Aids to navigation
      Airways
      Electronics in aeronautics
      Meteorology in aeronautics
      Navigation (Aeronautics)
— Defense measures
   xx War damage, Industrial
Aids to navigation *(Indirect)* *(Signaling,
   VK381-397; Lighthouse service,
   VK1000-1249)*
   sa Aids to air navigation
      Astronautics in navigation
      Beacons
      Buoys
      Electronics in navigation
      Fog-bells
      Fog-signals
      Ice breaking operations
      Lighthouses
      Nautical charts

1. This excerpt is from volume #_____.

2. The combination of capital letters and 3-
4 numbers which sometimes appears refers to

    a book number
    a call number
    a classification
    the location of a specific book-title
     on the library's shelves

3. Someone needing information about _____
A I D S disease
should look for subject cards with the 1st
line subject-heading wording_____
_____
_____

4. Airways
is an established subject-heading.

    TRUE   FALSE

5. If interested in _aids to navigation_____
_____
_____,
you should check that exact wording as·
well as _____
_____
_____in the subject catalog.

6. Electronics in aeronautics_____ is broader/narrower
than _Aids to air navigation_____.

7. There is a total of #_____ SEE ALSO-type cross references ("sa") indicated in
this excerpt; there is a total of #_____ SEE cross references.

8. An example of a subject-heading displayed in this excerpt which it's likely you
will find subdivided geographically in a library's catalog is _____
_____.

9. For publications about _lighthouse service aspects of aids to navigation_____,
you could check the library shelves in the vicinity of the Library of Congress
Classification _____.

10. Which one of the following is _not_ an established LCSH subject-heading?
    Aids to air navigation-- Defense measures   Navigational aids (Aeronautics)
    Lighthouses   Technical assistance

11. Defense measures_____ is
    a SEE ALSO cross reference   an established subject-heading
    a SEE cross reference   a subdivision of a subject-heading

Course Title, Date
Instructor

LCSH 10 ed.
KEY Vol. 1
Page 64

Practice Using the LCSH
Your Name _____

These questions relate to this excerpt from
the Library of Congress Subject Headings(LCSH)

Aid to underdeveloped areas
  See Economic assistance
    Technical assistance
AIDS (Disease)
  See Acquired immune deficiency syndrome
Aids (Horsemanship)
  See Riding aids
Aids to air navigation *(Indirect)*
  sa Aeronautical charts
    Airways
    Electronics in aeronautics
    Meteorology in aeronautics
    Radar in aeronautics
    Radio in aeronautics
    names of specific equipment and
      systems, e.g. Runway localizing
      beacons; Instrument landing systems
  x Air navigation aids
    Navigational aids (Aeronautics)
  xx Aids to navigation
    Airways
    Electronics in aeronautics
    Meteorology in aeronautics
    Navigation (Aeronautics)
  — Defense measures
    xx War damage, Industrial
Aids to navigation *(Indirect)* *(Signaling,*
    VK381-397; Lighthouse service,
    VK1000-1249)
  sa Aids to air navigation
    Astronautics in navigation
    Beacons
    Buoys
    Electronics in navigation
    Fog-bells
    Fog-signals
    Ice breaking operations
    Lighthouses
    Nautical charts

1. This excerpt is from volume # __1__ .

2. The combination of capital letters and 3-
   4 numbers which sometimes appears refers to

       a book number
       a call number
    X a classification
       the location of a specific book-title
       on the library's shelves

3. Someone needing information about _____
   A I D S disease
   should look for subject cards with the 1st
   line subject-heading wording_____
     ACQUIRED IMMUNE DEFICIENCY SYNDROME
   _____

4. Airways_____
   is an established subject-heading.

    X TRUE   FALSE

5. If interested in _aids to navigation____
   _____
   _____ ,
   you should check that exact wording as·
   well as AIDS TO AIR NAVIGATION; ASTRONAU-
   TICS IN NAVIGATION; BEACONS; BUOYS; ELECTRON-
   ICS IN NAVIGATION; FOG-BELLS; FOG-SIGNALS; ICE BREAKING OPERATIONS; LIGHTHOUSES; and
   NAUTICAL CHARTS in the subject catalog.

6. Electronics in aeronautics_____   is broader/~~narrower~~
                                                 X
   than Aids to air navigation_____ .

7. There is a total of # 16 SEE ALSO-type cross references ("sa") indicated in
   this excerpt; there is a total of # 4   SEE cross references.

8. An example of a subject-heading displayed in this excerpt which it's likely you
   will find subdivided geographically in a library's catalog is _____
   AIDS TO AIR NAVIGATION or AIDS TO NAVIGATION _____ .

9. For publications about lighthouse service aspects of aids to navigation _____ ,
   you could check the library shelves in the vicinity of the Library of Congress
   Classification _VK1000-VK1249_____ .

10. Which one of the following is <u>not</u> an established LCSH subject-heading?
        Aids to air navigation-- Defense measures Navigational aids (Aeronautics) X
        Lighthouses   Technical assistance

11. Defense measures_____ is

        a SEE ALSO cross reference   an established subject-heading
        a SEE cross reference   X a subdivision of a subject-heading

MORE LIBRARY BASICS

Assign study of "More Library Basics." On that date in the classroom, go over each of the points introduced on page 1. Having mastered the principles for locating periodical articles by use of Readers' Guide, students should be encouraged to recognize two other important things: (1) Readers' Guide is not subject-specialized. In doing research, they will need first to be able to identify the appropriate periodical index(es) in terms of their subject-specialization. (2) Applied Science & Technology, Humanities, and Social Sciences Indexes are semispecialized (see page 6). Within each of these three areas are numerous subjects (See page 1 of Assignment 4, which can be distributed now if you wish). Examples of the three semispecialized periodical indexes plus one subject-specialized index are provided on page 5. Ask class members to identify their scope and titles based on what they see in the excerpts.

#1 For example: Marx, crime, Economist, psychologist, labor, trade, United Nations
[Social Sciences Index April 1985-March 1986 volume 12, page 980]

#2 For example: history, film, god Hermes, God, euthanasia, a poem, Nineteenth Century Fiction, George Meredith [Humanities Index April 1985-March 1986 volume 12, page 662]

#3 For example: drug, Science, computer, air conditioning, drug factories, immunization
[Applied Science & Technology Index 1985, page 646]

#4 For example: Times Higher Education Supplement, curriculum, teaching, peers, home economics
[Education Index July 1984-June 1985 volume 35, page 542]

Discussion Questions:

Within which of the three large areas (#'s 1, 2 and 3; social sciences, humanities, applied sciences and technologies) would education be classified? Distinguish between the Library of Congress Classification and use of "classified" here.

Why is indexing under the subject GERMINATION present in #4--The Education Index? [It relates to teaching of this; note J of Biol Educ.] For each excerpt as time permits: Identify SEE and SEE ALSO cross references. Point out subject entries and especially those with subdivisions, e.g. #1 MIGRANT LABOR is a subject heading under which one article is cited, whereas MIGRANT LABOR--INTERNATIONAL ASPECTS is another subject heading, under which two articles are cited. Explain use of brackets [ ] for title enhancement (2 and 3).

Using #1 Social Sciences Index excerpt: Mies, Herbert is the first line.
It represents the author of the article, "'No!' to the traditions of German imperialism," which is an article also listed elsewhere in this same Index cumulation
under at least one subject entry--what might that subject heading sound like?
[GERMANY ... is a reasonable and reasoning response.] Miethe, Terance D. is
the author of the second article cited in this excerpt. Who is the author of the
third cited article? [F. T. Cullen and others.] So this "Consensus...." article
would be indexed under and for someone interested in the subject of MIETHE,
TERANCE D. Where is the author entry for it located, then? [In the C's under
Curren, F------ T.]

Do any of the Social Sciences Index excerpts contain bibliographic support--
a bibliography? Yes, two: "Treatment of childhood migraine using autogenic
feedback training" under the subject, MIGRAINE, and "International trade and
labor migration" under the subject MIGRANT LABOR--INTERNATIONAL ASPECTS.

How many articles about MIGRANT LABOR are listed? [one--"The new
economics of labor migration."]

If you needed more articles about MIGRANT LABOR, what would you look
under? [Any and all of the six SEE ALSO's: AGRICULTURAL LABORERS ...
CHILDREN OF MIGRANT LABORERS.]

Using the #2 Humanities Index excerpt: How would you transcribe to a bib
card the first article? [Do it on the board together, including the first two steps:
source and bibliographic data]

Suppose you needed more information such as that provided by F. E.
Devine's article, "Burke's reflections on criminal punishment." How many things
can you think of to do? Look under GOD--MERCY and SYMPATHY in this cumulation of the Humanities Index; look under them as well as MERCY in preceding
and subsequent Humanities Index cumulations; look under Devine, F. E. in this
cumulation, in the D's, to get her/his full name and possibly other articles under
that authorship; take author's full name to library card catalog for books; get
the article itself and check the bibliography (i.e., get from the library stacks the
bound volume containing the issue in which the article was published). How would
you go about getting the library call number for the volume? Suppose the library
doesn't subscribe to this periodical, how would you proceed?

HOW DO YOU FIND ARTICLES IN PERIODICALS? Use the right periodical index efficiently! Readers' Guide to Periodical Literature provides "subject access" to the contents of the periodicals it regularly indexes. Maga=zine and journal articles are usually useful because of their subject-matter, rather than who wrote them primarilly. Readers' Guide... also has author access, and sometimes you can find things under the title. Below is an excerpt from volume 44, which covered the period March 1984-February 1985, page 1105. If you are interested in very general information about Malaysia, the "See also" in Italics instructs you to look under the five subject headings listed, starting Agriculture-- Malaysia, elsewhere in this same, alphabetical, volume of Readers' Guide. Consider the first cited article, "The soul of a people":

Malaysia
See also
Agriculture—Malaysia
Anti-Semitism—Malaysia
Hotels, motels, etc.—Malaysia
Public health—Malaysia
Water supply—Malaysia
Civilization
The soul of a people [rice and civilization] Z. Kling. il *UNESCO Cour* 37:32-3 D '84
Industries
See also
Electronic industries—Malaysia
Politics and government
Malaysia: policies and leadership. R. S. Milne and D. K. Mauzy. bibl f *Curr Hist* 83:426-30+ D '84
Malcolm, Andrew H., 1943-
Dad. il *N Y Times Mag* p58 Ja 8 '84
In pursuit of the perfect cheeseburger. il *Read Dig* 124:171-4 My '84
On a wing and a computer. il *N Y Times Mag* p42-4+ F 12 '84
(jt. auth) See Morrison, Patt, and Malcolm, Andrew H., 1943-
Malcolm, Janet
about
Masson charges Knopf, New Yorker with libel. C. Goodrich. *Publ Wkly* 226:21 D 21 '84
Malcolm, Sara Jennifer
The truth about orgasm. *Ms* 13:67 O '84
Malcolm X, 1925-1965
about
Omaha, Neb. group seeking memorial honoring Malcolm X. por *Jet* 66:5 Je 4 '84
Malcomson, Scott L.
The high cost of helping Hassan. il *Nation* 239:674-5 D 22 '84
Malder, Francine
(ed) See Piazza, Kenneth M. The love debt: can you afford it?
Maldives
Underwater encounters in the Indian Ocean. B. Good. il *Oceans* 17:34-41 My/Je '84
Male psychology See Masculinity (Psychology); Men—Psychology
Male secretaries See Secretaries
Male striptease
A first-hand report on the silly, sexy, surprising scene at male strip clubs. M. A. Kellogg. il *Glamour* 82:200+ Ag '84

Malaysia-- Civilization is the specific subject heading under which it is found. (Civilization is the subdivision, similar to the subject heading structure used in the library catalog for books.)
Z. Kling is the author of our article. (Elsewhere, on page 1016 in the K's, is the author entry for this article; the author's full name is Zainal Kling.)
[rice and civilization]=Information in brackets is provided by the indexer so the user has a better idea of what the article contains; this is like the information sometimes found at the beginning of a magazine article, and is referred to as title enhancement.
il = The article is illustrated.
UNESCO Cour = The abbreviation of the periodical in which the article is published appears in Italics. Abbrev-iations are spelled out in the front of every volume and issue of the per-iodical index.
37 = volume # of the periodical
32-3 = The article begins on page 32, and ends on page 33.
D '84 = Date of the periodical issue: December 1984.

Malcolm, Andrew H., 1943- is not another subject entry; it is an author entry for 3 articles by him, which are probably also accessible elsewhere under at least one subject-heading.
Malcolm, Janet, however, is a subject heading leading to one article about her; C. Goodrich wrote it.
Male secretaries is a cross reference= For information about male secretaries, look under SECRETARIES when you use Readers' Guide.

Periodical indexing is constantly being made more accessible. While not changing the basic ground rules, the producers simplify and enhance the data display (and even make it retrievable in many libraries by computer.) Retrospective issues of periodicals contain valuable information, making it essential that you use back cumulations (volumes) of periodical indexes to access it. Below is an excerpt from volume 36, which covered the period March 1976-February 1977, page 1219. Consider the second cited article, "Republican politics-- let's make a deal; Equal Rights Amendment on the Republican platform".

WOMEN and politics
It's up to women to elect a good president. M. Mead. Redbook 146:38+ Mr '76
➤ Republican politics—let's make a deal: Equal rights amendment on the Republican platform. J. Freeman. il Ms 5:19-20 N '76
Something did happen at the Democratic national convention. J. Freeman. il Ms 5:74-6+ O '76
Womanpower! A new American doctrine. B. Abzug. por Redbook 146:34+ F '76
Women's planks in the party platforms: ERA, the issue for party platforms. M. McLaughlin. McCalls 103:36 Je '76

WOMEN and religion
Assertiveness for Christian women. J. Scanzoni. il Chr Today 20:16-18 Je 4 '76
Catholics and the E.R.A. A. Swidler. Commonweal 103:585-9 S 10 '76
Egalitarianism and scriptural infallibility. H. H. Lindsell. Chr Today 20:45-6 Mr 26 '76
Feminism: a new reformation; ed by F. X. Murphy. H. Küng. N Y Times Mag p34-5 My 23 '76
Gearing up for Portland; United Methodist church's annual meeting of the women's caucus. J. C. Lyles. Chr Cent 93:276-7 Mr 24 '76
Women and ministry. K. Gilfeather. America 135:101-4 O 2 '76
Women and missions. G. Hunt. Chr Today 20:37 Mr 26 '76
Women and the language of religion. C. Miller and K. Swift. Chr Cent 93:353-8 Ap 14 '76
Women in the church. T. Balasuriya. Commonweal 103:39-42 Ja 16 '76
Women in the limelight. il Chr Today 20:36 Je 18 '76
See also
Nuns
Ordination of women
Women—Religious life
Women clergy
Women in the Bible
WOMEN and the church. See Women and religion
WOMEN and the United Nations. See United Nations—Womens participation
WOMEN and war
See also
Vietnamese war, 1957-1975—Women
WOMEN architects
From high rises to restaurants: seven architects break ground. H. Rochlin. il Ms 5:10+ D '76
See also
Gray, E.
WOMEN artists
Art. See occasional issues of Ms.
Art: exhibition: 7 American women: the depression decade. L. Alloway. Nation 222:220-1 F 21 '76
Gallery (cont) il Ms 4:34+ Mr; 41-3 Je; 5:27-9 O '76
Great artists? Great women. J. Smyth. il Design 78:2-5 Wint '76
Pains and pleasures of rebirth: women's body art. L. R. Lippard. bibl il Art in Am 64:73-81 My '76

WOMEN and politics = the subject head for the first 5 cited articles.
"Republican politics-- let's make a deal; Equal rights amendment on the Republican platform." = the title of this article.
J. Freeman = author of the article.
il = article is illustrated.
Ms = abbrev. of title of magazine in which the article appeared.
5 = article appears in volume 5, on
19-20 = pages 19 and 20.
N '76 = article is in the November 1976 issue of Ms. magazine.

WOMEN and religion = the next (2nd) subject heading
See also (in Italics) = For additional articles related to WOMEN and religion and to aspects of this subject, see these 5 subject headings also, elsewhere in this Readers' Guide volume.
WOMEN and the United Nations = This is not an established subject heading, but for information, you can "See" United Nations--Womens participation", in the U's in this index.
For information about WOMEN architects, there is one article cited as well as a See also leading to a person associated with this subject: E. Gray may be an author of a related article, or an architect.

Always: 1. Look for the explanation at the front of the periodical index.
2. Locate the keys to abbreviations, usually found in the front of the index.
3. Find out exactly what time period is covered by each cumulation or issue of the periodical index you are using.
4. Search all relevant subject headings, paying attention to cross-references.
5. Copy all relevant information including author, title, periodical title, volume #, date of the periodical issue, inclusive pagination, etc.
6. To get the issue containing the article you want to read, consult the library's serials file under the title of the periodical.

GLOSSARY

CUMULATION: To keep up-to-date systematically with new magazine articles,
a periodical index cumulates. Readers' Guide, for example, is first
published in the form of temporary, paper supplements. Every few
months this indexing is interfiled into temporary-but-larger issues
called cumulations. At the end of the indexing period, all of
the entries appearing in all of the interim cumulations are interfiled into the one, big, permanent bound volume which replaces all
of the interim coverage. (In a library card catalog, the cards for
new books are interfiled right in among those already filed.)

JOURNAL: Scholarly periodicals are usually referred to as journals. Often
a newspaper will have the word journal in its name, reflecting the
original meaning of the word "jour"-- French for "day".

MAGAZINE: A periodical for general reading, containing articles on various subjects by different authors. Readers' Guide indexes the contents of popular magazines.

NEWSPAPER: A daily or weekly serial publication containing news and
opinion of current events, feature articles, and usually advertising.

PERIODICAL: A publication such as a newspaper, magazine, or journal,
that has a distinctive title and is intended to appear in successive
numbers or parts at stated or regular intervals ; as a rule, for an
indefinite period of time. It is usually issued with paper covers
and is later bound by libraries. Often periodicals, especially
newspapers, are microfilmed for library collections. (See also:
serial.)

SERIAL: A regularly issued publication ... newspapers, journals, magazines, annual reports, yearbooks, periodicals, monographic series ...; also

irregular publications. This is a more inclusive term than period-

ical. (See also periodical, journal, magazine, newspaper.)

VOLUME: Numerically, a volume is a full set of issues (or numbers)

which comprise a serial volume bound together. Two or three

numerical volumes are usually bound into one physical volume. Bib-

liographic citations use the term in the numerical sense. Most li-

braries'records utilize the serial volume number to locate their

holdings of periodicals. Readers' Guide and other periodical in-

dexes also refer to the volume number of a periodical in which an

issue was published which contains an article of interest.

These terms inter-relate and sometimes mean different things to differ-

ent people. The following guide to serials terminology and access may help:

SERIALS

Periodicals — Newspapers — Series

Magazines — Journals

Annuals / Sets / etc.

Access
example:
Readers'
Guide

Access(indexing)
examples:
Social Sciences Index
Education Index
America:History & Life
Psych Abstracts
Business Periodicals Index
Humanities Index
Art Index
RILM Abstracts of Music
Literature
Applied Science & Technol-
ogy Index
Science Citation Index
Excerpta Medica
Technical Book Review
Index
Agricultural Index
Biological Abstracts

Access(indexing)
example:
New York Times Index

Here are excerpts from 3 different semispecialized periodical indexes and 1 subject-specialized. Can you identify them?

The Applied Science & Technology Index   The Education Index

The Social Sciences Index   The Humanities Index

#1

Mies, Herbert
'No!' to the traditions of German imperialism. *World Marx Rev* 28:25-32 My '85

Miethe, Terance D.
Types of consensus in public evaluations of crime: an illustration of strategies for measuring "consensus". *J Crim Law Criminol* 75:459-73 Summ '84

about

Consensus in crime seriousness: empirical reality or methodological artifact? F. T. Cullen and others. bibl *Criminology* 23:99-118 F '85

Mifsud Bonnici, Karmenu

about

Malta: Mintoff's premature obituary. *World Today* 41:26 F '85

Mifune, Toshiro

about

The samurai who went solo. *Economist* 297:106-8 O 12 '85

Migraine
Fighting migraines with The Force. J. C. Horn. *Psychol Today* 19:74 N '85
Treatment of childhood migraine using autogenic feedback training. E. L. Labbé and D. A. Williamson. bibl *J Consult Clin Psychol* 52:968-76 D '84

Migrant labor

See also

Agricultural laborers
Agricultural laborers, Caribbean
Agricultural laborers, Mexican
Agricultural laborers, Saint Vincent and the Grenadines
Casual labor
Children of migrant laborers

The new economics of labor migration. O. Stark and D. E. Bloom. *Am Econ Rev* 75:173-8 My '85

International aspects

International trade and labor migration. W. J. Ethier. bibl *Am Econ Rev* 75:691-707 S '85

Migrant workers: recent trends. *UN Mon Chron* 22 no2:12 '85

#2

Merchants, East Indian
Merchants and kingship: an interpretation of Indian urban history. S. J. Lewandowski. *J Urban Hist* 11:151-79 F '85

Merchants, Indian (East Indian) *See* Merchants, East Indian

Merchants, Indic *See* Merchants, East Indian

Mercier, Jean A.

about

Film in a frame. il *Am Film* 11:39-41 N '85

Mercier, Laurie K.
(jt. auth) *See* Lang, William L., and Mercier, Laurie K.

Mercier, Louis-Sébastien, 1740-1814

about

L.-S. Mercier, Thomas Percival, and the anecdote of the prisoner preferring prison. E. W. Pitcher. *Am Notes Queries* 23:140-2 My/Je '85

Mercury (God)

See also

Hermes (God)

Mercy

See also

God—Mercy
Sympathy

Burke's reflections on criminal punishment. F. E. Devine. bibl *Midwest Q* 26:368-81 Spr '85

Mercy death *See* Euthanasia

Meredith, David
Government and the decline of the Nigerian oil-palm export industry, 1919-1939. *J Afr Hist* 25 no3:311-29 '84

Meredith, George, 1828-1909

about

George Meredith and Alice Meynell: a spurious attribution. A. D. Burnett. *Notes Queries* 31:501-2 D '84
Linguistic blindness and ironic vision in The egoist. G. J. Handwerk. *Nineteenth-Century Fict* 39:163-85 S '84

Meredith, Joseph
The old man in the garden [poem] *Southwest Rev* 70:244 Spr '85

#3

Drug abuse

See also

Drug withdrawal symptoms

ADAMHA funding pressed. C. Holden. *Science* 227:147-9 Ja 11 '85
A case for legal heroin. M. Cross. il *New Sci* 103:10-11 S 20 '84
Chemical abuse—unfit for fire duty. G. Carlson's. *Fire Eng* 137:8 D '84
Computer defects upset drugs crackdown. S. Connor. il *New Sci* 105:3 Mr 21 '85
Drug and alcohol problems in coal mines? D. Stritzel. *Min Eng* 37:583 Je '85
Drugged and victorious: doping in sport. P. Sperryn. il *New Sci* 103:16-19 Ag 2 '84
Getting straight again [Silicon Valley problems of drug and alcohol abuse] C. L. Howe. *Datamation* 31:32-4+ Ag 15 '85
Morphine analgesia potentiated but tolerance not affected by active immunization against cholecystokinin. P. L. Faris and others. bibl *Science* 226:1215-17 D 7 '84
New variety of street drugs poses growing problem. R. M. Baum. diags *Chem Eng News* 63:7-16 S 9 '85

Drug addiction *See* Drug abuse

Drug factories

Air conditioning

Down with dust [Torit "Downflo"] il *Pollut Eng* 17:22 Mr '85
HVAC systems for pharmaceutical clean room facilities. I. R. Meszaros. diags *Heat/Pip/Air Cond* 56:131-4+ N '84

Clean rooms

The effect of cleanroom design and manufacturing systems on the microbiological contamination of aseptically filled products. W. R. Frieben. bibl *J Environ Sci* 28:25-7 My/Je '85

#4

Germany (West). Federal Office of Languages *See* Germany (West). Bundessprachenamt

Germer, Paulette, and Miller, Richard E.
How peers perceive the female adolescent smoker. bibl *J Sch Health* 54:285-7 S '84

Germination
In vivo effects of barbiturates on seed germination and seedling growth. H. A. Kordan. bibl *J Biol Educ* 18:266-8 Wint '84
A winter sprout garden. H. Kim. il *Sci Child* 22:21-2 Ja '85

Germs *See* Microorganisms

Gerontology

See also

Aged

Ageism: a course of study. M. I. Sorgman and M. Sorensen. bibl *Theory Pract* 23:117-23 Spr '84
A question of decline or fall [interview with P. Rabbitt] P. Aspden. il por *Times Higher Educ Suppl* 642:12 F 22 '85

Curriculum

Intergenerational service-learning: contributions to curricula. J. Firman and others. *Educ Gerontol* 9:405-15 S/D '83

Subject matter

Death and dying: issues for educational gerontologists. H. Wass and J. E. Myers. bibl *Educ Gerontol* 10 no1-2:65-81 '84

Teaching

Clinical issues in the supervision of geriatric mental health trainees. R. W. Hubbard. *Educ Gerontol* 10 no4-5:317-23 '84
Home economics resources for the elderly: an integrative teaching approach. S. L. Van Zandt and others. *Ill Teach Home Econ* 28:11-14 S/O '84
Issues and implications of aging for home economics. G. F. Sanders. *Ill Teach Home Econ* 28:14-16 S/O '84

The scope of periodical indexes will be described in the introduction to each volume. The major areas covered by APPLIED SCIENCE & TEHCNOLOGY INDEX# include:

Aeronautics, Space Science	Mathematics
Chemistry	Metallurgy
Computer Technology	Meteorology
Construction	Mineralogy
Energy	Petroleum, Gas
Engineering	Physics
Fire Prevention	Robotics
Food	Solid State Technology
Geology	Telecommunications
Machinery	Textiles
Marine Technology, Oceanography	Transportation

The major areas covered by HUMANITIES INDEX* include:

Art	Language, Literature
Archaeology, Classical Studies	Music
Area Studies	Performing Arts
Folklore	Philosophy
History	Photography
Journalism, Communications	Religion, Theology

The major areas covered by SOCIAL SCIENCES INDEX* include:

Anthropology	Planning, Public Administration
Black Studies	Political Science
Economics	Psychology
Environmental Sciences	Sociology
Geography	Urban Studies
Health, Medicine	Women Studies
Law, Criminology	

----

* Before 1974, Humanities and Social Sciences Indexes were combined in the SOCIAL SCIENCES & HUMANITIES INDEX (1965-1974); this index was previously known as the INTERNATIONAL INDEX (1907-1965).

Before 1958, Applied Science and Technology Index and Business Periodicals Index were combined in the INDUSTRIAL ARTS INDEX (1913-1957).

SERIALS CATALOG, PARTS 1 and 2; and MORE LIBRARY BASICS

Serials Catalog, Part 1:

Assign in the previous class More Library Basics, especially pages 1-2; distribute Assignment 3 in the previous class (or earlier).

Part 1 is planned for in-class use. First discuss the layout of a periodical index subject-entry, using pages 1-2 of More Library Basics. Emphasize the basics. (Questions 1, 2 and 3 of Assignment 3 will help if you have not done this before.) Stress data in a periodical index citation which are essential for locating in your library's collection the volume in which the issue containing the cited article appears. In short, how one gets from a subject-entry for a particular article of interest, to the library's serials-holdings record, so one can then go to the shelves in the library and get the article to read.

Each form should be prepared (completed) by 1) adding (staple or tape, or duplicate if necessary) an excerpt such as the Social Sciences Index excerpt which appears on the first page of the Inventory, and 2) inserting the title of that index. Use Applied Science & Technology, Humanities, and Social Sciences Indexes as sources for this work. Select and mark an article in the excerpt with a red arrow, making sure it is 1) listed clearly under a subject-heading and includes an author's name and inclusive pagination, and 2) it is in the library's collection. The ideal is a worksheet for each student in terms of her/his interests as indicated in the autobiographical form completed at the same time as the Inventory. This necessitates having a large and varied file of excerpts derived from approximately the last ten years' cumulated volumes of these indexes and assigning each student her/his own example. At the other extreme is the possibility of a learning experience in which the worksheets are not personalized and even some duplicate excerpts used.

Having discussed the principles of a periodical index subject-entry layout, then (not before) distribute Serials Catalog, Part 1 (by name or en masse), ask the class to begin as soon as they receive theirs, put their name on it, complete it in five minutes, and turn it in at the end of class. Time this to end when the class is scheduled to end. Leave any absentees' forms in the box after class. If too many students are unable to accomplish this, you have an indication of how to adjust your lecture-discussion on interpreting a periodical index entry! Do not return them until the next class meeting in the library, probably the meeting after the next. Bring them to office hours in the meantime, however, in the event that students are concerned about how they did.

Serials Catalog, Part 2:

In the previous classroom class, use a multiple handout of a representative portion of the library's serials record. Duplicate it on color-coded paper if a color is associated with this file or with serials in your library. Instruct in interpretation. Emphasize volume number and making the transition from the periodical index, which is in any library, to the serials record, which is only in our library, and leads to our library's collection.

Part 2 is an in-library activity. Prepare (complete) it by duplicating it with a copy of the local serials charge-card on the verso. It is wise to staple together Parts 1 and 2.

Begin the class in the library by reviewing the routines for interpreting the library's serials file records in order to locate a volume or an issue of a given periodical title. (Begin to refer to "journals.") Before distributing their individual in-library work, also point out the locations of the various terminals, fiche files or whatever is used in your library, and that you will be moving about among them. Students should signal you if they are unable to find a record which communicates the location in our library of the volume of the periodical which includes the issue in which their article appears. If the class is large, point out they can begin work on Question 2 while waiting for a terminal, reader, whatever. Collect them five minutes before the end of class time.

In the next class, back in the classroom, return Parts 1 and 2. Discuss any "questions" or move directly into continuing, related work: page 5 of More Library Basics.

Here is a copy of an excerpt from a page of
the periodicals index titled _____

_____ .

You are concerned with the citation which
has the arrow. You do not need to refer to
the Index itself to do this work today.

Normally, when you have selected such a citation because of its relevance to your
work, you would transfer these data, together with the title and date of the source
Index itself, to a bib card. The next step
would then be to go to the Serials Catalog
in order to determine:

   1. All of the library locations on campus which have this issue of
      this periodical, and

   2. their call numbers, which may vary. Some libraries do not
      classify their periodicals.

In order to use the Serials Catalog efficiently, you will need to know
the exact wording of the periodical title and sometimes also of the
issuing agency (publisher, sponsor, whatever). For example, the "Journal"
of the American Medical Association.

Abbreviations for periodicals' titles are spelled out in every periodical
index, usually in an alphabetical list in the front of each index volume
or supplement. So, in the future, while you are still handling the periodical index and before going to the Serials Catalog, be sure to record
on your bib card the full accurate title of the journal or magazine.

From the excerpt above, get the following information:
1. The complete TITLE of the indexed-ARTICLE: "_____

   _____

                                                                      ".
                                                                       .
2. The SUBJECT of the article. What is the complete SUBJECT HEADING
    assigned to it by the Index? What is the article about? (Get into
    the habit of recording subject headings in ALL CAPS):

3. The TITLE of the periodical in which the indexed-article was published
    is abbreviated within the indexing. Record here exactly the way it
    appears abbreviated in the indexing._____
4. The AUTHOR's name as it appears within the indexing excerpt:

   _____ 5. The VOLUME NUMBER
   of the periodical in which the article was published:_____
6. The DATE of the issue of the periodical in which the article was pub-
    lished:_____ . 7. The number(s) of the first and last
    page of the article:_____   _____ .

Here is a copy of an excerpt from a page of the periodicals index titled _____

__SOCIAL SCIENCES INDEX__ .

You are concerned with the citation which has the arrow. You do not need to refer to the Index itself to do this work today.

Normally, when you have selected such a citation because of its relevance to your work, you would transfer these data, together with the title and date of the source Index itself, to a bib card. The next step would then be to go to the Serials Catalog in order to determine:

> Middle East—Industrialization—*cont.*
> The smaller they are [slump in construction market] P. Ensor. *Far East Econ Rev* 127:60 Ja 17 '85
> **Industries**
> *See also*
> Agriculture—Middle East
> **Politics**
> *See also*
> Terrorism—Middle East
> Britain: hope renewed for Mideast peace. Y. Li. *Beijing Rev* 28:12 O 7 '85
> Chronology. See issues of The Middle East Journal
> Jordan-Palestine: Middle East stalemate broken. *Beijing Rev* 28:12-13 Mr 11 '85
> Middle East: Arab nations set to solve disputes. J. Chen and G. Zhou. *Beijing Rev* 28:13 S 30 '85
> Middle East: behind the war of violence. J. Nan. *Beijing Rev* 28:11-12 O 28 '85
> The Middle East: from transition to development [symposium]; ed. by S. G. Hajjar. *J Asian Afr Stud* 19:3-272 Jl/O '84
> Middle East: Syrian-Soviet alliance faces test. *Beijing Rev* 27:14-15 O 29 '84

1. All of the library locations on campus which have this issue of this periodical, and

2. their call numbers, which may vary. Some libraries do not classify their periodicals.

In order to use the Serials Catalog efficiently, you will need to know the exact wording of the periodical title and sometimes also of the issuing agency (publisher, sponsor, whatever). For example, the "Journal" of the American Medical Association.

Abbreviations for periodicals' titles are spelled out in every periodical index, usually in an alphabetical list in the front of each index volume or supplement. So, in the future, while you are still handling the periodical index and before going to the Serials Catalog, be sure to record on your bib card the full accurate title of the journal or magazine.

From the excerpt above, get the following information:
1. The complete TITLE of the indexed-ARTICLE: " _____

_____

_____ ".

2. The SUBJECT of the article. What is the complete SUBJECT HEADING assigned to it by the Index? What is the article about? (Get into the habit of recording subject headings in ALL CAPS):

3. The TITLE of the periodical in which the indexed-article was published is abbreviated within the indexing. Record here exactly the way it appears abbreviated in the indexing. _____
4. The AUTHOR's name as it appears within the indexing excerpt:

_____ 5. The VOLUME NUMBER
of the periodical in which the article was published: _____
6. The DATE of the issue of the periodical in which the article was published: _____ . 7. The number(s) of the first and last page of the article: _____ _____ .

Here is a copy of an excerpt from a page of
the periodicals index titled _____

SOCIAL SCIENCES INDEX   .

You are concerned with the citation which
has the arrow. You do not need to refer to
the Index itself to do this work today.

Normally, when you have selected such a citation because of its relevance to your
work, you would transfer these data, together with the title and date of the source
Index itself, to a bib card. The next step
would then be to go to the Serials Catalog
in order to determine:

> Middle East—Industrialization—*cont.*
> The smaller they are [slump in construction market]
>   P. Ensor. *Far East Econ Rev* 127:60 Ja 17 '85
>   **Industries**
>   *See also*
>   Agriculture—Middle East
>   **Politics**
>   *See also*
>   Terrorism—Middle East
> Britain; hope renewed for Mideast peace. Y. Li. *Beijing
>   Rev* 28:12 O 7 '85
> Chronology. See issues of The Middle East Journal
> Jordan-Palestine: Middle East stalemate broken. *Beijing
>   Rev* 28:12-13 Mr 11 '85
> Middle East: Arab nations set to solve disputes. J. Chen
>   and G. Zhou. *Beijing Rev* 28:13 S 30 '85
> Middle East: behind the war of violence. J. Nan. *Beijing
>   Rev* 28:11-12 O 28 '85
> The Middle East: from transition to development [sym-
>   posium] ed. by S. G. Hajjar. *J Asian Afr Stud* 19:3-272
>   Jl/O '84
> Middle East: Syrian-Soviet alliance faces test. *Beijing
>   Rev* 27:14-15 O 29 '84

1. All of the library locations on campus which have this issue of
   this periodical, and

2. their call numbers, which may vary. Some libraries do not
   classify their periodicals.

In order to use the Serials Catalog efficiently, you will need to know
the exact wording of the periodical title and sometimes also of the
issuing agency (publisher, sponsor, whatever). For example, the "Journal"
of the American Medical Association.

Abbreviations for periodicals' titles are spelled out in every periodical
index, usually in an alphabetical list in the front of each index volume
or supplement. So, in the future, while you are still handling the periodical index and before going to the Serials Catalog, be sure to record
on your bib card the full accurate title of the journal or magazine.

From the excerpt above, get the following information:
1. The complete TITLE of the indexed-ARTICLE: " Middle East: behind

    the war of violence

                                                             ".

2. The SUBJECT of the article. What is the complete SUBJECT HEADING
    assigned to it by the Index? What is the article about? (Get into
    the habit of recording subject headings in ALL CAPS):
    MIDDLE EAST-- POLITICS
3. The TITLE of the periodical in which the indexed-article was published
    is abbreviated within the indexing. Record here exactly the way it
    appears abbreviated in the indexing. Beijing Rev
4. The AUTHOR's name as it appears within the indexing excerpt:

    J. Nan
                                                   5. The VOLUME NUMBER
    of the periodical in which the article was published: 28
6. The DATE of the issue of the periodical in which the article was pub-
    lished: October 28, 1985   . 7. The number(s) of the first and last
    page of the article: 11   12   .

This activity provides opportunity for supervised practice and review using the Serials Catalog. It should be possible to do this work quickly in the time remaining. Bring any questions directly to me; work independently. Turn this and Part 1 in 5 minutes before the end of class.

This continues your work on "Serials Catalog. Part 1".

1. In order to determine whether the library has THIS ISSUE of this periodical, you need to know:

    - the title of the periodical

    - the volume number of this periodical in which your issue appeared, and

    - the date of this issue.

    These are numbers 1, 5, and 6 of Part 1, which has been returned to you.

Now go to the Serials Catalog. Most, although not all, serials are main-entried by title and thus listed here alphabetically by title. Do not consider libraries which have some issues but not this issue of this serial. List one library which holds this specific issue according to the Serials Catalog.

If the periodical title abbreviation does not seem to provide you with sufficient information to utilize the Serials Catalog readilly, check with me.

Call Number_____ Library code _____

Name of the library. Consult the list of codes posted by the Serials Catalog._____
Building in which the library is located_____

2. Assume that : this issue circulates; it has already been bound with other issues from this time period (usually a year); the serial has been cataloged; it is classified and now shelved with books and other serials in the classification for this subject matter. Fill out the loan card reproduced on the verso.

Required Reading: "More Library Basics" handout.
- -

1. Use the glossary (and a dictionary) to differentiate among <u>series</u>,<u>journals</u>,
   <u>serials</u>, <u>periodicals</u>, <u>magazines</u> and <u>newspapers</u>. All of these are
   included within the scope of the serials catalog. Identify one <u>series</u>
   title referred to in Assignment 1: Question #____ . Series title (not
   the title of the portion of that series which is the part of assignment
   #1):"_____
   _____."

Now we'll concentrate on the kinds of serials with which you're probably
most familiar: <u>magazines</u> and <u>journals</u>. Indexes are as important for re-
trieving information from periodicals as the card catalog is for books.
The <u>Readers' Guide</u> is a good index to master now because once you learn
how to use it efficiently, you'll be able to find your way around more
specialized serials' indexes and abstracting services because many of
these are organized on the same principles. It is the specialized periodical indexes you'll need for college work in general and the Project in
particular. So we'll consider four H. W. Wilson Company periodical indexes
together: Location In the Reference Dept.:
   <u>READERS' GUIDE</u>, 1900-   . (1900 dash space means it began indexing in
       that year and continues to do so...)   _____
   <u>APPLIED SCIENCE & TECHNOLOGY INDEX</u>, 1958-   . _____
   <u>HUMANITIES INDEX</u>, 1974-   .   _____
   <u>SOCIAL SCIENCES INDEX</u>, 1974-   .   _____

2. <u>Readers' Guide</u> currently indexes (analyzes) the contents of approximately 181 of the most popular magazines to which most libraries subscribe. Magazines and newspapers emphasize SUBJECT-INFORMATION and
   the SUBJECT-APPROACH. So periodical indexes usually list articles
   mainly by subject... what they're about... but sometimes also under
   the author's name.

   <u>Readers' Guide</u> volume # _44_ covers what period of time? This means
   that the articles indexed in volume # _44_ were published approximately during the period of time between what two dates? _____
   and _____ . Turn to the most recent <u>Readers' Guide</u> major
   CUMULATION (bound volume) and study the "Suggestions For Use" in the
   front of the volume. ALWAYS DO THIS BEFORE YOU USE ANY REFERENCE TOOL
   FOR THE FIRST TIME. Then examine the volume over-all, cover-to-cover.
   What is the number of the most recent bound volume of <u>Readers' Guide</u>
   (not a paper supplement)? _____   What indexing period does it
   cover? _____

   Locate the subject-entry for an article approximately #_5_ pages
   long about the subject of RHETORIC_____ ,which
   appeared in the May 28, 1984_____ issue of a periodical which
   is regularly indexed in <u>Readers' Guide</u>. When you don't have the
   subject heading wording, first try the words you have.

2., contd.
Identify the R.G. volume dates: _____ - _____ and the
volume number:_____. Page numbers of the article itself (called
the "inclusive pagination"); the article begins on page ____ and
ends on page ____. R.G. Subject-heading under which you find the
article cited. Be sure to transcribe the complete subject-heading:

_____

These are not all Library of Congress subject headings. Try to realize why LC subject headings wouldn't always be exactly suitable here
in R.G. or periodical indexes in general.   Full title of the magazine article:
"
_____
_____".

Study the "Suggestions For Use" some more, as well as the lists of
abbreviations for magazine titles and for other things in the front
of each volume of R.G. and any periodical index. What is the magazine's full, real title?_____
The authorship exactly as it appears within the citation for the subject entry of the article is_____
The author's FULL NAME exactly as it appears in the AUTHOR ENTRY on
page # 672   is _____
To what does   190:15_____ refer-- exactly what does each of
these two sets of numbers mean in this arrangement?_____

_____

3. At this point you know that an article may have more than one approach
when using a periodical index such as R.G.: the SUBJECT and the author
approaches (entries.) But remember: R.G. is mainly a SUBJECT INDEX,
so there may be several subject entries for an article. R.G.'s scope
is popular, English-language magazines available in most libraries.

When "searching" a thesaurus for subject heading wordings, a library's
catalogs for publications on a subject of interest, or a periodical index
under subjects, some good ground-rules are:
   (1) Be specific.
   (2) Check under what you have-- the specific words you're thinking
       right then, and
   (3) then get creative.

Turn to page # 1533 of R.G. volume # 44 . (Usually expressed like this:
 44:1533   ). Approx.how many articles about RHODE ISLAND-- POLITICS & GOVT.
are cited here?_____   Suppose you were interested in locating more
magazine articles on this same subject. What additional subject heading
would you already now know from this indexing information that you could
go ahead and check for further information in R.G.?_____

_____

Yes, Readers' Guide uses some of the techniques a card catalog uses. These
include:
   (1) A subject heading system with subdivisions and with some cross
       references--SEE's and SEE ALSO's.
   (2) A magazine article may appear under more than one subject heading.

3., contd.
   (3) "Mc"was filed as if spelled Mac until recently;
   (4) Such useful things as bibliographies, maps. and _____
       accompanying the articles are pointed out within the indexing.

Although there are similarities between R.G. and the library catalog, a
subject heading system which organizes information contained in books
cannot always organize information contained in periodicals. R.G.'s main
subject headings appear in heavy darker print over to the left. SUB-
headings are centered... this is something like subject headings and their
SUB-divisions on catalog cards.

IMPORTANT. In a card catalog (and sometimes in online catalogs), the
cards and the entries for new books are interfiled right in among those
already filed. To keep up-to-date systematically with new magazine articles, a periodical index cumulates... it keeps coming out just as the
issues of the periodicals themselves keep coming out! This means R.G.
is first published in the form of temporary paper supplements. Every
few months this indexing is interfiled into temporary-but-larger issues,
or interim cumulations. At the end of the indexing period all of the
entries appearing in all of the cumulations are interfiled into the one,
"big", permanent bound volume replacing all of the interim coverage, and
known as "the" cumulation. Currently, these major, bound volume,final
cumulations of R.G. occur how often?_____

Notice that in the past, R.G. cumulated volumes have covered larger spans
of time-- as large as several years at times. Volume # 7   covered the
period from _____ to _____. There are two
main ways having such frequent RG supplements to the current issues
benefits you:
   (1) When accumulated materials (articles) are interfiled, the number
       of searches YOU have to make is cut down.
   (2) You get quick access to the latest articles and information,
       points-of-view.

Be sure you understand and can explain clearly the crucial difference
(significance) between a cumulation of a serial publication and a supplement to it. Why would you prefer a periodical index which you're going to
use a lot to cumulate perhaps each year, rather than just appear four
separate times (quarterly) a year, for example?_____

_____

4. MAKING A PERIODICAL INDEX WORK FOR YOU.
    In order to search all relevant Readers' Guides for articles on a
    given subject published and indexed from approximately 1925
    to   June 1935   , a total of how many searching steps would be
    necessary? _____   How do you reach this conclusion?_____

_____

For current topics and up-to-date information on any subject, begin your
search using periodical indexes with the LATEST, small, paperbound,

4., contd.

supplementary issue, and work BACKWARDS systematically into combined, cumulated issues (the bound, numbered volumes.) BUT, for information on a subject connected with a certain date or for specific issues of a magazine, first check the volume (cumulation) covering that time.

Locate the subject-indexing for an article about business use of COMPUTERS   , which appeared in the June 23, 1979 issue of Saturday Review magazine   , and which is approximately # 4   pages long.

You'll use R.G. because   .

You'll make your initial approach to volume #_____ of this periodical index because   .

What is the volume # of the magazine in which the article appeared?____

Locate in the same volume of the periodical index (R.G.) the author-entry for this article. The author's complete name is_____ Page# of this author entry is_____

Which libraries have this issue of this periodical? Include the call numbers. Do not abbreviate.

Library/Libraries	Call Number(s)
_____	_____
_____	_____

The permanent, bound, cumulated volumes of R.G. and other periodical indexes also provide RETROSPECTIVE INDEXING to articles written at the time an event took place long ago. When did R.G. begin, i.e. what period of time does volume one cover?_____

For articles written at the time of and about the TITANIC disaster, the sinking of this ship   , you'd BEGIN a R.G. search with R.G. volume #____ because it covers (period of time)_____ -_____ . If necessary, turn to one of the "first aids" of reference work: an unabridged dictionary, a general encyclopedia, the library catalog, or a world almanac-- to get the date of such an event. In this case, an encyclopedia indicates that the disaster lasted from April 14-15, 1912.

Older issues of periodicals may be bound into volumes and/or transferred to various microforms.

The comprehensive record of the locations of periodicals, both current and retrospective, and of the issues of the periodicals which are in our libraries' collections is contained in the file called _____. But remember: It does NOT list magazine ARTICLES. It DOES list most of the periodicals' ISSUES which R.G. indexed in the past and indexes now, IF they are in our libraries. It also includes periodicals' holdings for many other magazines, journals and series which are not indexed by R.G.. To gain access to the CONTENTS of periodicals indexed by indexes other than R.G., you must use other periodical indexes, depending upon the SUBJECT-specialization of the periodicals.

5. To locate a BOOK REVIEW, what do you need to find out FIRST in order to use RG or any periodical index most efficiently? (1) The author of the review? Or (2) What the book-reviewed is about-- its subject? Or

5.. contd.
(3)The year the book was published? _____ Why? Because _____

_____

_____

Locate a review of " Nam: the Vietnam War in Words of the Men and
   Women Who Fought There _____",
by Mark Baker _____, published around
19 81. In fact, locate, ALL IN ONE SPOT, citations to SEVERAL reviews
of this book by means of efficient use of Readers' Guide. If you
have trouble locating several reviews of this book by means of efficient use of R.G., then you should again study the Suggestions
for Using Readers' Guide. as well as the overall physical arrangement of the volume itself. (Book reviews are segregated in the back!)

Space for your answer: R.G. volume #_____, page #_____, under the head-
ing:_____. Who wrote the longest review
indexed there?_____Who wrote the
review which was published in   the New York Times Book Review   ?

_____

6. With the indexing of all of this material ready so closely to the
time it was published (by means of the frequent supplements and interim
cumulations before major cumulated volumes are published), it's possible to locate a variety of points-of-view on controversial timely
subjects, commentary on recent developments, texts of important speeches
and documents, etc. etc.   Locate the address, or speech, made by
   Jesse L. Jackson   , titled " The Rainbow Coalition
_____", on July
17, 1984   .

The term "lag" refers to the LENGTH OF TIME it takes between publication date of a magazine issue and the date of the issue of the
periodical index in which the magazine issue is indexed. The longer
this lag (delay), THE LESS USEFUL the indexing information becomes.
This would be especially critical in which field, do you think?
There are several; identify one:_____
Lag also relates to the length of time between the date of an event,
such as a speech, and the date of the magazine issue in which it is
published...

Space for your answer. Remember: The date the speech was made will precede the date of the issue of the magazine in which it was published. In
what R.G. volume do you find indexing for this pseech by (not about Jesse
L. Jackson   ? Volume #___; dates covered by this R.G. volume:_____
_____. On what page in that volume?#_____ Under what heading do you
find indexing for this speech? Exact, complete wording under which you
locate it:_____ Title of the periodical
in which the address appears._____ Issue of that
periodical (volume, inclusive pagination, date)_____ _____
Does the library have this issue?_____ If yes, list one of the libraries
and the call #:_____

Your Name_____
Assignment 3: Locating Periodical In-
formation & Articles (Mostly Serials).
Due: In class on date on your schedule.

Required Reading: "More Library Basics" handout.
----

1. Use the glossary (and a dictionary) to differentiate among series, journals,
   serials, periodicals, magazines and newspapers. All of these are
   included within the scope of the serials catalog. Identify one series
   title referred to in Assignment 1: Question #1,3 . Series title (not
   the title of the portion of that series which is the part of assignment
   #1):"Comparative studies in social and economic history" / "Clinics in
      endocrinology and metabolism   ".

Now we'll concentrate on the kinds of serials with which you're probably
most familiar: magazines and journals. Indexes are as important for re-
trieving information from periodicals as the card catalog is for books.
The Readers' Guide is a good index to master now because once you learn
how to use it efficiently, you'll be able to find your way around more
specialized serials' indexes and abstracting services because many of
these are organized on the same principles. It is the specialized periodical indexes you'll need for college work in general and the Project in
particular. So we'll consider four H. W. Wilson Company periodical indexes
together: Location In the Reference Dept.:
   READERS' GUIDE, 1900-   . (1900 dash space means it began indexing in
      that year and continues to do so...)
   APPLIED SCIENCE & TECHNOLOGY INDEX, 1958-   . _____
   HUMANITIES INDEX, 1974-   .   _____
   SOCIAL SCIENCES INDEX, 1974-   .   _____

2. Readers' Guide currently indexes (analyzes) the contents of approximately 181 of the most popular magazines to which most libraries subscribe. Magazines and newspapers emphasize SUBJECT-INFORMATION and
   the SUBJECT-APPROACH. So periodical indexes usually list articles
   mainly by subject... what they're about... but sometimes also under
   the author's name.

   Readers' Guide volume # 44 covers what period of time? This means
   that the articles indexed in volume # 44   were published approximately during the period of time between what two dates? March 1984
   and Feb. 1985 . Turn to the most recent Readers' Guide major
   CUMULATION (bound volume) and study the "Suggestions For Use" in the
   front of the volume. ALWAYS DO THIS BEFORE YOU USE ANY REFERENCE TOOL
   FOR THE FIRST TIME. Then examine the volume over-all, cover-to-cover.
   What is the number of the most recent bound volume of Readers' Guide
   (not a paper supplement)? _____   What indexing period does it
   cover? _____

   Locate the subject-entry for an article approximately # 5   pages
   long about the subject of ____RHETORIC_____,which
   appeared in the ____May 28, 1984_____ issue of a periodical which
   is regularly indexed in Readers' Guide. When you don't have the
   subject heading wording, first try the words you have.

2., contd.
   Identify the R.G. volume dates: <u>March 1984</u> - <u>Feb. 1985</u>   and the
   volume number: <u>44</u>   . Page numbers of the article itself (called
   the "inclusive pagination"); the article begins on page <u>15</u>   and
   ends on page <u>19</u>   . R.G. Subject-heading under which you find the
   article cited. Be sure to transcribe the complete subject-heading:

      RHETORIC

   These are not all Library of Congress subject headings. Try to realize why LC subject headings wouldn't always be exactly suitable here
   in R.G. or periodical indexes in general.   Full title of the magazine article:

   " <u>The decline of oratory" (Or, "The decline of oratory [political or-
   atory]". Bracketed information enhances the title indexed.</u>   .
   Study the "Suggestions For Use" some more, as well as the lists of
   abbreviations for magazine titles and for other things in the front
   of each volume of R.G. and any periodical index. What is the magazine's full, real title? <u>New Republic</u>
   The authorship exactly as it appears within the citation for the subject entry of the article is <u>H. Fairlie</u>
   The author's FULL NAME exactly as it appears in the AUTHOR ENTRY on
   page # <u>672</u>   is <u>Henry Fairlie (Or, Fairlie, Henry)</u>
   To what does <u>190:15</u>   refer-- exactly what does each of
   these two sets of numbers mean in this arrangement? <u>190 is the number of</u>
   <u>the New Republic volume in which the article was published; 15 is the</u>
   <u>number of the first page of the article in the issue in that volume.</u>

3. At this point you know that an article <u>may</u> have more than one approach
   when using a periodical index such as R.G.: the SUBJECT and the author
   approaches (entries.) But remember: R.G. is mainly a SUBJECT INDEX,
   so there may be several subject entries for an article. R.G.'s scope
   is popular, English-language magazines available in most libraries.

When "searching" a thesaurus for subject heading wordings, a library's
catalogs for publications on a subject of interest, or a periodical index
under subjects, some good ground-rules are:
   (1) Be specific.
   (2) Check under what you have-- the specific words you're thinking
       right then, and
   (3) then get creative.

Turn to page # <u>1533</u> of R.G. volume # <u>44</u> . (Usually expressed like this:
<u>44:1533</u>   ). Approx.how many articles about RHODE ISLAND-- POLITICS & GOVT.
are cited here? <u>2</u>   Suppose you were interested in locating more
magazine articles on this same subject. What additional subject heading
would you already now know from this indexing information that you could
go ahead and check for further information in R.G.? <u>PRESIDENTIAL PRI-
MARIES-- RHODE ISLAND is listed as a "See also" related to RHODE ISLAND--
POLITICS AND GOVERNMENT (just above the article titled "Facing the canons".</u>
Yes, <u>Readers' Guide</u> uses some of the techniques a card catalog uses. These
include:
   (1) A subject heading system with subdivisions and with some cross
       references--SEE's and SEE ALSO's.
   (2) A magazine article may appear under more than one subject heading.

3., contd.
   (3) "Mc"was filed as if spelled Mac until recently;
   (4) Such useful things as bibliographies, maps, and <u>illustrations</u>
       accompanying the articles are pointed out within the indexing.

Although there are similarities between R.G. and the library catalog, a
subject heading system which organizes information contained in books
cannot always organize information contained in periodicals. R.G.'s main
subject headings appear in heavy darker print over to the left. <u>SUB</u>-
headings are centered... this is something like subject headings <u>and</u> their
<u>SUB</u>-divisions on catalog cards.

IMPORTANT. In a card catalog (and sometimes in online catalogs), the
cards and the entries for new books are interfiled right in among those
already filed. To keep up-to-date systematically with new magazine articles, a periodical index <u>cumulates</u>... it keeps coming out just as the
issues of the periodicals themselves keep coming out! This means R.G.
is first published in the form of <u>temporary paper supplements.</u> Every
few months this indexing is interfiled into temporary-but-larger issues,
or interim cumulations. At the end of the indexing period all of the
entries appearing in all of the cumulations are interfiled into the one,
"big", permanent bound volume replacing all of the interim coverage, and
known as "the" cumulation. Currently, these major, bound volume,final
cumulations of R.G. occur how often? <u>Once each year</u>, i.e. every 12 months,
   March/February.

Notice that in the past, R.G. cumulated volumes have covered larger spans
of time-- as large as several years at times. Volume # <u>7</u> covered the
period from <u>1925</u>   to   <u>1928</u>   . There are two
main ways having such frequent RG supplements to the current issues
benefits you:
   (1) When accumulated materials (articles) are interfiled, the number
       of searches YOU have to make is cut down.
   (2) You get quick access to the latest articles and information,
       points-of-view.

Be sure you understand and can explain clearly the crucial difference
(significance) between a <u>cumulation</u> of a serial publication and a <u>supple-
ment</u> to it. Why would you <u>prefer</u> a periodical index which you're going to
use a lot to cumulate perhaps each year, rather than just appear four
separate times (quarterly) a year, for example? <u>The larger the number of</u>
   <u>issues (or supplements), the more searching steps.</u>

4. MAKING A PERIODICAL INDEX WORK FOR YOU.
   In order to search all relevant <u>Readers' Guides</u> for articles on a
   given subject published and indexed from approximately <u>1925</u>   .
   to <u>June 1935</u>   , a total of how many searching steps would be
   necessary? <u>at least 3</u> How do you reach this conclusion? <u>1925-1928 (vol. 7)</u>
   <u>are in one volume+ 1929-June 1932 (vol. 8)+ July 1932-June 1935) vol. 9)= 3.</u>
   <u>And you might want to play it sure by checking volume 10 too.</u>

For current topics and up-to-date information on <u>any</u> subject, begin your
search using periodical indexes with the LATEST, <u>small</u>, paperbound,

4., contd.

supplementary issue, and work BACKWARDS systematically into combined, cumulated issues (the bound, numbered volumes.) BUT, for information on a subject connected with a certain date or for specific issues of a magazine, first check the volume (cumulation) covering that time.

Locate the subject-indexing for an article about business use of COMPUTERS   , which appeared in the June 23, 1979 issue of Saturday Review magazine   , and which is approximately # 4   pages long.

You'll use R.G. because it was indexing Saturday Review in 1979 (still is!)

You'll make your initial approach to volume # 39   of this periodical index because volume 39 covers March 1979-Feb. 1980 which includes June 1979.

What is the volume # of the magazine in which the article appeared? 6

Locate in the same volume of the periodical index (R.G.) the author-entry for this article. The author's complete name is Jon Stewart

Page# of this author entry is 1302

Which libraries have this issue of this periodical? Include the call numbers. Do not abbreviate.

Library/Libraries	Call Number(s)
_____	_____
_____	_____

The permanent, bound, cumulated volumes of R.G. and other periodical indexes also provide RETROSPECTIVE INDEXING to articles written at the time an event took place long ago. When did R.G. begin, i.e. what period of time does volume one cover? Vol. 1=1900-1904.

For articles written at the time of and about the TITANIC disaster, the sinking of this ship   , you'd BEGIN a R.G. search with R.G. volume # 3   because it covers (period of time) 1910   - 1914   . If necessary, turn to one of the "first aids" of reference work: an unabridged dictionary, a general encyclopedia, the library catalog, or a world almanac-- to get the date of such an event. In this case, an encyclopedia indicates that the disaster lasted from April 14-15, 1912.

Older issues of periodicals may be bound into volumes and/or transferred to various microforms.

The comprehensive record of the locations of periodicals, both current and retrospective, and of the issues of the periodicals which are in our libraries' collections is contained in the file called _____

_____. But remember: It does NOT list magazine ARTICLES. It DOES list most of the periodicals' ISSUES which R.G. indexed in the past and indexes now, IF they are in our libraries. It also includes periodicals' holdings for many other magazines, journals and series which are not indexed by R.G.. To gain access to the CONTENTS of periodicals indexed by indexes other than R.G., you must use other periodical indexes, depending upon the SUBJECT-specialization of the periodicals.

5. To locate a BOOK REVIEW, what do you need to find out FIRST in order to use RG or any periodical index most efficiently? (1) The author of the review? Or (2) What the book-reviewed is about-- its subject? Or

5.. contd.

(3)The year the book was published? __YEAR__ Why? Because the year the book was published would be necessary in order to use Readers' Guide to locate book reviews for a specific book,, due to its overall chronological arrangement. (Within each volume or supplement, it is arranged alphabetically by subjects/ authors.)

Locate a review of " Nam: the Vietnam War in Words of the Men and Women Who Fought There   ," by Mark Baker   , published around 19 81 . In fact, locate, ALL IN ONE SPOT, citations to SEVERAL reviews of this book by means of efficient use of Readers' Guide. If you have trouble locating several reviews of this book by means of ef- ficient use of R.G., then you should again study the Suggestions for Using Readers' Guide. as well as the overall physical arrange- ment of the volume itself. (Book reviews are segregated in the back!)

Space for your answer: R.G. volume # 41 , page # 1845 , under the head- ing: Baker, M.   . Who wrote the longest review indexed there? T. Ensign and M. Uhl (3 pages)   Who wrote the review which was published in the New York Times Book Review   ? M. Leepson (The Newsweek review pagination, "78+",does not imply a lengthy

article,but simply a little more on a subsequent page).

6. With the indexing of all of this material ready so closely to the time it was published (by means of the frequent supplements and interim cumulations before major cumulated volumes are published), it's pos- sible to locate a variety of points-of-view on controversial timely subjects, commentary on recent developments, texts of important speeches and documents, etc. etc.   Locate the address, or speech, made by Jesse L. Jackson   , titled " The Rainbow Coalition   ", on July 17, 1984   .

The term "lag" refers to the LENGTH OF TIME it takes between publica- tion date of a magazine issue and the date of the issue of the periodical index in which the magazine issue is indexed. The longer this lag (delay), THE LESS USEFUL the indexing information becomes. This would be especially critical in which field, do you think? There are several; identify one: developments in disease treatments Lag also relates to the length of time between the date of an event, such as a speech, and the date of the magazine issue in which it is published...

Space for your answer. Remember: The date the speech was made will pre- cede the date of the issue of the magazine in which it was published. In what R.G. volume do you find indexing for this pseech by (not about Jesse L. Jackson   ? Volume # 44 ; dates covered by this R.G. volume: March '84- Feb. '85 . On what page in that volume?#965   Under what heading do you find indexing for this speech? Exact, complete wording under which you locate it: Jackson, Jesse L., 1941-   Title of the periodical in which the address appears. Vital Speeches of the Day   Issue of that periodical (volume, inclusive pagination, date) 51:77-81 Nov. 15, 1984 Does the library have this issue?____ If yes, list one of the libraries and the call #:_____ _____

IN-LIBRARY PRACTICE: NEWSPAPER INDEXES

Serials Catalog, parts 1 and 2, and Assignment 3 should have been completed and Assignment 4 should have been distributed prior to using this worksheet. It is intended to cap a class meeting in the Newspapers or Periodicals (if this includes newspapers) library unit, in which you first cover the scope of the local collection and routines of accessing it. Because many large libraries' general reference departments also have a New York Times Index set, and if it is located in the same building, some students in a large class might be asked to volunteer to go to the reference department to complete this work. New York Times Index problems are provided in Section III: Resources.

Use of the New York Times Index provides early opportunity for transition into the concept of a periodical index carrying some information as well as locating it, i.e. while not an abstracting service, it is nonetheless often possible to obtain content-information from the Index page beyond citations to articles in the New York Times newspaper. Use of this Index to lead to articles and information in other newspapers can also be communicated to students. Its indexing utility for leads to book reviews (in the New York Times), obituaries, and biographical information, and theatrical and other reviews is also comparable to many other periodical indexes.

In the time remaining today, use the <u>New York Times Index</u>, located

There is rarely a research topic which does not need use of newspapers.
It is essential that you also study the explanation and "Key" to abbreviations in the front/back of the volumes of this Index.
Remember: The indexing date represents the date on which a news item
appeared in the newspaper... not necessarilly the date on which the
event took place. This Index is both a "locator" and a "carrier" of information... notice that considerable information appears on the index
page in addition to the subject headings and bibliographic data which
constitute the indexing... like a reference book... even photos.

- In "January 1, 5:2" you'd interpret January 1 as the date on which
  the article appeared in the newspaper. Then 5 would represent_____
  _____, and 2 would refer to_____

- If you were writing a report on

  which <u>New York Times Index</u> volume would you consult first? The one
  for 19_____ .

- Now check there. Under what subject heading wording do you find an
  article or articles on this subject indexed?

  Page number(s) in the <u>New York Times Index</u> where you find indexing
  citation(s):_____

  News events frequently continue over several days (issues). Select
  the one best-sounding article and list:

  Date of issue of the <u>New York Times</u> in which it appeared_____

  _____
  Page(s) in that issue_____
  Column #_____

- Consult the Serials Catalog for the Library location of this issue
  of the <u>New York Times</u>:

  _____

Turn this in 5 minutes before the end of class today.

In the time remaining today, use the <u>New York Times Index</u>, located

There is rarely a research topic which does not need use of newspapers. It is essential that you also study the explanation and "Key" to abbreviations in the front/back of the volumes of this Index.
Remember: The indexing date represents the date on which a news item appeared in the newspaper... not necessarilly the date on which the event took place. This Index is both a "locator" and a "carrier" of information... notice that considerable information appears on the index page in addition to the subject headings and bibliographic data which constitute the indexing... like a reference book... even photos.

- In "January 1, 5:2" you'd interpret January 1 as the date on which the article appeared in the newspaper. Then 5 would represent_____ _____, and 2 would refer to_____

- If you were writing a report on   crime during The Depression in the United States, particularly "Public Enemy Number One" John Dillinger's activities in Spring 1934,

  which <u>New York Times Index</u> volume would you consult first? The one for 19_____ .

- Now check there. Under what subject heading wording do you find an article or articles on this subject indexed?

  Page number(s) in the <u>New York Times Index</u> where you find indexing citation(s):_____

  News events frequently continue over several days (issues). Select the one best-sounding article and list:

    Date of issue of the <u>New York Times</u> in which it appeared_____

    Page(s) in that issue_____
    Column #_____

- Consult the Serials Catalog for the Library location of this issue of the <u>New York Times</u>:

  _____

Turn this in 5 minutes before the end of class today.

Course
Instructor

<u>KEY</u>

In-Library Practice: Newspaper
Indexes.
Your Name_____

In the time remaining today, use the <u>New York Times Index</u>, located

There is rarely a research topic which does not need use of newspapers.
It is essential that you also study the explanation and "Key" to abbreviations in the front/back of the volumes of this Index.
Remember: The indexing date represents the date on which a news item
appeared in the newspaper... not necessarilly the date on which the
event took place. This Index is both a "locator" and a "carrier" of information... notice that considerable information appears on the index
page in addition to the subject headings and bibliographic data which
constitute the indexing... like a reference book... even photos.

- In "January 1, 5:2" you'd interpret January 1 as the date on which
  the article appeared in the newspaper. Then 5 would represent_____
  _____, and 2 would refer to_____

- If you were writing a report on   crime during The Depression in
  the United States, particularly "Public Enemy Number One" John
  Dillinger's activities in Spring 1934,

  which <u>New York Times Index</u> volume would you consult first? The one
  for 19<u> 34   </u> .

- Now check there. Under what subject heading wording do you find an
  article or articles on this subject indexed?
       DILLINGER, Jno.

  <u>Page number(s) in the New York Times Index where you find indexing</u>
  citation(s): <u>from page 710 through 713</u>

  News events frequently continue over several days (issues). Select
  the one best-sounding article and list: I selected the
  article about the car with the Illinois license plates scaring everyone
  in New York State because Dillinger was from Illinois!
       Date of issue of the <u>New York Times</u> in which it appeared <u>March 8,</u>
       <u> 1934 </u>
       Page(s) in that issue<u>   page 13   </u>
       Column #<u>   seven   </u>

- Consult the Serials Catalog for the Library location of this issue
  of the <u>New York Times</u>:

  _____

Turn this in 5 minutes before the end of class today.

Course, Date
Instructor
Page 1 (of 3)

Your Name_____
Assignment 4:Locating Periodical Information,contd. Due: Date on schedule.

Required reading: "More Library Basics", "Bib Cards & Style Manuals".

The basic principles you've acquired in practicing use of Readers' Guide
can now be applied to other, specialized periodical indexes. Always:
1. Look for the explanation at the front of any index or other reference tool.
2. Locate the key to abbreviations, etc., usually in the front of the
   volume. Learn them as much as possible because they are standardized.
3. Find out exactly what time period is covered by each issue, each
   cumulation, and each volume you're using.
4. Plan your strategy... don't jump in!
5. Search all relevant subject headings including the subdivisions
   and paying attention to cross references.
6. When in doubt how to start, look under the "words you have."

Can you differentiate among the APPLIED SCIENCES and TECHNOLOGIES, the
HUMANITIES, and the SOCIAL SCIENCES?   Within each of these very
broad areas of knowledge, specific subjects, fields and disciplines
are generally found.   But some, for example, history, may turn up in
more than one area, depending on a publisher's, editor's, or indexer's
perceptions; some see it as a social science, others among the humanities.
It's up to you to recognize such a potential overlap in order to enahance
your chances of finding information and publications you need. Provide
at least 4 additional subjects within each area on the diagram. An unabridged dictionary and the "Library Basics" may help, but this is largely
a thought question.

1.

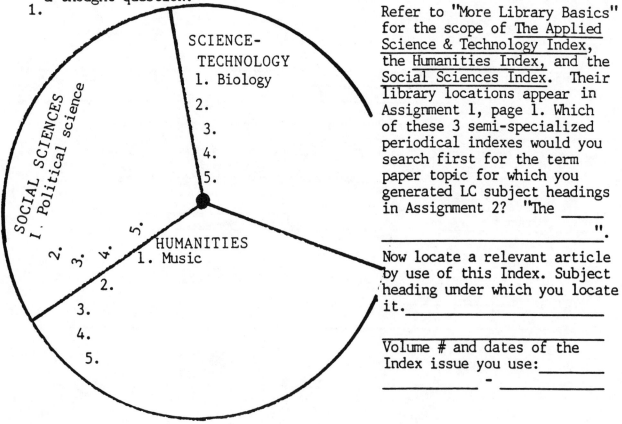

SCIENCE-
TECHNOLOGY
1. Biology
2.
3.
4.
5.

SOCIAL SCIENCES
1. Political science
2.
3.
4.
5.

HUMANITIES
1. Music
2.
3.
4.
5.

Refer to "More Library Basics"
for the scope of The Applied
Science & Technology Index,
the Humanities Index, and the
Social Sciences Index. Their
library locations appear in
Assignment 1, page 1. Which
of these 3 semi-specialized
periodical indexes would you
search first for the term
paper topic for which you
generated LC subject headings
in Assignment 2? "The _____

_____".

Now locate a relevant article
by use of this Index. Subject
heading under which you locate
it._____

Volume # and dates of the
Index issue you use:_____

_____ - _____

1., contd.
Complete title of the article "_____

_____"。

Full name of the author of the article (<u>Applied Science & Technology</u>
<u>Index</u> does not usually provide this information)?_____

_____

2. The following information[*] can be located by use of <u>Applied Science &</u>
<u>Technology Index</u>, or <u>Humanities Index</u>, or <u>Social Sciences Index, which</u>
are arranged on the same principles as Readers' Guide. Always strategize:
First, decide within the scope (subject) of <u>which index</u> the subject of
    the needed information falls.
Second, locate the appropriate volume (or issue) of the Index you've
    decided on, in terms of the <u>time scope</u>-- the period of time involved.
Third, take a <u>subject approach</u> to that Index volume (or issue). Try to
    think of and to locate a subject heading under which you can find the
    article providing the needed information.

* Locate bibliographically a <u>14</u> -page article published in <u>Fall</u>
    1979 in a Southern journal, about LOVE IN LITERATURE. Someone
    suggests it will be useful for a paper about the American West.

Space for your work: Title of the Index_____
    Time period covered by the Index volume you use:_____ - _____
    Page # on which you find the citation_____ Complete subject
    heading or other heading under which you find the needed information:

    _____
    Full name of the author of the article (if available within the Index)
    _____ Title of the
    article: "_____

    _____".
    Full title of the periodical in which the article was published.
    (Abbreviations are in the front of the volume):_____
    _____. Date the issue of the per-
    iodical was published_____. Volume #_____
    Which libraries have that issue of that periodical?
            Library/libraries   Call Number(s)

    _____   _____

    _____   _____

3. Series. The crucial ingredients of a series are SEPARATE works,
SUCCESSIVE, INDIVIDUAL TITLE, and SERIES TITLE. Series parts are usually
numbered. Refer to the beginning of Assignment 3 again. What is the
title of the series you identified in Assignment 1?_____
_____ What is the number of the book which
was part of that series? _____ When was it published?_____ Locate
that series in the library's serials record. Call # of the series:

4. THE NEW YORK TIMES INDEX, 1851-   . Library location:_____
    There is rarely a research topic which does not need use of news-
    papers and information provided by newspapers. It is essential that
    you study the explanation and key to abbreviations in front/back of
    the NYT Index volumes. This is another subject-approach index. A
    very useful feature is the fact that frequently there is additional
    information-- short statements of background information -- embedded
    in the indexing, making it occasionally unnecessary even to go to the
    newspaper itself.

Example:
    ILLINOIS ←—┌─Subject Heading

Subject Subdivision   Cross Reference
    └──→Elections. See also Pres Elect 76 - Primaries-Illinois   ←— Content
       2 Ill Dem primary races, 1 gubernatorial and other Cong,
       are regarded by politicians and pol observers as major tests
       of continuing strength of Chicago Mayor Richard J. Daley's
       powerful Cook County Dem machine; (L), F 8, 41:1

                              story length indicator   Date, page,
                              'L' means long article   column

Remember: The indexing date represents the date on which a news item
appeared in the newspaper itself, not necessarilly the date on which an
event took place. In "June 3, 2: 5," you'd interpret June 3 as the date
on which the article appeared in the newspaper. "2" would represent____
_____: and "5" refers to _____.

If you were writing a paper on the sinking of the Titanic steamship and
the TITANIC DISASTER , which New York Times Index volume would you check
first? The one for 19____ . Now check there. Under what subject heading
wording do you find articles on this subject?_____
_____ Page(s)_____

Using the New York Times Index, locate the following information:
Sonia Johnson was the candidate of which political Party in the 1984
PRESIDENTIAL ELECTION? The announcement of her nomination was made
in late October 1983.

Space for your work: Volume of the NYT Index which you use (year)_____
    Page # on which you find the needed citation, where you end up_____
    Heading under which you find the needed information on that page:
_____

Required reading: "More Library Basics", "Bib Cards & Style Manuals".

The basic principles you've acquired in practicing use of <u>Readers' Guide</u>
can now be applied to other, specialized periodical indexes. Always:
1. Look for the explanation at the front of any index or other reference tool.
2. Locate the key to abbreviations, etc., usually in the front of the
   volume. Learn them as much as possible because they are standard=
   ized.
3. Find out exactly what time period is covered by each issue, each
   cumulation, and each volume you're using.
4. Plan your strategy... don't jump in!
5. Search all relevant subject headings including the subdivisions
   and paying attention to cross references.
6. When in doubt how to start, look under the "words you have."

Can you differentiate among the APPLIED SCIENCES and TECHNOLOGIES, the
HUMANITIES, and the SOCIAL SCIENCES?   Within each of these very
broad areas of knowledge, specific subjects, fields and disciplines
are generally found.   But some, for example, history, may turn up in
more than one area, depending on a publisher's, editor's, or indexer's
perceptions; some see it as a social science, others among the humanities.
It's up to you to recognize such a potential overlap in order to enahance
your chances of finding information and publications you need.   Provide
at least 4 additional subjects within each area on the diagram.   An unabridged dictionary and the "Library Basics" may help, but this is largely
a thought question.

1.

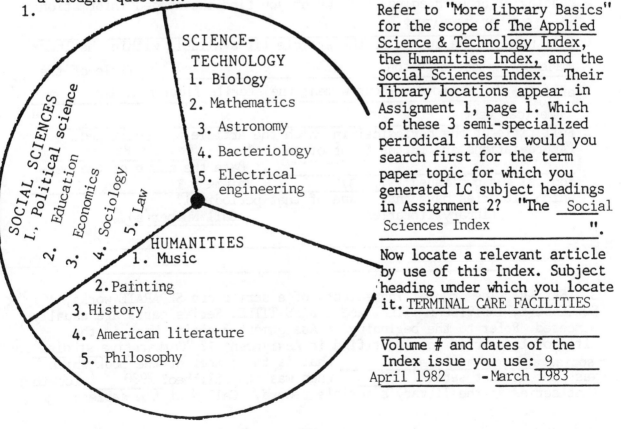

Refer to "More Library Basics"
for the scope of <u>The Applied
Science & Technology Index,</u>
the <u>Humanities Index,</u> and the
<u>Social Sciences Index.</u> Their
library locations appear in
Assignment 1, page 1. Which
of these 3 semi-specialized
periodical indexes would you
search first for the term
paper topic for which you
generated LC subject headings
in Assignment 2? "The <u>Social
Sciences Index   </u>".

Now locate a relevant article
by use of this Index. Subject
heading under which you locate
it. <u>TERMINAL CARE FACILITIES</u>

Volume # and dates of the
Index issue you use: <u>9</u>
<u>April 1982   </u> -March <u>1983</u>

SCIENCE-
TECHNOLOGY
1. Biology
2. Mathematics
3. Astronomy
4. Bacteriology
5. Electrical
   engineering

SOCIAL SCIENCES
I., Political science
2. Education
3. Economics
4. Sociology
5. Law

HUMANITIES
1. Music
2. Painting
3. History
4. American literature
5. Philosophy

1., contd.
Complete title of the article " The American way of hospice

                                                                    ".

Full name of the author of the article (<u>Applied Science & Technology</u>
<u>Index</u> does not usually provide this information)? David H. Smith and

 Judith A. Granbois

2. The following information*can be located by use of <u>Applied Science &</u>
<u>Technology Index</u>, or <u>Humanities Index</u>, or <u>Social Sciences Index</u>, which
are arranged on the same principles as Readers' Guide. Always strategize:
First, decide within the scope (subject) of <u>which index</u> the subject of
    the needed information falls.
Second, locate the appropriate volume (or issue) of the Index you've
    decided on, in terms of the <u>time scope</u>-- the period of time involved.
Third, take a <u>subject approach</u> to that Index volume (or issue). Try to
    think of and to locate a subject heading under which you can find the
    article providing the needed information.

* Locate bibliographically a 14   -page article published in Fall
    1979 in a Southern journal, about LOVE IN LITERATURE. Someone
    suggests it will be useful for a paper about the American West.

Space for your work: Title of the Index :Humanities Index
    Time period covered by the Index volume you use:April 1979 - March 1980
    Page # on which you find the citation 391   Complete subject
    heading or other heading under which you find the needed information:
         LOVE IN LITERATURE

Full name of the author of the article (if available within the Index)
Madelon E. Heatherington   Title of the

article: "   Romance without women: the sterile fiction of the

 American West   ".
Full title of the periodical in which the article was published.
(Abbreviations are in the front of the volume): Georgia Review

                                    . Date the issue of the per-
iodical was published Fall 1979   . Volume # 33
Which libraries have that issue of that periodical?
         Library/libraries   Call Number(s)

    _____   _____

    _____   _____

3. Series. The crucial ingredients of a series are SEPARATE works,
SUCCESSIVE, INDIVIDUAL TITLE, and SERIES TITLE. Series parts are usually
numbered. Refer to the beginning of Assignment 3 again. What is the
title of the series you identified in Assignment 1? "Comparative studies in
 social and economic history "   What is the number of the book which
was part of that series?   2   When was it published? 1980   Locate
that series in the library's serials record. Call # of the series:

Also, "Clinics in endocrinology and metabolism" 7 1978

4. THE NEW YORK TIMES INDEX, 1851-   . Library location:_____
   There is rarely a research topic which does not need use of newspapers and information provided by newspapers. It is essential that
   you study the explanation and key to abbreviations in front/back of
   the NYT Index volumes. This is another subject-approach index. A
   very useful feature is the fact that frequently there is additional
   information-- short statements of background information -- embedded
   in the indexing, making it occasionally unnecessary even to go to the
   newspaper itself.

Example: ━━━
     ILLINOIS ◄── ┌─Subject Heading

                          Cross Reference
Subject Subdivision   ↓
  └─►Elections. See also Pres Elect 76 - Primaries-Illinois   ◄── Content
     2 Ill Dem primary races, 1 gubernatorial and other Cong,
     are regarded by politicians and pol observers as major tests
     of continuing strength of Chicago Mayor Richard J. Daley's
     powerful Cook County Dem machine; (L), F 8, 41:1
                                         ↑   ↑
                        story length indicator   Date, page,
                        'L' means long article   column
     ━━━

Remember: The indexing date represents the date on which a news item
appeared in the newspaper itself, not necessarilly the date on which an
event took place. In "June 3, 2: 5," you'd interpret June 3 as the date
on which the article appeared in the newspaper. "2" would represent_____
the page   : and "5" refers to   the column   .

If you were writing a paper on   the sinking of the Titanic steamship and
the TITANIC DISASTER   , which New York Times Index volume would you check
first? The one for 1912   . Now check there. Under what subject heading
wording do you find articles on this subject? SHIPS-- TITANIC DISASTER
_____ Page(s) 293

Using the New York Times Index, locate the following information:
Sonia Johnson was the candidate of which political Party in the 1984
PRESIDENTIAL ELECTION? The announcement of her nomination was made
in late October 1983.

Space for your work: Volume of the NYT Index which you use (year) 1983
   Page # on which you find the needed citation, where you end up 994
   Heading under which you find the needed information on that page:
   PRESIDENTIAL ELECTION 1984 (begins on page 989)

   On page 994: "...Sonia Johnson to seek U.S. Presidential nomination
   of Citizens Party" (October 23, 1983 issue of the New York Times,
   Section I Page 41, column 5).

INTER-LIBRARY BORROWING & RELATED TOOLS

This activity is planned for part of a class held in the library. It should be supplemented with a question involving practice determining what library holds an issue of a periodical which is needed (bottom of the page). Alert students to the possibility that some libraries do not participate in inter-library borrowing-lending activities, and that while most do, it is normal for a library to require onsite use of some materials, e.g. rare books, one-of-a-kind, etc. Additional examples appear in Section III: Resources.

Suppose the library doesn't have a book you need.
Suppose the library doesn't have an issue of a periodical in which an
 article you need was published.
Consider an inter-library loan, a free library service in your behalf.

This involves your determining which other libraries do have it. To
do this, you need to use a UNION CATALOG to identify such libraries,
preferably within our state or region. After you have identified a
library which holds a book or issue of a periodical you need, take these
data together with full information about the publication itself, to
Interlibrary Borrowing. (Even if you aren't able to identify a holding
library, go to Interlibrary Borrowing and explain what you need and what
you have done so far.)

For your Project, you are asked to restrict yourself to publications you
are actually able to locate and use in the collections on campus.

BOOKS
Consult the National Union Catalog located _____
NUC volumes cumulate over periods of time and come right up to the present.
They constitute a BOOK CATALOG as well as a UNION CATALOG. Symbols for
participating libraries are listed inside some of the front/back covers
of the volumes.

Assume the Library does not have the following book in its collections:

Use the Pre-1956 basic set of the "NUC" to identify the nearest library
which has it. Use the list of symbols/codes inside the front/back covers
of the volume in which you locate the book bibliographically to get the
following information:

    NUC Volume #_____   Page #_____   Symbol of the library
    holding it which you select_____ _____
    Name of the holding library you select_____

    _____. City & state of the holding
    library_____

Still using a volume from the Pre-1956 cumulation, determine the symbol
(code) for _____,
located in the state of _____ in _____.

_____

PERIODICAL Issues
When our library does not have an issue of a periodical which you need,
you start by checking a union list of serials, which will be discussed
in class today.

Turn this in 5 minutes before the end of class today.

Course   Inter-Library Borrowing & Related
Instructor   Tools.
                                   Your Name_____

Suppose the library doesn't have a book you need.
Suppose the library doesn't have an issue of a periodical in which an
 article you need was published.
Consider an inter-library loan, a free library service in your behalf.

This involves your determining which other libraries do have it. To
do this, you need to use a UNION CATALOG to identify such libraries,
preferably within our state or region. After you have identified a
library which holds a book or issue of a periodical you need, take these
data together with full information about the publication itself, to
Interlibrary Borrowing. (Even if you aren't able to identify a holding
library, go to Interlibrary Borrowing and explain what you need and what
you have done so far.)

For your Project, you are asked to restrict yourself to publications you
are actually able to locate and use in the collections on campus.

BOOKS
Consult the National Union Catalog located _____
NUC volumes cumulate over periods of time and come right up to the present.
They constitute a BOOK CATALOG as well as a UNION CATALOG. Symbols for
participating libraries are listed inside some of the front/back covers
of the volumes.

Assume the Library does not have the following book in its collections:
"...A Study of Certain Factors Associated With Children's Play Interests...",
by James Daniel Wang, published in 1941.
Use the Pre-1956 basic set of the "NUC" to identify the nearest library
which has it. Use the list of symbols/codes inside the front/back covers
of the volume in which you locate the book bibliographically to get the
following information:

         NUC Volume #_____   Page #_____   Symbol of the library
         holding it which you select_____
         Name of the holding library you select_____

         _____. City & state of the holding
         library_____

Still using a volume from the Pre-1956 cumulation, determine the symbol
(code) for   Pennsylvania University_____,
located in the state of Pennsylvania_____ in Philadelphia_____.

_____

PERIODICAL Issues
When our library does not have an issue of a periodical which you need,
you start by checking a union list of serials, which will be discussed
in class today.

Turn this in 5 minutes before the end of class today.

Course   <u>K E Y</u>   Inter-Library Borrowing & Related
Instructor   Tools.
                                         Your Name _____

Suppose the library doesn't have a book you need.
Suppose the library doesn't have an issue of a periodical in which an article you need was published.
Consider an inter-library loan, a free library service in your behalf.

This involves your determining which other libraries <u>do</u> have it. To do this, you need to use a UNION CATALOG to identify such libraries, preferably within our state or region. After you have identified a library which holds a book or issue of a periodical you need, take these data together with full information about the publication itself, to Interlibrary Borrowing. (Even if you aren't able to identify a holding library, go to Interlibrary Borrowing and explain what you need and what you have done so far.)

For your Project, you are asked to restrict yourself to publications you are actually able to locate and use in the collections on campus.

BOOKS
Consult the National Union Catalog located _____
NUC volumes cumulate over periods of time and come right up to the present. They constitute a BOOK CATALOG as well as a UNION CATALOG. Symbols for participating libraries are listed inside some of the front/back covers of the volumes.

Assume the Library does not have the following book in its collections:
"...A Study of Certain Factors Associated With Children's Play Interests...", by James Daniel Wang, published in 1941.
Use the <u>Pre-1956 basic set</u> of the "NUC" to identify the nearest library which has it. Use the list of symbols/codes inside the front/back covers of the volume in which you locate the book bibliographically to get the following information:

      NUC Volume # <u>647</u>   Page # <u>598</u>   Symbol of the library
      holding it which you select <u>   O U   </u>
      Name of the holding library you select <u>Ohio State University</u>
      _____. City & state of the holding
      library <u>   Columbus, Ohio   </u>

Still using a volume from the Pre-1956 cumulation, determine the symbol (code) for <u>   Pennsylvania University   </u>,
located in the state of <u>Pennsylvania</u>   in <u>Philadelphia</u> .
<u>   P U   </u>

PERIODICAL Issues
When our library does not have an issue of a periodical which you need, you start by checking a union list of serials, which will be discussed in class today.

Turn this in 5 minutes before the end of class today.

Doing Library Research At XYZ University
&
Putting It All Together:
Project Guidelines

Calendar

By the 5th week:
Read Project Guidelines. Bring
Project-related questions to class.

During the 6th week:
Topic proposal due at your Project
conference. See pages 6 and 17 of
Project Guidelines.

8-10th weeks:
Project pathfinder assignment #'s
5 and 6.

10th week:
Do not change your topic after the
10th week. (Unwise to change it
after the 8th week.)

End of 12th - 15th weeks:
Work on Project. No other assignments in this course.

End of 13th week:
Rough draft.

14th week:
Type and proofread.

15th week:
Project due at beginning of first
class meeting.

INTRODUCTION

References
"Bibliography Cards & Style Manuals" handout. Pathfinder assignments
#'s 5 and 6.
Supplementary: Turabian style manual; Gates; Dwight and Speer.

Glossary
*Bibliography: Basically, a list of books. Library catalogs, for example,
are bibliographies of the books and other publications in the library's
collection. Bibliographies usually cover a particular subject area,
topic, period, place, or author. National bibliographies, for example,
attempt to include everything published in a particular country. Some
bibliographies attempt to list everything written by and about a particular author, e.g. Katherine Anne Porter or Henry James. Subject bibliographies can be very broad, listing material that falls within the boun-
daries of a particular discipline, e.g. McGraw-Hill Basic Bibliography of
Science and Technology, or they can be limited to books and articles on
a very narrow topic or issue such as the United States conversion to the
metric system.

*Comprehensive Bibliography: One which attempts to list everything which
has been written on the topic, or by the person, or in the location or
time period covered by the bibliography's scope. The current Books In
Print, for example, aims to list all books which are available on the
regular trade market in the United States.

*Selective Bibliography: One which lists the best and most representative
or useful materials in the area covered by the bibliography. The person
compiling it has selected the items from all of the material which has
been produced in the relevant area. The list of works referred to in a
term paper by the student or a text book by the author is one type of
selective bibliography.

*Annotated bibliography: One in which each entry is accompanied by des-
criptive or evaluative notes.

*Bibliographic citation: A note of reference to a book, periodical ar-
ticle, or other publication which includes the information required to
find that same item again.

The Project is intended to give you the opportunity to approach the job
of library research in a systematic and efficient way. You are not required actually to write a paper, but, rather, to give considerable
thought and time to the methods and materials of library research and to
show evidence of an understanding of sophisticated library use. Classes
and assignments will equip you with some of the basic concepts, tools
and skills of research methodology. Your Project should demonstrate
that you have gone beyond the basics to make a rigorous search of the
literature of your field. While it is important that you learn to use
particular reference and bibliographic sources, it is equally important
that you come to understand the principles of bibliographic organization

<u>INTRODUCTION</u>, contd.

and to develop a feel for the manner in which any topic can be researched
in most libraries.

A simple list of books and articles can easily be drawn up in half an
hour! It is not the purpose of the project merely to identify and compile a list of X number of titles on a given subject. This bibliography
should serve a specific purpose. You select titles of books and articles
to help do a specific job-- a selected and selective bibliography of
resources which are in our library. Do not rely on one or two sources
to find material on your topic. (It is often possible to find one very
good bibliography in a field which might contain most of the information
you would need on your topic.) The main object of this activity is to
expose yourself to a variety of bibliographic tools and to master the use
of some specific ones. Be sure, therefore, to consult as many types of
materials and sources as is reasonable.

In structuring your topic and following through with your literature
search, as well as preparing your Project, do not communicate your biases.
Everyone has them. The quality of your work should be such that it
could support "research." Provide for all sides and not merely <u>your</u>
attitude, opinion, and/or assumptions! Balance points of view.

Now and in the future, you will inevitably stumble across things as you
use libraries and close in on your subject's specialized resources, but
do not rely on browsing or serendipity as a source for your Project
bibliography selections.

<u>Sample Projects</u>
There are sample Projects on Reserve for this class in the library.
They are not intended to be models of perfection; they are representa-
tive.

<u>DEFINING A TOPIC</u>

Be prepared to settle on your topic before you begin pathfinder assignment #5. We can work on this together before then, but it is not possible for me to select, focus, or develop a topic for you. This is part
of bibliographic and research work. Do not expect to change your topic
after the 10th week of the term. (And it's unwise after the 8th week.)
Here are some examples of how students narrow and occasionally develop
their topics.

DEFINING A TOPIC, contd.

Original Topic Idea	FINAL DESCRIPTIVE TITLE, Including Key Words
Architecture, conservation	Architecture; Utilizing Passive Energy in Design.
Ann Rand	Objectivism: The Philosophy of Ayn Rand.
Women in Japan's economy	Japanese Women in Employment: A Struggle Against Societal Attitudes and Tradition.
Mrs. Franklin Roosevelt	Anna Eleanor Roosevelt and the United Nations.
Dolphins	Dolphins-- A Higher Form of Intelligence?
Solar energy	Solar Heating and Cooling of Residences.
Miscegenation	Black-White Marriages in the United States of America.
Russian japanese war	The Russo-Japanese War and American Public Opinion.
Communism, US history	Causes and Interpretations of the 'Red Scare' of 1919.
Cellular immunity	Immunology: The Effects and Treatments of Immunological Deficiency Syndromes in Humans.
Soldiers who said no	Disquiet in the Ranks; Organized Dissent in the United States Military During the Vietnam Era.
Disenfranchsiement of Blacks	An Effort to Disfranchise the Negro Voter in Maryland; the Poe Amendment of 1905.
Daniel Defoe and women	The Treatment of Women in 18th Century Literature by Daniel Defoe, Specifically in the Works, Moll Flanders and Roxana; Fiction or Feminism?
Marxism and Lenin in Africa	Marxist-Leninist Countries of Sub-Saharan Africa; A Search for Connections in Ideology and Practice.

Note that these titles are descriptive. They often utilize a colon or semi-colon to present a somewhat general subject or idea, followed by a subtitle which delineates the scope of the Project and of a paper which would be researched and then written using this bibliography. The key words and terms are in the titles. These are also usually in the subject headings used to access publications in the libraries' collections. You are fine-tuning a topic and then preparing a selective "subject bibliography" on which a paper could be based. Evolve a topic which would be very similar to something you would have in in a course, essay or thesis.

Do not be vague. For example, if you refer to "TV violence", make sure you communciate what you mean. Educational television? P B S? Commercial television? Violence in plot, action, commercials, dialog, in what? Covert or overt violence? U.S.A.? For another example: If you refer to "discrimination", are you using this noun negatively? If so, on what basis does the disparity you have in mind take place? (Sex or race or age or what?) Be specific and complete, and nonjudgmental.

A Project-title should communicate what you have in mind. Do not say merely "food additives" if you have in mind artifical sweeteners. Furthermore, don't say merely "artificial sweeteners' when you mean saccharin. Do not say "sex discrimination" when you have in mind, for

DEFINING A TOPIC, contd.

example, discrimination in education of contemporary high school-age American (U.S.A.) women based on their gender. Be specific.

Do not propose a topic because you're curious and want to explore. This is unproductive here. Propose a topic such as you would work on in connection with a course. Any research and a successful Project both involve more than production of a list of titles such as is possible to regurgitate by use of subject-entries in a college or university library's card or online catalog. You should already know (a little) something about what you are into. You must then either develop (broaden) or, more usually, focus (narrow) your subject and consider it in relation-ship to something else. Experience has shown that such words as "cul-ture", "condition of...", psychological or social "aspects", "role", etc. are worn-out, over-used and sometimes not clearly understood by the student. It is also wise to avoid topics which have frequently been done or are being done by other students.

There are several ways to develop or to focus on a topic. Someone choosing an historical incident might want to include a contemporary book or article. Contemporary publications would be those written at the time the event took place. In developing a subject to propose, you should evolve one which interests you and about which you have some, even a little, knowledge already. You should think in terms of a topic which argues, questions, inter-relates, contrasts, rather than merely reporting on a simple subject. For this reason, most topics which are initially simply about a person, for example, need to be developed. (Fortunately there are numerous tools supporting biographical research.) But most of our topics need to be focused rather than developed.

Since the objects of the Project are (1) to get you to use a variety of types of reference tools and sources, and (2) to become familiar with a variety of resources in the library, choose a topic which will enable these.

Here are some of the types of topics which do not always work:

  Sports, careers, recreation, hobbies, practical matters; e.g. tennis, surfing, judo, backpacking, how to get a job, how to fix your car, the "popular culture."
  Subjects which are too broad; e.g. astronomy, Japanese painting, Ren-aissance art, the Gold Rush, Chinese history. You'd find too much material and never be able to cover the subject adequately in a relatively brief paper. You wouldn't be able to locate articles in periodicals for too broad a subject.
  Subjects which are too narrow; e.g. the university's latest "affirma-tive action" program, how the government calculates the unemployment rate. A very few books, articles and reports may be available for some subjects, and sometimes one book might "cover" it. Too narrow or too specific.

DEFINING A TOPIC, contd.

   Subjects which are too recent. Although you probably could locate mag-
       azine articles, you'd have difficulty locating books written on a
       subject which is too recent.
   Occult, supernatural, exorcism, astrology.
   Religion and theology. Most of the related books and periodicals are in
       theological libraries.
   Subjects in which nearly everything will be written in a language you
       are not able to read.
   Pure science. Unless you have a very strong science background, you may
       find most of the periodical literature over your head.
   Subjects about which you already know nothing. This is not the occasion
       to propose a topic about which you "know nothing, are curious and
       would like to learn something." Read an encyclopedia survey-article
       or a book instead; ask me, and I'll recommend one!

CONFERENCES

By the time of your Project topic conference, you should have thought
about a "working title" which clearly communicates your topic, and you
should have checked out the LCSH and library's catalogs.

When you can identify a subject-heading which has been established by
the U.S. Library of Congress and is already in use in the library's subject
catalog with a substantial number of records there, you are probably on
your way. Then we'll check out a specialized periodicals index in the
field. However, one LC subject-heading rarely makes a good title or a
good topic for a Project or term paper! Aim for at least five entirely
different subject-headings when you actually get underway on your Project.
Pathfinder assignments # 5 and 6 will enable all of this. In proposing
your Project topic and a "working title", or in getting ready to do any
research in the future, you should be able to confirm all of these general things, as well as the classification(s) for most information on your
specific subject.

Be prepared the week previous to the Project conferences to schedule your
30-minute conference. Depending on the size of our class, this can mean
keeping free for library work at least three such spans of time, other
than class-time and regular office hours.

If you have the feeling that you have 'no questions or problems' to ask
and discuss at your Project conference, you definitely have a problem on
which we must work! Complete and bring to your Project conference the
Project Topic Proposal form which is the final page of these Project
Guidelines.

PROJECT REQUIREMENTS

+ Use XYZ University libraries. Select only publications which are in our
  library collections and in our library's catalogs.
+ Aim for at least one title from the main library collection.
+ Use at least one specialized branch library; include at least one title
  from its collection on your Project bibliography.
+ Use both the card catalog and online catalog as sources, and utilize at
  least two completely different subject-headings.
+ Use at least three (3) specialized periodical indexes as sources, one
  of which should be an abstracting service reflecting the subjects en-
  compassed by your Project.
     NOTE: Readers' Guide is limited in its potential at collegiate level;
     Project topics which are suitable learning experiences for this course
     require the types of journal articles which specialized indexes ac-
     cess. Therefore, do not use Readers' Guide as a source for the
     Project bibliography.
+ Select periodical articles which are substantial in length-- not a
  mere authorless, partial-page, news item!
+ Locate and include authors' full names wherever possible.
+ Include at least one book "part"-- possibly something you identify by
  use of Essay & General Literature Index. When only a portion of a book
  is relevant to something you're researching, by all means cite and
  use only that information. ADDRESSESS, ESSAYS & LECTURES also leads to these.
+ Try to include at least one government publication.
+ Demonstrate that you have identified and used in your search as a source
  at least one relevant selective guide to or bibliography of publications
  related to your topic.
+ Some other recommended sources include a newspaper index such as the
  'New York Times' Index, Comprehensive Dissertation Index, Monthly Catalog, citation indexes, etc.
+ Have a reasonable balance of books, periodical articles, book parts,
  and a variety of relevant sources represented.

If the nature of your topic seems to make one of these requirements impossible, we can work it out during office hours. If you encounter a
problem, it may be possible for you to convert it into a learning experience; describe how you coped with it in the strategy part of your essay.
With only twenty-five (25) titles, you will end up having a "problem" of
de-selection rather than of finding things to put on your bibliography.

Although in the future after this course, you may use as sources such
things as author entries in the library catalog, course lists, professors'
suggestions, Books In Print, Cumulative Book Index, a shelf list, or
browsing, it will not be necessary to do this for your Project. Likewise,
general encyclopedias can sometimes provide background information and
help in developing a term paper. Specialized encyclopedias can often
provide bibliographies, keywords, etc. Pamphlets and audiovisuals are
usually useful as supplementary material and occasionally as sources because of their bibliographic function. However, the idea of the Project
is to stretch yourself, maximize your library experience, and become selective. Therefore, do not use these as sources for the Project.

PROJECT REQUIREMENTS, contd.

Organization
Your term Project should have a title and be in two parts: an <u>essay</u> and a <u>bibliography</u>.

The essay is an introduction which is subdivided in two parts.

*<u>You first define and explain your topic</u>. The more clearly you can define at the beginning of research what you want to find and what you do not want to do, the easier, more productive, and less time-consuming work will be. Therefore, show reason and need for your Project, not merely a summary or history of a topic. This is the purpose of the bibliography you are selecting. Identify or explain for <u>what course</u> in which department you are or could be doing this report, paper, or thesis. Be sure to provide this connection by also describing and explaining the paper itself.

Include a <u>statement of purpose</u> (or a thesis statement); this will help you keep on target because it indicates what you intend to accomplish. If your purpose is to record, describe, or explain (an expository paper), you'll find the statement of purpose more useful. If your purpose is to support an idea or advance a proposition (an argumentative paper), you can also profit from a statement of purpose.

Conclude with a detailed <u>outline</u> of the paper which this bibliography would support. Because an outline of a paper is a crucial step in research and a library literature search, a sample is included here in your Project Guidelines. Dwight and Speer contains information about outlining if you have had no experience with this. Just as you can adjust your "working title", you will likely flesh out an outline as your work on a paper progresses.

*<u>The second part of the essay</u> is a thorough discussion of the <u>strategy and procedures you followed in using reference and bibliographical tools and materials</u>. How did you go about your research in the library? Which of the hundreds of resources available did you use most? Which ones worked for you and which ones did not? Which guide to the literature was most useful in leading you to more specialized tools? Is there a pattern of organization of information in your field that became clear to you as you went along? Do not describe your experience with an index, for example, as "I checked <u>Such 'N Such Index</u>, but it wasn't useful for my subject." Instead, describe which volumes and time spans you checked, what subject-headings you consulted, and what you found, demonstrating that you strategized and manipulated. If you had it to do over again, what changes would you make in your approaches to and use of reference and bibliographical resources and the library for this particular topic? (Do not say "I'd begin sooner.") Ample time has been provided at the end of the course during which no other assignments are required. See page 1, Calendar.

PROJECT REQUIREMENTS: Organization, contd.

This section is simply an account from you to me. It can be as long as you like. Suggestion: Keep a log of all the tools you consult and places where you work as you follow the plan related to researching your Project and provided by the pathfinder assignments.

The annotated bibliography is the second and main part of the Project. It consists of twenty-five (25) citations of publications you found particularly relevant to your subject. Include a variety of relevant publications. Do not include on the bibliography any of the reference tools (such sources as indexes, bibliographies, guides to the literature, abstracting services, etc.) which you discussed and used in the second, strategy account-part of the essay.

Normally the units within a bibliography can be organized by authors' names into one big alphabet, or by aspects of the topic, or by formats (books, articles, etc.), or however a prof recommends. For your Project, however, arrange all the units into one alphabetically-by-author or other main entry list. Number each unit consecutively from the beginning to the end of the bibliography: 1 through 25.

Each title selected for your bibliography should include the five things identified in the SAMPLE BIBLIOGRAPHY ENTRIES section of these Project Guidelines. You should be able to get the information for the first four things from your bib cards. The five parts of each entry are:

1. The source in which you initially found the item listed. Usually this will be a periodical index, library catalog, bibliography, or some other such reference tool. Include sufficient information so that you and someone else could locate the source of this selection in one step. Do not "select" any of these sources (tools such as periodical indexes, library catalog, bibliographies, etc.) for the bibliography itself. Some sources (such as periodical indexes) have call numbers of their own; do not put these call numbers on your selected bibliography. Instead, identify the call numbers of the titles you select by means of using these locators efficiently.

    With the source, e.g. Business Periodicals Index, list the date(s) of the volume or issue, and the complete subject-heading in ALL CAPS under which you first encountered it. You should record it initially on your bib card, and then you will have the information to put on your Project bibliography when you need it. This is very good practice for future research papers too.

2. The library call number of the book,or the periodical in which the article appears,which you have selected and used.

3. The library where you borrowed or used the book or article on campus.

4. A complete bibliographic citation typed in standard format according to Turabian's style manual, which is your authority for this work. See the "Bibliography Cards & Style Manuals" handout.

5. A brief annotation justifying inclusion of this selection on this
   particular bibliography for this particular purpose, which is the
   writing of a term paper.Re-read the first part of your essay, including the outline, which should clarify for you at the outset.
   These annotations are not simply summaries or descriptions-- they
   are also your personal perception of the publication. This bibliography is an enabler tied to a specific purpose: you find a reference
   to a book, for example; you get the call number, main entry and other
   data onto your bib card. Then you locate the book itself on the
   shelf in the library's collection. Examine and evaluate it and
   decide whether to select (or de-select) it for inclusion on the
   bibliography and future use. Include the publication's relevance
   to your topic, where and how you predict it would be supportive in
   writing the paper. Occasionally you might note some relationship
   to another item on the same bibliography. The annotation is derived
   from your reasons for including it on this bibliography. Thus, it
   is not simply a description.

   Remember: You are preparing a selected bibliography to support subsequent work on a paper which must accomplish some definite function.
   So your annotations communicate to the reader-user (you, me) the
   publication's content, potential, special utility in the context of
   this paper-- why you have selected it for this purpose. This "why"
   is your recommendation.

About Annotating

How is it possible to select and annotate without reading an entire book
cover to cover? The table of contents, introduction, appendices and even
the index can communicate a lot if you are thoughtFULL. As you look at
these and other aspects of the volume, ask yourself how they'd fit into
various parts of the paper's outline. You must handle it. Exploit all
of the information on the catalog record even before you examine the book,
however. Get the information down on your bib card to inspire your
annotating. For example, the series of which the book may be part can
influence your perception of it; whether there is significant bibliographic support in it; whether it is illustrated and these illustrations
are crucial in utilizing the publication; the added entries, etc.
Examine it physically. Scan it. Other sources of inspiration for the
neophyte selector are reviews. Check out what others whose purposes and
needs are similar to yours have already said and published about it.
Do not quote from annotations contained in a guide-to-the-literature or
from book reviews; it is, however, occasionally necessasry to quote
briefly within your annotation from the book or article itself. (Include the page nubmer on which your author makes the statement you quote.)

Annotating is a skill which you acquire by practicing it. Once it is
yours, you will also be able to scan and to read more rapidly for meaning.
The purpose of such an annotation is to provide useful information for
the reader-user. Annotations can compare, describe, evaluate, relate
(to each other), highlight, underscore, summarize... Sometimes they are
written in cryptic style (incomplete sentences), but your annotations
should consist of full sentences. They should be consistent. Do not

PROJECT REQUIREMENTS: About Annotating, contd.

fill space with generalizations. Avoid such adjectives as "excellent" and "good"-- rarely would you select a publication which was not "good", although it is concievable, in which case your annotation should justi-fy your having had to select it. Avoid the first person singular. It is not necessary to say "I included this because..." twenty-five times. Do not begin them all with "This book..." or "This article...". Don't use contractions (such as "don't"). In short, there are some specific requirements connected with this work, but there are also numerous bene-fits which you can, if you wish to, learn from this experience. Your Project annotations will not be evaluated for writing skills but, rather, for communication of information about the publication in relation to a term paper.

Some sample Project bibliography entries are provided on pages 14 and 15.

Mechanics

Type your Project; double space the essay and the annotations. Type all subject-headings in ALL CAPS. Number the pages. Proofread. Turn in an original and a copy; keep a copy. One of them will be returned to you with a grade and evaluative analysis after the end of the term. If you turn in only one, you will not receive a copy back.

Turn in all of the bib cards made in connection with your Project since you began work on it during pathfinder assignment #'s 5 and 6 and in-cluding those for publications you de-select. Do not re-do or fix them up. Twenty-five immaculate cards are not what you would end up with at the conclusion of this type of activity which involves de-selection at a rate of approximately three-to-one. Put your name on the outside of the pack; they will be returned to you.

Please do not use binders, folders, etc. for your Project, nor containers for the cards.

On the cover sheet, list your name, Project title, course and section, instructor's name, term and year.

EVALUATION

Your Project is due at the beginning of class on the date listed on your schedule. The Project is [%] of the course grade. The Project is required of all students in the course.

In fairness to other class members and because there is a deadline which instructors must meet in turning in course grades, because grading each Project involves considerable time in the library, because you are not required to turn in your Project until late in the term, because you have been aware of all due-dates since early in the course, etc., this will be strictly enforced. Please do not ask for special consideration.

EVALUATION, contd.

Page 16   consists of a copy of the CHECKLIST-EVALUATION OF PROJECT form
which will be used for your Project. You will receive a copy of this
form when your Project copy and bib cards are returned to you.

Frankenstein's Lonely Monster:

An Examination of Mary Shelley's <u>Frankenstein</u>

I. Introduction, Purpose

    A. Versions of the story of Frankenstein

        1. The novel

        2. Later plays and motion pictures

    B. Common meaning of term "Frankenstein"

        1. Derivation of populat concept

        2. Difference between popular concept and theme of novel

II. Background of Mary Shelley's social thought

    A. Mary Wollstonecraft and women's rights

    B. William Godwin's social philosophy

III. Creation of monster and Frankenstein's response

    A. Monster's moral sense and early tendencies

    B. Frankenstein's revulsion

IV. Horror of loneliness

    A. Importance of loneliness as theme

    B. Robert Walton's search for companionship

    C. Monster's loneliness

        1. His plea for acceptance

        2. Nature of relationship with Frankenstein

        3. His grief over Frankenstein's death

    D. Frankenstein's isolation

V. Frankenstein's tragic flaw

    A. His failure to love

    B. Mary Shelley's indictment of society

VI. Conclusions

    A. A novel with a strong moral and social theme

    B. Theme is the need for human fellowship

APPENDIX: SAMPLE PROJECT BIBLIOGRAPHY ENTRIES

     Key:
(1) =   Source
(2) =   Call Number
(3) =   Library
(4) =   Bibliographic citation according to Turabian's style manual
(5) =   Annotation

Sample for a one-author book selection:

(1) 9.   Subject catalog: WOMEN-- EMPLOYMENT-- U.S.
(2)   HD6095.H6
(3)   Business Library
(4)   Howe, Louise Kapp. Pink-Collar Workers; Inside the World of
          Women's Work. New York: Putnam, 1977.

(5)   Some of the books under this subject heading turned out to be

       merely series of anecdotes. Howe also supplies statistical

       data which I need and comments from industrial and academic

       experts. The people she considered pink collar workers in the

       "female job ghetto" in 1977 were beauticians, homemakers,

       office workers, sales workers, and waitresses. Economist John

       Kenneth Galbraith's recommendation of this book in a review I

       read also influenced me.

Sample for a book by two or more authors:

(1) 7.   "Sports" section, page 256, #1422 of Women in America; A Guide
         to Information Sources, by Virginia R. Terris.
(2)   GV709A64
(3)   Main library stacks
(4)   Gerber, Ellen W.; Felshin, Jan; Berlin, Pearl; and Wyrick, Waneen.
         The American Woman in Sport. Reading, Mass., Addison-Wesley,1974.

(5)   Sections deal with participation, social views of sports, the

       nature of women athletes, and biophysical perspectives. By sport,

       these authors mean activities of American females of college age

       and older which involve specific administrative organization,

       historical background of rules and customs which define it. Al-

       though more than ten years old, I plan on using this for its

APPENDIX: SAMPLE PROJECT BIBLIOGRAPHY ENTRIES, contd.

inclusion of coeducational sports, girls on so-called boys'

teams, and such things as women's football teams, which are

the elements in my report.

Sample for a journal article:

(1) 12. Education Index, July 1974-June 1975   WOMEN-- COUNSELING SERVICES
(2)   LB2301A3
(3)   Education-Psychology library
(4)   Friskey, Elizabeth A. "College Women and Careers". American
         Association of University Professors Bulletin 60 (September
         1974): 317-19.

(5)   Friskey's comments on student criticism of counseling at

Princeton University are accompanied by suggestions for improve-

ment. Information about specific institutions was not as avail-

able as generalized comments on counseling of college women, so

this article should provide a beginning from this perspective.I

expect to access some publications published after September

1974 which refer to this article (by using Social Science Cita-

tion Index)when I do this report because AAUP apparently is a mover.

Sample for a component part of a book:

(1) 1.   Essay & General Literature Index, 1970-1974   FOOD ADDITIVES
(2)   Q125.S714
(3)   Main library stacks
(4)   Lederberg, Joshua. "Food Additives." In The Social Responsibil-
         ity of the Scientist, pp. 121-30. Edited by Martin Brown. New
         York: Free Press, 1971.

(5)   These essays were lectures in the old Berkeley Science Students

for Social Responsibility course. I need this because, unlike

other publications, is is not an extreme call for legislation.

I later found this book under SCIENCE AND CIVILIZATION. I will

use this at the beginning survey part of my paper.

CHECKLIST-EVALUATION OF PROJECT

Student_____

Term _____ Year 19_____ Section #_____

Title of the Project as it appears on the Project:

" _____

_____

_____

_____ "

	OUTSTANDING	GOOD	SATISFACTORY	UNSATISFACTORY
OVERALL:				
Project conference_____				
Development and redevelopment of topic_____				
Title-construct, keywords, etc._____				
Correct identification of people's names and titles of publications. While grammar, punctuation, spelling, etc. <u>can</u> affect meaning, incorrect or vague usage have not had a conscious effect on grading._____				
Following instructions_____				
Independence of work._____	▓▓▓			
ESSAY:				
Background of topic_____				
Explanation of a paper which can be written based on this selected bibliography_____				
Outline of this paper_____				
Thorough discussion of research strategy and procedures followed in using references and bibliographic tools, libraries, resources. Demonstration that relevant basic and specialized tools have been considered, and, where feasible, used._____				
SELECTED BIBLIOGRAPHY:				
Accurately citing 25 appropriate publications____				
Bibliographic accessibility for each publication.Clear identification of sources, including subject-heading where applicable, call #, library location for each.____				
Following style manual_____				
Evidence of exploration & utilization of a reasonable # of potential approaches and significant tools____				
Annotations:				
Uniform style_____				
Demonstration that each publication has been located and examined_____				
Meaningful, revealing content of publication examined___				
Evaluation of each item in terms of relevance to coverage & support bibliography aims to provide term paper.				

_____ Failure to turn in   cards as assigned

_____ Failure to turn in 2 copies of Project (does not affect grade)

_____

_____ Project grade

_____ Course grade. (If A-, A or A+, your stack pass will be paper-clipped to this form.)

You will receive a copy of this form with your project

APPENDIX: PROJECT TOPIC PROPOSAL   Your Name_____
Due: Complete and bring to your Project conference.

Read <u>Project Guidelines</u> thoroughly; reread pages 1-6 concerning development of a topic. Construct an appropriate Project topic, one such as you
might be assigned for a term paper in a college course. Make a quick
survey (not an extensive search) of the LCSH to confirm the existence of
at least two different (they should begin with different words) subject
headings relevant to your tentative topic. Do not propose a Project
topic which "is" a subject heading.

Then confirm the presence in the library catalog of several books which
have been assigned these subject headings. It is not necessary to concern
yourself with periodical articles at this time. Record your work here:

At least two subject headings you locate using the LCSH:

    1. _____

    2. _____

At least one publication you find in the library catalog using one of your
subject headings:

    Subject heading:_____

    Full main entry (author):_____

    _____

    _____ _____

    Full title: "_____

    _____"

    _____._"

    Date of publication:_____ Call #_____ Library_____

Is the Project topic you're proposing in the social sciences, or sciences-
technologies, or the humanities? (See page 1 of assignment 4, if necessary).
_____
In what subject-area(s) is the topic? Not a branch of knowledge such as the
social sciences, but a subject-area within one of these branches, e.g.
anthropology, engineering, English literature, political sciences, zoology,
etc._____
What is the particular aspect of that subject (just above) with which you
propose to deal in your Project? Be as specific as possible?_____
_____
_____
On the verso of this page explain what you're interested in doing your
work on. "Something about..." time has passed. Do not propose in such a
way that I will have to ask "What about it?!" The ultimate in collegiate
work will be a topic expressed in some interrelationship.

BIBLIOGRAPHY CARDS

When using library catalogs and indexes for a literature search, record
each book, periodical article, or other publication on a separate bib
card. These can then be reorganized as necessary in a variety of ways.
Each card can be added to as you discover further information about the
publication and when you examine the book or article itself. This type
of card is part of the working bibliography process, and functions dif-
ferently from conventional "note cards", which are records of notes taken
from a book you have selected and are reading.

When you go FROM the Subject Catalog TO the Author-Title Catalog
in order to get complete information, you'd re-arrange your bib
cards so that they are alphabetical by what?_____

And, when you go FROM a library catalog TO the library stacks,
you'd re-arrange your bib cards so that they are arranged how?

Bib cards can support your library research:
You put on them data, discoveries and observations as you go along in
order to save back-tracking and to help yourself in several ways. Feel
free to abbreviate consistently, to develop your own style, shorthand and
layout codes ...   For example, you might decide to put all of your
call numbers in the upper right corner and all of your subject headings
in ALL CAPS. You might decide to put library locations in another corner,
with the date on which you place a "hold", etc. You can even get into
use of colors and cutting corners to signify your own procedure.

What needs to be gotten down on each bib card?
Maintain an ongoing, separate record (bib card) of your encounter with
each potentially useful book, article, etc. There are 3-4 basic types of
information and data which you need to obtain as you progress, so that
your search will be both productive and efficient. They are:
      -your source-- where you "discover" it.
      -bibliographic data you'd need in order to locate the publication
       in libraries and/or to cite it on a paper.
      -your library's locations.
      -any notes you make if you examine it.
Some publications you'll de-select as you go along, based on the compet-
itiveness of the other publications you discover as well as how your
topic develops; for these, you probably won't get to the 4th step.

1. A SOURCE STATEMENT
      Record on your bib cards where and how you discovered each publica-
      tion, i.e. in which library catalog or index or bibliography, etc.,
      and under exactly what heading. This information about your source
      may not be required in some research papers, but it is always
      useful in research. And it's required for your Project in this
      course. The source of your discovery is usually not the same as
      the location of the book or article itself in the collection.

2. THE ELEMENTS NEEDED IN THE BIBLIOGRAPHIC CITATION WHICH YOU ARE GOING TO PUT ON A BIBLIOGRAPHY

In any academic paper, however, it is important to "cite" publications in a standardized format, giving full bibliographic information without having to go back to the source-- to the library. Make it easy on yourself! Get the author's full name, the exact and complete title with accurate punctuation, and the imprint (place of publication, publisher, date of publication) and all the other data which can help you actually to locate and even to evaluate (select or de-select) the publication.

3. LOCATION(S) AND CALL NUMBER(S)

Also record on your bib cards the library location(s) of each item, the complete call number(s), etc., as you determine this information for each publication. Sometimes you'll acquire it gradually. Try to get as much and as soon as possible as you work along.

4. YOUR NOTES

At this point you will be able to evaluate comparatively the bibliographic information you have accumulated on your cards and to de-select, even before you go to the library stacks. You'll likely not have to pursue all of these publications, unless you've delayed too long, and it is the end of the term.

Once you have actually examined the publication, make notes on the back of the card. Get down the relevant things you find. These notes depend on your particular interests and purposes at the time-- that for which you are making a library literature search. You decide what additional things you're looking for. These notes should be functional for you-- they should help with annotating for your Project bibliography too. It helps if you have already developed the outline for a paper or report you must write, because you can refer to it for ideas about what specifics you're looking for and need.

Maximize the data and leads provided right in the catalog or fiche record without or before even handling the publication. These include the date of publication, place (nation) of publication, series of which the book may be a part, whether it's appropriately indexed or provided with such needed things as tables and illustrations, classification, author's reputation, subject headings in the tracings, length, keywords and message in the title and particularly the subtitle, etc.

If you are in the stacks and looking at the books and bound volumes of journals themselves, you can psych out (translation: examine them comparatively and critically). Scanning is an asset like typing. But with a book in hand, examine its table of contents, check out what the authors declare in the preliminary pages (the introduction, foreword or preface) they are going to do and not going to cover; sometimes the authors will tell you in the introduction what relationship this book or edition has to another one.

Locate and use such helpers as

- Book Reviews   Book Review Digest (Pathfinder assignment 6) is
                  especially useful because it provides selected
                  excerpts from a cross section of professional
                  reviewers' comments.
- Abstracts   Indexing-abstracting tools provide abstracts
                  of the contents of journal articles as well as
                  other types of publications. Individual journal
                  articles are often preceded by an abstract at
                  the beginning of the article itself. An abstract
                  is a nonevaluative summary of the crucial
                  ingredients.
- Guides-to-the-Literature of your topic or other selective (not
                  comprehensive) bibliographic support. These
                  are especially good for identifying "landmark"
                  publications in your field.

Some other considerations in evaluating the potential of a publication
include:

- How will it contribute specifically and uniquely to your topic?
- What are the author's qualifications?
- Does the publisher specialize in this field?
- Is the book or article frequently referred to by other authors?

STYLE MANUALS

We will use Kate L. Turabian's A Manual For Writers of Term Papers,
Theses, and Dissertations, 4th ed. (Chicago, Illinois: The University
of Chicago Press, c1973) as our authority. The three types of citing
rules provided by style manuals which are in use most are for:

- one-author books
- periodical articles
- component parts of books.
There are examples of each of these three most-used citing rules in your
Project Guidelines as well as Turabian's Manual.

In actual practice, your professor would indicate which style manual, if
any, was required in your class or discipline. The Random House Handbook, MLA Handbook, Chicago Style Manual, and the Publication Manual
of the APA are some standards. One uses the style manual which is oriented toward one's field or discipline. Actually, the bibliographic
formats of the various fields, especially the humanities and social
sciences, are being combined and simplified.

BIBLIOGRAPHY CARDS & USE OF STYLE MANUALS FOR BOOKS

Here's a sample bib card for a book discovered by use of the subject catalog. Someone took the "subject approach". Then s/he recorded the first three of the four basic steps.

Step 2:
BIBLIOGRAPHIC
DATA

Step 1:
SOURCE

Step 3:
LIBRARY
LOCATIONS

> Weibel, Kathryn
> "Mirror mirror; images of women reflected in popular culture " Garden City NY - Doubleday 1997
> Bib. → SEX ROLE-Subject Cat.
> HQ 14 26 W+231 Ungrad lib
> 6 Women in pop. culture
> 2. Women-US - Soc Condts
> *3. Sex Role
> 4. US - Popular culture

This person's shorthand includes using a "hook" to identify the main entry, and quotation marks around the book's title. S/he also considers it is important to get down right away the fact that this book has a bibliography, as well as the fact that it is in more than one campus library. This student also has developed a style which includes starring (*) the LC subject heading under which the book is initially discovered, as well as other subject headings assigned to it and listed in the tracings. Why might it be wise and necessary sometimes to resort to this? In what types of situations?_____

When this student discovered this book in the Subject Catalog, was s/he looking in the S's or U's or W's?_____ The reason for noting both the place of publication and publisher will become clear in the next phase-- use of the style manual.

Using Turabian's manual as your authority, prepare a bibliographic citation for Mirror Mirror... according to her "one author book" rule. (Note: three dots are used to indicate a word or words omitted by the writer. For this work don't indulge in this short cut!) Use correct style, punctuation, capitalization, underlining, indentation, spacing, etc., such as you would do for a book which you select for your Project bibliography or any collegiate work based on a style manual.

Remember: Library catalogs and style manual formats usually differ. Just compare the Turabian example in the Project Guidelines or the style manual itself (Chapter 8, page 132, 8:3B) with the data on your bib card, and then "translate" it carefully to the book on the sample bib card.

BIB CARDS AND USE OF STYLE MANUALS FOR PERIODICAL ARTICLES

When you are interested in an article cited in a periodical index, record the SOURCE (index title, periodical issue, and subject heading under which you discover the article initially) on a bib card. In most libraries in order to get the magazine or journal issue itself, you will need the full title and the volume number of the magazine containing the article in which you're interested. And, for your own use once you've obtained it from the library, you'll also need the full name of the author of the article, the title of the article, and the inclusive pagination of the article. (If the author's name isn't provided anywhere in the index, it will be among the first pieces of bibliographic data you will look for when you actually examine the periodical issue itself, so leave space for it on the bib card). Leave some space for your reaction (evaluation) later; the verso of each card is good for this purpose.

It is wise to transcribe to your bib card the date of the issue of the periodical and any other information the periodical index provides, for example, if the article is illustrated or contains a bibliography, etc. You would need some of these   data in order to request an interlibrary loan, in the event that our library does not have the issue of the periodical you need.

Below is a sample bib card on which someone has begun a periodical article's record. They have completed the first three of the four basic steps. Their SOURCE was this excerpt from a "page" in the April 1978-March 1979 Social Sciences Index.

Soc Sci I 4/78-3/79 UNMARRIED MOTHERS
Clapp, Douglas F & Rebecca S Rabb
"Follow up of unmarried adolescent mothers"
Social Work 23:149-153
March 1948

HV 1 S616

Unmarried mothers
 Follow-up of unmarried adolescent mothers. D. F. Clapp and R. S. Raab. Soc Work 23:149-53 Mr '78
Unpleasantness. See Pleasantness ar.d unpleasantness
Upper classes
  See also
Elite (social sciences)
        Great Britain
          History
Aristocratic indebtedness in the nineteenth century: the case re-opened. D. Cannadine. Econ Hist R s2 30:624-50 N '77
        United States
Inner group of the American capitalist class. M. Useem. bibl Soc Prob 25:225-40 F '78
Why the rich don't care. S. Burnham. il Washington M 10:10-16+ Ap '78

Using the bibliographic data provided by the <u>Social Sciences Index</u> and which have been transcribed to the bib card, but following Turabian's rule for citing journal articles, print a citation here for the periodical article such as you'd use on your Project bibliography or other college work. An example is provided in the Project Guidelines and the style manual itself (Chapter 8, page 139, 8:35B). Note that <u>Readers'</u> <u>Guide</u>'s use of the "+" is only one of several differences with which you must routinely cope. Data are not displayed in a periodical index in the same way they are in a bibliography. And use capital letters, underline, etc.

_____

_____

_____

_____

BIBLIOGRAPHY CARDS AND USE OF STYLE MANUALS FOR "COMPONENT

PARTS"

Only rarely, as for example, on your Project bibliography for this course, will you find it necessary to locate publications in various formats as well as on aspects of a specific subject. Usually when you are searching for subject-matter, you are not terribly concerned whether it consists of a book or an article in a periodical, or what the format is. It may consist of part of a book, in which case you need to cite only that relevant portion you use in your research... the component part of a collection of essays or an anthology, etc. Usually such a book consists of sections, articles, essays, chapters, plays, stories, etc. by various people, each writing on an aspect of a subject and coordinated, compiled or edited by another individual who may or may not also be a contributor.

Here is the source for a portion of a book which interested this student. The essays in the book are indexed by the <u>Essay & General Literature Index</u>, the 1975-1979 volume, on page 368 under the subject DECADENCE IN LITERATURE. The student was attracted by the second citation under that subject and transcribed all the available information onto the bib card which appears on the next page. The full names of the essay writer (Oberg) and book editor (Butscher) appear elsewhere in the same volume of the Index. S/he then checked the library's catalog for the book. (Practice in using <u>The Essay & General Literature Index</u>) will be provided in Assignment 7.)

> The management of complexity. *In* Benton, L. R. ed. Management for the future p77-86
> **Decadence in literature**
> Brombert, V. H. Huysmans: the prison house of decadence. *In* Brombert, V. H. The romantic prison p149-70
> Oberg, A. K. Sylvia Plath and the new decadence. *In* Butscher, E. ed. Sylvia Plath p177-85
> **De Caldes, Ramon.** See Ramon de Caldes
> **De Cecco, John P.** and Shively, Michael G.
> Conflicts over rights and needs in homosexual relationships. *In* Crew, L. ed. The gay academic p305-14
> **De Cecco, Marcello**
> The last of the Romans. *In* Skidelsky, R.J.A. ed. The end of the Keynesian era p18-24

And here is the bib card for the essay titled "Sylvia Plath and the New Decadence" by A. K. Oberg. Using the bibliographic data provided by the Index excerpt and which have been transcribed to the bib card by this student, but following Turabian's rule for citing component parts, print a citation here for the essay such as you'd use on your Project bibliography or other collegiate work. An example is provided in the Project Guidelines and the style manual (Chapter 8, page 137, 8:25B).

EGLI 1945-9 DECADENCE IN
LIT

Step 1:
SOURCE

Oberg, Arthur Kenneth "Sylvia Plath
+ the new decadence " In
Butscher, Edward . Sylvia
Plath ; the woman and
the work " ny : Dodd
1977   PP 177-185

Step 2:
BIBLIOGRAPHIC
DATA

PS 3566 Pl 27292

Step 3:LIBRARY
LOCATION

BIBLIOGRAPHY CARDS

When using library catalogs and indexes for a literature search, record
each book, periodical article, or other publication on a separate bib
card. These can then be reorganized as necessary in a variety of ways.
Each card can be added to as you discover further information about the
publication and when you examine the book or article itself. This type
of card is part of the working bibliography process, and functions dif-
ferently from conventional "note cards", which are records of notes taken
from a book you have selected and are reading.

> When you go FROM the Subject Catalog TO the Author-Title Catalog
> in order to get complete information, you'd re-arrange your bib
> cards so that they are alphabetical by what? main entries (authors)
>
> And, when you go FROM a library catalog TO the library stacks,
> you'd re-arrange your bib cards so that they are arranged how?
> by LC Classification, which is the first part of the call numbers

Bib cards can support your library research:
You put on them data, discoveries and observations as you go along in
order to save back-tracking and to help yourself in several ways. Feel
free to abbreviate consistently, to develop your own style, shorthand and
layout codes ...   For example, you might decide to put all of your
call numbers in the upper right corner and all of your subject headings
in ALL CAPS. You might decide to put library locations in another corner,
with the date on which you place a "hold", etc. You can even get into
use of colors and cutting corners to signify your own procedure.

What needs to be gotten down on each bib card?
Maintain an ongoing, separate record (bib card) of your encounter with
each potentially useful book, article, etc. There are 3-4 basic types of
information and data which you need to obtain as you progress, so that
your search will be both productive and efficient. They are:
       -your source-- where you "discover" it.
       -bibliographic data you'd need in order to locate the publication
        in libraries and/or to cite it on a paper.
       -your library's locations.
       -any notes you make if you examine it.
Some publications you'll de-select as you go along, based on the compet-
itiveness of the other publications you discover as well as how your
topic develops; for these, you probably won't get to the 4th step.

1. A SOURCE STATEMENT
       Record on your bib cards where and how you discovered each publica-
       tion, i.e. in which library catalog or index or bibliography, etc.,
       and under exactly what heading. This information about your source
       may not be required in some research papers, but it is always
       useful in research. And it's required for your Project in this
       course. The source of your discovery is usually not the same as
       the location of the book or article itself in the collection.

2. THE ELEMENTS NEEDED IN THE BIBLIOGRAPHIC CITATION WHICH YOU ARE GOING TO PUT ON A BIBLIOGRAPHY

In any academic paper, however, it is important to "cite" publications in a standardized format, giving full bibliographic information without having to go back to the source-- to the library. Make it easy on yourself! Get the author's full name, the exact and complete title with accurate punctuation, and the imprint (place of publication, publisher, date of publication) and all the other data which can help you actually to locate and even to evaluate (select or de-select) the publication.

3. LOCATION(S) AND CALL NUMBER(S)

Also record on your bib cards the library location(s) of each item, the complete call number(s), etc., as you determine this information for each publication. Sometimes you'll acquire it gradually. Try to get as much and as soon as possible as you work along.

4. YOUR NOTES

At this point you will be able to evaluate comparatively the bibliographic information you have accumulated on your cards and to de-select, even before you go to the library stacks. You'll likely not have to pursue all of these publications, unless you've delayed too long, and it is the end of the term.

Once you have actually examined the publication, make notes on the back of the card. Get down the relevant things you find. These notes depend on your particular interests and purposes at the time-- that for which you are making a library literature search. You decide what additional things you're looking for. These notes should be functional for you-- they should help with annotating for your Project bibliography too. It helps if you have already developed the outline for a paper or report you must write, because you can refer to it for ideas about what specifics you're looking for and need.

Maximize the data and leads provided right in the catalog or fiche record without or before even handling the publication. These include the date of publication, place (nation) of publication, series of which the book may be a part, whether it's appropriately indexed or provided with such needed things as tables and illustrations, classification, author's reputation, subject headings in the tracings, length, keywords and message in the title and particularly the subtitle, etc.

If you are in the stacks and looking at the books and bound volumes of journals themselves, you can psych out (translation: examine them comparatively and critically). Scanning is an asset like typing. But with a book in hand, examine its table of contents, check out what the authors declare in the preliminary pages (the introduction, foreword or preface) they are going to do and not going to cover; sometimes the authors will tell you in the introduction what relationship this book or edition has to another one.

Locate and use such helpers as

- Book Reviews   Book Review Digest (Pathfinder assignment 6) is
                    especially useful because it provides selected
                    excerpts from a cross section of professional
                    reviewers' comments.
- Abstracts   Indexing-abstracting tools provide abstracts
                    of the contents of journal articles as well as
                    other types of publications. Individual journal
                    articles are often preceded by an abstract at
                    the beginning of the article itself. An abstract
                    is a nonevaluative summary of the crucial
                    ingredients.
- Guides-to-the-Literature of your topic or other selective (not
                    comprehensive) bibliographic support. These
                    are especially good for identifying "landmark"
                    publications in your field.

Some other considerations in evaluating the potential of a publication
include:

- How will it contribute specifically and uniquely to your topic?
- What are the author's qualifications?
- Does the publisher specialize in this field?
- Is the book or article frequently referred to by other authors?

STYLE MANUALS

We will use Kate L. Turabian's A Manual For Writers of Term Papers,
Theses, and Dissertations, 4th ed. (Chicago, Illinois: The University
of Chicago Press, c1973) as our authority. The three types of citing
rules provided by style manuals which are in use most are for:

- one-author books
- periodical articles
- component parts of books.
There are examples of each of these three most-used citing rules in your
Project Guidelines as well as Turabian's Manual.

In actual practice, your professor would indicate which style manual, if
any, was required in your class or discipline. The Random House Handbook, MLA Handbook, Chicago Style Manual, and the Publication Manual
of the APA are some standards. One uses the style manual which is oriented toward one's field or discipline. Actually, the bibliographic
formats of the various fields, especially the humanities and social
sciences, are being combined and simplified.

BIBLIOGRAPHY CARDS & USE OF STYLE MANUALS FOR BOOKS

Here's a sample bib card for a book discovered by use of the subject catalog. Someone took the "subject approach". Then s/he recorded the first three of the four basic steps.

Step 2:
BIBLIOGRAPHIC
DATA

Step 1:
SOURCE

Step 3:
LIBRARY
LOCATIONS

> Weibel, Kathryn
> "Mirror mirror; images of women reflected in popular culture" Garden City NY - Doubleday 1977
> Bib. → SEX ROLE-Subject Cat.
> HQ 1426 W+231 Undergrad lib
> 1. Women in pop. culture
> 2. Women-US - Soc Condts
> *3. Sex Role
> 4. US - Popular culture

This person's shorthand includes using a "hook" to identify the main entry, and quotation marks around the book's title. S/he also considers it is important to get down right away the fact that this book has a bibliography, as well as the fact that it is in more than one campus library. This student also has developed a style which includes starring (*) the LC subject heading under which the book is initially discovered, as well as other subject headings assigned to it and listed in the tracings. Why might it be wise and necessary sometimes to resort to this? In what types of situations? new and changing fields and views; when it seems there are few publications in the library's collection; for whatever reason, you haven't been able to generate several good subject-heads. When this student discovered this book in the Subject Catalog, was s/he looking in the S's or U's or W's? S's   The reason for noting both the place of publication and publisher will become clear in the next phase-- use of the style manual.

Using Turabian's manual as your authority, prepare a bibliographic citation for Mirror Mirror... according to her "one author book" rule. (Note: three dots are used to indicate a word or words omitted by the writer. For this work don't indulge in this short cut!) Use correct style, punctuation, capitalization, underlining, indentation, spacing, etc., such as you would do for a book which you select for your Project bibliography or any collegiate work based on a style manual.

Remember: Library catalogs and style manual formats usually differ. Just compare the Turabian example in the Project Guidelines or the style manual itself (Chapter 8, page 132, 8:3B) with the data on your bib card, and then "translate" it carefully to the book on the sample bib card.

Weibel, Kathryn.   Mirror Mirror; Images of Women

Reflected in Popular Culture.   Garden City,

New York: Doubleday, 1977.

BIB CARDS AND USE OF STYLE MANUALS FOR PERIODICAL ARTICLES

When you are interested in an article cited in a periodical index, record the SOURCE (index title, periodical issue, and subject heading under which you discover the article initially) on a bib card. In most libraries in order to get the magazine or journal issue itself, you will need the full title and the volume number of the magazine containing the article in which you're interested. And, for your own use once you've obtained it from the library, you'll also need the full name of the author of the article, the title of the article, and the inclusive pagination of the article. (If the author's name isn't provided anywhere in the index, it will be among the first pieces of bibliographic data you will look for when you actually examine the periodical issue itself, so leave space for it on the bib card). Leave some space for your reaction (evaluation) later; the verso of each card is good for this purpose.

It is wise to transcribe to your bib card the date of the issue of the periodical and any other information the periodical index provides, for example, if the article is illustrated or contains a bibliography, etc. You would need some of these   data in order to request an interlibrary loan, in the event that our library does not have the issue of the periodical you need.

Below is a sample bib card on which someone has begun a periodical article's record. They have completed the first three of the four basic steps. Their SOURCE was this excerpt from a "page" in the April 1978- March 1979 Social Sciences Index.

Soc Sci I 4/78-3/79 UNMARRIED MOTHERS
Clapp, Douglas ← & Rebecca S Rabb
"Follow up of unmarried adolescent mothers"
Social Work 23:149-153
March 1948

HV 1 S616

> Unmarried mothers
> ←Follow-up of unmarried adolescent mothers. D. F. Clapp and R. S. Raab. Soc Work 23:149-53 Mr '78
> Unpleasantness. See Pleasantness and unpleasantness
> Upper classes
>   See also
> Elite (social sciences)
>   Great Britain
>   History
> Aristocratic indebtedness in the nineteenth century: the case re-opened. D. Cannadine. Econ Hist R s2 30:624-50 N '77
>   United States
> Inner group of the American capitalist class. M. Useem. bibl Soc Prob 25:225-40 F '78
> Why the rich don't care. S. Burnham. il Washington M 10:10-16+ Ap '78

Using the bibliographic data provided by the <u>Social Sciences Index</u>
and which have been transcribed to the bib card, but following Turabian's
rule for citing journal articles, print a citation here for the periodical article such as you'd use on your Project bibliography or other
college work. An example is provided in the Project Guidelines and the
style manual itself (Chapter 8, page 139, 8:35B). Note that <u>Readers'
Guide</u>'s use of the "+" is only one of several differences with which you
must routinely cope. Data are not displayed in a periodical index in the
same way they are in a bibliography. And use capital letters, underline, etc.

Clapp, Douglas F. and Rabb, Rebecca S.   "Follow-

up of Unmarried Adolescent Mothers."   <u>Social</u>

<u>Work</u> 23 (March 1978): 149-53.

BIBLIOGRAPHY CARDS AND USE OF STYLE MANUALS FOR "COMPONENT

PARTS"

Only rarely, as for example, on your Project bibliography for this course,
will you find it necessary to locate publications in various formats as
well as on aspects of a specific subject. Usually when you are searching
for subject-matter, you are not terribly concerned whether it consists of
a book or an article in a periodical, or what the format is. It may
consist of part of a book, in which case you need to cite only that relevant portion you use in your research... the component part of a collection
of essays or an anthology, etc. Usually such a book consists of sections,
articles, essays, chapters, plays, stories, etc. by various people, each
writing on an aspect of a subject and coordinated, compiled or edited by
another individual who may or may not also be a contributor.

Here is the source for a portion of a book which interested this student.
The essays in the book are indexed by the <u>Essay & General Literature Index</u>,
the 1975-1979 volume, on page 368 under the subject DECADENCE IN LITERATURE.

The student was attracted by the
second citation under that subject and transcribed all the available information onto the bib
card which appears on the next
page. The full names of the essay
writer (Oberg) and book editor
(Butscher) appear elsewhere in the
same volume of the Index. S/he
then checked the library's catalog for the book. (Practice in
using <u>The Essay & General Literature Index</u>) will be provided in
Assignment 7.)

The management of complexity. *In* Benton,
L. R. ed. Management for the future p77-86
Decadence in literature
  Brombert, V. H. Huysmans: the prison
house of decadence. *In* Brombert, V. H. The
romantic prison p149-70
  Oberg, A. K. Sylvia Plath and the new
decadence. *In* Butscher, E. ed. Sylvia Plath
p177-85
De Caldes, Ramon. See Ramon de Caldes
De Cecco, John P. and Shively, Michael G.
  Conflicts over rights and needs in homo-
sexual relationships. *In* Crew, L. ed. The gay
academic p305-14
De Cecco, Marcello
  The last of the Romans. *In* Skidelsky,
R.J.A. ed. The end of the Keynesian era p18-24

And here is the bib card for the essay titled "Sylvia Plath and the New Decadence" by A. K. Oberg. Using the bibliographic data provided by the Index excerpt and which have been transcribed to the bib card by this student, but following Turabian's rule for citing component parts, print a citation here for the essay such as you'd use on your Project bibliography or other collegiate work. An example is provided in the Project Guidelines and the style manual (Chapter 8, page 137, 8:25B).

EGLI 1945-9 DECADENCE IN LIT

Step 1: SOURCE

Oberg, Arthur Kenneth 'Sylvia Plath y the new decadence " In Butscher, Edward . Sylvia Plath ; the woman and the work" ny: Dodd 1977   PP 177-185

Step 2: BIBLIOGRAPHIC DATA

PS 3566 Pl 27292

Step 3: LIBRARY LOCATION

Oberg, Arthur Kenneth. "Sylvia Plath and the
New Decadence." In Sylvia Plath; the
Woman and the Work, pp. 177-85. Edited
by Edward Butscher.   New York: Dodd,
1977.

PRACTICE USING A PERIODICAL INDEX

Serials Catalog, parts 1 and 2, coverage of More Library Basics, and Assignment 3 (and 4 ideally) should precede this work. In order to complete question 7, the Bibliography Cards & Style Manuals handout should already have been distributed, assigned for study, and discussed, although pages 1, 2 and 5 cover the needed information. This worksheet is designed for in-class use, but is also useful as a source of test questions. Section III: Resources contains additional Practice Using A Periodical Index forms.

For in-class use, distribute the same form to each class member, and tell them they have fifteen minutes. Walk around to note who needs help. After fifteen minutes, ask for a volunteer to answer question 1, "and tell us why." After each question, ask if there are any questions. If you have time left, ask them to describe specifically how they would proceed if they were in the library and wanted to read this (question 7 perhaps) article. Collect the forms if they will be useful to you, e.g. for noting progress, recording attendance, etc. Return them at the next meeting, graded or not, depending on this class' needs.

Practice Using A Periodical Index
Your Name _____

1. These questions relate to using semi-specialized periodical indexes efficiently; this excerpt appears to be from The _____ Index.

    Applied Science & Technology
    Humanities
    Social Sciences

2. These subject headings are all derived from the LCSH.

    TRUE   FALSE

3. Someone interested in journal articles about dietary content of
  food
should look under the subject heading

_____ when they use this Index.

> Diet therapy
>   Dietary beliefs in health and illness among a Hong Kong community. S. S. Y. C. Ho. *Soc Sci Med* 20 no3:223-30 '85
>   Impact of a dietary change on emotional distress. L. Christensen and others. bibl *J Abnorm Psychol* 94:565-79 N '85
>   Reinstitution of diet therapy in PKU patients from twenty-two US clinics. V. E. Schuett and others. *Am J Public Health* 75:39-42 Ja '85
> Dietary content of food *See* Food—Fiber content
> Diethylene glycol *See* Glycols
> Diethylstilbestrol
>   Toxicology
>   "Gilding the Lilly": a DES update. A. M. Levine. *Trial* 20:18-22 D '84
> Dieting *See* Reducing
> Dietl, Dick
>   AT&T taking its own advice: "the commitment continues!". il *J Rehabil* 51:72-4 Ja/Mr '85
>   CRCA (Carondelet): an unfinished work of art. il *J Rehabil* 51:9-15 Ap/Je '85
>   The doctor made a house call. il *J Rehabil* 51:24-5 Jl/S '85

4. The excerpt displays #___ articles and #____ cross references.

5. The complete subject heading under which the article by A. M. Levine is entered is

_____

6. You've misplaced your bib cards! Now you've got to return to the Index volume to get some information. Based on the information contained in the excerpt, you'll approach first which volume of this Index? Put an X across it.

| APRIL 1984 - MARCH 1985 | APRIL 1985 - MARCH 1986 | APRIL 1986 - MARCH 1987 | APRIL 1987 - MARCH 1988 |

7. Record on the bib card all of the information possible for the article by V. E. Schuett

  and others

8. How many of these articles include some bibliographic support? #____

9. The complete title of the last cited article is " _____
_____ ", and it was
published in volume #____ of the periodical.

10. S.S.Y.C. Ho 's article begins and ends on pages _____;
it appeared in a periodical whose title is abbreviated _____

1. These questions relate to using semi-
   specialized periodical indexes
   efficiently; this excerpt appears to
   be from The _____ Index.

   ___ Applied Science & Technology
   ___ Humanities
   X   Social Sciences

> Diet therapy
>   Dietary beliefs in health and illness among a Hong Kong
>   community. S. S. Y. C. Ho. *Soc Sci Med* 20 no3:223-30
>   '85
>   Impact of a dietary change on emotional distress. L.
>   Christensen and others. bibl *J Abnorm Psychol* 94:565-79
>   N '85
>   Reinstitution of diet therapy in PKU patients from
>   twenty-two US clinics. V. E. Schuett and others. *Am
>   J Public Health* 75:39-42 Ja '85
> Dietary content of food *See* Food—Fiber content
> Diethylene glycol *See* Glycols
> Diethylstilbestrol
>   Toxicology
>   "Gilding the Lilly": a DES update. A. M. Levine. *Trial*
>   20:18-22 D '84
> Dieting *See* Reducing
> Dietl, Dick
>   AT&T taking its own advice: "the commitment con-
>   tinues!". il *J Rehabil* 51:72-4 Ja/Mr '85
>   CRCA (Carondelet): an unfinished work of art. il *J Rehabil*
>   51:9-15 Ap/Je '85
>   The doctor made a house call. il *J Rehabil* 51:24-5
>   Jl/S '85

2. These subject headings are all derived from the LCSH.

   ___ TRUE   X FALSE

3. Someone interested in journal articles about <u>dietary content of</u>
   <u>food</u>
   should look under the subject heading
   <u>FOOD-- FIBER CONTENT</u>   when they use this Index.

4. The excerpt displays #<u>7</u> articles and #<u>3</u> cross references.

5. The complete subject heading under which the article by <u>A. M. Levine</u>
   is entered is <u>DIETHYLSTILBESTROL-- TOXICOLOGY</u>

6. You've misplaced your bib cards! Now
   you've got to return to the Index
   volume to get some information.
   Based on the information contained in
   the excerpt, you'll approach first
   which volume of this Index? Put an X
   across it.

APRIL 1984 - MARCH 1985	X APRIL 1985 - MARCH 1986	APRIL 1986 - MARCH 1987	APRIL 1987 - MARCH 1988

7. Record on the bib
   card <u>all</u> of the information possible
   for the article
   by <u>V. E. Schuett</u>
   <u>and others</u>

   SOCIAL SCIENCES INDEX   Apr 85-March 86   DIET THERAPY

   Schuett, V   E., and others
   "Reinstitution of diet therapy in PKU patients
    from twenty-two US clinics."
   Am J Public Health 75:39-42   January 1985

8. How many of these articles include some bibliographic support? #<u>1</u>

9. The complete title of the <u>last cited</u> article is "The doctor
   <u>made a house call</u>", and it was
   published in volume #<u>51</u> of the periodical.

10. <u>S.S.Y.C. Ho</u>'s article begins and ends on pages <u>223-230</u> ;
    it appeared in a periodical whose title is abbreviated <u>Soc Sci Med</u>

Course
Instructor

Page -1-
of 6

Computer-Assisted Literature
Searching

Automation is apparent to library users in two main ways: in accessing (1) the library's own catalog of its holdings and (2) standard bibliographic reference tools found in most libraries, which have been stored in data bases. In some cases, the contents of reference books themselves have been stored and can be retrieved and read online. A computer-assisted search of records is quicker than a comparable search by hand; often the results will be better too.

Most academic libraries have begun to store in computerized files the records which in the past comprised their card catalogs. Although the card catalog is usually "closed" at the time the new storage-retrieval method begins, it remains in the library because retrospective conversion of records is not possible at the time, and in practice, the library begins to input records of acquisitions as of that date, making it necessary to search both "catalogs" occasionally. Even when the retrospective conversion has been accomplished, the card catalog --sometimes now referred to as Catalog One-- remains as a reliable back-up during power failure, or when Catalog Two is "down". Library online catalogs frequently function as union catalogs (see glossary, page 13 of Library Basics handout), providing holdings information about the collections of all the libraries on a campus and/or in a university system. They provide the same types of information access (e.g. author, subject, title) as conventional catalogs, in addition to such other "indexes" (types of access points) as periodicals, series, and others, depending on the catalog. Conventional card catalogs as well as online catalogs usually list the library's (or libraries') serials titles, but they do not analyze (index) the contents of the articles within the issues of the periodicals.

COMPUTER REFERENCE SERVICES IN LIBRARIES.

For a wide range of subjects in the humanities and the social, life, health, and physical sciences, the library offers for a fee the resources of the latest computer technology. Through direct (online telecommunication with computers that may be several thousand miles away, information retrieval systems sort through vast numbers of references (citations) to newspaper articles, journal articles, conference proceedings, articles in popular magazines, published reports, government documents, grants, dissertations, and research in progress. A computer print-out much like a bibliography and tailor-made to the patron's specifications is provided. The files which the computers scan are stored on magnetic tapes and discs and are referred to as databases.

You have already become aware of the various printed periodical indexes which are available for hand searching in libraries. Pathfinder Assignment 5, Step 3 referred you to <u>Periodical Indexes in the Social Sciences and Humanities...</u> by Lois Harzfeld and <u>Abstracts and Indexes in Science and Technology...</u> by Dolores Owen. They describe many of the standard periodical indexes commercially published as well as by professional organizations and government agencies. Harzfeld and Owen indicate which of these have also been stored in data bases and can be searched bibliographically by computer. In addition, there are some highly specialized data bases which are available only online, i.e. not in printed form. Computerized data bases (sometimes with varying titles) do analyze the contents of issues of serials especially in terms of their subject matter. Many of these data bases literally consist of printed periodical indexes which have been converted to computerized data bases in machine readable form. Most of the periodical indexes, citation indexes and abstracting tools considered in this course are available online, e.g. New York Times Index, Social Sciences Citation Index, Psychological Abstracts.

The advantages of online searching are:

(1) SPEED. The equivalent of many volumes of a printed periodical index can be searched in minutes. Usually 20-30 references (citations) can be printed out immediately when a search is done by a librarian who is a subject-specialist and whom you have provided with sufficient information about your needs.

(2) CURRENCY. Computer tapes are available before the printed index can be produced from them, dispatched to subscriber-libraries, processed and reach the reference department shelf.

(3) COORDINATE SUBJECT SEARCHING. It is possible to search for two or more subjects,or concepts, simultaneously. The computer can locate material on subjects in combinations which form such topics as "suicides among female college students", "dental plans provided by employers", "vitamin C and the common cold","disposable diapers as environmental pollutants", "self-concept therapies used with prisoners who have histories of drug abuse or addiction", "influenza viruses in humans", and "alcoholism among American adolescents and their rehabilitation." Finding this information by the conventional method of consulting printed indexes may be complicated, even impossible.

(4) LATEST INFORMATION. Online databases can be utilized through keywords and word combinations that do not appear in printed indexes. This is particularly useful for new topics and developments for which no printed subject headings have yet appeared or been established.

(5) NO PRINTED COUNTERPARTS. A computer data base may contain references which do not appear in any printed periodical index. Or, one data base may contain references which appear in several printed indexes.

(6) PRINTED ANNOTATIONS and ABSTRACTS are sometimes available, included in the list (bibliography) of references retrieved.

COMPARISON OF THE LIBRARY'S ONLINE CATALOG and COMPUTER-ASSISTED LITERATURE SEARCHING OF COMMERCIAL DATABASES:

	The Library's Online Catalog	Commercial Database Searching
Abstracts	No	Yes
Books	Mainly books	Mainly articles
Periodical Articles	No	Yes
Cost	No	Yes
Subject-headings	Yes	Sometimes
Permuted keywords	Sometimes	Yes
Call numbers	Yes	No
Worldwide information and scope	No	Yes
Book Reviews Cited	No	Yes
Subject-Coverage	LC Classification	Comprehensive, but strong in science, business.
Time Limitation	Must use other files with it	Approx. 1970-
Speed	Hmmmm	Yes, but can vary

Let's say someone is researching the subject of ALCOHOLISM among ADOLES-CENTS in the United States and is also interested in their REHABILITATION. S/he wants to know what type and amount of information and publications are available, especially from the educator's perspective. There are several indexes and data bases from various perspectives: ERIC (Educational Resources Information Center) is reliable and cheap. ERIC's indexes -- Current Index to Journals in Education (CIJIE), 1969-   , and Resources in Education (RIE), 1966-   , are also available in hard-copy, for hand searching in the library. The documents indexed in the ERIC RIE portion are also available in the library in fiche form. If interested in one of these publications, you'd need to look for the "ED number" which appears at the beginning of many of the ERIC citations.

Descriptors are like subject headings. The *'d ones are major ones. Some data bases are organized around structured subject-headings form various thesauri, much as the library's catalog is based on the LCSH. There are copies of the ERIC thesaurus in the library. But it's possible to query ERIC via computer using both descriptors (subject headings) and "free wording" (like keywords). "Identifiers" are similar to added entries in catalog cards' tracings (I, II, etc.)

ALCOHOLISM and DRINKING and REHABILITATION are established ERIC descriptors; they appear in the ERIC Thesaurus of Descriptors. Because this researcher is interested in adolescents, "ADOLES?" is truncated so that any title or abstract containing the various forms of this stem would be generated, e.g. adolescent, adolescents, adolesence. Likewise rehabilitation, rehabilitating, etc. Teenage will function somewhat like a synonym for adolescent, and drinking as related to alcoholism. By "OR-ing" we will get all the documents which have one or the other;

by "AND-ing" we will get (combine) all documents which have all three

concepts in them. This is a 3-faceted search using Boolean logic

(algebra). The operators are AND (decreases) and OR (increases).

Concept#1=adoles? [adolescent/adolescents/adolesence, etc.] OR teenage
     OR youth
Concept #2= Alcoholism OR Drinking
Concept #3= Rehabilitation

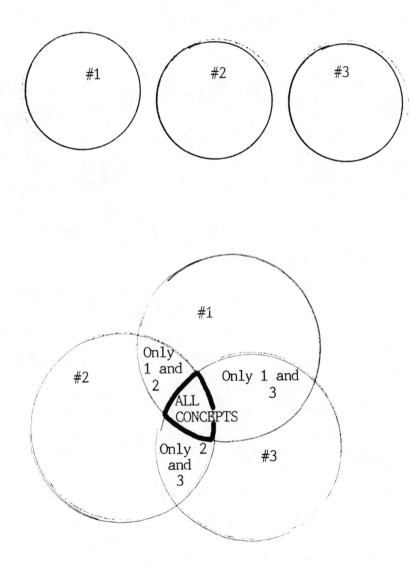

Course
Instructor
Page 1 of 2

Computer-Assisted Literature
Searching
Your Name _____

While there aren't sufficient funds in the treasury for everyone to have a computer-assisted literature search, it is possible to have a brief sample search demonstration done for you. And anyway, not all of the uses of this searching technique relate to generating lengthy bibliographies. People also use them to help:

>in identifying the relative number of publications available on a given topic
>in focusing (or broadening) research topics
>for current awareness
>to identify descriptors (subject-headings)
>to read the abstracts sometimes available

BEFORE YOUR SEARCH:
-A-
Go to the library and use the Thesaurus of ERIC Descriptors, which is located in the reference department and has the call number _____.
Consult the ERIC thesaurus to generate at least 4 descriptors relevant to your Project. Do not assume that simply because the "E" in ERIC stands for "Educational" that it is a pedagogue's tool! In fact, ERIC is a monumental data base for the social and behavioral sciences, and has some humanities, science, and technology-related publications recorded and abstracted in it too.

Note: Thesauri associated with specialized disciplines and fields do not have the flexibility of the LCSH ; use each descriptor "as is". Don't count on LCSH-type subdivisions.

(If you conclude that the ERIC data base is not relevant to your Project, then use one of the following topics, in which case, check the one you select:
____ Research in chemistry at private undergraduate colleges.
____ The portrayal of black women in the advertisements of popular magazines.
____ Toxic art materials and their effects on old adults.
____ Misconceptions about Einstein: his work and his views.)

Project-Related Descriptors	ERIC Thesaurus Page #
1. _____	_____
2. _____	_____
3. _____	_____
4. _____	_____
_____	_____
_____	_____

-B-
While in the library, examine the DIALOG DATABASE CATALOG located in the

_____

From it, identify at least 3 data bases (they refer to them as numbered "files"; for example ERIC is file 1) which are relevant to your Project's scope. You will actually be involved in the same type of survey as you did in pathfinder Assignment 5, Step 3, when you used Harzfeld and/or Owen to identify specialized periodical indexes, abstracting services, and citation indexes. So, therefore, you should start this work by trying to locate the data base-counterparts for the printed tools you located in Assignment5, Step 3. Some, although not all, have the identical titles online as they do in print form, e.g. <u>Sociological Abstracts</u>. Others have jazzed up titles, e.g. <u>Social Sciences Citation Index</u> in print becomes <u>Social SciSearch</u> online!

The 3 "best" tools identified in the <u>pathfinder Step 3</u>	Their DIALOG counterparts, if any. (If none, put "NA".)	The DIALOG File Number
1. "_____		
_____		
_____" _____	_____	# _____
2. "_____		
_____		
_____" _____	_____	# _____
3. "_____		
_____		
_____" _____	_____	# _____
Others:	_____	# _____
$--- ---\rightarrow$	_____	# _____
	_____	# _____
	_____	# _____

Your Name _____
Assignment 5: Working Through A Topic:
A Pathfinder for your Project.
Due: In class on date on your schedule.

Required Reading: "Project Guidelines". Bring Project topic proposal to
your Project conference. Return to "Bib Cards & Style Manuals" handout.

FOCUSING YOUR TOPIC

Is the Project topic you're proposing in the sciences-technologies, social
sciences, or humanities? _____

In what general subject areas is the Project? Not a branch of knowledge
    such as the sciences, social sciences or humanities, but a subject
    area within one or two of these. For example, anthropology, polit-
    ical science, English literature, engineering, etc. _____

What is the particular aspect of that subject (just above) with which your
Project will deal? Review the Project Guidelines. Be as specific as
possible. _____

_____

STEPS IN DOING MOST LIBRARY LITERATURE SEARCHES:
    1. Background reading, an outline, a "working title".
    2. Using a thesaurus efficiently to locate usable subject headings.
    3. Using a systematic methodology for locating articles in period-
       icals, i.e. identification of useful specialized periodical
       indexes, abstracting services and citation indexes.
    4. Locating and using a selective bibliography or "guide to the lit-
       erature" of your topic or field.
    5. Using some of the specialized periodical indexes identified.
    6. Evaluating your discoveries: selecting and de-selecting.

STEP #1 in doing library research for a term paper efficiently is BACK-
GROUND READING, an outline, and a "working title". Because locating an
appropriate background reading requires mastery of some library research
skills and some information about your topic itself which you may not yet
have, go to STEP #2 for now.

STEP #2 in doing library research for a term paper effectively is USING
A THESAURUS efficiently to locate usable subject headings. Do not expect
to find subject headings which are literally exactly a topic you're researching. You must manipulate and scrounge around, combine concepts and
subject headings, use sub-subject headings (subdivisions) and parts of
books-- literally, to re-search!

Refer to page 2: The sequence introduced here will "work" for any library
literature search. Complete the first step (column 1). Then move to the
second step (column 2), and so forth.

After you've completed the sequence on the next page, you'll have done much
of the basic work for your Project. Then you'll use these several subject
headings to discover relevant publications listed in the library catalogs.
Transcribe these onto bib cards. Consult the handout, "Bib Cards & Style
Manuals". Later you'll also apply the subject headings you settle on to
the catalog of the specialized branch library you use. Turn in with this
assignment all of the cards (at least 10) which you make in the course of
completing Step #2.

STEP #2. FIRST Generate all of the usable subject headings for your topic from the LCSH. List only and all established subject heads. Do NOT list broad ones which are really big fields (the ones with many See Also's). Be specific. Aim for several, totally different-from-each-other ones. Look for sub-divisions. Note any LC classification or other information.
Established Subject Headings

1 A. _____
_____

2 A. _____
_____

3 A. _____
_____

4 A. _____
_____

5 A. _____
_____

6 A. _____
_____

SECOND. Now check the library catalogs under subjects for each of the headings you've just generated in the first column. They may have, additionally, useful sub-divisions in the library catalog.

Is this subject heading (in the first column) present in the library catalog? Is the wording exactly the same? (Space is for your findings)

B. _____

B. _____

B. _____

B. _____

B. _____

B. _____

While you're doing this, do you discover any good subject headings in the library catalog which you had not already identified while searching the LCSH? _____ If yes, list them:

_____

THIRD. Which of these from the "B" column do you consider your best subject headings to explore further in the library catalog? They'll tend to be the #1 subject in the tracings, or to overlap in several tracings as "coordinates." Rank them!

First choice subject heading: ___
_____

2nd _____

3rd _____

4th _____

FOURTH You'll need access to bibliographies abstracts, etc. in your subject field. Do any of the subject headings you've listed above have the following valuable form-subdivisions in the library catalog? (Yes/No)
Your TOPIC dash:
BIBLIOGRAPHY ___
INDEXES ___
PERIODICALS ___
ABSTRACTS ___
HANDBOOKS, MANUALS, ETC. ___
DICTIONARIES AND ENCYCLOPEDIAS ___

STEP #3 involves a systematic methodology for LOCATING ARTICLES IN PERI-
ODICALS on your subject. The idea is not to locate periodicals, but
instead, to locate systematically indexes of numerous periodicals in your
specialized field or discipline.

Readers' Guide indexes only magazines which are general and "popular".
You need to be able to identify useful specialized periodical indexes for
whatever topic you're working on-- now for your Project and in the future.

Examine PERIODICAL INDEXES IN THE SOCIAL SCIENCES AND HUMANITIES: A SUB-
    JECT GUIDE, by Lois Harzfeld, and ABSTRACTS AND INDEXES IN SCIENCE
    AND TECHNOLOGY: A DESCRIPTIVE GUIDE, by Dolores Owen. They are on
    reserve and in the Reference Collection:
    Harzfeld's Call #: _____
    Owen's Call #: _____
You can tell that these two reference books complement each other by stud-
ying their titles. How do they complement each other? _____

_____
Which one, therefore, are you going to consult for your Project? _____

Study the TABLE OF CONTENTS (in the front) and consult the INDEX (in the
back) for subjects, disciplines, fields and areas which sound like they
have potential for your Project topic. Start with the groups in the CONTENTS
section. Analyze each group and each index title under that group-heading.
Then read her annotation for each likely-sounding index title, within the
body of the volume, where each periodical index is described.

Some of these indexes don't have the word "index" in their titles. Abstracting services and citation indexes are special types of periodical
indexes. Not all abstracting services have the word "abstract" in their
title; confirm whether the index you're interested in has abstracts by
reading her annotation. An "abstract" is a nonevaluative summary of the
contents of a publication.

These periodical indexes are "standards". In order to determine which libraries have a periodical index, it's a good idea to know when it started
indexing -- the date of the first volume or issue-- information which
both Harzfeld and Owen provide for each index. Consult the library serials
catalog for the library location of each periodical index in which you're
interested.

Using Harzfeld or Owen, generate a list of at least 5 specialized periodical indexes (not periodicals) in languages you can use bibliographically
which appear to have utility for your Project topic. Do not repeat The
Humanities Index, or the Social Sciences Index or The Applied Sciences &
Technology Index, which were introduced in Assignments 3 and 4. You do
not have to examine the actual index itself at this point; you do have to
search several systematically for your topic when you do your Project. Include one "citation index" and at least one "abstract service" among
your periodical indexes. There are 3 citation indexes: The Arts & Humanities
Citation Index, The Science Citation Index, and the Social Sciences
Citation Index.

STEP #3, contd.

Titles of Periodical Indexes from the Guide	Page #'s in the Guide	Library	Call #
1." _____ _____	_____	_____	_____
2." _____ _____	_____	_____	_____
3." _____ _____	_____	_____	_____
4." _____ _____	_____	_____	_____
5." _____ _____	_____	_____	_____
6." _____ _____	_____	_____	_____

X   X   X

Now back to STEP #1: BACKGROUND READING, AN OUTLINE, and a WORKING TITLE. Before you begin to organize a paper and after you have some idea of what the subject is all about, but before you begin a library literature search, it is essential that you start to work up an outline of the paper. A good "review article" in a journal or a specialized encyclopedia can help with this. Note that you are asked as part of the Project for an outline of a paper that your Project bibliography could support.

Even a general encyclopedia can sometimes provide references to "land-mark" publications, dates, events, persons and institutions (those cor- porate main entries, perhaps) associated with your subject, as well as outlines and keywords. An example of a general encyclopedia is the Encyclopaedia Britannica. Thus, reading an article can also help develop or focus a topic, as needed. Always use the latest edition of any reference book unless you have some particular reason. Select on the bases of such things as subjects covered in the scope of the title and subject headings assigned to it, the date and nation of publication, etc. Something published in 1910, for example, would be less useful for in- formation about World War I than something published in 1920... an en- cyclopedia created in England might be less useful on Custer's Last Stand than one originating in the United States; or, it might provide an additional perspective...

An encyclopedic work does not always have the word "encyclopedia" in its title; an encyclopedia is not always encyclopedic! Some standard subject- specialized encyclopedias in the Library reference collection are:

<u>Title</u>	<u>Call # In Reference</u>

Encyclopaedia Judaica
Encyclopedia of Philosophy
Encyclopedia of Psychology
Encyclopedia of World Art
International Encyclopedia of the
    Social Sciences
Kodansha Encyclopedia of Japan
McGraw Hill Encyclopedia of Sci-
    ence & Technology
McGraw Hill Encyclopedia of
    World Drama...
New Grove Dictionary of Music
    and Musicians.

A. One good way to locate reference books on many subjects is <u>The Guide
To Reference Books</u> by Eugene Sheehy, often referred to as "Sheehy".
The latest edition is in all libraries; between editions there will be
supplements.

Examine the basic volume of Sheehy cover-to-cover, including the Table
of Contents. Are the contents arranged according to the Library of
Congress Classification? (Yes/No)_____ How do you reach this conclusion? By comparing (be specic)_____

_____
Use the Index in the back to identify the "Sheehy code" (capital letters
and number) for the Encyclopaedia Britannica:_____ Read
the description on page_____.

Don't expect to find reference works exactly on your topic, although
it is always possible to find <u>some</u> reference book which relates to it
in <u>some</u> way. In which section(s) --other than "A: General Reference
Works"-- of Sheehy do you find most of the reference works relevant to
your topic?_____

B. Identify at least one specific <u>specialized</u> reference book, preferably
an encyclopedia or handbook, which you have not already selected in
STEP #3's work, which you predict would be helpful to researching your
Project. Base your prediction on such things as Sheehy's annotation of
it, if any, the code he assigns to it, the LC Classification he sometimes lists at the end of the entry, etc.

Main entry (author, if any; the author and the title may be the same because reference books tend to be main-entried by title)_____

_____

Title_____

_____
Page # in Sheehy_____ Specific Sheehy Code (letters & number) for
the publication you select_____ LC Classification if Sheehy pro-

B., contd.

vides it (at the end of the entry)_____ Now check
the catalog to confirm that the Library has this reference book. Call
#_____ (Do not select one of the relatively few
publications Sheehy lists but which is not in the Library).

C.   Identify a subject-specialized encyclopedia relevant to your subject.
Then locate and read an article at least one full page in length in
it which provides background related to your Project topic or to some
aspect of it. There are three ways you can locate such an article:

1. Consult Sheehy's Guide To Reference Books; see "B" above.

2. If you haven't found one that relates specifically to your topic by
   using Sheehy efficiently, take the subject-approach using the library catalog. For a subject heading use YOUR BEST SUBJECT (from
   STEP #2, page 2 of this assignment) dash FORM. Aim for as great a
   level of specificity as possible in your background article's coverage.

3. A combination of 1 and 2.

Did you locate your subject-specialized encyclopedia by using the catalog
or Sheehy?_____If the catalog, under what subject-heading
did you locate it?_____
Full title of the encyclopedic work you select _____

_____   _____

_____

Edition (e.g. number, revision)_____
Year of publication_____
Library Call #_____

D.   Get the following information from the encyclopedia which you just
   located in "C" above.   Always use the index
(volume or portion) of an encyclopedia first; then follow through on
all the entries related to your subject which you find listed in the
index. If there is an index volume, it is usually at the end of a
multi-volume set. Locate an article at least one full page long related
to your Project in some way. Since this is intended to provide the
experience as well as the information, the article need not be directly
on your Project, but you should communicate effort to locate such an
article, and you will ultimately need to do this for the Project. Index
volume or other index location, including page #_____ _____
Subject heading where you start in the index:_____

_____. This indexing
then referred you to a relevant article located in volume #____, on
pages _____ - _____. The article was titled (or captioned):"_____
_____."

D., contd.

      The article was written by _____
      (The article's author may be identified at the end of the article
      or elsewhere by use of initials in an encyclopedia.)

      Does your article have a bibliography? Does it provide, include, or
      is it accompanied by bibliographic citations?_____ Page # where
      the bibliographic support is located.____ Approximately how many
      citations in the bibliography?_____

E. "REVIEW ARTICLES"   The term review article or review essay does
not refer here to a review of a book, play, or motion picture, which
we'll consider in pathfinder assignment #6. What you need at this point
is a critical study which reviews and surveys the state-of-the-art
surrounding your specific topic, by an authority, but not book length.
Related subject heading sub-divisions leading to review articles are
LITERATURE REVIEW, YEARBOOKS, and SOURCES. You'd use a card catalog by
looking under YOUR BEST SUBJECT (from STEP #2) dash LITERATURE REVIEW,
for example.

Two major sources of REVIEW ARTICLES for background reading are REVIEW
SERIALS and JOURNAL ARTICLES. Review serials are mainly annuals published under such titles as "Advances In...", "Progress In...",
"Annual Review of...", etc. They may look like serials, and then again,
some appear to be a book, e.g. The Women's Annual, Number 4, 1983-
1984, published by the G. K. Hall Co., is part of The Women's Annual...
Year In Review series, which began in 1980. Number 4 contained ten
chapter-like articles by different specialists on such timely topics as
education, health, scholarship, communications, politics, etc. Each
chapter was accompanied by three resource lists: the writer's documentation, a selective bibliography of publications on that topic for further reading, and a selected list of such other types of resources as
audiovisuals, organizations, etc. To locate such a publication, you
would have to know how to establish   and use the subject heading
FEMINISM-- UNITED STATES-- YEARBOOKS.

Journals often include review articles in their contents. Signs
journal is an example of one which regularly publishes review essays.
The Index to Scientific Reviews, 1974-   , (Library location:
) provides multidisciplinary coverage of review articles
from every area of scientific endeavor: life, biomedical and behavioral sciences; physical and chemical sciences; agriculture, biology and
environmental sciences; engineering, technology and applied sciences.

The idea is to invest your new research skills and a little time in
locating and reading an article by an authority in your topic's field,
one which surveys the status quo and capsules it without taking sides
while interrelating points of view and recent developments.

Required Reading: "Project Guidelines"

STEP #4. Locate and use a SELECTIVE BIBLIOGRAPHY or "GUIDE TO THE LITER-
ATURE" of your topic early in your literature search. 2 ways to locate
a bibliography of publications selected by an authority in your field are:

(1) Use an Index to Bibliographies:

  "THE BIBLIOGRAPHIC INDEX; A Cumulative Bibliography of Bibliographies",
  1937-   . Library Location:_____

The Bibliographic Index is a subject-listing of bibliographies in both
English and some foreign languages, which are themselves bibliographies
or which are publications containing a bibliography which has 50 or more
bibliographic citations. BI covers bibliographies published as books, in
books, pamphlets and thousands of periodicals, and lists them under "modified" LC subject headings with cross references.

Bibliographies published separately are referred to as "separates". Bibs
appearing at the end of a magazine article, book or chapter are "parts".
BI is one of the first tools you'd search when starting a literature
search in a library. You might need to check out all volumes.

Women bank employees
  Dworaczek, Marian. Women in banking: a bibliography.
    (Public administration series, bibliography · P-1634)
    Vance Bibls. 1985 7p
Women bankers
  Dworaczek, Marian. Women in banking: a bibliography.
    (Public administration series, bibliography P-1634)
    Vance Bibls. 1985 7p
Women criminals *See* Female offenders
Women executives
  Davidson, Marilyn, and Cooper, Cary L. Stress and the
    woman manager. St. Martin's Press 1983 p217-25
  Tsui, A. S. and Gutek, B. A. A role set analysis of
    gender differences in performance, affective
    relationships, and career success of industrial middle
    managers. *Acad Manage J* 27:633-5 S '84
Women farmers
                    United States
  Bokemeier, J. L. and others. Labor force participation
    of metropolitan, nonmetropolitan, and farm women:
    a comparative study. *Rural Sociol* 48:536-9 Wint '83
Women homosexuals *See* Lesbians
Women in agriculture
      See also
      Women farmers
                    Botswana
  Fortmann, L. Economic status and women's participation
    in agriculture: a Botswana case study. *Rural Sociol*
    49:461-4 Fall '84
Women in Christianity
  McNamara, Jo Ann. A new song: celibate women in
    the first three Christian centuries. Institute for Res.
    in Hist.: Haworth Press 1983 p147-52

In this excerpt from volume 25/
1985 of the Bibliographic Index:
This book by Dworaczek is a bibliography; it is also P-1634 in
 the Public Administration Series,
 and seven pages in length. [A separate]
For bibliographies about Women
 criminals, look under(See) FE-
 MALE OFFENDERS in this Index.
Pages 217 through 225 consist of
 a bibliography in the Davidson
 & Cooper book. [A part]
The journal article by Bokemeier
 includes a bibliography of at
 least 50 units or citations.
For bibliographies about WOMEN IN
 AGRICULTURE, you should also
 look under WOMEN FARMERS.
WOMEN IN AGRICULTURE-- BOTSWANA
 is a subject heading leading to
 a journal article by Fortmann
 which includes a bibliography.

STEP #4.
(2) Go directly to the library catalog and take the subject approach.

> For a subject heading, use YOUR BEST SUBJECT HEADING (from STEP #2)
> dash BIBLIOGRAPHY.

Even better than using a bibliography at the start of a library literature search is the possibility of locating and using a guide to the literature of your field or topic. There are general guides, which may
include several fields, and there are subject guides which cover one
field, or even an aspect of it. Sometimes they also suggest methods of
doing library research in the field and describe the most important
reference sources for it. Many guides list books and articles on specific
topics within the subjects,which are very useful because they are selective,
rather than comprehensive. For all of these reasons, guides to researching the literature of various fields tend to have a variety of titles,
but they are typically shelved in Reference. Here are some examples of
recently-published guides to the literature :

> Davis, Elizabeth B. Using Biological Literature: A Practical Guide.
> Douglas, Nancy. Library Research Guide to Psychology: Illustrated
>   Search Strategy and Sources.
> Haas, Marilyn. Indians of North America; Methods and Sources for
>   Library Research.
> McMillan, Patricia. Library Research Guide to Sociology: Illus-
>   trated Search Strategy and Sources.
> Nelson, Barbara. American Women and Politics; A Selected Bibliog-
>   raphy and Resource Guide.
> Smith, Myron J., Jr. Watergate: An Annotated Bibliography of
>   Sources in English, 1972-1982.
> Trejo, Arnulfo D. Bibliografia Chicana; a Guide to Information Sources.

You can sometimes find a guide for your subject by using the subject card
catalog; unfortunately there's no special subject heading subdivision for
these guides. They are usually cataloged with bibliographies under the
heading: SUBJECT dash BIBLIOGRAPHY. They may have the words "research" and
"guide" in the title. Locate a guide to your Project topic's "literature"
or the field of which it is a part. Try to be as specific as possible.

Subject heading you use in the catalog:_____

_____

Main entry in the catalog for the guide:_____

_____

Complete title: _____

_____

Year of publication:_____ Call #_____

If you are unable to identify a guide-to-the-literature of your field,
be sure to talk with me before the date this assignment is due. A
guide-to-the-literature might not be a selector for your Project bibliography, although your experience with it as a source would be described in
your account of your strategy.

Using the Bibliographic Index, locate at least one bibliography on or related to your Project topic.   Index volume #_____. Year: 19_____. Page #_____. Complete subject heading under which you find your bibliography:_____

What form does your bib take... is it a book, or part of a book, or published in an issue of a journal as part of an article, or published in an issue of a journal as a bibliography, or what?   Hint: If inclusive pagination is listed in the indexing, the bib is likely a "part" of something else-- part of an article or part of a book.   A separate is cover-to-cover a bibliography itself, and usually longer.   The first citation in the excerpt on page 1 is a separate; the last citation in the excerpt is a part._____
Title of your bibliography or of the publication in which it appeared:

_____

_____

Now locate the bib (or the publication of which it is a part) in the library's collection using the appropriate catalog. Under what wording will you check in the library catalog?_____

_____

Call #_____. Inasmuch as this is a

pathfinder for your Project, select a bibliography which is in the

library. BI is designed to lead you to bibliographies and "guides to the literature" of your field, which you can then use as sources.   Do not use BI to discover books or articles other than bibliographies. In your Project essay, describe your experience searching for a selective bibliography; if you're successful, you can then use it as one of your sources.

Other bibliographies of bibliographies, such as Theodore Besterman's A World Bibliography of Bibliographies, are in the vicinity of the Bibliographic Index on the reference shelves in the library.

STEP #5: At this point, it's usually productive to use some of the specialized periodical indexes, abstracting services and citation indexes you identified using the Harzfeld/Owen methodology introduced in Assignment 5. Assignment 6 provides practice selecting and using several such periodical indexes. These are merely a few examples of the many standards found in college, university and public libraries. They provide subject and sometimes author points-of-access to the contents of serials in these fields, and are arranged basically the way Reader's Guide is arranged.

Use these four specialized periodical indexes (which may or may not relate to your Project) to locate the information needed in questions a - d. The call numbers provided are their locations in the Reference Dept., but these are so basic that they are in numerous libraries.

ART INDEX, 1929-   .   _____
BUSINESS PERIODICALS INDEX, 1958-   _____
EDUCATION INDEX, 1929-   .   _____
PAIS [Public Affairs Information
Service] BULLETIN, 1915-   .   _____

Follow the 3-step strategy introduced in Assignment 4 (page 2, #2).

a) You need to track down a 6-page article published in June 1981 about the NATIONAL FOOTBALL LEAGUE. You need it for a management course paper; someone says it's not only about winning based on organizational objectives, but is accompanied by tables and a bibliography.
Index title:_____
Index volume in terms of the time period it covers:_____ - _____
Under what heading wording do you locate your article?:

_____
Does the Index provide the author's full name?_____ If yes, page #_____
Title of the article"_____
_____."
Title (not abbreviation) of the periodical in which the article was published:_____
Issue date_____ Volume #_____ Inclusive pagination ____ - _____
Library call #_____

b) You need to track down a 15-page journal article published in 1981 about the heraldic LION in Akan art. You need it for an African Studies course paper; someone says it's illustrated and accompanied by a bibliography.
Index title:_____
Index volume in terms of the time period it covers:_____ - _____
Under what heading wording do you locate your article?:

_____
Does the Index provide the author's full name?_____ If yes, page #____
Title of the article "_____
_____."
Title (not abbreviation)of the periodical in which the article was published:_____
Issue date_____ Volume #_____ Inclusive pagination ____ - _____
Library call #_____

STEP #5, contd.

c) You need to track down a 12-page article published in April 1964 in a prestigious law review. It's about Supreme Court Justice Goldberg's questioning the propriety of the death penalty for persons convicted RAPE.

Index title:_____

Index volume in terms of the time period it covers:_____ - _____

Under what heading wording do you locate your article?:

_____

Does the Index provide the author's full name?_____ If yes, page #_____

Title of the article "_____

_____."

Title (not abbreviation) of the periodical in which the article was published:_____

Issue date_____ Volume #_____ Inclusive pagination _____ - _____

Library call #_____

d) You need to track down a 4-page article published in January 1975 about SEX ROLE IN LITERATURE. You need it for a psychology course paper, and since you've let things pile up, you hope it will also be helpful for a report about writing elementary school textbooks.

Index title:_____

Index volume in terms of the time period it covers:_____ - _____

Under what heading wording do you locate your article? :

_____

Does the Index provide the author's full name?_____ If yes, page #_____

Title of the article "_____

_____."

Title (not abbreviation) of the periodical in which the article was published:_____

Issue date_____ Volume #_____ Inclusive pagination _____ - _____

Library call #_____

STEP #6 EVALUATING YOUR DISCOVERIES: SELECTING AND DE-SELECTING

At this point in a library literature search, you'll have accumulated many bib cards for publications and should locate some of them in the library's collections. And you'd be wondering how to de-select... how to evaluate individual books and articles. One of the several ways to help yourself in this process is to use book reviews.

During the course we have already considered several indexing tools which refer you to ("cite") the locations of book reviews published in periodicals: Applied Science & Technology Index, Art Index, Business Periodicals Index, Education Index, Humanities Index, New York Times Index, PAIS, Readers' Guide, and Social Sciences Index. You could also consult Harzfeld and Owen, as well as what reference book to identify titles of book reviewing tools in various fields?"_____",

by _____.

STEP #6, contd. BOOK REVIEW DIGEST, 1905-   . _____

BOOK REVIEW DIGEST is unique because it indexes, or locates, book reviews as well as providing brief excerpts of the reviews, which are both evaluative and representative of general critical reaction.

From 1985 BOOK REVIEW DIGEST, pages 1125-6:

MROZEK, DONALD J. Sport and American mentality, 1880-1910. 284p il $24.95; pa $12.95 1983 University of Tenn. Press
    796 1. Sports—History 2. Sports—Social aspects 3. National characteristics, American 4. Social values
    ISBN 0-87049-394-9; 0-87049-395-7 (pa)
    LC 83-3667

"Exploring the social dynamics of sport, Mrozek [aims to show how] . . . 'sports gained increasing acceptance and respectability in the three decades covered. . . . [He discusses] how class distinctions and separations were reinforced by choices of sports, how certain collegiate sports began to emphasize victory and winning over the values of exercise and participation, how sports would be pressed into the service of military preparedness, and how sports . . . served as a national focal point for such . . . American forces as nationalism, secularism, and idealism." (Choice) Bibliography. Index.

_____

"[This] is a fine example of the social history of sport. The basic argument is that Americans approached their leisure with the same values that they brought to the rest of their concerns. . . . Mrozek's argument about sport as a form of increasingly secular regeneration through physical activity is persuasive. His characterizations are deft: Duncan Curry insisted that yachting was for 'practically everyone,' England's Sir Thomas Lipton was snubbed at Newport and J.P. Morgan grandly announced, 'You can do business with anyone, but you can go sailing only with a gentleman.' Mrozek's comments on the *Turnbewegung* in America and its relation to Swedish gymnastics are somewhat misleading (Ling's 'scientific' exercises were an alternative to and not simply a variation on German gymnastics), but minor errors of this sort are inevitable in a book as ambitious as [this one]."
    Am Hist Rev 89:1168 O '84. Allen Guttmann (450w)

"A work of considerable intellectual merit and high standards of interdisciplinary scholarship. . . . Mrozek draws extensively from a rich and varied periodical literature. . . . His work is enriched by his far-ranging familiarity with sociology, historiography, psychology, intellectual history, American studies, and economics. Especially noteworthy is his consideration of the introduction of more technical and specialized sports training. . . . [This] is an indispensable work dealing with the key transitional period in the evolution of sports as an American institution and secular faith."
    Choice 21:1339 My '84 (250w)

"Perhaps Mrozek's most intriguing proposition is that the unprecedented explosion in sports popularity was, at least in the United States, essentially a postreligious phenomenon. . . . This study is hardly without problems. Women and the idle rich formed important sporting constituencies, to be sure, but mostly influenced later decades, as might also be said of coaches and trainers. . . . Mrozek is therefore at times sensing the seeds of growth, rather than the growth itself, . . . and also at times arguing in circles. Further, he presents the ideas of elite spokesmen quite narrowly. There is no populace in this book, nor any spectators or even middle-level sports organizers. Yet the book has real strengths, particularly in specific areas: the military role in sports diffusion, the coaches' displacement of physical educators as authority figures, baseball's urban-industrial dimension, sports as force for nationalism, and, most provocatively, the sporting life as a search for order and meaning."
    J Am Hist 71:662 D '84. Ronald Story (500w)

If you wanted reviews of "Sport and American Mentality, 1880-1910" by Donald Mrozek, which was published in 1983, you'd start by looking in the 1983 BOOK REVIEW DIGEST under the author's surname, Mrozek, in the alphabetical main part of the volume. Not finding the book there might mean it was published too late that year for reviews (lag). If you're sure of the spelling of the author's name, you could continue forward into 1984. Not finding it there might mean that insufficient reviews had been published, or it was main-entried under some other wording; you could check the Title & Subject Index in the back of each volume. In this case, there was two years' lag. We find the entry in the body of the 1985 volume, under Morozek, Donald J.

Immediately following the heading, which consists of the author, title, imprint, subjects, etc., the first piece of information will be a brief description of the book. The centered, horizontal line is followed by the display of several (3 in this case) reviewers' reactions, each consisting of an excerpt quoted from the reviewer's opinion. Each excerpt is followed by a line consisting of: abbreviated title in Italics of the periodical in which the review was published, volume number, page, and issue date, using standard abbreviations, which are spelled out as usual in the front of the volume. The final, two pieces of information are the reviewer's name and the length of her/his review in terms of number of words. Choice in 1984 did not identify reviewers; it now does. The nonevaluative description at the beginning and preceding the 3 review excerpts is derived from Choice.

The address and other information about the University of Tenn. Press, the publisher, is on page 1939.

STEP #6, contd.

From 1985 BOOK REVIEW DIGEST, page 1859: Another way to use BRD is to start with the Title & Subject Index. Someone interested in identifying several recent books on American national characteristics, for example, as well as getting an idea of (1) what each was about and (2) the general critical reaction to it, could look under the subject, NATIONAL CHARACTERISTICS, AMERICAN, where 6 author-titles of books published and reviewed around or in 1985 are listed alphabetically by authors' surnames. By then turning to the front part of the same volume in the C's for Crozier, H for Habits of the heart (book main entried under title apparently), etc. the full display for each can be examined.

Someone who did not know the title of the reviewed-book, "The National Archives of the United States", by checking in the N's, for the first regarded word of the title, would learn that the next step is to check in the V's, for H. J. Viola, the author.

> Nation, state, and economy. Von Mises, L.
> **National Aeronautics and Space Administration (U.S.)** *See* United States. National Aeronautics and Space Administration
> **National Archives (U.S.)** *See* United States National Archives
> The National Archives of the United States. Viola, H. J.
> **National Broadcasting Co., Inc.**
>   Christensen, M. The sweeps
> **National characteristics, American**
>   Crozier, M. The trouble with America
>   Habits of the heart
>   Mrozek, D. J. Sport and American mentality, 1880-1910
>   Pugh, D. G. Sons of liberty
>   Shi, D. E. The simple life
>   Wilkinson, R. American tough
> **National characteristics, Canadian**
>   Malcolm, A. H. The Canadians
> **National characteristics, English**
>   Smith, G. The English companion
> **National characteristics, German**
>   Dundes, A. Life is like a chicken coop ladder
> **National characteristics, Japanese**
>   Courdy, J. C. The Japanese
>   Taylor, J. Shadows of the Rising Sun
> **National characteristics, Russian**
>   Fodor, A. Tolstoy and the Russians

BRD is a cumulative index to reviews of current fiction and nonfiction, including reference books, published in more than 80 periodicals. Its advantages include:

- SUBJECT-approach and title-access by means of the Title & Subject Index in the back of each volume-year.
- CUMULATIVE indexes to large periods of time distributed throughout the volumes. Check their spines for this coverage; also look for an Author/Title Index covering 1905-1974.
- A brief SUMMARY which appears right after the bibliographic data and just before the reviewers' excerpted comments.
- EXCERPTS from as many reviews as are necessary to reflect the balance of professional critical opinion.

Use BRD mainly to find out <u>more</u> about a book which you have already located by means of a locator-tool such as the catalog or a guide to the literature.

(A) Using the subject headings in the Title & Subject Index portion printed in the back of each BRD volume-year, identify one book on or related to your Project topic. Turn to the full display for your book, in the main part of the volume, where it is listed alphabetically under the author or other main entry with the full information.

STEP #6, contd. BOOK REVIEW DIGEST, (A)...

Read the "prefatory note" page in the front of the volume before doing
the following:

    Complete subject heading under which you first identify your book:
_____

Volume (year) you're using _____ Author or other main entry
for your book:_____
Page #'s for the full information about the book:_____
Complete title of your book :_____

_____

Year of publication:_____ Publisher_____
Original price according to Book Review Digest:$_____

(B) A book is "in print" when it is still generally available on the
trade market. Most such books are listed in the Author volumes of the
BOOKS IN PRINT series. Call #_____
The BIP "family" is not a book selector because it is comprehensive,
rather than selective. Use it to get prices and other data, and, mainly
to determine whether a book is available for purchase and all of the
various editions on the market, their prices, sources, etc. According
to the current edition of BIP, is your book still in print, or is it OP
(out of print)-- which?_____
(If it isn't listed, it's considered OP.) If it's still in print, how
much does it now cost? $_____

(C) Who reviewed the book published around 19_82_, written by_____
__John King Fairbank_____, and titled
___Chinabound; a fifty-year memoir_____;
the review in question was published in a periodical titled "the New
__York Review of Books_____".
_____
If you can't locate this book readily in BRD, perhaps you've forgotten
to take lag into consideration: a book published this year may not get
indexed in it until next year.

               *   *   *

SIZING UP A LIBRARY FOR YOUR RESEARCH NOW AND LATER. By now you have a
sense of which libraries have materials on your topic. They are the
branch libraries mentioned often in the catalog in connection with books
which relate to your topic. Visit one of these. Familiarize yourself with
its layout, resources, etc. You should be able to do all of the following
based on personal observation. Library:_____
Phone #_____ Normal hours_____ Building:_____
Consult the catalog. What is the title of one specialized periodical index
which you identified using Harzfeld or Owen (STEP #3) which is in this
library's collection?_____
In what part of the Classification do most of the materials appear to be
classified and shelved?_____ Is the shelf list access-
ible to the public?_____ Is there a vertical file?_____ What is the
current exhibit's theme or title?_____

# # #

What is the "working title" of your Project? Try to put together a preliminary phrase separated by a semicolon or other divider and followed
by a descriptive phrase. This is commended to you because it can help
you to focus (or to develop), and it tends to help you get in all of
the KEY WORDS. Suppose someone were attempting to retrieve the information contained in your Project bibliography or in a paper based on use
of that selective bibliography, perhaps by means of a computer-assisted
literature search relying only on key words you put into the title.

"_____

_____

_____

_____ . "

Suppose you get into this but find that, while you are still interested
in this topic (and it has been approved), you have taken on too much.
So you need to limit (focus) further the scope of your coverage. How
would you forsee doing this if necessasry? What are the possibilities for
doing this which you can now predict? Specify only one.

_____

_____

_____

_____

Required Reading: "Project Guidelines".

STEP #4. Locate and use a SELECTIVE BIBLIOGRAPHY or "GUIDE TO THE LITER-
ATURE" of your topic early in your literature search. 2 ways to locate
a bibliography of publications selected by an authority in your field are:

(1) Use an Index to Bibliographies:

"THE BIBLIOGRAPHIC INDEX; A Cumulative Bibliography of Bibliographies",
1937-   . Library Location:_____

The Bibliographic Index is a subject-listing of bibliographies in both
English and some foreign languages, which are themselves bibliographies
or which are publications containing a bibliography which has 50 or more
bibliographic citations. BI covers bibliographies published as books, in
books, pamphlets and thousands of periodicals, and lists them under "modified" LC subject headings with cross references.

Bibliographies published separately are referred to as "separates". Bibs
appearing at the end of a magazine article, book or chapter are "parts".
BI is one of the first tools you'd search when starting a literature
search in a library. You might need to check out all volumes.

Women bank employees
  Dworaczek, Marian. Women in banking: a bibliography.
    (Public administration series, bibliography P-1634)
    Vance Bibls. 1985 7p
Women bankers
  Dworaczek, Marian. Women in banking: a bibliography.
    (Public administration series, bibliography P-1634)
    Vance Bibls. 1985 7p
Women criminals See Female offenders
Women executives
  Davidson, Marilyn, and Cooper, Cary L. Stress and the
    woman manager. St. Martin's Press 1983 p217-25
  Tsui, A. S. and Gutek, B. A. A role set analysis of
    gender differences in performance, affective
    relationships, and career success of industrial middle
    managers. Acad Manage J 27:633-5 S '84
Women farmers
            United States
  Bokemeier, J. L. and others. Labor force participation
    of metropolitan, nonmetropolitan, and farm women:
    a comparative study. Rural Sociol 48:536-9 Wint '83
Women homosexuals See Lesbians
Women in agriculture
        See also
    Women farmers
            Botswana
  Fortmann, L. Economic status and women's participation
    in agriculture: a Botswana case study. Rural Sociol
    49:461-4 Fall '84
Women in Christianity
  McNamara, Jo Ann. A new song; celibate women in
    the first three Christian centuries. Institute for Res.
    in Hist.: Haworth Press 1983 p147-52

In this excerpt from volume 25/
1985 of the Bibliographic Index:
This book by Dworaczek is a bibliography; it is also P-1634 in
  the Public Administration Series,
  and seven pages in length. [A separate]
For bibliographies about Women
  criminals, look under(See) FE-
  MALE OFFENDERS in this Index.
Pages 217 through 225 consist of
  a bibliography in the Davidson
  & Cooper book. [A part]
The journal article by Bokemeier
  includes a bibliography of at
  least 50 units or citations.
For bibliographies about WOMEN IN
  AGRICULTURE, you should also
  look under WOMEN FARMERS.
WOMEN IN AGRICULTURE-- BOTSWANA
  is a subject heading leading to
  a journal article by Fortmann
  which includes a bibliography.

STEP #4.
(2) Go directly to the library catalog and take the subject approach.

> For a subject heading, use YOUR BEST SUBJECT HEADING (from STEP #2)
> dash BIBLIOGRAPHY.

Even better than using a bibliography at the start of a library literature search is the possibility of locating and using a guide to the literature of your field or topic. There are general guides, which may
include several fields, and there are subject guides which cover one
field, or even an aspect of it. Sometimes they also suggest methods of
doing library research in the field and describe the most important
reference sources for it. Many guides list books and articles on specific
topics within the subjects,which are very useful because they are selective,
rather than comprehensive. For all of these reasons, guides to researching the literature of various fields tend to have a variety of titles,
but they are typically shelved in Reference. Here are some examples of
recently-published guides to the literature :

> Davis, Elizabeth B. Using Biological Literature: A Practical Guide.
> Douglas, Nancy. Library Research Guide to Psychology: Illustrated
>   Search Strategy and Sources.
> Haas, Marilyn. Indians of North America; Methods and Sources for
>   Library Research.
> McMillan, Patricia. Library Research Guide to Sociology: Illus-
>   trated Search Strategy and Sources.
> Nelson, Barbara. American Women and Politics; A Selected Bibliog-
>   raphy and Resource Guide.
> Smith, Myron J., Jr. Watergate: An Annotated Bibliography of
>   Sources in English, 1972-1982.
> Trejo, Arnulfo D. Bibliografia Chicana; a Guide to Information Sources.

You can sometimes find a guide for your subject by using the subject card
catalog; unfortunately there's no special subject heading subdivision for
these guides. They are usually cataloged with bibliographies under the
heading: SUBJECT dash BIBLIOGRAPHY. They may have the words "research" and
"guide" in the title. Locate a guide to your Project topic's "literature"
or the field of which it is a part. Try to be as specific as possible.

Subject heading you use in the catalog:_____

_____

Main entry in the catalog for the guide:_____

_____

Complete title: _____

_____

Year of publication:_____ Call #_____

If you are unable to identify a guide-to-the-literature of your field,
be sure to talk with me before the date this assignment is due. A
guide-to-the-literature might not be a selector for your Project bibliography, although your experience with it as a source would be described in
your account of your strategy.

Using the Bibliographic Index, locate at least one bibliography on or related to your Project topic. Index volume #_____. Year: 19_____. Page #_____. Complete subject heading under which you find your bibliography:_____

What form does your bib take... is it a book, or part of a book, or published in an issue of a journal as part of an article, or published in an issue of a journal as a bibliography, or what? Hint: If inclusive pagination is listed in the indexing, the bib is likely a "part" of something else-- part of an article or part of a book. A separate is cover-to-cover a bibliography itself, and usually longer. The first citation in the excerpt on page 1 is a separate; the last citation in the excerpt is a part._____
Title of your bibliography or of the publication in which it appeared:

_____

_____

Now locate the bib (or the publication of which it is a part) in the library's collection using the appropriate catalog. Under what wording will you check in the library catalog?_____

_____

Call #_____. Inasmuch as this is a

pathfinder for your Project, select a bibliography which is in the

library. BI is designed to lead you to bibliographies and "guides to the literature" of your field, which you can then use as sources. Do not use BI to discover books or articles other than bibliographies. In your Project essay, describe your experience searching for a selective bibliography; if you're successful, you can then use it as one of your sources.

Other bibliographies of bibliographies, such as Theodore Besterman's A World Bibliography of Bibliographies, are in the vicinity of the Bibliographic Index on the reference shelves in the library.

STEP #5: At this point, it's usually productive to use some of the specialized periodical indexes, abstracting services and citation indexes you identified using the Harzfeld/Owen methodology introduced in Assignment 5. Assignment 6 provides practice selecting and using several such periodical indexes. These are merely a few examples of the many standards found in college, university and public libraries. They provide subject and sometimes author points-of-access to the contents of serials in these fields, and are arranged basically the way Reader's Guide is arranged.

Use these four specialized periodical indexes (which may or may not relate to your Project) to locate the information needed in questions a - d. The call numbers provided are their locations in the Reference Dept., but these are so basic that they are in numerous libraries.

ART INDEX, 1929-   .   _____
BUSINESS PERIODICALS INDEX, 1958-   _____
EDUCATION INDEX, 1929-   .   _____
PAIS [Public Affairs Information
Service] BULLETIN, 1915-   .   _____

Follow the 3-step strategy introduced in Assignment 4 (page 2, #2).

a) You need to track down a 6-page article published in June 1981 about the NATIONAL FOOTBALL LEAGUE. You need it for a management course paper; someone says it's not only about winning based on organizational objectives, but is accompanied by tables and a bibliography.
Index title: Business Periodicals Index
Index volume in terms of the time period it covers: Aug.1981 - July 1982
Under what heading wording do you locate your article?:
    NATIONAL FOOTBALL LEAGUE   (page 941)
Does the Index provide the author's full name?   no If yes, page #_____
Title of the article" Organizational objectives and winning: an
    examination of the N F L   ."
Title (not abbreviation) of the periodical in which the article was published: Academy of Management Journal
Issue date June 1981 Volume # 24   Inclusive pagination 403 - 408
Library call #_____

b) You need to track down a 15-page journal article published in 1981 about the heraldic LION in Akan art. You need it for an African Studies course paper; someone says it's illustrated and accompanied by a bibliography.
Index title: Art Index
Index volume in terms of the time period it covers: Nov. 1983- Oct. 1984
Under what heading wording do you locate your article?:
    LIONS
Does the Index provide the author's full name? yes If yes, page # 698
Title of the article " Heraldic lion in Akan art: a study of motif
    assimilation in southern Ghana.   ."
Title (not abbreviation) of the periodical in which the article was published: Metropolitan Museum Journal
Issue date 1981   Volume # 16   Inclusive pagination 165 - 180
Library call #_____

STEP #5, contd.

c) You need to track down a 12-page article published in April 1964 in a prestigious law review. It's about Supreme Court Justice Goldberg's questioning the propriety of the death penalty for persons convicted of RAPE.

Index title: ___PAIS [Index]___

Index volume in terms of the time period it covers: Oct.1963 - Sept. 1964

Under what heading wording do you locate your article?:

RAPE

Does the Index provide the author's full name? _yes_ If yes, page #696

Title of the article " _Making the punishment fit the crime[critical comment_ on Justice Arthur Goldberg's questioning of the propriety ... ."

Title (not abbreviation) of the periodical in which the article was published: _Harvard Law Review_

Issue date _Apr. '64_ volume # _77_ Inclusive pagination _1071_ - _1082_

Library call # _____

d) You need to track down a 4-page article published in January 1975 about SEX ROLE IN LITERATURE. You need it for a psychology course paper, and since you've let things pile up, you hope it will also be helpful for a report about writing elementary school textbooks.

Index title: ___Education Index___

Index volume in terms of the time period it covers: July 1974 - June 1975

Under what heading wording do you locate your article? :

SEX ROLE IN LITERATURE

Does the Index provide the author's full name? _yes_ If yes, page #406,656

Title of the article " _Sexism in the language of elementary_

school textbooks ."

Title (not abbreviation) of the periodical in which the article was published: _Science and Children_

Issue date _Jan.'75_ Volume # _12_ Inclusive pagination _22_ - _25_

Library call # _____

STEP #6 EVALUATING YOUR DISCOVERIES: SELECTING AND DE-SELECTING

At this point in a library literature search, you'll have accumulated many bib cards for publications and should locate some of them in the library's collections. And you'd be wondering how to de-select... how to evaluate individual books and articles. One of the several ways to help yourself in this process is to use book reviews.

During the course we have already considered several indexing tools which refer you to ("cite") the locations of book reviews published in periodicals: Applied Science & Technology Index, Art Index, Business Periodicals Index, Education Index, Humanities Index, New York Times Index, PAIS, Readers' Guide, and Social Sciences Index. You could also consult Harzfeld and Owen, as well as what reference book to identify titles of book reviewing tools in various fields?" _____ " ,

by _____ .

STEP #6, contd. BOOK REVIEW DIGEST, 1905-   . _____

BOOK REVIEW DIGEST is unique because it indexes, or locates, book reviews as well as providing brief excerpts of the reviews, which are both evaluative and representative of general critical reaction.

From 1985 BOOK REVIEW DIGEST, pages 1125-6:

MROZEK, DONALD J. Sport and American mentality, 1880-1910. 284p il $24.95; pa $12.95 1983 University of Tenn. Press
796 1. Sports—History 2. Sports—Social aspects 3. National characteristics, American 4. Social values
ISBN 0-87049-394-9; 0-87049-395-7 (pa)
LC 83-3667

"Exploring the social dynamics of sport, Mrozek [aims to show how] . . . sports gained increasing acceptance and respectability in the three decades covered. . . . [He discusses] how class distinctions and separations were reinforced by choices of sports, how certain collegiate sports began to emphasize victory and winning over the values of exercise and participation, how sports would be pressed into the service of military preparedness, and how sports . . . served as a national focal point for such . . . American forces as nationalism, secularism, and idealism." (Choice) Bibliography. Index.

―――――

"[This] is a fine example of the social history of sport. The basic argument is that Americans approached their leisure with the same values that they brought to the rest of their concerns. . . . Mrozek's argument about sport as a form of increasingly secular regeneration through physical activity is persuasive. His characterizations are deft: Duncan Curry insisted that yachting was for 'practically everyone,' England's Sir Thomas Lipton was snubbed at Newport and J.P. Morgan grandly announced, 'You can do business with anyone, but you can go sailing only with a gentleman.' Mrozek's comments on the *Turnbewegung* in America and its relation to Swedish gymnastics are somewhat misleading (Ling's 'scientific' exercises were an alternative to and not simply a variation on German gymnastics), but minor errors of this sort are inevitable in a book as ambitious as [this one]."
Am Hist Rev 89:1168 O '84. Allen Guttmann (450w)

"A work of considerable intellectual merit and high standards of interdisciplinary scholarship. . . . Mrozek draws extensively from a rich and varied periodical literature. . . . His work is enriched by his far-ranging familiarity with sociology, historiography, psychology, intellectual history, American studies, and economics. Especially noteworthy is his consideration of the introduction of more technical and specialized sports training. . . . [This] is an indispensable work dealing with the key transitional period in the evolution of sports as an American institution and secular faith."
Choice 21:1339 My '84 (250w)

"Perhaps Mrozek's most intriguing proposition is that the unprecedented explosion in sports popularity was, at least in the United States, essentially a postreligious phenomenon. . . . This study is hardly without problems. Women and the idle rich formed important sporting constituencies, to be sure, but mostly influenced later decades, as might also be said of coaches and trainers. . . . Mrozek is therefore at times sensing the seeds of growth, rather than the growth itself, . . . and also at times arguing in circles. Further, he presents the ideas of elite spokesmen quite narrowly. There is no populace in this book, nor any spectators or even middle-level sports organizers. Yet the book has real strengths, particularly in specific areas: the military role in sports diffusion, the coaches' displacement of physical educators as authority figures, baseball's urban-industrial dimension, sports as force for nationalism, and, most provocatively, the sporting life as a search for order and meaning."
J Am Hist 71:662 D '84. Ronald Story (500w)

If you wanted reviews of "Sport and American Mentality, 1880-1910" by Donald Mrozek, which was published in 1983, you'd start by looking in the 1983 BOOK REVIEW DIGEST under the author's surname, Mrozek, in the alphabetical main part of the volume. Not finding the book there might mean it was published too late that year for reviews (lag). If you're sure of the spelling of the author's name, you could continue forward into 1984. Not finding it there might mean that insufficient reviews had been published, or it was main-entried under some other wording; you could check the Title & Subject Index in the back of each volume. In this case, there was two years' lag. We find the entry in the body of the 1985 volume, under Morozek, Donald J.

Immediately following the heading, which consists of the author, title, imprint, subjects, etc., the first piece of information will be a brief description of the book. The centered, horizontal line is followed by the display of several (3 in this case) reviewers' reactions, each consisting of an excerpt quoted from the reviewer's opinion. Each excerpt is followed by a line consisting of: abbreviated title in Italics of the periodical in which the review was published, volume number, page, and issue date, using standard abbreviations, which are spelled out as usual in the front of the volume. The final, two pieces of information are the reviewer's name and the length of her/his review in terms of number of words. Choice in 1984 did not identify reviewers; it now does. The nonevaluative description at the beginning and preceding the 3 review excerpts is derived from Choice.

The address and other information about the University of Tenn. Press, the publisher, is on page 1939.

STEP #6, contd.

From 1985 BOOK REVIEW DIGEST, page 1859: Another way to use BRD is to start with the Title & Subject Index. Someone interested in identifying several recent books on American national characteristics, for example, as well as getting an idea of (1) what each was about and (2) the general critical reaction to it, could look under the subject, NATIONAL CHARACTERISTICS, AMERICAN, where 6 author-titles of books published and reviewed around or in 1985 are listed alphabetically by authors' surnames. By then turning to the front part of the same volume in the C's for Crozier, H for Habits of the heart (book main entried under title apparently), etc. the full display for each can be examined.

Someone who did not know the title of the reviewed-book, "The National Archives of the United States", by checking in the N's, for the first regarded word of the title, would learn that the next step is to check in the V's, for H. J. Viola, the author.

> Nation, state, and economy. Von Mises, L.
> **National Aeronautics and Space Administration (U.S.)** *See* United States. National Aeronautics and Space Administration
> **National Archives (U.S.)** *See* United States National Archives
> The National Archives of the United States. Viola, H. J.
> **National Broadcasting Co., Inc.**
>   Christensen, M. The sweeps
> **National characteristics, American**
>   Crozier, M. The trouble with America
>   Habits of the heart
>   Mrozek, D. J. Sport and American mentality, 1880-1910
>   Pugh, D. G. Sons of liberty
>   Shi, D. E. The simple life
>   Wilkinson, R. American tough
> **National characteristics, Canadian**
>   Malcolm, A. H. The Canadians
> **National characteristics, English**
>   Smith, G. The English companion
> **National characteristics, German**
>   Dundes, A. Life is like a chicken coop ladder
> **National characteristics, Japanese**
>   Courdy, J. C. The Japanese
>   Taylor, J. Shadows of the Rising Sun
> **National characteristics, Russian**
>   Fodor, A. Tolstoy and the Russians

BRD is a cumulative index to reviews of current fiction and nonfiction, including reference books, published in more than 80 periodicals. Its advantages include:

- SUBJECT-approach and title-access by means of the Title & Subject Index in the back of each volume-year.
- CUMULATIVE indexes to large periods of time distributed throughout the volumes. Check their spines for this coverage; also look for an Author/Title Index covering 1905-1974.
- A brief SUMMARY which appears right after the bibliographic data and just before the reviewers' excerpted comments.
- EXCERPTS from as many reviews as are necessary to reflect the balance of professional critical opinion.

Use BRD mainly to find out more about a book which you have already located by means of a locator-tool such as the catalog or a guide to the literature.

(A) Using the subject headings in the Title & Subject Index portion printed in the back of each BRD volume-year, identify one book on or related to your Project topic. Turn to the full display for your book, in the main part of the volume, where it is listed alphabetically under the author or other main entry with the full information.

STEP #6, contd. BOOK REVIEW DIGEST, (A)...

Read the "prefatory note" page in the front of the volume before doing the following:

Complete subject heading under which you first identify your book:

_____

Volume (year) you're using _____   Author or other main entry

for your book:_____

Page #'s for the full information about the book:_____

Complete title of your book :_____

_____

Year of publication:_____   Publisher_____

Original price according to Book Review Digest:$_____

(B) A book is "in print" when it is still generally available on the trade market. Most such books are listed in the Author volumes of the BOOKS IN PRINT series. Call #_____
The BIP "family" is not a book selector because it is comprehensive, rather than selective. Use it to get prices and other data, and, mainly to determine whether a book is available for purchase and all of the various editions on the market, their prices, sources, etc. According to the current edition of BIP, is your book still in print, or is it OP (out of print)-- which?_____
(If it isn't listed, it's considered OP.) If it's still in print, how much does it now cost? $_____

(C) Who reviewed the book published around 19__82__, written by_____
    John King Fairbank
_____, and titled
_____Chinabound; a fifty-year memoir_____;
the review in question was published in a periodical titled "___the____
    New York Review of Books_____".   D. S. Nivison_____
If you can't locate this book readily in BRD, perhaps you've forgotten to take lag into consideration: a book published this year may not get indexed in it until next year.

＊   ＊   ＊

SIZING UP A LIBRARY FOR YOUR RESEARCH NOW AND LATER. By now you have a sense of which libraries have materials on your topic. They are the branch libraries mentioned often in the catalog in connection with books which relate to your topic. Visit one of these. Familiarize yourself with its layout, resources, etc. You should be able to do all of the following based on personal observation. Library:_____
Phone #_____   Normal hours_____   Building:_____
Consult the catalog. What is the title of one specialized periodical index which you identified using Harzfeld or Owen (STEP #3) which is in this library's collection? _____
In what part of the Classification do most of the materials appear to be classified and shelved?_____   Is the shelf list accessible to the public?_____   Is there a vertical file?_____   What is the current exhibit's theme or title?_____

# # #

What is the "working title" of your Project? Try to put together a preliminary phrase separated by a semicolon or other divider and followed
by a descriptive phrase. This is commended to you because it can help
you to focus (or to develop), and it tends to help you get in all of
the KEY WORDS. Suppose someone were attempting to retrieve the information contained in your Project bibliography or in a paper based on use
of that selective bibliography, perhaps by means of a computer-assisted
literature search relying only on key words you put into the title.

"
_____

_____

_____

_____ . "

Suppose you get into this but find that, while you are still interested
in this topic (and it has been approved), you have taken on too much.
So you need to limit (focus) further the scope of your coverage. How
would you forsee doing this if necessasry? What are the possibilities for
doing this which you can now predict? Specify only one.

_____

_____

_____

_____

The United States federal government is a major publisher. County, state, and federal governments issue government publications. Each year millions of government publications are issued by them as well as by regional bodies and international organizations such as the United Nations. United States government publications are not copyrighted and may be reprinted and quoted. Government documents usually consist of information printed at government expense or as required by a government's law. Governments, then, are publishers.

The use of government documents in research is almost limitless. The following four broad areas are especially well covered by such materials and information:

STATISTICAL INFORMATION AND SOURCES

Major basic tools include:
The Statistical Abstract of the United States
The Statistical Yearbook [of the United Nations]
The American Statistics Index

SOCIAL POLICY AND PUBLIC AFFAIRS

HISTORICAL RESEARCH

For example, The Serial Set, 1789- of the U.S. Govt.

TECHNICAL INFORMATION

Meet in the corridor outside the Government Documents Department, located

_____, on the date which

appears on the schedule. The Government Documents Department collects official publications of state, federal, foreign and international governments and organizations. The subject matter is diverse and includes publications on defense, population, vital statistics, and all of the many concerns and activities of governments. Because many documents are "findable" only through specialized bibliographies and indexes, it is especially important to consult a reference librarian when you use

any government documents collection anywhere.

What To Do When The Class Is In The Government Documents Department:

We will focus on The Monthly Catalog, an index which accesses many, but

not all, federal government publications of the U.S.A.

THE MONTHLY CATALOG, 1895-   . Call Number: _____

>   Each monthly issue has separate author, title, subject, and key
>   word indexes. There is an annual cumulated bound volume. The
>   main, or first, part of the Monthly Catalog for whatever period
>   you're using is arranged by ENTRY NUMBERS. (Note: entry number
>   and accession number are more or less interchangeable terms in
>   using indexes.) Keep in mind that the subject index, for example,
>   will refer you to an entry number where the full information is
>   displayed, rather than to an author. There are two steps involved.

Beginning with the July 1976 Monthly Catalog issue, layout of this
index was simplified, so we will use recent issues dating back to
July 1976 while in the Government Documents library. Notice that
the sample entry (page 3) is much like a catalog entry. If you
needed information about the Cotopaxi Mountain in Ecuador's representation in art, and particularly the 1985 exhibition at the
National Museum of American Art, you should consider (1) U.S. federal government documents, and (2) therefore, The Monthly Catalog.

The first step would be to consult the LCSH for subject headings,
where you'd be able to generate COTOPAXI MOUNTAIN (ECUDAOR) IN
ART-- EXHIBITIONS. You could use this in the Subject Index portion
of the MOnthly Catalog around 1986, which provides entry number 86-
1621. You'd then move to the numerically arranged volume for the
same time period, where you'd find the sample entry display (page 3.)

Annual Index 1986
Subject section, page I-1068

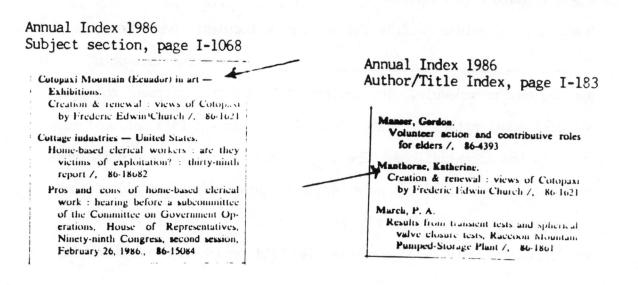

Annual Index 1986
Author/Title Index, page I-183

MONTHLY CATALOG Sample Entry

Annual Index 1986, January-March 1986 / Entries 1-7742 . Page 200.

MONTHLY CATALOG Entry
Number

ISSUING AGENCY Part of the Government

SMITHSONIAN INSTITUTION
Washington, DC 20560

SI 1.2:C 86

(Supt. of Documents'
Class # assigned
by the GPO Library)

86-1621

MAIN ENTRY (Personal
author in this
case)

Manthorne, Katherine.
    Creation & renewal : views of Cotopaxi by Frederic Edwin

TITLE

Church / Katherine Manthorne. — Washington, D.C. : Published for the National Museum of American Art by the Smithsonian Institution Press, c1985.

IMPRINT: Place,
Publisher, Date
of publication

viii, 88 p. : ill. (some col.), 2 maps ; 22 x 28 cm. Catalogue
of an exhibition organized and held at the Museum, Mar. 29-
July 14, 1985. Bibliography: p. 65-68.

SUBJECT HEADINGS (2)
Arabic numeraled
tracings.

1. Church, Frederick Edwin, 1826-1900 Exhibitions. 2. Cotopaxi Mountain (Ecuador) in art — Exhibitions. I. Church,
Frederick Edwin, 1826-1900. II. National Museum of American Art (U.S.) III. Smithsonian Institution. Press. IV. Title.
V. Title: Creation and renewal. ND237.C52A4 1985 84-

ADDED ENTRIES (5)
Roman numeraled
tracings.

(Dewey Decimal Class)   600358 759.13 /19 OCLC 11519066

235

PRACTICE GETTING AROUND THE MONTHLY CATALOG.

Search the Monthly Catalog bound volumes and paper supplements issued
beginning July 1976 to locate references to federal government publications related to your Project. Use the LC subject headings you generated
in pathfinder Assignment 5, Step #2. If you conclude that no issue of
the Monthly Catalog from July 1976 to the present contains any
citations under LC subject headings related to your Project, select one
of the topics listed below. (Check the one you settle on).

_____ Project topic: _____

_____ Abortion	_____ Pollution (air, land or sea)
_____ Agriculture	_____ Printing of currency
_____ Crime increases recently	_____ Energy
_____ "Victimless" crimes	_____ National health (or medicine)

To do this work, use SUBJECT INDEX volumes of the Monthly Catalog since
July 1976. For the topic you checked above, use LC subject headings to
search for documents. For one such publication, list which Monthly
Catalog you used:

Date_____ Page # on which you locate the appropriate subject-entry:_____ Subject heading under which you
found it:_____

Entry # which is listed there   -- it's the HYPHENATED NUMBER at
the end of the brief entry. (In the Cotopaxi Mountain publication, it
is "86-1621 ".) _____

Now move to the main part of the Monthly Catalog for the same
year to the numbered entries portion. Locate the full informational display for that publication by following through on the entry
number you've just identified for the subject above. You're looking at something like a main entry catalog card. It's on page
#_____ of the main part of the Monthly Catalog for that year.

What is the main entry (or author) of your publication?_____

_____The
authorship may be listed as a corporate main entry, or by a personal author or authors, or be a main-entry-by-title, especially
if it's a serial. Title: "_____
_____".

Reference Books

So far this term we have considered "locators" of information. "Carriers" of information --or reference books, as they are usually called-- also can help in getting information related to doing research. Examples of five standards in most libraries' collections of reference tools are described below. They just happen to relate to knowing about and using government publications too. They are by, about, or from governments and international organizations of governments. With such reference books, you usually need to look for and use the latest, current edition, which may be kept at the reference desk. (Older editions may be available in the library's stacks).

After you have looked them over, strategize which of them you would try first in order to locate the information in the questions which follow.

THE UNITED STATES CONGRESSIONAL QUARTERLY ALMANAC, 1945-   .
Call #_____

    Here's a handy condensation of federal government information.

THE UNITED STATES GOVERNMENT MANUAL, 1935-   .
Call #_____

    There are several indexes in the back of this volume. You must select the best one for your purpose. This manual relates to the organization of the federal government and its bureaucracy. It is an indispensable, annually-revised source of information about the nation's chief officials, and it is therefore in most libraries. A very useful feature is the list of agencies which have been abolished, transferred or terminated.

THE STATISTICAL ABSTRACT OF THE UNITED STATES, 1878-   .
Call #_____

    Here's a brief, annual, one-volume "partner" to the U.S. GOVERNMENT MANUAL. It is a digest of data collected by all of the statistical agencies of the U.S. Government as well as some collected by private agencies. It covers population, vital statistics, immigration, finance, railroads, commerce, etc.

THE [UNITED NATIONS] STATISTICAL YEARBOOK, 1948-   .
Call #_____

    Since 1948 the UNESCO has provided this annual compilation of political, scientific, educational and cultural data for more than two hundred nations; included is information about book production and the mass media.

Our state's statistical abstract, e.g. THE CALIFORNIA STATISTICAL ABSTRACT
Call #_____

Reference Books, contd.

Analyze the question first.

1. What percent of the United States population before the Civil War was black and what percent after?

2. Who is the current architect of the Capitol (the one in Washington, D.C.)?

3. What are the main objectives of the Bureau of Indian Affairs today?

4. The United States decennial census began in 1790. In what year or census did the number of females for the first time exceed males?

5. What police, subpena and/or law enforcement powers, if any, does the C I A have?

6. To whom does the director of the Drug Enforcement Administration report?

7. What was the Consumer Price Index for San Francisco in 1975?

8. What is the responsibility of the Center for Disease Control?

9. What is the highest temperature recorded in New York City?

10. Where is the West Coast office of the United States Department of Transportation?

11. What percentage of the nation's farmers filed for bankruptcy in 1982?

12. Which nation published the most books in the field of history and geography for the last year this information was reported?

13. How many acres of kiwifruit are in production in California?

GOVERNMENT PUBLICATIONS

Page 7. Instructor's Key:

1. The Statistical Abstract of the United States

2. United States Government Manual

3. United States Government Manual

4. The Statistical Abstract of the United States

5. United States Government Manual

6. United States Government Manual

7. The Statistical Abstract of the United States

8. United States Government Manual

9. The Statistical Abstract of the United States

10. United States Government Manual

11. The Statistical Abstract of the United States

12. The [United Nations] Statistical Yearbook

13. The California Statistical Abstract

ASSIGNMENT 7; PRACTICE USING ABSTRACTING SERVICES;
PRACTICE USING CDI/DAI:

Assignment 7 consists of instructional material and practice related to several different types of research techniques: locating parts of books in collections, using abstracting tools and abstracts, and locating dissertations. You may prefer to use these separately, perhaps in the library. They all require previous experience with local library accessing techniques and basic concepts, and they are therefore most appropriately scheduled in the latter part of the term. It is well to plan the term so that students have two weeks with no other out-of-class assignments following completion of pathfinder Assignments 5 and 6 and before the Project due-date.

"Practice Using Abstracting Services" is an in-library worksheet which can be used to reinforce this skill. "Practice Using Comprehensive Dissertation Index/ Dissertation Abstracts International" is also provided for supervised in-library work. Problems which can be used with each are included in Section III: Resources. It is well to duplicate on the verso of "Practice Using Abstracting Services" Owen/Harzfeld's description of the abstracting service being used.

Course, Date
Instructor
Page 1 (of 7)

Your Name_____
Assignment 7: Identifying and Using
Some Specialized Sources. Due: In
class on date on your schedule.

Assignment 7 is devoted to some specialized and special sources: parts of books (essays) which have been published in collections ; abstracting tools, services or journals, as they're variously referred to; and doctoral dissertations. There will be in-library work related to each of these, so that this assignment may function as introduction, practice, review, or self-testing.

I. Parts of books (essays). Required reading: <u>Bib Cards & Style Manuals</u>, pages 6 and 7.
You may have noticed occasional "Contents" notes on cataloging for books. Usually they consist of the titles of plays or short stories included in a book which is a literary or other type of collection. Only occasionally are titles and authors of essays identified. "Analytics" are too infrequently provided for you to be able to exploit parts of books. You can utilize your best SUBJECT HEADING dash ADDRESSES, ESSAYS AND LECTURES subdivision. And for essays in non-technical subjects, you can also use a very important index:

<u>THE ESSAY & GENERAL LITERATURE INDEX</u>, 1900-   ._____
Use it to know about parts of books which are themselves collections or anthologies. EGLI is, however, not a book "selector". It is an AUTHOR and SUBJECT index to collections of essays and works of a composite nature which have reference value in many areas of knowledge, particularly in the <u>humanities</u> and <u>social sciences</u>. <u>Literary criticism</u> is especially emphasized. Authors from every period and nation are included; however, only 20th Century publications are indexed. Volume # 9 covers what period of time? _____ - _____

You need information about <u>development of Black studies in early 1970's.</u>
Someone commends to you an essay published in a 19 75 book published by <u>Prentice-Hall</u>_____ . They can recall only that the essay in the book was approximately five pages in length. Locate the essay.
You use EGLI volume # _____ covering the time span _____ - _____.
On page #_____ of EGLI you find the citation leading to the needed essay under the subject heading _____

The title of the essay is "_____
_____
_____"
The inclusive pagination of the essay is _____ - _____. The full name of the author of the essay is _____
_____. Page # where the essay author's full name is found:_____. Editor (or author) of the book in which the essay appears is _____.
(It sometimes happens that the editor of the book wrote an essay which appears in the book.)

I. THE ESSAY & GENERAL LITERATURE INDEX, contd.

Get the full bibliographical information for the books indexed by EG
LI, in which the essays, chapters, articles, "parts", etc. appear,
from the List Of Books Indexed Section in the back of each EGLI
cumulated volume (or interim supplement.)
   Page # in the List Of Books Indexed Section in the back of the
   EGLI volume you have been using where you find the book in which
   the essay appears listed:_____. Full title of the book
   in which the essay was published:_____

   _____

   _____

Library call # for the book_____
While getting this information, also note the place of publication,
which you'd need in order to cite the essay for a bibliography.

   _____

Depending on your Project topic, you will need to check all volumes or
just certain time-spans of Essay & General Literature Index when you
complete your literature search. Even scientific and technical subjects
have social and humanistic implications...

II. Practice Using ABSTRACTING TOOLS, SERVICES, and JOURNALS

An abstract is a nonevaluative summary of a document. Most abstracts summarize long journal articles, but there are, fortunately, abstracts of dissertations available in reference books. Sometimes an abstract appears right at the beginning of an article itself in the journal issue where the article is published.

Locating and reading an abstract of any publication can be helpful when doing research. It is advantageous to have access to an abstract of a publication, whether or not the complete publication itself is part of the library's collection, because:

(1) Based on this information about what's contained in the publication, you can "de-select" on the spot, while using the index in the reference department, and not have to go to the catalog and then to the stacks.

(2) You can decide whether it is worthwhile then to go to the interlibrary loan department if the library doesn't have this publication.

Think of a tool such as America: History & Life (not all abstracting tools have that word in their titles), Psychological Abstracts, or Sociological Abstracts as a periodical index which also provides abstracts as a bonus, right in the index. And they index dissertations, proceedings, book reviews, etc. in their field as well as articles.

You must use an appropriate abstracting tool as a source in your Project, but do not cite or rely on just an abstract on the Project bibliography itself. In short, you must also track down and evaluate the original, abstracted-publication itself. Identify the title of one abstracting-index in your Project's field. (If necessary, refer to Assignment 5, STEP #3)." _____ "

The following is an abstract sample entry derived from Women Studies Abstracts:

Abstract number	┌─Author	Title of the article	Magazine	Volume	Pages	Issue date

1221A Loftus, Elizabeth. Follies of Affirmative Action. SOCIETY 14:21-4 Ja-F '77
    "Whether one feels that affirmative action programs have or have not been successful, it is reasonable to ask why they have not been more successful. One possible reason is that the punishment--the removal of federal funds--is so severe that it is almost never invoked. Universities know that it is unlikely that this 'atom bomb' will ever be dropped. It is no wonder that women and minorities who are protected by affirmative action feel frustrated by the state of affairs." Alternatives to the practice used in the present system are suggested.

Abstract ⌐ [The name or initials of the abstractor may appear.]

II. ABSTRACTS, Contd.

Important: Using any abstracting tool is a TWO STEP process, unlike <u>Readers' Guide</u>, for example, where you found everything (authors and subjects) <u>interfiled</u> in one neat A-Z volume. Tools with abstracts always involve an ABSTRACT NUMBER assigned to the abstracted-document, and at least two steps.

> FIRST: Use the INDEX Volume for the appropriate time-period to locate the alphabetical subject-entry, which will include the abstract number at its end.
>
> SECOND: Use that Abstract number to move to the appropriate volume within the same time period to get all the needed information about the publication and to read the abstract. This volume (or section of a volume) will be arranged numerically by abstract numbers, not alphabetically.

Do the following problem using <u>PSYCHOLOGICAL ABSTRACTS</u>

You desperately need to read the abstract of a long (about 75 pages) journal article published in November 1979 about such variables effecting the academically elite as their BIRTH ORDER. How large was the authors' sample, i.e. how many usable replies did they receive? Who were their sample, i.e. what group of people? Were their findings in agreement with Manaster's? How many references in the authors' documentation? Who abstracted the article? Where were the author-researchers based or located?

On what page in the INDEX VOLUME do you locate your initial clue, under what subject-heading? _____ _____
Abstract #_____   On what page in the corresponding ABSTRACTS VOLUME do you find the full, author-entry with the abstract following it? _____ Author[s]' name[s]: _____

Title of the journal article "_____
_____
_____
                                                                    "
Title of the serial in which the article was published "_____
_____
                                                                    "
    Issue of the serial: Volume #_____ Date of publication_____
    Inclusive pagination of the article in that issue _____ - _____
Library Call #_____
Answers to the questions:_____
_____
_____
_____

Many of the dissertation and thesis-locators are shelved together for reference use in libraries. These two basics in university libraries complement each other:

COMPREHENSIVE DISSERTATION INDEX (CDI), 1861-1972, 1973-

Location: _____

and

DISSERTATION ABSTRACTS INTERNATIONAL (DAI), 1938-

Location: _____

CDI indexes DAI.
CDI is one of the library tools which organizes information by means of KEYWORDs, rather than subject-headings. The keywords are derived from the indexed-publication's title. If the word isn't in the dissertation title, it will not turn up in CDI.

A dissertation research-report typically includes an extensive bibliography, surveys and reviews the literature of its topics, and/or reports on the "state of the art." If the doctorate was completed at the university you are using, there will likely be an author entry in the catalog. If it was not done there, you should check the catalog under that writer's name anyway, because the library might have acquired (1) the dissertation itself, and (2) the trade version of a book possibly subsequently published and based on it.

1A. Using the alphabetical AUTHOR volumes and sections at the end of each CDI cumulated time-period, identify the dissertation of an author, scholar, professor or other personality associated with your Project's field. If someone doesn't readily come to mind, check your bib cards for writers of books (mainly) and journal articles. Keep in mind that someone receiving their PhD. or other type of doctoral degree in 1972, for example, completed the dissertation around that year.

Here is a sample excerpt from CDI:

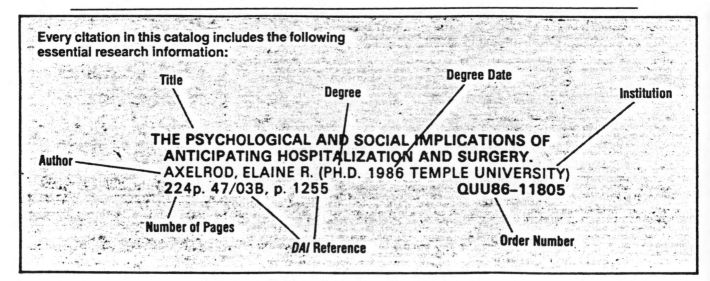

1., contd.

1A. If you are unable to locate someone from your Project's field in CDI
    author volumes, for purposes of this assignment, use one of the
    following members of our faculty:
               Name   Field within CDI Subjects

    _____   _____

    _____   _____

    _____   _____

    Note: Contrary to what some might assume, this information isn't
    always included in biographical directories;in any event, a tool such
    as Who's Who In America would list only the title, etc. and not pro-
    vide the abstract.

    Your person's name_____
    CDI Volume #_____, which covers year(s)_____. Page #_____
    Title of her/his dissertation:

       "_____

    _____

    _____."

    Type of degree awarded (e.g. PhD., EdD., etc.)_____
    Year awarded_____. Granting institution_____

    Abstract # (Not the "order number"; see sample CDI excerpt on previous
    page: "DAI Reference" 47/03B is the abstract number-location. "p.
    1255" refers to the number of the DAI page on which 47/03B is located,
    and as such, is very useful information, so when making bib cards
    and using CDI/DAI, include it with the abstract number.)As you see, a
    CDI/DAI abstract number consists of digits-slash-digits + an A or B.

    _____   _____

1B. Using the abstract number, move to the DAI volume which includes this
    number. Turn to the appropriate page, and read the abstract of the
    dissertation.   [If CDI appears not to provide an abstract number
    and page number such as that in the process described for the scholar
    in your Project field, see me during office hours or try another
    person from your field, preferably one whose dissertation was written
    more recently.]

    Does the abstract information provide the name of the thesis advisor
    or chairperson?_____ If yes, what is it?_____

    _____

2A. Warren Farrell's 1974 book was published by Random and titled <u>The</u>
    <u>Liberated Man; Beyond Masculinity...</u> . It was a trade-revision of
    his doctoral thesis apparently, which was also completed that year.
    Locate the dissertation in the AUTHOR volumes of CDI for that time
    coverage.

    CDI Author Volume where you start:#_____; Date(s) of that vol-
    ume's coverage:_____. Page # in the CDI author
    volume where you find Warren Farrell's dissertation mentioned:_____.
    What is the name of the institution which granted Farrell's doctoral
    degree?_____
    How many pages in length was the dissertation?_____
    What type of doctorate did he receive?_____
    What is the full title of the dissertation?
       "_____

    _____

    _____."

    [Any of the information which you are unable to locate using CDI,
    you can pick up when you move to DAI.]

    What is the ABSTRACT NUMBER which CDI provides?_____

2B. Using the abstract number (and page number), move to the DAI volume
    which includes this number. Turn to the appropriate page, and read
    the abstract of the dissertation.

    In what field was it earned (for example,sociology, political science,
    biology, etc.)?_____

    Use the abstract to locate the following information:

    Who was the dissertation advisor?_____

    How many men scored?_____

Course, Date   KEY   Your Name _____
Instructor   Assignment 7: Identifying and Using
Page 1 (of 7)   Some Specialized Sources.   Due; In
                               class on date on your schedule.

Assignment 7 is devoted to some specialized and special sources: parts of books (essays) which have been published in collections ; abstracting tools, services or journals, as they're variously referred to; and doctoral dissertations. There will be in-library work related to each of these, so that this assignment may function as introduction, practice, review, or self-testing.

I.   Parts of books (essays).   Required reading: <u>Bib Cards & Style Manuals</u>, pages 6 and 7.

You may have noticed occasional "Contents" notes on cataloging for books. Usually they consist of the titles of plays or short stories included in a book which is a literary or other type of collection. Only occasionally are titles and authors of essays identified. "Analytics" are too infrequently provided for you to be able to exploit parts of books. You can utilize your best SUBJECT HEADING dash ADDRESSES, ESSAYS AND LECTURES subdivision. And for essays in non-technical subjects, you can also use a very important index:

<u>THE ESSAY & GENERAL LITERATURE INDEX</u>, 1900-   . _____
Use it to know about <u>parts</u> of books which are themselves collections or anthologies. EGLI is, however, not a book "selector". It is an AUTHOR and SUBJECT index to collections of essays and works of a composite nature which have reference value in many areas of knowledge, particularly in the <u>humanities</u> and <u>social sciences</u>. <u>Literary criticism</u> is especially emphasized. Authors from every period and nation are included; however, only 20th Century publications are indexed.
Volume #<u> 9 </u> covers what period of time? <u> 1975 </u> - <u> 1979 </u>

You need information about <u>development of Black studies in early 1970's</u>. Someone commends to you an essay published in a <u>1975</u> book published by <u>Prentice-Hall</u>   . They can recall only that the essay in the book was approximately <u> five </u> pages in length. Locate the essay.
    You use EGLI volume #<u> 9 </u> covering the time span<u>1975</u> - <u>1979</u> .
    On page #<u> 20 </u> of EGLI you find the citation leading to the needed essay under the subject heading <u>AFRO-AMERICAN STUDIES</u> (A "SEE" reference from Black studies to <u>AFRO-AMERICAN STUDIES</u> should precede.)
The title of the essay is "<u>Black studies and changing times</u> _____
_____ ".
The inclusive pagination of the essay is <u> 134 </u> - <u> 138 </u> . The full name of the author of the essay is <u>Alston Brower</u> _____ . Page # where the essay author's full name is found: <u> 192 </u> . Editor (o̸r̸/a̸u̸t̸h̸o̸r̸) of the book in which the essay appears is <u>Roy P. Fairfield</u>   .
(It sometimes happens that the editor of the book wrote an essay which appears in the book.)

II. Practice Using ABSTRACTING TOOLS, SERVICES, and JOURNALS

An abstract is a nonevaluative summary of a document. Most abstracts summarize long journal articles, but there are, fortunately, abstracts of dissertations available in reference books. Sometimes an abstract appears right at the beginning of an article itself in the journal issue where the article is published.

Locating and reading an abstract of any publication can be helpful when doing research. It is advantageous to have access to an abstract of a publication, whether or not the complete publication itself is part of the library's collection, because:

> (1) Based on this information about what's contained in the publi-
> cation, you can "de-select" on the spot, while using the index in
> the reference department, and not have to go to the catalog and
> then to the stacks.

> (2) You can decide whether it is worthwhile then to go to the
> interlibrary loan department if the library doesn't have this
> publication.

Think of a tool such as America: History & Life (not all abstracting tools have that word in their titles), Psychological Abstracts, or Sociological Abstracts as a periodical index which also provides abstracts as a bonus, right in the index. And they index dissertations, proceedings, book reviews, etc. in their field as well as articles.

You must use an appropriate abstracting tool as a source in your Project, but do not cite or rely on just an abstract on the Project bibliography itself.   In short, you must also track down and evaluate the original, abstracted-publication itself. Identify the title of one abstracting-index in your Project's field. (If necessary, refer to Assignment 5, STEP #3)."_____"

The following is an abstract sample entry derived from Women Studies Abstracts:

Abstract number	Author	Title of the article	Magazine	Volume	Pages	Issue date

1221A Loftus, Elizabeth. Follies of Affirmative Action. SOCIETY 14:21-4 Ja-F '77
     "Whether one feels that affirmative action programs have or have not been successful, it is reasonable to ask why they have not been more successful. One possible reason is that the punishment--the removal of federal funds--is so severe that it is almost never invoked. Universities know that it is unlikely that this 'atom bomb' will ever be dropped. It is no wonder that women and minorities who are protected by affirmative action feel frustrated by the state of affairs." Alternatives to the practice used in the present system are suggested.

Abstract   [The name or initials of the abstractor may appear.]

I. THE ESSAY & GENERAL LITERATURE INDEX, contd.

Get the full bibliographical information for the books indexed by EG
LI, in which the essays, chapters, articles, "parts", etc. appear,
from the List Of Books Indexed Section in the back of each EGLI
cumulated volume (or interim supplement.)
   Page # in the List Of Books Indexed Section in the back of the
   EGLI volume you have been using where you find the book in which
   the essay appears listed: 1704   . Full title of the book
   in which the essay was published: "Humanistic Frontiers in
      American Education, 2nd edition."

   _____

Library call # for the book_____
While getting this information, also note the place of publication,
which you'd need in order to cite the essay for a bibliography.

   _____

Depending on your Project topic, you will need to check all volumes or
just certain time-spans of Essay & General Literature Index when you
complete your literature search. Even scientific and technical subjects
have social and humanistic implications...

II. ABSTRACTS, Contd.

Important: Using any abstracting tool is a TWO STEP process, unlike <u>Readers' Guide</u>, for example, where you found everything (authors and subjects) <u>interfiled</u> in one neat A-Z volume. Tools with abstracts always involve an ABSTRACT NUMBER assigned to the abstracted-document, and at least two steps.

> FIRST: Use the INDEX Volume for the appropriate time-period to locate the alphabetical subject-entry, which will include the abstract number at its end.
> SECOND: Use that Abstract number to move to the appropriate volume within the same time period to get all the needed information about the publication and to read the abstract. This volume (or section of a volume) will be arranged numerically by abstract numbers, not alphabetically.

Do the following problem using <u>PSYCHOLOGICAL ABSTRACTS</u>

You desperately need to read the abstract of a long (about 75 pages) journal article published in November 1979 about such variables effecting the academically elite as their BIRTH ORDER. How large was the authors' sample, i.e. how many usable replies did they receive? Who were their sample, i.e. what group of people? Were their findings in agreement with Manaster's? How many references in the authors' documentation? Who abstracted the article? Where were the author-researchers based or located?

On what page in the INDEX VOLUME do you locate your initial clue, under what subject-heading? <u>171</u>   BIRTH ORDER [Jan-June 1982 vol. #67]
Abstract # <u>3444</u>   On what page in the corresponding ABSTRACTS VOLUME do you find the full, author-entry with the abstract following it?
<u>369</u>   Author[s]' name[s]: Roslyn F. Hayes and Arline L.
Bronzaft [Jan.-March 1982 vol. #67]

Title of the journal article "Birth order and related variables in an academically elite sample.
                                                                          "

Title of the serial in which the article was published " Journal of Individual Psychology
                                                                          "

Issue of the serial: Volume # <u>35</u>   Date of publication Nov. 1979
   Inclusive pagination of the article in that issue <u>214</u> - <u>224</u>
Library Call #
Answers to the questions: 529 / current members aged 20-95 years of Phi Beta Kappa Assoc. of New York / yes / 13 / J. L. Driscoll / Educational Records Bureau, Wellesley Hills, MA.

Many of the dissertation and thesis-locators are shelved together for reference use in libraries. These two basics in university libraries complement each other:

COMPREHENSIVE DISSERTATION INDEX (CDI), 1861-1972, 1973-

Location: _____

and

DISSERTATION ABSTRACTS INTERNATIONAL (DAI), 1938-

Location: _____

CDI indexes DAI.
CDI is one of the library tools which organizes information by means of KEYWORDs, rather than subject-headings. The keywords are derived from the indexed-publication's title. If the word isn't in the dissertation title, it will not turn up in CDI.

A dissertation research-report typically includes an extensive bibliography, surveys and reviews the literature of its topics, and/or reports on the "state of the art." If the doctorate was completed at the university you are using, there will likely be an author entry in the catalog. If it was not done there, you should check the catalog under that writer's name anyway, because the library might have acquired (1) the dissertation itself, and (2) the trade version of a book possibly subsequently published and based on it.

1A. Using the alphabetical AUTHOR volumes and sections at the end of each CDI cumulated time-period, identify the dissertation of an author, scholar, professor or other personality associated with your Project's field. If someone doesn't readilly come to mind, check your bib cards for writers of books (mainly) and journal articles. Keep in mind that someone receiving their PhD. or other type of doctoral degree in 1972, for example, completed the dissertation around that year.

Here is a sample excerpt from CDI:

Every citation in this catalog includes the following essential research information:

Title   Degree   Degree Date   Institution

THE PSYCHOLOGICAL AND SOCIAL IMPLICATIONS OF
ANTICIPATING HOSPITALIZATION AND SURGERY.
Author — AXELROD, ELAINE R. (PH.D. 1986 TEMPLE UNIVERSITY)
224p. 47/03B, p. 1255   QUU86-11805

Number of Pages   DAI Reference   Order Number

1., contd.

1A. If you are unable to locate someone from your Project's field in CDI author volumes, for purposes of this assignment, use one of the following members of our faculty:

         <u>Name</u>   <u>Field within CDI Subjects</u>

_____   _____

_____   _____

_____   _____

Note: Contrary to what some might assume, this information isn't always included in biographical directories; in any event, a tool such as <u>Who's Who In America</u> would list only the title, etc. and not provide the abstract.

Your person's name_____
CDI Volume #_____, which covers year(s)_____. Page #_____
Title of her/his dissertation:

    "_____

_____

_____."

Type of degree awarded (e.g. PhD., EdD., etc.)_____
Year awarded_____. Granting institution_____

Abstract # (Not the "order number"; see sample CDI excerpt on previous page: "DAI Reference" 47/03B is the abstract number-location. "p. 1255" refers to the number of the DAI page on which 47/03B is located, and as such, is very useful information, so when making bib cards and using CDI/DAI, include it with the abstract number.)As you see, a CDI/DAI abstract number consists of digits-slash-digits + an A <u>or</u> B.

_____   _____

1B. Using the abstract number, move to the DAI volume which includes this number. Turn to the appropriate page, and read the abstract of the dissertation. [If CDI appears not to provide an abstract number and page number such as that in the process described for the scholar in your Project field, see me during office hours or try another person from your field, preferably one whose dissertation was written more recently.]

Does the abstract information provide the name of the thesis advisor or chairperson?_____ If yes, what is it?_____

_____

2A. Warren Farrell's 1974 book was published by Random and titled The
    Liberated Man; Beyond Masculinity... .   It was a trade-revision of
    his doctoral thesis apparently, which was also completed that year.
    Locate the dissertation in the AUTHOR volumes of CDI for that time
    coverage.

    CDI Author Volume where you start:# 34_____ ; Date(s) of that vol-
    ume's coverage:____1973-82_____ . Page # in the CDI author
    volume where you find Warren Farrell's dissertation mentioned: 523 .
    What is the name of the institution which granted Farrell's doctoral
    degree? New York University_____
    How many pages in length was the dissertation?   560_____
    What type of doctorate did he receive?   Ph.D._____
    What is the full title of the dissertation?

    "The Political Potential of the Women's Liberation Movement as Indi-
    cated By Its Effectiveness in Changing Men's Attitudes_____
    _____ ."

    [Any of the information which you are unable to locate using CDI,
    you can pick up when you move to DAI.]

    What is the ABSTRACT NUMBER which CDI provides? 37/06A p.3872_____

2B. Using the abstract number (and page number), move to the DAI volume
    which includes this number. Turn to the appropriate page, and read
    the abstract of the dissertation.

    In what field was it earned (for example, sociology, political science,
    biology, etc.)?   Political Science_____

    Use the abstract to locate the following information:

    Who was the dissertation advisor? James T. Crown_____
    How many men scored?   240_____

The abstract service titled "_____

_____" is here in the Reference Department's col-
lection. This is one of the tools which you (or I) identified in your
pathfinder Assignment #3, STEP #3 for accessing periodical literature.

You need information about

Someone refers you to a publication

LOCATE THIS PUBLICATION BIBLIOGRAPHICALLY AND USE ITS ABSTRACT:
1. Normally, you would begin by quickly getting the abstract service's
    call number from the catalog. However, you already know it is

    _____. Go to that
    location in the Reference Dept. (If in doubt at this point, come
    directly to me).
2. Decide which volume of the set will be a logical starting point
    TIMEWISE, considering the date of publication involved in "your pub-
    lication".
3. Consult the SUBJECT INDEXING. Most abstracting services have SUBJECT
    indexes scattered through each issue and volume. But the subject-
    index in the BACK OF THE ANNUAL VOLUME is often a CUMULATED SUBJECT
    INDEX for the entire time span and volume, saving you searching steps.
    Using that subject-approach, locate a reference to the publication
    that meets the needs of the problem. Keep notes of where you are...
    volume, time-period, page, etc., so you don't get lost or repeat steps.
    Space for your notes:

4. What is the abstract number of "your publication"? _____
    In what # volume of the abstracting tool did you find it? _____
    What is the date of that volume of the abstract tool? _____
    Under what keywords or subject did you find reference to it? _____

    _____

5. Move from the subject indexing to the abstracts, numerically displayed,
    for your publication's abstract. This usually involves moving from
    one volume to another, or from one section to another section of a
    supplement. Two separate volumes (or issues) within the same time
    period are usually involved.
6. According to the abstract,

    _____

    _____

    _____

Turn this in five minutes before the end of class today.

Practice Using Abstracting Services
Your Name_____

The abstract service titled "_____America: History and Life

_____" is here in the Reference Department's col-
lection. This is one of the tools which you (or I) identified in your
pathfinder Assignment #3, STEP #3 for accessing periodical literature.

You need information about the impact of deregulation of air transportation industry on labor union power. You'd like to know what unions were
involved too.

Someone refers you to a publication in 1983 about airlines deregulation
and labor unions, a fourteen-page (or so) article in the Industrial and
Labor Relations journal or "something like that".

LOCATE THIS PUBLICATION BIBLIOGRAPHICALLY AND USE ITS ABSTRACT:
1. Normally, you would begin by quickly getting the abstract service's
    call number from the catalog. However, you already know it is

    _____. Go to that
    location in the Reference Dept. (If in doubt at this point, come
    directly to me).
2. Decide which volume of the set will be a logical starting point
    TIMEWISE, considering the date of publication involved in "your pub-
    lication".
3. Consult the SUBJECT INDEXING. Most abstracting services have SUBJECT
    indexes scattered through each issue and volume. But the subject-
    index in the BACK OF THE ANNUAL VOLUME is often a CUMULATED SUBJECT
    INDEX for the entire time span and volume, saving you searching steps.
    Using that subject-approach, locate a reference to the publication
    that meets the needs of the problem. Keep notes of where you are...
    volume, time-period, page, etc., so you don't get lost or repeat steps.
    Space for your notes:

4. What is the abstract number of "your publication"?_____
    In what # volume of the abstracting tool did you find it?_____
    What is the date of that volume of the abstract tool?_____
    Under what keywords or subject did you find reference to it?_____

    _____

5. Move from the subject indexing to the abstracts, numerically displayed,
   for your publication's abstract. This usually involves moving from
   one volume to another, or from one section to another section of a
   supplement. Two separate volumes (or issues) within the same time
   period are usually involved.
6. According to the abstract, what are the names of 2 unions involved?
   Does the writer conclude that the impact of deregulation had been
   significant? What factors does he consider (problems does he examine)?

   _____

   _____

   _____

Turn this in five minutes before the end of class today.

Course _____ KEY ___ Practice Using Abstracting Services
Instructor   Your Name _____

The abstract service titled " ___ America: History and Life ___

_____ " is here in the Reference Department's collection. This is one of the tools which you (or I) identified in your
pathfinder Assignment #3, STEP #3 for accessing periodical literature.

You need information about the impact of deregulation of air transportation industry on labor union power. You'd like to know what unions were
involved too.

Someone refers you to a publication in 1983 about airlines deregulation
and labor unions, a fourteen-page (or so) article in the Industrial and
Labor Relations journal or "something like that".

LOCATE THIS PUBLICATION BIBLIOGRAPHICALLY AND USE ITS ABSTRACT:
1. Normally, you would begin by quickly getting the abstract service's
    call number from the catalog. However, you already know it is

    _____ . Go to that
    location in the Reference Dept. (If in doubt at this point, come
    directly to me).
2. Decide which volume of the set will be a logical starting point
    TIMEWISE, considering the date of publication involved in "your pub-
    lication".
·3. Consult the SUBJECT INDEXING. Most abstracting services have SUBJECT
    indexes scattered through each issue and volume. But the subject-
    index in the BACK OF THE ANNUAL VOLUME is often a CUMULATED SUBJECT
    INDEX for the entire time span and volume, saving you searching steps.
    Using that subject-approach, locate a reference to the publication
    that meets the needs of the problem. Keep notes of where you are...
    volume, time-period, page, etc., so you don't get lost or repeat steps.
    Space for your notes:

4. What is the abstract number of "your publication"? _20A : 7515_
    In what # volume of the abstracting tool did you find it? v.20 of '83 Subj.Index
    What is the date of that volume of the abstract tool? _1983_
    Under what keywords or subject did you find reference to it? _____
    AIR LINES. DEREGULATION.LABOR UNIONS AND ORGANIZATIONS...

5. Move from the subject indexing to the abstracts, numerically displayed,
    for your publication's abstract. This usually involves moving from
    one volume to another, or from one section to another section of a
    supplement. Two separate volumes (or issues) within the same time
    period are usually involved.
6. According to the abstract, what are the names of 2 unions involved?
    Does the writer conclude that the impact of deregulation had been
    significant? What factors does he consider (problems does he examine)?
    In 1983 Abstracts volume 20, Part A (USA 1945-present), I found 20A:7515,page 517:
    The 2 unions: Air Line Pilots Assoc., International Assoc. of Machinists
    and Aerospace Workers. Yes,the writer uses the word "significant". He
    considers the entry of nonunion carriers into the market,the flight control-

Turn this in five minutes before the end of class today. lers' strike, the
    decline of traffic during the then-recent recession,and the differing union
    approaches to the industry's problems.

Course   <u>Practice</u> <u>Using</u> <u>Comprehensive</u>
Instructor   <u>Dissertation</u> <u>Index/Dissertation</u>
                                    <u>Abstracts</u> <u>International</u>
Turn this in 5 minutes before
the end of class today.   Your Name_____

These two tools are usually used together and shelved nearby. CDI has the
abstract numbers and indexes DAI; DAI has the abstracts of the dissertations.

Normally, you would begin by quickly getting their call numbers from the
catalog. However, you already know their location:

     Comprehensive Dissertation Index: _____

     Dissertation Abstracts International: _____

CDI is chronologically arranged by periods of time covered. Within each
time period, the set of volumes is provided with AUTHOR volumes located
at the end of that set. The balance of the set consists of volumes which
provide SUBJECT-access by use of KEYWORDS, rather than subject-headings.
Today, use the KEYWORD subject-access volumes.

Start by examining them closely. As is usually the case with "reference
books", the first few pages of the[first]volume provide basic HOW TO.
CDI batches subjects within large subject-fields. For examples:

     BUSINESS & ECONOMICS: MEDICAL SCIENCES:
        Accounting   Audiology & Speech Pathology
        Agriculture   Chemotherapy
        Business Administration   Genetics
        Business Education   Health Education
        Commerce/Business   Hospital Management
        Economics   Immunology
        Finance   Medicine & Surgery
        Finance in Education   Neuroscience
        Labor   Nursing
        Management   Nutrition
        Marketing   Pharmaceutical Chemistry
        Theory   etc. etc.

Look for the front page which lists <u>all</u> of these break-downs. Select
at least two which sound like they have potential for your Project topic:

MAIN SUBJECT FIELD:_____
     Subdivision: _____
MAIN SUBJECT FIELD:_____
     Subdivision:_____
Stay within a time-span. Locate the volumes and pages which list dissertations under these two groups. Scan all of the titles. Do they sound as if
you made the right selection(s)?____ If so, list one dissertation title,
author, degree date, and abstract number for it:_____
_____
_____

259

PRACTICE STRATEGIZING A LIBRARY LITERATURE SEARCH

The "standard library resources" can be varied. Other useful possibilities include the Encyclopedia of Associations, Current Biography, a citation index, Comprehensive Dissertation Index and Dissertation Abstracts International, Books in Print, etc.

Ideas for additional subjects for the paper in question can be derived from Section III: Resources Multiple Subject Topics.... Most nineteenth- and twentieth-centuries major authors of both fiction and nonfiction are productive. The following format is illustrative: "...a paper on the subject of novelist Olive Schreiner and her influence during her lifetime on feminism and after her death on economic thought and scholarship. Schreiner lived from 1855 to 1920, and was a South African-English author of both fiction and nonfiction." Some others which will work are these:

William Carlos Williams, 1883-1963, American poet and physician.
Joseph Pulitzer, 1847-1911, Hungarian-born American journalist and newspaper publisher.
Ralph Johnson Bunche, 1904-1971, American diplomat and United Nations Undersecretary.
Oliver Wendell Holmes, 1809-1894, American author of verse, essays and novels.
Sun Yat-sen, 1866-1926, Chinese statesman and leader.
Josephine Elizabeth Butler, 1828-1906, English philanthropist and social reformer.
Isabella Lucy Bird Bishop, 1831-1904, English geographer and author.
Joy Gessner Adamson, 1910-1980, Austrian conservationist and writer.
Simone de Beauvoir, 1908-1986, French philosopher.
Margaret Higgins Sanger, 1883-1966, American social reformer, lecturer and author.
Helen Adams Keller, 1880-1968, American author, lecturer, and educator.
Florence Rena Sabin, 1871-1953, American anatomist, author, educator.
Charlotte Perkins Gilman, 1860-1935, American author, lecturer, social reformer.
Margaret Bateson Mead, 1901-1977, American anthropologist.

Using the library's resources, you're going to write a paper on the subject of NOISE AS A FORM OF POLLUTION. From the list of twenty standard library resources below, select TEN and number them in the order you'd consult them-- first, second, third, etc.

There's no law requiring use of all of them, or each only once, or in one-and-only-one particular sequence. But there is a logical overall approach, and some things must precede or follow effective use of others. (Like getting dressed: you might not wear socks and shoes today, but you would likely put on the socks before the shoes if you did!)

_____ ABSTRACTS AND INDEXES IN SCIENCE AND TECHNOLOGY, by D. B. Owen

_____ APPLIED SCIENCE & TECHNOLOGY INDEX

_____ BIBLIOGRAPHIC INDEX

_____ BIOGRAPHY INDEX

_____ DICTIONARY OF AMERICAN BIOGRAPHY

_____ DICTIONARY OF NATIONAL BIOGRAPHY

_____ Government Documents Department

_____ GUIDE TO REFERENCE BOOKS, by E. Sheehy

_____ a guide to the literature

_____ HUMANITIES INDEX

_____ LCSH

_____ Library serials catalog

_____ Library stacks

_____ Library subject catalog

_____ MONTHLY CATALOG

_____ PAIS BULLETIN

_____ PERIODICAL INDEXES IN THE SOCIAL SCIENCES AND HUMANITIES, by L. Harzfeld

_____ SOCIAL SCIENCES INDEX

_____ a specialized index with abstracts

_____ WHO'S WHO

USING WHAT YOU KNOW: LOCATORS AND
CARRIERS OF INFORMATION

This is intended for in-class use following lecture-discussion about "reference
books" (carriers of information), many of which also function as locators of information. Among the specific titles discussed will be biographical tools. It also
provides a take-off point for emphasis of the three-step, analytical process:
which, why, and how. Normally, it would be useful at the end of the term; it
must follow a discussion of the purpose of reference books and their distinct
characteristics as compared to indexes, abstracts, etc. (locators of information
and publications). Biographical tools support research, and should be emphasized.
In fact, this exercise could be built around the four biographical reference works
and tools. Additional problems are part of Section III: Resources.

1. WEBSTER'S THIRD NEW INTERNATIONAL DICTIONARY OF THE ENGLISH
   LANGUAGE [Unabridged]

2. CURRENT BIOGRAPHY [1969]

3. BIOGRAPHY INDEX [Vol. 7, Sept. 1964-August 1967]

4. WORLD ALMANAC

5. NEW YORK TIMES INDEX [1965]

6. DICTIONARY OF NATIONAL BIOGRAPHY

7. DICTIONARY OF AMERICAN BIOGRAPHY

8. ENCYCLOPEDIA OF ASSOCIATIONS

9. CURRENT BIOGRAPHY [1963]

Practice Locating Periodical Articles and Information

This is for in-class use following the introduction of abstracting tools. The information or publication can be obtained by use of the tool whose title is listed.
In some cases, additional ways or examples could be found; these are examples.

1. BUSINESS PERIODICALS INDEX [July 1965-June 1966, Vol. 8; Duesenberry]

2. PSYCHOLOGICAL ABSTRACTS [July-December 1978, Vol. 60 Index SIGN
   LANGUAGE; Abstract #11205]

262

3. EDUCATION INDEX [July 1982-June 1983, Vol. 33; TESTS AND SCALES--SOCIAL ASPECTS]

4. SOCIOLOGICAL ABSTRACTS [1983, Vol. 31 Index DRUG/DRUGS; Abstract #1787]

5. BOOK REVIEW DIGEST [1962-1966 Cumulative Subject & Title Index; 1963 Lipman, Eugene J.]

6. HISTORICAL ABSTRACTS [1982, Vol. 33 Index SADAT, ANWAR; Abstract #3179]

7. ART INDEX [November 1977-October 1978 CLOCKS AND WATCHES--EXHIBITIONS]

8. PHYSICAL EDUCATION INDEX [Cumulation covering 1980 ATHLETES--ELITE]

9. BUSINESS PERIODICALS INDEX [July 1965-June 1966, Vol. 8; EARLS, WILLIAM A.]

10. EDUCATION INDEX [July 1964-June 1965, Vol. 15; KNEE]

11. BUSINESS PERIODICALS INDEX [July 1965-June 1966, Vol. 8; DRUGS--LAWS AND REGULATIONS]

So far you have had situations structured where you knew which library

tool to use. All you had to do was use it efficiently. Today, based on

the information contained in each "situation" on the attached sheet,

strategize:

First:

Which specialized periodical index you'd try first. **

Second:

In which volume (time period) you'd start your search.

Third:

The wording (subject-heading possibly) you'd look under.

** Your Reference Library for this work consists of:

ART INDEX, 1929-

BOOK REVIEW DIGEST, 1905-

BUSINESS PERIODICALS INDEX, 1958-

EDUCATION INDEX, July 1929-

HISTORICAL ABSTRACTS, 1955-

PHYSICAL EDUCATION INDEX, 1978-

PSYCHOLOGICAL ABSTRACTS, 1927-

SOCIOLOGICAL ABSTRACTS, 1963-

WOMEN STUDIES ABSTRACTS, 1972-

1. You need information about banker James Stembel Dusenberry, but
    you're not 100% sure of how his name is spelled. He was in the news
    in the mid-sixties.

2. You need a journal article about Koko, the gorilla at Stanford Un-
    iversity who, it is said, can use sign language. You also hope for
    an abstract of this article, inasmuch as journal articles can be
    very long.

3. You want information about non-biased tests used in counseling--
    fairly recent too, published in the 1980's.

4. Your friends contend that "sports-and-clean-living is a useful myth".
    They declare that a Pennsylvania State University researcher named
    Rooney published proof of this in 1983. You are interested in docu-
    menting your belief that the greater the number of sports participated
    in, the lower the rate of illegal substance use. You want to read an
    abstract before you get deeper into it, however.(They might be right!)

5. You're preparing a bibliography to support a paper on the subject of
    factors which divide Americans. You need a capsule evaluation as well
    as a brief summary of the book, A Tale of Ten Cities: The Triple
    Ghetto In American Religious Life, which was published some time be-
    tween 1962 and 1966. Unfortunately you don't know the author's
    name.

6. You need an article about Anwar Sadat's negotiating techniques-- his
    diplomacy. And you want to read an abstract before you bother locating
    the article itself in the stacks or getting an inter-library loan.

7. You need information about an exhibition of European and American
    clocks which was held in 1977 at the Museum of Our National Heritage
    in Lexington, Massachusetts.

8. An issue of the Journal of Sport and Social Issues had an article in
    1980 about social disorganizational aspects of professional sports
    careers. It included some discussion about something called "elite
    athletes".

9. You need information about the death of insurance man William A.
    Earls in 1966.

10. You need information about the effect of walking in cowboy boots on
    knee action! Someone says the American Association for Health,
    Physical Education, and Creation's Research Quarterly contained such
    an article in   late   1964 .

11. You need information about the 1966 warning to drug companies about
    glaucoma and the labeling of their products composed of belladona.

Source materials are good old-fashioned reference books, located in the
Reference Departments of many libraries.

If you need...	Try looking in...	For examples...
An OVERVIEW, survey or short explanation giving key events, dates, people involved, concepts	General encyclopedias Subject encyclopedias	Encyclopedia Americana Ency. of Philosophy Internatl. ency. of the Social Sciences
EVENTS of the past or current year(s)	Annuals, Yearbooks	Britannica Yearbook Annual Register of World Events Facts on File New York Times Index
BIOGRAPHICAL information	General encyclopedias Subject encyclopedias Directories Specialized biographical sources Biography indexes	Encyclo. Britannica Encyclo. Judaica Who's Who of...; in... Directory of American Scholars. In Black And White Contemporary Authors Internatl. Dictionary of Women's Biography Biography Index Biography Almanac
ADDRESSES of people and organizations	Directories	Telephone books Official Congressional Directory Current Biography
Information about ORGANIZATIONS	Directories	Encyclopedia of Associations World of Learning Literary Market Place
GEOGRAPHICAL information -- climate, population density, mineral resources and products. History	Atlases Gazetteers Geographical dictionaries Historical atlases	Times Atlas ... Columbia Lippincott... Webster's New Geographical Dictionary Shepherd's Historical Atlas

If you need...	Try looking in...	For examples...
STATISTICAL information on people, education, elections, government, transportation, law, etc.	Almanacs: facts, statistics and basic data, events of the preceding year(s)	World Almanac Europa Yearbook
	Statistical abstracts	Statistical abstract of the U.S.
	Annuals & Yearbooks	Statesman's Yearbook
WORDS History-- where they came from, how used.	Etymology dictionaries	Oxford English Dict.
Definitions, spelling, meaning, pronunciation	Language dictionaries Subject dictionaries	American Heritage Dict. Black's Law Dict.
Synonyms	A thesaurus	Roget's Thesaurus
Quotations	A quotations "dictionary"	Bartlett's Familiar Quotations
	Concordances	Complete Concordance to Shakespeare Nelson's Complete Concordance of the ... Bible.
HOW TO do something, or to cope. Guidance or instruction	Manuals	Turabian's [Style] Manual...
FACTS Quick & Easy to get!	Handbooks	Handbook of Classical Mythology. New Columbia Ency. Physician's Desk Reference Oxford Companion to Music (etc.) Fodor's Modern Guides

So far you've had situations structured where you knew which library tool to use, or at least which type of tool to use. All you had to do was use it efficiently.

Based on the information contained in each "situation" on the next page, strategize:

1. WHICH tool would be most useful? Your Reference Library for this work consists of the tools listed below. ⁂

2. WHY you select it... what's in the problem or informational need that suggests that particular tool?

3. HOW would you go about using it efficiently?

⁂ Your Reference Library for this work consists of:

Biography Index, 1947-

Current Biography, 1940-

Dictionary of American Biography ("DAB")

Dictionary of National Biography ("DNB")

Encyclopedia of Associations

New York Times Index, 1851-

Webster's Third New International Dictionary of the English Language

Who's Who

Who's Who In America

World Almanac & Book of Facts

1. What is Hoshana Rabbah? What does joukery-pawkery mean? What do the three letters -- Beta, Kappa and Phi -- each stand for? What is laced coffee? What is an amicus curiae? How many gallons in a barrel? (The information is all in one source throughout these questions.)

2. What is former Congressional Representative Shirley Chisholm's highest academic degree (for example, the doctorate), and is it true that she is a contest-winning amateur ballroom dancer? How does she pronounce her surname?

3. You're looking for the title of a biography of Elizabeth Cady Stanton which is suitable for children as well as a novel about Cleopatra.

4. What are the dates for the Ming Dynasty? Who holds the world's swimming record for women's back stroke? What were the gold reserves of the U.S.A. in 1970? On what dates were four of Lincoln's alleged assassins executed, and by what means? How many representatives are there from Northern Ireland in the British Parliament?

5. There was considerable speculation and inuendo at the time of American reporter Dorothy Kilgallen's death around 1965. Of what did she die?

6. "Sister" Edith Cavell was executed as a British spy in 1915. There was a little newspaper "coverage" at the time, and you could probably track down some reference to it in newspapers. But you need authoritative biographical material which will also provide some bibliographic support as well as discuss her life and answer these two questions: How was she executed? How much time elapsed between her arrest and her execution?

7. Adolph Sutro was elected mayor of San Francisco in 1894 on which political ticket? Were the Sutro Baths named after him? Sutro was known as a bibliophile... Of what did his valuable collection of books consist... what did it feature, specialize in? Where is it now located? Was he born in the U.S.A.?

8. You've heard that the National Football League Players Association's official charity is the Better Boys Foundation. Is this accurate? Where is this Foundation located? If it is not accurate, who does sponsor the Foundation?

9. Is it true that Senator Edward Kennedy was suspended from Harvard for cheating? Confirm or disprove. If it is true, what was the outcome, i.e. how did he manage to graduate from college, assuming he did so. If it is not true, how did this rumor get started? You need documentation for this type of information, of course.

1. WEBSTER'S THIRD NEW INTERNATIONAL DICTIONARY OF THE ENGLISH
   LANGUAGE

2. Current Biography 1969

3. Biography Index

4. World Almanac & Book of Facts

5. New York Times Index

6. Dictionary of National Biography

7. Dictionary of American Biography

8. Encyclopedia of Associations

9. Current Biography 1963

"CARRIERS" OF BIOGRAPHICAL INFORMATION ABOUT INDIVIDUALS

Generally, use the latest, current edition.

	Arrangement / Includes / frequency	Scope Living/ Deceased	Nationality/ Residence	Occupation/ Field,etc.	Bibl. Pers.	Pronunci- ation	Cumulates?	Other
Who's Who	1849-	Living	English,Gr Br.,C'wealth					Directory-type data
Who's Who In America	1899/1900-	living	USA +	"notable"				IN BioBase
International Who's Who	1935-							IN BioBase Cumulated Index
Current Biography	1940- Monthly, annual.	Living	world	"notable"	x x	x	x	Articles
McGraw-Hill Encyclopedia of World Biography					x x			Articles
Dictionary of National Biography (DNB)		deceas.	British Isles & Colonies		bibs	no	Index	Authority Articles
Dictionary of American Biography (DAB)		deceased			bibs		Indexed	Articles Accuracy Authority
Contemporary Authors	1962-	living					index cumulates	revisions, sketches self-input
Webster's Biographical Dictionary	"dictionary"							

EXAMPLES OF SOME "CARRIERS" OF BIOGRAPHICAL INFORMATION IN REFERENCE LIBRARIES

American Men & Women of Science
American Women Artists...
Appleton's Cyclopedia of American Biography
Biography Almanac
Civil Rights Struggle:Leaders in Profile
Dictionary of International Biography
Directory of Blacks in Performing Arts
European Authors, 1000-1900
International Dictionary of Women's Biography

Internatl. Dictionary of Women Workers in Decorative Arts
Internatl. Dictionary of Women's Biography
National Directory of Women Elected Officials
New York Times Biographical Edition
Notable American Women...
Something About the Author
Who's Who Among Black Americans
Who's Who in American Politics
Who's Who of American Women

Author-Title Catalogs:

    For autobiographical material, look under the writer's name, i.e. the
    biographee is the author.

SUBJECT Catalogs:

    Look under the name of any person, organization, tribe, etc. You may not
    find it listed in the LCSH. For examples:

1. BROWNING, ROBERT, 1812-1889
    CHICAGO, JUDY, 1939-
    GARCIA MARQUEZ, GABRIEL
    JOSEPH, NEZ PERCE CHIEF, 1840-1904
    KING, MARTIN LUTHER, 1929-1964
    RAPHAEL, 1483-1520 PORTRAIT OF POPE JULIUS II
    ULLMANN, LIV
    WINTERS, SHELLEY
    WOLLSTONECRAFT, MARY, 1759-1797-- BIOGRAPHY-- LAST YEARS AND SUDDEN DEATH

2. AFROAMERICANS   MEXICAN AMERICANS *
    CAMBRIDGE PLATONISTS   MEXICANS IN CALIFORNIA*
    BLACK MUSLIMS   SOCIALISTS--GREAT BRITAIN--BIOGRAPHY
    CHINESE IN CALIFORNIA *   TONKAWA INDIANS
    CHOCTAW INDIANS
    FILIPINOS IN THE U.S.
    INDIANS OF NORTH AMERICA*
    INDIANS, TREATMENT OF--U.S.*
    JAPANESE IN THE U.S.*
        (* Can be subdivided geographically and chronologically)

3. ABOLITIONISTS   MEN--FRANCE--HISTORY--19th CENTURY
    ABUSED WIVES--WISCONSIN--BIOGRAPHY   MEN--PSYCHOLOGY
    ACTORS--NORWAY--BIOGRAPHY   MOTHERS
    BASEBALL PLAYERS -U.S.--BIOGRAPHY   MOVING PICTURE ACTORS AND ACTRESSES
    BUSINESSMEN--EUROPE--HISTORY   MURDER--INDIANA
    EXECUTIVES   OFFENSES AGAINST THE PERSON--U.S.
    HUSBAND AND WIFE--TAXATION--CANADA   SON OF MAN--BIBLICAL TEACHING
    LABOR AND LABORING CLASSES--U.S.   TRAVELERS, WOMEN-- BIOGRAPHY
    MAMMALS--BEHAVIOR   UNDERDEVELOPED AREAS--WOMEN'S EMPLOYMENT
    MAN--INFLUENCE ON NATURE   VICTIMS OF CRIMES--U.S.
                                          WIVES--BIOGRAPHY
                                          WOMEN

BioBase
Biography Almanac, edited by Susan L. Stetler.
Biography Index
Research Guide to Biography and Criticism, ed. by Walton Beacham.
New York Times Index
Readers' Guide

You need information about LEONARD WOOLF and about VIRGINIA STEPHEN WOOLF.
If possible, you would like to use an index which will provide citations
leading to information in several formats -- books, journal articles,
bibliographies, book reviews, illustrations, popular magazine articles,
etc -- in one step!   You pick Volume 13 of BIOGRAPHY INDEX, the September 1982-August 1984 cumulation, off the shelf, and turn to the W's. On
pages 626-7 under the two biographees' (subjects') names, you find:

WOODY, Russell, art expert 　Bios of the demonstrators. Am Artist 47:S42 N '83 WOOLDRIDGE, Rhoda, 1906- teacher and author 　Commire, Anne. Something about the author; v22. Gale 　'81 p249-50 bibl il por WOOLF, Leonard Sidney, 1880-1969. English historian 　Kenney, S. M. and Kenney, E. J. Jr. Virginia Woolf and 　the art of madness. Mass R 23:161-85 Spr '82 WOOLF, Virginia (Stephen) 1882-1941. English author 　Alley, H. M. Rediscovered eulogy: Virginia Woolf's Miss 　Janet Case: classical scholar and teacher [with text] bibl 　20th Cent Lit 28:290-301 Fall '82 　Baker, D. V. From Bloomsbury to Cornwall. il map 　Geog Mag 54:169-70 Mr '82 　Blackstone, Bernard. Virginia Woolf. (In British writers. v7. 　Scribner '84 p 17-39) bibl 　Dahl, C. C. Virginia Woolf's Moments of being and auto- 　biographical tradition in the Stephen family. il por J 　Mod Lit 10:175-96 Je '83 　DeSalvo, L. A. Lighting the cave: the relationship between 　Vita Sackville-West and Virginia Woolf. Signs 8:195-214 　Wint '82 　Fleishman, A. To return to St Ives: Woolf's autobiographi- 　cal writings. bibl ELH 48:606-18 Fall '81 　Fleishman, Avrom. Figures of autobiography. Univ. of 　Calif. Press '83 p454-70 　Hasler, J. Virginia Woolf and the chimes of Big Ben. 　Engl Stud 63:145-58 Ap '82 　Hyman, V. R. Reflections in the looking-glass: Leslie 　Stephen and Virginia Woolf. pors J Mod Lit 10:197-216 　Je '83 　Jones, M. Happy literary event! il por Redbook 　159-90+ Jl '82 　Kenney, S. M. and Kenney, E. J. Jr. Virginia Woolf and 　the art of madness. Mass R 23:161-85 Spr '82 　Kiely, R. Years of maturity. il pors N Y Times Book 　Rev p3+ Jl 11 '82 　Runyan, William McKinley. Life histories and psychobiog- 　raphy. Oxford Univ. Press '82 p04-7 bibl 　Silver, Brenda R. Virginia Woolf's reading notebooks. 　Princeton Univ. Press '83 384p bibl facsim 　Steinberg, E. R. Mrs Dalloway and T. S. Eliot's personal 　waste land. J Mod Lit 10:3-25 Mr '83	WOOLF, Virginia (Stephen)—Continued 　Stewart, J. F. Impressionism in the early novels of Virginia 　Woolf. il J Mod Lit 9:237-66 My '82 　Stone, L. Virginia Woolf. il pors Ms 11:59-60+ N '82 　Strawson, G. Interests of the patient. Times Lit Supp 　no4109:15-16 Ja 1 '82 　　　　　Bibliography 　Brown, Christopher, C. and Thesing, William B. English 　prose and criticism, 1900-1950. Gale '83 p470-87 WOOLLCOTT, Alexander (The Town Crier, pseud) 　1887-1943, journalist 　Hopkins, E. Where they lived. il por N Y 16:51-2 Mr 7 　'83 WOOLLEN, Kim, 1958?- dancer and wife of Glen 　Campbell 　Lague, L. Couples. il pors People Wkly 19:63-4+ Ja 31 　'83 WOOLLETT, Ralph, 1917?-1984, physicist 　Obituary 　　N Y Times p B-12 Mr 15 '84 WOOLLEY, Hannah, fl 1670, English governess and 　author 　Smith, Hilda L. Reason's disciples. Univ. of Ill. Press '82 　p 105-9 bibl WOOLLEY, Knight, 1895-1984, banker 　Obituary 　　N Y Times por p19 Ja 21 '84 　　N Y Times Biog Service por 15:156 Ja '84 WOOLLEY, Monty, 1888-1963, actor 　Biography 　　NCAB 62:271-2 '84 WOOLLEY, Paul, 1902?-1984, clergyman and professor of 　church history 　Obituary 　　N Y Times p32 Ap 7 '84 WOOLSON, Constance Fenimore, 1840-1894, author 　Boren, Lynda S. Constance Fenimore Woolson. (In Dictio- 　nary of literary biography, v 12. Gale '82 p456-63) bibl 　il por facsims autog

The articles by D. V. Baker, A. Fleishman, and J. Hasler about Virginia
Stephen Woolf are of particular interest to you, so you turn to page ix
of the same BIOGRAPHY INDEX and look at the KEY TO PERIODICAL ABBREVIA-
TIONS under the abbreviations for the periodicals: Geog Mag, ELH, and
Engl Stud, for their full titles. (Turn to page 2)

The book by Avrom Fleishman, Figures of Autobiography, has a portion
(pages 454-470) about Virginia Woolf, so you turn to page xvi and look
at the CHECKLIST OF COMPOSITE BOOKS ANALYZED for full information about
this book. (Turn to page 2)

And you could proceed like this for all nineteen of the publications
listed about Virginia Woolf, and the one listed for Leonard Woolf.

EDN—EDN
ELH—ELH: a Journal of English Literary History
EPA Journal—E P A Journal
E Eur Q—East European Quarterly
Early Am Lit—Early American Literature
Early Yrs—Early Years
Ebony—Ebony
Econ Bot—Economic Botany
Econ Devel Cult Change—Economic Development and Cultural Change
Econ Geol—Economic Geology and the Bulletin of the Society of Economic Geologists
Econ Hist R—Economic History Review
Economist—Economist
Ed Publ Fourth Estate—Editor & Publisher. The Fourth Estate
Educ & Train Men Retard—Education and Training of the Mentally Retarded
Educ Dig—Education Digest
Educ Forum—Educational Forum
Educ Lead—Educational Leadership
Educ Stud—Educational Studies
Educ Tech—Educational Technology
Educ Theory—Educational Theory
18th Cent Stud—Eighteenth-Century Studies
Ekistics—Ekistics
Electr Perspect—Electric Perspectives
Electron & Power—Electronics & Power
Electron Bus—Electronic Business
Electron News—Electronic News
Electronics—Electronics
Encounter—Encounter
Eng J (Can)—Engineering Journal (Montreal, Quebec)
Eng Min J—Engineering and Mining Journal
Eng News-Rec—Engineering News-Record
Engineer—Engineer
Engl Hist R—English Historical Review
Engl J—English Journal
Engl Lang Notes—English Language Notes
Engl Lang Teach J—English Language Teaching Journal
Engl Lit in Trans—English Literature in Transition
Engl Stud—English Studies
Environ Ethics—Environmental Ethics
Esquire—Esquire
Essays Crit—Essays in Criticism
Essence—Essence
Ethnic & Racial Stud—Ethnic and Racial Studies

Ga R—Georgia Review
Garden (Engl)—The Garden (London, England)
Garden (U S)—Garden (Bronx, N.Y.)
Gaz Beaux Arts—Gazette des Beaux-Arts
Genetics—Genetics
Geog J—Geographical Journal
Geog Mag—Geographical Magazine
Geog R—Geographical Review
Geol Soc Am Bull—Geological Society of America. Bulletin
German Q—German Quarterly
Gesta—Gesta
Gifted Child Q—Gifted Child Quarterly
Glamour—Glamour
           Incorporating: Charm
Glass Ind—Glass Industry
Glean Bee Cult—Gleanings in Bee Culture
Good Housekeep—Good Housekeeping
Gourmet—Gourmet
Govt & Oppos—Government and Opposition
Goya—Goya
Graph Arts Mon Print Ind—Graphic Arts Monthly and the Printing Industry
Graphic Des—Graphic Design
Graphis—Graphis
Greek Rom & Byz Stud—Greek, Roman and Byzantine Studies

H Sch J—High School Journal
Handl Shipp Manage—Handling & Shipping Management
Harpers—Harper's
Harpers Bazaar—Harper's Bazaar
Harv J Asiatic Stud—Harvard Journal of Asiatic Studies
Harv Theol R—Harvard Theological Review
Harvard Bus R—Harvard Business Review
Hastings Center Rept—Hastings Center Report
Health—Health (New York, N.Y.)
Health Care Manage Rev—Health Care Management Review
Healthcare Financ Manage—Healthcare Financial Management
High Fidel—High Fidelity (Musical America edition)
Hispan Am Hist R—Hispanic American Historical Review
Hispan R—Hispanic Review
Hispania—Hispania
Hist & Theory—History & Theory
Hist Educ Q—History of Education Que...
Hist J—Historical Journal
Hist Photo—History of Ph...

CHECKLIST OF COMPOSITE BOOKS ANALYZED

xvi

...tems; with a new
...of N.Mex. Press '82 338p

...to ballet. Guinness Superlatives Ltd. '81
...pors facsims
..., John Owen
Iron of melancholy: structures of spiritual conversion in America from the Puritan conscience to Victorian neurosis. Wesleyan Univ. Press '83 457p bibl
KING, Norman
• Money messiahs. Coward-McCann '83 221p
KLAMER, Arjo
• Conversations with economists: new classical economists and opponents speak out on the current controversy in macroeconomics. Rowman & Allanheld '84 265p bibl
KUFRIN, Joan
• Uncommon women. New Century Pubs. '81 173p il pors
• LAS VEGAS celebrity cookbook; v 1: the private recipes of 50 international entertainers; presented by Hollybrooke House; ed. by Jo Smith. Creel Printing '83 206p il pors autog
LECLAIR, Tom, and McCaffery, Larry
• Anything can happen: interviews with contemporary American novelists. Univ. of Ill. Press '83 305p pors
LEHMANN, John
• Three literary friendships: Byron & Shelley, Rimbaud & Verlaine, Robert Frost & Edward Thomas. Holt, Rinehart & Winston '84 184p bibl

...[interviews]
...es; popular writers
...ors
... Middle Ages and the Renais-
... H. Jackson and George Stade. v 1
...oner '83 2v bibl
...Doris
Love & rivalry: three exceptional pairs of sisters. Viking Press '83 200p bibl il pors
FLEISHMAN, Avrom
Figures of autobiography: the language of self-writing in Victorian and modern England. Univ. of Calif. Press '83 486p
• FOUR modern masters: De Chirico, Ernst, Magritte, and Miro. Glenbow Museum/Museum of Modern Art '83 123p bibl il
FROM Hester Street to Hollywood: the Jewish-American stage and screen; ed. by Sarah Blacher Cohen. Indiana Univ. Press '83 278p bibl

BIOGRAPHY INDEX is also useful in another way. It leads to publications and information about people in various professions, occupations, walks of life, activities, etc. For example, if a list of ASSASSINS AND MURDERERS would be useful in your work, you would be able to generate a lengthy list by turning to page 648 of the INDEX TO PROFESSIONS AND OCCUPATIONS (still using BIOGRAPHY INDEX Sept. 1982-August 1984 cumulation, Volume 13). And further more, you could also find the dates of birth and death and references to publications about each, back in the main part of the volume.

If you wanted names of ASTRONAUTS, you would find a lengthy list on page 648. One of these is Sally Ride. On page 482 of the main part of the volume, is information about her and numerous citations to periodical articles, poetry, an interview, a government publication, and a <u>Current Biography</u> <u>article about her.</u>

648 INDEX TO PROFESSIONS AND OCCUPATIONS	
ASBESTOS industry Manville, Hiram Edward ASSASSINS and murderers Adkins, Wayne Agca, Mehmet Ali Autry, J. D. Báthory, Elizabeth Booth, John Wilkes Bown, Gary Bremer, Arthur Herman Breslin, Joseph Franklin Brooks, Charles Bundy, Theodore Robert Byck, Samuel Joseph Chapman, Mark David Collazo, Oscar Crowley, Francis Czolgosz, Leon F. Dracula, Prince of Hungary Everson, Paul Fain, William Archie Frank, Theodore Fromme, Lynette Alice Gacy, John Wayne Gilmore, Gary Mark Groseclose, Bill Guiteau, Charles Julius Gunness, Belle Harris, Jean Witte Struven Hartman, Lawrence Hauptmann, Bruno Richard Hellier, Thomas Herrin, Richard James Houston, Richard Irvin, Leslie Jahnke, Richard C. Kennedy, Shane King, Geoffrey Leonski, Edward Joseph Linscott, Steven McCray, James MacDonald, Jeffrey R. Miller, Jim Moore, Sara Jane Oswald, Lee Harvey Peltier, Leonard Princip, Gavrilo Quartararo, Michael Quartararo, Peter Rais, Gilles de Laval, Seigneur de Ray, James Earl Schrank, John Nepomuk Sirhan, Sirhan Bishara Sullivan, Robert Austin Sweeney, John Thomas Torresola, Griselio Watts, Coral Eugene Weiss, Carl Austin White, Daniel James Williams, Wayne B.	Yanikian, Gourgen Migirdic Zangara, Giuseppe ASSYRIOLOGISTS Smith, George ASTROBIOLOGISTS Sagan, Carl ASTROLOGERS Jillson, Joyce Notredame, Michel de ASTRONAUTS Allen, Joseph P. Armstrong, Neil Alden Bluford, Guion S. Bolden, Charles F. Borman, Frank Brand, Vance DeVoe Brandenstein, Daniel Charles Carpenter, Malcolm Scott Chretien, Jean-Loup Cooper, Leroy Gordon Crippen, Robert L. Dwight, Edward Joseph Engle, Joe Henry Fabian, John M. Fullerton, Charles Gordon Gardner, Dale A. Garnott, Owen Glenn, John Herschel Gregory, Frederick D. Grissom, Virgil Ivan Hartsfield, Henry W. Hauck, Frederick H. Lawrence, Robert Henry Lenoir, William B. Lichtenberg, Byron Lousma, Jack R. McNair, Ronald Erwin Mattingly, Thomas Kenneth Merbold, Ulf Overmyer, Robert F. Parker, Robert Allan Ridley Ride, Sally Savitskaya, Svetlana Schirra, Walter Marty Schmitt, Harrison Hagan Schweickart, Russell L. Shaw, Brewster Shepard, Alan Bartlett Slayton, Donald Kent Swigert, John L. Thagard, Norman Thornton, William E. Truly, Richard Harrison Young, John Watts ASTRONOMERS See also Astrobiologists Astrophysicists Abell, George O. Abetti, Giorgio

482 BIOGRAPHY INDEX

RIDDLEBERGER, James W. 1904-1982, diplomat
Obituary
  Chicago Tribune p 13 O 20 '82
  Cur Biog 44:48 Ja '83
  Cur Biog Yrbk 1983:472 '84
RIDE, Sally, 1951- astronaut
Adler, J. and Abramson, P. Sally Ride: ready for liftoff. il pors Newsweek 101:36-8+ Je 13 '83
Begley, S. and others. Challenger: ride. Sally Ride. il por Newsweek 101:20-1 Je 27 '83
Biography
  Cur Biog bibl por 44:27-9 O '83
  Cur Biog Yrbk 1983:318-21 '84 bibl por
Broad, W. Cool, versatile astronaut. il por N Y Times Biog Service 14:729-30 Je '83
Bruning, F. Ticket to a boring Sally Ride. Macleans 96:9 Jl 25 '83
Golden, F. Sally's joy ride into the sky. il pors Time 121:56-8 Je 13 '83
Hill, C. Hero for our time. Vogue 174:86+ Ja '84
Lowther, W. High ride through the sex barrier. il pors Macleans 96:40-1 Je 27 '83
Peterson, S. Breaking through: women on the move. por U S News World Rep 93:50-1 N 29 '82
Raiston, J. Sally Ride breaks the space barrier. por McCalls 110:60-1 My '83
Ryan, M. Ride in space. il pors People Wkly 19:82-4+ Je 20 '83
Sanborn, S. Sally Ride, astronaut: the world is watching. il pors Ms 11:45-8+ Ja '83
Steinem, G. Sally Ride on the future in space [interview] por Ms 12:86 Ja '84
Uhrbrock, M. Sally Ride, first woman astronaut, blasts off. por Seventeen 42:101 Ap '83
U.S. Congress. House. Committee on Science and Technology. Hearing before the Committee. . .U.S. House of Representatives, 98th Congress, 1st session, on Flight of STS-7 with Dr Sally K. Ride [and others] July 19, 1983. U.S. G.P.O. '83 22p
Poetry
Knox, H. Sally's ride. il por Space World T-10-238:2 O '83
RIDER-RIDER, William Frederick, 1914?-1982, English photojournalist
Obituary
  N Y Times p A-10 Ag 27 '82
RIDGE, Antonia Florence, d 1981, English author and dramatist
Commire, Anne. Something about the author; v27. Gale '82 p 170 bibl
RIDGE, Julie, 1956- actress and swimmer
Levin, D. Big designs on the Big Apple. pors Sports Illus 59:36-8+ Jl 11 '83
Vecsey, G. Pain caused by terra firma. por N Y Times Biog Service 14:985 Ag '83
RIDGE, Major, 1771?-1839, Cherokee chief
Strickland, W. M. Rhetoric of removal and the Trail of tears: Cherokee speaking against Jackson's Indian removal policy, 1828-1832. South Speech Comm J 47:292-309 Spr '82

Interested in locating names and information about people who are FARMERS, FASHION DESIGNERS, FATHERS OF PROMINENT WOMEN, or FEMINISTS? The INDEX TO PROFESSIONS AND OCCUPATIONS, page 702, lists the names of such persons. Full information and publications about farmer Charles Savage, fashion designer Arnold Scassi, father of prominent woman Irby Mandrell, and feminist Louise Bryant appear on pages 508, 373, and 78. (See page 5.)

---

702   INDEX TO PROFESSIONS AND OCCUPATIONS

EXPLOSIVES industry
Du Pont, Irénée
Gottshall, Ralph Kerr
EXPORTERS and importers
Boles, Jack
Chew, Ralph H.
Dobkin, Eleonora
Elliot, Inger McCabe
Keitlen, Phyllis
Rose, Sherman E.
Segerman, Herbert H.
Smith, Clare

F

FBI agents
See also
Intelligence service
Davis, Wayne
Gibson, Johnnie M. M.
Glover, John D.
Hoover, John Edgar
Mehegan, Albert D.
Sullivan, Daniel P.
Webster, William H.
Yablonsky, Joseph
FACTORY workers
See also
Automobile workers
FAITH healers
Edwards, Harry
Greatrakes, Valentine
Milingo, Emmanuel
Roberts, Oral
Roberts, Richard
Stapleton, Ruth (Carter)
FARM leaders
Chavez, Librado Hernandez
Williams, Aubrey Willis
FARM machinery industry. See Agricultural machinery industry
FARMERS
See also
Cattle ranchers
Planters
Albosta, Don
Bickel, John Clarence James
Buckli, Mayo Greenleaf
Gublin, John
Rodale, Jerome Irving
Savage, Charles
Scott, Mac
Singer, John
Smart, John Henry
Stovin, Cornelius
Utsunomiya, Haruko
Waring, P. Alston
Wong, Lee Kim Lee
FASHION agents. See Model and fashion agents
FASHION critics
Bacharach, Bert
FASHION designers
Aldredge, Theoni (Vachliotis)
Armani, Giorgio
Azzedine
Balmain, Pierre
Beene, Geoffrey
Bernstein, Aline (Frankau)
Biagiotti, Laura
Bijan, Pakzad
Bohan, Marc
Bundick, Tessie
Cardin, Pierre

Cassini, Oleg Loiewski
Chanel, Gabrielle
Copeland, Jo
De La Renta, Oscar
Delaunay-Terk, Sonia
Echevarria, Pilar Crespi
Eiseman, Florence
Erté
Exter, Aleksandra Aleksandrovna
Fabrice
Fletcher, Robert
Freis, Diane
Fürstenberg, Diana (Halfin)
Galitzine, Irene
Girbaud, François
Girbaud, Marithé
Givenchy, Hubert de
Grès, Alix
Guild, Tricia
Halston
Head, Edith
Herrera, Carolina
James, Charles
Jeffries, Wes
Kamali, Norma
Karinska, Barbara
Kawakubo, Rei
Klein, Calvin Richard
Kostrukoff, Pola
Lagerfeld, Karl
Lanvin, Bernard
Lanvin, Maryll
Lauren, Ralph
Lechmere, Kate
Leigh, Kristian
Leslie, Diana
Little, Carole
Long, William I.
Lubove-Klein, ...
McFadden, ...
Mc..., Bernard
Laurent, Yves Mathieu
Scassi, Arnold
Seven Seven, Nike Olanyi
Smith, Willi
Spadea, Jean Miller
Sprouse, Stephen
Tilley, Monika
Von Mayrhauser, Jennifer
Weiss, Darran
Wolsky, Albert
Worth, Charles Frederick
Yamamoto, Yohji
FATHERS of prominent men
Chavez, Librado Hernandez
Giamatti, Valentine
Guys, François Lazare
Mancini, Lenny
Rampal, Joseph
Steinbrenner, Henry George
Stevens, Garrett Barcalow
Wain, Arnold
FATHERS of prominent women
Mandrell, Irby
Martin, Louis Joseph Aloys Stanislaus
Robbins, Kenneth
FATS and oils industry. See Oils and fats industry
FAVORITES, Royal
Chaceporc, Peter
Maintenon, Françoise d'Aubigné
Montex, Lola
Schratt, Katharina
Shore, Jane
Vetsera, Marie Alexandrine, Baronesse

FELT industry
Dolge, Alfred
FEMINISTS
Abzug, Bella (Savitsky)
Anthony, Susan Brownell
Astell, Mary
Beauvoir, Simone de
Betcherman, Barbara
Bird, Caroline
Blackwell, Elizabeth
Brown, Helen (Gurley)
Brown, Rita Mae
Brownmiller, Susan
Bryant, Louise
Duniway, Abigail Jane (Scott)
Egerton, Sarah
Flexner, Helen (Thomas)
Foat, Ginny
Friedan, Betty
Godwin, Mary (Wollstonecraft)
Goldsmith, Judith Becker
Grahn, Judy
Grand, Sarah
Greer, Germaine
Griffin, Susan
Grimké, Angelina E.
Grimké, Sarah (Lucas)
Hallinan, H.
Height, ...
He..., Margaret (Fuller) Marcy
Julia (Garnett)
..rcy, Marge
Reuss, Pat
Richards, Ann
Robinson, Harriet Jane (Hanson)
Rokeya, Begum
Sagan, Miriam
Schwimmer, Rosika
Seton, Cynthia (Propper)
Shouse, Catherine Filene
Smeal, Eleanor Marie Cutri
Stanton, Elizabeth (Cady)
Steinem, Gloria
Stone, Lucy
Terrell, Mary Eliza (Church)
Unksova, Kari
Waite, Catharine (Van Valkenburg)
Weiss, Louise
Whitton, Charlotte Elizabeth
Willard, Frances Elizabeth
Wilson, Elizabeth
Wilson, Kathy
FENCERS
Kogler, Aladar
Monates, Stacey
Saint-Georges, Chevalier de
Santelli, Giorgio
Westbrook, Peter
FENCING coaches
Kogler, Aladar
Santelli, Giorgio
Sieja, Stanley S.
FIELD marshals, British
Alanbrooke, Alan Francis Brooke, 1st Viscount
Montgomery of Alamein, Bernard Law Montgomery, 1st Viscount
Wavell, Archibald Percival Wavell, 1st Earl
FIELD marshals, Chinese
Chu, Teh
FIELD marshals, French
Foch, Ferdinand
Rais, Gilles de Laval, Seigneur de
FIELD marshals, German
Rommel, Erwin

BRYANT, Kelvin.   football player
   McDermott. B.   Man who makes the Stars shine. pors
      Sports Illus 58:26-7 Ap 25 '83
   Moran. M.   Bryant forgets the what if's. il pors N Y
      Times Biog Service 13:970-1 Ag '82
BRYANT, Louise, 1887-1936. feminist and journalist
   Gardner. Virginia.   Friend and lover: the life of Louise Bry-
      ant. Horizon Press '82 390p bibl il pors
   Schneir. M.   Meet the real Louise Bryant. pors Ms
      10:43+ Ap '82
BRYANT, Paul William (Bear Bryant) 1913-1983. football
      coach
   Callahan. T.   Not your average Bear. il por Time 120:80
      D 27 '82
   Ford. Tommy.   Bama under Bear: Alabama's family tides.
      rev ed. Strode '83 288p il
   Master of success. il N Y Times Biog Service 13:1569-70
      D '82
   Obituary
         Cur Biog 44:43 Mr '83
         Cur Biog Yrbk 1983:461 '84
         Macleans 96:4 F 7 '83
         N Y Times il pors p D-25 Ja 27 '83
         N Y Times Biog Service il pors 14:9-11 Ja '83
         Natl Rev 35:165 F 18 '83
         New Yorker 58:35-6 F 14 '83
         Sports Illus il 58:11 F 7 '83
         Time por 121:87 F 7; 122:48 D 26 '83
   Peterson. James A. and Cromartie. Bill. Bear Bryant:
      countdown to glory: a game-by-game history of Bear Bry-
      ant's 323 career victories: rev ed. Leisure Press '83 431p
      il pors facsims autog

MANDRELL, Barbara, 1948- singer
   Anderson. N. A visit with Barbara Mandrell. il pors
      Good Housekeep 194:108+ My '82
   Biography
         Cur Biog bibl por 43:33-6 Ag '82
         Cur Biog Yrbk 1982:263-7 '83 bibl por
   Hildreth. J. and others.   When a dad's dream finally comes
      true. il por U S News World Rep 94:36 Je 20 '83
   Las Vegas celebrity cookbook. Creel Printing '83 p 119-22
      il por
   Mandrell. Louise. and Collins. Ace.   Mandrell family album.
      Nelson '83 192p il pors
MANDRELL, Irby, 1926?- father of Barbara Mandrell
   Hildreth. J. and others.   When a dad's dream finally comes
      true. il por U S News World Rep 94:36 Je 20 '83
MANDRELL, Irlene, 1955?- singer
   Mandrell. Louise. and Collins. Ace.   Mandrell family album.
      Nelson '83 192p il pors

SAUVÉ, Jeanne, 1922- Canadian government official
   Kaufman. M. T. Canada's next Governor General. por
      N Y Times Biog Service 14:1485 D '83
SAVAGE, Charles, 1917?- farmer
   Means. H. Last farm. il por Blair Ketchums Ctry J
      9:44-9 N '82
SAVAGE, Peter, 1934?-1982. editor
   Obituary
         PS 15:672-3 Fall '82

SBARRO, Franco, 1937?- Italian automobile executive
   O'Rourke. P. J. Sweet dreams with Franco Sbarro. il
      pors Car Driv 28:62-5+ Ap '83
SCAASI, Arnold, 1930?- fashion designer
                  Pictorial works
   Collectors: ed. by Paige Rense (Worlds of Architectural
      Digest) Knapp Press '82 p 12-17 il
SCALIGER, Joseph Juste, 1540-1609. Italian philologist
                     Bibliography
   Grafton. Anthony. Joseph Scaliger. a bibliography,
      1852-1982: comp. by A. T. Grafton and H. J. de Jonge.
      Cristal-Montana Press '82 27p

In addition to knowing about people's lives, the researcher uses library
biographical works for such things as "by-and-about" bibliographies,
portraits, pronunciation, addresses, dates, etc. Biographical reference
works tend to be either

   (1) who's-who-type directories, e.g. Who's Who In America, pro-
       viding such data as addresses, date of birth, etc., with
       no discussion or analysis, or
   (2) compilations of articles, e.g. Current Biography, Dictionary
       of American Biography, discussing individuals. The need for
       authority is important with such a tool. The person writing
       should be identified, and s/he should identify sources used.
   (3) There is always need for indexes to locate publications... in
       this case about people. These biographees are the subjects.

Biographical reference tools are usually considered in terms of their SCOPE...

   By the period of time in which people written about lived, whether
       they're deceased or living; for example, all of the biographees
       described in Current Biography are living (or were at the time
       the volume was written.)
   By the geographical area involved; for example, Who's Who In
       America.
   By occupation or other specialization which all of the biographees
       have in common; for example, Directory of Blacks in Performing
       Arts.

The following examples of basics in biographical research are in the Reference Departments of most libraries, accessible to the public:
                                      Location
CURRENT BIOGRAPHY, 1940-   .   _____

DICTIONARY OF AMERICAN BIOGRAPHY _____
   ("DAB")
DICTIONARY OF NATIONAL BIOGRAPHY _____
   ("DNB")
BIOGRAPHY INDEX, 1946-   .   _____

BioBASE   _____

CURRENT BIOGRAPHY and DICTIONARY OF AMERICAN BIOGRAPHY have cumulated in-
dex volumes. DAB's indexes volumes 1-20 and Supplements 1-7. CURRENT
BIOGRAPHY's indexes 1940-1985. DNB has a "Corrections & Additions" volume.
(See diagram of organization of these types of sets.)

Check the BioBASE fiche file for "your" biographee at the beginning of a
literature search. If s/he's listed there, consult the BioBASE-related
list of indexed-works by their codes, which will lead you to call numbers
in our reference department's collection.

A typical pattern of organization for standard, ongoing biographical sets
updates all indexing in the latest volume. The next page illustrates this
with two examples. It is important that you understand and apply these
principles to all such tools in order to cut down on multiple searching
steps and to get maximum information.

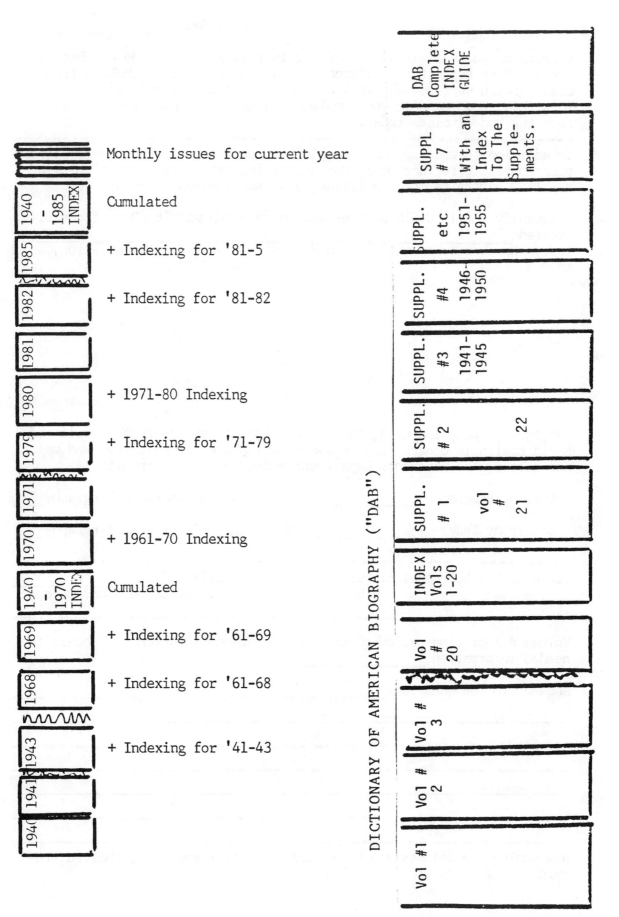

CURRENT BIOGRAPHY, 1940-

Monthly issues for current year

Cumulated

+ Indexing for '81-5

+ Indexing for '81-82

+ 1971-80 Indexing

+ Indexing for '71-79

+ 1961-70 Indexing

Cumulated

+ Indexing for '61-69

+ Indexing for '61-68

+ Indexing for '41-43

DICTIONARY OF AMERICAN BIOGRAPHY ("DAB")

Your Name_____

Everything you need is on this floor in this room. You do not need to
use anything kept at the Reference Desk. Consult your handouts from
class if you want to, but work as rapidly and efficiently as possible.
Turn this in as soon as you complete it, no later than five minutes before the end of class today.

In addition to knowing about people's lives, the researcher uses library
biographical reference tools for such things as "by-and-about" bibliographies, portraits, pronunciation, addresses, dates of events, etc.

Frequently you'll BEGIN people-related research with BioBase fiche file,
located _____.
Today, however, skip that step and go directly on to your question, which
is

Get this information using the appropriate one of the four examples of
basic basics in biographical research which are listed below, and which
are here in the Reference Department accessible to the public :

  Current Biography _____   Dictionary of American Biography____

  Biography Index _____   Dictionary of National Biography____

Title of the biographical reference work you select "_____
_____." Why did you select it of these four? Because
it _____

Volume # &/or time-period covered by the volume in which you locate the
needed information _____ _____

Answer to the question:_____

_____

_____

_____

_____

_____

_____

Now shelve the volumes you have used where they should be shelved, regardless of where you found them.

Your Name_____

Everything you need is on this floor in this room. You do not need to
use anything kept at the Reference Desk. Consult your handouts from
class if you want to, but work as rapidly and efficiently as possible.
Turn this in as soon as you complete it, no later than five minutes before the end of class today.

In addition to knowing about people's lives, the researcher uses library
biographical reference tools for such things as "by-and-about" bibliographies, portraits, pronunciation, addresses, dates of events, etc.

Frequently you'll BEGIN people-related research with <u>BioBase</u> fiche file,
located _____.
Today, however, skip that step and go directly on to your question, which
is about the contemporary controversial psychologist associated with
the subject of death and dying, Elizabeth Kubler Ross. She has identified stages that terminally-ill patients pass through in reacting to
the knowledge of their own death. How many stages? Can you locate a quick
summary-list of them too? And what is the full title of her 1975 book
about her ideas? Is she a psychiatrist or a psychologist according to your
source? Is her name Kubler or Ross or Kubler Ross or Kubler-Ross or what?
Where does she live? What types of sources (reference tools) does your
source use in gathering this information-- newspapers, other types of
periodicals, reference books, "reading books"?

Get this information using the appropriate one of the four examples of
basic basics in biographical research which are listed below, and which
are here in the Reference Department accessible to the public :

  Current Biography _____   Dictionary of American Biography____

  Biography Index _____   Dictionary of National Biography____

Title of the biographical reference work you select "_____
_____." Why did you select it of these four? Because
it _____

Volume # &/or time-period covered by the volume in which you locate the
needed information _____ _____

Answer to the question:_____
_____
_____
_____
_____
_____
_____

Now shelve the volumes you have used where they should be shelved, regardless of where you found them.

Your Name _____

Everything you need is on this floor in this room. You do not need to
use anything kept at the Reference Desk. Consult your handouts from
class if you want to, but work as rapidly and efficiently as possible.
Turn this in as soon as you complete it, no later than five minutes before the end of class today.

In addition to knowing about people's lives, the researcher uses library
biographical reference tools for such things as "by-and-about" bibliographies, portraits, pronunciation, addresses, dates of events, etc.

Frequently you'll BEGIN people-related research with <u>BioBase</u> fiche file,
located _____ .
Today, however, skip that step and go directly on to your question, which
is about the contemporary controversial psychologist associated with
the subject of death and dying, Elizabeth Kubler Ross. She has identified stages that terminally-ill patients pass through in reacting to
the knowledge of their own death. How many stages? Can you locate a quick
summary-list of them too? And what is the full title of her 1975 book
about her ideas? Is she a psychiatrist or a psychologist according to your
source? Is her name Kubler or Ross or Kubler Ross or Kubler-Ross or what?
Where does she live? What types of sources (reference tools) does your
source use in gathering this information-- newspapers, other types of
periodicals, reference books, "reading books"?

Get this information using the appropriate one of the four examples of
basic basics in biographical research which are listed below, and which
are here in the Reference Department accessible to the public :

  Current Biography _____   Dictionary of American Biography_____

  Biography Index _____   Dictionary of National Biography_____

Title of the biographical reference work you select " CURRENT BIOGRAPHY
_____ ." Why did you select it of these four? Because
it ___is the only one of the 4 reference books whose scope includes "contemporary" (living) people, and includes references (sources).
Volume # &/or time-period covered by the volume in which you locate the
needed information _1980_ _____

Answer to the question: 5 stages / yes, on page 193 / "Death: The Final
Stage of Growth" / "psychiatrist" in the article (pp. 191-4); "psychologist" in the subject index (p. 474)/ Kubler-Ross / Escondido, Calif. /
The writer of the article lists periodicals, newspaper, Contemporary Authors
(reference book), and 2 other books as sources, on page 194, at the end
of the article.

Now shelve the volumes you have used where they should be shelved, regardless of where you found them.

CITATION INDEXES

The five-page handout can be distributed at the previous meeting and the class asked to read it over before the next meeting in the classroom. The course-program administrator may be able to obtain for ongoing use a set of 15-30 copies of the same issue of the same citation index from superseded supplements. Social Sciences Citation Index provides the most productive learning experience in this situation. Contact the Institute for Scientific Information regional representative. (See Section III: Resources--Audiovisuals). A master schedule posted in the program office for sign-up use by each instructor will ensure efficient use and preservation of the set. At the previous class ask for two or three volunteers who do not have a class which meets before "ours" to stop by the office to pick them up and take them to "our classroom."

Before the class begins, sketch on the board the "spines" of several cumulations, so that the similarities and contrasts with Readers' Guide, for example, come across: chronological and cumulative, but within each time period of a citation index the several "functions." Focus on three: source, citing, permuted index.

Develop a worksheet which can be used in class to demonstrate the Permuterm Subject Index and the Citation Index. In the following sample, productive keyword combinations in question 1 include:

NEW-DEAN + AMERICAN   ANGLO-AMERICAN + POLITICS

RACE-RELATED + DIFFERENCES   TAX REFORM + PROPOSALS

RACE-RELATIONS + HISTORY   TAX SHELTERS + PARTNERSHI

TEACHER-EDUCATION + CHANGE   ENERGY CRISIS + WORLD

TEEN AGE + BEHAVIOR   TEENAGE + BEHAVIOR

MARKETING RESEARCH + ADVERTISING.

1. Use the volume which has the PERMUTERM SUBJECT INDEX in it to locate
   a publication about

   Then consult the SOURCE INDEX to obtain full information about
   that publication.

SPACE FOR YOUR WORK:
PERMUTERM SUBJECT INDEX column number in which you find the initial clue
   to this publciation:_____. Under what key word (It's in all
   caps)?_____. It's combined with what other
   key word (It's in smaller caps, indented underneath)?_____
   _____. This combination is tied to what
   author (Surname + Initials)?_____
SOURCE INDEX column number in which you find the display providing full
   information for the publication you've just discovered by taking a
   keyword-subject approach._____. Author of the article

   _____. If there are
   joint authors, list her/his name(s) here: _____

   _____

   _____
   Title of the article "_____

   _____
   _____."
   Abbreviation of the title of the journal in which the article was
   published._____ Volume number of the journal._____
   Pagination of the article:_____ Year of publication:_____
   How many references (R's), if any, are provided by this article's
   bibliography?_____ Who is the author of the first publication by a
   person in that bibliography?_____

2. Use the CITATION INDEX to locate a reference to a publication by____
   _____ published in_____

   _____.

SPACE FOR YOUR WORK:
Column number in the CITATION INDEX portion where you locate the above
   reference under the author's surname, which is in ALL CAPS to the
   left, with her/his publications indented underneath:_____
Now locate, underneath the author's name, the reference to the publication DATE and to the publication itself, both on one line. Underneath that line will be information about the writer(s) who have
   cited this publication (who have referred to it in their writing)
   since it was published. The name of the first citing author is
   _____. The abbreviation for
   the citing-journal's title is_____. The volume
   number of the journal is_____. The year in which the citing
   article was published in that journal was _____. The
   number of the first page of the article is_____.

Citation indexes are another "keyword" tool available in the library for
searching by hand as well as online for computer-assisted literature
searching.

> The KEYWORD CONCEPT is very important for all types of research
> and library work. Keywords are not the same as subject-headings.
> Some library catalogs now have keyword indexes, which is not the
> same thing as the Subject Catalog. The titles of books are alpha-
> betically arranged by all of the key words contained in their ti-
> tles. In other words, a book titled Sign Language for the Deaf
> would be listed three times: under DEAF, under LANGUAGE, and under
> SIGN, and in that alphabetical order, in the D's, L's and S's.

> Computer-assisted literature searching of online data bases relies
> on both subject headings (called descriptors) and keywords.

Two slide-tape kits are available in the library for individual use:

> "Introduction to the SCIENCE CITATION INDEX"
> "Introduction to the SOCIAL SCIENCES CITATION INDEX"

There are three citation indexes:

Library Location

> THE SCIENCE CITATION INDEX, 1955-
> THE SOCIAL SCIENCES CITATION INDEX, 1966-
> THE ARTS & HUMANITIES CITATION INDEX, 1976-

How do you decide whether to use a "straight" periodical index such as
The Social Sciences Index or The Art Index, etc., instead of a citation
index such as The Social Sciences Citation Index or The Arts & Humanities
Citation Index?
> Since citation indexes are a relatively new concept, you would
  have to use Art Index, for example, for coverage of the 1930's.
> Use conventional periodical indexes to locate articles on a
  topic, especially if you've established a great subject-heading,
  within a specific period of time.
> Use citation indexes to find articles directly related to another
  article which you've already discovered and read and found very
  useful.
> Use citation indexes when you want to know all of the articles
  which were published after "your" one great article was published
  and which rely on "your" author's article, discovery, etc. (Or
  perhaps disagree with, or quote her/him.)
> Use citation indexes generally when you want a large harvest of
  citations of articles-- emphasis on quantity.
> Sometimes citation indexes must be used because, although you
  are aware of the existence of a specific article, you are unable
  to locate it using conventional periodical indexes mainly because you're unable to verbalize the subject-heading(s). Citation indexes rely on KEY WORDS, which are automatic.

In class you'll receive a brochure related to one of the three citation indexes, depending on your Project interest --social sciences, arts and humanities, or science-- as well as a sample search process related to it. Keep in mind that you may sometimes need to use two --for example, if you were concerned with the effects of some science or technological development on the lives of people, you might consider using both Science Citation Index and one of the other two. If you were researching something historical, you might need both the Arts & Humanities Citation Index and the Social Sciences Index.

A citation index is based on the concept that authors' references (or citations) to previously-published material indicate subject-relationships between their current articles and older publications. In addition to subject-relationships with the earlier publications, articles that refer to (or cite) the same publications usually have subject-relationships with each other. Cited and citing articles have a potentially useful relationship involving your starting with the citation index (portion) and then referring to the source index (portion) of whichever citation index you're using.

Each of the three citation indexes cumulates and is divided into alphabetically-arranged volumes (and parts of volumes.) Each of these is, in turn, called and serves as:

    a citation index
    a source index
    a permuted subject index (A permuted index is one in which words
            are rearranged)
Be sure to check inside front and back covers of the volume you're using for "HOW TO".

THE SCIENCE CITATION INDEX, 1955-64, 1965-69, 1970-74, 1975-79, 1980-

    Most scientific articles carry citations to pertinent articles previously published. The SCI through its computerized indexing of the citations in thousands of journals has become an important research tool in science and technology. Disciplines represented include:

    clinical medicine   technology & applied sciences
    physical sciences   engineering
    chemistry   environmental sciences
    life sciences   earth sciences
    agriculture

The behavioral sciences are more fully treated in The Social Sciences Citation Index. By checking the author of a cited item in the citation index portion of SCI, additional articles which cite any publications by this author in the period covered by the Index may be identified. These citing items may report the latest developments in a particular field, corroborate or refute earlier studies, identify scientists investigating similar phenomena, etc. Or the citing author may in turn be traced in the citation index portion for another gathering of related references. Full bibliographic information for the citing items is provided in the source index portion. Other indexes include the Permuterm Subject Index section, which consists of alphabetically-arranged paired keywords from the title of each citing article, the Corporate Index, and the Patent Citation Index.

THE SOCIAL SCIENCES CITATION INDEX, 1966-70, 1971-75, 1976-80, 1981-

Disciplines represented include:

anthropology & archaeology	area and ethnic group studies
business & finance	communications
community health	criminology & penology
demography	economics
educational research	geography
international relations	law
management & marketing	political science
psychology & psychiatry	sociology
urban planning & development	information & library sciences

Based upon the citations appearing in articles from 1,000+ journals concerned with social, behavioral and related sciences, SSCI uses the same general plan and purpose as SCI. Cited authors are centered in the citation index portion, together with a list of abbreviated references to all articles citing the author's publications in the period covered by the Index. In the source index portion, complete bibliographic information is provided for the citing items. A Permuterm Subject Index utilizing paired keywords from the titles of citing articles, and a Corporate Author Index are also part of each supplement, which are incorporated into the annual cumulation.

ARTS & HUMANITIES CITATION INDEX, 1976-

Disciplines represented include journals and some books in the fields of:

archaeology	architecture
art	classics
dance	film, TV & radio
folklore	history
language & linguistics	literature
music	philosophy
theater	theology & religious studies

Ways To Use Citation Indexes:

Try looking in the PERMUTERM SUBJECT INDEX volume (or part of a volume) under your Project topic. The main keyword you select to use should combine well with one subdivision (another keyword). Opposite it will be an author's name. You can then move to that author in the Source Index (volume) for the same time period. The Source Index provides the complete bibliographical citation for the article on your subject which you've just discovered. It also provides the number of References which the author cited in that article and usually cites some or even all of them. Thus you locate much more than just one new article related to your topic.

Another approach to citation indexes is to look in the CITATION INDEX portion under the author of an article you have previously read and decided is a great one for your purposes. You are therefore interested in knowing of articles published subsequently in which other writers cite it or rely on it to document their contentions. And if researchers refute "your author's" contentions, you'd need to know!

Or, you might be interested in knowing about articles in which an author's book is referenced. (Arts & Humanities Citation Index indexes parts of some books as well as periodical articles). This provision of citations of articles published AFTER and REFERRING BACK to a publication with which you are already very familiar is the really unique thing about citation indexes.

Choose one of the three citation indexes. Each cumulates and is divided into alphabetical volumes (and parts of volumes) called and serving as a citation index, a source index, and a permuted subject index.

Title of the Index you select: "_____

_____ Citation Index". (If in doubt, it will likely be the one which you or I included in pathfinder Assignment 5, STEP #3.)

A. Try looking in the PERMUTERM SUBJECT INDEX volume (or part of a volume) under your Project topic. Main keyword you select to use:

_____. In column #(s): _____.
One subdivision (another keyword) which combines well with that main keyword you've selected and found is _____.
The/An author opposite that subdivision:_____
The period of time covered by the volume you're using: _____

B. You could then move to that author in the SOURCE INDEX volume for that same year or period of time (cumulation). The Source Index gives the complete bibliographical citation of the article on your subject which you've discovered in "A" above. It also provides other information including the number of R's (references) which the author cited in that article and displays them in a list like a bibliography directly below.

Who is the author (main entry) of the article, and where do you find the information in the Source Index volume?_____
_____. Column #_____
Who is the co-author, if any?_____

Abbreviation of the journal title:_____. Full title of the journal (Lists of journals are in front of some volumes; also try beginning of Sources.) "_____
_____"

Volume # of the journal in which the article was published_____
Pagination of the article:_____. Year it was published: 19_____. How many R's (references) are cited in the article, if any?_____.

C. Another approach to citation indexes -- its most unique function, in fact -- is to look in the CITATION INDEX portion under the AUTHOR of an article you have previously read and decided is a good one for your purposes. You are, therefore, interested in knowing of articles published SUBSEQUENTLY in which writers cite it or rely on it to document their contentions. Or, you might be interested in knowing about articles in which an author's book is referred to.

Here's a demonstration: You know that in 1968 Thomas Stephen Szasz published a paper (article) with someone else titled "Mental-Illness as an Excuse for Civil Wrongs" in the Journal of Nervous and Mental Disease (147). You want to know of writers who subsequently cited Szasz's paper, and you want to update your existing knowledge in the field of contemporary perception of "mental illness".

First take a look at the indexing which Social Sciences Citation Index provides for the Szasz article-- the SOURCE. Check the Source Index, volume 8 Prin-Z, 1966-1970 cumulation, for this display. You find it in column #_____. You learn there that Szasz's co-writer is _____,
and that the two authors relied on how many "references"?_____
(All of which are detailed beneath the entry itself.) Their article begins on page #_____ of the Journal of Nervous and Mental Disease.

Now follow through on the CITATION indexing... to learn of articles in which writers subsequently cite the source-article by Szasz and colleague. Enter the Citation Index section of the 1971-1975 cumulation of SSCI via the entry for this item under SZASZ, TS. Check column # 36546 , which indicates that TS Szasz's article written with joint author, published in 1968 in the Journal of Nervous and Mental Disease has in the meantime been referred to (cited) by the following writers (notice that their articles were published after 1968, when Szasz's paper was published):_____

_____

And you could re-cycle back and find a citing author in the source index.

REVIEWING AND TESTING

Two tests are recommended: one at the mid-term point and one at the conclusion of the course, covering "everything" since the first test. They should be uniform throughout all sections and consistent from term to term. The first test may also be useful in generating a mid-term grade, which, even if not required by the institution, is useful information. The second test should be part of the institution's Final Examinations period.

Aside from the fact that subjective essay-type questions are less popular than objective-type questions (true or false, multiple choice, completion, etc.), achievement and learning in this type of course are more efficiently tested by means of well constructed, valid and reliable objective-type questions. Aim to construct each question so that it:

- tests acquisition and mastery of specific and significant aspects of the course;

- tests more than one such concept, skill, accomplishment, fact, etc.;

- does so in a true-to-life context.

Multiple choice questions which include "all of these [choices]" and "none of these [choices]" ask too much of freshmen and are often unjustified. When using true or false questions, have students circle, rather than check, the relevant one, and never use plus and minus.

A functional testing situation is fifty minutes/fifty questions, particularly for the first test. Begin the test with all of the ground rules. Well before the test date, go over in class the scope and format of the questions. Especially in the fall term, when there will be numerous new-to-college students, build in guidance and general test-taking. Stress not lingering on any one question. Suggest that instead they feel free to put a mark in the margin, move on to the next question, and return to it after having steadily gone through the entire test once. A surprising number of these students will not be aware of the fact that any answer is better than no answer on this test. They should learn as part of this course the importance of reading and following directions. All of the questions provided have been validated, and they can test teaching as well as learning.

Point out to them at the end of the previous class meeting that the test will begin when they are seated in every-other seat, with their possessions in the front of the room, and there is silence. There should be no need for students who have been attending regularly and doing a fair amount of work to question any of these questions during the examination. Because there may be instructors who do not permit students to retain their examinations (they usually let them see them and then collect them), clarify in advance that you will be returning their first examination, which will literally become theirs. (This means of course that you do not use the same question wording more than once.) Do not go over the test during the class at the end of which you return the first test; rather, urge them first to bring questions to office hours. The second test, or Final Examination, can also be returned to them together with their Projects and Project Evaluations following the end of the term. (Recycle a large envelope for each student's materials.) The Final Examination should be somewhat longer and more difficult than the first test.

Approximately 10-20 percent of both tests should involve local arrangements, i.e. knowledge of the organization of the college library or the university library system. Such questions require skill in construction if they are to be more than picky points or orientation teasers. Construct them to combine and apply skills and knowledge that can be extrapolated elsewhere in the course.

During the early phase of the program, these and other such questions also have potential for constructing an "exit" examination, if one is needed. Incorporate with them local questions and information to construct a valid pretest which identifies students who might be exempted from ("test out" of) a course required of all new students. Other sources of test questions include the Library Basics and More Library Basics handouts and Assignments 1-7, as well as all of the materials provided in this chapter and Section III: Resources.

Reviewing

Some institutions have regulations which require the provision of some review prior to a test. How this is interpreted varies. I counsel the following as most educative. Day One course information should provide brief information about the testing component of the course. Most new undergraduate students want to know then and/or just before a test:

- how much "it" counts towards the course grade;

- how many questions there will be;

- whether you grade on the curve. Usually they ask this after the fact, and they rarely know what the term means exactly.

Review should be offered for anyone who wants to come to office hours. From time to time you may recognize need, especially with larger classes, to schedule an hour review session, but stress that it is voluntary. Reentry and transfer students tend to welcome this and to attend. One or two of the best students will also show up, but so will lagging students who have simply not caught on to study habits or for other reasons did not get off to a great start in college. Multiple copies of an old examination are useful for review. Select the most crucial questions and go through it, explaining the reasons for the answers. Another useful review medium at the end of the term is a duplicate handout composed of ten excerpts from such tools as the local online computerized catalog display, the local serials file, a citation index, periodical indexes (see page 5 of More Library Basics), Book Review Digest, Essay and General Literature Index, National Union Catalog, Books in Print, Bibliographic Index, Biography

Index, BioBase, LCSH, an abstract, New York Times Index, etc. Carefully select each excerpt to convey a unique aspect of that tool's function. Paste the numbered excerpts on one or two pages, and provide an alphabetically-arranged list of their titles for use in identification and discussion.

Quizzes

You may want to have a "pop" quiz or an announced quiz--perhaps one each half of the term. The following are five-minute quiz possibilities:

Describe how an "abstracting service" differs from a "periodical index." Include examples.

Describe how the library's online catalog differs from the computer-assisted literature searching of commercial data bases such as discussed in class and demonstrated in the library recently.

Identify 3 specific ways in which the library's online catalog and the computer-assisted literature searching of commercial data bases ("DIALOG") differ from or closely resemble each other, from your perspective as a library patron.

Clearly identify and describe one unique advantage of online searching over manual (hand) searching of printed periodical indexes.

Clearly identify and describe one possible advantage of manual (hand) searching of a conventional library card catalog over online searching of a computerized catalog listing the library's holdings.

Compare and contrast truncation in DIALOG and in the library's online catalog.

Citation indexes can be useful in several ways. However, they have a unique function. Clearly identify and discuss this unique function.

A computer-assisted literature search of commercial data bases, available through the library reference department, is very useful for quickly generating a current bibliography on your topic. However, it can also be useful in several other ways. Clearly identify and discuss one of these other ways.

Feedback

It is essential that you provide students with the opportunity to evaluate your teaching and the course, and that you take responsibility for assuring anonymity. This is an opportunity to determine what aspects of the course they would like to have had less or more concentration.

INSTRUCTIONS Sit in every-other seat. Do not use the
handouts or any other resource. If you have a question,
raise your hand. Plan your time. You have until the
usual end of class-time today. Do not linger on any one
question. Do read carefully. Before you begin, check
that you have __7__ pages and 50 questions. In questions where there is a statement followed by a question
(for example, # __7__), consider the last part
"questionable". Select the one, "best answer" where there's a choice.
Be specific when answering open-ended "completion questions." Pen or
pencil is ok. Good luck. Begin now.

1-6 relate to this
catalog card.

1. Add the call number
to the card.

2. Convert the card to
the third subject-
tracing.

3. What type of main
entry has been assigned
to this publication?

_____

MacGregor, David, 1943-
    The Communist ideal in Hegel and Marx / David MacGregor.
 — Toronto ; Buffalo : University of Toronto Press, c1984.

        viii, 312 p. ; 24 cm.

        Bibliography: p. ₍264₎-295.
        Includes index.

    1. Hegel, Georg Wilhelm Friedrich, 1770-1831.   2. Marx, Karl, 1818-1883.
3. Hegel, Georg Wilhelm Friedrich, 1770-1831—Influence.   I. Title.
    B2948.M14   1984   83-168024
                                ●   335.4'1'0922—dc19
                                                        AACR 2   MARC

    Library of Congress

4. The Library of Congress classification is _____ ; for
other books like this, you could check the library stacks' shelves for
books with what LC classification? _____

5. There would be a total of #_____ cards filed for this book in a
dictionary catalog.

6. Subject cards (access points) for this publication would be found
alphabetically as follows: two in the H's, one in the I's, and one in
the M's.
            TRUE   FALSE

7. Readers' Guide and many other periodical indexes use some of the techniques a card catalog uses. These include:
        - a subject-heading system with subdivisions and cross-references;
        - a magazine article may appear under more than one subject-heading;
        - "Mc" may be filed as if it is spelled out "MAC"; and
        - _____

8. A campus library which currently subscribes to a magazine or journal
will always have all issues of it including and since volume #1.

        TRUE   FALSE

293

9 -14 relate to your efficient use of this LCSH excerpt.

Cables, Electric
  See Cables, Submarine
    Electric cables
    Telegraph cables
    Telephone cables
Cables, Submarine (*Economics, HE7709-7741; Military art and science, UG607; Technology, TK5605-5681)*
  sa Cable ships
    Telegraph cables
  x Cables, Electric
    Ocean cables
    Submarine cables
    Submarine telegraph
    Telegraph, Submarine
  xx Communication and traffic
    Electric cables
    Telecommunication
    Telegraph
— Code addresses
    See Telegraph code addresses
— Directories (*HE7710)*
    x Cable directories

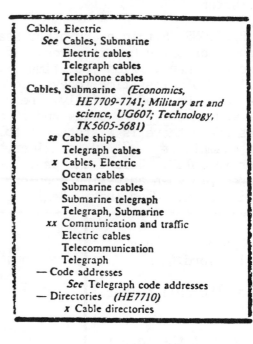

9. For books about technological aspects of submarine cables, one could check the library shelves in the vicinity of the Library of Congress Classification

from HE7009 through HE7741
from TK5605 through TK5681
UG607
VM791

10. Which one of the following is not an established subject-heading?

Cables, Electric
Cables, Submarine
Cables-- Directories
Telegraph code addresses

11. If you need a lot of information and publications about submarine telegraph, using the LCSH, you should check the display for the subject heading ______________________________

12. Cables, Submarine is _____ Electric cables

broader than   narrower than

13. There is a total of #______ "See also" cross references in this excerpt.

14. This excerpt is from volume #____ of the LCSH.

15. Some would say that the two lists (A and B) below are both filed (top-to-bottom) "alphabetically". One is filed "letter by letter", the other "word by word". Which is filed "word by word"-- List A or B?____

-A-	-B-
Hydrogen	Hydrogen
Hydrogenase	Hydrogen conversion
Hydrogenation	Hydrogen economy
Hydrogen economy	"A Hydrogen Energy System"
"A Hydrogen Energy System"	Hydrogenase
Hydrogen homestead	Hydrogenation

And which way is the way library catalogs are alphabetized? A or B?____

16. Using the periodical indexes we've considered so far this term, you need to locate journal articles published in 1979 about economic conditions in the South. What is the title of the periodical index other than Readers' Guide which you'll consult first?" ______________________
____ "

17- 27 relate to this excerpt from one of the semispecialized periodical indexes considered in the course.

17. The excerpt displays 9 articles and 1 cross reference.

TRUE   FALSE

18. "HOWELLS, William Dean" (the first line of the excerpt) is used in this indexing as

   an author
   a subject
   a title

19. These subject-headings are all derived from the LCSH.

TRUE   FALSE

20. Someone interested in locating journal articles about the Hsi-Hsia language should look under the subject heading, _____
_____, when they use this Index.

21. This indexing excerpt appears to be from The

   Applied Science & Technology Index
   Humanities Index
   Social Sciences Index

22. To identify the full name of the author of "Discourse of Persuasion in Hrafnkatla", your first step would be to consult the

   Authors Section of this Index for the same time period
   D's section of this Index for the same time period
   H's section of this Index for the same time period

23. "rediscovering a novel of the Orkneys" is a

   subject-heading
   subtitle
   title
   title enhancement

24. Indexing indicates that none of these articles includes some bibliographic support.

TRUE   FALSE

25. The frequency of the journal in which James Hoyt's article appears is probably

   weekly   quarterly
   monthly   annual

Sidebar excerpt:

HOWELLS, William Dean
  Different view of the iron madonna: William Dean Howells and his magazine readers. L. T. Goldman. New Eng Q 50:563-86 D '77
  Reality that can't be quite definitely spoken: sexuality in Their wedding journey. G. A. Hunt. Stud Novel 9:17-32 Spr '77
  William Dean Howells and the American Hebrew. G. Monteiro. New Eng Q 50:515-16 S '77
HOYT, James L.
  Courtroom coverage: the effects of being televised. J Broadcasting 21:487-95 Fall '77
HOYT, Robert G.
  Call to reflection. Chr & Crisis 37:253-5, 264-6 O 31-N 14 '77
  Columbia U: the Korean collection. Chr & Crisis 37:210-11 O 3 '77
HRAFNKELS saga Freysgoða
  Discourse of persuasion in Hrafnkatla. K. E. Duhs. Scand Stud 49:464-73 Aut '77
HSI-HSIA language. See Tangut language
HSÜN-tzu, 340-245 B.C.
  Conceptual aspect of Hsün Tzu's philosophy of human nature. A. S. Cua. Philos East & West 27:373-89 O '77
HUBERMAN, Elizabeth
  Mackay Brown's Greenvoe: rediscovering a novel of the Orkneys. Critique 19 no2:33-43 '77

26. Huberman's article appeared in a periodical whose title is (or is abbreviated as) "_____", ending on page #_____.

27. You've misplaced your bib cards. Now you've got to return to the periodical index volume to get some information. Based on the information contained in the excerpt, you'll approach first which one of these five volumes? Volume #_____.

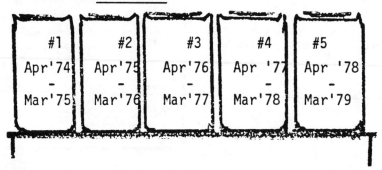

28- 31 Judy Chicago's autobiography was published by the New York publisher, Doubleday. Its title is <u>Through the Flower; My Struggle as a Woman Artist</u>. Its call number is N6537.C48A2/1982. There are two subject points-of-access for this book; the second is ARTISTS-- U.S.-- BIOGRAPHY. Fill in the four first lines for these "cards", which should also be alphabetically filed as in a dictionary catalog.

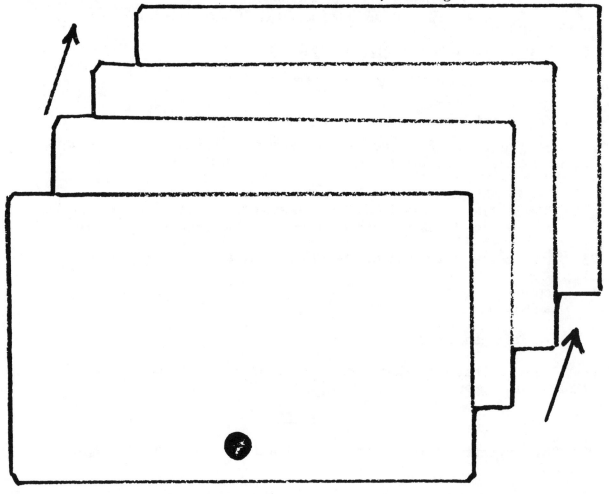

32. If you could use only <u>Readers' Guide</u> and were thus restricted to
accessing the contents of articles in periodicals which Readers' Guide
indexes, and if you were looking for articles about phobias, you'd
start your search by looking under:

        magazine articles-- phobias
        mental problems-- phobias
        phobia
        phobias

33. Based on efficient interpretation of the following reproduction of an
excerpt from the <u>New York Times Index</u>, complete the statement which
follows it:

> LAMPS and Lampshades
>   R Reif on Emeralites, green-glass-shaped, brass-
> based desk lamps that dominated lamp design from
> about 1910 to 1940; lamps are on display at Phyllis
> Elliot Gallery (M), F 19,II,30:3

The New York Times article cited here is of _____length and
can be read by referring to the issue of the New York Times published
on (date)_____, in column #_____, on
page #_____of section #_____.

34. A divided catalog has three separate parts or files: (1) authors,
(2) subjects, and (3) titles.

        TRUE   FALSE

35. Here is a partial outline of the Library of Congress Classification
system:
A General Works   M Music
B Philosophy, Psychology, Religion N Fine Arts
C History (Auxiliary Sciences)   P Language and Literature
D History (except America)   Q Science
E & F America   R Medicine
G Geography, Anthropology   S Agriculture, Plant & Animal Industry
H Social Sciences   T Technology
J Political Science   U Military Science
K Law   V Naval Science
L Education   Z Bibliography & Library Science
   You are employed by a large library to shelve books. The library uses
   the LC Classification. Someone who thought s/he was helping, arranged
   the following books alphabetically by their titles! So now you have to
   rearrange them in a pre-sort before you can shelve them. (We can assume
   that the authors titled them accurately and fully!)

Cambridge History of India   History of Nursing from Ancient Times...
Dictionary of American Naval Ships Index to Art Reproductions in Books
Encyclopaedia Britannica   International Encyclopedia of the
The Gifted Student   Social Sciences
The first book to be shelved is the one titled"_____"

36-43 relate to this pile of periodical indexes piled on the table. Use them to locate the following information.

36-7. You need citations to several reviews (including those in Esquire and Business Week) of Charles Silberman's book published in late 1978. So you check volume #____ of the index titled "_____" under the

wording_____.

38-9. You want to read about Marie Curie's winning the Nobel Prize reported at the time it was presented to her in Stockholm, December 1911. You check volume #____ of the index titled "_____"

under the wording_____.

[pile of index books illustrated]

NEW YORK TIMES INDEX
1911 Volume

SOCIAL SCIENCES INDEX Vol.6
April 1979-March 1980

NEW YORK TIMES INDEX
1912 Volume

READERS' GUIDE Vol. 39
March 1979-Feb. 1980

READERS' GUIDE Vol.38
March 1978- Feb. 1979

HUMANITIES INDEX Vol. 6
April 1979 - March 1980

40-1. In May 1979 actor Alan Alda made the Commencement Address for the Columbia University College of Physicians and Surgeons. You want to read it, so you consult volume #____ of the index titled "_____", under the wording _____.

42-3. You're trying to track down an article about "rights of the unborn" said to have been published in the January 1979 issue of the American Journal of Psychology. You don't know the article's title, but you do know the author's name is Paul H. Soloff. You check volume #____ of the index titled "_____" under the wording_____.

44. When using periodical indexes for locating information on current topics and up-to-date information on any subject, begin your search with the _____ issues, and then work your way _____ systematically.

    latest / backwards
    old / forwards

45. In a card catalog and fiche files, the entries for new books are interfiled right in among those already filed-listed. To keep up-to-date systematically with newly published magazine articles, a periodical index

    binds
    cumulates
    supplements and then cumulates

46. 4 types of "first aids" of reference work were commended to you: an unabridged dictionary, a general encyclopedia, an almanac, and _____

_____.

47-50 Here are definitions for 3 terms listed below. Following each
definition, insert the term it defines.

A direction from a term or name under which entries are listed to a-
nother term(s) or name(s) under which additional or allied information
may be found. _____

An inclusive term referring to regularly issued publications which
comprises newspapers, annual reports, yearbooks, periodicals, monographic series, etc. _____

A list, often found at the end of a catalog entry, which traces all the
subject and added entries for a particular book in a catalog or other
file. _____

Terms

cross reference   "See" reference
cumulation   "See also" reference
imprint   serial
magazine   tracings
periodical   volume

Select one of the left-over, remaining terms and define it clearly in
one sentence:
Term you select:_____

Your definition:_____

_____
_____
_____
_____
_____.

END of test. The test will be returned within a week, possibly at the
next class meeting. It is your test, so you will be able to keep it;bring
it to class as we'll discuss it later.Meantime, it is graded in such a
way that you will be able to know the correct answers. You are urged
to bring your individual questions about the test to office hours, or,
if you have a class or lab then, to make an appointment.

INSTRUCTIONS Sit in every-other seat. Do not use the
handouts or any other resource. If you have a question,
raise your hand. Plan your time. You have until the
usual end of class-time today. <u>Do not</u> linger on any one
question. <u>Do</u> read carefully. Before you begin, check
that you have __7__ pages and 50 questions. In questions where there is a statement followed by a question
(for example, #__7__), consider the last part
"questionable". Select the one, "best answer" where there's a choice.
Be specific when answering open-ended "completion questions." Pen or
pencil is ok. Good luck. Begin now.

1-6 relate to this
catalog card.

1. Add the call number
to the card.

2. Convert the card to
the third subject-
tracing.

3. What type of main
entry has been assigned
to this publication?

  by personal AUTHOR

HEGEL, GEORG WILHELM FRIEDRICH, 1770-1831-- INFLUENCE

B2948   **MacGregor, David,** 1943-
M14   The Communist ideal in Hegel and Marx / David MacGregor.
1984   — Toronto ; Buffalo : University of Toronto Press, c1984.

         viii, 312 p. ; 24 cm.

         Bibliography: p. [264]-295.
         Includes index.

         1. Hegel, Georg Wilhelm Friedrich, 1770-1831. 2. Marx, Karl, 1818-1883.
         3. Hegel, Georg Wilhelm Friedrich, 1770-1831—Influence.   I. Title.

         B2948.M14   1984   83-168024
                                          335.4'1'0922—dc19
                                                                   AACR 2   MARC
         Library of Congress

4. The Library of Congress classification is __B2948__ ; for
other books like this, you could check the library stacks' shelves for
books with what LC classification? __B2948__

5. There would be a total of #__5__ cards filed for this book in a
dictionary catalog. Main entry(author) + 3 subject cards + 1 added entry (ti-
                       tle) card= 5
6. Subject cards (access points) for this publication would be found
alphabetically as follows: two in the H's, one in the I's, and one in
the M's.
       TRUE   FALSE   (none in the I's)
7. Readers' Guide and many other periodical indexes use some of the techniques a card catalog uses. These include:
       - a subject-heading system with subdivisions and cross-references;
       - a magazine article may appear under more than one subject-heading;
       - "Mc" may be filed as if it is spelled out "MAC"; and
       - <u>indication of such things as bibliographies and illustrations in</u>
              the publication.
8. A campus library which currently subscribes to a magazine or journal
will always have all issues of it including and since volume #1.

       TRUE   FALSE

                                          Not <u>always</u>.

9 -14 relate to your efficient use of this <u>LCSH</u> excerpt.

9. For books about technological aspects of submarine cables, one could check the library shelves in the vicinity of the Library of Congress Classification

       from HE7009 through HE7741
  X from TK5605 through TK5681
       UG607
       VM791

10. Which one of the following is not an established subject-heading?

  X Cables, Electric
    Cables, Submarine
    Cables-- Directories
    Telegraph code addresses

> Cables, Electric
>   *See* Cables, Submarine
>   Electric cables
>   Telegraph cables
>   Telephone cables
> Cables, Submarine *(Economics, HE7709-7741; Military art and science, UG607; Technology, TK5605-5681)*
>   *sa* Cable ships
>   Telegraph cables
>   *x* Cables, Electric
>   Ocean cables
>   Submarine cables
>   Submarine telegraph
>   Telegraph, Submarine
>   *xx* Communication and traffic
>   Electric cables
>   Telecommunication
>   Telegraph
> — Code addresses
>   *See* Telegraph code addresses
> — Directories *(HE7710)*
>   *x* Cable directories

11. If you need a lot of information and publications about submarine telegraph, using the LCSH, you should check the display for the subject heading <u>CABLES, SUBMARINE</u>

12. Cables, Submarine is _____ Electric cables

  broader than   (narrower than)

13. There is a total of # <u>2</u> "See also" cross references in this excerpt.
                    [and 5 See's]

14. This excerpt is from volume # <u>1</u> of the LCSH.

15. Some would say that the two lists (A and B) below are both filed (top-to-bottom) "alphabetically". One is filed "letter by letter", the other "word by word". Which is filed "word by word"-- List A or B? <u>B</u>

-A-	-B-
Hydrogen	Hydrogen
Hydrogenase	Hydrogen conversion
Hydrogenation	Hydrogen economy
Hydrogen economy	"A Hydrogen Energy System"
"A Hydrogen Energy System"	Hydrogenase
Hydrogen homestead	Hydrogenation

And which way is the way library catalogs are alphabetized? A or B? <u>B</u>

16. Using the periodical indexes we've considered so far this term, you need to locate journal articles published in 1979 about economic conditions in the South. What is the title of the periodical index <u>other than Readers' Guide</u> which you'll consult first?" <u>Social Sciences Index</u> "

17-27 relate to this excerpt from one
of the semispecialized periodical
indexes considered in the course.

17. The excerpt displays 9 articles
and 1 cross reference.

      FALSE

18. "HOWELLS, William Dean" (the
first line of the excerpt) is used in
this indexing as

    an author
  X a subject
    a title

HOWELLS, William Dean
  Different view of the iron madonna: William
  Dean Howells and his magazine readers. L. T.
  Goldman. New Eng Q 50:563-86 D '77
  Reality that can't be quite definitely spoken:
  sexuality in Their wedding journey. G. A.
  Hunt. Stud Novel 9:17-32 Spr '77
  William Dean Howells and the American He-
  brew. G. Monteiro. New Eng Q 50:515-16 S '77
HOYT, James L.
  Courtroom coverage: the effects of being tele-
  vised. J Broadcasting 21:487-95 Fall '77
HOYT, Robert G.
  Call to reflection. Chr & Crisis 37:253-5, 264-6
  O 31-N 14 '77
  Columbia U: the Korean collection. Chr & Crisis
  37:210-11 O 3 '77
HRAFNKELS saga Freysgoða
  Discourse of persuasion in Hrafnkatla. K. E.
  Duhs. Scand Stud 49:464-73 Aut '77
HSI-HSIA language. See Tangut language
HSÜN-tzu, 340-245 B.C.
  Conceptual aspect of Hsün Tzu's philosophy of
  human nature. A. S. Cua. Philos East &
  West 27:373-89 O '77
HUBERMAN, Elizabeth
  Mackay Brown's Greenvoe: rediscovering a novel
  of the Orkneys. Critique 19 no2:33-43 '77

19. These subject-headings are all
derived from the LCSH.

    TRUE   FALSE

20. Someone interested in locating journal articles about the Hsi-Hsia
language should look under the subject heading, TANGUT LANGUAGE
_____, when they use this Index.

21. This indexing excerpt appears to be from The

    Applied Science & Technology Index
  X Humanities Index
    Social Sciences Index

22. To identify the full name of the author of "Discourse of Persuasion
in Hrafnkatla", your first step would be to consult the

    Authors Section of this Index for the same time period
  X D's section of this Index for the same time period
    H's section of this Index for the same time period

23. "rediscovering a novel of the Orkneys" is a

    subject-heading
  X subtitle
    title
    title enhancement

24. Indexing indicates that none of these articles includes some bibliographic support.

      FALSE

25. The frequency of the journal in which James Hoyt's article appears
is probably

    weekly   X quarterly
    monthly   annual

26. Huberman's article appeared in a periodical whose title is (or is abbreviated as) " <u>Critique</u>   ", ending on page # <u>43</u> .

27. You've misplaced your bib cards. Now you've got to return to the periodical index volume to get some information. Based on the information contained in the excerpt, you'll approach first which one of these five volumes? Volume # <u>4</u> .

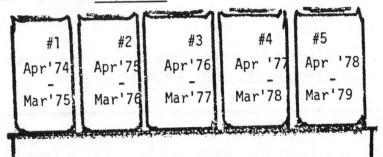

#1	#2	#3	#4	#5
Apr'74 - Mar'75	Apr'75 - Mar'76	Apr'76 - Mar'77	Apr '77 - Mar'78	Apr '78 - Mar'79

28-31 Judy Chicago's autobiography was published by the New York publisher, Doubleday. Its title is <u>Through the Flower; My Struggle as a Woman Artist</u>. Its call number is <u>N6537.C48A2/1982</u>. There are two subject points-of-access for this book; the second is ARTISTS-- U.S.-- BIOGRAPHY. Fill in the four first lines for these "cards", which should also be alphabetically filed as in a dictionary catalog.

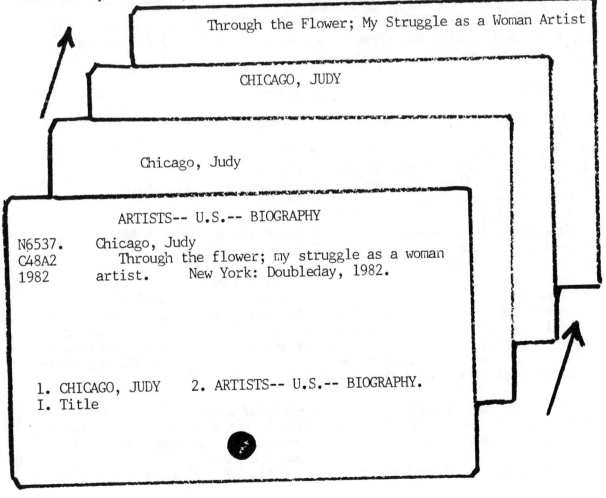

Through the Flower; My Struggle as a Woman Artist

CHICAGO, JUDY

Chicago, Judy

ARTISTS-- U.S.-- BIOGRAPHY

N6537.   Chicago, Judy
C48A2   Through the flower; my struggle as a woman
1982   artist.   New York: Doubleday, 1982.

1. CHICAGO, JUDY   2. ARTISTS-- U.S.-- BIOGRAPHY.
I. Title

32. If you could use only <u>Readers' Guide</u> and were thus restricted to accessing the contents of articles in periodicals which Readers' Guide indexes, and if you were looking for articles about phobias, you'd start your search by looking under:

       magazine articles-- phobias
       mental problems-- phobias
       phobia
  X phobias

33. Based on efficient interpretation of the following reproduction of an excerpt from the <u>New York Times Index</u>, complete the statement which follows it:

> LAMPS and Lampshades
>   R Reif on Emeralites, green-glass-shaped, brass-based desk lamps that dominated lamp design from about 1910 to 1940; lamps are on display at Phyllis Elliot Gallery (M), F 19,II,30:3

The New York Times article cited here is of <u> medium </u> length and can be read by referring to the issue of the New York Times published on (date) <u>Feb. 19th   </u>, in column # <u> 3   </u>, on page # <u>   30   </u> of section # <u> II   </u>.

34. A divided catalog has three separate parts or files: (1) authors, (2) subjects, and (3) titles.

    TRUE  FALSE

35. Here is a partial outline of the Library of Congress Classification system:

A General Works
B Philosophy, Psychology, Religion
C History (Auxiliary Sciences)
D History (except America)
E & F America
G Geography, Anthropology
H Social Sciences
J Political Science
K Law
L Education
M Music
N Fine Arts
P Language and Literature
Q Science
R Medicine
S Agriculture, Plant & Animal Industry
T Technology
U Military Science
V Naval Science
Z Bibliography & Library Science

You are employed by a large library to shelve books. The library uses the LC Classification. Someone who thought s/he was helping, arranged the following books alphabetically by their titles! So now you have to rearrange them in a pre-sort before you can shelve them. (We can assume that the authors titled them accurately and fully!)

Cambridge History of India
Dictionary of American Naval Ships
Encyclopaedia Britannica
The Gifted Student
History of Nursing from Ancient Times...
Index to Art Reproductions in Books
International Encyclopedia of the Social Sciences

The first book to be shelved is the one titled "<u>Encyclopaedia Britannica</u>"

36-43 relate to this pile of periodical indexes piled on the table. Use them to locate the following information.

36-7. You need citations to several reviews (including those in Esquire and Business Week) of Charles Silberman's book published in late 1978. So you check volume #_38_ of the index titled " Readers' Guide " under the

wording BOOK REVIEWS [section in back of volume] Silberman, C.

| NEW YORK TIMES INDEX |
| 1911 Volume |

| SOCIAL SCIENCES INDEX Vol.6 |
| April 1979-March 1980 |

| NEW YORK TIMES INDEX |
| 1912 Volume |

| READERS' GUIDE Vol. 39 |
| March 1979-Feb. 1980 |

| READERS' GUIDE Vol.38 |
| March 1978- Feb. 1979 |

HUMANITIES INDEX Vol. 6
April 1979 - March 1980

38-9. You want to read about Marie Curie's winning the Nobel Prize reported at the time it was presented to her in Stockholm, December 1911. You check volume #_1911_ of the index

titled "New York Times Index"

under the wording Curie, Marie .

40-1. In May 1979 actor Alan Alda made the Commencement Address for the Columbia University College of Physicians and Surgeons. You want to read it, so you consult volume #_39_ of the index titled " Readers' Guide ", under the wording Alda , Alan .

42-3. You're trying to track down an article about "rights of the unborn" said to have been published in the January 1979 issue of the American Journal of Psychology. You don't know the article's title, but you do know the author's name is Paul H. Soloff. You check volume #_6_ of the index titled " Social Sciences Index " under the wording Soloff, Paul H. .

44. When using periodical indexes for locating information on current topics and up-to-date information on any subject, begin your search with the _____ issues, and then work your way _____ systematically.

    X latest / backwards
      old / forwards

45. In a card catalog and fiche files, the entries for new books are interfiled right in among those already filed-listed. To keep up-to-date systematically with newly published magazine articles, a periodical index

      binds
      cumulates
    X supplements and then cumulates

46. 4 types of "first aids" of reference work were commended to you: an unabridged dictionary, a general encyclopedia, an almanac, and _____ the library's catalog .

47-50 Here are definitions for 3 terms listed below. Following each
      definition, insert the term it defines.

A direction from a term or name under which entries are listed to a-
nother term(s) or name(s) under which additional or allied information
may be found. ___SEE ALSO___

An inclusive term referring to regularly issued publications which
comprises newspapers, annual reports, yearbooks, periodicals, monographic series, etc. _____SERIAL___

A list, often found at the end of a catalog entry, which traces all the
subject and added entries for a particular book in a catalog or other
file. ___TRACINGS___

Terms

cross reference	"See" reference
cumulation	"See also" reference
imprint	serial
magazine	tracings
periodical	volume

Select one of the left-over, remaining terms and define it clearly in
one sentence:

Term you select:_____

Your definition:_____

_____

_____

_____

_____

_____

_____.

END of test. The test will be returned within a week, possibly at the
next class meeting. It is your test, so you will be able to keep it; bring
it to class as we'll discuss it later. Meantime, it is graded in such a
way that you will be able to know the correct answers. You are urged
to bring your individual questions about the test to office hours, or,
if you have a class or lab then, to make an appointment.

-1-   Your Name_____

Final Examination

INSTRUCTIONS: Do not use the course handouts or any other resource. Plan your time. Do not linger on any one question. Do read carefully. Before you begin, check that you have 9 pages and 50 questions. In questions where there is a statement followed by a question (for example, #7), consider the last part "questionable". Select the one, "best answer" where there's a choice. Be specific when answering open-ended "completion questions".

----

1. Four broad areas are especially well covered by government publications: statistical information and sources, technical information, social policy and public affairs, and [what type of]_____

_____ research.

2. Most back issues of periodicals in the library's collection are arranged alphabetically by title, and then chronologically by date of publication.

    TRUE   FALSE

If false, correct the statement by adjusting it.

3. You are attracted by the keywords in this excerpt derived from the 1982 Sociological Abstracts. To pursue this publication, how would you proceed? Describe your next step specifically:

> INSTITUTIONAL/INSTITUTIONALISM
> institutional racism/sexism, US;
> parallels, particularities; possible solutions (M 6916)

_____

_____

_____

4. You are attracted by this entry derived from the 1982 Psychological Abstracts. To read this publication, how would you proceed? Describe your next step specifically:

> 3445. Hildebrandt, Katherine A. & Fitzgerald, Hiram E. (State U New York, Buffalo) Mothers' responses to infant physical appearance. Infant Mental Health Journal, 1981 (Spr), Vol 2(1), 56-64.   ....

_____

_____

_____

5. You need to read several brief summaries of professional evaluations from varied perspectives of a book you're reading and which was a 1975 best-seller and published that year. So you start by consulting

    Book Review Digest for 1975 under the author's surname.
    Book Review Digest for 1976 under the first word of the title.
    Book Review Index in the cumulation covering 1974-6 under main entry.

6. A magazine or journal article will appear under only one subject-heading in a periodical index, whereas a book will appear under one or more subject headings "as needed" in a library catalog.

     TRUE   FALSE

If false, correct the statement by rewriting it in the space below:

_____

_____

_____

_____

7. After you've gotten well along in a library literature search and have a handful of bib cards for publications and have located them in the libraries' collections, you're wondering how to de-select-- how to evaluate books especially. One way at this point is to consult:

      Bibliographic Index   Book Review Digest
      Book Review Index   Books In Print

8. A "review article" refers to a

      book by an authority in your field
      critical study which reviews and surveys the "state of the art"
      a nonevaluative summary of the publication
      a review of a book, play or motion picture.

9. If you query the library's online catalog for a particular book, and if it responds that we don't have it, you know that the next logical step is to

      arrange for an inter-library loan
      buy it
      consult the library card catalog
      consult the National Union Catalog main set, pre 1956 volumes

10. When "searching" a thesaurus for subject-heading wordings (descriptors), for a library's catalogs for publications on a subject of interest, or a periodical index for articles on a subject of interest, some good ground rules are:
      (1) Be general rather than specific.
      (2) Check what you have-- the actual words you're thinking.
      (3) And then get creative as necessary.
The three steps in the ground rules sequence contain an error; correct the sequence by making necessary adjustment.

11. You need material about the background of the novel, Emma, written by Jane Austen (1775-1817). You're looking for books of criticism and commentary. So you check the library card catalog under the subject-heading (PRINT):

_____

12-13 relate to the reproduction below of an entry from_____.

      Comprehensive Dissertation Index
      Dissertation Abstracts International
      Political Science Abstracts

13. It consists of 3 citations which have in common the title keyword

_____.

```
┌──────────────────────────────────────────────────────┐
│                   POLITICAL SCIENCE                    │
│ THE POLITICAL ECONOMY OF U.S. TRADE POLICY:  AN EVALUATION │
│    OF THEORY (TRANSNATIONALS, THE STATE, TAXES, TARIFFS, │
│    UNITED STATES.)                                     │
│    ALGER, KEITH NORMAN  (PH.D.   1985   THE UNIVERSITY OF │
│    WISCONSIN - MADISON)   325p.   47/03A, p. 1038      │
│                     QUU86-01523                        │
│ POLITICAL REASON AND PUBLIC FREEDOM:  A CRITIQUE OF MAX │
│    WEBER'S POLITICAL THEORY.                           │
│    BREINER, PETER DAVID  (PH.D.   1986   STANFORD UNIVERSITY) │
│    261p.   47/03A,  p. 1039   QUU86-12717              │
│ UNDERSTANDING EFFECTIVE POLITICAL LEADERSHIP IN THE THIRD │
│    WORLD  - AN ALTERNATIVE APPROACH:  THE CASES OF FIDEL │
│    CASTRO AND INDIRA GANDHI.                           │
│    BROTHERTON, FESTUS, JR.  (PH.D.   1985   UNIVERSITY OF │
│    CALIFORNIA, LOS ANGELES)   674p.   47/02A,  p. 641  │
│                     QUU86003937                        │
└──────────────────────────────────────────────────────┘
```

14. When you have a handful of bib cards following a search on your topic of periodical indexes, in order to proceed with getting complete information, you'd arrange these bib cards so that they are

      alphabetical by authors' surnames
      alphabetical by periodical titles' first regarded words
      chronological by dates of publication
      grouped by subjects

15. Always use the latest edition of an encyclopedia unless you have some particular reason. Select the encyclopedia you use on the bases of such things as subjects covered in the scope of the title, and

_____.

16. An indexing tool which cumulates usually utilizes temporary paper supplements as part of this technique. Every so often this indexing is then _____ into larger issues or cumulations. The new "big" permanent bound volume then ____ all of the interim coverage. An example is____.

      alphabetized / becomes / Sheehy's Guide To Reference Books
      interfiled / replaces / Humanities Index
      weeded / replaces / Readers' Guide

17-26. Which one of the library tools would you consult if you could use only one such resource and you needed all of the following information in one spot? Record the letter of the resource, referring to the "COLLECTION (CHOICES)" which follows the informational needs and which begins on page 5. Be sure to print the capital letter clearly. ANSWER ONLY TEN OF THE "needs"; ANSWER ONLY 10; DO ANY BUT ONLY TEN OF THEM!

You need to...

_____ get the exact date of the abdication of King Edward VIII of Great Britain.

_____ identify quickly 4-5 specialized periodical indexes relevant to the topic (Should prostitution in the U.S.A. be de-regularized/legalized? For a sociology course) on which you're doing a library literature search.

_____ locate (get the library's call number, title, bibliographic data) a great, up-to-date, background reading, possibly less than book length, on the status of the contemporary women's movement.

_____ compile a fairly lengthy bibliography of books by and about American writer Carson McCullers (1917-1967) which are in the library's collection.

_____ know which libraries in Illinois have the 1902 book, "Child Labour Legislation Handbook" by Josephine Goldmark.

_____ compile a bibliography of biographies relating to Karl Marx appearing in books as well as in magazines.

_____ get some authoritative background information about Afra Behn (born 1640), "the first female writer who had lived by her pen in England." You also need to clear up the question of "Why did she attempt to write in a style that should be mistaken for that of a man" and to have access to a list of all of her works.

_____ identify the titles of several recommended (by an expert) bibliographies, handbooks, and other reference books related to your specialized field or topic.

_____ identify the titles, compilers and publishers of several recently published (approximately within the last three years) bibliographies of book length on an important subject which you're researching.

_____ compile a list of bibliographies published in the 1930's and 1940's on the subject of pottery; you'd like it to encompass a variety of formats-- books, parts of books, parts of articles, etc.

17-26, contd.

You need to...

____ compile a bibliography of articles published in popular magazines
about Gertrude Ederle at the time she swam the English Channel,
August 1926.

____ know what % of the U.S. population before the Civil War was black

____ get titles of several specialized periodical indexes and abstracting services in the field of nuclear and space science.

____ compile bibliographies of U.S. government documents published at
the time(s) of each of the following: World War I, the passage of
the Constitutional Amendment providing women the right to vote (1920)
and the Great Depression of the 1930's.

____ You need a journal article about Koko, the gorilla at Stanford University, who, it is said, can use sign language. Because a scholarly journal article is likely to be lengthy, you would like to
read an abstract of the article before pursuing the issue of the
periodical itself.

COLLECTION (CHOICES)

A. "Abstracts and Indexes in Science & Technology: A Descriptive Guide", by
Dolores Owen

B. "Bibliographic Index"

C. "Biography Index"

D. "Cumulative Subject Index to the Monthly Catalog, 1900-1971"

E. "Dictionary of National Biography"

F. "Guide to Reference Books", by Eugene Sheehy

G. the library's catalog

H. "The Monthly Catalog"

I. "National Union Catalog" pre 1956 basic set

J. "New Columbia Encyclopedia"

K. "Periodical Indexes in the Social Sciences and Humanities: A Subject
Guide", by Lois Harzfeld

L. "Psychological Abstracts"

M. "Readers' Guide"

N. "The Statistical Abstract of the United States"

27. Six steps involved in doing library research for a term paper were commended to you: [fill in the two blanks]

#1 Background reading, an _____, and a "working title".
#2 Using a thesaurus efficiently to locate usable subject headings.
#3 A systematic methodology for locating articles in periodicals.
#4 Using a selective _____ or "guide to the literature".
#5 Using some specialized periodical indexes and abstracting services.
#6 Evaluating your discoveries: selecting and de-selecting.

28-31 Cards for these books are filed together with one cross reference card alphabetically in a library card catalog. (There are no subject cards here). The 20 "cards" have been randomly listed below:

"84, Charing Cross Road" [a title card]
"The Dalhousie Journals" [a title card] by Louise Dalhousie [an author card]
"Dr. Jekyll and Mr. Hyde" [a title card]
"El Cazador Oculto" [a title card]
A SEE card from DeBalzac, Honore to Balzac, Honore de, 1799-1850
"Eugene Grandet" [a title card] by Honore DeBalzac [an author card]
"Shoulder to Shoulder" [a title card] by Midge Mackenzie [an author card]
"The Psychology of Sex Differences" [a title card] by Eleanor Maccoby [an author card]
"The Power Lovers" [a title card] by Myra MacPherson [an author card]
"Memories of a Catholic Girlhood" [a title card] by Mary McCarthy [an author card]
"The Doctor Takes a Wife" [a title card] by Elizabeth Seifert [an author card]
"The Group" [a title card] by Mary McCarthy [an author card]

The first line of the 5th card reads _____

The first line of the 15th card reads _____

Feel free to use the space below for working out your response. It will not be regarded in connection with your answers to the two questions above.

-7-

32.
Reproduced to the right is an
excerpt derived from a _____
which appeared within the
"_____".

Check one of the following:
-list of descriptors/ Arts &
  Humanities Citation Index
-permuted subject index/ Social
  Sciences Citation Index
-thesaurus / Science Citation
  Index

```
PORK
  BARRELL ---- GRAFTON CT  +
          ---- NATION
          ---- REICHARD GW
          ---- RICE RR
  EMPTY   ---- NATION
  POLITICS --- GRAFTON CT +
           --- REICHARD GW
           --- RICE RR +
PORNOGRAPHY
  ATTACK ---- COURT JH
  CONTROVERSY  STEVENDS JD +
  DEVIANCE --- ELLIS A +
  LAW  ------ EICKHOFF LF
  MENTAL-HEA      "
  SEXUAL ---- ELLIS A +
  WOMEN  ---- COURT JH
```

33. Reproduced to the right is

  a Books In Print entry
  the verso of the title page of a
    book
  a catalog card
  the title page of Woman's Work

34. You need to discover publications which refer to (cite) an
article about English history
which you have read and found
very useful. So you start by consulting the _____ in
"_____".

Check one of the following:

  - abstract / Historical
    Abstracts
  - citation index portion /
    Arts & Humanities Citation
    Index
  - source index portion /
    Social Sciences Citation
    Index

Copyright © 1974 by Ann Oakley

All rights reserved under International and Pan-American Copyright Conventions. Published in the United States by Pantheon Books, a division of Random House, Inc., New York.

Originally published in Great Britain as *Housewife* by Allen Lane, Penguin Books Ltd., London.

Library of Congress Cataloging in Publication Data

Oakley, Ann.
  Woman's Work.

British ed. published in 1974 under title: Housewife.
  Bibliography: pp. 251–68
  Includes index.
  1. Wives—Case studies. 2. Mothers—Case studies. 3. Home economics. I. Title
HQ759.03   1975   301.41'2   74-4765
ISBN 0-394-46097-9

Manufactured in the United States of America

First American Edition

35-37 relate to this excerpt from

    the Bibliographic Index
    the Biography Index
    the Humanities Index
    a Wordsworth bio-bibliography

36. It includes 7 citations to publications on the subject of

_____

37. "Wives of famous men" (the sixth line) refers to the title of

    a book by Eda Howink
    a book by Dorothy Wordsworth
    part (pages 35-40) of a book
    poetry by Eda Howink

38. Five publications are cited in the excerpt reproduced to the right which is from one of the basic tools considered in this course. These five publications have in common the fact that they _____

_____

_____ .

39-40 relate to this excerpt from

    the Bibliographic Index
    the Biography Index
    Women Studies Abstracts

40. The citations relating to publications about Bangladesh women in rural development and about women in science conclude with a reference to an inclusive pagination. To what do these pairs of numbers refer?

    the length of the publication itself
    the location of a bibliography within the publication
    the location of an article within another publication

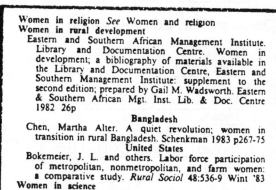

41-43 relate to this excerpt from

    Essay & General Literature Index
    Social Sciences Citation Index
    Social Sciences Index
    Sociological Abstracts

42. Elinor Ostrom and _____

43. wrote "_____

_____

_____ ,

which was published in a book edited by W. D. Hawley and D. Rogers.

> Ostrom, Elinor, and Parks, Roger B.
> Suburban police departments: too many and too small?
> *In* Masotti, L. H. and Hadden, J. K. eds. The urbanization of the suburbs p367-402
> Ostrom, Elinor, and Whitaker, Gordon Prevo
> Community control and governmental responsiveness: the case of police in Black neighborhoods
> *In* Hawley, W. D. and Rogers, D. eds. Improving the quality of urban management p303-34

44-50. Mary Therese McCarthy (1912-   ) is an American writer of fiction and nonfiction. Her most famous novel is probably The Group, one of several made into motion pictures. Her nonfiction has included Sights and Spectacles ; an autobiography titled Memories of a Catholic Girlhood; and travel books. She is known for her "searching social comment and keen wit, which has reflected her hatred of hypocrisy, and commitment to radical causes".   You have to report on the effect, if any, of attending a liberal, women's college and of having had a convent education. This might be for an education, psychology, Women's studies, or other course. In column #1, list ten specific library resources you would use. Then, in column #2, number them in the order you would consult them.

      #1   #2

END OF EXAMINATION. The test will be returned during office hours next week. If you do not pick it up then, it will be in the envelope with your Project.

INSTRUCTIONS: Do not use the course handouts or any other resource. Plan your time. <u>Do not</u> linger on any one question. Do read carefully. Before you begin, check that you have 9 pages and 50 questions. In questions where there is a statement followed by a question (for example, #7), consider the last part "questionable". Select the one, "best answer" where there's a choice. Be specific when answering open-ended "completion questions".

----

1. Four broad areas are especially well covered by government publications: statistical information and sources, technical information, social policy and public affairs, and [what type of]_____

                  statistical   research.

2. Most back issues of periodicals in the library's collection are arranged alphabetically by title, and then chronologically by date of publication.

    TRUE   (FALSE)   They're arranged according to the Library of Congress Classification (and within that, each periodical title is chronological.)

If false, correct the statement by adjusting it.

3. You are attracted by the keywords in this excerpt derived from the 1982 <u>Sociological Abstracts</u>. To pursue this publication, how would you proceed? Describe your next step specifically:

> INSTITUTIONAL/INSTITUTIONALISM institutional racism/sexism, US; parallels, particularities; possible solutions (M 6916)

I'd need to get the full bibliographic data for this particular publication; it's probably a journal article. Anyway, I'd move FROM this keyword index TO the abstracts. Staying within the same time period, I'd look for the abstract # M6916, where the author, title, issue, etc. would be listed.

4. You are attracted by this entry derived from the 1982 <u>Psychological Abstracts</u>. To read this publication, how would you proceed? Describe your next step specifically: I'd look up in the library's

> 3445. Hildebrandt, Katherine A. & Fitzgerald, Hiram E. (State U New York, Buffalo) Mothers' responses to infant physical appearance. Infant Mental Health Journal, 1981 (Spr), Vol 2(1), 56-64. ....

serials holdings record to find out if we have volume 2 of the "Infant Mental Health Journal", specifically Spring 1981 issue. If we do, I'd take down the call number and then go to the shelves in the stacks where that part of the LC Classification is.

5. You need to read several brief summaries of professional evaluations from varied perspectives of a book you're reading and which was a 1975 best-seller and published that year. So you start by consulting

X   Book Review Digest for 1975 under the author's surname.
    Book Review Digest for 1976 under the first word of the title.
    Book Review Index in the cumulation covering 1974-6 under main entry.

6. A magazine or journal article will appear under only one subject-heading in a periodical index, whereas a book will appear under one or more subject headings "as needed" in a library catalog.

TRUE   (FALSE)

If false, correct the statement by rewriting it in the space below:
Both magazine/journal articles AND books are assigned one or more

subjects "as needed" normally.

_____

7. After you've gotten well along in a library literature search and have a handful of bib cards for publications and have located them in the libraries' collections, you're wondering how to de-select-- how to evaluate books especially. One way at this point is to consult:

Bibliographic Index   X Book Review Digest
Book Review Index   Books In Print

8. A "review article" refers to a

    book by an authority in your field
  X critical study which reviews and surveys the "state of the art"
    a nonevaluative summary of the publication
    a review of a book, play or motion picture.

9. If you query the library's online catalog for a particular book, and if it responds that we don't have it, you know that the next logical step is to

    arrange for an inter-library loan
    buy it
  X consult the library card catalog
    consult the National Union Catalog main set, pre 1956 volumes

10. When "searching" a thesaurus for subject-heading wordings (descriptors), for a library's catalogs for publications on a subject of interest, or a periodical index for articles on a subject of interest, some good ground rules are:
   →(1) Be general rather than specific. Be SPECIFIC rather than general.
    (2) Check what you have-- the actual words you're thinking.
    (3) And then get creative as necessary.
The three steps in the ground rules sequence contain an error; correct the sequence by making necessary adjustment.

11. You need material about the background of the novel, _Emma_, written by Jane Austen (1775-1817). You're looking for books of criticism and commentary. So you check the library card catalog under the subject-heading (PRINT):
    AUSTEN, JANE, 1775-1817. EMMA.

12-13 relate to the reproduction below of an entry from_____.

  X Comprehensive Dissertation Index
      Dissertation Abstracts International
      Political Science Abstracts

13. It consists of 3 citations which have in common the title keyword
    POLITICAL_____.

```
┌─────────────────────────────────────────────────────────┐
│                   POLITICAL SCIENCE                       │
│ THE POLITICAL ECONOMY OF U.S. TRADE POLICY:  AN EVALUATION│
│   OF THEORY (TRANSNATIONALS, THE STATE, TAXES, TARIFFS,   │
│   UNITED STATES.)                                         │
│   ALGER, KEITH NORMAN  (PH.D.  1985   THE UNIVERSITY OF   │
│   WISCONSIN - MADISON)   325p.  47/03A, p. 1038           │
│                     QUU86-01523                           │
│ POLITICAL REASON AND PUBLIC FREEDOM:  A CRITIQUE OF MAX   │
│   WEBER'S POLITICAL THEORY.                               │
│   BREINER, PETER DAVID  (PH.D.  1986   STANFORD UNIVERSITY)│
│   261p.  47/03A, p. 1039   QUU86-12717                    │
│ UNDERSTANDING EFFECTIVE POLITICAL LEADERSHIP IN THE THIRD │
│   WORLD  -  AN ALTERNATIVE APPROACH:  THE CASES OF FIDEL  │
│   CASTRO AND INDIRA GANDHI.                               │
│   BROTHERTON, FESTUS, JR.  (PH.D.   1985   UNIVERSITY OF  │
│   CALIFORNIA, LOS ANGELES)   674p.  47/02A,  p. 641       │
│                     QUU86003937                           │
└─────────────────────────────────────────────────────────┘
```

14. When you have a handful of bib cards following a search on your
topic of periodical indexes, in order to proceed with getting complete
information, you'd arrange these bib cards so that they are

      alphabetical by authors' surnames
  X alphabetical by periodical titles' first regarded words
      chronological by dates of publication
      grouped by subjects

15. Always use the latest edition of an encyclopedia unless you have
some particular reason. Select the encyclopedia you use on the bases
of such things as subjects covered in the scope of the title, and

    place of publication._____.

16. An indexing tool which cumulates usually utilizes temporary paper
supplements as part of this technique. Every so often this indexing is
then_____ into larger issues or cumulations. The new "big" permanent
bound volume then ____ all of the interim coverage. An example is_____.

      alphabetized / becomes / Sheehy's Guide To Reference Books
  X interfiled / replaces / Humanities Index
      weeded / replaces / Readers' Guide

17-26. Which one of the library tools would you consult if you could use only one such resource and you needed all of the following information in one spot? Record the letter of the resource, referring to the "COLLECTION (CHOICES)" which follows the informational needs and which begins on page 5.   Be sure to print the capital letter clearly. ANSWER ONLY TEN OF THE "needs"; ANSWER ONLY 10; DO ANY BUT ONLY TEN OF THEM!

You need to...

J ___ get the exact date of the abdication of King Edward VIII of Great Britain. ["E" would be a reasonable answer; "J" would be better.]

K ___ identify quickly 4-5 specialized periodical indexes relevant to the topic (Should prostitution in the U.S.A. be de-regularized/legalized? For a sociology course) on which you're doing a library literature search.

G ___ locate (get the library's call number, title, bibliographic data) a great, up-to-date, background reading, possibly less than book length, on the status of the contemporary women's movement.

G ___ compile a fairly lengthy bibliography of books by and about American writer Carson McCullers (1917-1967) which are in the library's collection.

I ___ know which libraries in Illinois have the 1902 book, "Child Labour Legislation Handbook" by Josephine Goldmark.

C ___ compile a bibliography of biographies relating to Karl Marx appearing in books as well as in magazines.

E ___ get some authoritative background information about Afra Behn (born 1640), "the first female writer who had lived by her pen in England." You also need to clear up the question of "Why did she attempt to write in a style that should be mistaken for that of a man" and to have access to a list of all of her works.

F ___ identify the titles of several recommended (by an expert) bibliographies, handbooks, and other reference books related to your specialized field or topic.

B ___ identify the titles, compilers and publishers of several recently published (approximately within the last three years) bibliographies of book length on an important subject which you're researching.

B ___ compile a list of bibliographies published in the 1930's and 1940's on the subject of pottery; you'd like it to encompass a variety of formats-- books, parts of books, parts of articles, etc.

17-26, contd.

You need to...

M____ compile a bibliography of articles published in popular magazines about Gertrude Ederle at the time she swam the English Channel, August 1926.

N____ know what % of the U.S. population before the Civil War was black and what % after.

A____ get titles of several specialized periodical indexes and abstracting services in the field of nuclear and space science.

D____
[Not H] compile bibliographies of U.S. government documents published at the time(s) of each of the following: World War I, the passage of the Constitutional Amendment providing women the right to vote (1920) and the Great Depression of the 1930's.

L____ You need a journal article about Koko, the gorilla at Stanford University, who, it is said, can use sign language. Because a scholarly journal article is likely to be lengthy, you would like to read an abstract of the article before pursuing the issue of the periodical itself.

COLLECTION (CHOICES)

A. "Abstracts and Indexes in Science & Technology: A Descriptive Guide", by Dolores Owen

B. "Bibliographic Index"

C. "Biography Index"

D. "Cumulative Subject Index to the Monthly Catalog, 1900-1971"

E. "Dictionary of National Biography"

F. "Guide to Reference Books", by Eugene Sheehy

G. the library's catalog

H. "The Monthly Catalog"

I. "National Union Catalog" pre 1956 basic set

J. "New Columbia Encyclopedia"

K. "Periodical Indexes in the Social Sciences and Humanities: A Subject Guide", by Lois Harzfeld

L. "Psychological Abstracts"

M. "Readers' Guide"

N. "The Statistical Abstract of the United States"

27. Six steps involved in doing library research for a term paper were commended to you: [fill in the two blanks]

#1 Background reading, an ___OUTLINE___, and a "working title".
#2 Using a thesaurus efficiently to locate usable subject headings.
#3 A systematic methodology for locating articles in periodicals.
#4 Using a selective ___BIBLIOGRAPHY___ or "guide to the literature".
#5 Using some specialized periodical indexes and abstracting services.
#6 Evaluating your discoveries: selecting and de-selecting.

28-31 Cards for these books are filed together with one cross reference card alphabetically in a library card catalog. (There are no subject cards here). The 20 "cards" have been randomly listed below:

"84, Charing Cross Road" [a title card]
"The Dalhousie Journals" [a title card] by Louise Dalhousie [an author card]
"Dr. Jekyll and Mr. Hyde" [a title card]
"El Cazador Oculto" [a title card]
A SEE card from DeBalzac, Honore to Balzac, Honore de, 1799-1850
"Eugene Grandet" [a title card] by Honore DeBalzac [an author card]
"Shoulder to Shoulder" [a title card] by Midge Mackenzie [an author card]
"The Psychology of Sex Differences" [a title card] by Eleanor Maccoby [an author card]
"The Power Lovers" [a title card] by Myra MacPherson [an author card]
"Memories of a Catholic Girlhood" [a title card] by Mary McCarthy [an author card]
"The Doctor Takes a Wife" [a title card] by Elizabeth Seifert [an author card]
"The Group" [a title card] by Mary McCarthy [an author card]

The first line of the 5th card reads___DeBalzac, See Balzac___

The first line of the 15th card reads___MacPherson, Myra___

Feel free to use the space below for working out your response. It will not be regarded in connection with your answers to the two questions above.

10 The Group
9 Eugene Grandet
8 84, Charing Cross Road
7 The Doctor Takes a Wife
6 Dr. Jekyll and Mr. Hyde
5 DeBalzac, See Balzac
4 The Dalhousie Journals
3 Dalhousie, Louise
2 El Cazador Oculto
1 Balzac, Honore

20 Shoulder to Shoulder
19 Seifert, Elizabeth
18 The Psychology of Sex Differences
17 The Power Lovers
16 Memories of a Catholic Girlhood
15 MacPherson, Myra
14 Mackenzie, Midge
13 Maccoby, Eleanor
12 McCarthy, Mary [Memories...]
11 McCarthy, Mary [The Group]

32.
Reproduced to the right is an
excerpt derived from a _____
which appeared within the
"_____".

Check one of the following:
-list of descriptors/ Arts &
  Humanities Citation Index
X-permuted subject index/ Social
  Sciences Citation Index
-thesaurus / Science Citation
  Index

```
PORK
   BARRELL ---- GRAFTON CT   +
           ---- NATION
           ---- REICHARD GW
           ---- RICE RR
   EMPTY   ---- NATION
   POLITICS --- GRAFTON CT   +
            --- REICHARD GW
            --- RICE RR      +
PORNOGRAPHY
   ATTACK    ---- COURT JH
   CONTROVERSY  STEVENDS JD +
   DEVIANCE --- ELLIS A     +
   LAW     ------ EICKHOFF LF
   MENTAL-HEA       "
   SEXUAL   ---- ELLIS A     +
   WOMEN    ---- COURT JH
```

33. Reproduced to the right is

  a Books In Print entry
X the verso of the title page of a
  book
  a catalog card
  the title page of Woman's Work

34. You need to discover publications which refer to (cite) an
article about English history
which you have read and found
very useful. So you start by consulting the _____ in
"_____".

Check one of the following:

  - abstract / Historical
    Abstracts
X - citation index portion /
    Arts & Humanities Citation
    Index
  - source index portion /
    Social Sciences Citation
    Index

Copyright © 1974 by Ann Oakley

All rights reserved under International and Pan-
American Copyright Conventions. Published in
the United States by Pantheon Books, a division of
Random House, Inc., New York.

Originally published in Great Britain as *Housewife*
by Allen Lane, Penguin Books Ltd., London.

Library of Congress Cataloging in Publication Data

Oakley, Ann.
  Woman's Work.

British ed. published in 1974 under title: Housewife.
  Bibliography: pp. 251-68
  Includes index.
  1. Wives—Case studies. 2. Mothers—Case
studies. 3. Home economics. I. Title
HQ759.O3   1975   301.41'2   74-4765
ISBN 0-394-46097-9

Manufactured in the United States of America

First American Edition

35-37 relate to this excerpt from

    the Bibliographic Index
X   the Biography Index
    the Humanities Index
    a Wordsworth bio-bibliography

36. It includes 7 citations to publications on the subject of

<u>William Wordsworth</u>

37. "Wives of famous men" (the sixth
line) refers to the title of

X a book by Eda Howink
    a book by Dorothy Wordsworth
    part (pages 35-40) of a book
    poetry by Eda Howink

38. Five publications are cited in
the excerpt reproduced to the right
which is from one of the basic
tools considered in this course.
These five publications have in common the fact that they _____

   <u>are all bibliographies or</u>
   <u>include bibliographies</u> .

39-40 relate to this excerpt from

X   the Bibliographic Index
    the Biography Index
    Women Studies Abstracts

40. The citations relating to publications about Bangladesh women in
rural development and about women
in science conclude with a reference to an inclusive pagination.
To what do these pairs of numbers
refer?

    the length of the publication itself
X the location of a bibliography with-
    in the publication
    the location of an article within
    another publication

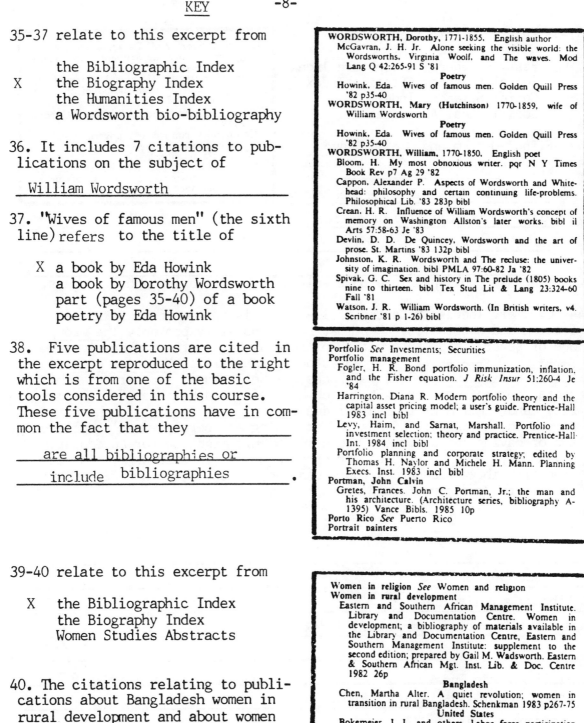

WORDSWORTH, Dorothy, 1771-1855. English author
  McGavran, J. H. Jr. Alone seeking the visible world: the
  Wordsworths, Virginia Woolf, and The waves. Mod
  Lang Q 42:265-91 S '81
              Poetry
  Howink, Eda. Wives of famous men. Golden Quill Press
  '82 p35-40
WORDSWORTH, Mary (Hutchinson) 1770-1859, wife of
  William Wordsworth
              Poetry
  Howink, Eda. Wives of famous men. Golden Quill Press
  '82 p35-40
WORDSWORTH, William, 1770-1850. English poet
  Bloom, H. My most obnoxious writer. pqr N Y Times
  Book Rev p7 Ag 29 '82
  Cappon, Alexander P. Aspects of Wordsworth and White-
  head: philosophy and certain continuing life-problems.
  Philosophical Lib. '83 283p bibl
  Crean. H. R. Influence of William Wordsworth's concept of
  memory on Washington Allston's later works. bibl il
  Arts 57:58-63 Je '83
  Devlin, D. D. De Quincey, Wordsworth and the art of
  prose. St. Martins '83 132p bibl
  Johnston, K. R. Wordsworth and The recluse: the univer-
  sity of imagination. bibl PMLA 97:60-82 Ja '82
  Spivak, G. C. Sex and history in The prelude (1805) books
  nine to thirteen. bibl Tex Stud Lit & Lang 23:324-60
  Fall '81
  Watson, J. R. William Wordsworth. (In British writers, v4.
  Scribner '81 p 1-26) bibl

Portfolio *See* Investments; Securities
Portfolio management
  Fogler, H. R. Bond portfolio immunization, inflation,
  and the Fisher equation. *J Risk Insur* 51:260-4 Je
  '84
  Harrington, Diana R. Modern portfolio theory and the
  capital asset pricing model; a user's guide. Prentice-Hall
  1983 incl bibl
  Levy, Haim, and Sarnat, Marshall. Portfolio and
  investment selection; theory and practice. Prentice-Hall
  Int. 1984 incl bibl
  Portfolio planning and corporate strategy; edited by
  Thomas H. Naylor and Michele H. Mann. Planning
  Execs. Inst. 1983 incl bibl
Portman, John Calvin
  Gretes, Frances. John C. Portman, Jr.; the man and
  his architecture. (Architecture series, bibliography A-
  1395) Vance Bibls. 1985 10p
Porto Rico *See* Puerto Rico
Portrait painters

Women in religion *See* Women and religion
Women in rural development
  Eastern and Southern African Management Institute.
  Library and Documentation Centre. Women in
  development; a bibliography of materials available in
  the Library and Documentation Centre, Eastern and
  Southern Management Institute: supplement to the
  second edition; prepared by Gail M. Wadsworth. Eastern
  & Southern African Mgt. Inst. Lib. & Doc. Centre
  1982 26p
             Bangladesh
  Chen, Martha Alter. A quiet revolution; women in
  transition in rural Bangladesh. Schenkman 1983 p267-75
           United States
  Bokemeier, J. L. and others. Labor force participation
  of metropolitan, nonmetropolitan, and farm women:
  a comparative study. *Rural Sociol* 48:536-9 Wint '83
Women in science
  Keller, Evelyn Fox. Reflections on gender and science.
  Yale Univ. Press 1985 p181-9

41-43 relate to this excerpt from

   X   Essay & General Literature Index
       Social Sciences Citation Index
       Social Sciences Index
       Sociological Abstracts

> Ostrom, Elinor, and Parks, Roger B. Suburban police departments: too many and too small? *In* Masotti, L. H. and Hadden, J. K. eds. The urbanization of the suburbs p367-402
> Ostrom, Elinor, and Whitaker, Gordon Prevo Community control and governmental responsiveness: the case of police in Black neighborhoods *In* Hawley, W. D. and Rogers, D. eds. Improving the quality of urban management p303-34

42. Elinor Ostrom and <u>Gordon Prevo</u>
43. wrote " _____ Whitaker _____

Community control and governmental responsiveness: the case of police in Black neighborhoods"

_____

which was published in a book edited by W. D. Hawley and D. Rogers.

44-50. Mary Therese McCarthy (1912-   ) is an American writer of fiction and nonfiction. Her most famous novel is probably <u>The Group</u>, one of several made into motion pictures. Her nonfiction has included <u>Sights and Spectacles</u>; an autobiography titled <u>Memories of a Catholic Girlhood</u>; and travel books. She is known for her "searching social comment and keen wit, which has reflected her hatred of hypocrisy, and commitment to radical causes". You have to report on the effect, if any, of attending a liberal, women's college and of having had a convent education. This might be for an education, psychology, Women's studies, or other course. In column #1, list ten specific library resources you would use. Then, in column #2, number them in the order you would consult them.

#1	#2
LCSH	1
Subject catalog	2
Library's online catalog	3
Harzfeld's book of periodical indexes in soc scis/humanities	4
Book Review Digest	10
Bibliographic Index	6
Arts & Humanities Citation Index	9
Biography Index	5
Essay & General Literature Index	8
Women Studies Abstracts	7

END OF EXAMINATION. The test will be returned during office hours next week. If you do not pick it up then, it will be in the envelope with your Project.

Department   <u>Guidelines for Discussing the</u>
Senior Thesis Seminar   <u>Prospectus</u>
Date   Instructor

Some Related Terminology:

<u>Prospectus</u>: A formal summary of a proposed commercial, literary, or
       other venture. (<u>American Heritage Dictionary of the English</u>
       <u>Language</u>)

       Abstract   Primary source
       Action research   Research
       Bibliography   Review article
       Dissertation   Search strategy
       Guide to the literature   Selective/comprehensive
       Hypothesis(es)/assumption; to   Style manual
         hypothesize   Thesis(es)
       Key words   Working title

Add others:

_____

Here are some considerations for each prospectus we discuss:

1. Is the TITLE a good indicator of the content of the proposed paper?
    Are all of the essential key words in the title? Ask yourself,
    if you could have only three key words, which would rank most
    importantly? At this point, this is a "working title."

2. What is your evaluation of the HYPOTHESIS? Not all research in-
    volves an hypothesis. Is it workable? Is it biased? Has anything
    been omitted? How much and what type of research would be needed
    to prove it [true or false]?

3. Are the direction and point of view of the paper clear? For what
    AUDIENCE is the scholar-colleague writing?

4. What kinds of TERMS are being used? Are they defined clearly?

5. Does the OPENING sentence catch your attention? What expectations
    does it raise?

6. What type of DATA should be collected in order to carry out the
    research or prove the argument (thesis) of the paper?

7. Will a QUESTIONNAIRE be involved? (Social sciences field?) Inter-
    views?

8. What is new, different, SIGNIFICANT about the proposed research?
    Ask, why bother?! Is plagiarism (unintentional or otherwise) a
    possibility? Of ideas or words? With what other work by what
    other researcher is there any RELATIONSHIP? Why is this going to

matter? For whom will it be significant?

9. What ASSUMPTIONS are involved? What assumptions are forthright-
    ly expressed?

10. What do you like about it, and why? What is FEASIBLE about the
    prospectus?

11. How does the writer of the prospectus define her/his research in
    terms of whatever s/he is, e.g. scholar, scientist, civil rights
    activist? Is the definition of whatever that commitment or
    PERSPECTIVE is expressed? Implied? Do you agree with it?

12. The MECHANICS of communication: pages numbered, directions
    followed, appropriate style manual identified, etc.

13. Evaluate the selective, annotated (albeit preliminary) BIBLIOG-
    RAPHY.

14. What did you learn from this reading and critique that you might
    apply to your own work?

Space for notes:

Chapter 4

The University of California System: A Case Study

Background

A positive, pragmatic approach to the near-future, based on practice and experience, is the intent of this book. It proposes, recommends, and enables. The experiences of a state university system are of interest to many readers of a book about coursework which includes bibliographic instruction. Another reason for their inclusion is the limited amount in the literature about undergraduate bibliographic instruction courses involving the University of California system's campuses, departments, and libraries. This chapter is not a case study in the sense of detailed analysis of a particular program as an exemplary social phenomenon; it is provided to illustrate.

In 1978 I had seemingly been unemployable for five years, dating from the time when my employment on the graduate faculty at the main campus of another land grant state university ceased. I had filed a civil rights action against a fellow institution, and numerous female-sex discrimination charges had followed. [1] I heard about a recruitment process for Bibliography 1 teachers from a University of California, Berkeley, School of Library and Information Studies alumna; there was no open advertising. My first letter was unanswered. In the margin of my University of California system Academic Personnel application form (which stipulates provision of age, marital status, and salary history), someone fearlessly commented in ink, "From Associate Professor to associate!!!???" One question during my interview related to how I would deal with plagiarism. Although they were unable to provide information and lapsed into a hazy conversation among themselves about the decision making process, it was stressed by the chairman of the interview committee that they were not the decision makers. I was employed as an associate to teach one section of Bibliography 1 for less than the academic year. Associate is a job title just above teaching assistant and below lecturer, although salary ranges overlap, so that I was initially placed lower than some TA's whom I later met. The dean volunteered attribution of the lowness of my salary to Proposition 13, a recent initiative affecting California taxation. Later, my employment was extended to the end of that academic year, and thereafter year-by-year. I was usually notified in midsummer about the following academic year. During the third week of the first term, the dean brought into a casual conversation that I should not expect to become a member of the School faculty "ever."

While working alone in the Bibliography 1 room between terms, I was approached by visiting academics. An Australian educator asked about the course's "history and workings." She subsequently provided me with the following list of the things she wanted to know about Bib 1, as it is known.

Basic status: Number of years
   Number of students per course and per year
   Duration, periodicity
   Number of courses

Objectives, goal statements: Original and current
   Changes over time and why

Students: Attitudes, evaluations, participation
   Choice of topics
   Increasing, more sophisticated use of reference staff and facilities?

Staff: Staff/student ratio
   Recruitment, qualifications, experience, sources
   Autonomy, standardization with reference to content, methodology, and who decides?
   Means of communication between instructors--mandatory regular meetings, informal, none

Budget: Staff salaries, materials, costs, come from where?

Methods and Materials: What were/are they. Changes and why?
   Who decides?

Content: Ditto

Fitting into academic structure: Credit and noncredit
   Faculty links, attitudes
   Specific PR and promotion efforts
   Relationship to library and library staff in general and the administration
   What other bibliographic instruction activities available on campus?
   Has anything else been tried and discarded?

By 1980 I was receiving direct inquiries from persons in professional education, education for librarianship, Women studies, undergraduate education, and librarianship. In the intervening years I have received more generalized questions about this type of course rather than Bibliography 1 in particular. International interest in the bibliographic instruction course concept led me while a Visiting Scholar in Summer 1984 to several presentations in Japanese academe.

In 1979 the dean mentioned the desirability of "a Bib 1 journal article."
As a published academic who by then was enthusiastic about the course concept, I volunteered, not knowing that this bait had previously been cast. I worked out with him a preliminary draft titled "9,000 [as of 1980] Undergraduates Later; a Case Study in Bibliographic Instruction at the University of California, Berkeley."
During the dean's sabbatical abroad, the "paper" served him as raw material at professional meetings. Four revisions later, it dawned on me that I had reached the point beyond which I was unable to incorporate further adjustments without deterioration of both my authorship and integrity. But I had chosen to limit further my utility to the School and the University by not cooperating--especially

unwise for an old woman with my "history." As a campus newspaper reporter put it in an article titled "Women Still Fighting For Job Equality," "...although she has extensive experience teaching library science as an associate professor, her active involvement in filing sex discrimination charges has prevented her from maintaining a full-time level of employment. Her current position at UC Berkeley is part-time and temporary." [2]

The System

California public higher education is provided by two-year community colleges, a system of state colleges and universities, and the research-oriented nine-campus University of California system. These institutions' many libraries offer a variety of bibliographic instructional services. BI courses as part of library programming exist in all three systems. Indeed, transfer credit is possible from a community college library self-paced workbook "course" toward the University of California baccalaureate degree! Specialized bibliographic and research methodology courses are found among some graduate level departmental offerings. Universities in California which offer professionally-accredited graduate-level degrees in library-information science, separate from the libraries of these institutions, are San José State University and the University of California at Los Angeles and at Berkeley.

The University of California is composed of nine campuses, dominated by UC Berkeley and UC Los Angeles. Three large campuses--UC Davis, San Diego at LaJolla, and Santa Barbara--are complemented by four smaller institutions--UC Irvine, Riverside, San Francisco, and Santa Cruz, with their various strengths and specializations. Systemwide administration is located in Berkeley. Throughout the UC system, in order for a course to generate credit for the student, it must be sponsored by or administered through an academic department; at UC, the library is not a department. Curricular matters and approval of courses are generally within the domain of each campus' Academic Senate. These governing bodies are composed of Academic Senate faculty, who are administrators, full-time Lecturers, Instructors, and professorial faculty, i.e. Assistant, Associate, Acting, and full Professors, and no professional librarians other than the University Librarian. A large number of teaching assistants, associates, part-time lecturers, and all professional librarians other than the director--who submit the same Academic Personnel application as "regular" faculty--are excluded from membership in their Academic Senate and participation in its influential committees.

Problems involved in establishing formal library instruction courses for undergraduate students on University of California campuses were discussed by a UC Berkeley libraries' professional staff member, who described courses offered in 1975 throughout the UC system. In her paper, Toy urged two changes. Each University library should be recognized as an academic department in its own right, responsible for initiating and conducting courses taught by librarians using their own academic titles, and subject to normal academic review. Library budget formulation should be examined and revised to identify and provide for such courses. [3]

The Nine Campuses' Courses

In 1975 Toy described UC Davis' newly constituted three unit BI course, English

28: Introduction to Library Research and Bibliography, an elective taught by campus librarians designated "lecturers without stipend" in the English Department. It continues to be offered each quarter during the academic year, i.e. not during the summer quarter. Two sections were offered in Fall 1986, with sixty students enrolled in each. One is considered the general section and focuses on humanities and social sciences; the other, on biology and agriculture. (The UC Davis campus has veterinary and medical schools and is a leader in agriculture.) English 28 meets once a week and is now offered both for a grade or Pass/Not Pass, for two credits. Passed/Not Passed is an option UC undergraduates often apply to letter-graded courses they judge will require little of their time. Letter grades of all the students in the class are presumably computed together, with students who have designated P/NP (the cut-off declaration date is well into the term) considered to have passed, with credit, if their achievement is the equivalent of C-minus or better. UC-B undergraduates, for example, receive credit for such courses to a limit of one-third of the total units undertaken and passed. The units are accepted for credit but are not used in computing grade-point average. In general, students may not apply this option to courses required for their majors. A locally created handbook is used. The English Department provides a one quarter time Teaching Assistant.

With the retirement of a librarian who has been committed to the course, there appears to be a move toward a self-paced course, despite the fact that students are described as requesting "some personal contact, rather than having it all automated" and "would like to have the University require it." Each student prepares a twenty-item bibliography of books and articles. [4]

• • •

The University of California, Irvine in 1975 was in its third quarter of provision of a two-unit research methods course called Biblio-Strategy. The librarians had recently been granted an extension of approval by the sponsoring Humanities Department to enable their continued teaching of the course.

In 1986 Humanities 75: Bibliostrategy survives as an elective, two-credit course taught by librarians, offered in one section and sponsored by the now-School of Humanities. It is available for Pass/Not Pass option. A bibliographic project is a requirement. There is no locally-produced handbook. Bibliostrategy meets twice weekly for fifty minutes. Writing a Research Paper, Or How I Learned to Stop Worrying and Love the Library, a videotape produced by the library for use with an undergraduate writing class, has been shown at the end of the quarter for Bibliostrategy class members' critique. The UC-I library does not provide a self-paced "course."

• • •

UCLA and UC-B are able to conduct undergraduate "service courses" for credit through their graduate, professionally-accredited library schools, but they are the only two University of California system campuses having library schools. The UCLA Graduate School of Library and Information Science is said to have observed the UC-B Bibliography 1 course-program, founded in 1968, and to have evolved their program, beginning in 1976 with Information Resources and Libraries. It was to be a strongly academic course carrying four units credit, with faculty consisting of lecturers already faculty members of the Graduate School of Library and Information Science, which offered the course, and librarians from the General Library staff, who carried the designation Librarian-Teacher. Only the library school faculty were able to grade students' work, because their titles did not qualify librarians to act as "officers of instruction." The UCLA "methods course" was designed to teach upper division students access to the library in a field of study as well as to the basic resources of any library. Sophomore standing or instructor's consent was required. The librarians appointed to teach were assisted by second-year Master's degree library school students employed as 25 per cent time Teaching Assistants. Four sections of about twenty students each were offered each quarter, reaching some two hundred students. The course met for two hours twice a week. Sections focused on specific subject areas, e.g. science and technology. Similarities to the UC-B Bibliography 1 course reported in a 1979 interview included the annotated bibliography requirement, a handbook, considerable independence for each instructor, and a demonstration of online reference service retrieval for each section. Separate but related undergraduate materials courses (GSLIS 111A-D: Ethnic Groups and Their Bibliography) went into such fields as American Indian and Afro-American bibliography. [5] The UCLA Undergraduate Library workbook BI provision was discontinued.

In 1986, the course GSLIS 110: Information Resources and Libraries continues to be administered by the graduate, professional library school and offered every quarter for four units. It is available for Pass/Not Pass, and satisfies no undergraduate requirements. Focus is on social sciences and humanities, with one section taught as an adjunct to Political Science 20; a section in the fall focuses on science and technology. Requirements include a bibliographic project. A Syllabus/Workbook and Turabian style manual are "required texts"; recommended "texts" are Richard Lanham's Revising Prose (New York: Scribner's, 1979) and John R. Trimble's Writing With Style: Conversations on the Art of Writing (Englewood Cliffs, New Jersey: Prentice-Hall, 1975). It meets twice weekly, two hours per class. Although the course announcement distributed in Fall 1986 by the School did not refer to prerequisites, another source described GSLIS 110 as an upper division course. Graduate students enrolled in the library school courses, Training and Supervision of Teaching Asistants and Teaching Apprentice Practicum, serve as teaching assistants for it. It can be seen that the UCLA Graduate School of Library and Information Science is enhancing its primary mission of provision of professional, graduate level training for librarians-information scientists while making available an undergraduate service course to some UCLA undergraduate students as well as much of the staff support for the course. [6]

•   •   •

Requests from UC Riverside faculty for librarians to provide lectures in the bibliography of various subject fields quadrupled in 1975. One librarian, endowed with the title of temporary associate-without-stipend, conducted a four unit course for the Music Department.

The Library Instruction Coordinator described the UC Riverside library's credit course, "Library Research Strategies," in Fall 1986. Two thirds of the class meetings are taught by him, and he is also responsible for the grading. The other classes are taught by librarians as guest lecturers. "Library Research Strategies" is now offered only in the spring quarter, although it had been offered until recently during two of the three principle quarters, for two Pass/Not credits, i.e. not for a letter-grade. It is administered through the Humanities and Social Sciences Interdisciplinary Program and focuses on these areas. All of the instructional personnel are full-time professional librarians employed on the UC Riverside library staff. A bibliographic project of at least ten pages is a requirement. Students do not purchase a locally produced handbook nor use a trade book. The course meets twice a week for fifty minutes and satisfies no undergraduate requirements. Rather low enrollment (fifteen students during Spring 1986 quarter) has led UC-R librarians to "wonder about the future of this course." Through it, they have attempted to reach students who want to go beyond the basics and learn a considerable amount about library resources. Basic library instruction is provided by the library's involvement with the English 1 program, the composition course which most undergraduates must take. [7]

• • •

The UC San Diego library began in 1973 a two-unit course in an interdisciplinary sequence called Contemporary Issues. Librarians who had been teaching this successful library instruction course looked forward to prolonged use of the accommodating "lecturer without stipend" designation. Their Academic Senate's Committee on Educational Policy approved the course for an indefinite period. By 1980, UC San Diego library's undergraduate BI course was well known. Administered by the interdisciplinary Contemporary Issues Department, Information and Academic Libraries was an elective introduction to research strategies, directed at satisfying the information needs of the students using academic libraries, with emphases on the UC San Diego library system. Virginia Sherwood, of the library staff, coordinated the program in the first phase. Classes were taught by librarians, who received ten hours released time each week. For the quarter that the librarian taught, s/he was appointed as a temporary lecturer through the Contemporary Issues office. A classroom in the undergraduate library was used; sections were also taught at the main and science libraries. Specialized sections on science and in ethnic studies were offered. Finding Information in the University of California, San Diego Libraries was used as a text and given to students. An administrative assistant and two students provided support.

An interview in 1986 confirmed that Contemporary Issues 50: Information and Academic Libraries and the locally produced handbook continue at UC-SD. One section is offered in each of the three main quarters of the academic year, providing two units credit. The course, taught by librarians, satisfies no undergraduate requirements. Library Search Strategy, a slide tape, has been produced.

• • •

In 1975 a librarian at the University of California, San Francisco provided a two unit course for the Department of the History of Health Sciences titled Introduction to the History and Bibliography of the Health Sciences. A graduate level course, Historical Methods and Bibliography of Health Sciences, is currently (1986) offered at least once a year. Team-taught by a librarian and faculty members, it provides four units credit.

• • •

The University of California, Santa Barbara in 1975 offered a two unit course in the campus' Interdisciplinary Studies program taught by librarians who had no special titles. The University Librarian (director) was required to sign their grade sheets. Other librarians at UC-SB served as lecturers-without-stipend in the departments of chemistry, music, and political science, for which they provided subject bibliography courses.

In 1987 Coordinator of Library Instruction Patricia Gebhard listed several UC-SB credit courses for which librarians are responsible:

Interdisciplinary 1: Library Skills, for 1 unit; not prerequisite of:
Interdisciplinary 100: Library Research, for 2 units
Black Studies 196: Bibliographic Method in Black Studies
Chemistry 184: Chemical Literature
Chicano Studies 110: Research Methods in Chicano Studies
Music 111: Music Library Research Techniques
Political Science 49: Library Research Methods in Political Science

Both Interdisciplinary 1: Library Skills and 100: Library Research texts have been stored in ERIC and are also on file at the California Clearinghouse on Library Instruction. The latest editions are available at the campus bookstore. Interdisciplinary 1: Library Skills is a self-paced course offered by librarians for one Pass or Not Pass credit every term in ten sections. It consists of an initial class, a review session, and a final meeting. A bibliographic project is not a requirement. Library Skills and Library Skills Exercises are purchased by the student.

Interdisciplinary 100: Library Research is also offered only for Pass or Not Pass, but provides two credits. Two sections are offered in both fall and winter quarters, three in the spring. A short bibliographic project is required. Completion of both courses is required for students majoring in Speech and Hearing. Library Research contains assignments and is purchased at the Bookstore. A diagnostic test and evaluation form have been developed for use in connection with Interdisciplinary 100. Gebhard describes the course as differing from both the UC Berkeley and Los Angeles courses in that "it emphasizes the problem solving skills necessary to do library research rather than emphasizing bibliography." However, the UC-B School of Library and Information Studies' Bibliography 1 is similar to UC-SB's Interdisciplinary 1: Library Skills in that Bb 1, although open to all undergraduates (despite its course number) attracts many lower division students.

Among UC-SB bibliographic instruction subject courses, Introduction to Music Research Techniques is offered only for a grade (Pass/Not Pass is not an option), and for two or three credits. One section is offered each year in the spring quarter by the Music Department and taught by music librarians, meeting once a week for two hours. A short bibliographic project is required. This course is said to be "in transition."

• • •

In 1975 the UC Santa Cruz library was presenting a new series of seminars in social sciences, humanities, and science. It provided no credit, and librarians, with credit courses in view, were involved in discussions with their Academic Senate's Committee on Educational Policies. In 1986, the University Librarian (director) indicated that the UC-SC library does not "give a credit course in library instruciton ... but rather takes other approaches to library instruction."

Also in California...

San José State University is part of the state college and university system in California, but is mentioned here because of its library school--the Division of Library Science. In 1982 a Pass/Fail credit course covering DIALOG, BRS, basic search strategy, and Boolean logic for San José State University undergraduates and community members was proposed by librarians Osegueda and Reynolds. [8] LS 1, Use of Books and Libraries, a general lower division course on the use of books and library facilities, open to all college students, and LS 101: Use of Library Materials, an upper division general course on the use of books and library facilities, with some emphasis on techniques of research, were increased from one to two credits each. These elective BI courses were administered through the Division of Library Science. Various text books were tried, with Katz's Your Library a required purchase. An "EOP" version of the course was offered during summer 1985 by Reynolds as part of a team which included tutors, to enhance the possibility of students' library skills being extrapolated into their writing and other academic work. LS 1 and 101 have not been offered for several years, and the Division of Library Science no longer lists them. Students are reported to "have too many other units to fit in any extras. The library's 'one-hour stand' in freshman and junior writing courses is now our major focus ... few students want to know that much about the library."

A House Is Not a Habitat: Getting Around the System

Persistence and ingenuity have dealt with the problem of finding an acceptable academic home--a department, program, or school to house University of California libraries' undergraduate BI courses so that they can provide academic credit, which is to say, so that students can take the courses. At two of the nine campuses, Los Angeles and Berkeley, the presence of graduate professional schools of library-information science suggested the "logical" sponsors. Notably, there are no representatives from either the UC Berkeley or Los Angeles library school faculties on the "front line" steering committees of the California Clearing-house on Library Instruction. Library school faculty are, however, members of their campuses' influential Academic Senates, while librarians other than the director are not eligible. Such departments as English, Contemporary Issues, and Interdisciplinary Studies have provided solutions on other UC campuses. Other considerations of interest to the educator concerned with an undergraduate research course of which libraries are an important, but nonetheless only one, part have emerged. They include:

- The amount of credits and whether the course is offered for both a grade and Pass/Not Pass option, or only Passed/Not Passed.

- Whether completion of the course satisfies any degree requirements, e.g. breadth, general education, departmental, core, etc., or alternatively, is required.

- The "text," if any, and whether it is locally-created or a trade publication, as well as its nature, e.g. workbook, assignments, syllabus, etc.

- Course-related audiovisual media--locally-produced or commercial.

- Structure of the course: self-paced, team taught, multisection, etc.

- Whether there is a bibliographic project as a requirement, its significance in terms of such things as length, strategy essay, proportion of course grade, selection of topic.

- Attendance

- Whether there is an examination or testing process, uniformly utilized; if there is a final examination, whether it is part of Examination Week.

- Attitude of the library administration and librarians not involved in the libraries' BI program.

The University of California-Berkeley and Bibliography 1

"Undergraduate Courses. Bibliography 1. Methods of Library Use. (2) Two hours of lecture per week. Students will learn how to approach the UC Library's resources in a systematic way to meet their needs, via lecture, section, problem sets, examinations, and a term paper. They will learn to extend these techniques to future independent research." [9]

Prehistory

By May 1985 approximately twelve thousand students had completed the under-graduate course on methods of library use at the University of California Berkeley (UC-B). The scale and sustained existence of this course program make it of unusual interest; its decline must also be considered. A four-and-a-half page case study published in 1985 concerning Bibliography 1 is inevitably an account of one instructor's section; its author overlooked some history, due perhaps to reliance on information provided her and to her relatively recent entrance into and occasional teaching in the program. [10] Bibliography 1 has been one of the most successful and longest-lived of the experimental courses introduced into the University curriculum via this route. Librarians noticed a marked increase in the sophistication of undergraduates' use of reference collections after it was in-troduced.

It has been suggested by the graduate UC-B School of Library and Infor-mation Studies that Bib 1's roots reach back to academic year 1933-1934, when Peyton Hurt was employed by the School to teach Librarianship 101: Library Use and General Bibliography. Hurt was listed as that course's instructor for the next three years, while employed by the Library. It continued to be listed, although not offered, until 1940. It appears to have been a library school bib-liography course provision, unrelated to the contemporary undergraduate BI course concept.

In June 1966 City and Regional Planning Librarian Charles H. Shain sought University Librarian Donald C. Coney's approval of a proposal for an experimental undergraduate elective course which would teach the use of the Library and be taught by librarians, as a precondition for its submittal to the Board of Educational Development. It had been spurred by a report of the Academic Senate Committee on Education ("The Muscatine Report," March 1966) and encouraged by discussions with Librarianship Associate Professor Ray Held, who volunteered to serve as the requisite Faculty Sponsor (without salary) for the course, and English Professor Charles Muscatine. Muscatine was to become a member of the Association of American Colleges' Project on Redefining the Meaning and Purpose of Baccalaureate Degrees Committee responsible for the 1984 report, Integrity in the College Curriculum (See Chapter One). He predicted an initial attendance of approximately one hundred fifty students were the course offered on a Tuesday or Thursday. The proposal also alluded to the possibility of a second course, Bibliography 2, to permit a more nearly adequate treatment of the subject in a more reasonable amount of time. [11]

Coney's approval was immediate, and the Board authorized an experimental two-year instruction period preceded by a two-quarter planning period. Instruction began in Fall 1968, with Shain serving as Bibliography 1-X's coordinator and one of the instructors. In a paper prepared for the 1969 California Library Association conference, he reviewed the history of the young course. Including a shorter pilot version taught in the Educational Opportunity Program of summer 1968, sixteen librarians had taught some five hundred ninety UC-B undergraduates enrolled in twenty-seven sections beginning in fall 1968 and continuing through fall 1969. The Muscatine Report, in the aftermath of the Free Speech Movement and concern for the content of the University's curriculum, including its relevance to current social problems and the processes for introducing educational innovations, had proposed a Board of Educational Development to authorize temporary, experimental courses. The original proposal had grown out of Shain's "realization of this serious gap in my own undergraduate education at U.C., as soon as I had taken my first reference course in the U.C. School of Librarianship. Sensing the new climate of experimentation I brought my proposal to the librarian's union at U.C., the only forum then existing for professional discussion by staff librarians."

In practice, instructors employed a common list of twenty-four reference titles to illustrate the broad variety of reference tools that a student might use in a search strategy to find library material on a given topic. These tools were related to the broader world of information, which is only partially approached through even the largest university library. Following Patricia Knapp's example, they referred to the sociology of a particular discipline, including its formal and informal information exchange processes, which extend beyond traditional library sources. [12] Most of their assignments were geared toward the final term project--an annotated bibliography of approximately twenty-five citations. (They had originally thought in terms of fifty citations.) The student was required to identify the specific source, including page number, where that item was located, and to write a brief annotation on each citation describing its use for a topical paper. A brief outline of the projected paper was also required. Finally and, they considered, most importantly, the student was required to write a three to five page introductory essay describing the individual search strategy which s/he had employed within the library. "We do require that the student actually examine the citations used ... rather than relying upon the 'dry lab' procedure of simply listing likely sounding titles.... This forces him to fill out cards, wait in line, place 'holds' on circulating books, and substitute for missing items--all real problems in doing library research." Some term project titles illustrate the variety of subjects students selected circa 1968-1969:

Researching a paper on California railroads
Economic development in Arnhem land due to contact with the white man
Japanese immigration to California, 1890-1924
The Scopes trial
From spirituals to "soul music"
Women's liberation as a social movement
The legal aspects of the consumer in automobile warranties
Education of the blind child with the seeing child in public schools
A general history of American folk and country music since 1900
The art and history of astrology
Angular momentum in quantum theory
Slavery in Brazil and the United States

There were "many problems" facing them in improving the course. An "ideal textbook," for example. They had tried Jean Gates' Guide to the Use of Books and Libraries and Daniel Gore's Bibliography for Beginners: Form A. They had also evolved their own handbook, which was useful mainly for bringing out the location of the UC-B branch libraries' holdings and some of the problems of the catalogs. And they considered there was need to develop a syllabus which would gather the more useful problem sets, handouts, and additional texts they wished to present to their students. Another problem already identified in connection with the neophyte Bib 1 was "the wide range of library experiences among our students, who are almost equally distributed from freshmen to seniors, predominantly in the social sciences and humanities." While they recognized this phenomenon existed in other courses as well, it was especially noticeable in Bib 1. Most of their administrative problems were associated with the experimental nature of the course and their anomalous situation outside the established University departments. Not having any space of their own was a problem. Instructors were granted ten hours released time per week from their library positions, plus a total of twenty hours advance preparation for each new instructor. A second major pressure upon a conscientious instructor, particularly one employed as a subject specialist or in an institute library (a campus library outside of the General Library system), was the growing backlog of work at the primary job. Finding an academic home without departing from the character of the course was a key problem. The School of Librarianship was considering adopting the course, but was concerned over an assured level of funding, so that they could supervise it without jeopardizing their own programs. One of the strongest factors enabling Bib 1's survival had been the continued commitment of the Library administration. The Reference Department in particular was commended for having borne up under a wave of added inquiries resulting from the innovative course. A final problem was identified, that of management. Coordinators "...should have the recent experience of teaching the course in order to understand its problems and to avoid the bureaucratization that comes with distance. They should also be willing to accept change, respect the various talents of the instructors, and bring new material to the course in hopes of improving it...." Shain believed that Bib 1's logical future home, spiritually and physically, should be in the undergraduate library, while its administrative home should be in the library school.

He considered the possibility of computer-assisted instruction in combination, he stressed, with enough personal contact to provide a learning environment. But he cautioned that the elements should be introduced gradually and carefully, so as to avoid destroying an "imperfect but functioning program." Also mentioned for the future was the possibility of broad sections specializing in the natural sciences, social sciences, and humanities. [13]

It was proposed in 1969 that the experimental course be regularized. It continued to be taught by librarians, but, because all courses must be sponsored by a teaching department if credit is to be awarded, the School of Librarianship undertook sponsorship. The School faculty had been reluctant. They feared adverse financial effects, and they were wary of Bib 1's being an opening wedge for undergraduate courses. Early in 1970 they voted to adopt Bibliography 1. Shain announced his "temporary (?) withdrawal" from Bibliography 1 in Spring 1971. Librarian Joan Berman, who had taught the course, replaced him as coordinator. [14] Dr. Fay Blake represented the School's faculty, both directing and teaching the course, which by the mid-1970's decade had become a multi-section program. One instructor from this period who continued to teach Bib 1 occasionally into the 1980's decade recalled nostalgically a collective-like staff structure, with meetings she eagerly anticipated. Dean Patrick Wilson declared that the School could take "no credit at all for the success of the course," and that during the entire time of Shain's association with it, the School's attitude had been one of "at most a reluctant approval of its existence." [15]

Bibliography 1: How to Use the U.C. Library was a learn-by-doing approach for the undergraduate, or amateur library researcher, taught by professional librarians who were largely amateur instructors. The first cycle of the course--preplanning, planning, and instruction--ended in spring 1971. From fall 1968 through winter 1971, Bibliography 1 (formerly 1X) had involved twenty-four librarian-instructors teaching three hundred forty eight sections of 1,100 students. [16] Its goal was to start students using the libraries by informing them of the various kinds of tools they might utilize, including librarians, and then having them apply that knowledge using a search strategy to compile a subject bibliography.

The School continued to sponsor Bib 1 through the 1970's and into the 1980's. Bibliography 1 is recognized as a major contribution to education on the Berkeley campus. A much closer connection between the now-School of Library & Information Studies and the libraries system resulted from additional library staff members serving as part-time teachers associated with the School through it, several of whom then taught on the School faculty. Students in Bib 1, as it became known, have become candidates for its graduate programs. The School became better known generally on campus, and its responsibility for a valuable service offering to undergraduates materially improved its general campus position. [17]

College and university BI courses became increasingly important during this period. Nationally, BI integrated with instruction continues to be the provision by librarians for students' needs, but it has become evident that self-paced workbooks, visits to classes, etc. are frequently second best offerings in lieu of a BI course. Library instruction encompasses more than orientation--it involves fostering actual and effective use of libraries. Most large universities do not have large programs of BI. There are relatively few campuses with great research

libraries which have large numbers of undergraduates. At Berkeley they have
been combined. UC-B enrolled 22,131 undergraduates and 9,332 graduate students
in fall 1986. This means that there is an unusual combination of very research-
and course-oriented faculty, who cannot understand giving credit for something
like a self-paced workbook ... some who believe that a respectable student needs
no formal training in library use, and that the interest should come from a need
to use the library. In a university of such size, many students are taking
courses which are built around large lectures, and they may or may not attend
sections. At UC-B, Bib 1 has been based on relatively small, self-contained sections (contrary to what is implied in the course catalog annotation). The amount
of personal contact has often been unusual for these undergraduate students.

Fall Quarter 1968-Spring Semester 1985

From student response, it quickly became apparent that Bibliography 1 was useful.
It was approved as an elective for undergraduate majors in the College of Letters
and Science, which dominates the undergraduate and especially the lower division
program at Berkeley. For the first few years, total enrollment continued to be
limited to just over one hundred students, but heavy preenrollment warranted
expansion. Several needed modifications had been recognized during the experimental phase. Rote memory was deemphasized. The unit value was increased to
four quarter units. One of the great appeals of Bib 1, an eight-day main library
stacks pass, evolved into a "permanent" (for the balance of their undergraduate
career) stacks pass as a reward to students achieving A-, A or A+ in the course.
The undergraduate and most other campus libraries have open stacks.

When the new Moffitt Library building opened in 1970, Bib 1 obtained use of
one of the classrooms for some of its sections. In addition to classes in the Undergraduate Library building classrooms section, Bib 1 classes have been scheduled in
locations throughout campus in a variety of times-and-days combinations, which
have not always been conducive to increasing enrollment, e.g. three sections meeting at 3 p.m. on Monday, Wednesday and Friday. The Bib 1 office has consisted
of a small basement room in South Hall, a splendid Second Empire building reno-
vated and used entirely by the School of Library and Information Studies, its library, and its computer laboratory. The main Doe, Bancroft, and Business and
Social Sciences libraries, as well as the Women's Resource Center library (not part of
the UC-B Library System) are adjacent. The Undergraduate Library is nearby, and
all are centrally located on campus. But asbestos questions have been raised
about South Hall, and it has been perceived by many to be among the most
earthquake-prone buildings on campus. It was closed in December 1986 to be
made "seismic-safe."

Instructors have been on their own to develop approaches and materials
and have not been required to follow uniform lesson plans, assignments, or lectures. Most have developed a series of assignments involving the use of a variety
of library tools. New instructors have access to a collection of these assignments
and handouts. There is, however, no uniform list of library tools to be "covered"
in Bibliography 1. The lack of a very standardized curriculum is countered by
the requirement that all students purchase the current Bibliography 1 Handbook,
which is sold at the campus bookstore.

When Bib 1 was first offered at the University of California-Berkeley, students were attracted by posters, information sheets at campus libraries' reference desks, mention during library tours, and by the listing in the University Bulletin (catalog). Subsequent experience showed that advertising in the campus newspaper, the Daily Californian, was also productive, although costly. Recently, word-of-mouth recommendation and commendation during the summer orientation program have constituted the publicity. The student counter-catalog commented that "... students find this course invaluable; many upper division students say that they wish they had taken it earlier and suggest that it should be required (or at least strongly recommended) for freshmen since the library skills developed in the course are indispensable for upper division work." Distribution of fliers by some Bib 1 instructors in large undergraduate courses at the end of the semester is potentially the most effective advertising, but it is difficult to rally the extra effort from part-time instructors.

"Reach an Accommodation ..."

Concentration on the individual term project continued to be a distinctive feature of Bib 1, with students asked to identify and use a range and variety of materials to demonstrate their grasp of systematic use of library resources. Much of the original description of 1970 practice continued to be observable in many Bib 1 sections in the 1980's:

> We must prepare students for the realities of using a complex library system, finding alternatives when first efforts fail. Students are encouraged to find the ... best locations, among ... department libraries, and to consult specialist librarians to round out their search. Such guidance is not designed as a substitute for individual study, but is a realistic supplement, particularly when the subject appears prematurely exhausted or after encountering numerous blind alleys ... assignments using a variety of representative reference materials should have turned up some material and established a pattern for finding additional material later. In practice, however, students tend to delay their research and do not take the opportunity to discuss their problems with their instructors because of a lack of time or a misplaced confidence ... there are a great many competent and even distinguished papers ... turned in. The latter often come from quiet students who simply have been learning to use the library via assignments, preparation for quizzes, and by individual work in the library. [18]

The student can choose a topic assigned in a concurrent class; occasionally it may relate to a future course, perhaps in her or his major. Some instructors have worked with students individually in conferences and have involved them in the libraries which provide specialized bibliographical and reference sources relevant to the particular topic. The typical project requirement came to be a bibliography of twenty items, accompanied by an account of the search strategy and experiences the student had along the way. Some instructors have also requested a description of a research paper which the bibliography might support and an outline of it. The project has constituted varying proportions of the course grade; I have assigned approximately one third. Some instructors have accepted a brief pathfinder in the guise of a project. UC B undergraduates' interests are reflected in some of my students' project titles:

By Freshmen:

"Determination of the Rates of Chemical Reactions by Computer Simulation."
(1985)
"Cohabitation of Unmarried Couples With Children: Families Without Mar-
riage in the United States." (1982)
"The Vocational Education and Work Release Programs Offered to Male Felons
in the United States in the 1970's: Can They Provide a Foundation for
Effective Functioning in Contemporary Society?" (1981)
"Immunology: The Effects and Treatments of Immunological Deficiency
Syndromes in Humans." (1979)

By Sophomores:

"Peer Counseling: A Study of the Last Ten Years of United States College
Freshmen." (1984)
"American Women and Politics: Their Exclusion From the Traditional
Avenues of Full Participation." (1981)
"A Look at International and Transnational Terrorism Since 1968: Goals,
Effects, and the Future." (1983)
"Solar Energy Policy in the Carter and Reagan Administrations: Politics-
as-Usual and Contrasting Goals." (1984)

By Juniors:

"Nicholas II and the Radical Transformation of Russia: The Tsar's Policies
and Their Failure to Appease a Population in Revolt." (1983)
"Theories of Carcinogenesis; The Latest Research Findings on the Cancer
Cell, Including Genetics and Oncogenes."
"The Silent Invasion; A Look at the Development of Communication and
Understanding Between the Deaf and Hearing Populations of the United
States." (1980)
"Josephine Miles--How the Sixties Affected Her Art or Craft." (1980)

By Seniors:

"Stalking the Irreducible Biological Gender Components: Sex Dimorphic
Brain Structure in Humans--The Association of Biology and Behavior in
Shaping Structure and Function." (1983)
"Dialectics in the Novels of Ann Petry." (1981)
"The New 'Spinsters': A Modern Assessment of the Never-Married Woman."
(1982)
"Asian Americans: A Historical Comparison of Various Asian Ethnic Com-
munities in California." (1984)

Post-Doctoral Auditor:

"Translating Literature; Art or Science?" (1982)

Master's-Program Foreign Student:

"Is There a Successful Afforestation in Communist China?" (1985)

But the ongoing requirement of term papers, frequently on the same topics, in several large required courses is conducive to the cheating which is a problem on many campuses. [19] And Bib 1 has encouraged students to do their projects on subjects of their own choosing.... Informants tell us that some fraternity houses maintain their own Bib 1 projects files. Until 1985 each student was required to turn in an original and a copy of the project; the copy was retained on file in the Bib 1 office. Some of the too often recurring or simplistic topics have been:

Annorexia nervosa or bulimia	D day
Battle of Britain	Euthanasia
California gold rush	Japanese-America relocation camps
Child abuse	Physiological effects of marijuana
Children and divorce	Schizophrenia
Chimpanzees	Solar energy
Cold war	Subliminal advertising

"Reach an accommodation" was the Bib 1 coordinator's response when I approached him about a situation clearly involving cheating by two colluding students in one of my sections--freshmen roommates who attended class alternately, and who were athletes; I consulted the dean--"Person in Charge of Bibliography 1"--providing him with an envelope of evidence, which was returned unopened. "Can't you do something for this guy?" was another coordinator's request in behalf of a student who had gone directly to the power structure to get his grade upped. Two team members who sensed they might not get the automatic Bib 1 A brought the coach to office hours "to deal with" me; when I would not assure him that all would ultimately be well, they were transferred to the coordinator's section. But even the grades they were given were unsatisfactory to them, they petitioned, and the grades were upped.

It was not feasible to deduct credit for excessive spelling, grammar, and punctuation errors, or neglect. My compromise consisted of a statement on my Checklist-Evaluation of Project, a copy of which was included in the Project Guidelines distributed early in the term: "While grammar, punctuation, spelling, etc. can affect meaning, incorrect or vague usage has not had a conscious effect on grading." Nevertheless, students frequently demanded assurance that I indeed had not "taken off" for such considerations.

The projects file was a useful resource in several ways. New Bib 1 instructors and visitors turned to it for insights. Originally organized by Sheehy codes, a computer-based, cumulative, keyword index was subsequently innovated, but School office personnel time for inputting this information became unavailable, and it too was discontinued (Bib 1 has no clerical staff). Instructor-approval of the proposed topic and use of a course-related topic (even if the course must be hypothetical) appear conducive to honest, productive project work when standards are uniform throughout all sections and terms. Most Bib 1 instructors have referred students to a folder of a sample projects on reserve in the Undergraduate Library; some provide their own folder or simply refer to the folders.

A project-related problem which none of my colleagues ever mentioned gnawed at my conscience: the need to let stand some of the students' rigid ideas, mistaken contentions, and serious assumptions which were clearly bigoted, nonfactual, or prejudgmental. Part of this problem is the role of the instructor of such a course, compounded by a staff consisting of less prestigious personnel--part-time, temporary, not regular faculty, mostly female, librarians. In such a situation, it can be difficult to motivate students to work which will develop or focus their initial project interests into productive learning experiences. It becomes less time-consuming and less stressful for some instructors simply to poll their students' topics and proceed, particularly when the instructors rarely see each other and there is little continuity. It takes considerable effort, persistence, and, as it may have seemed to some students, unjustified requirements, to bring them along. One proposed "hitler" as a project topic. At her project conference, I learned that her parents were from Germany, so she was going to do her project on Adolf Hitler inasmuch as she already knew all about him. When freshmen propose a single concept or one word project topic, I have a line that goes, "What about it?" Ultimately, she declared she would do "Hitler's contributions." We progressed to a project titled "Adolf Hitler: Actions That Benefitted Germany's People, Government, and Economy in the Years 1919-1945." Her background essay included:

> Obviously, Hitler had to do some things right or else the people would have forced him out. It is only fair for people to know that despite of Hitler's cruel actions [she had mentioned that just at the end of World War II, he had been "cruel" to the Jewish people], he did help Germany get through crisis that occured after the Weimar Republic ended in 1933 up to most of World War II. [She cited] ... the achievements of his leadership, such as abolishing unemployment and military victories and foreign policy.... [sic]

The not infrequent project defending and elaborating the contention that the United States' use of the atom bomb was malicious and unnecessary usually contended that it was designed to "get even for Pearl Harbor." For the first time, I was unable to influence the student to evolve it into a learning experience. The student's background essay was drawn verbatim from a paper for another course. Titled "Wrong decision to use the atom bomb," the project introduction included:

> During world War II the Japaneses' attack on Pearl Harbor led the United States to drop the atomic bomb in japan   The United States thought dropping the atomic bomb would make up for the damages and injuries in Pearl Harbor. In the attack of Pearl Harbor, the Japanese used non-atomic bombs to destroy the military warships. The damage from Pearl Harbor was not as bad as the damages in Hiroshima and Nagasaki." (I had introduced her to the fact that not only Hiroshima had been bombed.) [sic]

The Graduate Research University Setting

Bib 1 has encompassed much more than bibliography--both in course description and in what many students typically say they got out of it beyond the basic commitment. Its subtitle was changed from "How to Use the U.C. Library" to "Methods of Library Use." It had evolved into a course designed to offer undergraduates opportunity to develop their ability to solve information problems independently as well as to utilize the immense and complex libraries, the variety of library tools, and the expertise of the campus library personnel to plan and evaluate search strategies and to discover information sources. It has been more

"Librarians, secretaries, and laborers
don't mix ... "

From the UC Employee, a publication of the Berkeley Campus Personnel Office

than a remedial or a simple skills course. No UC-B undergraduate is likely to have had access, in either a school or community library, to the variety and number of library resources available at the University of California--Berkeley. Despite its "bibliography" title, the emphasis has been placed by many of the instructors on teaching students the processes involved in finding information, rather than on introducing specific library tools or types of tools, and thus, on techniques and principles transferrable to all aspects of their current and future information-finding needs. Undergraduate students like to use the word "research" in connection with their assignments, papers, and library use. Bib 1 has enabled some of them to justify that term.

Other benefits which were derived by some students from the course and more or less related to library use have included annotating, documenting (using a style manual), judging critically (using reviews, identifying authority), selecting rather than merely locating, classifying, using thesauri, and researching per se. It is typical for an upper division Bib 1 student to report a new, expanded perception of her/his major field of interest.

Bibliography 1's spectacular growth, from seven sections in its first quarter during the 1968 experimental phase to almost five hundred students in Fall 1975, leveled off at 865 in academic year 1978-1979. In fall 1980 the College of Letters & Sciences' "breadth requirements" (something like general education) came into effect. Bib 1 could not be taken to fulfill them. Bib 1 was offered during five summers: 1972, and 1981-1984. From fall quarter 1969 through spring semester 1985, a total of 12,177 students completed Bib 1. [20] It was the largest such bibliographic instruction course known to Michael K. Buckland, Dean of the School of Library and Information Studies until 1984. [21] Sixteen sections became standard. Bib 1's stabilization at this level was due in part to a commitment to keeping section sizes relatively small. Preenrollment was instituted. The need for specialized Bib 1 sections was articulated by the staff. They suggested the possibility of sections for: freshmen; prospective graduate students, with emphases on the disciplines they intended to follow; and specific disciplines themselves, e.g. engineering, ethnic studies, health sciences, literature, and Women's studies. But the school administration held that, as long as the course was fully enrolled, it was best to provide multiple sections of a nonspecialized Bib 1 for all undergraduates, allowing students to pursue their interests by means of the project. Reference to "resources" and "funding" were occasionally heard, but no budget nor related policy was provided Bib 1 staff.

•   •   •

Some Bib 1 instructors have used, been involved in production of, and evaluated audiovisual media, and some University librarians involved in audiovisual media development have taught Bib 1. As part of the University General Library's bibliographic instruction program, librarians produced slide-tape, twenty-minute color presentations, "The Author, The Title and You; What to Do About the Subject Catalog Until the Librarian Comes" and "In Pursuit of Periodicals," which are available in the main library reference department. They are commended to some Bib 1 sections and required viewing-listening in the Audiovisual Media Center, located in the Undergraduate Library building, where duplicate sets are available, in others. Some of the Bib 1 staff (a term I use to encompass the various persons who have taught Bib 1) cooperated in gathering feedback from their students, contributing to documentation needed in obtaining grant monies for the project. As part of its BI program, the Undergraduate Library developed a self-administered, portable cassette tour and a worksheet exercise, which most Bib 1 instructors assign their students. Both the Undergraduate Library and the General Library system have assigned personnel the role of library instruction coordinators, who communicate with and sometimes teach a Bib 1 section.

A 1980 documentary film focused on the daily life of a UC-B disabled undergraduate student who was in my Bib 1 class. I was apparently the instructor willing to have the production crew come into our classroom. I have regularly held office hours in the wheel-chair accessible main library. Rights of Passage, the award-winning film, has since been on PBS throughout the United States.

•   •   •

Bibliography 1: Methods of Library Use has been concerned with developing library skills and ability to use efficiently a variety of library tools in whatever format they may appear. Obvious constraints, mainly cost combined with hundreds of students enrolled annually, made it impossible to move beyond twenty-minute class demonstrations of the applications of computer technology to library research, and these were discontinued in 1984.

The University of California system libraries plan not to rely on the traditional card catalogs for primary access to library publications. Members of the public are already consulting computer terminals to access information about them. The UC system libraries' online catalog is known as "Melvyl." Since Bib 1 has been the only large-scale introductory course in library use available on the campus, asking students who were actually enrolled to help evaluate the impact of computer-assisted literature searching on bibliographic research skills was an effective way of determining the best approaches for helping students understand most fully the advantages and limitations of the technology with which they will inevitably be confronted in the future. The University Council on Educational Development funded an instructional improvement project designed to provide funds during 1979-1980 to begin expanding student contact with this process and opportunity to measure students' response and learning gains as a result of the increased contact. Bib 1 students were thusly provided with individual searches of several DIALOG files and their own printouts. A chapter of the Handbook has been devoted to literature searching of commercial data bases. Most Bib 1 staff were able to provide such a demonstration, but if they were unable or reluctant, another instructor would provide it. A class prior to the demonstration usually included discussion of the advantages of computer-assisted over manual literature searching.

• • •

The Bib 1 course, as some School faculty had feared, led to several undergraduate, elective service and cultural courses offered by the School of Library and Information Studies. Their frequency and credits have varied, but they have encompassed computer literacy (now offered regularly), the book as an artefact, and a children's literature survey, and they can be used to meet "breadth" requirements. The School, "believing immodestly that librarianship has much to offer nonlibrarians, has built up a range of undergraduate offerings. There is no intention of making mini-librarians or even of offering a 'Major,' but the campus undergraduate experience is enriched by some eight hundred students a year taking a for-credit elective on methods of library use [Bibliography 1], and more who sample specifically tailored courses on children's literature, on the history of the book and problems of information retrieval." [22] It has been many years since undergraduate library science majors were offered in the United States. The professional accrediting body that accredits UC-B School of Library and Information Studies professional degree programs accredits graduate-level programs only. The infusion of FTE (full-time equivalent) data into the School's statistical picture is a fact of life which has never been fully acknowledged, at least beyond the School administration's door, and Bib 1 instructors are not part of the School faculty. Moreover, the Bib 1 students and staff have been visibly more representative than those of the School.

Teachers and Teaching

During the early years of the Bibliography 1 course at the UC-B, an average of five instructors devoted twenty-five percent of their time to the course, theoretically ten hours a week, and the balance to their regular University Library jobs. In addition to the three hours of class each week, one office hour was required, and there were staff meetings, preparations, grading, individually-scheduled project conferences, etc. University librarians were released at the rate of thirty-three percent time, so that a notional 13.3 hours weekly were assigned. This was the case for both campus librarians and the other Bib 1 instructors-- those employed from outside the University library family in order to provide for all sections. Bib 1 is perceived as competing for FTE (full-time equivalent) academic positions and other funds within the School. Bib 1 instructors are now employed one quarter time to teach one section and are placed on the associate or other scale. Thus individual stipends vary. There are no "benefits." To teach such a course well, especially the first few times, requires considerable time. And yet retention and any increment for "outsider" librarians employed to teach Bib 1 are said to be based solely on students' evaluations. Many University librarians consider the amount of their released time unrealistic and, moreover, that "replacement" personnel-time has not been provided. Some report that teaching Bib 1 is no longer a highly valued contribution to one's library promotion portfolio.

University librarians have a great deal to give and to receive from a course such as Bib 1: their familiarity with the campus libraries, their relationships with faculty, and their daily contact with students on campus before and after teaching cannot help but improve the course. And when University librarians teach a section of such a course, their recognition as part of the instructional team, their work with individual students and the bibliographic project, and their development of innovative instructional techniques cannot help but improve library services on campus. For the men who have taught Bib 1, the experience has led to teaching on the School's faculty. A campus librarian declared that he had "learned and relearned a great deal. In a complex, decentralized campus library system, a Bib 1 teaching experience is a great way to gain a fresh overview of the system and to learn about the specific resources of the libraries. I'm able to make more informed referrals to other campus libraries because of my Bib 1 experience."

Because of the rapid growth of Bib 1 enrollment, inadequate funding, and the fluctuating interest of campus librarians, it soon became impossible to continue to implement the original concept that it be taught entirely by University librarians. At one time the course benefited from a continuing arrangement through which the undergraduate library regularly provided two librarians to teach a section each, but it went back to one person each term because of the heavy demands on its staff. A similar arrangement with the General Library was tried and discontinued. Librarians recruited from off campus have until recently constituted approximately half of the Bib 1 staff. Bib 1 teachers have increasingly been from the School's doctoral programs, for whom income and teaching experience are attractions. Minority persons also receive priority in staff selection. [23] The School faculty, according to the 1986-1987 Announcement, consists of seven tenured white males, six of whom have the Ph.D degree, in the rank of full Professor; one white male Ph.D. Acting Associate Professor; two white females with the Ph.D. degree and one white male, with no degrees listed, in the rank of Assistant Professor; one white female Lecturer with the M.L.S. degree; and two female Visiting Lecturers with the M.L.S. degree, one a minority person. [24]

The recruitment announcement declared that qualifications for teaching Bib 1 "include an MLIS, a working knowledge of libraries on the campus, and an interest in library instruction and in teaching undergraduates. Reference work, experience with on-line computer searching, and teaching or related experience are ordinarily expected. Appointments will normally be made on the Associate scale...." [25] The experienced academic personnel manager will recognize several flexible aspects of such a description, subject to narrow and wide interpretation and variable application. The School's self-study report prepared for professional reaccreditation by the American Library Association referred to the "criteria for appointments"

for Bib 1 as "An MLIS degree, two years of experience in reference work, familiarity with campus libraries, interest in undergraduate bibliographical instruction,
and teaching ability." This is the only direct reference to Bib 1 in the Self-
Study. [26]

Bib 1 instructors have been hired on a part-time, temporary basis. There
was intermittent discussion of developing a full-time career track for Bib 1, which
would be welcomed by some and possibly have influenced many who have passed
through and departed. A core of "continuing staff" would, it seems, provide
certain advantages. Dean Buckland acknowledged a University career track "Lecturer with Security of Employment," but stressed that the criteria for security of
employment are very severely written: not only is outstanding excellence in
teaching required but also relevant expertise not otherwise available in the school
or department. Bib 1 instructors have the MLS degree, generally from UC-B or
another California program. "Instructor" here refers not to the academic tenure-
track sometimes followed in academe by Assistant, Associate, and full Professor,
but simply conveys responsibility and role. Most Bib 1 instructors have held the
"associate" title, which is a University academic title between "teaching assistant"
and "lecturer", providing no career status or benefits for someone who is 50 percent time employed. Teaching more than one Bibliography 1 section does not meet
the definition of more than 50 percent time employment. The coordinator has
usually been one of the instructors, who may or may not teach a section. Although the School administration has alluded to a vast pool of potential off-campus
Bib 1 instructors, one or more sections has regularly become vacant at the last
minute, providing employment for someone from the existing Bib 1 staff who is
awarded the section's employment. Several years ago the Bib 1 staff prepared a
report to the School Dean, noting that the commitment to the purposes of the
course, the career potential, and the value of experience in teaching the course
had produced a dedicated, skillful, and enthusiastic collective. It now appears
that, while staff members are generally able and committed, some do not perceive
career potential in this experience, and an enthusiastic collective no longer exists.

Bibliography 1 has been seen by the administration as an anomaly in that
it is a mass, multisection undergraduate course that would, they contend, ordinarily be taught by graduate teaching assistants. The School has preferred
and been able to use librarians and others usually paid slightly more than teaching assistants. With good performance, which is not defined in any policy document, instructors are generally rehired for the following year, usually at a
higher stipend. Once, I did not receive a salary increase due to "the unusually
wide spread of evaluations." Awarding teaching of an extra section, i.e. salary,
was a decision said to be have been based solely on student evaluations which
had been averaged. Aside from the fact that my sections generally were relatively large (there are ways to pare down the size of classes), I later compared
the ratings of another applicant for the additional section's employment and discovered it was not a possible computation. Reference to a personnel committee,
said to be elected, began to be heard more frequently in recent years, although
elections were never held in the presence of the Bib 1 staff as a faculty, and a
count was never revealed. Everyone "elected" to it was always a member of the
University library staff or teaching on the School faculty, often "elected" while
not teaching Bibliography 1. No minutes were available. It was not until spring
1986, when an effort to curtail University part-time visiting lecturers resulted in
the campus newspaper publishing a series about a popular young man who was
not being continued by his department despite his evaluations, book publications,

etc., that I discovered that my evaluations were well above his. No one from the administration ever visited my class, although it was the only section regularly visited, videotaped, and observed by visitors and guests, and I was asked by my colleagues to cover their sections.

Throughout my eight years on the Bibliography 1 teaching staff, I heard and overheard allusions to the course's requiring too much of the students' time, the possibility of students complaining, etc. There was, however, never any coordinated effort to deal with the situation, e.g. staff meetings, if indeed there was a situation. I included a statement on the course information sheet, which they received at the first meeting, that "The University considers that a 3-credit course requires 9 hours (including classes) a week of a student's time. Therefore you will need to plan 6 hours a week for work in libraries and reading." Some instructors adjusted their requirements downward at the first sign of discontent. While declaring the course to be popular and unique (it had required preenrollment), the administration periodically alluded to the need to avoid requiring too much work. The "Course Evaluation" was structured to ask how "time-consuming" Bibliography 1 was as compared with other UC-B courses they had taken. A feminist student interested in the effect on all women of the "course evaluation" methodology, made a carbon copy of her very favorable evaluation [of a woman instructor], which did not turn up among those presented for viewing by the Bibliography 1 instructor following that term. [27]

Beginning in 1985, Bibliography 1 staff were required to complete the An-nual Supplement to the Bio-Bibliography, the updating of accomplishments and other qualifications used for regular UC-B faculty. (Those of us who taught more than one section had been subject to this requirement previously.) Clarification as to how a Bib 1 associate (or even a Visiting Lecturer) has access to experiences which would enable her/him to chair doctoral theses, supervise post-doctoral scholars, institute new courses, serve on Academic Senate committees, present papers at meetings, and function as such things as department officer-- all mentioned in the form--has not been provided. A few Bib 1 staff members have been able to list publications. In practice, there has been some continuity, but teaching Bib 1 is clearly not structured as a career position. Nor is it clear to the University administration that full-time career positions would be beneficial to, or necessary to maintain, the program. (Of course it has not been tried.) It contends that a career teaching Bib 1 full-time would lead to exhaustion and staleness. Bib 1 staff are referred to in the School Self Study... as "temporary faculty."

Bib 1 has no budget of its own, according to former Dean Buckland, during preparation of an earlier paper. The coordinator and staff (usually about fifteen persons) have an electric typewriter and a telephone extension. The Bib 1 program grew tremendously with no office staff. It has never had clerical personnel of its own, although the part-time coordinator can draw upon some School office staff support, and assignments are processed by University duplicating if thirty or more copies are needed and sufficient time is scheduled by the instructor.

• • •

The Bibliography 1 Handbook--not a workbook--devised by some of the instructors and produced by the University's central duplication service, is sold at the University bookstore. [28] In view of the vast changes going on in the

University libraries, such a tool needs ongoing revision, which has usually involved payment to selected instructors for their time during the summer. The Handbook provides information on the organization and accessing of UC-B libraries as well as standard tools and techniques, but "local" information enabling access to UC-B libraries' files and collections is stressed. It is not organized by types of formats, e.g. dictionaries, encyclopedias, handbooks, etc., nor by types of library divisional structure, e.g. the card catalog, periodical indexes, etc. Rather, these are integrated to provide for the needs of highly qualified undergraduates learning to use university libraries to do library research and to develop strategies appropriate to their majors and courses. Excerpts from Turabian's A Manual For Writers of Term Papers, Theses, and Dissertations, 4th ed. [29] and a glossary of terms is appended; Juta Savage prepared an index to the 1984 printing. Information concerning some basic principles of organization of information and publications is included, e.g. main entry concept, classification, filing, etc. Chapters are devoted to such things as government publications, computer-assisted literature searching of commercial data bases (although this instruction is no longer provided), the subject approach, and planning the "term project."

Provision of a regular itemized Bib 1 budget might have supported current and developmental needs as well as enabled more effective planning. Some of the occasional instructors who are based in the Undergraduate Library are active in the California Clearinghouse for Library Instruction, which provides samples of materials and demonstrates teaching techniques in its workshops. Members of the Undergraduate Library staff are also active in the Association of College & Research Libraries' Bibliographic Section. Instructors may visit each other's classes, although they rarely do. Some share sections unofficially. Bib 1 instructors were encouraged to attend the University teaching assistants' training program at the beginning of the academic year. I did so and found in the inevitable packet a reading list of titles from the Middle Ages of pedagogy. Committee work was encouraged; committees varied, but have included concern for handbook revision, grants, teaching aids, "AFT," publicity, and instructional support.

A small collection of mostly-standard, related tools located in the Bib 1 room has included:

Bischof, Phyllis. Afro-Americana; a Research Guide to Collections at the University of California, Berkeley. (The General Library & The Afro-American Studies, 1984).

California Clearinghouse on Library Instruction. Directory of Library Instruction Programs in California Academic Libraries. (The Clearinghouse; see Clearinghouses section of Part III for latest edition and acquisition information.)

DIALOG Data Base Catalog.

Gates, Jean Key. Guide to the Use of Libraries and Information Sources. (See Texts ... section of Part III for latest edition.)

Goniwiecha, Mark, et al. Guide to Ethnic Sources at UC Berkeley, 1973-1983, compiled by Members of the Class LS 259: Ethnic Bibliography. (Spring 1982). (Chicano Studies Library Publications, 1983.)

Harzfeld, Lois A. Periodical Indexes in the Social Sciences and Humanities; A Subject Guide. (Scarecrow Press, 1978.)

Library Orientation for Academic Libraries. Papers of Annual Conference[s].

Lubans, John, Jr. <u>Educating the Library User</u>. (Bowker, 1974.)

Owen, Dolores B. <u>Abstracts and Indexes in Science and Technology, a Descriptive Guide, 2nd edition</u>. (Scarecrow Press, 1985.)

Sheehy, Eugene. <u>Guide to Reference Books, 9th edition</u>. (American Library Association, 1976.)

<u>Thesaurus of ERIC Descriptors, 10th edition</u>. (Oryx Press.)

Woodbury, Marda A. <u>A Guide to Sources of Educational Information, 2nd edition</u>. (Information Resources Press, 1982.)

Lois Harzfeld's <u>Periodical Indexes in the Social Sciences and Humanities; A Subject Guide</u> derived directly from her experience as a Bib 1 instructor explaining to Bib 1 students how to identify periodical indexes and abstracts appropriate to their topics and the multiplicity of different sources that might need to be examined as well as the various shortcomings these sources had. Through the students' use of the indexes, she identified their assumptions in understanding their scope and use, and she designed the annotations accordingly. For example, they frequently overlooked cumulated indexes, they thought the word "modern" in M[odern] L[anguage] A Bibliography meant twentieth-century literature, they assumed Historical Abstracts would encompass United States history, etc. Since the book was published, most Bib 1 instructors have used or mentioned it in the course. I find it works well in tandem with the complementary science and technology title by Owen, although it needs updating when used in the context of the magnitude of a university library system's resources.

Students and Learning

The Teaching Innovation and Evaluation Services, whose goal is to assist faculty, teaching assistants, programs, and departments to innovate, evaluate, and improve instruction on the Berkeley campus, distributed questionnaires to students of some Bib 1 sections. Their report to Bib 1 instructors provides a picture of students circa 1977-1978. Most were enrolled in the College of Letters and Science, representing a diverse group of major fields ranging from biology to philosophy to physical education. Although all classes were represented in TIES' survey, most Bib 1 students were relatively new to the campus--about half freshmen and most of the upper-division transfer students. Social science majors have been the largest number (31 percent in this survey). In response to open-ended items asking what they had hoped to learn from Bib 1, most mentioned need for familiarity with the library's resources in relationship to "research papers." Students gave the course high marks in TIES' survey: 99 percent agreed that they would make better use of library resources in the future; 30 percent had already used their Bib 1 project as the basis for a paper in another course or planned to utilize it subsequently in some way. The term project clearly was considered a most useful aspect of the course, with library tours and assignments also important. While every part of the course was rated as being at least somewhat useful, classroom lectures, quizzes, and discussions (which vary in amounts included by instructors) were not considered as useful as other parts. These results were consistent across sections, which, according to TIES' interpretation, means that they are independent of the classroom teaching skills of the various Bib 1 instructors.

There was also interest in attempting to assess <u>increase in student knowledge and skills in the context of subsequent coursework or personal and career achieve-</u>

ments. Former School faculty sponsor Fay Blake, who also taught Bib 1, was an advocate of both need and feasibility of "action research" which would track Bib 1 students' use of techniques learned in the course and its effect on other information-gathering activities. I asked several Bib 1 students from previous terms, two then in graduate school, one a junior, and one a senior, to complete a questionnaire in 1981 about ways in which Bib 1 had met their expectations. They commented in retrospect:

- It gave me tools to find information and made me familiar with libraries I now use regularly; helped me to think for myself, saves me time I would otherwise waste standing in line or groping.

- Highly useful in researching my History 101 topic. Gave greater sense of proficiency to me.

- Learned more about UC libraries, research, writing a research paper.

Before taking Bib 1, two had used the undergraduate library "somewhat," one "almost never," and one "regularly." Their uniform experience at the UC-B was that instructors "gave assignments involving library use only for required, 'reserve reading,'" with one adding that they "expect library use without assigning." All asserted that "every student" should take Bib 1, agreeing that the individual project was an important part of the course and that they "got a lot out of it." All subsequently used libraries in connection with courses much more than they used to. Their responses to "If you were a member of a search committee for selecting faculty, what special qualifications would you put into a description listing minimum requirements for Bib 1 instructors?" were

- enthusiasm, treating people equally, knowledge of UC libraries, had done research;

- extensive experience in research, organized teaching techniques, willing to listen and help;

- Master's degree, desire to teach for the purpose of students learning, not his/her own power presentation;

- has it together, experience with UC library system and or similar systems.

New college students vary greatly in their preparation. A television announcement in behalf of California community colleges concludes with a community college graduate's triumphant declaration, "UC, here I come!" There are twenty-four community junior colleges within commuting distance of the campus, and many more institutions offer transferrable credit from elsewhere within the state. One former Bib 1 instructor has referred to "a wide disparity in the interest and ability displayed by the students.... Some were highly interested and able and some were not--a few seemed barely literate. I felt those in the 'not' category needed the class most and put a lot of effort in helping them learn something ... some did learn something, but some of the more able students probably found the class too elementary."

Bibliography 1 Students, 1981-1985: "It should be required"

During my eight years teaching Bibliography 1, 50 percent of my students were freshmen. The balance consisted of sophomores, juniors, and seniors, as well as accelerated high school and graduate students. Regularly among my students were disabled and re-entry persons. From 1981 to 1985 a questionnaire was distributed to Bib 1 students in some sections, usually at the beginning of the term. The plan appears to have been to generate data that would improve and secure the program. It might have been conducive to placement of Bib 1 on the list of courses fulfilling the College of Letters and Sciences' breadth requirements, a goal considered by some staff as desirable as well as justifiable, but which the School administration and faculty seemed unwilling to push. During this period, Bib 1 was diminished in several obvious ways: despite continued demand, the number of sections offered and the amount of credits provided were decreased, and the summer section was discontinued. In December 1985 the accumulated questionnaires were offered by the coordinator to anyone who would remove them.

Although not systematically administered, validated, or tabulated, 1,877 students' questionnaires beginning with fall 1981 quarter and continuing more or less regularly through fall 1985 semester, including 1982 and 1983 summer sessions, help us to know about University of California, Berkeley students who elected Bibliography 1 during this period of its history:

Freshmen	1,005
Sophomores	350
Juniors	360
Seniors	150
Graduate	4
Unidentified	8
TOTAL	1,877

Freshmen include the advanced-placement high school students who identify themselves thusly, which they technically are under this program.

Of the Bib 1 students completing questionnaires, 53 percent were freshmen, with all four class levels well represented. In the fall term, freshmen regularly outnumber members of other classes enrolled. The information gathering and decision making processes of freshmen, who typically are newcomers to both college and campus, are of particular interest. Freshmen have constituted approximately half the students electing Bib 1. The survey asked "How or where did you learn about Bib 1?" and provided these choices:

Former Bib 1 students	116
Friends who had not taken it	75
UC-B course catalog	70
Summer orientation program [on campus]	50
Leaflet or poster	46
Freshman orientation [tours, etc. after the term has begun]	8
Faculty	8
Academic advisor or counselor	1

The "poster" referred to was an 8½ x 11" duplicated announcement (see elsewhere in this chapter) prepared by the Bib 1 program staff and distributed throughout the campus, often available and posted in some libraries, especially the undergraduate and main reference libraries, and in classroom buildings, student learning center, and women's center. Few freshmen indicated "Faculty" or "Academic advisor or counselor" as sources of access to Bib 1 because most had not yet encountered these persons. They will not have academic advisors until they are juniors involved in majors. Those they listed here were librarians, history, and geography teachers, athletics coaches, and admissions and EOP counselors. About their awareness of Bib 1, freshmen commented: "Someone told me about it and said it was a helpful class to take." "Brother specified the title of the class." "A mailing." "I saw it on the blackboard in the pre-enrollment room." [S/he had been in the classroom where Bib 1 pre-enrollment had taken place, saw our instructions left-over on the board, and, required pre-enrollment notwithstanding, apparently then got into Bib 1. Beginning about the time it was offered for two instead of three credits, pre-enrollment was no longer necessary.] "Mother said it was excelent." [sic] "Sister." "Parent." "Professor at Merritt College." [A local community college]. "My American Government teacher at Skyline high in 12th grade." "I heard about Bib 1 in Massachusetts. I used to canvass for MassPirg, a political environmental organization related to CalPirg, and I canvassed a couple who were alumnae, and who recommended that I take this course."

The frequent responses to what had been heard said about Bib 1 by those who had not and did not plan to take it were "It's useful for research in other classes," and "I can get into the stacks anyway."

Freshmen and sophomore classes constitute the collegiate lower division, which is of great concern to many bibliographic instruction course developers. Sophomores have been on campus long enough to have acquired some insights and strategies. BI courses are usually elective. A particularly relevant question, therefore, is "When choosing any elective, what factors affect your choice?" The Bib 1 survey provided the following choices:

The course fulfills L & S breadth requirements.
The course fits into my schedule.
The course is related to or useful for my future career.
The course broadens my general education.
The course is highly recommended by an academic advisor.
The course is recommended by someone who has taken it.
The course offers a challenge.
The course requires a minimum of work.
The course allows me to raise my grade point average, i.e. it is easy or is
    known for high grades.
The subject matter interests me.
The instructor is known to be excellent.

That a course fulfills Letters & Sciences' breadth requirements was listed as important by more than half the sophomores. That it requires a minimum of work and/or allows for raising one's grade point average was important to about 20 percent. That the instructor is known to be excellent was important to about 10 percent and of some importance to another 15 percent. (Bibliography 1 sections' instructors' names did not appear in the course schedule.)

Throughout American collegiate education, the junior class level tends to include students who are new to upper division work and to a major field, and perhaps new to campus, being away from home, university life and an academic setting with a library system. Sixty percent of the Bib 1 juniors surveyed were transfer students. Many had likely spent approximately two years at a California community junior college. Some noted that they were returning to the University of California--Berkeley or "to college," a few "after many years." By the junior year, most college students are no longer in the "undecided major" category, and are able to express their subject interests in terms of existing majors. These junior class members' major subject interests were:

History	63
English	33
Political science	29
Psychology	17
Economics	16
Business	15

Other majors attracting substantial interest were geography, architecture, computer science, sociology, biology, rhetoric, anthropology, and microbiology. Fifteen (4 percent) of the juniors were still undecided about a major. None listed Asian American Studies as a major subject interest; Chicano Studies was listed by two students, Women's Studies by four, and Native American Studies by one. Such interdisciplinary programs offer majors as well as featuring provision of elective courses which can be used to meet the College of Letters & Science's breadth requirements.

Students surveyed were asked about their reasons "in addition to wanting to use the library effectively" for enrolling in Bib 1 and to rate them from the following list in terms of important, of some importance, or of no importance: to ...

- gain a stack pass to Doe Library [the main campus collection, restricted to graduate students since the opening in 1969 of the undergraduate library building]

- write better term papers

- find information in the library for outside interests

- be in a class with friends who are taking it also

- prepare for graduate studies

- improve my grade point average

- have enough units this term [in order to maintain enrollment in College]

To write better term papers was listed among the important reasons they had enrolled in Bib 1 by 65 percent of the 360 juniors involved in this survey. It was by far the most important of the important reasons. Next were "to prepare for graduate studies" and "to find information in the library."

To gain a stack pass to Doe Library was an important reason for taking Bib 1 at all four class levels. It was rated important or of some importance by most of these juniors, the majority of whom are transfer newcomers and less likely to know that almost any undergraduate can wangle a stack pass authorization from a professor. But 40 percent of the juniors surveyed had been on campus for two or more years and were still so unfamiliar with the library scene that they had not discovered this fact of library-related life.

"To improve my grade point average" and "To have enough units this term" were each indicated as important reasons for having enrolled in Bib 1 by 12 percent of the juniors. Only three juniors ranked as important "being in a class with friends," although many considered it of some importance.

Several juniors volunteered comments. "I think this is an incredibly valuable course that should undeniably be required. It's the student's loss that it's not." (Likely the questionnaires had been administered at the end of the term in her/his section). Two of the three "alternative formats" to Bib 1 (self-paced with conferences; televised or taped lab sessions in the library) which were suggested for reaction drew scornful comments. "Too stale" and "Should you fill Bib 1 with these frills, I most assuredly would not take it," for example. "A subject oriented Bibliography 1 course" as an alternative, however, elicited numerous positive comments. Of the juniors, 34 percent indicated that they would take "a subject oriented Bib 1 course." One suggested, "Ideas: possibly change the title to a more descriptive or imaginative title. Faculty cooperation in pushing course." "Faculty" likely refers here to regular faculty, i.e. not to Bib 1 instructors, who are often assumed to be teaching assistants. "This course should be required, I think." "I got comments [from former Bib 1 students] that the course is useful, not excessively difficult but required legwork and a significant amount of time."

The one hundred fifty seniors taking Bib 1, who had been around long enough to have heard from students who have been enrolled in it, reported that Bib 1 was rumored

very valuable	90 (60 percent)
of some value	26
not very valuable	none
left it blank or indicated they hadn't heard anything	34
	150

Grading had been described to them as

easy	18
average	85 (57 percent)
hard	11
left it blank or indicated they hadn't heard anything	36
	150

They had heard that Bib 1 required

a lot of time	74 (49 percent)
average amount of time	30
very little time	5
left it blank or indicated they hadn't heard anything	41
	——
	150

Seniors turned up in their greatest percentages in spring and summer terms, attributed by some staff to their needing last-minute credits or improved grade point averages in order to graduate. Seniors in my sections usually mentioned to me during the course that they had just heard about it, couldn't fit it in until then, or were going to graduate school. Their questionnaire comments were generally more focused than those of the other students. Their comments regarding their personal reasons for having enrolled in Bib 1 included:

"to help me learn how to research for my senior thesis is Number One reason"
"I'm writing a thesis this year and I'm taking Humanities 100--It's time I learned the libraries."
"to help me to learn how to research for my senior thesis" and numerous such comments including the word "research."
"I love libraries--I love getting lost in stacks"
"In four years I have never used the UC-B library, I wanted to learn how to use it for future reference" [sic]
"to break up the academic monotony (I have 3 physical science courses and Bib 1 as my schedule this quarter)"
"to help re-acquaint myself after being out of school for 10 years"

Regarding alternative formats (audiovisual, subject-oriented course, etc.) and whether Bib 1 should meet three times a week for one hour or twice weekly for one and a half hours:

"Just fine the way it is"
"A Bib 1 course for varied units, for an option of units obtainable"
"This was a very difficult 3 units to earn, I feel it would be a mistake to lower the units received for taking Bibliography 1, this is expecially true when one considers the difficulty involved of completing a bibliography to an instructors exact specification." [sic]
"freshmen should be strongly advised to take it, if only to get the stack pass in the main library, for it's extremely useful in research"
"You run around the library looking for information it's a lot of fun, I heard. Based on the first lecture I am very much excited about the course and would not change the format but rather the work load that's ahead of us."
"One less homework or a smaller project could make a big difference."

Would s/he have taken a semester version? [asked at the end of a quarter apparently.] "Only if the course required more in terms of writing papers." Throughout Bib 1, students typically referred to the bibliographic project as writing a term paper.

About graduate students enrolled in Bib 1: Each year a graduate student asked to audit my section. I also had a graduate student whose Department arranged for her to take it for credit. She had just arrived from China and had had little experience speaking or hearing English, although she had completed graduate level work at home. While commuting and keeping house for her family, she came regularly to office hours (we met in the library) and asked for one special consideration--use of her bilingual dictionary during the tests. She achieved A-. Bib 1 is listed as an undergraduate course; in fact, the number makes it a lower division course. I routinely granted the occasional graduate student's request to audit, although I pointed out that mere auditing this type of course is unrealistic.

Students choose UC-B because of its academic reputation, special educational programs, and overall institutional image, according to annual surveys by the Office of Student Research. Berkeley undergraduates are said to be more autonomous and intellectual than students nationally, but otherwise share the same general characteristics of students in comparable fields of study elsewhere. They are scholastically strong and have high academic aspirations. More Berkeley students go on to earn doctorates than students from any other university in the United States. A total of 26,185 students applied for undergraduate admission for fall 1986; 9,280 were admitted to Berkeley. Total campus enrollment consisted of 22,131 undergraduates, of whom 21 percent were new to the campus, and 9,332 graduate students. Fifty-three percent of the undergraduates were male; 55 percent were Caucasian (non Hispanic). [30] UC-B is essentially a conservative environment, notwithstanding media events. [31]

Recruitment: The Academic Facts of Life

During the years 1981-1985 some Bib 1 teachers during the final two weeks of fall terms occasionally organized what I perceive to be the most potentially productive recruitment methodology for a course such as Bibliography 1. For merely the cost of the announcement reproduced on the following page and some staff effort, the most directly potential market--lower division students in a captive audience situation--can be systematically reached at the very moment when they are considering electives for the following term. It is a simple matter to identify lower division undergraduate courses with large enrollments. They often fulfill degree requirements or are prerequisites for entrance into majors; they may be associated with a TA population, undergraduate library reserves, or the large lecture halls and auditoria, etc. where a Professor lectures. At UC-B they include biology, physics, anthropology, sociology, geography, and economics courses, as well as a sort of remediation course administered by the English Department and known as Subject A. A few weeks into the second half of the term, a call during the Professor's office hours to request permission to distribute the Bib 1 announcement to students in her/his course always, with one exception, resulted in prompt consent. I would arrive five minutes before class and introduce myself to the Professor, who usually suggested that I wait until the class began, at which time, s/he identified what they were receiving and blessed the course while I rapidly distributed the announcements at the head of each row. That these Professors typically stressed the conventional goodness of knowing how to find a book in such a large library, evidenced no real idea of what many Bib 1 sections provided, and rarely connected it with a report or requirement in their class is not the point here.

The Academic Facts of Life:

- Grades
- Term papers
- 6,000,000+ books in the UCB Libraries
- 100,000+ periodicals in the UCB libraries
- 60+ libraries on the UCB campus
- 300+ periodical indexes and abstracts
- Newspaper indexes
- Catalogs on microfiche
- Melvyl: an experimental computer catalog for all UC campuses
- Government publications in the UCB libraries
- Computer literature searching

Bibliography 1: Methods of Library Use
3 units

Three hours of class per week. Learn how to approach the
UCB Library's resources in a systematic way via lectures,
problem sets, individual conferences, on-line database
searching, and a term project. Develop a search strategy
and list of sources on a topic of your choice. Utilize the
results for a paper in another course.

BIBLIOGRAPHY 1 offers many sections to fit your schedule
BIBLIOGRAPHY 1 gives you a Main Library Stack pass while taking the course
BIBLIOGRAPHY 1 gives you a permanent Stack pass if you earn an A or A-
BIBLIOGRAPHY 1 helps you succeed at UCB

Pre-enroll at the first class meeting
Sections listed in the Schedule of Classes under Library & Information
    Studies
Bibliography 1 office: 19 South Hall. Phone 642-1087 or 642-1464

A few students when completing the questionnaire in my sections would naively report that "the leaflet you gave me in Professor XYZ's class" was the way they heard about Bib 1. A biology Professor suggested that I deliver 1,500 fliers to the Department secretary, and offered to have her collate them into the packets distributed at students' required, weekly sections and to coordinate their distribution with the fifteen TA's.

"Special" Students and Subjects

By 1980 a surprising number of seniors took Bib 1 after they discovered they needed three (and later, two) additional credits or to improve their average in order to graduate. Some Bib 1 students anticipated literally being given an automatic A or Incomplete. It is possible to require and enable respectable levels of achievement in such a course. The presence of EO, re-entry, transfer, and disabled students or athletes, minorities, whatever need not justify disparate expectations for various groups within the student body by various instructors.

A campus admissions officer slowly working her way through the B.A. degree and I met when she elected Bib 1. Her employment has involved counseling reentry students, to whom she stresses taking Bib 1 during their first term on campus, based in part on her personal experience. She perceives this course as an excellent way for new or returning students to learn the campus and to have access to a sort of counselor. Usually there was an advanced placement high school student in my class. (I realize in retrospect that they were all females.) They are students attending nearby high schools who have already been admitted to the University freshman class and who can take one course each term. They tend to identify Bib 1 as a course needed during their first term on campus despite the great attraction for them of other University courses. In fall 1984, seated next to each other in the front row were an APHS student and a re-entry student with fifty years between them. She had enrolled in Bib 1 based on her reading of the UC-B catalog shared with her by her high school counselor and a peer's endorsement of the course. He had taken a few courses on the GI Bill following World War II, then married and raised a family. Now a widower residing with his married granddaughter, he had begun to complete his B.A. degree. As usual for students in these two groups, they were never absent and achieved course grades in the A range. He had been processed by the admissions officer, who counseled him to take Bib 1.

The disabled students program has also referred students to Bib 1. A partially-sighted, community college transfer, Latin American history major made a difficult personal transition to campus life; he continued to come to office hours "to talk." The 1980 documentary film, Rights of Passage, focused on the dormitory and classroom life of a black UC-B student confined to a wheel-chair. (I realize in retrospect that all such disabled students in my classes were males.) In recent years a number of young women with herpes, chlamydia, and similar problems usually as yet undiagnosed would stop me as I crossed campus with "I want to make an appointment," which meant they did not want to wait until office hours and wanted to schedule a tête-à-tête. And recently there was a former student of mine who was waiting when I arrived for office hours, with a grim look instead of his usual cheerful, almost clown self. Normally his expensive clothes were neat and clean. Today his looked seedy. This very young man, a minority honors alumnus of a "selective" parochial school, who insisted that he had taken "the family life course" there, was in bad shape ... not just because of the way he felt, but because there was no one to his knowledge to whom he could turn. He was, he thought, in love. And there were several recovering alcoholics as well as a veteran with (documented) cancer--people who were not hiding their conditions, but who wanted to pick the time, place and person with whom to talk about them.

Subject A (Basic Writing) is a large remedial course-program administered by the English Department. Freshmen endeavor to test out of it and go directly into a "regular" English course. Transfers are exempt. Because there are no prerequisites for Bib 1, a student has the right to take it and Subject A during the same term, which experience clearly demonstrated to Bib 1 instructors, was counterproductive. They dealt with it in varying, even contradictory, ways. With a large class, they might stress on Day One that the two courses should not be taken together and even that Subject A should be taken first. Aside from being dishonest, this often resulted in intimidated inexperienced, unsophisticated students, some of whom had already tested out of Subject A. Some students continued in both Subject A and Bib 1, simply moving to another Bib 1 section, which was theoretically not possible. Doubtless the School administration and some individual instructors did not want to lose any of the "market," as Bib 1 students were referred to on one occasion by an administrator who spoke to us about grading. In short, remediation courses should be completed before taking a course such as Bib 1. Both should be completed early, and there should be consistency in management.

Some UC-B undergraduate majors require a senior thesis, e.g. history, humanities, and Women's studies, and most departments provide opportunity to achieve honors by means of similar endeavors and topical seminars. These students often take Bib 1 followed by the senior thesis seminar. I encouraged but did not require Bib 1 students to relate their projects to other college course requirements. This can be a turn-on if the instructor is willing to supervise closely and require a level of achievement which indeed does not amount to triumphant double-dipping. A feminist Women's studies major utilized Bib 1 to evolve her senior thesis topic and her project to begin work on it. Later, when she was enrolled in the thesis seminar, I served as the "outside advisor," which each such student must recruit, for "The New 'Spinsters': A Modern Assessment of the Never-Married Woman." Not all gender-related projects are pursued in Women's studies majors or courses, however. A UC-B sophomore told me that, although a feminist, she was majoring in political science because she planned to enter law school. She applied her project work, titled "American Women in Politics; Their Exclusion from the Traditional Avenues of Full Participation" to a concurrent political science course. This type of student often needs reference letters which, to be functional, require considerable effort on the part of the writer. She recently completed Boalt School of Law.

Not all gender-related project topics are pursued by feminists. A physically-disabled, single head of family re-entered college via an experimental program in the Bay Area. During her senior year there she was involved in frustrating discussions with a physiology professor regarding dimorphic brain structure. She arranged to take Bib 1 at UC-B for transfer credit back to her college, from which she then graduated. Her Bib 1 project was titled "Stalking the Irreducible Biological Gender Components: Sex Dimorphic Brain Structure in Humans--The Association of Biology and Behavior in Shaping Structure and Function." Her

UC-B experience led to her realization that she had underestimated herself in not applying there, and brought to her attention the real possibility of graduate work at UC-B, which she completed in the School of Library and Information Studies. At the opposite end of the social poles was a well-to-do, re-entry student whose attention had been drawn to Bib 1 during admissions counseling. Her project was the foundation for an assignment in a concurrent history course. The evolution of the wording of her topic demonstrates learned-research techniques possible in such a course. Early in the semester, she indicated interest in "something connected with Sonoma Country [California] research." By mid-semester, when I queried tentative project working-titles, she was overwhelmed by the resources opening up to her, but she applied skills, tools, and strategies acquired in Bib 1 in the interim to submit "The Reluctant Sarah Rayse & The Robust Saray Royal: An Examination of the Reasons Women Came West." This evolved into her final title: "Sarah Royce and Louisa Clapp: The Differences in Two Women's Values and the Influence Their Values Had on California's Developing Social Conditions, 1850-1870." She is now completing a Master's degree elsewhere in public history.

Occasionally criticism of Bib 1 has been heard from outside that the projects are not "scholarly"; on the other hand, the School at times has objected to use of the word "research" in relationship to the project. A student wrote in the introduction to and strategy for her bibliography on hyperkinesis in children, which later evolved into a pamphlet written for a semiprofessional, coping group:

> My nine-year-old son is hyperkinetic. He plagues our family, his classmates, teachers and the occasional temporary friend that he may have.... The purpose of this project is to compile a selected bibliography of material that will assist me ... to understand the problem of hyperkinesis in education, to cope with the problems incurred by our child at home, and to inform me as to some of the controversies on the subject and what is being done. I hope to equip myself to discuss the problem with other concerned parents and ... to offer them sources of information. A number of sources of help for parents have come to my attention and through this project I am less inclined to blame myself for my son's problem. In the interim, I dispelled inhibitions for using a variety of libraries which I now manipulate comfortably.

The possibility of serving the needs of special interest groups and subject-matters exists in bibliographic instruction. Such interdisciplinary programs as Black, Ethnic, and Women studies provide the potential on college and university campuses for contributing to nondiscriminatory "affirmative action" in that they can be enablers and are not literally blacks' studies, or ethnics' studies, or women's studies (a potentially proscriptive perspective). With the example on which I have focused here--feminist perspectives, women students' needs, gender equity, Title IX, Women's studies majors and courses, etc.--students face, additionally, a special need to deal with conventional, existing tools and library structures while identifying innovative, feminist/nonsexist techniques, resources, and tools. My article, "A Feminist Researcher's Guide to Periodical Indexes, Abstracting Services, Citation Indexes and Online Databases," derived from my experience as a Bib 1 instructor working with such students and their projects. [32]

<u>Epilog: July 1985</u>

This has been an account of a rare successful experimental course which survived. Bibliography 1 made history as a unique and durable bibliographic instruction course of interest to higher education personnel, educators, and librarians concerned with enabling. Its main goal has been provision of instruction for all University of California--Berkeley undergraduates in efficient use of libraries and information in the UC-B libraries system. The program also served as an inspiration and a model.

An effort to curtail Bibliography 1 appeared to begin circa fall 1981. A decline in Bib 1 enrollment was attributed by the School administration in part to the introduction of the "breadth" requirements. But there was also criticism because the number of undergraduate students on campus was said to have "been increasing substantially." [33] In point of fact, fall 1981 University overall undergraduate enrollment was down from 1980 and 1979. I urged that we in Bib 1 actively recruit students for the winter quarter by distributing announcements in the manner previously described. Effective fall 1983 the Berkeley campus converted from quarter to semester system, with two semesters spanning the portion of the academic year previously occupied by three quarters; even with this fact, fall 1983 semester's count showed an increase in Bib 1 enrollment. In July 1984, UC-B School of Library and Information Studies Dean Michael Buckland became University of California [system-wide] Assistant Vice President for Library Plans and Policies. Academic year 1984-1985 was one of confusion and contradictions for the Bib 1 staff. In September 1984 the acting dean directed a memo to School Faculty, of which Bib 1 teachers were not a part, proposing a review of Bib 1, "the oldest and most expensive of our undergraduate courses...." Despite former Dean Buckland's counsel with regard to Bib 1 as the source of infusion of FTE into the school's data picture and with no involvement of any of the then-current Bib 1 instructors, he appointed a member of the School faculty to chair the review and make recommendations regarding Bib 1. Two other school faculty members, who also had not taught the course, constituted the committee. (The one School faculty member who had taught and coordinated Bib 1 was not involved.) In a fall 1985 letter to the editor of <u>American Libraries</u>, former Bib 1 coordinator (now California Historical Society Library Director and occasional School faculty member) Bruce Johnson referred inaccurately to the "declining student demand" for Bibliography 1. It was a seemingly spontaneous response to a June 1985 report that "U Cal/Berkeley Downgrades Respected Bib 1 Course." [34]

Following a period of rumored discontinuance by the school, it was learned in late spring 1985 that the course would be "revised." There would be no summer session, fewer sections, and it would provide only two weekly contact (fifty minutes) hours and credits, a unit difficult for many UC-B undergraduates to schedule. Instructors were to be derived from School doctoral candidates and the UC-B Library staff. Some aspects of the revised curtailed Bib 1 were conveyed informally by the coordinator to the Bib 1 staff by the administration. They included: elimination of DIALOG demonstrations and systematic instruction concerning computer-assisted literature data base searching; "no more than two hours on the subject of the University system's online catalog" (one of the elements of the school's recently introduced, undergraduate computer-literacy course); "reduction or elimination of tours"; elimination of instruction related to the National Union Catalog and Library of Congress subject catalog volumes; only "basic filing rules"; and elimination of connections between library research and "writing a term paper." [35] Considerations which appeared to have been over-looked included the feasibility of the requirement of a bibliographic project of the caliber of many past Bib 1 projects for a UC-B undergraduate student in a non-major, two-credit elective course. The likelihood was that individual conferences would not attract Bib 1 students, because a two-credit course merits a minimum of their time. The catalog description of Bibliography 1: Methods of Library Use was changed only in the number of credits, from three to two.

Several facts cannot be overlooked. The recently-introduced, undergraduate School computer literacy course did not receive the same treatment. Indeed, it is offered regularly in multiple sections, for three credits, and another, advanced undergraduate, three-credit course in information access and retrieval is also of-fered by the School. [36] Some Bib 1 instructors have been associated with a union recently introduced into the UC System whose membership consists of non-Academic Senate Faculty members. In 1985 it filed a Bibliography 1-related, un-fair labor practice suit against the University. [37] During spring 1986, some Bib 1 staff members met with Professor Muscatine regarding the relocation of the Bib 1 course-program in another department to prevent its gradual demise. Such a location would be based on precedent of other departments at other UC campuses. He suggested a petition, directed to the Committee on Educational Policy and ad-vocating such a move, signed by regular Faculty, to be circulated among them by Bib 1 staff members. I had no difficulty in filling my copy of the petition with signatures of Academic Senate faculty members. In each case, she hesitated briefly, asked a thoughtful question or two, listened, and then signed my petition-copy. The other members of the spring 1986 semester Bib 1 staff thought better of it, and did not circulate the petition. It read:

> We, the undersigned faculty at the University of California, Berkeley, are writing in strong support of the faculty of Bibliography 1, School of Library and Information Studies, in their efforts to restore the educational value and quality to the program commensurate with the breadth of subject matter covered, workload and intellectual content.
>
> The Bibliography 1 course has won recognition throughout the country for innovative development in teaching bibliographic research methodology on the undergraduate level. Begun in the late 1960's as a precedent setting, experimental program designed to cope with the rapid expansion of information resources, Bibliography 1 has gone from a 3-quarter unit to a 4-quarter unit course to better adjust its unit Award to its content and workload.
>
> In the fall of 1985, the credit units and course itself were seriously eroded. The course has been reduced to 2-semester units; much of its major emphasis, content, and effectiveness are being gutted. The 2 unit course does not allow faculty to prepare the students for the variety of bibliographic and reference resources they will encounter in their under-graduate career at UC-B. Ironically, this has occurred at a time when the undergraduate must cope with new, more sophisticated information re-sources, a bewildering array of reference tools, a university library sys-tem with richly diverse collections and formidable technologies that re-quire awareness of alternate research strategies.
>
> The mission of the School of Library and Information Studies--to pre-pare its graduate students for the library and information profession--has, to a large extent, diverted it from its earlier involvement in undergraduate education. In this process, it can no longer accomodate sympathetically

a program developed specifically for a general undergraduate population. It is imperative that Bibliography 1 find a favorable and hospitable sponsor, one committed to excellence in undergraduate education. It is to this purpose that we urge the Academic Senate Committee on Educational Policy both to reconsider the unit value of Bibliography 1, as well as to ensure an appropriate departmental affiliation.

In October 1986 the Associated Students of the University of California's response to a UC-B Academic Senate Planning committee report noted that it is important to restore a balance between preprofessional training and liberal education, and that "too many students graduate who have achieved competency in technical subjects, but have never studied ... subjects that expose people to different thoughts and ideas." The ASUC urged the establishment of a common core curriculum to guarantee that students take a wide variety of courses. [38] Ironically, it was left to the Associated Students to provide in Fall 1987 a course, "Senior Thesis Workshop," "designed to offer structure, assistance and support to students presently engaged in the research ... of a ... Senior Thesis ... to work on bibliography, topic questions, thesis development, outlines...." These student-initiated classes, called Democratic Education at Cal or DE-Cal, work "to reshape education at U.C. Berkeley to be socially responsible and based on critical thinking, participation, and dialogue.... We encourage the initiation of classes and internships which 1) do not fit neatly into the compartmentalization of study into "disciplines"; or 2) are usually ignored as legitimate fields of academic inquiry." [39]

Notes

1. Wheeler, Helen. "Delay, Divide, Discredit; How Uppity Women Are Kept Down, Apart and Out of Academe." WLW Journal 8 (July-September 1983): 1-5. Reprinted in Alternative Library Literature, 1982/1983: Biennial Anthology, edited by Sanford Berman and James Danky. Phoenix, Arizona: Oryx Press, 1984.

2. Barton, Laurie. "Women Still Fighting for Job Equality." The Daily Californian 14 (April 26, 1983): 14.

3. Toy, Beverly M. Library Instruction at the University of California: Formal Courses. ERIC ED 116 649 1975 8 pages.

4. Librarians with bibliographic instruction responsibility at all University of California system campuses were contacted in fall 1986. Adams includes accounts of bibliographic instruction at UC--Berkeley and Irvine, and San José State University.

5. Eisenbach, Elizabeth. "Bibliographic Instruction from the Other Side of the Desk." RQ 17 (1978): 312-316. Eisenbach was also interviewed in 1979.

6. A two-page statement of "GSLIS 110 General Information and Course Requirements" provides information about its objectives, organization, requirements, grading, etc.; contact course coordinator Connie Nyhan, Adjunct Lecturer, Graduate School of Library and Information Science, Room 300H Powell Library Building, University of California--Los Angeles, Los Angeles, California 90024.

7. A one-page course syllabus for "Library Research Strategies" is available from Peter Bliss, University of California--Riverside Library, Riverside, California 92521.

8. Osegueda, Laura and Judy Reynolds. "Introducing Online Skills into the University Curriculum." RQ 22(1982):10-11.

9. California, University--Berkeley. [School of] Library and Information Studies Announcement 1986-7. (Volume 80, No. 16, September 1986). Page 10.

10. Vanderberg, Patricia S. "Case Study #4: University of California-Berkeley" in Teaching Library Skills for Academic Credit, pp. 111-115, by Mignon S. Adams and Jacquelyn M. Morris. Phoenix, Arizona: Oryx Press, 1985.

11. Memo dated 6 June 1966 to Professor Donald C. Coney, University Librarian; from Charles H. Shain, City & Regional Planning Librarian, Environmental Design Library; Subject: A proposal for an experimental undergraduate course teaching the use of the library--to be taught by librarians.

12. Knapp, Patricia. The Monteith College Library Experiment. Metuchen, New Jersey: Scarecrow Press, 1966.

13. Shain, Charles. "A Bibliography Course at U.C. Berkeley; a Paper Submitted to the California Library Association Conference in San Francisco, December 11, 1969." Also "Bibliography I: The UC Berkeley Experience." In Instruction in the Use of the College and University Library. ERIC ED 045 103 1970.

14. University of California--Berkeley General Library. "On Leaving Bibliography 1." CU News 26 (April 8, 1971): 1.

15. Letter dated January 7, 1975, to Library Personnel Officer William E. Wenz; from Patrick Wilson, Dean, School of Librarianship; cc: Charles Shain.

16. University of California--Berkeley General Library.

17. Letter dated January 7, 1975.

18. Shain. p. 2 of ERIC document version.

19. Heinrich, Teresa. "Cheating on Campus Grows Dramatically; Investigation Uncovers Widespread and Varied Tricks Used by Students." Daily Californian 17 (October 8, 1985): 1.

20. Data may not be exact due to such things as my regard for statistics from Bib 1's inception and the School's sometime regard for data since it came under its jurisdiction.

21. University policy requires a school faculty member, identified as "Person in Charge," to sponsor Bibliography 1. Dr. Fay Blake sponsored and sometimes taught Bib 1 from 1972 to 1976; Dean Buckland served as sponsor from 1976 to 1984 except during his sabbatical, when Prof. William Cooper was Acting Dean. Prof. Robert Harlan was Acting Dean several times, including 1984-January

1986, when Law School Librarian/Professor Robert Berring added the School deanship to his responsibilities.

22. Buckland, Michael K. "Library Education--Meeting the Needs of the Future." Catholic Library World 50 (May-June 1979): 424-426. Page 425.

23. Dean Buckland at spring 1981 staff meeting.

24. California, University--Berkeley. Page 15.

25. "Part-Time Teaching Positions in Bibliography I (SLIS), 1984-85." CU News 39 (March 8, 1984): 4. This format was the same until reference to one-third time was changed to one-quarter time, Bibliography 1 was referred to as a 2 unit course, and "experience with on-line computer searching" was changed to "acquaintance with...." in 1986: CU News 41 (March 20, 1986): 1.

26. "A Self-Study of the Master of Library and Information Studies Degree Program at the School of Library and Information Studies, University of California, Berkeley." 1980. Page 32.

27. Psychologist Susan Basow (Lafayette College, Easton, Pennsylvania 18042)'s research concerning why students give female professors lower ratings has been mentioned in the AFL/CIO newspaper, On Campus 6 (December 1986-January 1987): 6, for example.

28. Johnson, Bruce L. Methods of Library Use: Handbook for Bibliography I. Berkeley, California: University School of Librarianship, 1976. ERIC ED 129 340.

29. Turabian, Kate. A Manual for Writers of Term Papers, Theses, and Dissertations, 4th ed. Chicago, Illinois: University of Chicago Press, 1973.

30. California, University--Berkeley. Office of Student Research. A Profile of the Students at Berkeley, November 1986. 4 pages.

31. A two-year survey at the University of California--Berkeley reported in the Daily Californian and the Chronicle of Higher Education, 33 (January 7, 1987): 33, suggests that most students still believe in a traditional marriage "where the husband brings home the bacon and the wife stays home with the kids. Two-thirds of the men and half of the women interviewed said the husband's career comes first and most men said they were unwilling to do laundry or cook dinner. Missing ... from both the women and the men is a sense that joint incomes increasingly are necessary in order to maintain a middle-class life style."

32. Wheeler, Helen R. "A Feminist Researcher's Guide to Periodical Indexes, Abstracting Services, Citation Indexes and Online Databases." Collection Building: Studies... 5 (Winter 1983/1984): 3-24. This has since been revised and is regularly updated for inclusion in the "Getting Published" workshop packet.

33. October 21, 1981 memorandum.

34. Johnson, Bruce L. "Bib 1, American Libraries 0." Letter to the Editor. American Libraries 16 (September 1985): 546. "U Cal/Berkeley Downgrades Respected Bib 1 Course." American Libraries 16 (June 1985): 370.

35. July 2, 1985 memorandum to "Bibliography 1 Faculty, Fall 1985 Semester" from the coordinator. At a March 19, 1985 meeting with some Bibliography 1 staff members, (Acting) School Dean Harlan, Associate Dean Cook, and faculty member Braunstein "presented the findings of the committee that reviewed Bib I. [Braunstein] said ... A two-person committee reviewed Bib I ... Bib I will be reduced to 2 units, subject to review of the standing committee.... The committee felt that there were 'inappropriate' areas of instruction included in the Bib. I curriculum, based on examination of the syllabus and a few term projects." No one has ever observed a Bib. I class or spoken with the instructors to get a true sense of what is taught. "Inappropriate" areas mentioned were "extensive" coverage of government documents and "advanced" MELVYL techniques. The committee felt that Bib. I should be a "fundamental use course" without teaching the students to do research and to use "sophisticated" tools such as indexes and abstracts. We should not be teaching them how to do research, only to use the library...." Minutes of Bibliography I meeting, 19 March 1985.

36. California, University--Berkeley. Page 10.

37. "University of California--Berkeley Downgrades Respected Bib I Course." American Libraries 16 (June 1985): 370; Cavanaugh, Gerald, "Undergraduate Teaching at University of California." Letter to the Editor. Chronicle of Higher Education 31 (December 11, 1985): 36; McLaughlin, Sigrid. "The Dilemma of the Temporary Lecturer." Off the Track, Bulletin of Non Academic Senate Faculty of the University of California 1 (Fall 1981): 5,7 (published under the auspices of University Council, A.F.T. AFL-CIO); Heinrich, Teresa. "Library Profs May Lose Pay, Board Hears." Daily Californian 17 (January 20, 1986): 1, 3.

38. In August 1986 the University of California--Berkeley Academic Senate's planning committee released a faculty report, referred to as The Elberg Report (the Committee was chaired by Professor Emeritus Sanford Elberg), which made recommendations including guaranteeing that students take a wide variety of courses by establishing a common core curriculum. In October 1986, the ASUC's response in essence was agreement, but that a committee should be established to re-examine the undergraduate curriculum, that the core curriculum should include an ethnic studies requirement, and the advisory system be strengthened. Kazmin, Amy Louise, "ASUC Responds to Elberg Report." Daily Californian 19 (October 30, 1986): 5.

Earlier, in response to three national reports criticizing quality of undergraduate education, the Californian legislature "launched a major review of the state's master plan for higher education." McCurdy, Jack. "University of California Faculty Panel Proposes Smaller Classes." Chronicle of Higher Education 33 (September 24, 1986): 3.

39. Student Initiated Classes. ASUC Sponsored DE-Cal Supplement to the General Catalog. Spring 1987. 4 pages.

Bibliography

See also Section III: Resources.

Adams, Mignon S. and Jacquelyn M. Morris. Teaching Library Skills for Academic

Credit. Phoenix, Arizona: Oryx, 1985. Case studies # 4 (University of California--Berkeley) pp. 111-115; 13 (San José State University) pp. 155-158; and 118 (University of California--Irvine) pp. 179-184.

American Libraries 16 (June 1985): 370. "University of California--Berkeley Downgrades Respected Bib I Course."

Barton, Laurie. "Women Still Fighting for Job Equality." Daily Californian 14 (April 26, 1983): 8.

Berry, John. "'Pilgrim's Progress' & 'The Bible.'" Editorial. Library Journal 106 (April 15, 1981): 831.

Buckland, Michael K. "Bibliography 1 Not Remedial," Letter to the Editor. Library Journal 106 (September 15, 1981): 1659.

_____. "Library Education--Meeting the Needs of the Future." Catholic Library World 50 (May-June 1979): 424-426.

California. University. Conference Workshop, July 13-14, 1970. Instruction in the Use of the College and University Library. Selected Conference Papers. ERIC ED 045-103 1970.

Cavanaugh, Gerald. "Undergraduate Teaching at University of California." Letter to the Editor. Chronicle of Higher Education 31 (December 11, 1985): 36.

Collard, R. Michael. "Illinois' 'Foundations' Course." Letter to the Editor. Library Journal 107 (January 1, 1982): 3.

Dudley, Miriam. "Chicano Library Project, Based on the 'Research Skills in the Library Context' Program Developed for the Chicano High Potential Students in the Department of Special Education Programs." UCLA Occasional Paper, No. 17. Los Angeles, California: University of California--Los Angeles Library, 1970. ERIC ED 045 105.

_____. "A Self-Paced Library Skills Program at UCLA's College Library" in Educating the Library User, pp. 330-335. Edited by John Lubans, Jr. New York: Bowker, 1974.

Dyson, Allan J. "Organizing Undergraduate Library Instruction: The English and American Experience." Journal of Academic Librarianship 1 (March 1975): 9-13.

Eisenbach, Elizabeth. "Bibliographic Instruction from the Other Side of the Desk." RQ 17 (1978): 312-316.

Heinrich, Teresa. "Library Profs May Lose Pay, Board Hears." Daily Californian 17 (January 20, 1986): 1, 3.

Johnson, Bruce L. "Bib 1, American Libraries 0." Letter to the Editor. American Libraries 16 (September 1985): 546.

Knapp, Patricia B. The Library, The Undergraduate and the Teaching Faculty. San Diego, California: University of California Library, 1970. ERIC ED 042 475.

Osegueda, Laura and Judy Reynolds. "Introducing Online Skills Into the University Curriculum." RQ 22 (1982): 10-11.

Peterschmidt, Mary J. "Experiences Team Teaching Library Instruction at San Jose State College." In Instruction in the Use of the College and University Library. Selected Conference Papers. ERIC ED 045 103 1970.

Rader, Hannelore B. "Formal Courses in Bibliography." In Educating the Library User, pp. 279-285. Edited by John Lubans, Jr. New York: Bowker, 1974.

Shain, Charles H. "Bibliography 1 Pioneer." Letter to the Editor. Library Journal 106 (September 15, 1981): 1659.

_____. "Bibliography I: The UC Berkeley Experience." In Instruction in the Use of the College and University Library. Selected Conference Papers. ERIC ED 045 103 1970.

Toy, Beverly M. Library Instruction at the University of California: Formal Courses. Berkeley, California: University of California--Berkeley University Libraries, 1975. ERIC ED 116 649 8 pages.

"University of California Faulted on Affirmative Action." Chronicle of Higher Education 24 (July 21, 1982): 3.

Vanderberg, Patricia S. "Case Study #4: University of California--Berkeley." In Teaching Library Skills for Academic Credit, pp. 111-115. Edited by Mignon S. Adams and Jacquelyn M. Morris. Phoenix, Arizona: Oryx, 1985.

Wheeler, Helen Rippier. For-Credit, Undergraduate, Bibliographic Instruction Courses in the University of California System; With Consideration of the Berkeley Campus' "Bibliography 1" Course-Program's History as a Model. ERIC ED 266 799 1986 43 pages.

SECTION III

RESOURCES

Bibliographic and Library Instruction Courses Bibliography

[See Also: "Texts, Handbooks, Workbooks...." Section and Chapter 4 Bibliography]

Adams, Mignon S. and Jacquelyn M. Morris. Teaching Library Skills for Academic Credit. Phoenix, Arizona: Oryx, 1985.

Aluri, Rao. "Application of Learning Theories to Library-Use Instruction." Libri 31 (August 1981): 140-152.

Aluri, Rao and June Engle. "Bibliographic Instruction and Library Education," in Bibliographic Instruction (Mellon, ed.). Libraries Unlimited, 1987.

Association of College & Research Libraries. Bibliographic Instruction Handbook. Chicago, Illinois: American Library Association, 1979.

_____. Evaluating Bibliographic Instruction: A Handbook. Chicago, Illinois: American Library Association, 1983. [See also Tiefel, V.]

_____. "Guidelines for Bibliographic Instruction in Academic Libraries." C&RL News 38 (April 1977): 92.

_____. "Standards for College Libraries, 1986 edition." C&RL News 47 (March 1986): 189-200.

_____. "Think Tank Recommendations for Bibliographic Instruction." C&RL News 42 (December 1981): 394-398. See also: Euster, J.

Beaubien, Anne K., et al. Learning the Library: Concepts and Methods for Effective Bibliographic Instruction. New York: Bowker, 1982. Companion to Oberman's Theories of Bibliographic Education. "Between the three major books on the subject--those by Breivik, Beaubien/George/Hogan, and Rice-- everything that could be said about BI has been." (LOEX)

Bhullar, Pushpajit and Harry V. Hosel, Eds. Library Skills. Columbia, Missouri: University of Missouri School of Library & Information Science, 1979. ERIC ED 190 083.

Bhullar, Pushpajit and P. P. Timberlake. "Library Skills: An Undergraduate Course at the University of Missouri--Columbia." Show-Me Libraries 36 (October-November 1984): 70-74.

Biggins, Jeanne. A Study of the Administration of Library Use Instruction Courses by Committee. ERIC ED 171 241 1979.

Blum, Mark E. and Stephen Spangehl. Introducing the College Student to Academic Inquiry: An Individualized Course in Library Research: Paper Presented at the International Congress for Individualized Instruction. ERIC ED 152 315, November 1977, 35 pages.

Breivik, Patricia Senn. Planning the Library Instruction Program. Chicago, Illinois: American Library Association, 1982. [See note under Beaubien.]

Brownson, C. W. "Strategies for Promoting Instruction." In Reform and Renewal in Higher Education: Implications for Library Instruction.... pp. 73-87. Edited by Carolyn A. Kirkendall. Ann Arbor, Michigan: Pierian Press, 1980.

Brundin, Robert E. "Education for Instructional Librarians; Development and Overview." Journal of Education for Library and Information Science 25 (Winter 1985): 177-189.

DeHart, Florence E. The Library-College Concept: For the Want of a Horse Shoe Nail. Emporia, Kansas: Kansas State Teachers College, Graduate Library School. ERIC ED 098 995 1974.

Dougherty, Robert and Lois M. Pausch. Bibliographic Instruction in Illinois Libraries: A Survey Report. Illinois Library Statistical Report No. 11. Springfield, Illinois: Illinois State Library. ERIC ED 238 454, 1983, 96 pages.

Droog, J. "The Education of the Information Users." International Forum on Information and Documentation 1 (1976): 26-32.

Dudley, Miriam S. "The State of Library Instruction Credit Courses and the State of the Use of Library Skills Workbooks." In Library Instruction in the Seventies: State of the Art.... pp. 79-84. Edited by Hannelore B. Rader. Ann Arbor, Michigan: Pierian Press, 1977.

_____. "Teaching Library Skills to College Students." In Advances in Librarianship 3, pp. 83-105. Edited by Melvin J. Voigt. New York: Seminar Press, 1972.

Dunlap, Connie R. "Library Services to the Graduate Community: The University of Michigan." College & Research Libraries 37 (1976): 247-251.

Dyer, Esther. "The Visible College." Journal of Education for Librarianship 18 (Spring 1978): 359-361.

Euster, Joanne R. "Reactions to the Think Tank Recommendations: A Symposium." Journal of Academic Librarianship 9 (March 1983): 4-14. [See Also: Association of College & Research Libraries.]

Eyman, David H. and Alvin C. Nunley, Jr. The Effectiveness of Library Science 1011 in Teaching Bibliographic Skills. Tahlequah, Oklahoma: Northeastern Oklahoma State University, 1978. ERIC ED 150 962.

Farber, Evan. "Teaching the Use of the Library: Part II Implementation." Library Issues 2 (January 1982): 3-4.

Franco, Elaine A., Ed. Improving the Use of Libraries. Proceedings from the

Spring Meeting of the Nebraska Library Association.... ERIC ED 234 817, 1983, 115 pages.

Galloway, Sue. "Nobody Is Teaching the Teacher." Booklegger 3 (1976): 29-31.

Getchell, C. M. "Bibliographic Instruction: A Non-Credit/Non-Graded Course at the University of Kansas." C&RL News 6 (June 1981): 173-174.

Gore, Daniel. "A Course in Bibliography for Freshmen at Asheville-Biltmore College." North Carolina Libraries 23 (1965): 80.

Hales, Celia and D. Catlett. "The Credit Course: Reaffirmation From Two University Libraries' Methodology: East Carolina University." Research Strategies 2 (Fall 1984): 156-165.

Head, S. L. Evaluation of the Library Skills Course at the University of Missouri, Columbia. Columbia, Missouri: University of Missouri--Columbia, 1980.

Howarth, Lisa and Donald Kenney. "Education for Bibliographic Instruction: A Syllabi Project." C&RL News 44 (November 1983): 379-380.

Johnson, P. T. "The Latin American Subject Specialist and Bibliographic Instruction." Seminar on the Acquisition of Latin American Library Materials: Final Report and Working Papers 19 (1974): 203-221.

Jones, G. "Using the Chemical Literature--An Undergraduate Course?" Education in Chemistry 10 (1973): 11.

Kennedy, James R. "Question: A Separate Course in Bibliography or Course-Related Instruction?" In Library Orientation.... pp. 18-28. Edited by Sul H. Lee. Ann Arbor, Michigan: Pierian Press, 1972.

Kibby, R. A. and A. M. Weiner. "U.S.F. Library Lectures, Revisited." RQ 13 (1983): 139-142.

Kirkendall, Carolyn, Ed. "Library Instruction: A Column of Opinion." In Journal of Academic Librarianship 2 (November 1976): 240-241; 3 (1977): 94-95.

_____. Putting Library Instruction in its Place: In the Library and in the Library School. (Seventh Annual Conference on Library Orientation for Academic Libraries Series, #8). Ann Arbor, Michigan: Pierian Press, 1978.

_____. "A Review of the Past.... A Call for the Future." Research Strategies 1 (Winter 1983): 83, 36-37.

Knapp, Patricia B. The Monteith College Library Experiment. Metuchen, New Jersey: Scarecrow Press, 1966.

Krzywkowski, Valerie I. "Bibliographic Instruction for Undergraduate Students: Development of a One Credit Course." In Improving the Use of Libraries. Proceedings.... 1983. #2. Edited by Elaine A. Franco. ERIC ED 234 817.

LaRose, Al and Barbara Young. "A Librarian in the Classroom." In Bibliographic Instruction. pp. 12-19. Compiled by Barbara Mertins. West Virginia Library

Assn. Conf. of the College and University Section. ERIC, ED 144 582, 1977.

Larson, Mary Ellen and Ellen Meltzer. "Education for Bibliographic Instruction." Journal of Education for Library and Information Science 28 (Summer 1987): 9-16.

Lee, J. W. and R. L. Read. "Making the Library Good for Business." Learning Today 6 (1973): 36-41.

McQuistion, Virginia Frank. "The Credit Course: Reaffirmation from Two University Libraries' Measurement: Millikin University." Research Strategies 2 (Fall 1984): 166-171.

Marshall, A. P., Issue Editor. "Current Library Use Instruction" [Issue]. Library Trends 39 (Summer 1980).

Martin, J. et al. "Teaching of Formal Courses by Medical Librarians." Journal of Medical Education 50 (1975): 883-887.

Miller, Wayne Stuart. "Library Use Instruction in Selected American Colleges." Occasional Papers No. 134. Urbana, Illinois: University of Illinois Graduate School of Library Science, August 1978.

Morris, Jacquelyn M. Bibliographic Instruction in Academic Libraries. A Review of the Literature and Selected Bibliography. ERIC ED 180 505, 1979. 54 pages.

_____. "Gaining Faculty Acceptance and Support of Library Instruction: A Case Study." In Faculty Involvement in Library Instruction.... pp. 57-73. Edited by Hannelore B. Rader. Ann Arbor, Michigan: Pierian Press, 1976.

_____. "A Philosophical Defense of a Credit Course." In Proceedings from the Second Southeastern Conference on Approaches to Bibliographic Instruction, pp. 11-18. Edited by Cerise Oberman. Charleston, South Carolina: College of Charleston Library Associates, 1980.

Nettlefold, B. A. "A Course in Communication and Information Retrieval for Undergraduate Biologists." Journal of Biological Education 9 (1975): 201-205.

New York. State University (SUNY). Library Skills Course for EOP Students [At SUNY Plattsburgh.] ERIC ED 202 459, 1981.

Oberman, Cerise. Petals Around a Rose: Abstract Reasoning and Bibliographic Instruction. Chicago, Illinois: Association of College & Research Libraries, 1981. Also available as ERIC ED 229 013, 1980, 25 pages.

_____ and Katina Spraugh. Theories of Bibliographic Education. New York: Bowker, 1982. [A companion volume to Beaubien.]

Palmer, V. E. "Bibliographic Instruction for the Invisible University." C&RL News 43 (1982): 12-13.

Pastine, Maureen and Karen Seibert. "Update on the Status of Bibliographic Instruction in Library School Programs." Journal of Education for Librarianship 21 (Fall 1980): 169-171.

Paugh, S. L. and Guy A. Marco. "Music Bibliography Course: Status and Quo." Music Library Association Notes 30 (1973): 260-262.

Peele, David. "Librarians as Teachers; Some Reality, Mostly Myth." Journal of Academic Librarianship 10 (November 1984): 267-270.

Person, Roland. "Long-Term Evaluation of Bibliographic Instruction: Lasting Encouragement." College & Research Libraries 42 (January 1981): 19-25.

Rader, Hannelore B. "Formal Courses in Bibliography." In Educating the Library User, pp. 279-285. Edited by John Lubans, Jr. New York: Bowker, 1975.

Reeves, Pamela. Library Services for Non-Traditional Students. Final Report. Ypsilanti, Michigan: Eastern Michigan University, 1979. ERIC ED 184 550.

Renford, Beverly and Linnea Hendrickson. Bibliographic Instruction: A Handbook. New York: Neal-Schuman, 1980. (See especially Chapter 6, "Credit Instruction," pp. 121-149.)

Rettig, James. "General Library Skills Credit Courses." In State of the Art of Academic Library Instruction, 1977 Update, pp. 79-113. Edited by Thomas Kirk. Chicago, Illinois: American Library Association, 1977. Also available as ERIC ED 171 272. (Updates a 1973 Report).

Rice, James. Teaching Library Use: A Guide for Library Instruction. Contributions in Librarianship and Information Service Series, 37. Westport, Connecticut: Greenwood Press, 1981. [See note under Beaubien.]

Roberts, Anne. Library Instruction for Librarians. Littleton, Colorado: Libraries Unlimited, 1982.

_____. A Study of Ten SUNY Campuses Offering an Undergraduate Credit Course in Library Instruction. Albany, New York: SUNY University Libraries, 1978. ERIC ED 157 529, 81 pages.

_____ and Frances L. Hopkins. "Can Bibliographic Instruction Be Considered a Separate Discipline?" Journal of Academic Librarianship 8 (1982): 160-161.

Selegean, John C., et al. "Long-Range Effectiveness of Library Use Instruction." College & Research Libraries 44 (1983): 476-480.

Smalley, Topsy N. Bibliographic Instruction for Undergraduates: An Example of a One-Unit Required Library Research Skills Course. Plattsburgh, New York: SUNY College, 1983. ERIC ED 232 656, 116 pages.

_____. "Bibliographic Instruction in Academic Libraries: Questioning Some Assumptions." Journal of Academic Librarianship 3 (November 1977): 280-283.

Stillerman, Sophia J. Format for Library Instruction: Stated Student Preferences at a Community College. ERIC ED 115 294 1975.

Sugranes, Maria P. and James A. Neal. "Evaluation of a Self-Paced Bibliographic Instruction Course." College & Research Libraries 44 (November 1983): 444-457.

Tiefel, Virginia and David King. "Evaluating Bibliographic Instruction: A Handbook." C&RL News 44 (September 1983): 271-273. (A reprint of the contents, preface and introduction of the Association of College & Research Libraries' Evaluating Bibliographic Instruction: A Handbook.)

Turner, P. M. "Instructional Design Competencies Taught at Library Schools." Journal of Education for Librarianship 22 (Spring 1982): 275-282.

Walser, Katina P. and Kathryn W. Kruse. "A College Course for Nurses on the Utilization of Library Resources." Bulletin of the Medical Library Association 65 (April 1977): 265-267.

Will, L. D. "Finding Information: A Course for Physics Students." Physics Bulletin 23 (1972): 539-540.

Wilson, Pauline. "Librarians As Teachers: The Study of an Organization Fiction." Library Quarterly 49 (April 1979): 146-152.

Wood, Richard J. "The Impact of a Library Research Course on Students at Slippery Rock University." Journal of Academic Librarianship 10 (1984): 278-284.

_____. A One Credit, Self-Paced Library Research Course and Its Impact on The Knowledge and Attitude Base of Slippery Rock University Students. ERIC ED 241 026 1983.

Texts, Handbooks, Workbooks, Self-Paced
Courses and Manuals

Adalian, P. T. and I. F. Rockman. BLISS: Basic Library Information Sources and Strategies; A Handbook for Library 101. San Luis Obispo, California: California Polytechnic State University. ERIC ED 20Q 202 1981.

Argall, Rebecca and Janell Rudolph. Library Skills Handbook. Memphis, Tennessee: Metropolitan Books, 1983.

Baker, Robert K. Doing Library Research: An Introduction for Community College Students. Boulder, Colorado: Westview Press, 1981.

Bodien, C. and M. K. Smith. Developing Library Skills: How to Use the University Library. Bemidji, Minnesota: Bemidji State University, A. C. Clark Library. ERIC ED 153 656 1978.

Breyson, E. M. and W. Kelly. Library Research Manual: History. ERIC ED 229 011 1982.

California University. Los Angeles. Graduate School of Library & Information Science. Syllabus/Workbook for GSLIS 110. Available from UCLA Bookstore, Los Angeles, CA 90024.

California University. San Diego. University Library Instructional Services Office. Finding Information in the U.C.S.D. Libraries, Revised 1977.

Clement, Russell T., et al. Using the Joseph F. Smith Library. Laie, Hawaii. Brigham Young University--Hawaii: Joseph F. Smith Library, 1981. ERIC ED 201 328.

Cohen, David. Library Skills. A Self-Paced Program in the Use of Stockton State College Library. Workbook, Handbook, and Program. Pomona, New Jersey: Stockton State College, 1982. ERIC ED 253 226.

Cook, Margaret G. The New Library Key, 3rd Edition. New York: H. W. Wilson Co., 1975.

Devine, Marie E. Guide to Library Research; A Basic Text for the Undergraduate, 2nd Edition. Asheville, North Carolina: University of North Carolina Ramsey Library. ERIC ED 258 578.

Dialog Information Services, Inc. User's Workbook [with] Knowledge Index. Palo Alto, California, DIALOG Information Services, Inc., November 1982.

Downs, Robert Bingham and Clara D. Keller. How to do Library Research, 2nd Edition. Urbana, Illinois: University of Illinois Press, 1975.

Dwight, John A. & Dana C. Speer. How to Write a Research Paper. Mentor, Ohio: Learning Concepts, Inc., 1979.

Els, P. and K. L. Amen. Introduction to Bibliography. San Antonio, Texas: St. Mary's University. ERIC ED 156 107 1978.

Fenner, Peter and Martha C. Armstrong. Research: A Practical Guide to Finding Information. Los Angeles, California: William Kaufmann, 1981.

Frick, Elizabeth. Library Research Guide to History: Illustrated Search Strategy and Sources. (Library Research Guides Series, 4). Ann Arbor, Michigan: Pierian, 1980.

Gates, Jean Key. Guide to the Use of Libraries and Information Sources, 5th Edition. New York: McGraw-Hill, 1983.

Gavryck, J., et al. Library Research Curriculum Materials for a One Credit Course. Albany, New York: SUNY. ERIC ED 203 884 1981.

Gebhard, Patricia. Library Research, Fall 1985. Available from the University of California--Santa Barbara Bookstore, Santa Barbara, CA 93106.

_____. Library Skills, Fall 1986. Available from the University of California--Santa Barbara Bookstore, Santa Barbara, CA 93106.

Gilmer, Wesley, Jr. Legal Research Writing & Advocacy; Paralegal Instructor's Manual. Cincinnati, Ohio: Anderson Publishing Co. For use with his Legal Research, Writing & Advocacy; a Sourcebook. 1978.

Gorden, Charlotte. How to Find What You Want in the Library. Woodbury, New York: Barron's Educational Series, 1978.

Gore, Daniel. Bibliography for Beginners: Form A. New York: Appleton-Century-Crofts, 1968.

Gover, Harvey R. Keys to Library Research on the Graduate Level: A Guide to Guides. Washington, DC: University Press of America, 1981.

Graham, Christine, Ed. Library Resources: A Self-Paced Workbook, 3rd Edition. San Francisco, California: San Francisco State University Leonard Library, 1983. ERIC ED 248 899.

Hales, Celia, et al. Strategies for Search. A Self-Paced Workbook for Basic Library Skills, 2nd Edition. ERIC ED 252 228 1984.

Hauer, Mary G., et al. Books, Libraries, and Research, 2nd Edition. Dubuque, Iowa: Kendall and Hunt, 1983.

Hodina, A., et al. Information Resources in the Sciences and Engineering: A Laboratory Workbook. California, Santa Barbara: University of California--Santa Barbara University Library, 1981. ERIC 205 178.

Resources

Honigsblum, Bonnie. See Turabian, Kate.

Huston, Mary M. and D. M. Robinson. Library Research Source Curricular
    Package [Designed for a course at Evergreen State College, Washington].
    ERIC ED 213 416 1981.

Johnson, Bruce L. Methods of Library Use: Handbook for Bibliography I.
    Berkeley, California: School of Librarianship, 1976. ERIC ED 219 340.

Katz, William A. Introduction to Reference Work, Volume II: Reference Services
    and Reference Processes, 2nd Edition. New York: McGraw-Hill, 1974.

_____. Your Library: A Reference Guide, 2nd Edition. New York: Holt,
    Rinehart & Winston, 1984.

Kennedy, James Randolph. Library Research Guide to Education: Illustrated
    Search Strategy and Sources. (Library Research Guides Series, 3). Ann
    Arbor, Michigan: Pierian, 1979.

Guide to the Use of Kentucky Libraries [Workbook]. ED 126 901.

Knight, Hattie M. The 1-2-3 Guide to Libraries, 5th Edition. Dubuque, Iowa:
    Brown, 1976.

Kirk, Thomas. Library Research Guide to Biology: Illustrated Search Strategy
    and Sources. (Library Research Guides Series, 2). Ann Arbor, Michigan:
    Pierian, 1978.

Lass, Abraham H. "How to Do Research." In World Book Encyclopedia, Volume
    22, 1981.

Library Research Guides Series. Ann Arbor, Michigan: Pierian Press. [See:
    Frick, Kennedy, Kirk, and McMillan.]

Lolley, John L. Your Library--What's in it for You? New York: Wiley, 1974.

McMillan, Patricia and James Randolph. Library Research Guide to Sociology:
    Illustrated Search Strategy and Sources. (Library Research Guides Series, 5.)
    Ann Arbor, Michigan: Pierian, 1981.

Library Instruction Series Workbook [At the University of Maine, Orono]. ERIC
    ED 162 667; also 664, 665 and 666.

Meyer, Michael. The Little, Brown Guide to Writing Research Papers, 2nd
    Edition. Boston, Massachusetts: Little, Brown, 1985.

Moore, Nick. How to Do Research, 2nd Edition. Chicago, Illinois: American
    Library Association, 1986.

Morris, Jacquelyn and Elizabeth A. Elkins. Library Searching: Resources and
    Strategies ... Environmental Sciences. New York: Jeffrey Norton, 1978.

Morse, Grant W. Concise Guide to Library Research, Revised Edition. New York:
    Fleet Academic Editions, 1975.

_____. Guide to the Incomparable New York Times Index. New York: Fleet Academic Editions, 1980.

New York. State University. Buffalo. Workbook for Library Research in Psychology. ERIC ED 151 025.

_____. Potsdam. Library Resources in Education: An Introductory Module for Students and Teachers. ERIC ED 124 129.

Pikoff, H. Workbook for Library Research in Psychology. ERIC ED 151 025 1978.

Reed, Jeffrey G. and Pam M. Baxter. Library Use: A Handbook for Psychology. Washington, D.C: American Psychological Association, 1983.

Renford, Beverly L. "A Self-Paced Workbook Program for Beginning College Students." Journal of Academic Librarianship 4 (September 1978): 200-205.

Rice, S. Workbook for the Introduction to the Library. Ann Arbor, Michigan: University of Michigan Libraries. ERIC ED 163 953 1979.

Rominger, C. A. Handbook for English 48: Introduction to Library Research and Bibliography. Davis, California: University of California, University Library. ERIC ED 108 670. 1975.

Smalley, Topsy N. Basic Reference Tools for Nursing Research: A Work Book with Explanation and Examples. Plattsburgh, New York: SUNY. ERIC ED 197 071 1978.

Texas. University at Austin. A Module for Training Library Researchers [In Educational Psychology]. ERIC ED 145 849.

Tierney, Judith. Basic Library Skills: A Self-Paced Workbook. ERIC ED 247 941 1984.

Turabian, Kate. A Manual for Writers of Term Papers, Theses, and Dissertations, 4th Edition. Chicago, Illinois: University of Chicago Press, 1977. 5th Edition (1987) by Bonnie Honigsblum.

_____. Student's Guide for Writing College Papers, 3rd Revised Expanded Edition. Chicago, Illinois: University of Chicago Press, 1977.

Walsh, P. and H. Giessen. Research in Practice: A Workbook for the College Student. Redding Ridge, Connecticut: Professional Services Publishing Co., 1983.

Wheeler, Helen R. ERIC and Equity: Using ERIC Products for Information and Publications Affirming Gender Equity. ERIC ED 219 076 1982.

_____. "A Feminist Researcher's Guide to Periodical Indexes, Abstracting Services, Citation Indexes and Online Databases." Collection Building: Studies.... (Winter 1983/1984): 3-24.

Resources

Wisconsin. University, Parkside. <u>Basic Library Skills: A Self-Paced Introduc-</u>
<u>tion to the Use of the Library Learning Center</u>.... 8th Edition, Revised.
Kenosha, Wisconsin: University of Wisconsin--Parkside, 1983.

Wolf, Carolyn and Richard R. Wolf. <u>Basic Library Skills</u>, 2nd Edition. Jefferson,
North Carolina: McFarland, 1981.

Bibliographic and Library Instruction Clearinghouse Information

Ariel, Joan. Library Instruction Clearinghouses: 1985, A Directory, Revised.... Chicago, Illinois: American Library Association, 1985.

Beaubien, Anne K. Bibliographic Instruction Within Library and Discipline Associations: A Survey of Contact Persons and Committees. ERIC ED 175 468, 1979, 31 pages.

California Clearinghouse on Library Instruction. For current-year personnel, contact California Library Association, 717 K Street, #300, Sacramento, California 95814. The California Clearinghouse on Library Instruction has a Newsletter, Northern and Southern Regional sections, and depositories. See also: Grassian, Esther.

Coleman, Kathleen, Ed. The Bibliographic Instruction Clearinghouse: A Practical Guide. Chicago, Illinois: American Library Association, 1984.

Costa, Joseph J., Comp. A Directory of Library Instruction Programs in Pennsylvania Academic Libraries. Pittsburgh, Pennsylvania: Pennsylvania Library Association, 1980. ERIC ED 200 225.

Dantin, Doris B., Comp. Bibliographic Instruction Programs in Louisiana Academic Libraries: A Directory. Baton Rouge, Louisiana: Louisiana Library Association, 1983.

Engelbrecht, Pamela. It Really Works: A Directory of Programs, Courses, and Resource People for Bibliographic Instruction Librarians. Library Instruction Round Table, 1985. Contact Engelbrecht at Newman Library, Virginia Tech, Blacksburg, Virginia 24061.

Grassian, Esther, Ed. [The 1986 CCLI] Directory of Library Instruction Programs in California Academic Libraries. California Clearinghouse on Library Instruction. Contact: Irene Hoffman, 10624 Regent Street, Los Angeles, California 90034.

Kirkendall, Carolyn A. "Improving Teaching: How a Clearinghouse Helps." New Directions for Teaching and Learning 18 (June 1984): 79-84.

_____. "Library Instruction Organizations and Clearinghouses." Education Libraries 7 (Fall 1982): 45-60.

Lester, Linda, et al., Comps. List of Library Instruction Clearinghouses, Directories, and Newsletters. ACRL Bibliographic Instruction Section, June 1978. Contact Association of College & Research Libraries, 50 East Huron Street, Chicago, Illinois 60611.

Library Orientation-Instruction Exchange (LOEX). Center for Educational Resources, Eastern Michigan University, Ypsilanti, Michigan 48197. Has LEOX
News newsletter.

Marlow, Celia Ann & Robert C. Thomas, Eds. The Directory of Directories,
1987, 4th ed. Detroit, Michigan: Gale Research Co., 1986.

Miller, B. "The Bibliographic Instruction Clearinghouse--A Practical Guide."
Journal of Academic Librarianship 11 (1985).

"New York Library Instruction Clearinghouse." Information Hotline 8 (September
1976): 10.

"Orientation Clearinghouse Set Up at SUNY--Syracuse." Library Journal 101
(March 1, 1976): 649-650.

Prince, William W. Directory of Academic Library Instruction Programs in Virginia.
Richmond, Virginia: Virginia Library Association, 1977. ERIC ED 175 475
43 pages.

Quiring, Virginia, et al., Comps. Academic Library Instruction in Kansas, A
Directory. Manhattan, Kansas: Kansas University Library, 1980. ERIC ED
206 308.

Rettig, James. General Library Skills Courses Offered for Credit, 1977. Contact
LOEX.

Robison, D. "Institutions Offering a Formal Course With or Without Credit."
In Academic Libraries Bibliographic Instruction: Status Report, pp. 8-18.
Edited by Thomas Kirk. Chicago, Illinois: Association of College & Research
Libraries, 1973. From ERIC, ED 072 823.

Skinner, Jane and Judith Violette, Comps. A Directory of Library Instruction
Programs in Indiana Academic Libraries. Indiana Library Association, 1980.
ERIC 191 487.

Stockard, Joan. A Directory of Bibliographic Instruction Programs in New
England Academic Libraries. Association of College & Research Libraries,
New England Chapter, 1978. ERIC ED 171 259 188 pages.

Stoffle, Carla J., et al., Comps. Library Instruction Programs, 1975: A
Wisconsin Directory. Madison, Wisconsin Library Assoc., 1975.

Ward, James. Southeastern Activities in Bibliographic Instruction. Proceedings
from Southeastern Conference on Approaches to Bibliographic Instruction,
March 16-17, 1978. Southeastern Bibliographic Instruction Clearinghouse
(SEBIC).

Audiovisuals

Business Periodicals Index. (See Readers' Guide)

Current Index to Journals in Education. (See ERIC)

Education Index. (See Readers' Guide)

ERIC. 6 slide tapes on various ERIC products. Oak Woods Media, 2243 South
   11th Street, Kalamazoo, Michigan 49009.

Essay & General Literature Index. (See Readers' Guide)

Guide to the Incomparable "New York Times Index," by Grant W. Morse. New
   York: Fleet Academic Editions, 1980.

HOW TO USE THE "Social Sciences Citation Index." Poster. Contact the Institute
   for Scientific Information, 3501 Market Street, Philadelphia, Pennsylvania 19104.
   Telephone 800/523-1851.

Humanities Index. (See Readers' Guide)

Introduction to the "Science Citation Index." Slide-Tape. Contact the Institute
   for Scientific Information.

Introduction to the "Social Sciences Citation Index." Slide-Tape. Contact the
   Institute for Scientific Information.

Library Reference Information: How to Locate and Use It. Filmstrips, sound,
   Handbook, Guides, transparencies. Includes: "Information, Please! The Sub-
   ject Approach to the Card Catalog and Information"; "Let's Look It Up in
   Reference Books; Getting Your Facts Straight"; "Locating Information:
   Magazines and The Readers' Guide"; "Putting It All Together." Freeport, New
   York: Educational Activities, Inc.

Library Search Strategy. Color slide-tapes, 10 minutes each on "Sex Roles" and
   "Nuclear Arms Control Disarmament." Interlibrary loan, University of
   California--San Diego Undergraduate Library, La Jolla, California 92093.

"The Monthly Catalog" of United States Government Publications. 43 slides.
   Contact Pittsburgh Regional Library Center, Beatty Hall, Chatham College,
   Pittsburgh, Pennsylvania 15232.

<u>New York Times Index</u>.   37 slides.   Contact Pittsburgh Regional Library Center.

<u>Readers' Guide</u>.   Slide tapes on Wilson Company indexes.   Oak Woods Media,
2243 South 11th Street, Kalamazoo, Michigan 49009.

<u>Resources in Education</u>.   (See ERIC)

<u>Social Sciences Index</u> (See Readers' Guide)

<u>Writing a Research Paper, or How I Learned to Stop Worrying and Love the
Library</u>.   Videotape.   University of California--Irvine Undergraduate Library,
Irvine, California 92717.

<u>Your Search Key to L.C.: Library of Congress Classification</u>, by Jovian P. Lang.
Bronx, New York: Fordham Publishing Company, 1980.   "Library Instruction
Program IV."   Has Teacher's Edition.

Mediated, Computer-Assisted, and Programmed Instruction Information Published in the 1980's

Barry, Carol, Comp. An Illinois Union List of Commercially-Produced Audio-visual Materials for Bibliographic Instruction. ERIC ED 203 881 1980. 16 pages.

Bayer, Bernard and Sharon W. Schwerzel. "A Comparison of Online and Manual Searching in Selected Areas of Research." In Proceedings National Online Meeting, pp. 23-28. Ohio State University, 1982.

Collins, John. "Non-Print Materials for College and University Bibliographic Instruction," In "Bibliographic Instruction: A Guide" Special Issue. Education Libraries 7 (Fall 1982): 45-60.

Haynes, E. "Computer Assisted Library Instruction; An Annotated Bibliography." Colorado Libraries 11 (March 1985): 31-35.

Jacobson, G. N. and M. J. Albright. "Motivation Via Video-Tape: Key to Undergraduate Library Instruction in the Research Library." Journal of Academic Librarianship 9 (November 1983): 270-275.

Kenney, Patricia Ann and Judith N. McArthur. "Designing and Evaluating a Programmed Library Instruction Text." College & Research Libraries 45 (January 1984): 35-42.

Koelewyn, A. C. and K. Corby. "Citation; A Library Instruction Computer Game." RQ 22 (Winter 1982): 171-174.

Leeper, Dennis P. and John B. Hall, Issue Editors. Drexel Library Quarterly [Issue devoted to mediated approaches to library instruction.] 16 (January 1980): 1-133.

Lowry, G. R. Online Document Retrieval System Education for Undergraduates: Rationale, Content, and Observations. ERIC ED 183 176 1980.

McDonald, D. R. and Susan E. Searing. "Bibliographic Instruction and the Development of Online Catalogs." College & Research Libraries 44 (January 1983): 5-11.

Osegueda, Laura and Judy Reynolds. "Introducing Online Skills Into the University Curriculum." RQ 22 (1982): 10-11.

Shearer, B., et al. Bibliographic Instruction Through the Related Studies Division in Vocational Education: LRC Guide, Pathfinders, and Script for Slide Presentation. ERIC ED 205 171 1980.

Resources

Surprenant, Thomas. "Learning Theory, Lecture, and Programmed Instruction Text; An Experiment in Bibliographic Instruction." College & Research Libraries 43 (January 1982): 31-37.

"University of Delaware Uses PLATO For Bibliographic Instruction." Library Journal 106 (June 15, 1981): 1266.

Whitson, Donna L. "A Comparison of Microcomputer-Assisted Instruction and the Traditional Lecture Approach to Bibliographic Instruction in Higher Education." Ph.D. Thesis. Laramie, Wyoming: University of Wyoming, 1982.

For filing in "dictionary" one-alphabet files, moderate degree of difficulty:

1. American author Sarah Orne Jewett's (1849-1909) <u>Letters of Sarah Orne</u> <u>Jewett</u> was edited by Annie Fields and published in 1911 in a 259-page edition by Houghton Mifflin Company of Boston, Massachusetts.

2. Judy Chicago's autobiography was published by the New York publisher Doubleday Company. Its title is <u>Through the Flower; My Struggle as a</u> <u>Woman Artist</u>. Its call number is N6537C48A2/1982. There are two subject-points of access for this book; the second is ARTISTS--U.S.--BIOGRAPHY.

3. Kate Millett's 1982 book was illustrated with photographs by Sophie Keir and was about their experiences in Iran at that time. The New York company Coward McCann & Geoghegan published it. Call number HQ1735.2M53/1982. She titled it <u>Going to Iran</u>.

4. <u>Loving Warriors: Selected Letters of Lucy Stone and Henry B. Blackwell</u> was published in 1981 by Dial Press of New York and edited and introduced by Leslie Wheeler. Lucy Stone (1818-1893) wrote most of the letters; call number HQ1413.S73A4.

5. Arnold Eric Sevareid's <u>Not So Wild a Dream</u> is autobiographical; the "New edition" was published in 1976 by the New York publisher, Atheneum. It is indexed and has 522 pages. Three subject headings were assigned to it: the second is JOURNALISTS--CORRESPONDENCE, REMINISCENCES, ETC.; the third is WORLD WAR, 1939-1945--PERSONAL NARRATIVES, AMERICA. The call number is PN487.4S3A3/1976.

6. <u>The Naked Civil Servant</u>, by Quentin Crisp, is autobiographical. It was published by the London publisher Cape in 1968. The call number is HQ75.8.C74A35. It was assigned two subject headings; the second is HOMO-SEXUALS, MALE--ENGLAND--LONDON--BIOGRAPHY.

The following pages provide exercises in filing in a dictionary file which are of considerable difficulty.

There are 4 access points in a one-alphabet DICTIONARY catalog (such
as that in the   Library) for this book. Record here
the first two lines for each of them , in order.

Ewers, John Keith, 1904-
    Long enough for a joke : an autobiography / John K. Ewers.
— Fremantle, W.A. : Fremantle Arts Centre Press, 1983.

    308 p. : ill. ; 25 cm.

    Bibliography: p. [305]
    Includes index.
    ISBN 0-909144-72-9 (pbk.) : $15.00

    1. Ewers, John Keith, 1904-   —Biography.   2. Authors, Australian—
20th century—Biography.   I. Title.

PR9619.3.E89Z466   1983   828—dc19   84-168575
                     [B]   AACR 2   MARC

Library of Congress

There are 4 access points in a one-alphabet DICTIONARY catalog (such
as that in the   Library) for this book. Record here
the first two lines for each of them , in order.

Long enough for a joke: an autobiography

PR9619. Ewers, John Keith, 1904-

EWERS, JOHN KEITH, 1904-   -- BIOGRAPHY

PR9619. Ewers, John Keith, 1904-

PR9619. Ewers, John Keth, 1904-
          Long enough for a joke: an autobiography.

AUTHORS, AUSTRALIAN-- 20th CENTURY-- BIOG-
RAPHY

PR9619. **Ewers, John Keith, 1904-**
          Long enough for a joke : an autobiography / John K. Ewers.
— Fremantle, W.A. : Fremantle Arts Centre Press, 1983.

308 p. : ill. ; 25 cm.

Bibliography: p. ₁305₁
Includes index.
ISBN 0-909144-72-9 (pbk.) : $15.00

1. Ewers, John Keith, 1904-   —Biography. 2. Authors, Australian—
20th century—Biography.   I. Title.

PR9619.3.E89Z466   1983   828—dc19   84-168575
                                ₁B₁   AACR 2   MARC

Library of Congress

There are 5 access points in a one-alphabet DICTIONARY catalog (such as
that in the   Library) for this book. Record the first
two lines for each of them, in order, here.

BQ972.   **Miyamoto, Kazuo, 1900-**
I937A36   One man's journey : a spiritual autobiography / Kazuo
              Miyamoto. — Honolulu : Buddhist Study Center, 1981.

                  ISBN 0-938474-01-4 : $5.95

                  1. Miyamoto, Kazuo, 1900-   . 2. Shin Buddhists—United States—Bi-
              ography.   3. Physicians (General practice)—United States—Biography.   I.
              Title.

              BQ972.I937A36   294.3'92—dc19   81-21572
                                               ₍B₎   AACR 2   MARC CIP

              Library of Congress

There are 5 access points in a one-alphabet DICTIONARY catalog (such as
that in the   Library) for this book. Record the first
two lines for each of them, in order, here.

SHIN BUDDHISTS-- UNITED STATES-- BIOGRAPHY

BA972.   Miyamoto, Kazuo, 1900-

PHYSICIANS (GENERAL PRACTICE)-- UNITED
STATES-- BIOGRAPHY
BA972.   Miyamoto, Kazuo, 1900-

One man's journey: a spiritual autobiography.
BA972.   Miyamoto, Kazuo, 1900-

MIYAMOTO, KAZUO, 1900-
BQ972.   Miyamoto, Kazuo, 1900-

BQ972.   **Miyamoto, Kazuo, 1900-**
I937A36   One man's journey : a spiritual autobiography / Kazuo
Miyamoto. — Honolulu : Buddhist Study Center, 1981.

         ISBN 0-938474-01-4 : $5.95

      1. Miyamoto, Kazuo, 1900-   . 2. Shin Buddhists—United States—Bi-
ography.   3. Physicians (General practice)—United States—Biography.   I.
Title.

     BQ972.I937A36   294.3'92—dc19   81-21572
                                  [B]   AACR 2   MARC CIP

    Library of Congress

There are 6 access points in a one-alphabet DICTIONARY catalog (such as that in the ＿＿＿＿＿＿＿＿＿＿＿ Library) for this book. Record the first two lines for each of them, in order, here.

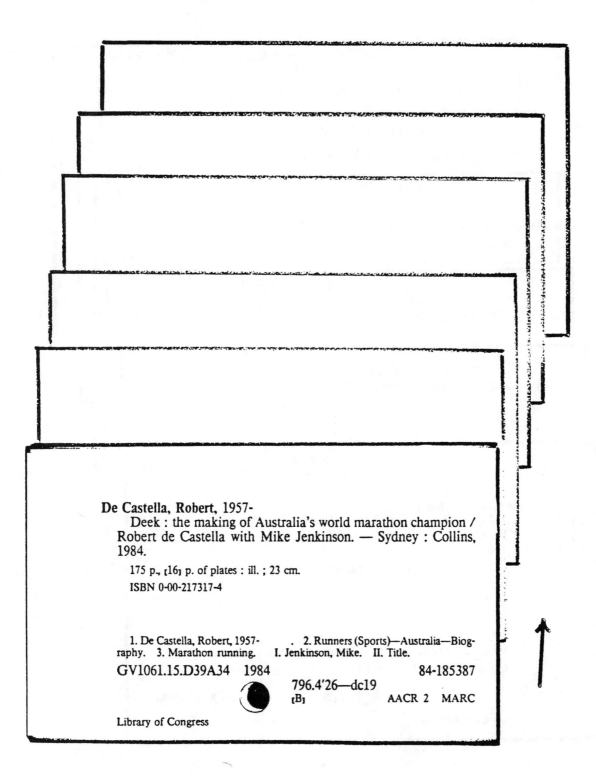

De Castella, Robert, 1957-
    Deek : the making of Australia's world marathon champion / Robert de Castella with Mike Jenkinson. — Sydney : Collins, 1984.

      175 p., ₍16₎ p. of plates : ill. ; 23 cm.

      ISBN 0-00-217317-4

    1. De Castella, Robert, 1957-   . 2. Runners (Sports)—Australia—Biography. 3. Marathon running. I. Jenkinson, Mike. II. Title.

GV1061.15.D39A34 1984   84-185387

                 796.4'26—dc19
                 ₍B₎   AACR 2 MARC

Library of Congress

There are 6 access points in a one-alphabet DICTIONARY catalog (such as
that in the   Library) for this book. Record the first
two lines for each of them, in order, here.

RUNNERS (SPORTS)-- AUSTRALIA-- BIOGRAPHY

GV1061. De Castella, Robert, 1957-

MARATHON RUNNING

GV1061. De Castella, Robert, 1957-

Jenkinson, Mike

GV1061. De Castella, Robert, 1957-

Deek: the making of Australia's world
    champion
GV1061. De Castella, Robert, 1957-

DE CASTELLA, ROBERT, 1957-
GV1061. De Castella, Robert, 1957-

GV1061. 15.D39 A34 1984	**De Castella, Robert, 1957-** Deek : the making of Australia's world marathon champion / Robert de Castella with Mike Jenkinson. — Sydney : Collins, 1984.
	175 p., [16] p. of plates : ill. ; 23 cm.
	ISBN 0-00-217317-4

    1. De Castella, Robert, 1957-   . 2. Runners (Sports)—Australia—Biog-
raphy. 3. Marathon running.   I. Jenkinson, Mike. II. Title.

GV1061.15.D39A34   1984   84-185387

                         796.4'26—dc19
                         [B]   AACR 2 MARC

Library of Congress

There are 5 access points in a one-alphabet DICTIONARY catalog (such as that in the   Library) for this book. Record the first two lines for each of them, in order, here.

PN5516.
G76A34
1983

Grosvenor, G. Arch (Gregor Arch)
   A long way from "Tipperary" : 58 years of South Australian journalism / by G. Arch Grosvenor. — Hawthorndene, S. Aust. : Investigator Press, 1983.

   160 p. : ill. ; 22 cm.
   ISBN 0-85864-075-9 (pbk.)

   1. Grosvenor, G. Arch (Gregor Arch)   2. Journalists—Australia—South Australia—Biography.   3. South Australia—Biography.   I. Title.
PN5516.G76A34   1983   070'.92'4—dc19   84-173165
                           [B]   AACR 2   MARC

Library of Congress

There are 5 access points in a one-alphabet DICTIONARY catalog (such as that in the   Library) for this book. Record the first two lines for each of them, in order, here.

SOUTH AUSTRALIA-- BIOGRAPHY

PN5516. Grosvenor, G. Arch (Gregor Arch)

A long way from "Tipperary": 58 years of
South Australian journalism

PN5516. Grosvenor, G. Arch (Gregor Arch)

JOURNALISTS-- AUSTRALIA-- SOUTH AUSTRALIA--
BIOGRAPHY

PN5516. Grosvenor, G. Arch (Gregor ARch)

GROSVENOR, G. ARCH (GREGOR ARCH)

PN5516. Grosvenor, G. Arch (Gregor Arch)

PN5516. **Grosvenor, G. Arch (Gregor Arch)**
G76A34   A long way from "Tipperary" : 58 years of South Australian
1983   journalism / by G. Arch Grosvenor. — Hawthorndene, S. Aust.
              : Investigator Press, 1983.

    160 p. : ill. ; 22 cm.

    ISBN 0-85864-075-9 (pbk.)

    1. Grosvenor, G. Arch (Gregor Arch)   2. Journalists—Australia—South
Australia—Biography.   3. South Australia—Biography.   I. Title.

PN5516.G76A34   1983   070'.92'4—dc19   84-173165
               [B]   AACR 2   MARC

Library of Congress

FILING PART 3: ADDITIONAL DEMONSTRATION SETS

1. 18 "cards"

   (1) "The Dalhousie Journals"   by (2) Louise Dalhousie
   (3) "Dr. Jekyll and Mr. Hyde"
   (4) "El Cazador Oculto"
   (5) is a SEE card <u>from</u> De Balzac <u>to</u> Balzac
   (6) "Shoulder to Shoulder"   by (7) Midge Mackenzie
   (8) "The Psychology of Sex Differences" by (9) Eleanor Maccoby
   (10) "The Power Lovers"   by (11) Myra MacPherson
   (12) "Memories of a Catholic Girlhood" by (13) Mary McCarthy
   (14) "The Doctor Takes a Wife"
   (15) "The Group"   by (16) Mary McCarthy
   (17) "Eugene Grandet"   by (18) Honore de Balzac

The group	9	Shoulder to shoulder	18
Eugene Grandet	8	The psychology of sex differences	17
The doctor takes a wife	7	The power lovers	16
Dr. Jekyll and Mr. Hyde	6	Memories of a Catholic Girlhood	15
DeBalzac, SEE Balzac	5	MacPherson, Myra	14
The Dalhousie Journals	4	Mackenzie, Midge	13
Dalhousie, Louise	3	Maccoby, Eleanor	12
El cazador oculto	2	McCarthy, Mary Memories of a Catholic...	11

Balzac, Honore de
    Eugene Grandet
	1	McCarthy, Mary
		    The group
			10

FILING PART 3: ADDITIONAL DEMONSTRATION SETS

2. 18 "cards"

    (1) "Woman's Art Journal
    (2) is a SEE card from Thanet, Octave, pseud., to French, Alice
    (3) "One Hundred Fifty Years of Arithmetic Books"
    (4) "Woman Engineer"
    (5) "From Stoney Creek to Whakarongo..."   by (6) Vera McLennan
    (7) "Stories of a Western Town"   by (8) Alice French
    (9) "A Cost Analysis Model..."   by (10) Grace Lowe MacNab
    (11) "Ten Years in Washington..."
    (12) "Our Bodies, Ourselves"   by (13) the Boston Women's
                                                       Health Book Collective
    (14) the McGraw-Hill Encyclopedia of World Biography
    (15) "Knitters in the Sun"   by (16) Alice French
    (17) "A Moral Tale..."   by (18) Anne Scott MacLeod

MacLeod, Anne Scott	9	Woman's Art Journal	18
McLennan, Vera	8	Woman Engineer	17
McGraw-Hill Encyclopedia of World Biography	7	Thanet, Octave See French, Alice	16
Knitters in the Sun	6	Ten Years in Washington...	15
From Stoney Creek...	5	Stories of a Western Town	14
French, Alice Stories of a Western Town	4	Our Bodies, Ourselves	13
French, Alice Knitters in the Sun	3	One Hundred Fifty Years of Arithmetic Books	12
A Cost Analysis Model...	2	A Moral Tale...	11
Boston Women's Health Book Collective	1	MacNab, Grace Lowe	10

400

FILING PART 3: ADDITIONAL DEMONSTRATION SETS

3. 18 "cards"

    (1) "Ten Korean Short Stories"   comp. by (2) Kevin O'Rourke
    (3) is a SEE card from Lucas, Victoria, pseud. to Plath, Sylvia
    (4) "Tristes Tropiques"   by (5) Claude Levi-Strauss
    (6) "Johnny Panic..."   by (7) Sylvia Plath
    (8) "A Journey to Ohio in 1810" by (9) Margaret V. H. Bell
    (10) "TDR: The Drama Review"
    (11) "100 Nineteenth-Century Rhyming Alphabets in English"
    (12) "The Liberal Education of Women" by (13) James Orton
    (14) "The Bell Jar"   by (15) Sylvia Plath
    (16) "The Open Door Colleges..." by (17) the Carnegie Commission on
                                        Higher Education
    (18) "One Hundred Fifty Years of Arithmetic Books"

One Hundred Fifty Years of Arithmetic Books	9	Tristes Tropiques	18
Lucas, Victoria, pseud., SEE Plath, Sylvia	8	Ten Korean Short Stories	17
The Liberal Education of Women	7	TDR: The Drama Review	16
Levi-Strauss, Claude	6	Plath, Sylvia Johnny Panic...	15
A Journey to Ohio in 1810	5	Plath, Sylvia The Bell Jar	14
Johnny Panic...	4	Orton, james	13
Carnegie Commission on Higher Education	3	O'Rourke, Kevin	12
The Bell Jar	2	The Open Door Colleges...	11
Bell, Margaret V. H.	1	100 Nineteenth-Century Rhyming Alphabets in English	10

FILING   PART 2:   "FILING IN DICTIONARY AND DIVIDED FILES"
                   DEMONSTRATIONS

For filing in "dictionary" one-alphabet files, least degree of difficulty:

1. Educator and author Helen Adams Keller's 1929 book, titled <u>Midstream; My
    Later Life</u>, was published by Doubleday Company located in Garden City,
    New York. It is 362 pages long, and its call number is HV1624K4A15.
    Keller was born in 1880 and died in 1968.

2. American author and lecturer Lillian Hellman's 1973 book, titled <u>Pentimento</u>,
    was published by Little, Brown and Company located in Boston, Massachusetts.
    It is 297 pages long, and its call number is PS3515He52Z498.

3. Playwright Neil Simon's <u>Brighton Beach Memoirs</u> is autobiographical. It was
    published in 1984 by Random House, call number PS3537I663B7.

4. Jessica Mitford's 1977 book, <u>A Fine Old Conflict</u>, is autobiographical. It was
    published by Knopf in 1977. She was born in 1917. The call number is
    HX84.M55A341/1977.

5. Sonia Johnson's 1981 book was titled <u>From Housewife to Heretic</u> and was pub-
    lished by the New York company Doubleday. It has 406 pages, call number
    BX8695J65A34.

6. Maya Angelou's 1976 autobiographical book, titled <u>Singin' and Swingin' and
    Gettin' Merry Like Christmas</u>, was published by Random House in New York.
    It has 269 pages, and the call number is E185.97.A56A33.

LIBRARY OF CONGRESS SUBJECT HEADINGS (LCSH):
"See" REFERENCES

In doing Assignment 2, page 1, it is most productive to provide the student with a subject interest which leads to one established subject heading, rather than to several. The following appear in the LCSH 10th edition, *'d subjects appear in both 9th and 10th editions.

Interested In?	See
AIDS (Disease)	ACQUIRED IMMUNE DEFICIENCY SYNDROME
*Abandonment of family	DESERTION AND NON-SUPPORT
Abominable snowman	YETI
Abortion, Spontaneous	MISCARRIAGE
Absahrokee Indians	CROW INDIANS
Aikidoists	MARTIAL ARTISTS
Aiko language	MORI LANGUAGE
*Anthracosis	LUNGS--DUST DISEASE
Ashanti women	WOMEN, ASHANTI
*Baleen	WHALEBONE
*Bomb-proof building	BUILDING, BOMBPROOF
*Book awards	LITERARY PRIZES
*Catastrophes	DISASTERS
*Cathode ray picture tubes	TELEVISION PICTURE TUBES
Chicano authors	MEXICAN AMERICAN AUTHORS
*Chicanos	MEXICAN AMERICANS
*Christian theologians	THEOLOGIANS
Comparable worth (Compensation management)	EQUAL PAY FOR EQUAL WORK
*Criminal insane	INSANE, CRIMINAL AND DANGEROUS
*Delinquency prediction	CRIMINAL BEHAVIOR, PREDICTION OF
*Doomsday	JUDGMENT DAY
*Employer-employee relations	INDUSTRIAL RELATIONS
Equal educational opportunity	EDUCATIONAL EQUALIZATION
*Farm laborers	AGRICULTURAL LABORERS
Female studies	WOMEN'S STUDIES
Females	WOMEN
Feminist studies	WOMEN'S STUDIES
*Food processing	FOOD INDUSTRY AND TRADE

General aviation   PRIVATE FLYING
General practitioners   PHYSICIANS (GENERAL PRACTICE)
*Grade crossings   RAILROADS--CROSSINGS
*Grape culture   VITICULTURE

*Incentives in education   REWARDS AND PUNISHMENTS IN EDUCA-
         TION

*Kaapor Indians   URUBU INDIANS
*Karma yoga   YOGA, KARMA
*Kiosks   PAVILLIONS

*Lake disposal of radioactive wastes   RADIOACTIVE WASTE DISPOSAL IN
         RIVERS, LAKES, ETC.

*Marionettes   PUPPETS AND PUPPET-PLAYS
*Minerals in soils   SOIL MINERALOGY

*Neoprene   RUBBER, ARTIFICIAL

*Orgone energy   ORGONOMY

*Papal infallibility   POPES--INFALLIBILITY
*Paramedics   ALLIED HEALTH PERSONNEL
*Persians   IRANIANS
*Petty larceny   LARCENY
*Pigeon English   PIDGIN ENGLISH
*Planned parenthood   BIRTH CONTROL
Press censorship   CENSORSHIP

*Queen bees   BEE CULTURE--QUEEN REARING

*Reactor fuels   NUCLEAR FUELS

*Satan   DEVIL
*Saulteaux Indians   CHIPPEWA INDIANS
Sex and drugs   DRUGS AND SEX
Sex bias   SEXISM
Sex determinant antigen   H-Y ANTIGEN

Sex glands   GONADS
Sex hormones   HORMONES, SEX
Sex in art   EROTIC ART
Sex in plants   PLANTS, SEX IN

*Tape recorders   MAGNETIC RECORDERS AND RECORDING
Text compression (Computer science)   DATA COMPRESSION (COMPUTER
         SCIENCE)

*Utilization of waste products   SALVAGE (WASTE, ETC.)

*Vanishing birds   RARE BIRDS
*Victimless crimes   CRIMES WITHOUT VICTIMS

Womb	UTERUS
Women camp followers	CAMP FOLLOWERS
Women in war	WAR--WOMEN'S WORK
Women deans	DEANS OF WOMEN
Women homosexuals	LESBIANS
Women saints	SAINTS, WOMEN
Women workers	WOMEN--EMPLOYMENT
Women, Asian American	ASIAN AMERICAN WOMEN
Women's autobiography	AUTOBIOGRAPHY--WOMEN AUTHORS
Women's liberation movement	FEMINISM

PRACTICE USING THE LCSH

The exercises which follow relate to the Library of Congress Subject Headings, 10th edition, published in 1986. Additional forms based on the 9th edition follow. The wording and order of the questions can be rearranged when you use these questions; they are not presented in a particular sequence.

1. Answer: 1 or 2 (I or II). The appropriate answer will signify understanding of the LCSH thesaurus' alphabetical arrangement and possibly having examined it.

2. Answer: a classification. You may elect not to teach (include) book number, or perhaps it has not been introduced or mastered yet, in which case, simply omit it as a choice.
In going over this in class together, stress that the LCSH does not provide call numbers or refer to specific books. This underscores the ideas that: the Library of Congress classifications begin with capital letters and may include additional letters, e.g. WOLVES (QL737.C2); the LCSH sometimes provides a range within the LC classifications which it sometimes provides, e.g. FEMINISM (HQ 1101-HQ2030.7); there may be a decimal point within a classification, e.g. EQUALITY (ISLAM) (BP173.45).

3. Answer: the subject heading referred to by a See reference is generally the route here. The objective is to underscore and practice the utility of starting by looking under the words "you have." Depending on local arrangements, you may wish to substitute "should look under the subject-entry" for "should look for subject cards with the first line subject-heading wording."

4. Answer: true. In constructing this type of question, insert a XX.

5. Answer: a subject-heading referred to by a See Also (sa).
Insert: any established subject heading followed by one or more Sa's. Depending on the sophistication of the class, you might insert one of the See Also's (sa's) which is not preceded by the "sa," i.e. in a case where there are several listed together, such as "ABORS sa Gallongs, Pailibo (Indic people), and Shimongs," from which you would insert Shimongs, rather than Gollongs.

6. Answer: broader.
First insert: xx; second insert: the established subject heading to which it refers.

7. Answer: See individual exercises. These reponses relate to interpreting xx's as See Also's, and not x's as See's.

8. Answer: Any subject heading accompanied by "(Indirect)" is the goal. Omit this question if you do not teach this.

9. For an upper division course, consider upgrading the question to "... library shelves and the shelf list in the vicinity...."
    Answer: See individual exercises; there is at least one LC Classification indicated in each.

10. Answer: x'd or See-related "choice." The three maximum learning choices include: a subdivided subject heading, a subject heading to See, and an x or See-related item.

11. Answer: a subdivision of an established subject-heading.

These questions relate to this excerpt from
the Library of Congress Subject Headings(LCSH).

The excerpt (right column):

Aborian Tagbanwa language
  See Tagbanua language
Aborn family
  x Abern family
Abors *(DS485.A86)*
  sa Gallongs
    Pailibo (Indic people)
    Shimongs
  x Adis
    Tangams
  xx Ethnology—India
  — Anthropometry
  — Rites and ceremonies
    sa Mopin
Abortifacients *(Indirect)* *(RG734.4-734.5)*
  xx Abortion
    Obstetrical pharmacology
Abortion *(Indirect)* *(Birth control,*
  HQ767-767.7; Medical
  jurisprudence, RA1067; Obstetrical
  operations, RG734; Obstetrics,
  RG648)
  sa Abortifacients
    Menstrual regulation
  x Feticide
    Pregnancy termination
    Termination of pregnancy
  xx Birth control
    Fetal death
    Infanticide
    Obstetrics
    Pregnancy, Unwanted
  — Complications and sequelae
  — Government policy *(Indirect)*
  — — Citizen participation
    sa Pro-choice movement
      Pro-life movement
  — Law and legislation *(Indirect)*
    xx Offenses against the person
      Sex and law
  — Moral and ethical aspects *(HQ767.3)*
    sa Pro-choice movement
      Pro-life movement
  — Religious aspects
    sa Fetal propitiatory rites
      Pro-choice movement
      Pro-life movement

1. This excerpt is from volume #_____.

2. The combination of capital letters and 3-
   4 numbers which sometimes appears refers to

      a book number
      a call number
      a classification
      the location of a specific book-title
      on the library's shelves

3. Someone needing information about _____
   Aborian Tagbanwa language
   should look for subject cards with the 1st
   line subject-heading wording_____
   _____
   _____

4. Sex and law
   is an established subject-heading.

    TRUE   FALSE

5. If interested in _____
   Abortion-- Religious aspects
   _____,
   you should check that exact wording as·
   well as _____

   _____in the subject catalog.

6. Obstetrical pharmacology is broader /
   narrower than Abortifacients.

7. There is a total of #_____ SEE ALSO-type cross references ("sa") indicated in
   this excerpt; there is a total of #_____ SEE cross references.

8. An example of a subject-heading displayed in this excerpt which it's likely you
   will find subdivided geographically in a library's catalog is _____
   _____ _____.

9. For publications about Obstetrical aspects of Abortion _____,
   you could check the library shelves in the vicinity of the Library of Congress
   Classification _____.

10. Which one of the following is not an established LCSH subject-heading?
      Abortion-- Government policy-- Citizen participation
      Tagbanua language
      Termination of pregnancy

11. Rites and ceremonies _____ is

    a SEE ALSO cross reference   an established subject-heading
    a SEE cross reference   a subdivision of a subject-heading

Course Title, Date
Instructor

LCSH 10 ed.
KEY Vol. 1
Page 6

Practice Using the LCSH
Your Name_____

These questions relate to this excerpt from
the Library of Congress Subject Headings(LCSH)

1. This excerpt is from volume # 1 _____.

2. The combination of capital letters and 3-
   4 numbers which sometimes appears refers to

      a book number
      a call number
   X a classification
      the location of a specific book-title
      on the library's shelves

3. Someone needing information about _____
   Aborian Tagbanwa language
   should look for subject cards with the 1st
   line subject-heading wording_____
   TAGBANUA LANGUAGE
   _____

4. Sex and law
   is an established subject-heading.

     X TRUE   FALSE

5. If interested in _____
   Abortion-- Religious aspects
   _____,
   you should check that exact wording as
   well as FETAL PROPITIATORY RITES; PRO-
   CHOICE MOVEMENT; and PRO-LIFE MOVEMENT
   _____in the subject catalog.

6. Obstetrical pharmacology is broader / (X)
   narrower than Abortifacients.

Aborian Tagbanwa language
  See Tagbanua language
Aborn family
  x Abern family
Abors *(DS485.A86)*
  sa Gallongs
    Pailibo (Indic people)
    Shimongs
  x Adis
    Tangams
  xx Ethnology—India
  — Anthropometry
  — Rites and ceremonies
    sa Mopin
Abortifacients *(Indirect) (RG734.4-734.5)*
  xx Abortion
    Obstetrical pharmacology
Abortion *(Indirect) (Birth control,
  HQ767-767.7; Medical
  jurisprudence, RA1067; Obstetrical
  operations, RG734; Obstetrics,
  RG648)*
  sa Abortifacients
    Menstrual regulation
  x Feticide
    Pregnancy termination
    Termination of pregnancy
  xx Birth control
    Fetal death
    Infanticide
    Obstetrics
    Pregnancy, Unwanted
  — Complications and sequelae
  — Government policy *(Indirect)*
  — — Citizen participation
    sa Pro-choice movement
      Pro-life movement
  — Law and legislation *(Indirect)*
    xx Offenses against the person
      Sex and law
  — Moral and ethical aspects *(HQ767.3)*
    sa Pro-choice movement
      Pro-life movement
  — Religious aspects
    sa Fetal propitiatory rites
      Pro-choice movement
      Pro-life movement

---

7. There is a total of #13___ SEE ALSO-type cross references ("sa") indicated in
   this excerpt; there is a total of #_1_____ SEE cross references.

8. An example of a subject-heading displayed in this excerpt which it's likely you
   will find subdivided geographically in a library's catalog is ABORTIFACIENTS;___
   ABORTION; ABORTION-- GOVERNMENT POLICY; or ABORTION-- LAW AND LEGISLATION._____.

9. For publications about Obstetrical aspects of Abortion_____,
   you could check the library shelves in the vicinity of the Library of Congress
   Classification _RG648_____ (Or RG648 and RG734)_____.

10. Which one of the following is not an established LCSH subject-heading?
        Abortion-- Government policy-- Citizen participation
        Tagbanua language
     X Termination of pregnancy

11. Rites and ceremonies
    _____ is

       a SEE ALSO cross reference   an established subject-heading
       a SEE cross reference   X a subdivision of a subject-heading

These questions relate to this excerpt from
the Library of Congress Subject Headings(LCSH)

The excerpt (right side):

> Abortion facilities
>   *See* Abortion services
> **Abortion in animals**   *(SF871)*
>   *sa* Brucellosis in cattle
>   Brucellosis in goats
>   *xx* Cattle—Diseases
>   Horses—Diseases
>   Veterinary medicine
> **Abortion services** *(Indirect) (RG734)*
>   *sa* Abortion counseling
>   Strikes and lockouts—Abortion services
>   *x* Abortion clinics
>   Abortion facilities
>   *xx* Birth control clinics
>   Clinics
>   Women's health services
>   — Employees
>   *sa* Strikes and lockouts—Abortion
>   services
>   Trade-unions—Abortion service
>   employees
>   — Law and legislation   *(Indirect)*
>   *xx* Medical laws and legislation
> Abot family
>   *See* Abbott family
> Abott family
>   *See* Abbott family
> Aboukir, Battle of, 1798
>   *See* Nile, Battle of the, 1798
> Aboukir, Battle of, 1801
>   *See* Alexandria, Battle of, 1801
> **Abraham family**
>   *sa* Abrams family

1. This excerpt is from volume #_____.

2. The combination of capital letters and 3-
   4 numbers which sometimes appears refers to

       a book number
       a call number
       a classification
       the location of a specific book-title
       on the library's shelves

3. Someone needing information about _____
   _Abortion facilities_____
   should look for subject cards with the 1st
   line subject-heading wording_____
   _____
   _____

4. _Women's health services_____
   is an established subject-heading.

       TRUE   FALSE

5. If interested in _____
   _Abortion in animals_____

   _____,
   you should check that exact wording as
   well as _____

   _____in the subject catalog.

6. _Veterinary medicine_____   is broader/narrower
   than _Abortion in animals_____.

7. There is a total of #_____ SEE ALSO-type cross references ("sa") indicated in
   this excerpt; there is a total of #_____   SEE cross references.

8. An example of a subject-heading displayed in this excerpt which it's likely you
   will find subdivided geographically in a library's catalog is _____
   _____.

9. For publications about _Abortion in animals_____,
   you could check the library shelves in the vicinity of the Library of Congress
   Classification _____.

10. Which one of the following is _not_ an established LCSH subject-heading?
        Abortion clinics   Abbott family
        Abortion services-- Employees   Nile, Battle of the, 1798

11. _Law and legislation_____ is

        a SEE ALSO cross reference   an established subject-heading
        a SEE cross reference   a subdivision of a subject-heading

These questions relate to this excerpt from
the Library of Congress Subject Headings(LCSH)

1. This excerpt is from volume # 1   .

2. The combination of capital letters and 3-
   4 numbers which sometimes appears refers to

       a book number
       a call number
   X a classification
       the location of a specific book-title
       on the library's shelves

3. Someone needing information about _____
   <u>Abortion facilities</u>
   should look for subject cards with the 1st
   line subject-heading wording_____
   <u>ABORTION SERVICES</u>
   _____

4. <u>Women's health services</u>
   is an established subject-heading.

   X TRUE   FALSE

5. If interested in _____
   <u>Abortion in animals</u>
   _____,
   you should check that exact wording as
   well as <u>BRUCELLOSIS IN CATTLE</u> and
   <u>BRUCELLOSIS IN GOATS</u>
   _____in the subject catalog.

6. <u>Veterinary medicine</u>   X
                                          is broader/narrower
   than <u>Abortion in animals</u>   .

7. There is a total of # 7   SEE ALSO-type cross references ("sa") indicated in
   this excerpt; there is a total of # 5   SEE cross references.

8. An example of a subject-heading displayed in this excerpt which it's likely you
   will find subdivided geographically in a library's catalog is _____
      ABORTION SERVICES or ABORTION SERVICES-- LAW AND LEGISLATION   .

9. For publications about <u>Abortion in animals</u>_____,
   you could check the library shelves in the vicinity of the Library of Congress
   Classification   <u>SF871</u>_____.

10. Which one of the following is <u>not</u> an established LCSH subject-heading?
      X Abortion clinics   Abbott family
        Abortion services-- Employees   Nile, Battle of the, 1798

11. <u>Law and legislation</u>_____ is

      a SEE ALSO cross reference   an established subject-heading
      a SEE cross reference   X a subdivision of a subject-heading

Excerpt box:

Abortion facilities
  See Abortion services
Abortion in animals *(SF871)*
  sa Brucellosis in cattle
    Brucellosis in goats
  xx Cattle—Diseases
    Horses—Diseases
    Veterinary medicine
Abortion services *(Indirect)* *(RG734)*
  sa Abortion counseling
    Strikes and lockouts—Abortion services
  x Abortion clinics
    Abortion facilities
  xx Birth control clinics
    Clinics
    Women's health services
  — Employees
    sa Strikes and lockouts—Abortion
      services
      Trade-unions—Abortion service
      employees
  — Law and legislation *(Indirect)*
    xx Medical laws and legislation
Abot family
  See Abbott family
Abott family
  See Abbott family
Aboukir, Battle of, 1798
  See Nile, Battle of the, 1798
Aboukir, Battle of, 1801
  See Alexandria, Battle of, 1801
Abraham family
  sa Abrams family

These questions relate to this excerpt from
the Library of Congress Subject Headings(LCSH)

1. This excerpt is from volume #_____.

2. The combination of capital letters and 3-
   4 numbers which sometimes appears refers to

        a book number
        a call number
        a classification
        the location of a specific book-title
          on the library's shelves

3. Someone needing information about _____
   <u>Acoustooptical effects</u>
   should look for subject cards with the 1st
   line subject-heading wording_____
   _____
   _____

4. <u>Immunological deficiency syndromes</u>
   is an established subject-heading.

        TRUE   FALSE

5. If interested in _____
   <u>Acoustooptics</u>
   _____,
   you should check that exact wording as·
   well as _____

   _____in the subject catalog.

6. <u>Adjustment (Psychology)</u>_____   is broader/narrower
   than ___<u>Acquiescence (Psychology)</u>_____.

7. There is a total of #____ SEE ALSO-type cross references ("sa") indicated in
   this excerpt; there is a total of #_____   SEE cross references.

8. An example of a subject-heading displayed in this excerpt which it's likely you
   will find subdivided geographically in a library's catalog is _____
   _____.

9. For publications about <u>Acoustooptics</u>_____,
   you could check the library shelves in the vicinity of the Library of Congress
   Classification _____.

10. Which one of the following is <u>not</u> an established LCSH subject-heading?
    Acquiescence (Psychology)-- Religious aspects-- Buddhism
    AIDS (Disease)
    Target acquisition
11. <u>Religious aspects</u>_____ is

        a SEE ALSO cross reference   an established subject-heading
        a SEE cross reference   a subdivision of a subject-heading

Acoustooptical effects
    See Acoustooptics
Acoustooptics   *(QC220.5)*
    sa Acoustic imaging
       Acoustooptical devices
    x Acoustooptical effects
    xx Optics
       Sound-waves
Acquiescence (International law)
    xx International law
Acquiescence (Law)   *(Indirect)*
    xx Civil procedure
       Consent (Law)
       Silence (Law)
Acquiescence (Psychology)
    x Agreement (Psychology)
    xx Adjustment (Psychology)
    — Religious aspects
    —— Buddhism, [Christianity, etc.]
Acquired characters, Heredity of
    See Inheritance of acquired characters
Acquired characters, Inheritance of
    See Inheritance of acquired characters
Acquired immune deficiency syndrome
        (Indirect)
    x Acquired immunodeficiency syndrome
      Acquired immunological deficiency
         syndrome
      AID syndrome
      AIDS (Disease)
    xx Immunological deficiency syndromes
Acquired immunodeficiency syndrome
    See Acquired immune deficiency syndrome
Acquired immunological deficiency syndrome
    See Acquired immune deficiency syndrome
Acquisition, Target
    See Target acquisition
Acquisition of African publications
    x African publications, Acquisition of
    xx Acquisitions (Libraries)

Course Title, Date   LCSH 10 ed.
Instructor   KEY Vol. 1   Practice Using the <u>LCSH</u>
                       Page 17   Your Name _____

These questions relate to this excerpt from
the Library of Congress Subject Headings(LCSH)

The excerpt (boxed):

Acoustooptical effects
   See Acoustooptics
Acoustooptics *(QC220.5)*
   sa Acoustic imaging
      Acoustooptical devices
   x Acoustooptical effects
   xx Optics
      Sound-waves
Acquiescence (International law)
   xx International law
Acquiescence (Law) *(Indirect)*
   xx Civil procedure
      Consent (Law)
      Silence (Law)
Acquiescence (Psychology)
   x Agreement (Psychology)
   xx Adjustment (Psychology)
  — Religious aspects
  — — Buddhism, ₍Christianity, etc.₎
Acquired characters, Heredity of
   See Inheritance of acquired characters
Acquired characters, Inheritance of
   See Inheritance of acquired characters
Acquired immune deficiency syndrome
      (Indirect)
   x Acquired immunodeficiency syndrome
      Acquired immunological deficiency
        syndrome
      AID syndrome ·
      AIDS (Disease)
   xx Immunological deficiency syndromes
Acquired immunodeficiency syndrome
   See Acquired immune deficiency syndrome
Acquired immunological deficiency syndrome
   See Acquired immune deficiency syndrome
Acquisition, Target
   See Target acquisition
Acquisition of African publications
   x African publications, Acquisition of
   xx Acquisitions (Libraries)

1. This excerpt is from volume # __1__ .

2. The combination of capital letters and 3-
   4 numbers which sometimes appears refers to

       a book number
       a call number
   X a classification
       the location of a specific book-title
       on the library's shelves

3. Someone needing information about _____
      Acoustooptical effects
   should look for subject cards with the 1st
   line subject-heading wording_____
      ACOUSTOOPTICS
   _____

4. Immunological deficiency syndromes
   is an established subject-heading.

     X TRUE   FALSE

5. If interested in _____
    Acoustooptics
   _____,
   you should check that exact wording as
   well as ACOUSTIC IMAGING and
   ACOUSTOOPTICAL DEVICES
   _____in the subject catalog.

6. Adjustment (Psychology)_____   X
                                         is broader/narrower
   than   Acquiescence (Psychology)_____.

7. There is a total of #_2_ SEE ALSO-type cross references ("sa") indicated in
   this excerpt; there is a total of #_6____ SEE cross references.

8. An example of a subject-heading displayed in this excerpt which it's likely you
   will find subdivided geographically in a library's catalog is _____
     ACQUIESCENCE (LAW) OR ACQUIRED IMMUNE DEFICIENCY SYNDROME_____.

9. For publications about Acoustooptics_____,
   you could check the library shelves in the vicinity of the Library of Congress
   Classification _____QC220.5_____.

10. Which one of the following is <u>not</u> an established LCSH subject-heading?
        Acquiescence (Psychology)-- Religious aspects-- Buddhism
     X AIDS (Disease)
        Target acquisition

11. _Religious aspects_____ is

        a SEE ALSO cross reference   an established subject-heading
        a SEE cross reference   X a subdivision of a subject-heading

These questions relate to this excerpt from
the Library of Congress Subject Headings(LCSH)

1. This excerpt is from volume #_____.

2. The combination of capital letters and 3-
   4 numbers which sometimes appears refers to

    a book number
    a call number
    a classification
    the location of a specific book-title
    on the library's shelves

3. Someone needing information about _____
   <u>Ainu art</u>
   should look for subject cards with the 1st
   line subject-heading wording_____
   _____
   _____

4. <u>Ethnology-- Japan</u>
   is an established subject-heading.

    TRUE   FALSE

5. If interested in _____
   <u>the Ainu</u>
   _____,
   you should check that exact wording as
   well as _____
   _____in the subject catalog.

```
Ainu
     sa Emishi
      x Ainos
     xx Ethnology—Japan
   — Anthropometry
   — Ethnic identity
   — Implements
   — Medicine  (DS832)
       xx Medicine, Primitive
Ainu art
   See Art, Ainu
Ainu decoration and ornament
   See Decoration and ornament, Ainu
Ainu decorative arts
   See Decorative arts, Ainu
Ainu dog  (SF429.A58)
      x Hokkaidō dog
     xx Spitz dogs
Ainu epic poetry
   See Epic poetry, Ainu
Ainu folk poetry
   See Folk poetry, Ainu
Ainu in art
Ainu language  (PL495)
      x Aino language
     xx Hyperborean languages
   — Etymology
   — — Names
         sa Names, Ainu
   — Names
       See Names, Ainu
Ainu names
   See Names, Ainu
Ainu poetry  (Indirect)
     sa Epic poetry, Ainu
        Folk poetry, Ainu
Aiolopus  (QL508.A2)
     xx Acrididae
```

6. <u>Acrididae</u>   is broader/narrower
   than <u>Aiolopus</u>   .

7. There is a total of #_____ SEE ALSO-type cross references ("sa") indicated in
   this excerpt; there is a total of #_____   SEE cross references.

8. An example of a subject-heading displayed in this excerpt which it's likely you
   will find subdivided geographically in a library's catalog is _____
   _____.

9. For publications about <u>Ainu-- Medicine</u>_____,
   you could check the library shelves in the vicinity of the Library of Congress
   Classification _____.

10. Which one of the following is <u>not</u> an established LCSH subject-heading?
       Ainu language   Hokkaidō dog
       Ainu language-- Etymology-- Names Spitz dogs

11. <u>Ethnic identity</u>   is

    a SEE ALSO cross reference   an established subject-heading
    a SEE cross reference   a subdivision of a subject-heading

Course Title, Date   LCSH 10 ed.   Practice Using the <u>LCSH</u>
Instructor   KEY Vol. 1   Your Name_____
                             Page 64

These questions relate to this excerpt from
the Library of Congress Subject Headings (LCSH)

> **Ainu**
>   *sa* Emishi
>   *x* Ainos
>   *xx* Ethnology—Japan
> — Anthropometry
> — Ethnic identity
> — Implements
> — Medicine   *(DS832)*
>   *xx* Medicine, Primitive
> **Ainu art**
>   *See* Art, Ainu
> **Ainu decoration and ornament**
>   *See* Decoration and ornament, Ainu
> **Ainu decorative arts**
>   *See* Decorative arts, Ainu
> **Ainu dog**   *(SF429.A58)*
>   *x* Hokkaidō dog
>   *xx* Spitz dogs
> **Ainu epic poetry**
>   *See* Epic poetry, Ainu
> **Ainu folk poetry**
>   *See* Folk poetry, Ainu
> **Ainu in art**
> **Ainu language**   *(PL495)*
>   *x* Aino language
>   *xx* Hyperborean languages
> — Etymology
> —— Names
>   *sa* Names, Ainu
> — Names
>   *See* Names, Ainu
> **Ainu names**
>   *See* Names, Ainu
> **Ainu poetry**   *(Indirect)*
>   *sa* Epic poetry, Ainu
>   Folk poetry, Ainu
> **Aiolopus**   *(QL508.A2)*
>   *xx* Acrididae

1. This excerpt is from volume #__1__ .

2. The combination of capital letters and 3-
   4 numbers which sometimes appears refers to

        a book number
        a call number
   X   a classification
        the location of a specific book-title
        on the library's shelves

3. Someone needing information about _____
   __Ainu art__
   should look for subject cards with the 1st
   line subject-heading wording_____
   __ART, AINU__
   _____

4. __Ethnology-- Japan__
   is an established subject-heading.

   X   TRUE   FALSE

5. If interested in _____
   __the Ainu__
   _____,
   you should check that exact wording as
   well as _____EMISHI_____
   _____
   _____in the subject catalog.

6. __Acrididae_____   X
                                          is broader/narrower
   than __Aiolopus_____ .

7. There is a total of #_4_ SEE ALSO-type cross references ("sa") indicated in
   this excerpt; there is a total of #_7_____ SEE cross references.

8. An example of a subject-heading displayed in this excerpt which it's likely you
   will find subdivided geographically in a library's catalog is _____
   __AINU POETRY_____ .

9. For publications about __Ainu-- Medicine_____ ,
   you could check the library shelves in the vicinity of the Library of Congress
   Classification _____DS832_____ .

10. Which one of the following is <u>not</u> an established LCSH subject-heading?
        Ainu language   X Hokkaidō dog
        Ainu language-- Etymology-- Names   Spitz dogs

11. __Ethnic identity_____ is
         _____

         a SEE ALSO cross reference   an established subject-heading
         a SEE cross reference   X a subdivision of a subject-heading

These questions relate to this excerpt from
the Library of Congress Subject Headings (LCSH):

1. This excerpt is from volume #_____.

2. The combination of capital letters and 3-
   4 numbers which sometimes appears refers to

       a book number
       a call number
       a classification
       the location of a specific book-title
         on the library's shelves

3. Someone needing information about _____
   Execution in effigy
   _____
   should look for subject cards with the 1st
   line subject-heading wording_____
   _____
   _____

4. International law_____
   is an established subject-heading.

       TRUE   FALSE

5. If interested in _____
   Executions (Law)_____
   _____,
   you should check that exact wording as
   well as _____
   _____
   _____ in the subject catalog.

6. Sanctions (International law)_____ is broader/narrower
   than   Executions (International law)_____.

7. There is a total of #____ SEE ALSO-type cross references ("sa") indicated in
   this excerpt; there is a total of #_____   SEE cross references.

8. An example of a subject-heading displayed in this excerpt which it's likely you
   will find subdivided geographically in a library's catalog is _____
   _____.

9. For publications about   Execution sermons_____,
   you could check the library shelves in the vicinity of the Library of Congress
   Classification _____.

10. Which one of the following is not an established LCSH subject-heading?
        Conflict of laws-- Executions   Poor debtor's oath
        Executions (Law)-- Cases-- Digests   Sermons

11. Executions _____ is

        a SEE ALSO cross reference   an established subject-heading
        a SEE cross reference   a subdivision of a subject-heading

---

Execution in effigy
    See Executions in effigy
Execution of Tennessee militiamen, 1815
    See Tennessee militiamen, Execution of,
        1815
Execution sermons (BV4262)
        Here are entered sermons preached at the
            execution of criminals.
    xx Sermons
Executions (Administrative law) *(Indirect)*
    xx Administrative law
Executions (Ancient law)
Executions (Canon law)
Executions (Greek law)
Executions (International law)
    xx International law
        Sanctions (International law)
Executions (Islamic law)
Executions (Law) *(Indirect)*
    sa Attachment and garnishment
        Creditors' bills
        Distress (Law)
        Exemption (Law)
        Extent (Writ)
        Foreclosure
        Judicial sales
        Poor debtor's oath
        Supplementary proceedings
        Tax-sales
    xx Civil procedure
        Debtor and creditor
        Judgments
        Writs
— Cases
— — Digests
        See Executions (Law)—Digests
— Conflict of laws
        See Conflict of laws—Executions

Course Title, Date
Instructor

LCSH 10 ed.
KEY Vol.1
Page 1106

Practice Using the <u>LCSH</u>
Your Name _____

These questions relate to this excerpt from
the Library of Congress Subject Headings(LCSH)

1. This excerpt is from volume # __1__.

2. The combination of capital letters and 3-
   4 numbers which sometimes appears refers to

           a book number
           a call number
   X   a classification
           the location of a specific book-title
           on the library's shelves

3. Someone needing information about _____
   <u>Execution in effigy</u>
   _____
   should look for subject cards with the 1st
   line subject-heading wording_____
   <u>EXECUTIONS IN EFFIGY</u>
   _____

4. <u>International law</u>_____
   is an established subject-heading.

   X TRUE   FALSE

5. If interested in _____
   <u>Executions (Law)</u>_____
   _____,
   you should check that exact wording as
   well as ATTACHMENT AND GARNISHMENT; CREDITORS' BILLS; DISTRESS (LAW); EXEMPTION
   (LAW); EXTENT (WRIT); FORECLOSURE; JUDICIAL SALES; POOR DEBTOR'S OATH; SUPPLEMENTARY
   PROCEEDINGS; and TAX-SALES in the subject catalog.

Excerpt box:

Execution in effigy
   See Executions in effigy
Execution of Tennessee militiamen. 1815
   See Tennessee militiamen. Execution of.
     1815
Execution sermons   *(BV4262)*
    Here are entered sermons preached at the
    execution of criminals.
  xx Sermons
Executions (Administrative law)   *(Indirect)*
  xx Administrative law
Executions (Ancient law)
Executions (Canon law)
Executions (Greek law)
Executions (International law)
  xx International law
    Sanctions (International law)
Executions (Islamic law)
Executions (Law)   *(Indirect)*
  sa Attachment and garnishment
    Creditors' bills
    Distress (Law)
    Exemption (Law)
    Extent (Writ)
    Foreclosure
    Judicial sales
    Poor debtor's oath
    Supplementary proceedings
    Tax-sales
  xx Civil procedure
    Debtor and creditor
    Judgments
    Writs
 — Cases
 — — Digests
    See Executions (Law)—Digests
 — Conflict of laws
    See Conflict of laws—Executions

---

6. <u>Sanctions (International law)</u>_____ is broader/narrower [X above narrower]
   than   <u>Executions (International law)</u>_____.

7. There is a total of # _10_ SEE ALSO-type cross references ("sa") indicated in
   this excerpt; there is a total of #_4_____ SEE cross references.

8. An example of a subject-heading displayed in this excerpt which it's likely you
   will find subdivided geographically in a library's catalog is _____
   <u>EXECUTIONS (ADMINISTRATIVE LAW) or EXECUTIONS (LAW)</u>
   _____.

9. For publications about   <u>Execution sermons</u>_____,
   you could check the library shelves in the vicinity of the Library of Congress
   Classification   <u>BV 4262</u>_____.

10. Which one of the following is <u>not</u> an established LCSH subject-heading?
        Conflict of laws-- Executions   Poor debtor's oath
    X Executions (Law)-- Cases-- Digests   Sermons

11. <u>Executions</u>_____ is

        a SEE ALSO cross reference   an established subject-heading
        a SEE cross reference   X a subdivision of a subject-heading

These questions relate to this excerpt from
the Library of Congress Subject Headings(LCSH)

1. This excerpt is from volume #_____.

2. The combination of capital letters and 3-
   4 numbers which sometimes appears refers to

   > a book number
   > a call number
   > a classification
   > the location of a specific book-title
   >   on the library's shelves

3. Someone needing information about _____
   Eptatetridae
   should look for subject cards with the 1st
   line subject-heading wording_____
   _____
   _____
   _____

4. Wages_____
   is an established subject-heading.

   TRUE   FALSE

5. If interested in _____
   Equal pay for equal work
   _____
   _____,
   you should check that exact wording as
   well as _____
   _____in the subject catalog.

Eptatetridae
   See Myxinidae
Eptatretus *(QL638.15.M9)*
   xx Myxinidae
Eptatretus stouti *(QL638.15.M9)*
Epulum (The Latin word)
   xx Latin language—Church Latin—
      Etymology
Epuran Cave (Romania)
   x Peştera Epuran (Romania)
   xx Caves—Romania
Equal educational opportunity
   See Educational equalization
Equal employment opportunity
   See Affirmative action programs
      Discrimination in employment
Equal opportunity in employment
   See Affirmative action programs
      Discrimination in employment
Equal pay for equal work *(Indirect)*
   sa Women—Employment
   x Comparable worth (Compensation
      management)
      Pay equity
   xx Discrimination in employment
      Wages
      Women—Employment
— Law and legislation *(Indirect)*
   xx Labor laws and legislation

6. Caves-- Romania _____   is broader/narrower
   than Epuran Cave (Romania)_____.

7. There is a total of #_____ SEE ALSO-type cross references ("sa") indicated in
   this excerpt; there is a total of #_____   SEE cross references.

8. An example of a subject-heading displayed in this excerpt which it's likely you
   will find subdivided geographically in a library's catalog is _____
   _____.

9. For publications about_____Eptatretus stouti_____,
   you could check the library shelves in the vicinity of the Library of Congress
   Classification _____.

10. Which one of the following is not an established LCSH subject-heading?
    Affirmative action programs   Equal pay for equal work-- Law and legislation
    Equal pay for equal work   Pay equity

11. ____Church Latin_____ is

    a SEE ALSO cross reference   an established subject-heading
    a SEE cross reference   a subdivision of a subject-heading

Course Title, Date   Practice Using the LCSH
Instructor   Your Name_____

These questions relate to this excerpt from
the Library of Congress Subject Headings(LCSH)

1. This excerpt is from volume #___1___.

2. The combination of capital letters and 3-
   4 numbers which sometimes appears refers to

   ___ a book number
   ___ a call number
   X a classification
   ___ the location of a specific book-title
       on the library's shelves

3. Someone needing information about _____
   Eptatetridae
   _____
   should look for subject cards with the 1st
   line subject-heading wording_____
   MYXINIDAE
   _____

   _____

4. Wages
   _____
   is an established subject-heading.

   X TRUE   FALSE

5. If interested in _____
   Equal pay for equal work
   _____

   _____,
   you should check that exact wording as
   well as   WOMEN-- EMPLOYMENT
   _____

   _____in the subject catalog.

Eptatetridae
   See Myxinidae
Eptatretus   *(QL638.15.M9)*
   xx Myxinidae
Eptatretus stouti   *(QL638.15.M9)*
Epulum (The Latin word)
   xx Latin language—Church Latin—
       Etymology
Epuran Cave (Romania)
   x Peştera Epuran (Romania)
   xx Caves—Romania
Equal educational opportunity
   See Educational equalization
Equal employment opportunity
   See Affirmative action programs
       Discrimination in employment
Equal opportunity in employment
   See Affirmative action programs
       Discrimination in employment
Equal pay for equal work   *(Indirect)*
   sa Women—Employment
   x Comparable worth (Compensation
       management)
       Pay equity
   xx Discrimination in employment
       Wages
       Women—Employment
   — Law and legislation   *(Indirect)*
       xx Labor laws and legislation

6. Caves-- Romania   X
   _____   is broader/narrower
   than Epuran Cave (Romania)
   _____.

7. There is a total of #_1___ SEE ALSO-type cross references ("sa") indicated in
   this excerpt; there is a total of #_5_____   SEE cross references.

8. An example of a subject-heading displayed in this excerpt which it's likely you
   will find subdivided geographically in a library's catalog is
   EQUAL PAY FOR EQUAL WORK or EQUAL PAY FOR EQUAL WORK-- LAW AND LEGISLATION   .

9. For publications about_____Eptatretus stouti_____,
   you could check the library shelves in the vicinity of the Library of Congress
   Classification ___QL638.15.M9_____.

10. Which one of the following is not an established LCSH subject-heading?
    ___ Affirmative action programs ___ ___ Equal pay for equal work-- Law and legislation
    ___ Equal pay for equal work   X Pay equity

11. ___Church Latin_____ is

    ___ a SEE ALSO cross reference   ___ an established subject-heading
    ___ a SEE cross reference   X a subdivision of a subject-heading

Course Title, Date   Practice Using the LCSH
Instructor   Your Name _____

These questions relate to this excerpt from
the Library of Congress Subject Headings(LCSH)

1. This excerpt is from volume #_____.

2. The combination of capital letters and 3-
   4 numbers which sometimes appears refers to

        a book number
        a call number
        a classification
        the location of a specific book-title
        on the library's shelves

3. Someone needing information about _____
   Equal protection of the law
   should look for subject cards with the 1st
   line subject-heading wording_____
   _____
   _____

4. Justice
   _____
   is an established subject-heading.

        TRUE   FALSE

5. If interested in _____
   Equality before the law
   _____,
   you should check that exact wording as·
   well as _____
   _____
   _____in the subject catalog.

> Equality (Islam) *(BP173.45)*
>   *xx* Islam—Doctrines
>   Islam—Relations
>   Islam and social problems
>   Sociology, Islamic
> **Equality before the law** *(Indirect)* *(JC578;*
>   *United States, JK1001; K)*
>   Here are entered discussions of the prin-
>   ciple of just legislation and administra-
>   tion of justice, and its application in
>   various constitutional systems.
>   Works on the doctrine of equal protection
>   of the law are entered under the head-
>   ing Equality before the law—United
>   States. Works on the doctrine of due
>   process of law are entered under the
>   heading Due process of law.
>   *sa* Due process of law
>   Race discrimination—Law and
>   legislation
>   Reverse discrimination—Law and
>   legislation
>   Sex discrimination—Law and legislation
>   Sex discrimination against men—Law
>   and legislation
>   Sex discrimination against women—
>   Law and legislation
>   *xx* Civil rights
>   Constitutional law
>   Justice
>   — Biblical teaching
>   *xx* Jewish law
>   GEOGRAPHIC SUBDIVISIONS
>   — United States
>   *x* Equal protection of the law
>   *Note under* Equality before the law

6. Jewish law _____ is broader/narrower
   than Equality before the law-- Biblical teaching _____.

7. There is a total of #_____ SEE ALSO-type cross references ("sa") indicated in
   this excerpt; there is a total of #_____   SEE cross references.

8. An example of a subject-heading displayed in this excerpt which it's likely you
   will find subdivided geographically in a library's catalog is _____
   _____.

9. For publications about Equality (Islam) _____,
   you could check the library shelves in the vicinity of the Library of Congress
   Classification _____.

10. Which one of the following is **not** an established LCSH subject-heading?
        Equal protection of the law
        Islam and social problems
        Sex discrimination against women-- Law and legislation

11. Biblical teaching _____ is

        a SEE ALSO cross reference   an established subject-heading
        a SEE cross reference   a subdivision of a subject-heading

These questions relate to this excerpt from
the Library of Congress Subject Headings(LCSH)

1. This excerpt is from volume # 1_____.

2. The combination of capital letters and 3-
   4 numbers which sometimes appears refers to

      ___ a book number
      ___ a call number
    X   a classification
      ___ the location of a specific book-title
          on the library's shelves

3. Someone needing information about _____
   Equal protection of the law
   should look for subject cards with the 1st
   line subject-heading wording
      EQUALITY BEFORE THE LAW-- UNITED STATES
   _____

4. Justice
   is an established subject-heading.

    X TRUE   ___ FALSE

5. If interested in _____
   Equality before the law
   _____ ,
   you should check that exact wording as
   well as DUE PROCESS OF LAW; RACE DISCRIMINATION--
LAW AND LEGISLATION; REVERSE DISCRIMINATION-- LAW AND
LEGISLATION; SEX DISCRIMINATION-- LAW AND LEGISLATION; SEX DISCRIMINATION AGAINST MEN-- LAW AND LEGISLATION;
SEX DISCRIMINATION AGAINST WOMEN-- LAW AND LEGISLATION in the subject catalog.

                                                          X
6. Jewish law _____ is broader/narrower
   than Equality before the law-- Biblical teaching _____.

7. There is a total of # 6___ SEE ALSO-type cross references ("sa") indicated in
   this excerpt; there is a total of # 0____   SEE cross references.

8. An example of a subject-heading displayed in this excerpt which it's likely you
   will find subdivided geographically in a library's catalog is _____
      EQUALITY BEFORE THE LAW
   _____.

9. For publications about _____Equality (Islam)_____ ,
   you could check the library shelves in the vicinity of the Library of Congress
   Classification _____BP173.45_____.

10. Which one of the following is not an established LCSH subject-heading?
    X Equal protection of the law
       Islam and social problems
       Sex discrimination against women-- Law and legislation

11. Biblical teaching _____ is

      ___ a SEE ALSO cross reference   ___ an established subject-heading
      ___ a SEE cross reference   X a subdivision of a subject-heading

---

Equality (Islam) (BP173.45)
  xx Islam—Doctrines
     Islam—Relations
     Islam and social problems
     Sociology, Islamic
Equality before the law (Indirect) (JC578;
     United States, JK1001; K)
     Here are entered discussions of the prin-
     ciple of just legislation and administra-
     tion of justice, and its application in
     various constitutional systems.
     Works on the doctrine of equal protection
     of the law are entered under the head-
     ing Equality before the law—United
     States. Works on the doctrine of due
     process of law are entered under the
     heading Due process of law.
  sa Due process of law
     Race discrimination—Law and
       legislation
     Reverse discrimination—Law and
       legislation
     Sex discrimination—Law and legislation
     Sex discrimination against men—Law
       and legislation
     Sex discrimination against women—
       Law and legislation
  xx Civil rights
     Constitutional law
     Justice
  — Biblical teaching
     xx Jewish law
          GEOGRAPHIC SUBDIVISIONS
  — United States
     x Equal protection of the law
     Note under Equality before the law

These questions relate to this excerpt from
the Library of Congress Subject Headings(LCSH)

1. This excerpt is from volume #_____.

2. The combination of capital letters and 3-
   4 numbers which sometimes appears refers to

        a book number
        a call number
        a classification
        the location of a specific book-title
          on the library's shelves

3. Someone needing information about _____
   Females
   _____
   should look for subject cards with the 1st
   line subject-heading wording_____
   _____
   _____

4. Women in art
   is an established subject-heading.

        TRUE   FALSE

5. If interested in _____
   Femininity of God_____
   _____,
   you should check that exact wording as
   well as _____
   _____
                             in the subject catalog.

6. Women--Psychology is broader/narrower
   _____
   than Femininity (Psychology)_____

7. There is a total of #_____ SEE ALSO-type cross references ("sa") indicated in
   this excerpt; there is a total of #_____   SEE cross references.

8. An example of a subject-heading displayed in this excerpt which it's likely you
   will find subdivided geographically in a library's catalog is _____
   _____.

9. For publications about Feminism_____,
   you could check the library shelves in the vicinity of the Library of Congress
   Classification _____.

10. Which one of the following is not an established LCSH subject-heading?
    Feminism-- Religious aspects-- Baptists Women-- Social conditions
    Sex (Psychology)   Women's lib

11. Attributes
    _____ is

        a SEE ALSO cross reference   an established subject-heading
        a SEE cross reference   a subdivision of a subject-heading

Females
    See Women
Feminine beauty (Aesthetics) (Indirect)
        Here are entered works on the attractive-
        ness of women as a philosophic or ar-
        tistic concept. Practical works on per-
        sonal grooming and appearance are en-
        tered under Beauty, Personal.
    sa Beauty, Personal
     x Ideal beautiful women
    xx Aesthetics
        Women in art
    Note under Beauty, Personal
Femininity (Philosophy) (BD450)
    xx Philosophical anthropology
        Philosophy
Femininity (Psychology)
    xx Sex (Psychology)
        Women—Psychology
Femininity of God
    sa God—Motherhood
     x God—Femininity
    xx God—Attributes
        God—Motherhood
Feminism (Indirect) (HQ1101-2030.7)
    sa Bible and feminism
        Feminist motion pictures
        Feminist theater
        Feminist therapy
        Feminists
        International Women's Year, 1975
        Radical therapy
        Sex discrimination against women
        Women—History
        Women—Legal status, laws, etc.
        Women—Social conditions
        Women's rights
     x Women's lib
        Women's liberation movement
    xx Women
    — Bibliography
        sa Feminist literature
        xx Feminist literature
    — Religious aspects
    — — Baptists [Catholic Church, etc.]
    — — Buddhism [Christianity, etc.]

Course Title, Date
Instructor

LCSH 10 ed.
KEY Vol. 1
Page 1146

Practice Using the LCSH
Your Name _____

These questions relate to this excerpt from
the Library of Congress Subject Headings (LCSH)

1. This excerpt is from volume # __1__ .

2. The combination of capital letters and 3-
   4 numbers which sometimes appears refers to

          a book number
          a call number
    X a classification
          the location of a specific book-title
          on the library's shelves

3. Someone needing information about _____
   Females _____
   should look for subject cards with the 1st
   line subject-heading wording_____
        WOMEN

4. Women in art _____
   is an established subject-heading.

    X TRUE   FALSE

5. If interested in _____
   Femininity of God _____
   _____ ,
   you should check that exact wording as
   well as   GOD-- MOTHERHOOD
   _____
   _____ in the subject catalog.

                             X

6. Women-- Psychology is broader/narrower
   than Femininity (Psychology) _____

Excerpt (right column):

Females
   See Women
Feminine beauty (Aesthetics) *(Indirect)*
      Here are entered works on the attractive-
      ness of women as a philosophic or ar-
      tistic concept. Practical works on per-
      sonal grooming and appearance are en-
      tered under Beauty, Personal.
   sa Beauty, Personal
   x Ideal beautiful women
   xx Aesthetics
      Women in art
   Note under Beauty, Personal
Femininity (Philosophy) *(BD450)*
   xx Philosophical anthropology
      Philosophy
Femininity (Psychology)
   xx Sex (Psychology)
      Women—Psychology
Femininity of God
   sa God—Motherhood
   x God—Femininity
   xx God—Attributes
      God—Motherhood
Feminism *(Indirect) (HQ1101-2030.7)*
   sa Bible and feminism
      Feminist motion pictures
      Feminist theater
      Feminist therapy
      Feminists
      International Women's Year, 1975
      Radical therapy
      Sex discrimination against women
      Women—History
      Women—Legal status, laws, etc.
      Women—Social conditions
      Women's rights
   x Women's lib
      Women's liberation movement
   xx Women
   — Bibliography
     sa Feminist literature
     xx Feminist literature
   — Religious aspects
   — — Baptists [Catholic Church, etc.]
   — — Buddhism [Christianity. etc.]

7. There is a total of # __15__ SEE ALSO-type cross references ("sa") indicated in
   this excerpt; there is a total of # __1__   SEE cross references.

8. An example of a subject-heading displayed in this excerpt which it's likely you
   will find subdivided geographically in a library's catalog is _____
   FEMININE BEAUTY (AESTHETICS) or FEMINISM   .

9. For publications about Feminism _____ ,
   you could check the library shelves in the vicinity of the Library of Congress
   Classification HQ1101-HQ2030.7 _____ .

10. Which one of the following is <u>not</u> an established LCSH subject-heading?
     Feminism-- Religious aspects-- Baptists   Women-- Social conditions
     Sex (Psychology)   X Women's lib

11. _____ Attributes _____ is

     a SEE ALSO cross reference   an established subject-heading
     a SEE cross reference   X a subdivision of a subject-heading

These questions relate to this excerpt from
the Library of Congress Subject Headings(LCSH)

1. This excerpt is from volume #_____.

2. The combination of capital letters and 3-
   4 numbers which sometimes appears refers to

       a book number
       a call number
       a classification
       the location of a specific book-title
       on the library's shelves

3. Someone needing information about _____
   Feminist studies
   should look for subject cards with the 1st
   line subject-heading wording_____
   _____
   _____

4. Social reformers_____
   is an established subject-heading.

       TRUE   FALSE

5. If interested in _____
   Feminist theater _____
   _____,
   you should check that exact wording as
   well as _____

   _____in the subject catalog.

6. Arteries _____ is broader/narrower
   than ____Femoral artery_____.

7. There is a total of #_____ SEE ALSO-type cross references ("sa") indicated in
   this excerpt; there is a total of #_____   SEE cross references.

8. An example of a subject-heading displayed in this excerpt which it's likely you
   will find subdivided geographically in a library's catalog is _____
   _____.

9. For publications about ___Femmes fatales in art_____,
   you could check the library shelves in the vicinity of the Library of Congress
   Classification _____.

10. Which one of the following is <u>not</u> an established LCSH subject-heading?
    Femoral hernia   Vamps
    Miro, Joan, 1893-   . Woman   Women-- Mental health

11. _Surgery_____ is

        a SEE ALSO cross reference   an established subject-heading
        a SEE cross reference   a subdivision of a subject-heading

Feminist studies
    See Women's studies
Feminist theater (Indirect) (United States.
    PN2270.F45)
    sa Women in the theater
    x Women's theater
    xx Feminism
       Theater
       Women in the theater
Feminist therapy (RC489.F45)
       Here are entered works on psychotherapy
          for women which focuses on the ef-
          fects of sexism on their mental health.
    x Therapy, Feminist
    xx Feminism
       Psychotherapy
       Women—Mental health
Feminists (Indirect)
    sa Suffragettes
       Women social reformers
    xx Feminism
       Social reformers
Femme (Tapestry)
    See Miró, Joan, 1893- . Woman
Femmes fatales (Indirect)
    x Adventuresses
       Seductresses
       Vamps
    xx Women
Femmes fatales in art (NX650.F46)
Femoral artery
    x Femur—Artery
    xx Arteries
Femoral epiphysis
    See Femur—Epiphysis
Femoral hernia
    xx Hernia
Femoral nerve
  — Surgery

Course Title, Date
Instructor

LCSH 10 ed.
KEY Vol. 1
Page 1146

Practice Using the LCSH
Your Name _____

These questions relate to this excerpt from
the Library of Congress Subject Headings(LCSH)

1. This excerpt is from volume # __1__ .

2. The combination of capital letters and 3-
4 numbers which sometimes appears refers to

      a book number
      a call number
  X a classification
      the location of a specific book-title
      on the library's shelves

3. Someone needing information about _____
Feminist studies
should look for subject cards with the 1st
line subject-heading wording_____
   WOMEN'S STUDIES

_____

4. Social reformers
is an established subject-heading.

  X TRUE   FALSE

5. If interested in _____
Feminist theater
_____
_____ ,
you should check that exact wording as
well as _____ WOMEN IN THE THEATER
_____
_____in the subject catalog.

Feminist studies
   See Women's studies
Feminist theater *(Indirect)* *(United States,*
     PN2270.F45)
   sa Women in the theater
   x Women's theater
  xx Feminism
     Theater
     Women in the theater
Feminist therapy *(RC489.F45)*
    Here are entered works on psychotherapy
     for women which focuses on the ef-
     fects of sexism on their mental health.
   x Therapy, Feminist
  xx Feminism
     Psychotherapy
     Women—Mental health
Feminists *(Indirect)*
   sa Suffragettes
     Women social reformers
  xx Feminism
     Social reformers
Femme (Tapestry)
   See Miró, Joan, 1893-   Woman
Femmes fatales *(Indirect)*
   x Adventuresses
     Seductresses
     Vamps
  xx Women
Femmes fatales in art *(NX650.F46)*
Femoral artery
   x Femur—Artery
  xx Arteries
Femoral epiphysis
   See Femur—Epiphysis
Femoral hernia
  xx Hernia
Femoral nerve
  — Surgery

6. Arteries
_____   X
                                      is broader/narrower
   than ___ Femoral artery _____ .

7. There is a total of #_3__ SEE ALSO-type cross references ("sa") indicated in
this excerpt; there is a total of #__3__ SEE cross references.

8. An example of a subject-heading displayed in this excerpt which it's likely you
will find subdivided geographically in a library's catalog is FEMINIST THEATER;
FEMINISTS; or FEMMES FATALES
_____ .

9. For publications about ___ Femmes fatales in art _____ ,
you could check the library shelves in the vicinity of the Library of Congress
Classification _____ NX650.F46 _____ .

10. Which one of the following is not an established LCSH subject-heading?
   Femoral hernia   X Vamps
   Miró, Joan, 1893- . Woman   Women-- Mental health

11. Surgery
_____ is

    a SEE ALSO cross reference   an established subject-heading
    a SEE cross reference   X a subdivision of a subject-heading

These questions relate to this excerpt from
the Library of Congress Subject Headings(LCSH)

1. This excerpt is from volume #_____.

2. The combination of capital letters and 3-
   4 numbers which sometimes appears refers to

       a book number
       a call number
       a classification
       the location of a specific book-title
        on the library's shelves

3. Someone needing information about _____
   <u>General Dynamics B-58</u>
   should look for subject cards with the 1st
   line subject-heading wording_____
   _____
   _____

4. <u>Historic districts-- New York (State)</u>
   is an established subject-heading.

      TRUE   FALSE

5. If interested in _____
   <u>General educational development tests</u>
   _____,
   you should check that exact wording as
   well as _____
   _____
   _____in the subject catalog.

Excerpt box:

General confession (Prayer)
  xx Confession (Prayer)
    Prayers
General Convention of the Christian Church
    (Indirect) (BX6751-6793)
  xx Christian sects
 — United States
    sa Afro-American Christians (General
       Convention of the Christian
       Church)
General Dynamics B-58
  See B-58 bomber
General educational development tests
  sa High school equivalency examination
  x GED tests
  xx Achievement tests
    United States. Army—Examinations
General Electric Realty Plot Historic District
(Schenectady, N.Y.)
  x GE Plot (Schenectady, N.Y.)
    GE Realty Plot (Schenectady, N.Y.)
    Schenectady (N.Y.). General Electric
      Realty Plot Historic District
  xx Historic districts—New York (State)
General equilibrium (Economics)
  See Equilibrium (Economics)
General Game Playing Program
  See GGPP (Computer program)
General Information Processing System
  See GIPSY (Information retrieval system)
General Integrated Programming System
  See GIPS (Electronic computer system)
General judgment
  See Judgment Day
General Ledger Accounting System (Computer
    system)
  See GLAS (Computer system)

---

6. <u>Achievement tests</u> _____ is broader/narrower
   than <u>General educational development tests</u> _____.

7. There is a total of #_____ SEE ALSO-type cross references ("sa") indicated in
   this excerpt; there is a total of #_____ SEE cross references.

8. An example of a subject-heading displayed in this excerpt which it's likely you
   will find subdivided geographically in a library's catalog is _____
   _____.

9. For publications about <u>General Convention of the Christian Church</u>,
   you could check the library shelves in the vicinity of the Library of Congress
   Classification _____.

10. Which one of the following is <u>not</u> an established LCSH subject-heading?
      Afro-American Christians (General   Judgment Day
        Convention of the Christian Church)
      GED tests   Prayers

11. <u>New York (State)</u> _____ is

      a SEE ALSO cross reference   an established subject-heading
      a SEE cross reference   a subdivision of a subject-heading

Course Title, Date
Instructor

LCSH 10 ed.
KEY Vol. 1
Page 1286

Practice Using the LCSH
Your Name _____

These questions relate to this excerpt from
the Library of Congress Subject Headings(LCSH)

1. This excerpt is from volume # _1____ .

2. The combination of capital letters and 3-
   4 numbers which sometimes appears refers to

       a book number
       a call number
   X   a classification
       the location of a specific book-title
       on the library's shelves

3. Someone needing information about _____
   General Dynamics B-58
   should look for subject cards with the 1st
   line subject-heading wording_____
   B-58 BOMBER
   _____

4. Historic districts-- New York (State)
   is an established subject-heading.

      X TRUE   FALSE

5. If interested in _____
   General educational development tests
   _____,
   you should check that exact wording as
   well as _____
   HIGH SCHOOL EQUIVALENCY EXAMINATION
   _____in the subject catalog.

6. Achievement tests _____ is broader/narrower
   than _General educational development tests_____ .

7. There is a total of # 2___ SEE ALSO-type cross references ("sa") indicated in
   this excerpt; there is a total of # 7_____ SEE cross references.

8. An example of a subject-heading displayed in this excerpt which it's likely you
   will find subdivided geographically in a library's catalog is _____
   GENERAL CONVENTION OF THE CHRISTIAN CHURCH
   _____ .

9. For publications about General Convention of the Christian Church _____ ,
   you could check the library shelves in the vicinity of the Library of Congress
   Classification _____BX6751-BX6793_____ .

10. Which one of the following is not an established LCSH subject-heading?
      Afro-American Christians (General   Judgment Day
        Convention of the Christian Church)
     X GED tests   Prayers

11. _New York (State)_____ is

        a SEE ALSO cross reference   an established subject-heading
        a SEE cross reference   X a subdivision of a subject-heading

---

General confession (Prayer)
  xx Confession (Prayer)
    Prayers
General Convention of the Christian Church
    (Indirect) (BX6751-6793)
  xx Christian sects
  — United States
    sa Afro-American Christians (General
        Convention of the Christian
        Church)
General Dynamics B-58
  See B-58 bomber
General educational development tests
  sa High school equivalency examination
  x GED tests
  xx Achievement tests
    United States. Army—Examinations
General Electric Realty Plot Historic District
    (Schenectady, N.Y.)
  x GE Plot (Schenectady, N.Y.)
    GE Realty Plot (Schenectady, N.Y.)
    Schenectady (N.Y.). General Electric
        Realty Plot Historic District
  xx Historic districts—New York (State)
General equilibrium (Economics)
  See Equilibrium (Economics)
General Game Playing Program
  See GGPP (Computer program)
General Information Processing System
  See GIPSY (Information retrieval system)
General Integrated Programming System
  See GIPS (Electronic computer system)
General judgment
  See Judgment Day
General Ledger Accounting System (Computer
    system)
  See GLAS (Computer system)

These questions relate to this excerpt from
the Library of Congress Subject Headings(LCSH)

1. This excerpt is from volume #_____.

2. The combination of capital letters and 3-
   4 numbers which sometimes appears refers to

      a book number
      a call number
      a classification
      the location of a specific book-title
       on the library's shelves

3. Someone needing information about _____
   Oral diagnosis
   should look for subject cards with the 1st
   line subject-heading wording_____
   _____
   _____

4. Contraceptive drugs _____
   is an established subject-heading.

      TRUE   FALSE

5. If interested in _____
   Oral contraceptives
   _____,
   you should check that exact wording as
   well as _____

   _____in the subject catalog.

6. Contraceptive drugs _____   is broader/narrower
   than _____Oral contraceptives, Male_____.

7. There is a total of #_____ SEE ALSO-type cross references ("sa") indicated in
   this excerpt; there is a total of #_____   SEE cross references.

8. An example of a subject-heading displayed in this excerpt which it's likely you
   will find subdivided geographically in a library's catalog is _____
   _____.

9. For publications about_____Oral contraceptives_____,
   you could check the library shelves in the vicinity of the Library of Congress
   Classification _____.

10. Which one of the following is not an established LCSH subject-heading?
       Birth control pills, Male
       Oral contraceptives-- Religious aspects
       Teeth-- Diseases-- Diagnosis

11. Examination _____ is

       a SEE ALSO cross reference   an established subject-heading
       a SEE cross reference   a subdivision of a subject-heading

---

Oral contraceptives *(Indirect) (RG137.5)*
   sa Ethinyl estradiol
        Mestranol
        Norethindrone
   x Anovulants, Oral
       Birth control pills
       Contraceptives, Oral
       Oral anovulants
       Oral contraceptives, Female
       Pill, Birth control
       Pill, The
   xx Contraceptive drugs
        Contraceptives
        Gynecologic drugs
        Progestational hormones
   — Religious aspects
   — — Baptists, [Catholic Church, etc.]
   — — Buddhism, [Christianity, etc.]
   — Side effects *(Indirect)*
       Example under Drugs—Side effects
   — Social aspects *(Indirect)*
       x Society and oral contraceptives
Oral contraceptives, Female
   See Oral contraceptives
Oral contraceptives, Male
   x Birth control pills, Male
      Male birth control pills
      Male oral contraceptives
   xx Contraceptive drugs
        Fertility, Effect of drugs on
Oral diagnosis
   See Mouth—Diseases—Diagnosis
          Teeth—Diseases—Diagnosis
Oral examination (Medicine)
   See Mouth—Examination

Course Title, Date
Instructor

LCSH 10 ed.
KEY VOL. 2
Page 2294

Practice Using the LCSH
Your Name _____

These questions relate to this excerpt from
the Library of Congress Subject Headings(LCSH)

1. This excerpt is from volume # 2 ____.

2. The combination of capital letters and 3-
   4 numbers which sometimes appears refers to

   _____ a book number
   _____ a call number
   X a classification
   _____ the location of a specific book-title
   on the library's shelves

3. Someone needing information about _____
   Oral diagnosis
   should look for subject cards with the 1st
   line subject-heading wording _____
   MOUTH-- DISEASES-- DIAGNOSIS and
   TEETH-- DISEASES-- DIAGNOSIS

4. Contraceptive drugs
   is an established subject-heading.

   X TRUE   FALSE

5. If interested in _____
   Oral contraceptives
   _____,
   you should check that exact wording as
   well as ETHINYL ESTRADIOL; MESTRANOL;
   and NORETHINDRONE
   _____in the subject catalog.

Oral contraceptives *(Indirect)* *(RG137.5)*
  sa Ethinyl estradiol
     Mestranol
     Norethindrone
   x Anovulants, Oral
     Birth control pills
     Contraceptives, Oral
     Oral anovulants
     Oral contraceptives, Female
     Pill, Birth control
     Pill, The
  xx Contraceptive drugs
     Contraceptives
     Gynecologic drugs
     Progestational hormones
— Religious aspects
— — Baptists, [Catholic Church, etc.]
— — Buddhism, [Christianity, etc.]
— Side effects *(Indirect)*
     Example under Drugs—Side effects
— Social aspects *(Indirect)*
   x Society and oral contraceptives
Oral contraceptives, Female
  See Oral contraceptives
Oral contraceptives, Male
   x Birth control pills, Male
     Male birth control pills
     Male oral contraceptives
  xx Contraceptive drugs
     Fertility, Effect of drugs on
Oral diagnosis
  See Mouth—Diseases—Diagnosis
     Teeth—Diseases—Diagnosis
Oral examination (Medicine)
  See Mouth—Examination

6. Contraceptive drugs
   _____   X
                                     is broader/narrower
   than ____Oral contraceptives, Male_____.

7. There is a total of # 3 SEE ALSO-type cross references ("sa") indicated in
   this excerpt; there is a total of # 4   SEE cross references.

8. An example of a subject-heading displayed in this excerpt which it's likely you
   will find subdivided geographically in a library's catalog is ORAL CONTRACEPTIVES;
   ORAL CONTRACEPTIVES-- SIDE EFFECTS; ORAL CONTRACEPTIVES-- SOCIAL ASPECTS.

9. For publications about   Oral contraceptives
   _____,
   you could check the library shelves in the vicinity of the Library of Congress
   Classification   RG137.5
   _____.

10. Which one of the following is not an established LCSH subject-heading?
    X Birth control pills, Male
      Oral contraceptives-- Religious aspects
      Teeth-- Diseases-- Diagnosis

11. Examination _____ is

      a SEE ALSO cross reference   an established subject-heading
      a SEE cross reference   X a subdivision of a subject-heading

These questions relate to this excerpt from
the Library of Congress Subject Headings(LCSH)

> Sex change *(Indirect)* *(RC560.C4)*
>   sa Transsexuals
>   x Change of sex
>   Sex. Change of
>   Sex-role inversion
>   Transexualism
>   Transsexualism
>   xx Gender identity disorders
>   Generative organs
>   Sex role
>   — Law and legislation *(Indirect)*
>   xx Medical laws and legislation
>   Persons (Law)
> **Sex chromatin**
>   x Barr bodies
>   xx Chromatin
>   Sex chromosomes
> **Sex chromosome abnormalities**
>   sa Ectodermal dysplasia
>   Klinefelter's syndrome
>   X chromosome—Abnormalities
>   xx Chromosome abnormalities
>   Sexual disorders
> **Sex chromosome abnormalities in children**
>   *(Indirect)* *(RJ47.4)*
>   xx Children—Diseases—Genetic aspects
>   Human chromosome abnormalities
>   Sexual disorders in children
> **Sex chromosomes**
>   sa Sex chromatin
>   Sex determination, Genetic
>   Sex differentiation
>   Sex-linkage (Genetics)
>   X chromosome
>   x Gonosomes
>   Y chromosome
>   xx Chromosomes
> Sex control (Preselection)
>   *See Sex preselection*

1. This excerpt is from volume #_____.

2. The combination of capital letters and 3-
   4 numbers which sometimes appears refers to

        a book number
        a call number
        a classification
        the location of a specific book-title
        on the library's shelves

3. Someone needing information about _____
   Sex control (Preselection)
   _____
   should look for subject cards with the 1st
   line subject-heading wording_____
   _____
   _____

4. Chromatin
   _____
   is an established subject-heading.

       TRUE   FALSE

5. If interested in _____
   Sex change
   _____
   _____,
   you should check that exact wording as
   well as _____
   _____
   _____in the subject catalog.

6. Medical laws and legislation _____   is broader/narrower
   than ___Sex change-- Law and legislation_____.

7. There is a total of #_____ SEE ALSO-type cross references ("sa") indicated in
   this excerpt; there is a total of #_____   SEE cross references.

8. An example of a subject-heading displayed in this excerpt which it's likely you
   will find subdivided geographically in a library's catalog is _____
   _____.

9. For publications about ___Sex chromosome abnormalities in children_____,
   you could check the library shelves in the vicinity of the Library of Congress
   Classification _____.

10. Which one of the following is **not** an established LCSH subject-heading?
        Barr bodies
        Children-- Diseases-- Genetic aspects
        Chromosome abnormalities

11. Diseases _____ is

        a SEE ALSO cross reference   an established subject-heading
        a SEE cross reference   a subdivision of a subject-heading

Course Title, Date   LCSH 10 ed.   Practice Using the LCSH
Instructor   KEY Vol. 2   Your Name _____
                         Page 2888

These questions relate to this excerpt from
the Library of Congress Subject Headings (LCSH)

1. This excerpt is from volume #__2__.

2. The combination of capital letters and 3-
   4 numbers which sometimes appears refers to

         a book number
         a call number
   X   a classification
         the location of a specific book-title
         on the library's shelves

3. Someone needing information about _____
   Sex control (Preselection)
   ─────────────────────────────────────
   should look for subject cards with the 1st
   line subject-heading wording_____
   SEX PRESELECTION
   ─────────────────────────────────────
   ─────────────────────────────────────

4. Chromatin
   ─────────────────────────────────────
   is an established subject-heading.

   X TRUE   FALSE

5. If interested in _____
   Sex change
   ─────────────────────────────────────
   ───────────────────────────────────── ,
   you should check that exact wording as
   well as _____
   TRANSSEXUALS
   ─────────────────── in the subject catalog.

6. Medical laws and legislation _____   is broader/~~narrower~~ X
   than ___Sex change-- Law and legislation_____ .

7. There is a total of #9___ SEE ALSO-type cross references ("sa") indicated in
   this excerpt; there is a total of #1_____   SEE cross references.

8. An example of a subject-heading displayed in this excerpt which it's likely you
   will find subdivided geographically in a library's catalog is
   SEX CHANGE; SEX CHANGE-- LAW AND LEGISLATION; or SEX CHROMOSOME ABNORMALITIES
   IN CHILDREN.

9. For publications about Sex chromosome abnormalities in children _____ ,
   you could check the library shelves in the vicinity of the Library of Congress
   Classification ____RJ47.4_____ .

10. Which one of the following is not an established LCSH subject-heading?
    X Barr bodies
       Children-- Diseases-- Genetic aspects
       Chromosome abnormalities

11. Diseases
    ─────────────────────────────────────── is

         a SEE ALSO cross reference   an established subject-heading
         a SEE cross reference   X   a subdivision of a subject-heading

---

Sex change *(Indirect)* *(RC560.C4)*
   sa Transsexuals
   x Change of sex
     Sex, Change of
     Sex-role inversion
     Transexualism
     Transsexualism
   xx Gender identity disorders
     Generative organs
     Sex role
 — Law and legislation *(Indirect)*
     xx Medical laws and legislation
      Persons (Law)
Sex chromatin
   x Barr bodies
   xx Chromatin
     Sex chromosomes
Sex chromosome abnormalities
   sa Ectodermal dysplasia
     Klinefelter's syndrome
     X chromosome—Abnormalities
   xx Chromosome abnormalities
     Sexual disorders
Sex chromosome abnormalities in children
      (Indirect) *(RJ47.4)*
   xx Children—Diseases—Genetic aspects
     Human chromosome abnormalities
     Sexual disorders in children
Sex chromosomes
   sa Sex chromatin
     Sex determination, Genetic
     Sex differentiation
     Sex-linkage (Genetics)
     X chromosome
   x Gonosomes
     Y chromosome
   xx Chromosomes
Sex control (Preselection)
   See Sex preselection

These questions relate to this excerpt from
the Library of Congress Subject Headings(LCSH)

1. This excerpt is from volume #_____.

2. The combination of capital letters and 3-
   4 numbers which sometimes appears refers to

   a book number
   a call number
   a classification
   the location of a specific book-title
     on the library's shelves

3. Someone needing information about _____
   Textile creasing
   should look for subject cards with the 1st
   line subject-heading wording_____
   _____
   _____

4. Textile industry
   is an established subject-heading.

   TRUE   FALSE

5. If interested in _____
   Textile design
   _____,
   you should check that exact wording as·
   well as _____

   _____in the subject catalog.

Textile crafts *(Indirect) (TT699-854.5)*
  sa Burlap craft
    Color in textile crafts
    Fancy work
    Felt work
    Fiberwork
    Hand spinning
    Hand weaving
    Marine canvas work
    Needlework
    Panty hose craft
    Sprang
    Tassels
  x Fabric crafts
    Textile arts
    Textile fiber crafts
  xx Fancy work
    Fiberwork
    Handicraft
Textile creasing
  See Creasing of textiles
Textile design *(Indirect) (Art industries,*
    NK8800-8999; Textile industries,
    TS1475)
  sa Resist-dyed textiles
    Textile designers
    Textile painting
  xx Decoration and ornament
    Design
    Textile industry
  — Japan
  — — History
  — — — To 794
  — — — To 1868
  — — — Kamakura-Momoyama periods,
      1185-1600
  — — — Edo period, 1600-1868

6. Handicraft _____ is broader/narrower
   than   Textile crafts _____.

7. There is a total of #____ SEE ALSO-type cross references ("sa") indicated in
   this excerpt; there is a total of #_____   SEE cross references.

8. An example of a subject-heading displayed in this excerpt which it's likely you
   will find subdivided geographically in a library's catalog is _____
   _____.

9. For publications about Textile industries' relationship to Textile design ,
   you could check the library shelves in the vicinity of the Library of Congress
   Classification _____.

10. Which one of the following is not an established LCSH subject-heading?
    Creasing of textiles   Textile arts
    Panty hose craft   Textile design-- Japan-- History

11. Edo period, 1600-1868
   _____ is

       a SEE ALSO cross reference   an established subject-heading
       a SEE cross reference   a subdivision of a subject-heading

These questions relate to this excerpt from
the Library of Congress Subject Headings(LCSH)

1. This excerpt is from volume # __2__ .

2. The combination of capital letters and 3-
   4 numbers which sometimes appears refers to

   _____ a book number
   _____ a call number
     X   a classification
   _____ the location of a specific book-title
         on the library's shelves

3. Someone needing information about _____
   Textile creasing
   _____
   should look for subject cards with the 1st
   line subject-heading wording_____
   __CREASING OF TEXTILES_____
   _____

4. Textile industry_____
   is an established subject-heading.

     X   TRUE   _____ FALSE

5. If interested in _____
   Textile design
   _____
   _____ ,
   you should check that exact wording as
   well as RESIST-DYED TEXTILES; TEXTILE
   DESIGNERS; and TEXTILE PAINTING
   _____in the subject catalog.

| Textile crafts *(Indirect)* *(TT699-354.5)* |
| sa Burlap craft |
| Color in textile crafts |
| Fancy work |
| Felt work |
| Fiberwork |
| Hand spinning |
| Hand weaving |
| Marine canvas work |
| Needlework |
| Panty hose craft |
| Sprang |
| Tassels |
| *x* Fabric crafts |
| Textile arts |
| Textile fiber crafts |
| *xx* Fancy work |
| Fiberwork |
| Handicraft |
| Textile creasing |
| *See* Creasing of textiles |
| **Textile design** *(Indirect)* *(Art industries,* |
| *NK8800-8999; Textile industries,* |
| *TS1475)* |
| sa Resist-dyed textiles |
| Textile designers |
| Textile painting |
| *xx* Decoration and ornament |
| Design |
| Textile industry |
| — Japan |
| — — History |
| — — — To 794 |
| — — — To 1868 |
| — — — Kamakura-Momoyama periods, |
| 1185-1600 |
| — — — Edo period, 1600-1868 |

6. Handicraft_____   X
   _____is broader/narrower
   than ____Textile crafts_____.

7. There is a total of #_15__ SEE ALSO-type cross references ("sa") indicated in
   this excerpt; there is a total of #__1___ SEE cross references.

8. An example of a subject-heading displayed in this excerpt which it's likely you
   will find subdivided geographically in a library's catalog is _____
   TEXTILE CRAFTS or TEXTILE DESIGN_____.

9. For publications about _Textile industries' relationship to Textile design___ ,
   you could check the library shelves in the vicinity of the Library of Congress
   Classification ___TS1475_____.

10. Which one of the following is not an established LCSH subject-heading?
    _____ Creasing of textiles   X   Textile arts
    _____ Panty hose craft   _____ Textile design-- Japan-- History

11. __Edo period, 1600-1868_____ is

    _____ a SEE ALSO cross reference   _____ an established subject-heading
    _____ a SEE cross reference   X   a subdivision of a subject-heading

These questions relate to this excerpt from
the Library of Congress Subject Headings(LCSH)

Wolverines, Fossil *(QE882.C15)*
    sa Plesioguio
    xx Carnivora, Fossil
Wolverton family
    x Woolverton family
Wolves *(Indirect)* *(QL737.C2)*
    sa Coyotes
        Red wolf
        Wolfdogs
    x Canis lupus
  — Control *(Indirect)* *(SB994.W7)*
    x Wolves—Extermination
  — Extermination
    See Wolves—Control
  — Folklore *(GR730.W6)*
    sa Roman she-wolf (Legendary
        character)
        Werewolves
  — Food
Wolves as pets *(SF459.W63)*
Wolves in art
Wolworth family
    See Woolworth family
Womac family
    See Womack family
Womach family
    See Womack family
Womack family
    x Wamack family
        Wammock family
        Wamock family
        Womac family
        Womach family
        Wommack family
        Wommoch family
        Wormack family
Woman
    See Women
Woman (Buddhism) *(BQ4570.W6)*
    x Women (Buddhism)
    xx Man (Buddhism)
        Women in Buddhism

1. This excerpt is from volume #_____.

2. The combination of capital letters and 3-
   4 numbers which sometimes appears refers to

       a book number
       a call number
       a classification
       the location of a specific book-title
       on the library's shelves

3. Someone needing information about _____
   <u>woman</u>_____
   should look for subject cards with the 1st
   line subject-heading wording_____
   _____
   _____

4. <u>Man (Buddhism)</u>_____
   is an established subject-heading.

      TRUE   FALSE

5. If interested in <u>Wolves</u>_____
   _____
   _____,
   you should check that exact wording as
   well as _____
   _____in the subject catalog.

6. <u>Carnivora, Fossil</u>_____   is broader/narrower
   than _____<u>Wolverines, Fossil</u>_____.

7. There is a total of #_____ SEE ALSO-type cross references ("sa") indicated in
   this excerpt; there is a total of #_____ SEE cross references.

8. An example of a subject-heading displayed in this excerpt which it's likely you
   will find subdivided geographically in a library's catalog is _____
   _____.

9. For publications about <u>Folklore of Wolves</u>_____,
   you could check the library shelves in the vicinity of the Library of Congress
   Classification _____.

10. Which one of the following is <u>not</u> an established LCSH subject-heading?
        Wolves   Wolves in art
        Wolves-- Extermination   Women

11. <u>Food</u>_____ is

        a SEE ALSO cross reference   an established subject-heading
        a SEE cross reference   a subdivision of a subject-heading

Course Title, Date   LCSH 10 ed.   Practice Using the LCSH
Instructor   KEY Vol. 2   Your Name _____
      Page 3481

These questions relate to this excerpt from
the Library of Congress Subject Headings(LCSH)

1. This excerpt is from volume # __2__ .

2. The combination of capital letters and 3-
   4 numbers which sometimes appears refers to

       a book number
       a call number
   X   a classification
       the location of a specific book-title
       on the library's shelves

3. Someone needing information about _____
   woman
   should look for subject cards with the 1st
   line subject-heading wording_____
   WOMEN

   _____

4. Man (Buddhism)
   is an established subject-heading.

   X TRUE   FALSE

5. If interested in Wolves
   _____
   _____,
   you should check that exact wording as
   well as COYOTES; RED WOLF; and
   _____
   WOLFDOGS
   _____ in the subject catalog.

Wolverines. Fossil *(QE882.C15)*	
sa Plesiogulo	
xx Carnivora. Fossil	
Wolverton family	
x Woolverton family	
Wolves *(Indirect)* *(QL737.C2)*	
sa Coyotes	
Red wolf	
Wolfdogs	
x Canis lupus	
—Control *(Indirect)* *(SB994.W7)*	
x Wolves—Extermination	
—Extermination	
See Wolves—Control	
—Folklore *(GR730.W6)*	
sa Roman she-wolf (Legendary	
character)	
Werewolves	
—Food	
Wolves as pets *(SF459.W63)*	
Wolves in art	
Wolworth family	
See Woolworth family	
Womac family	
See Womack family	
Womach family	
See Womack family	
Womack family	
x Wamack family	
Wammock family	
Wamock family	
Womac family	
Womach family	
Wommack family	
Wommoch family	
Wormack family	
Woman	
See Women	
Woman (Buddhism) *(BQ4570.W6)*	
x Women (Buddhism)	
xx Man (Buddhism)	
Women in Buddhism	

6. Carnivora, Fossil _____   X
                                is broader/narrower
   than _____ Wolverines, Fossil _____ .

7. There is a total of # _6_ SEE ALSO-type cross references ("sa") indicated in
   this excerpt; there is a total of # _5_ SEE cross references.

8. An example of a subject-heading displayed in this excerpt which it's likely you
   will find subdivided geographically in a library's catalog is _____
   WOLVES or WOLVES-- CONTROL
   _____ .

9. For publications about Folklore of Wolves
   _____,
   you could check the library shelves in the vicinity of the Library of Congress
   Classification _____ GR730.W6 _____ .

10. Which one of the following is not an established LCSH subject-heading?
        Wolves   Wolves in art
    X Wolves-- Extermination   Women

11. Food
    _____ is

        a SEE ALSO cross reference   an established subject-heading
        a SEE cross reference   X a subdivision of a subject-heading

These questions relate to this excerpt from
the Library of Congress Subject Headings(LCSH)

1. This excerpt is from volume #_____.

2. The combination of capital letters and 3-
   4 numbers which sometimes appears refers to

   a book number
   a call number
   a classification
   the location of a specific book-title
     on the library's shelves

3. Someone needing information about _____
   Women police officers
   should look for subject cards with the 1st
   line subject-heading wording_____
   _____
   _____

4. Poets
   is an established subject-heading.

       TRUE   FALSE

5. If interested in _____
   Women poets
   _____,
   you should check that exact wording as
   well as _____
   _____
   _____in the subject catalog.

> Women physicians *(Indirect) (R692)*
>   *sa* Women medical students
>   Women surgeons
>   *x* Physicians, Women
>   Women as physicians
>   *xx* Physicians
>   Women in medicine
> Women physicists *(Indirect) (QC15-16.2)*
>   *xx* Physicists
> Women physiologists *(Indirect)*
>   *xx* Physiologists
>   Women scientists
> Women pioneers *(Indirect)*
>   *sa* Explorers, Women
>   *xx* Explorers, Women
>   Pioneers
> Women plantation owners *(Indirect)*
>   *xx* Plantation owners
>   Women in agriculture
> Women poets *(Indirect)*
>   *sa* Women hymn writers
>   *x* Poetesses
>   Poets, Women
>   Women as poets
>   *xx* Poets
>   Women authors
> Women poets, American, [Urdu, etc.]
>   — 20th century
> Women poets, Arab *(Indirect)*
>   *x* Arab women poets
> Women poets, Chinese *(Indirect)*
>   *x* Chinese women poets
> Women poets, Japanese *(Indirect)*
>   *x* Japanese women poets
>   *xx* Poets, Japanese
> Women police officers
>   *See* Policewomen

6. _Physicians_____ is broader/narrower
   than ___Women physicians_____.

7. There is a total of #_____ SEE ALSO-type cross references ("sa") indicated in
   this excerpt; there is a total of #_____ SEE cross references.

8. An example of a subject-heading displayed in this excerpt which it's likely you
   will find subdivided geographically in a library's catalog is _____
   _____.

9. For publications about___Women physicists_____,
   you could check the library shelves in the vicinity of the Library of Congress
   Classification _____.

10. Which one of the following is not an established LCSH subject-heading?
        Explorers, Women
        Poetesses
        Women poets, American-- 20th century

11. _20th century_____ is

        a SEE ALSO cross reference   an established subject-heading
        a SEE cross reference   a subdivision of a subject-heading

Course Title, Date
Instructor

LCSH 10 ed.
KEY Vol. 2
Page 3489

Practice Using the LCSH
Your Name_____

These questions relate to this excerpt from
the Library of Congress Subject Headings(LCSH)

1. This excerpt is from volume # 2____.

2. The combination of capital letters and 3-
   4 numbers which sometimes appears refers to

         a book number
         a call number
    X   a classification
         the location of a specific book-title
         on the library's shelves

3. Someone needing information about _____
   Women police officers
   should look for subject cards with the 1st
   line subject-heading wording_____
   POLICEWOMEN
   _____
   _____

4. Poets
   _____
   is an established subject-heading.

      X TRUE   FALSE

5. If interested in _____
   Women poets
   _____,
   you should check that exact wording as·
   well as _____
   __WOMEN HYMN WRITERS_____
   _____in the subject catalog.

| Women physicians *(Indirect)* *(R692)* |
| sa Women medical students |
| Women surgeons |
| x Physicians, Women |
| Women as physicians |
| xx Physicians |
| Women in medicine |
| **Women physicists** *(Indirect)* *(QC15-16.2)* |
| xx Physicists |
| **Women physiologists** *(Indirect)* |
| xx Physiologists |
| Women scientists |
| **Women pioneers** *(Indirect)* |
| sa Explorers, Women |
| xx Explorers, Women |
| Pioneers |
| **Women plantation owners** *(Indirect)* |
| xx Plantation owners |
| Women in agriculture |
| **Women poets** *(Indirect)* |
| sa Women hymn writers |
| x Poetesses |
| Poets, Women |
| Women as poets |
| xx Poets |
| Women authors |
| **Women poets, American,** [Urdu, etc.] |
| — 20th century |
| **Women poets, Arab** *(Indirect)* |
| x Arab women poets |
| **Women poets, Chinese** *(Indirect)* |
| x Chinese women poets |
| **Women poets, Japanese** *(Indirect)* |
| x Japanese women poets |
| xx Poets, Japanese |
| Women police officers |
| *See* Policewomen |

6. __Physicians_____   is broader/̶n̶a̶r̶r̶o̶w̶e̶r̶ ^X
   than ___Women physicians_____.

7. There is a total of # 4__ SEE ALSO-type cross references ("sa") indicated in
   this excerpt; there is a total of #___1____ ` SEE cross references.

8. An example of a subject-heading displayed in this excerpt which it's likely you
   will find subdivided geographically in a library's catalog is __WOMEN PHYSICIANS;
   WOMEN PHYSICISTS; WOMEN PHYSIOLOGISTS; WOMEN PIONEERS;WOMEN PLANTATION OWNERS;WOMEN
   POETS; WOMEN POETS,ARAB;WOMEN POETS,CHINESE; or WOMEN POETS,JAPANESE

9. For publications about __Women physicists_____,
   you could check the library shelves in the vicinity of the Library of Congress
   Classification ___QC15-QC16.2_____.

10. Which one of the following is <u>not</u> an established LCSH subject-heading?
        Explorers, Women
     X Poetesses
        Women poets, American-- 20th century

11. _20th century_____   is

        a SEE ALSO cross reference   an established subject-heading
        a SEE cross reference   X a subdivision of a subject-heading

Practice Using the <u>LCSH</u>

Your Name_____

These questions relate to this excerpt from
the Library of Congress Subject Headings(LCSH)

> Women's education
>> See Women—Education
>
> Women's education, Medieval
>> See Women—Education, Medieval
>
> **Women's encyclopedias and dictionaries**
>> *xx* Encyclopedias and dictionaries
>
> **Women's encyclopedias and dictionaries,**
> **Chinese**
>> *x* Chinese women's encyclopedias and
>> dictionaries
>
> **Women's encyclopedias and dictionaries,**
> **Japanese, [etc.]**
>
> Women's etiquette
>> See Etiquette for women
>
> **Women's exchanges** *(HD6076)*
>> *xx* Women—Employment
>
> **Women's health services** *(Indirect)*
>> *(General, RA564.85; Gynecology,*
>> *RG12-16; Obstetrics, RG500-501)*
>> *sa* Abortion services
>> Hospitals, Gynecologic and obstetric
>> Maternal health services
>> *x* Health services for women
>> Women—Medical care
>> *xx* Gynecology
>> Medical care
>> Public health
>> Women—Health and hygiene
>> Women—Services for
>> — Utilization
>>> *x* Utilization of women's health
>>> services
>
> **Women's institutes** *(Indirect)* *(England,*
> *HQ1946)*
>> *xx* Women—Societies and clubs
>
> Women's lib
>> See Feminism
>
> Women's liberation
>> See Women's rights

1. This excerpt is from volume #_____.

2. The combination of capital letters and 3-
   4 numbers which sometimes appears refers to

   > a book number
   > a call number
   > a classification
   > the location of a specific book-title
   > on the library's shelves

3. Someone needing information about _____
   <u>Women's etiquette</u>
   should look for subject cards with the 1st
   line subject-heading wording_____
   _____
   _____

4. <u>Gynecology</u>
   is an established subject-heading.

   TRUE   FALSE

5. If interested in <u>Women's health</u>
   <u>services</u>
   _____,
   you should check that exact wording as·
   well as _____
   _____
   _____in the subject catalog.

6. <u>Encyclopedias and dictionaries</u>_____   is broader/narrower
   than ____<u>Women's encyclopedias and dictionaries</u>_____.

7. There is a total of #_____ SEE ALSO-type cross references ("sa") indicated in
   this excerpt; there is a total of #_____ SEE cross references.

8. An example of a subject-heading displayed in this excerpt which it's likely you
   will find subdivided geographically in a library's catalog is _____
   _____.

9. For publications about <u>obstetrical aspects of Women's health services</u>_____,
   you could check the library shelves in the vicinity of the Library of Congress
   Classification _____.

10. Which one of the following is <u>not</u> an established LCSH subject-heading?
    > Chinese women's encyclopedias and dictionaries
    > Feminism
    > Women's health services-- Utilization

11. <u>Education, Medieval</u>_____ is

    > a SEE ALSO cross reference   an established subject-heading
    > a SEE cross reference   a subdivision of a subject-heading

Course Title, Date
Instructor

LCSH 10 ed.
KEY Vol. 2,
Page 3490

Practice Using the LCSH
Your Name _____

These questions relate to this excerpt from
the Library of Congress Subject Headings(LCSH)

Women's education
　　See Women—Education
Women's education, Medieval
　　See Women—Education, Medieval
Women's encyclopedias and dictionaries
　　xx Encyclopedias and dictionaries
**Women's encyclopedias and dictionaries,
　　Chinese**
　　　x Chinese women's encyclopedias and
　　　　dictionaries
**Women's encyclopedias and dictionaries,
　　Japanese, [etc.]**
Women's etiquette
　　See Etiquette for women
Women's exchanges *(HD6076)*
　　xx Women—Employment
Women's health services *(Indirect)*
　　　*(General, RA564.85; Gynecology,
　　　RG12-16; Obstetrics, RG500-501)*
　　sa Abortion services
　　　Hospitals, Gynecologic and obstetric
　　　Maternal health services
　　x Health services for women
　　　Women—Medical care
　　xx Gynecology
　　　Medical care
　　　Public health
　　　Women—Health and hygiene
　　　Women—Services for
　　— Utilization
　　　x Utilization of women's health
　　　　services
Women's institutes *(Indirect)* *(England,
　　HQ1946)*
　　xx Women—Societies and clubs
Women's lib
　　See Feminism
Women's liberation
　　See Women's rights

1. This excerpt is from volume # _2_____.

2. The combination of capital letters and 3-
   4 numbers which sometimes appears refers to

   _____ a book number
   _____ a call number
   X   a classification
   _____ the location of a specific book-title
          on the library's shelves

3. Someone needing information about _____
   _Women's etiquette_____
   should look for subject cards with the 1st
   line subject-heading wording_____
   _ETIQUETTE FOR WOMEN_____
   _____

4. _Gynecology_____
   is an established subject-heading.

   X   TRUE   _____ FALSE

5. If interested in _Women's health_____
   _services_____
   _____,
   you should check that exact wording as
   well as ABORTION SERVICES; HOSPITALS,
   GYNECOLOGIC AND OBSTETRIC; and MATERNAL
   HEALTH SERVICES_____ in the subject catalog.

6. _Encyclopedias and dictionaries_____ is b̌roader/narrower
   than _____Women's encyclopedias and dictionaries_____.

7. There is a total of #_3__ SEE ALSO-type cross references ("sa") indicated in
   this excerpt; there is a total of #__5____ SEE cross references.

8. An example of a subject-heading displayed in this excerpt which it's likely you
   will find subdivided geographically in a library's catalog is _____
   WOMEN'S HEALTH SERVICES; or WOMEN'S INSTITUTES_____.

9. For publications about _obstetrical aspects of Women's health services_____,
   you could check the library shelves in the vicinity of the Library of Congress
   Classification _____RG500 - RG501_____.

10. Which one of the following is _not_ an established LCSH subject-heading?
    X   Chinese women's encyclopedias and dictionaries
    _____ Feminism
    _____ Women's health services-- Utilization

11. _Education, Medieval_____ is

    _____ a SEE ALSO cross reference   _____ an established subject-heading
    _____ a SEE cross reference   X a subdivision of a subject-heading

These questions relate to this excerpt from
the Library of Congress Subject Headings(LCSH)

1. This excerpt is from volume #_____ .

2. The combination of capital letters and 3-
4 numbers which sometimes appears refers to

    a book number
    a call number
    a classification
    the location of a specific book-title
     on the library's shelves

3. Someone needing information about _____
the Wonnell family_____
should look for subject cards with the 1st
line subject-heading wording_____
_____
_____

4. Buddhist sects_____
is an established subject-heading.

    TRUE   FALSE

5. If interested in Wood-- Anatomy_____
_____
_____ ,
you should check that exact wording as
well as _____
_____
_____in the subject catalog.

6. Trees_____ is broader/narrower
than _____Wood_____ .

The boxed excerpt:

Wŏnhyo (Sect)
   x Haedong (Sect)
  xx Buddhist sects
 — Sacred books
Wonnell family
  See Warnell family
Wood, Grant, 1892-1942.   American Gothic
  x American Gothic (Painting)
Wood *(Indirect)* *(Properties and testing,*
    TA419-424; Structural botany,
    QK647; Wood supply, SD431-536)
  sa Bark
    Burl
    Excelsior
    Forests and forestry
    Hardwoods
    Laminated wood
    Lumber
    Lye
    Plywood
    Pulpwood
    Ships, Wooden
    Simulated wood
    Timber
    Wood, Compressed
    Wood waste
    Woodwork
    Woody plants
    kinds of woods, e.g. Mahogany, Walnut
  xx Bark
    Building materials
    Forest products
    Forests and forestry
    Fuel trade
    Timber
    Trees
 — Analysis
    See Wood—Chemistry
 — Anatomy
   sa Spiral grain

7. There is a total of #_____ SEE ALSO-type cross references ("sa") indicated in
this excerpt; there is a total of #_____   SEE cross references.

8. An example of a subject-heading displayed in this excerpt which it's likely you
will find subdivided geographically in a library's catalog is _____
_____ .

9. For publications about Structural botanical aspects of wood_____ ,
you could check the library shelves in the vicinity of the Library of Congress
Classification _____ .

10. Which one of the following is not an established LCSH subject-heading?
   American Gothic (Painting)   Wood-- Chemistry
   Wonhyo (Sect)-- Sacred books   Wood, Grant, 1892-1942. American Gothic

11. ___Anatomy_____ is

   a SEE ALSO cross reference   an established subject-heading
   a SEE cross reference   a subdivision of a subject-heading

Course Title, Date / Instructor

LCSH 10 ed. KEY Vol. 2 Page 3491

Practice Using the LCSH / Your Name ___

These questions relate to this excerpt from the Library of Congress Subject Headings(LCSH)

```
Wŏnhyo (Sect)
    x Haedong (Sect)
    xx Buddhist sects
    — Sacred books
Wonnell family
    See Warnell family
Wood, Grant, 1892-1942.  American Gothic
    x American Gothic (Painting)
Wood  (Indirect)  (Properties and testing,
        TA419-424; Structural botany,
        QK647; Wood supply, SD431-536)
    sa Bark
       Burl
       Excelsior
       Forests and forestry
       Hardwoods
       Laminated wood
       Lumber
       Lye
       Plywood
       Pulpwood
       Ships, Wooden
       Simulated wood
       Timber
       Wood, Compressed
       Wood waste
       Woodwork
       Woody plants
       kinds of woods, e.g. Mahogany, Walnut
    xx Bark
       Building materials
       Forest products
       Forests and forestry
       Fuel trade
       Timber
       Trees
    — Analysis
        See Wood—Chemistry
    — Anatomy
        sa Spiral grain
```

1. This excerpt is from volume # 2 .

2. The combination of capital letters and 3-4 numbers which sometimes appears refers to
   - a book number
   - a call number
   - X a classification
   - the location of a specific book-title on the library's shelves

3. Someone needing information about ___ the Wonnell family should look for subject cards with the 1st line subject-heading wording___ WARNELL FAMILY

4. Buddhist sects is an established subject-heading.
   - X TRUE   FALSE

5. If interested in Wood-- Anatomy ___, you should check that exact wording as well as SPIRAL GRAIN ___ in the subject catalog.

6. Trees ___ is broader/narrower X than Wood .

7. There is a total of #18 SEE ALSO-type cross references ("sa") indicated in this excerpt; there is a total of #2 SEE cross references. (See also "kinds of woods, e.g. Mahogany, Walnut" as well)

8. An example of a subject-heading displayed in this excerpt which it's likely you will find subdivided geographically in a library's catalog is ___ WOOD .

9. For publications about Structural botanical aspects of wood , you could check the library shelves in the vicinity of the Library of Congress Classification QK647 .

10. Which one of the following is not an established LCSH subject-heading?
    - X American Gothic (Painting)   Wood-- Chemistry
    - Wonhyo (Sect)-- Sacred books   Wood, Grant, 1892-1942. American Gothic

11. Anatomy ___ is
    - a SEE ALSO cross reference   an established subject-heading
    - a SEE cross reference   X a subdivision of a subject-heading

440

These questions relate to this excerpt from
the Library of Congress Subject Headings(LCSH)

1. This excerpt is from volume #_____.

2. The combination of capital letters and 3-
   4 numbers which sometimes appears refers to

        a book number
        a call number
        a classification
        the location of a specific book-title
        on the library's shelves

3. Someone needing information about _____
         Housing for the aged
   _____
   should look for subject cards with the 1st
   line subject-heading wording_____
   _____
   _____

4. _Management_____
   is an established subject-heading.

        TRUE   FALSE

5. If interested in _____
   _housing management_____
   _____,
   you should check that exact wording as
   well as _____
   _____in the subject catalog.

6. _Forecasting_____   is broader/narrower
   than _Housing forecasting_____.

7. There is a total of #_____ SEE ALSO-type cross references ("sa") indicated in
   this excerpt; there is a total of #_____   SEE cross references.

8. An example of a subject-heading displayed in this excerpt which it's likely you
   will find subdivided geographically in a library's catalog is _____
   _____

9. For publications about _Housing management_____,
   you could check the library shelves in the vicinity of the Library of Congress
   Classification _____.

10. Which one of the following is _not_ an established LCSH subject-heading?
        Housing finance
        Housing management-- Accounting
        Target Projects Program

11. _Accounting_____ is

        a SEE ALSO cross reference   an established subject-heading
        a SEE cross reference   a subdivision of a subject-heading

The excerpt from the LCSH reads:

Housing finance
    See Housing—Finance
        Housing. Rural—Finance
        Public housing—Finance
Housing for government employees
    See subdivision Officials and employees—
        Housing _under names of countries._
        cities. etc.
Housing for physically handicapped
    (Indirect)
        _xx_ Architecture and the physically
            handicapped
        Physically handicapped
Housing for the aged
    See Aged—Dwellings
Housing forecasting _(Indirect)_
    _x_ Forecasting. Housing
    _xx_ Forecasting
Housing management _(Indirect)_ _(TX960)_
    _sa_ Landlord and tenant
    _x_ Housing—Management
    _xx_ Apartment houses
        Housing
        Management
        Real estate management
    — Accounting
        _x_ Housing—Accounting
    — Law and legislation _(Indirect)_
            GEOGRAPHIC SUBDIVISIONS

    — United States
        _sa_ Target Projects Program

These questions relate to this excerpt from
the Library of Congress Subject Headings(LCSH)

1. This excerpt is from volume # ___1___ .

2. The combination of capital letters and 3-
   4 numbers which sometimes appears refers to

      a book number
      a call number
   X a classification
      the location of a specific book-title
      on the library's shelves

3. Someone needing information about _____
        Housing for the aged
   _____
   should look for subject cards with the 1st
   line subject-heading wording_____
   AGED-- DWELLINGS
   _____
   _____

4. __Management_____
   is an established subject-heading.

      X TRUE   FALSE

5. If interested in _____
   __housing management_____
   _____,
   you should check that exact wording as
   well as __LANDLORD AND TENANT_____
   _____
   _____in the subject catalog.

The excerpt (boxed):

Housing finance
   See Housing—Finance
            Housing. Rural—Finance
            Public housing—Finance
Housing for government employees
   See subdivision Officials and employees—
            Housing *under names of countries.
            cities. etc.*
Housing for physically handicapped
            (Indirect)
      xx Architecture and the physically
            handicapped
            Physically handicapped
Housing for the aged
   See Aged—Dwellings
Housing forecasting *(Indirect)*
      x Forecasting. Housing
      xx Forecasting
Housing management *(Indirect) (TX960)*
      sa Landlord and tenant
       x Housing—Management
      xx Apartment houses
            Housing
            Management
            Real estate management
   — Accounting
       x Housing—Accounting
   — Law and legislation *(Indirect)*
            GEOGRAPHIC SUBDIVISIONS
   — United States
            sa Target Projects Program

6. __Forecasting_____   is broader/narrower X
   than __Housing forecasting_____.

7. There is a total of # _2_ SEE ALSO-type cross references ("sa") indicated in
   this excerpt; there is a total of # ___4___ SEE cross references. (or 5 SEE's
   including subdivision OFFICIALS AND EMPLOYEES-- HOUSING under names of countries, etc.)

8. An example of a subject-heading displayed in this excerpt which it's likely you
   will find subdivided geographically in a library's catalog is HOUSING FOR PHYSICALLY
   HANDICAPPED; HOUSING FORECASTING; HOUSING MANAGEMENT; or HOUSING MANAGEMENT-- LAW AND
   LEGISLATION.

9. For publications about Housing management
   you could check the library shelves in the vicinity of the Library of Congress'
   Classification TX960
   _____.

10. Which one of the following is not an established LCSH subject-heading?
       X Housing finance
         Housing management-- Accounting
         Target Projects Program

11.__Accounting_____ is

      a SEE ALSO cross reference   an established subject-heading
      a SEE cross reference   X a subdivision of a subject-heading

These questions relate to this excerpt from
the Library of Congress Subject Headings(LCSH)

1. This excerpt is from volume #_____.

2. The combination of capital letters and 3-
   4 numbers which sometimes appears refers to

   a book number
   a call number
   a classification
   the location of a specific book-title
     on the library's shelves

3. Someone needing information about _____
   Mothers-- Biblical teaching
   should look for subject cards with the 1st
   line subject-heading wording_____
   _____
   _____

4. Married people-- Employment
   is an established subject-heading.

       TRUE   FALSE

5. If interested in_____
   Mother-of-pearl
   _____
   _____,
   you should check that exact wording as
   well as _____

   _____in the subject catalog.

> Mother-of-pearl *(Fisheries, SH377.5;*
>   *Zoology, QL432)*
>   *sa* Pearl button industry
>   Trochus shell fisheries
> Mother tongue
>   *See* Native language
> Motherhood insurance
>   *See* Insurance, Maternity
> Mothers *(Indirect) (Literary extracts,*
>   *PN6071.M7; Social sciences,*
>   *HQ759)*
>   *sa* Adolescent mothers
>   Grandparents
>   Housewives
>   Love, Maternal
>   Maternal age
>   Maternal and infant welfare
>   Maternal deprivation
>   Mother's Day
>   Pregnant women
>   Single parents
>   Stepmothers
>   *xx* Eugenics
>   Family
>   Housewives
>   Parent and child
>   Parents
>   Pregnant women
>   Women
> — Biblical teaching
>   *See* Women in the Bible
> — Employment *(Indirect)*
>   *sa* Children of working mothers
>   *x* Working mothers
>   *xx* Married people—Employment
> — Medical care
>   *See* Maternal health services
> — Mortality
>   *x* Maternal mortality

6. Married people-- Employment   is broader/narrower
   than   Mothers-- Employment   .

7. There is a total of #____ SEE ALSO-type cross references ("sa") indicated in
   this excerpt; there is a total of #_____   SEE cross references.

8. An example of a subject-heading displayed in this excerpt which it's likely you
   will find subdivided geographically in a library's catalog is _____
   _____.

9. For publications about____ social sciences aspects of mothers _____,
   you could check the library shelves in the vicinity of the Library of Congress
   Classification _____.

10. Which one of the following is not an established LCSH subject-heading?
       Grandparents   Mothers-- Medical care
       Insurance, Maternity   Mothers-- Mortality

11. Mortality _____ is

       a SEE ALSO cross reference   an established subject-heading
       a SEE cross reference   a subdivision of a subject-heading

Course Title, Date   KEY Vol.2   Practice Using the LCSH
Instructor   Your Name _____

These questions relate to this excerpt from
the Library of Congress Subject Headings(LCSH)

1. This excerpt is from volume # __2__ .

2. The combination of capital letters and 3-
   4 numbers which sometimes appears refers to

       a book number
       a call number
   X a classification
       the location of a specific book-title
       on the library's shelves

3. Someone needing information about _____
   __Mothers-- Biblical teaching__
   should look for subject cards with the 1st
   line subject-heading wording_____
   __WOMEN IN THE BIBLE__
   _____

4. __Married people-- Employment_____
   is an established subject-heading.

   X TRUE   FALSE

5. If interested in _____
   __Mother-of-pearl__
   _____ ,
   you should check that exact wording as
   well as __PEARL BUTTON INDUSTRY and___
   __TROCHUS SHELL FISHERIES__
   _____in the subject catalog.

6. __Married people-- Employment_____   X
   than __Mothers-- Employment_____ is broader/narrower .

7. There is a total of #_14_ SEE ALSO-type cross references ("sa") indicated in
   this excerpt; there is a total of #__4__ SEE cross references.

8. An example of a subject-heading displayed in this excerpt which it's likely you
   will find subdivided geographically in a library's catalog is _____
   __MOTHERS or MOTHERS-- EMPLOYMENT_____ .

9. For publications about___social sciences aspects of mothers_____ ,
   you could check the library shelves in the vicinity of the Library of Congress
   Classification ___HQ759_____ .

10. Which one of the following is not an established LCSH subject-heading?
        Grandparents   X Mothers-- Medical care
        Insurance, Maternity   Mothers-- Mortality

11. __Mortality_____ is

        a SEE ALSO cross reference   an established subject-heading
        a SEE cross reference   X a subdivision of a subject-heading

---

Mother-of-pearl *(Fisheries, SH377.5;*
*   Zoology, QL432)*
   sa Pearl button industry
     Trochus shell fisheries
Mother tongue
   See Native language
Motherhood insurance
   See Insurance, Maternity
Mothers *(Indirect)* *(Literary extracts,*
*   PN6071.M7; Social sciences,*
*   HQ759)*
   sa Adolescent mothers
     Grandparents
     Housewives
     Love, Maternal
     Maternal age
     Maternal and infant welfare
     Maternal deprivation
     Mother's Day
     Pregnant women
     Single parents
     Stepmothers
   xx Eugenics
     Family
     Housewives
     Parent and child
     Parents
     Pregnant women
     Women
 — Biblical teaching
    See Women in the Bible
 — Employment *(Indirect)*
    sa Children of working mothers
    x Working mothers
    xx Married people—Employment
 — Medical care
    See Maternal health services
 — Mortality
    x Maternal mortality

These questions relate to this excerpt from
the Library of Congress Subject Headings(LCSH)

```
Mother's Day sermons
    x Mother's Day—Sermons
    xx Sermons
Mothers general
    xx Convents and nunneries
        Monasticism and religious orders for
        women
Mothers in art  (N7630)
    sa Mothers—Portraits
    x Mother and child in art
    xx Art
        Women in art
Mothers-in-law
    x Mother-in-law
    xx Family
        Parents-in-law
Mothers in literature
Mothers in poetry
    See Mothers—Poetry
Mothers' pensions  (Indirect)  (HV697-700)
    sa Child welfare
        Family allowances
    x Widows—Pensions
        Widows' pensions
    xx Child welfare
        Maternal and infant welfare
        Pensions
        Widows
Mothproofing  (TS1523)
    xx Insecticides
        Moths
Moths  (Indirect)  (QL541-562)
    sa Ailanthus moth
        Brown-tail moth
        Bud-moth
        Caterpillars
        Cecropia moth
```

1. This excerpt is from volume #_____.

2. The combination of capital letters and 3-
4 numbers which sometimes appears refers to

    a book number
    a call number
    a classification
    the location of a specific book-title
    on the library's shelves

3. Someone needing information about _____
   Mothers in poetry
   should look for subject cards with the 1st
   line subject-heading wording_____
   _____
   _____

4. ___Mothers in art_____
   is an established subject-heading.

       TRUE   FALSE

5. If interested in _____
   Mothers' pensions
   _____,
   you should check that exact wording as
   well as _____
   _____in the subject catalog.

6. ___Moths_____ is broader/narrower
   than ____Mothproofing_____.

7. There is a total of #_____ SEE ALSO-type cross references ("sa") indicated in
   this excerpt; there is a total of #_____   SEE cross references.

8. An example of a subject-heading displayed in this excerpt which it's likely you
   will find subdivided geographically in a library's catalog is _____
   _____.

9. For publications about_____Moths_____,
   you could check the library shelves in the vicinity of the Library of Congress
   Classification _____.

10. Which one of the following is <u>not</u> an established LCSH subject-heading?
    Maternal and infant welfare   Mother's Day sermons
    Mother's Day-- Sermons   Mothers-- Portraits

11. Portraits_____ is
    a SEE ALSO cross reference   an established subject-heading
    a SEE cross reference   a subdivision of a subject-heading

Course Title, Date
Instructor

Practice Using the <u>LCSH</u>
Your Name _____

These questions relate to this excerpt from
the Library of Congress Subject Headings(LCSH)

1. This excerpt is from volume # 2_____ .

2. The combination of capital letters and 3-
   4 numbers which sometimes appears refers to

   _____ a book number
   _____ a call number
   X _____ a classification
   _____ the location of a specific book-title
        on the library's shelves

3. Someone needing information about _____
   _Mothers in poetry_____
   should look for subject cards with the 1st
   line subject-heading wording_____
   MOTHERS-- POETRY_____

   _____

4. __Mothers in art_____
   is an established subject-heading.

   X   TRUE   FALSE

5. If interested in _____
   __Mothers' pensions_____

   _____,
   you should check that exact wording as
   well as _CHILD WELFARE and FAMILY_____
   ALLOWANCES_____
   _____in the subject catalog.

Mother's Day sermons
   x Mother's Day—Sermons
   xx Sermons
Mothers general
   xx Convents and nunneries
      Monasticism and religious orders for
      women
Mothers in art   (N7630)
   sa Mothers—Portraits
   x Mother and child in art
   xx Art
      Women in art
Mothers-in-law
   x Mother-in-law
   xx Family
      Parents-in-law
Mothers in literature
Mothers in poetry
   See Mothers—Poetry
Mothers' pensions   (Indirect)   (HV697-700)
   sa Child welfare
      Family allowances
   x Widows—Pensions
      Widows' pensions
   xx Child welfare
      Maternal and infant welfare
      Pensions
      Widows
Mothproofing   (TS1523)
   xx Insecticides
      Moths
Moths   (Indirect)   (QL541-562)
   sa Ailanthus moth
      Brown-tail moth
      Bud-moth
      Caterpillars
      Cecropia moth

---

6. __Moths_____   X
   than ___Mothproofing_____   is broader/narrower ____.

7. There is a total of # _8__ SEE ALSO-type cross references ("sa") indicated in
   this excerpt; there is a total of # __1__   SEE cross references.

8. An example of a subject-heading displayed in this excerpt which it's likely you
   will find subdivided geographically in a library's catalog is _____
   MOTHERS' PENSIONS or MOTHS_____ .

9. For publications about_____Moths_____,
   you could check the library shelves in the vicinity of the Library of Congress
   Classification ____QL541-QL562_____ .

10. Which one of the following is <u>not</u> an established LCSH subject-heading?
    _____ Maternal and infant welfare   _____ Mother's Day sermons
    X _____ Mother's Day-- Sermons   _____ Mothers-- Portraits

11. _Portraits_____ is

    _____ a SEE ALSO cross reference   _____ an established subject-heading
    _____ a SEE cross reference   X _____ a subdivision of a subject-heading

446

These questions relate to this excerpt from
the Library of Congress Subject Headings(LCSH)

> Press clubs
>   *See* Journalism—Societies, etc.
> Press conferences
>   *sa* Presidents—United States—Press
>   conferences
>   *xx* Journalism
>   Press releases
>   Public relations
>   Publicity
> Press councils *(Indirect)*
>   *x* Councils, Press
>   *xx* Journalism
> Press fits *(TS172)*
>   *x* Fits, Press
>   Force fits
>   Press fitting
>   *xx* Joints (Engineering)
>   Tolerance (Engineering)
> Press fitting
>   *See* Press fits
> Press forming of metals
>   *See* Metal stamping
> Press-gangs
>   *See* Impressment

1. This excerpt is from volume #_____.

2. The combination of capital letters and 3-
   4 numbers which sometimes appears refers to

         a book number
         a call number
         a classification
         the location of a specific book-title
          on the library's shelves

3. Someone needing information about _____
        Press clubs
   _____
   should look for subject cards with the 1st
   line subject-heading wording_____
   _____
   _____

4.   Tolerance (Engineering)_____
   is an established subject-heading.

        TRUE   FALSE

5. If interested in _____
        Press conferences
   _____
   _____,
   you should check that exact wording as
   well as _____
   _____
                      in the subject catalog.

6.   Journalism_____   is broader/narrower
   than _____Press conferences_____.

7. There is a total of #_____ SEE ALSO-type cross references ("sa") indicated in
   this excerpt; there is a total of #_____   SEE cross references.

8. An example of a subject-heading displayed in this excerpt which it's likely you
   will find subdivided geographically in a library's catalog is _____
   _____.

9. For publications about___Press fits_____,
   you could check the library shelves in the vicinity of the Library of Congress
   Classification _____.

10. Which one of the following is <u>not</u> an established LCSH subject-heading?
        Councils, Press   Metal stamping
        Journalism-- Societies, etc.   Public relations

11.   United States_____ is

        a SEE ALSO cross reference   an established subject-heading
        a SEE cross reference   a subdivision of a subject-heading

Course Title, Date
Instructor

LCSH 9th ed.
KEY

Practice Using the <u>LCSH</u>
Your Name _____

These questions relate to this excerpt from
the Library of Congress Subject Headings(LCSH)

1. This excerpt is from volume # __2__ .

2. The combination of capital letters and 3-
   4 numbers which sometimes appears refers to

   ___ a book number
   ___ a call number
   X a classification
   ___ the location of a specific book-title
       on the library's shelves

3. Someone needing information about _____
   __Press clubs__
   should look for subject cards with the 1st
   line subject-heading wording_____
   JOURNALISM-- SOCIETIES, etc._____
   _____

4. ___Tolerance (Engineering)_____
   is an established subject-heading.

   X   TRUE   FALSE

5. If interested in _____
   __Press conferences_____

   _____ ,
   you should check that exact wording as
   well as _____
   PRESIDENTS-- UNITED STATES-- PRESS CONFERENCES
   _____in the subject catalog.

6. ___Journalism_____   X
   than ____Press conferences____   is broader/narrower
   _____.

7. There is a total of #_1__ SEE ALSO-type cross references ("sa") indicated in
   this excerpt; there is a total of #___4___ SEE cross references.

8. An example of a subject-heading displayed in this excerpt which it's likely you
   will find subdivided geographically in a library's catalog is _____
   PRESS COUNCILS
   _____.

9. For publications about __Press fits_____,
   you could check the library shelves in the vicinity of the Library of Congress
   Classification __TS172__
   _____.

10. Which one of the following is <u>not</u> an established LCSH subject-heading?
    X Councils, Press   Metal stamping
      Journalism-- Societies, etc.   Public relations

11. ___United States_____ is

    ___ a SEE ALSO cross reference   ___ an established subject-heading
    ___ a SEE cross reference   X   a subdivision of a subject-heading

---

Press clubs
   See Journalism—Societies, etc.
Press conferences
   sa Presidents—United States—Press
          conferences
   xx Journalism
        Press releases
        Public relations
        Publicity
Press councils *(Indirect)*
   x Councils, Press
   xx Journalism
Press fits *(TS172)*
   x Fits, Press
       Force fits
       Press fitting
   xx Joints (Engineering)
        Tolerance (Engineering)
Press fitting
   See Press fits
Press forming of metals
   See Metal stamping
Press-gangs
   See Impressment

These questions relate to this excerpt from
the Library of Congress Subject Headings(LCSH)

1. This excerpt is from volume #_____.

2. The combination of capital letters and 3-
   4 numbers which sometimes appears refers to

      a book number
      a call number
      a classification
      the location of a specific book-title
      on the library's shelves

3. Someone needing information about _____
   <u>Sink holes</u>
   should look for subject cards with the 1st
   line subject-heading wording_____
   _____
   _____

4. <u>Forest reserves-- Bulgaria</u>
   is an established subject-heading.

    TRUE   FALSE

5. If interested in _____
   <u>Singularities (Mathematics)</u>
   _____,
   you should check that exact wording as
   well as _____
   _____in the subject catalog.

6. <u>Erosion</u>   is broader/narrower
   than <u>Sinkholes</u>   .

7. There is a total of #____ SEE ALSO-type cross references ("sa") indicated in
   this excerpt; there is a total of #_____   SEE cross references.

8. An example of a subject-heading displayed in this excerpt which it's likely you
   will find subdivided geographically in a library's catalog is _____
   _____.

9. For publications about <u>historical aspects of Sinhalese poetry</u> ,
   you could check the library shelves in the vicinity of the Library of Congress
   Classification _____.

10. Which one of the following is <u>not</u> an established LCSH subject-heading?
      Sinhalese literature   Sinyard family
      Sinhalese literature-- To 1500   Succession, Singular

11. <u>20th century</u>   is

      a SEE ALSO cross reference   an established subject-heading
      a SEE cross reference   a subdivision of a subject-heading

---

Singular succession *(Indirect)*
   sa Assignments
      Transfer (Law)
   x Succession, Singular
   xx Acquisition of property
Singularities (Mathematics)
   sa Catastrophes (Mathematics)
   xx Geometry, Algebraic
Singultus
   See Hiccups
Sinhalese *(DS489.2)*
   x Cingalese
      Singhalese
Sinhalese drama (Comedy)
Sinhalese fiction *(PK2850-2888)*
Sinhalese language *(PK2801-2845)*
   xx Indo-Aryan languages, Modern
Sinhalese literature *(PK2850-2888)*
  —To 1500
Sinhalese philology
Sinhalese poetry *(Collections, PK2856;*
         History, PK2852)
  — 20th century
Sinhalese prose literature *(Indirect)*
Siniard family
   See Sinyard family
Sinite Kamuni Forest Park, Bulgaria
    (SB485.B)
   x Lesopark Sinite kamüni
   xx Forest reserves—Bulgaria
      National parks and reserves—Bulgaria
Sink holes
   See Sinkholes
Sinkholes *(Indirect)*
   x Sink holes
      Sinks (Geology)
   xx Erosion
      Karst

Course Title, Date   LCSH 9th ed.   Practice Using the <u>LCSH</u>

Instructor   KEY   Your Name_____

                            Vol.2

These questions relate to this excerpt from
the Library of Congress Subject Headings(LCSH)

1. This excerpt is from volume # __2__ .

2. The combination of capital letters and 3-
   4 numbers which sometimes appears refers to

       a book number
       a call number
    X   a classification
       the location of a specific book-title
       on the library's shelves

3. Someone needing information about _____
   Sink holes_____
   should look for subject cards with the 1st
   line subject-heading wording_____
   SINKHOLES_____
   _____

4.   Forest reserves-- Bulgaria_____
   is an established subject-heading.

    X TRUE   FALSE

5. If interested in _____
   Singularities (Mathematics)_____
   _____ ,
   you should check that exact wording as
   well as <u>CATASTROPHES (MATHEMATICS)</u>_____
   _____in the subject catalog.

6. __Erosion_____ is broader/<u>narrower</u>
   than __Sinkholes_____ .

7. There is a total of #_3__ SEE ALSO-type cross references ("sa") indicated in
   this excerpt; there is a total of #__3___ SEE cross references.

8. An example of a subject-heading displayed in this excerpt which it's likely you
   will find subdivided geographically in a library's catalog is _____
   __SINGULAR SUCCESSION or SINKHOLES or SINHALESE PROSE LITERATURE_____ .

9. For publications about __historical aspects of Sinhalese poetry_____ ,
   you could check the library shelves in the vicinity of the Library of Congress
   Classification _PK2852_____ .

10. Which one of the following is <u>not</u> an established LCSH subject-heading?
    Sinhalese literature   Sinyard family
    Sinhalese literature-- To 1500   X Succession, Singular

11. __20th century_____ is

       a SEE ALSO cross reference   an established subject-heading
       a SEE cross reference   X a subdivision of a subject-heading

---

Singular succession   *(Indirect)*
   sa Assignments
      Transfer (Law)
   x Succession, Singular
   xx Acquisition of property
Singularities (Mathematics)
   sa Catastrophes (Mathematics)
   xx Geometry, Algebraic
Singultus
   See Hiccups
Sinhalese   *(DS489.2)*
   x Cingalese
     Singhalese
Sinhalese drama (Comedy)
Sinhalese fiction   *(PK2850-2888)*
Sinhalese language   *(PK2801-2845)*
   xx Indo-Aryan languages, Modern
Sinhalese literature   *(PK2850-2888)*
   —To 1500
Sinhalese philology
Sinhalese poetry   *(Collections, PK2856;*
       History, PK2852)
   —20th century
Sinhalese prose literature   *(Indirect)*
Siniard family
   See Sinyard family
Sinite Kamuni Forest Park, Bulgaria
     (SB485.B)
   x Lesopark Sinite kamŭni
   xx Forest reserves—Bulgaria
     National parks and reserves—Bulgaria
Sink holes
   See Sinkholes
Sinkholes   *(Indirect)*
   x Sink holes
     Sinks (Geology)
   xx Erosion
     Karst

These questions relate to this excerpt from
the Library of Congress Subject Headings(LCSH)

1. This excerpt is from volume #_____.

2. The combination of capital letters and 3-
   4 numbers which sometimes appears refers to

       a book number
       a call number
       a classification
       the location of a specific book-title
        on the library's shelves

3. Someone needing information about _____
    Reproductions of sailing ships   _____
   should look for subject cards with the 1st
   line subject-heading wording_____

   _____

4. __Herpetology_____
   is an established subject-heading.

       TRUE   FALSE

5. If interested in _____
    Reptiles _____

   _____,
   you should check that exact wording as
   well as _____

   _____
   _____in the subject catalog.

| Reproduction of works of art |
| *See* Art—Reproduction |
| Arts—Reproduction |
| Reproduction paper *(TS1167)* |
| *x* Duplicating paper |
| *xx* Copying processes |
| Paper |
| Reproduction processes |
| *See* Copying processes |
| Reproductions of boats |
| *See* Boats and boating—Reproductions |
| Reproductions of sailing ships |
| *See* Sailing ships—Reproductions |
| Reproductive behavior |
| *See* Sexual behavior in animals |
| Reproductive cells |
| *See* Germ cells |
| Reproductive organs |
| *See* Generative organs |
| Reprographic art |
| *See* Copy art |
| Reprography |
| *See* Copying processes |
| Reptile cages |
| *x* Cages, Reptile |
| *xx* Animal housing |
| Pets—Housing |
| Reptile populations *(Indirect)* |
| *xx* Animal populations |
| Reptiles *(Indirect)* *(QL641-669; Folk-lore, GR740)* |
| *sa* Crocodilia |
| Rhynchocephalia |
| Squamata |
| *xx* Herpetology |
| Vertebrates |
| —Anatomy *(QL669)* |
| *sa* Salt gland |
| Scales (Reptiles) |
| *subdivision* Reptiles *under* Digestive organs |

6. __Pets-- Housing_____   is broader/narrower
   than ___Reptile cages_____.

7. There is a total of #_____ SEE ALSO-type cross references ("sa") indicated in
   this excerpt; there is a total of #_____   SEE cross references.

8. An example of a subject-heading displayed in this excerpt which it's likely you
   will find subdivided geographically in a library's catalog is _____

   _____.

9. For publications about_____folk-lore aspects of reptiles_____,
   you could check the library shelves in the vicinity of the Library of Congress
   Classification _____.

10. Which one of the following is not an established LCSH subject-heading?
    Boats and boating-- Reproductions   Paper
    Duplicating paper   Reptile populations

11. __Anatomy_____ is

       a SEE ALSO cross reference   an established subject-heading
       a SEE cross reference   a subdivision of a subject-heading

Course Title, Date   Practice Using the <u>LCSH</u>
Instructor   Your Name _____

These questions relate to this excerpt from
the Library of Congress Subject Headings(LCSH)

1. This excerpt is from volume # __2__ .

2. The combination of capital letters and 3-
   4 numbers which sometimes appears refers to

        a book number
        a call number
   X   a classification
        the location of a specific book-title
        on the library's shelves

3. Someone needing information about _____
   <u>Reproductions of sailing ships</u>
   should look for subject cards with the 1st
   line subject-heading wording _____
   <u>SAILING SHIPS-- REPRODUCTIONS</u>
   _____

4. <u>Herpetology</u>
   is an established subject-heading.

   X   TRUE   FALSE

5. If interested in _____
   <u>Reptiles</u>
   _____ ,
   you should check that exact wording as
   well as <u>CROCODILIA; RHYNCHOCEPHALIA; and</u>
   <u>SQUAMATA</u>
   _____ in the subject catalog.

Reproduction of works of art
    See Art—Reproduction
    Arts—Reproduction
Reproduction paper *(TS1167)*
    x Duplicating paper
    xx Copying processes
    Paper
Reproduction processes
    See Copying processes
Reproductions of boats
    See Boats and boating—Reproductions
Reproductions of sailing ships
    See Sailing ships—Reproductions
Reproductive behavior
    See Sexual behavior in animals
Reproductive cells
    See Germ cells
Reproductive organs
    See Generative organs
Reprographic art
    See Copy art
Reprography
    See Copying processes
Reptile cages
    x Cages, Reptile
    xx Animal housing
    Pets—Housing
Reptile populations *(Indirect)*
    xx Animal populations
Reptiles *(Indirect) (QL641-669; Folk-lore,*
    GR740)
    sa Crocodilia
    Rhynchocephalia
    Squamata
    xx Herpetology
    Vertebrates
    —Anatomy *(QL669)*
    sa Salt gland
    Scales (Reptiles)
    subdivision Reptiles *under* Digestive
    organs

6. <u>Pets-- Housing</u> _____   X
   _____   is broader/narrower
   than ___<u>Reptile cages</u>_____ .

7. There is a total of # _5_ SEE ALSO-type cross references ("sa") indicated in
   this excerpt; there is a total of #___10____ SEE cross references.

8. An example of a subject-heading displayed in this excerpt which it's likely you
   will find subdivided geographically in a library's catalog is _____
   <u>REPTILE POPULATIONS or REPTILES</u>
   _____ .

9. For publications about_____<u>folk-lore aspects of reptiles</u>_____ ,
   you could check the library shelves in the vicinity of the Library of Congress
   Classification __<u>GR740</u>
   _____ .

10. Which one of the following is <u>not</u> an established LCSH subject-heading?
        <u>Boats and boating-- Reproductions</u>   Paper
    X   <u>Duplicating paper</u>   Reptile populations

11. <u>Anatomy</u>
    _____ is

        a SEE ALSO cross reference   an established subject-heading
        a SEE cross reference   X   a subdivision of a subject-heading

These questions relate to this excerpt from
the Library of Congress Subject Headings(LCSH)

> **Single people** *(Indirect)*
>   *sa* Bachelors
>   Church work with single people
>   Divorcees
>   Single men
>   Single women
>   Social work with single people
>   Unmarried couples
>   *x* People, Single
>   People, Unmarried
>   Persons, Single
>   Persons, Unmarried
>   Single persons
>   Unmarried people
>   Unmarried persons
>   *xx* Marital status
>   — Sexual behavior *(HQ800)*
>   *xx* Sex
>   — Taxation *(Indirect)*
>   *xx* Income tax—Law
> **Single persons**
>   *See* Single people
> **Single point moorings (Oil terminals)**
>   *See* Petroleum shipping terminals
> **Single-rail railroads**
>   *See* Monorail railroads
> **Single-sideband radio**
>   *See* Radio, Single-sideband
> **Single-stick** *(GV1141)*
>   *xx* Fencing
>   Staffs (Sticks, canes, etc.)
>   Stick fighting

1. This excerpt is from volume #_____ .

2. The combination of capital letters and 3-
   4 numbers which sometimes appears refers to

       a book number
       a call number
       a classification
       the location of a specific book-title
       on the library's shelves

3. Someone needing information about _____
   Single-rail railroads
   should look for subject cards with the 1st
   line subject-heading wording_____
   _____
   _____

4. Stick fighting_____
   is an established subject-heading.

       TRUE   FALSE

5. If interested in Single people_____
   _____
   _____ ,
   you should check that exact wording as
   well as _____
   _____in the subject catalog.

6. Income tax-- Law_____ is broader/narrower
   than _Single people-- Taxation_____ .

7. There is a total of #_____ SEE ALSO-type cross references ("sa") indicated in
   this excerpt; there is a total of #_____ SEE cross references.

8. An example of a subject-heading displayed in this excerpt which it's likely you
   will find subdivided geographically in a library's catalog is _____
   _____ .

9. For publications about sexual behavior of single people_____ ,
   you could check the library shelves in the vicinity of the Library of Congress
   Classification _____ .

10. Which one of the following is not an established LCSH subject-heading?
        Fencing
        Income tax-- Law
        Unmarried people

11. Sexual behavior_____ is

        a SEE ALSO cross reference   an established subject-heading
        a SEE cross reference   a subdivision of a subject-heading

Course Title, Date
Instructor

LCSH 9th ed.
KEY vol.2

Practice Using the LCSH
Your Name_____

These questions relate to this excerpt from
the Library of Congress Subject Headings(LCSH)

1. This excerpt is from volume #___2___.

2. The combination of capital letters and 3-
   4 numbers which sometimes appears refers to

       a book number
       a call number
    X a classification
       the location of a specific book-title
       on the library's shelves

3. Someone needing information about _____
   Single-rail railroads
   should look for subject cards with the 1st
   line subject-heading wording_____
       MONORAIL RAILROADS
   _____

4. Stick fighting
   is an established subject-heading.

    X TRUE   FALSE

5. If interested in Single people _____
   _____
   _____,
   you should check that exact wording as
   well as BACHELORS; CHURCH WORK WITH SINGLE PEOPLE; DIVORCEES; SINGLE MEN; SINGLE
   WOMEN; SOCIAL WORK WITH SINGLE PEOPLE; and UNMARRIED
   COUPLES_____ in the subject catalog.

The excerpt (card) reads:

Single people (Indirect)
    sa Bachelors
       Church work with single people
       Divorcees
       Single men
       Single women
       Social work with single people
       Unmarried couples
    x People, Single
       People, Unmarried
       Persons, Single
       Persons, Unmarried
       Single persons
       Unmarried people
       Unmarried persons
    xx Marital status
   — Sexual behavior (HQ800)
       xx Sex
   — Taxation (Indirect)
       xx Income tax—Law
Single persons
    See Single people
Single point moorings (Oil terminals)
    See Petroleum shipping terminals
Single-rail railroads
    See Monorail railroads
Single-sideband radio
    See Radio, Single-sideband
Single-stick (GV1141)
    xx Fencing
       Staffs (Sticks, canes, etc.)
       Stick fighting

6. Income tax-- Law _____ X   is broader/narrower
   than __Single people-- Taxation_____.

7. There is a total of #_7__ SEE ALSO-type cross references ("sa") indicated in
   this excerpt; there is a total of #___4___ SEE cross references.

8. An example of a subject-heading displayed in this excerpt which it's likely you
   will find subdivided geographically in a library's catalog is _____
       SINGLE PEOPLE or SINGLE PEOPLE-- TAXATION_____.

9. For publications about sexual behavior of single people _____,
   you could check the library shelves in the vicinity of the Library of Congress
   Classification _HQ800_____.

10. Which one of the following is not an established LCSH subject-heading?
         Fencing
         Income tax-- Law
     X   Unmarried people

11. Sexual behavior _____ is

        a SEE ALSO cross reference   an established subject-heading
        a SEE cross reference   X a subdivision of a subject-heading

MULTIPLE-SUBJECT TOPICS WITH DEVELOPED
LITERATURE SEARCHES

The following topics are planned to span several assignments, and thus steps, in the general library research process. Each begins with Assignment 2, Catalogs and Related Tools (Mostly Books), questions 3 and 4. The student should continue with the same topic in Assignment 4, Locating Periodical Information & Articles (Mostly Serials), question 1. At least one relevant periodical article has been identified using Applied Science & Technology Index, Humanities Index, or Social Sciences Index. The topics (and Assignments 3 and 4) are constructed so that they could be extended beyond the semi-specialized level to Art Index, Business Periodicals Index, Education Index, etc. An upper division course based on this experience could "take off" from Arts & Humanities Citation Index, Science Citation Index, or Social Sciences Citation Index, and continue through the level of abstracting tools.

The topics are usually interdisciplinary and provide geographical and time or period scope aspects. They can also be utilized for topic ideas for the final question on the course Inventory and for teaching use of the LCSH. Each is posed in the following form:

> For a paper for a 20th Century American history, psychology, or sociology course, you need publications which provide information about _____.

Subject-headings in use in the LCSH and periodical indexes are expressed in ALL CAPS. LC classification is included if indicated by LCSH. Throughout, references to "Women studies" can also be considered as Women's studies and/or Men's studies.

1. For a paper for a public health, sociology, or other course, you need publications which provide information about care of people with chronic diseases in the United States, including information about the hospice movement. Note: Assignment 2, page 2, question 3's "key" lists useful subject headings derived from the LCSH 9th edition. The following also includes subject headings from the 10th edition.

LCSH	LC Class
HOSPICE CARE	R726.8
HOSPICES (TERMINAL CARE)	R726.8
CHRONIC DISEASES	RA642.2-.5; BR156; RA644.5-645 Public health
TERMINAL CARE FACILITIES	
TERMINAL CARE	

TERMINAL CARE--LAW AND LEGISLATION
TERMINAL CARE--RELIGIOUS ASPECTS
TERMINAL CARE--SOCIAL ASPECTS
TERMINALLY ILL
TERMINALLY ILL CHILDREN
SOCIAL WORK WITH THE TERMINALLY ILL
VOLUNTEER WORKERS IN TERMINAL
   CARE
HOSPITALS
DEATH--PSYCHOLOGICAL ASPECTS   BF789.D4
LIFE AND DEATH, POWER OVER   RJ1469
RIGHT TO DIE
YOUTH AND DEATH

Social Sciences Index April 1982-March 1983 (Volume 9):

    1150 TERMINAL CARE FACILITIES
          The American way of hospice. D. H. Smith and J. A. Granbois.
          Hastings Center Report 12:8-10 Apr '82

    1059 Hastings Center Report

2.   ... U.S. history, Women studies, or other course ... information about the
    history of midwifery, focusing on its status in our state's health system.
    ["... the history of midwifery in Appalachia" is an alternative.]

LCSH   LC Class

OBSTETRICS   RG
MIDWIVES   RG950
MIDWIVES--SUPPLY AND DEMAND
MEDICAL PERSONNEL
CHILDBIRTH AT HOME
OBSTETRICAL NURSING   RG951, RG741
NATURAL CHILDBIRTH   RG661

Social Sciences Index April 1985-March 1986 (Volume 12):

    980 MIDWIVES
         The nature and style of practice of immigrant midwives in early
         twentieth century Massachusetts. E. R. Declercq
         J Soc Hist 19:113-29 Fall '85

    384 Declercq, Eugene
         Journal of Social History

Social Sciences Index April 1983-March 1984 (Volume 10):

    791 MIDWIFERY
         Midwives in transition: the structure of a clinical review.
         B. K. Rothman. Social Prob 30:262-71 F '83
   1045 Rothman, Barbara Katch
         Social Problems

3. ... music, humanities, or other course ... information about rock music and musicians in contemporary U.S.A. and England including the part they play in national life.

LCSH

ROCK MUSIC
ROCK MUSIC--U.S.
REGGAE MUSIC
ROCK GROUPS
DRUM--STUDIES AND EXERCISES (ROCK)
PIANO--STUDIES AND EXERCISES (ROCK)
AFRO-AMERICAN MUSIC
MUSIC, POPULAR (SONGS, ETC.)
MUSIC--JAMAICA
ROCK MUSICIANS
ROCK MUSICIANS--ENGLAND--BIOGRAPHY
ROCK AND ROLL DANCING
RADIO STATIONS--SOCIAL ASPECTS--U.S.
U.S.--POPULAR CULTURE

Social Sciences Index April 1982-March 1983 (Volume 9):

    986 ROCK MUSIC--PUBLIC OPINION
         Popular music: resistance to new wave. J. Lull. bibl J Com 32:
         121-31 Wint '82

    687 Lull, James
         Journal of Communication

4. ... European history, public health, or sociology course ... information about the social consequences of the "Black Death" (plague) in Europe, especially Medieval Britain. ["... the 'Black Death' (plague) and its influence on the history of Spain" is an upper division course alternative.]

LCSH	LC Class
BLACK DEATH	RC171-9
EPIDEMICS	RA649-53
PLAGUE	RC171-9
GREAT BRITAIN--HISTORY--MEDIEVAL PERIOD, 1066-1485	
COMMUNICABLE DISEASES	
PLAGUE IN LITERATURE	
BLACK DEATH--GREAT BRITAIN	
PLAGUE--GREAT BRITAIN	
MEDICINE, MEDIEVAL	R128
MANORS	
MANORS--ENGLAND	
ANIMALS AS CARRIERS OF DISEASE	
RODENTS AS CARRIERS OF DISEASE	
HOSPITALS, MEDIEVAL	RA964

The Bibliographic Instruction-Course Handbook

Humanities Index April 1981-March 1982 (Volume 8):

547   PLAGUE
      Black death and western European eschatological mentalities.
      R. E. Lerner. il Am Hist R 86:533-52 Je '81

398   Lerner, Robert E
      American Historical Review

Humanities Index April 1981-March 1982 (Volume 8):

547   PLAGUE
      Plague, melancholy and the devil; tr by J Ferguson. F. Azouvi.
      Diogenes no 108:112-30 Wint '79

52   Azouvi, Francois
      Diogenes

5. ... psychology, public health, or Women studies ... "painless childbirth,"
    especially in U.S. history--reasons for progress (or lack of progress) in
    its development, status of research. [Note: Students may equate painless
    and natural childbirth.]

Painless labor (Obstet); Labor, Painless (Obstet), See:
NATURAL CHILDBIRTH   RG661
LABOR (OBSTETRICS)   RG651-791
HYPNOTISM IN OBSTETRICS
ANESTHESIA IN OBSTETRICS   RG732
LABOR, COMPLICATED   RG701-721
Psychoprophylactic childbirth, See:
OBSTETRICAL NURSING   RG951
OBSTETRICAL PHARMACOLOGY   RG125
MATERNAL HEALTH SERVICES   RG940-991
OBSTETRICS, HOMEOPATHIC   RX476
WOMEN'S HEALTH SERVICES   RG12-16 gynecology;
                                        obstetrics RG500-501
CHILDBIRTH DELIVERY (OBSTETRICS)

Social Sciences Index April 1982-March 1983 (Volume 9):

184   CHILDBIRTH--PSYCHOLOGICAL ASPECTS
      Anxiety associated with birth trauma. E. V. Gemmette.
      Psychol Rept 40:942 Je pt 1 '82

445   Gemmette, Elizabeth V
      Psychological Reports

Social Sciences Index April 1983-March 1984 (Volume 10)

196   CHILDBIRTH--STUDY AND TEACHING
      Self-efficacy expectancies, outcome expectancies, and the persistence
      of pain control in childbirth. M. M. Manning and T. L. Wright.

458

bibl   J Personal & Soc Psychol 45: 421-431 Ag '83

746   Manning, Martha M. and Wright, Thomas L
Journal of Personality and Social Psychology

6. ... education, psychology, or sociology course, information about the "only
child" in today's world, especially in, but not restricted to, the U.S.A.

FAMILY   GT2420 manners and customs aspects
                                                of family; GNH80 primitive aspect;
                                                HQ sociological aspects

FAMILY--RESEARCH
BIRTH ORDER
BROTHERS AND SISTERS
SINGLE PARENT FAMILY
CHILDREN, FIRST-BORN   HQ754.1F5
YOUNGEST CHILD
PRIMOGENITURE
REDEMPTION OF THE FIRST BORN   BM720.R

Social Sciences Index April 1981-March 1982 (Volume 8):

782   ONLY CHILD
Only isn't lonely (or spoiled or selfish). M. Pines. il
Psychol Today 15:15-16+ Mr '81

825   Pines, Maya
Psychology Today

7. ... biology, economics, or geography course, information about the ecology
of the palm oasis.

PALMS   QK495.P17
OASES   GB611-618
SUCCULENT PLANTS
SAND DUNE FAUNA
DESERT KANGAROO RAT
DESERT ECOLOGY   QH541.5.D4
DESERT BIOLOGY
DESERT FAUNA
DESERT FLORA

Social Sciences Index April 1985-March 1986 (Volume 12):

398   DESERT ECOLOGY
Sahara and Sahel [review article] A. T. Grove.
Geogr J 247-8 Jl '85

634   Grove, A. T. (This author uses her/his initials.)
Geographical Journal

8. ... Women studies, nutrition, or psychology course, information about nutritionally-induced diseases--Why now?

NUTRITIONALLY INDUCED DISEASES   RC622
CARBOHYDRATES, REFINED
DEFICIENCY DISEASES   RC620-632
DEFICIENCY DISEASES--DIAGNOSIS
DIET THERAPY
DISEASES--CAUSES AND THEORIES OF
    CAUSATION
NUTRITION DISORDERS
NUTRITION DISORDERS IN CHILDREN
ANOREXIA IN CHILDREN   RJ399.N8
OBESITY IN CHILDREN

Social Sciences Index April 1985-March 1986 (Volume 12):

    307   DEFICIENCY DISEASES
           Women's preponderance in possession cults: the calcium-deficiency hypothesis extended. A. B. Kehoe & D. H. Giletti. bibl Am Anthrop 82: 549-61 S '81; Disc 85:412-17 Je '83

    649   Kehoe, Alice B and Giletti, Dodhy H
           American Anthropology

9. ... English literature, English history, or humanities course, information about Shakespeare's "problem" with women, as seen in his life and works.

SHAKESPEARE, WILLIAM, 1564-1616   PR2750-3112
    --ALLEGORY AND SYMBOLISM
    --KNOWLEDGE
    --RELATIONS WITH WOMEN
    --RADIO AND TV PLAYS
    --CHARACTERS--WOMEN   PR2991
    --POLITICAL AND SOCIAL VIEWS   PR3017,3024
    --PHILOSOPHY
    --BIOGRAPHY--MARRIAGE
DRAMA--17th CENTURY
WOMEN IN LITERATURE   PN 56W6
SEX IN LITERATURE   PN56.S5; PR149.S5
                        English literature

AUTHORS AND THE THEATER
THEATER--CENSORSHIP   PN2042-5
DRAMA--TECHNIQUE   PN1660-1692
TELEVISION PLAYS
ENGLISH DRAMA   Collections PR1241-73
DRAMA--15th and 16th CENTURIES   PN1831

Humanities Index April 1981-March 1982 (Volume 8):

    651   SHAKESPEARE, WILLIAM--POLITICAL AND SOCIAL VIEWS
           Marriage and mercifixion in The Merchant of Venice: the casket scene

revisited. H. Berger, jr.
Shakespeare Q 32: 155-62 Summ '81

64 Berger, Harry, Jr.
Shakespeare Quarterly

10. ... philosophy, health sciences, or ethics course, information about the role of the modern physician--healer or businessman?; the "Hippocratic imperative" in the nuclear age. [It is well to include the following statement with the topic: The Hippocratic Oath is taken by most physicians as they begin their professional careers; it dates back to ancient times and relates to the healer's responsibility and integrity.]

MEDICAL ETHICS	R724-5
PHYSICIANS--DISCIPLINE	
PHYSICIANS--MALPRACTICE	
CONFIDENTIAL COMMUNICATIONS-- PHYSICIANS	
PHYSICIAN AND PATIENT	R727.3
WOMEN PHYSICIANS	
ADVERTISING--MEDICINE	
EUTHANASIA	
HUMAN EXPERIMENTATION IN MEDICINE	
INFORMED CONSENT (MEDICAL LAW)	

Humanities Index April 1984-March 1985 (Volume 7):

684-5 PHYSICIAN AND PATIENT
When a doctor hates a patient; case history, literary histories.
R. E. Peschel & E. R. Peschel.
Michigan Q Rev 23: 402-10 Summ '84

674 Peschel, Richard E & Peschel, Enid Rhodes
Michigan Quarterly Review

11. ... biology, Women studies, or sociology course, information about sexually transmissible diseases--laypeople's current concerns. [Alternatives might be pre-20th Century or pre-World War I concerns and insights. Note: Students may equate sexually transmissible diseases and AIDS.]

VENEREAL DISEASES	RC200-203
GONORRHEA	
GRANULOMA VENEREUM	
HYGIENE, SEXUAL	
LYMPHOGRANULOMA VENEREUM	
SPERMATORRHEA	
SYCOSIS (HOMEOPATHY)	
SYPHYLLIS	RC201
SEX INSTRUCTION	
CONDOMS	
ACQUIRED IMMUNE DEFICIENCY SYNDROME	

Social Sciences Index April 1985-March 1986 (Volume 12):

    1602 VENEREAL DISEASES--PREVENTION [Sexually transmitted diseases, See...]
           Progress toward the 1990 objectives for sexually transmitted diseases: good news and bad. W. C. Parra and W. Cates, Jr. Public Health Rep 100:261-9 My/Je '85.

    1108 Parra, William C. and Cates, Willard, Jr.
          Public Health Reports.

12. ... sociology, psychology, or Women studies course, information about domestic violence in the current decade, focusing on females and the U.S.A. [Alternative: focusing on males.]

FAMILY VIOLENCE	Psychiatry RC569.5.F3; Sociology HQ809-809.3
CONJUGAL VIOLENCE	
CHILD ABUSE	
CHILD ABUSE--LAW AND LEGISLATION	
CHILD ABUSE--SERVICES	HV701-803
HUSBAND AND WIFE	
BATTERED CHILD SYNDROME	
WIFE ABUSE	HV6626
ABUSED WIVES	
ABUSED PARENTS	
WOMEN--CRIMES AGAINST	

Social Sciences Index April 1984-March 1985 (Volume 7):

    1277-8 WIFE ABUSE

          Aggression in battered and non-battered women as reflected in the hand test. D. A. Dalton & J. E. Kanter. bibl Psychol Rep 53 pt 1:703-9 D '83

    291 Dalton, Debra A. and Kanter, James E
         Psychological Reports

13. ... political science, U.S. history, or other course, information about "Watergate," official secrets and involvement of the press.

WATERGATE AFFAIR, 1972-1974	E860
WATERGATE TRIAL, WASHINGTON, D.C. 1973	KF224.W
OFFICIAL SECRETS	
DEFENSE INFORMATION, CLASSIFIED	
EXECUTIVE PRIVILEGE (GOVERNMENT INFORMATION)	
SECURITY CLASSIFICATION (GOVERNMENT DOCUMENTS)	

GOVERNMENT AND THE PRESS
EXECUTIVE POWER
PRESS AND POLITICS
CABINET OFFICERS   U.S.A.: JK610-616
REPUBLICAN PARTY

Social Sciences Index April 1985-March 1986 (Volume 12):

   1634   WATERGATE CASE--PUBLIC OPINION
          Selective exposure: voter information preferences and the Watergate
          affair. P. D. Sweeney and K. L. Gruber. bibl J Pers Soc Psychol
          46:1208-21 Je '84

   1489   Sweeney, Paul D. and Gruber, Kathy L.
          Journal of Personality and Social Psychology

                OTHER COURSE/TOPIC POSSIBILITIES INCLUDE

Courses   Topics

Development studies,   Establishing a commercial jojoba (an oilseed
   Business.   plant) plantation

Communications,   The Freedom of Information Act--its history,
   Legal studies.   use and non-use in the lives of reporters and
                                 citizens. (The Freedom of Information Act is
                                 a law enacted by the U.S. federal government
                                 originally in 1966.)

Education, Legal studies,   Blacklisting and harassment of, retaliation and
   Ethnic studies, Women   reprisal against private citizens who have
   studies.   attempted to bring charges under Title VII of
                                 the Civil Rights Act.

U.S. history, Ethnic studies.   Policy and provision for schooling in relocation
                                 camps for Japanese and Japanese-American
                                 children during World War II.

History, Sociology,   Slavery throughout the world today [focusing,
   Women studies.   for example, on Africa.]

History.   Japanese policy and provision for and treatment
                                 of prisoners taken during World War II.

Communications,   Control of communication as political power
   Political science.   [Alternative: Control of mass media....]

Business, Psychology,   Psychological issues in administration. [Alter-
   Management.   native: ... in organizational administration.]

Legal studies, Education,   A survey of sexual harassment of male college
   Women studies, Sociology.   and university students [or employees] in the

Courses	Topics
	U.S.A. during the past twenty-five years. [Alternative: female....]
Communications.	Do the mass media communicate the activity and beliefs of the Ku Klux Klan fairly?
U.S. history, Women studies.	Women in the military during World War II. [Alternative for upper division course: during World War I; alternative: women in U.S.A. military.]
Sociology, Women studies, Ethnic studies, Legal studies.	Should prostitution be deregularized? (So that it becomes a person's occupational choice.) [An alternate word might be "decriminalized."]
Sociology, Women studies, Ethnic studies.	Egalitarianism in middle (or working) class families.
Sociology, Women studies, Ethnic studies.	Career aspirations of girls and boys of different social classes. [ages, races, religious groups] Validity and use of the Scholastic Aptitude Test ("SAT").
English literature, Popular culture, Women studies, Mass media.	Dorothy Leigh Sayer's (1893-1957) strong characters.
Sociology, Journalism, Mass media.	Margaret Fuller; a life for a movie scenario (Sarah Margaret Fuller, Marchioness Ossoli, 1810-1850.)
Economics, English and South African literature(s)	Olive Schreiner (1855-1920) and Ralph Iron.
Ethnic studies, Women studies, Sociology, Social welfare, Public policy.	The mental hospital as prison and custodian.
Various	Crimes without victims?: Abortion [or] Drug addiction [or] Homosexuality

The following problem situations are derived from Readers' Guide To Periodical Literature (not Abridged Readers' Guide.) They have been selected for use in teaching the several conceptual aspects of periodical indexing which are introduced starting with Assignment 3. The principles on which these are based carry over to other periodical indexes and Assignment 4.

It may be useful to note that:

• Beginning with Readers' Guide volume 45, major cumulations encompass a calendar year. Volume 45 is labeled "1985." In the recent past dating back to volume 25, which covered March 1965-February 1966, the publisher's March-February year has been the major cumulated volume period, with larger time spans previously.

• Beginning with volume 43 (March 1983-February 1984), Readers' Guide introduced a clearer, enhanced display-arrangement and new typography. By and about are explicit, whereas in the past the articles by an individual were simply grouped first under her/his name.

• The subdivision ADDRESSES, MESSAGES, ETC. leads to citations of magazine articles about a speech. Reference to the speech (or extract, excerpt, etc.) itself would be locatable among the creative works by the speaker-as-author.

• For accessing book reviews, particularly several citations from varied periodicals for one book in one location, Readers' Guide beginning volume 36 (March 1976-February 1977) is useful as an introductory learning experience. Beginning with volume 36, citations to book reviews are segregated in the back of the volume (or supplement). Previously they were and are bibliographically accessible under authors' names, within the index-alphabet.

READERS' GUIDE: ASSIGNMENTS 3 AND 4

The following examples can be used with Assignment 3 and in other situations. The data are presented in the following order:

Readers' Guide volume number and dates:
Page number and SUBJECT HEADING (in all caps)
    Title of the article with bibliographic data
Page number of the author entry, if any
    Author's full name
Full title of the periodical (derived from preliminary pages of the index)
Other information.

• • •

Useful for Assignment 3, Question 2:

Volume 44   March 1984-February 1985:

1533   RHETORIC
The decline of oratory [political oratory].   H. Fairlie.   il   New Repub
190:15-19   My 28 '84
672   Fairlie, Henry
New Republic

1267   NEUROTRANSMITTERS
The ultimate head waiter: how the brain controls diet.   R. J. Wurtman.   il   Technol Rev 87:42-51   Jl '84
2016   Wurtman, Richard J.
Technology Review

1145   MEDICAL EDUCATION
The training of a gynecologist.   D. Hellerstein.   il   Ms 13:136-7
N '84
854   Hellerstein, David
Ms

Volume 43 March 1983-February 1984:

425   CONTRACEPTIVES
The pill for men: bad news, good news--or no news?   J. Kelly.
Mademoiselle 89:210-11+   S '83
897   Kelly, John
Mademoiselle

Volume 42 March 1982-February 1983:

1453-4 1454:   SPERMATOZA
Sex preselection in mammals? Separation of sperm bearing Y and O
chromosomes in the vole microtus oregoni.   D. Pinkel and others.
bibl f   il   Science 218:904-6   N 26 '82
1201   Pinkel, Daniel and others
Science

Volume 39   March 1979-February 1980

431-2 432:   DIVORCEES
What every divorced woman should know about taxes.   G. F. Hanks.
Essence 9:66-7+   Mr '79
627   Hanks, George F. and others
Essence

1262   SMOKING

Smoking; how real are the dangers for women? L. Cherry. il
Glamour 77:250-1+ O '79
284 Cherry, Laurence
Glamour

1302 STILBESTROLS
DES: the drug with unexpected legacies. A. Hecht. il FDA Consumer 13:14-17 My '79
639 Hecht, Annabel
FDA Consumer

Volume 38 March 1978-February 1979:

1131 REFORESTATION
Canada; moth war still rages. R. Paehlke. il Environment 20:2-4
S '78
995 Paehlke, Robert C.
Environment

1245-6 1246: SMOKING
Women and cigarettes: the deadly new evidence. B. Ford. Good H
187:301-2 N '78
533 Ford, Barbara
Good Housekeeping

1234 SINGLE PARENT FAMILIES
Going it alone. M. Slavin. il por Work Wom 3:42-4 F '78
1240 Slavin, Maeve
Working Woman

321 COLLEGE OFFICIALS
How administrators get their jobs. D. J. Socolow. Change 10:42-3+
My '78
1252 Socolow, Daniel J.
Change

Volume 37 March 1977-February 1978:

849 PHOBIAS
AGORAPHOBIA: life rule by panic. J. Baumgold. il N Y Times
Mag p46-8+ D 4 '77
123 Baumgold, Julie
New York Times Magazine

911 PURDAH
Purdah in India; life behind the veil. D. W. Jacobson. il por map
Nat Geog Mag 152:270-86 Ag '77
592 Jacobson, Doranne Wilson
National Geographic Magazine

999 SEX ROLE
Changing male roles. J. Harrison. il Am Educ 13:20-6 Jl '77

513   Harrison, James
        American Education

1249   YOUNG WOMEN
        Loneliness of a teenage feminist. D. Shaw. il por Ms 6:112-13
        N '77
1002   Shaw, Diana
        Ms

Volume 36   March 1976-February 1977:

463   GINSENG
        Ginseng, folklore cure-all, is being regarded seriously. J. S. Massey.
        il bibl (p122) Smithsonian 6:104-11 F '76
684   Massey, John Stewart
        Smithsonian

1220   WOMEN IN LITERATURE
        Chaste pornography: romantic suspense novels. S. S. McDonald.
        Nat Rev 28:958-9 S 3 '76
663   McDonald, Susan Schwartz
        National Review

Volume 34   March 1974-February 1975:

1191   WEATHER
        Circulation and weather of 1973. A. J. Wagner. il Weatherwise 27:
        24-35 F '74
1176   Wagner, A. James
        Weatherwise

Volume 32   March 1972-February 1973:

957   PRONOUNS
        What about new human pronouns? C. Miller and K. Swift. il Current
        138:43-5 Mr '72
758   Miller, Casey and Swift, Kate
        Current

Volume 27   March 1967-February 1968:

578   INSOMNIA
        Long day's journey into the insomniac's night. E. Diamond. il N Y
        Times Mag p30-1+ 0 1 '67; Same abr. with title Inside Insomnia.
        Read Digest 92:131-4 Ja '68

335   Diamond, Edwin
        New York Times Magazine; Readers' Digest

•   •   •

<u>Useful for Assignment 3, Question 3:</u>

Volume 44   March 1984-February 1985:

    1533   RHODE ISLAND--POLITICS AND GOVERNMENT   (2 articles)
          Facing the canons [nuns A. Violet and E. Morancy run for office]
          D. R. Carlin, Jr. Commonweal 111:38 Ja 27 '84
    334   Carlin, David R., Jr.
          Commonweal
  SEE ALSO   PRESIDENTIAL PRIMARIES--RHODE ISLAND

    1533   RHETORIC   (8 articles)
          The decline of oratory [political oratory]. H. Fairlie. il New Repub
          190:15-19 My 28 '84
    672   Fairlie, Henry
          New Republic
  SEE ALSO   IRONY

    1267   NEUROTRANSMITTERS   (5 articles)
          The ultimate head waiter: how the brain controls diet. R. J. Wurt-
          man. il Technol Rev 87:42-51 Jl '84
    2016   Wurtman, Richard J.
          Technology Review
  SEE ALSO   ACETOLCHOLINE; CHOLECYSTOKININ; DOPAMINE; SEROTONIN;
      SUBSTANCE P

    1145   MEDICAL EDUCATION   (5 articles)
          The training of a gynecologist. D. Hellerstein. il Ms 13:136-7 N
          '84
    854   Hellerstein, David
          Ms
  SEE ALSO   BLACK MEDICAL STUDENTS; INTERNS (MEDICINE); MEDICAL
      COLLEGES; MEDICAL STUDENTS

  1145-6 1145:   MEDICAL ETHICS   (7 articles on page 1145, 5 on 1146)
          Healing before birth: an ethical dilemma. J. C. Fletcher. il
          Technol Rev 87:26-30+ Ja '84
    709   Fletcher, John C.
          Technology Review
  SEE ALSO   BABY DOE RULES; BABY JANE DOE CASE 1983; FERTILIZATION
      IN VITRO--ETHICAL ASPECTS, etc.

Volume 43   March 1983-February 1984:
    425   CONTRACEPTIVES   (approximately 30 articles on this page)
          The pill for men: bad news, good news--or no news? J. Kelly.
          Mademoiselle 89:210-11+ S '83
    897   Kelly, John
          Mademoiselle
  SEE ALSO   CONTRACAP INC.; DEPO-PROVERA

Volume 42   March 1982-February 1983:

    1453-4 1454:   SPERMATOZA   (2 articles on page 1453; 2 on page 1454)

Sex preselection in mammals? Separation of sperm bearing Y and O chromosomes in the vole microtus oregoni. D. Pinkel and others. bibl f il Science 218:904-6 N 26 '82
1201 Pinkel, Daniel and others
      Science
SEE ALSO SEMEN

Volume 39 March 1979-February 1980:

431-2 432: DIVORCEES (5 articles on page 431; two on page 432)
       What every divorced woman should know about taxes. G. F. Hanks.
       Essence 9:66-7+ Mr '79
627   Hanks, George F. and others
       Essence
SEE ALSO DISPLACED HOMEMAKERS; SINGLE PARENT FAMILIES

1262   SMOKING (approximately 25 articles)
       Smoking; how real are the dangers for women? L. Cherry. il
       Glamour 77:250-1+ O '79
284   Cherry, Laurence
       Glamour
SEE ALSO CIGARS; FETUS, EFFECT OF SMOKING ON THE

348   COMPUTERS--BUSINESS USE (10 articles)
       Computer shock; the inhuman office of the future. J. Stewart il
       Sat R 6:14-17 Je 23 '79; Same with title: Inhuman office of the
       future. Current 214:30-8 Jl '79
1302   Stewart, Jon
       Saturday Review; Current (Washington, D.C.)
SEE ALSO COMPUTERS--EXPORT-IMPORT TRADE USE; OFFICES--AUTO-
       MATION; WORD PROCESSING; WORD PROCESSING EQUIPMENT

1449   U.S.--HEALTH, EDUCATION & WELFARE, DEPARTMENT OF (approx.
       45 articles)
       Sex equity in education, Title IX. B. Stein. Today's educat
       68:18-19 N '79
1299   Stein, Barbara A.
       Today's Education
SEE ALSO U.S.--AGING, ADMINISTRATION; U.S.--ALCOHOL, DRUG
       ABUSE & MENTAL HEALTH ADMINISTRATION; U.S.--EDUCATION,
       OFFICE OF

Volume 38 March 1978-February 1979:

1245-6 1246: SMOKING (24/14 articles)
        Women and cigarettes: the deadly new evidence. B. Ford. Good H
        187:301-2 N '78
533   Ford, Barbara
        Good Housekeeping
SEE ALSO FETUS, EFFECT OF SMOKING ON THE; U.S.--HEALTH, EDU-
       CATION & WELFARE, DEPARTMENT OF--SMOKING AND HEALTH,
       OFFICE ON.

1234 SINGLE PARENT FAMILIES (8 articles)
      Going it alone. M. Slavin. il por Work Wom 3:42-4 F '78
1240 Slavin, Maeve
      Working Woman
SEE ALSO PARENTAL DEPRIVATION

321 COLLEGE OFFICIALS (3 articles)
     How administrators get their jobs. D. J. Socolow. Change 10:42-3+
     My '78
1252 Socolow, Daniel J.
      Change
SEE ALSO COLLEGE PRESIDENTS; WOMEN COLLEGE OFFICIALS

760 LABOR LAWS AND LEGISLATION--U.S. (numerous articles; 1 column)
     Guaranteeing workers' rights. M. Humphrey. il New Leader 61:
     14-15 Je 5 '78
662 Humphrey, Muriel
     New Leader
SEE ALSO ARBITRATION, INDUSTRIAL--U.S.; MINIMUM WAGE--U.S.

Volume 37 March 1977-February 1978:

849 PHOBIAS (10 articles)
     Agoraphobia: life rule by panic. J. Baumgold. il N Y Times Mag
     p46-8+ D 4 '77
123 Baumgold, Julle
     New York Times Magazine
SEE ALSO SCHOOL PHOBIA

999 SEX ROLE (15 articles)
     Changing male roles. J. Harrison. il Am Educ 13:20-6 Jl '77
513 Harrison, James
     American Education
SEE ALSO WOMEN AND MEN

1249 YOUNG WOMEN (2 articles)
      Loneliness of a teenage feminist. D. Shaw. il por Ms 6:112-13
      N '77
1002 Shaw, Diana
      Ms
SEE ALSO YOUTH

Volume 34 March 1974-February 1975:

1191 WEATHER (9 articles)
      Circulation and weather of 1973. A. J. Wagner il Weatherwise 27:
      24-35 F '74
1176 Wagner, A. James
      Weatherwise
SEE ALSO CLIMATE; DROUGHTS; HOT WEATHER; RAIN AND RAINFALL;
      SNOW; STORMS; TEMPERATURE; WINDS

Volume 27   March 1967-February 1968:

> 578   INSOMNIA (3 articles)
> Long day's journey into the insomniac's night. E. Diamond. il N Y
> Times Mag p30-1+ O 1 '67; Same abr. with title Inside Insomnia.
> Read Digest 92:131-4 Ja '68
> 335   Diamond, Edwin
> New York Times Magazine; Readers' Digest
> SEE ALSO SLEEP

Volume 14   July 1943-April 1945:

> 1902-3 1903: WORLD WAR, 1939- --ATROCITIES
> Surrender at Corregidor. R. A. Gunnison. il Colliers 113:13+
> Mr 18 '44
> 704   Gunnison, Royal Arch
> Colliers
> SEE ALSO WORLD WAR, 1939- --WAR CRIMINALS

•   •   •

Useful for Assignment 3, Question 4 having "New York Times Index" counterparts
in Assignment 4:

Volume 3   1910-1914:

> 2568-9 TITANIC (STEAMSHIP)
> [The sinking of the Titanic took place on April 14-15, 1912.]

> 2596 TRIANGLE WAIST COMPANY, NEW YORK
> 936   FIRES--U.S. provides leads, but not as specific.
> [The event referred to as the infamous Triangle Shirtwaist Fire began on
> March 26, 1911; it was also referred to as The Triangle Fire Scandal for
> purposes of the 1979 television movie. Shirtwaists were what women's
> blouses were generally called at the time.]

Volume 4   1915-1918:

> 296   CAVELL, EDITH LOUISA
> Last hours of Edith Cavell. H. Gibson. por World's work 34:
> 650-9 O '17
> 843   Gibson, Hugh S.
> World's Work
> [Cavell was executed in October 1915.]

> 1199-1200 LUSITANIA (STEAMSHIP)
> [The Lusitania was sunk on May 7, 1915.]

Volume 5   1919-1921:

> 1800 WOMAN SUFFRAGE--UNITED STATES--FEDERAL AMENDMENT

Is the 19th Amendment legal? G. S. Brown. Rev 4:54-5 Jan 19 '21
194 Brown, George Stewart
Review
[The 19th Amendment to the U.S. Constitution, known as the Suffrage
Amendment, was ratified on August 26, 1920.]

Volume 7 1925-1928:

733 EDERLE, GERTRUDE CAROLINE
How a girl beat Leander at the hero game. por Lit digest 90:
52-67 Ag 21 '26
Literary Digest
[Ederle swam the English Channel on August 6, 1926.]

Volume 8 January 1929-June 1932:

390 CARAWAY, MRS. THADDEUS H.
[Hattie Caraway became the first female member of the U.S. Senate in early
1932, following the death of Senator Thaddeus H. Caraway.]

Volume 9 July 1932-June 1935:

1687-8 PERKINS, FRANCES (MRS. PAUL WILSON)
[Perkins was selected by President Franklin D. Roosevelt to serve as Secretary of Labor in March 1933.]

Volume 10 July 1935-June 1937:

567-9 568: EDWARD VIII KING OF GREAT BRITAIN
His will is not his own: events leading to the abdication of Edward
VIII. S. Baldwin. Vital speeches 3:189-92 Ja 1 '37
136 Baldwin, Stanley Baldwin, 1st earl
Vital Speeches
[Parliament passed the Bill of Abdication on December 11, 1936.]

Volume 11 July 1937-June 1939:

32 AIRSHIPS
125 AVIATION--ACCIDENTS
[The Hindenburg, sometimes referred to as the VonHindenburg zeppelin,
burned in Lakehurst, New Jersey in May 1937.]

Volume 20 March 1955-February 1957:

538 COLLISIONS AT SEA
[The Andrea Doria and the Stockholm collision at sea took place during
summer 1956.]

•   •   •

Exercises Useful for Assignment 3, Question 5 about book reviews:

Volume 44   March 1984-February 1985:

Randall Rothenberg's The Neoliberals, published in 1984.
2069 Rothenberg, R.   The neoliberals.   1984
R. M. Kaus wrote the longest review cited.
R. Reeves wrote the review in the New York Times Book Review.

Salman Rushdie's Shame, published around 1983.
2069 Rushdie, S.   Shame
J. W. Crowley wrote the longest review cited.
C. Medwick wrote the review in Vogue.

William A. Rusher's The Rise of the Right, published around 1984.
2069 Rusher, W. A.   The rise of the right
W. F. Rickenbacker wrote the longest review cited.
J. Zukowsky wrote the review in Business Week.

Oliver W. Sacks' A Leg to Stand On, published in 1984.
2069 Sacks, O. W.   A leg to stand on.   1984
J. S. Bruner wrote the longest review cited.
D. X. Freedman wrote the review in the New York Times Book Review.

Volume 41   March 1981-February 1982

Mark Baker's NAM: The Vietnam War in Words of the Men and Women Who Fought There, published around 1981.
1845 Baker, M.   Nam: the Vietnam war in words of the men and women who fought there
T. Ensign and M. Uhl wrote the longest review cited.
P. S. Prescott wrote the review in Newsweek.

Volume 39   March 1979-February 1980:

Barbara Jordan's Barbara Jordan; A Self-Portrait, published in 1979.
1575 Jordan, B. C. and Hearon, S.   Barbara Jordan; a self-portrait.
      1979
J. Nocera wrote the longest review cited.
C. Hunter-Gault wrote the review in Ms.

Vivian Gornick's Essays in Feminism, published around 1979.
1570 Gornick, V.   Essays in feminism
E. Posner wrote the longest review cited.
E. Posner wrote the review in New Republic.

Mary Churchill Soames' Clementine Churchill: The Biography of a Marriage, published around 1979.
1594 Soames, M.   Clementine Churchill: the biography of a marriage

M. Panter-Downes wrote the longest review cited.
F. Taliaferro wrote the review in Harpers.

Peter Steinfels' Neo-Conservatives: The Men Who Are Changing America's Politics, published in 1979.
1595 Steinfels, P. Neo-conservatives: the men who are changing America's politics.
L. Goodwyn wrote the longest review cited.
A. Fremantle wrote the review in America.

Volume 38   March 1978-February 1979:

Tillie Olson's Silences, published around 1978.
1566 Olsen, T. Silences
J. C. Oates wrote the longest review cited.
M. Atwood wrote the review published in the New York Times Book Review.

Volume 36   March 1976-February 1977:

Lillian Hellman's Scoundrel Time, published in 1976.
1257 Hellman, L. Scoundrel time
W. F. Buckley, Jr. wrote the longest review cited.
B. Cook wrote the review in Saturday Review.

Adrienne Rich's Of Woman Born: Motherhood as Experience and Institution, published around 1976.
1277 Rich, A. Of woman born: motherhood as experience and institution.
J. T. Weedie wrote the longest review cited.
N. Newton wrote the review in Psychology Today.

Christina Stead's Miss Herbert (The Suburban Wife), published in 1976.
1283 Stead, C. Miss Herbert (the suburban wife)
J. Updike wrote the longest review cited.
E. Connell wrote the review in Harpers

Volume 32   March 1972-February 1973   [Book reviews are not in the back of the volume; they are in the volume-alphabet, under author of the book.]

Margaret Mead's Blackberry Winter, published around 1972.
734   MEAD, MARGARET
A. Fremantle wrote the longest review cited.
A. Cooper wrote the review for Newsweek.

•   •   •

Exercises Useful for Assignment 3, Question 6 about speeches, addresses, remarks, etc., including "excerpts."

Volume 44   March 1984-February 1985:

Address made by Jesse L. Jackson titled "The Rainbow Coalition," on July 17, 1984.

965   Jackson, Jesse L., 1941-
      The Rainbow Coalition [Address July 17, 1984] Vital Speeches Day
      51: 77-81 N 15 '84
      Vital Speeches of the Day

Address made by Jeane Kirkpatrick titled "The Atlantic Alliance and the
American National Interest," on April 30, 1984.
1012 Kirkpatrick, Jeane J., 1926-
      The Atlantic Alliance and the American national interest [address,
      April 30 1984] Dep St Bull 84:70-4 Jl '84
      Department of State Bulletin
1290 NORTH ATLANTIC TREATY ORGANIZATION

Volume 41 March 1981-February 1982:

Inaugural address made by President Reagan in January 1981.
1339 Reagan, Ronald
      Inaugural Address of President Reagan, January 20, 1981. il pors
      US News 90:70-2 F 2 '81; same Vital Speeches 47:258-60 F 15 '81;
      Dept State Bull 81:36A-36C F '81
      U S News; Vital Speeches; Department of State Bulletin

Address made by Prime Minister Margaret Thatcher on November 10, 1980,
titled "West: In Good Shape to Face International Upheavals."
1610 Thatcher, Margaret
      West: in good shape to face international upheavals [address, Nov.
      10, 1980] Vital speeches 47:194-6 Ja 15 '81
      Vital Speeches of the Day

Address made by Alexander Haig on September 13, 1981, titled "Democratic
Revolution and Its Future."
733   Haig, Alexander Meigs, 1924-
      Democratic rev. and its future [address, Sept. 13, 1981]
      Vital speeches 48:66-8 N 15 '81
      Vital Speeches of the Day

Volume 40 March 1980-February 1981:

Remarks made by Rosalynn Carter in November 1979 during her Thailand
visit.
290   Carter, Rosalynn (Smith)
      Mrs. Carter visits Thailand [remarks, November 1979] Dept. of State
      Bull 80:6-7 Ja '80
      Department of State Bulletin

Address made by George Meany on November 15, 1979, titled "Trade Union
Movement."
945   Meany, George
      Trade union movement [address, November 15, 1979] Vital Speeches
      46:164-6 Ja 1 '80
      Vital Speeches of the Day

Volume 39   March 1979-February 1980:

Commencement Address made by Alan Alda in May 1979 for the Columbia
University College of Physicians & Surgeons.
43   Alda, Alan
      M*A*S*H notes for docs: Columbia University College of Physicians
      & Surgeons commencement address, May 1979. por Good H 189:
      78+ O '79; Excerpts Time 113:68 My 28 '79.
      Good Housekeeping; Time

Volume 38   March 1978-February 1979:

Excerpts from Egyptian President Sadat's address to the Knesset on November 20, 1977.
1175   Sadat, Anwar
       Egyptian President Sadat speaks to the Knesset; excerpts from
       address Nov. 20, 1977. Cur Hist 74:34+ Ja '78
       Current History

Volume 37   March 1977-February 1978:

Excerpts from Phyllis Schlafly's April 1977 statement on the ERA.
977   Schlafly, Phyllis
       Excerpt from statement on the ERA, April 1977. Cong Dig 56:89+
       Je '77
       Congressional Digest

Excerpts from Bella Abzug's April 1, 1976 debate on the Federal Elections
Campaign Act Amendments.
3   Abzug, Bella
       Excerpts from debate on Federal Elections Campaign Act Amendments,
       April 1, 1976. Cong Digest 56:88+ Mr '77
       Congressional Digest

Volume 36   March 1976-February 1977:

Hubert Humphrey's October 1975 address titled "... In the Courts, Or in
the Woods?"
534   Humphrey, Hubert Horatio, 1911-
       ... In the courts, or in the woods? address. October 1975. il por
       Am For 82:14-15+ Ja '76
       American Forests

Volume 35   March 1975-February 1976:

Lillian Hellman's May 14, 1975 address titled "On Jumping Into Life."
498   Hellman, Lillian
       On jumping into life; address May 14, 1975. Mademoiselle 81:166-7
       Ag '75
       Mademoiselle

Excerpts from Hubert Humphrey's February 5, 1975 debate on changes in the Food Stamp Program.
525   Humphrey, Hubert Horatio, 1911-
       Excerpt from debate on changes in the Food stamp program: February 5, 1975. Cong Dig 54:145+ My '75
       Congressional Digest

Volume 34   March 1974-February 1975:

Richard Nixon's farewell address, August 8, 1974.
773   Nixon, Richard Milhous
       Nixon's farewell: address, August 8, 1974. il pors US News 77:71-2 Ag 19 '74 Same Vital Speeches 40:643-4 Ag 15 '74
       US News; Vital Speeches of the Day

Volume 33   March 1973-February 1974:

Wilma Heide's February 1973 address, titled "Revolution."
492   Heide, Wilma Scott
       Revolution; address. February 1973. Vital Speeches 39:424-8 My 1 '73
       Vital Speeches of the Day

Volume 32   March 1972-February 1973:

Margaret Mead's address (adapted) titled "Future Family," delivered on February 12, 1970.
734   Mead, Margaret
       Future family; adapt of address, Feb. 12, 1970. il Trans-Action 8:50-3 S '71
       Trans-Action

Volume 31   March 1971-February 1972:

Excerpt from Galo Plaza's April 14, 1971 address titled "Beyond the Alliance."
907   Plaza, Galo
       Beyond the Alliance; excerpt from address. April 14, 1971. il Americas 23:2-4 My '71
       Americas

Excerpt from Patsy Takemoto Mink's remarks made on February 10, 1971.
743   Mink, Patsy (Takemoto)
       Excerpt from remarks, Feb. 10, 1971. Cong Dig 50:119+ Ap '71
       Congressional Digest

Volume 24   March 1963-February 1965:

Nelson Rockefeller's address titled "Inter-Continental Unity," delivered November 20, 1964.

1732 Rockefeller, Nelson Aldrich
     Inter-continental unity; address. Nov. 20, 1964. Vital Speeches
     31:132-5 D 15 '64
     Vital Speeches of the Day

•   •   •

The following problem situations do not relate directly to an Assignment question or library activity using Readers' Guide. They provide opportunity to practice various aspects of periodical indexing.

Following Through on "SEE" Cross-references:

YOU NEED INFORMATION ABOUT...

... Inez Garcia's trial for murder which took place in the 1970's decade. Someone tells you about a very useful article at least six pages long published in Ms magazine in 1975, which was illustrated, including a portrait of Inez Garcia.

Volume 35 March 1975-February 1976:

  443   Garcia, Inez, Murder Trial. See TRIALS (MURDER)
 1093   TRIALS (MURDER) Several articles include:
         Inez Garcia on trial. N. Blitman and R. Green. pors Ms 3:49-54+
         My '75
  140   Blitman, Nan and Green, Robin
         Ms

... DES. Someone tells you about a very useful article about four pages long published in spring 1979, which was illustrated and in FDA Consumer.

Volume 39 March 1979-February 1980:

  398   DES (diethylstilbestrol). See STILBESTROLS
 1302   STILBESTROLS. Several articles include:
         DES: the drug with unexpected legacies. A. Hecht. il FDA
         Consumer 13:14-17 My '79
  639   Hecht, Annabel
         FDA Consumer

... Title IX regulations. Someone tells you about a very useful article about two pages long published in late 1979 in Today's Education.

Volume 39 March 1979-February 1980:

 1375   Title IX regulations. See U.S.--HEALTH, EDUCATION & WELFARE,
         DEPARTMENT OF
 1449   U.S.--HEALTH, EDUCATION & WELFARE, DEPARTMENT OF.
         Numerous articles include:

479

Sex equity in education, Title IX. B. Stein. Today's educa 68: 18-19 N '79
1299 Stein, Barbara A.
Today's Education

... Administrators of colleges and how they get their jobs. Someone tells you about a very useful article but can recall only that it was published in spring 1978 in <u>Change</u> magazine and was about two pages long.

Volume 38 March 1978-February 1979:

9 Administrators, College. See COLLEGE OFFICIALS
321 COLLEGE OFFICIALS. Several articles include:
How administrators get their jobs. D. J. Socolow. Change 10: 42-3+ My '78
1252 Socolow, Daniel J.
Change

... the WACs during World War II, including their training routine. Someone tells you about a very useful article published in July 1943 in <u>Newsweek</u> magazine, but can recall only that it was about a page in length and was <u>illustrated</u>.

Volume 14 July 1943-April 1945
1811 W.A.C. See WOMEN'S ARMY CORPS (WACS)
1886 WOMEN'S ARMY CORPS (WACS)
Newsweek synthetic Waac samples six-day slice of training routine.
V. Clay. il Newsweek 22: 44+ Jl 5 '43
333 Clay, Vera
Newsweek

... women and smoking, particularly some evidence that the dangers were recognized in the 1970's. Someone tells you about a useful article published in fall 1979 in <u>Glamour</u>, which was illustrated and about two pages long.

Volume 39 March 1979-February 1980:

1531 Women and smoking. See SMOKING
1262 SMOKING
Smoking; how real are the dangers for women? L. Cherry. il
Glamour 77: 250-1+ O '79
284 Cherry, Laurence
Glamour

... the Equal Rights Amendment at the time it was proposed. Someone tells you about a useful article "from a Christian perspective" published in March 1981, but can recall only that it was about two pages long and by a man.

Volume 41 March 1981-February 1982:

578　Equal rights amendment (proposed).　See UNITED STATES--CONSTI-
　　　TUTION--AMENDMENTS
1690　UNITED STATES--CONSTITUTION--AMENDMENTS
　　　New wisdom from Rosie the Riveter [Equal Rights Amendment].
　　　J. M. Wall.　Christian Century 98:219-20　Mr 4 '81
1768　Wall, James M. is listed as the author of two other articles in
　　　Christian Century.

... the Suffrage amendment's legality.　Someone tells you about a useful article
published in Review magazine early in 1921, which was about two pages long, and
referred to the 19th Amendment's legality.

Volume 5　1919-1921:

1588　Suffrage amendment.　See WOMAN SUFFRAGE--UNITED STATES--
　　　FEDERAL AMENDMENT
1800　WOMAN SUFFRAGE--UNITED STATES--FEDERAL AMENDMENT
　　　Is the 19th Amendment legal?　G. S. Brown.　Rev 4:54-5　Jan 19
　　　'21
194　Brown, George Stewart
　　　Review

... moving pictures, specifically plot information and critical opinion such as a
professional reviewer of motion pictures provided, and even more to the point ...
about Five Easy Pieces, which came out in the early 1970's.　Klute, too.
Someone tells you about using Readers' Guide for leads to reviews of moving pictures.

Volume 31　March 1971-February 1972:

981　Reviews of moving pictures.　See MOVING PICTURE PLAYS--
　　　CRITICISM, PLOTS, ETC.
766　MOVING PICTURE PLAYS--CRITICISM, PLOTS, ETC.--SINGLE WORKS
　　　Five easy pieces:　Several citations, including Harpers 242:113-4
　　　My '71
　　　Klute:　Several citations, including Film Q 25:55-6　F '71

... to know whether there were any reviews of the motion picture Bell Jar
around 1979, when you think it came out, and particularly whether Time magazine
published one; and what did America think of Norma Rae?

Volume 39　March 1979-February 1980

909　MOTION PICTURE REVIEWS--SINGLE WORKS--BELL JAR
　　　Reviews in several popular magazines indexed by Readers' Guide are
　　　cited, including Time il 113:105　Ap 2 '79
912　MOTION PICTURE REVIEWS--SINGLE WORKS--NORMA RAE
　　　America 140:286　Ap 7 '79

•　　•　　•

Some Readers' Guide Challenges. You need to locate references (citations) to magazine articles which will lead to the following information or answer this question:

When Maureen Reagan married a "young third husband" in 1981, who played the big supporting role?

Volume 41 March 1981-February 1982:

> 1338 REAGAN, MAUREEN
> Mother Jane Wyman played the big supporting role as Maureen Reagan took a young third husband. D. Wallace. il pors People 15:42-3 My 11 '81 [An example of the occasional article for which an author entry is not provided.]
> People Weekly

Is it true that in 1984 someone was conducting a seminar on how to flirt?!

Volume 44 March 1984-February 1985:

> 709 FLIRTING
> Learning to flirt [seminar conducted by C. Flashner]. D. K. Mano. Natl rev 36:59-60 My 4 '84
> 1110 Mano, D. Keith is listed as the author of other articles
> National Review

What is or was "Jensenism"? Someone says it's controversial and was in the news around 1969 or 1970 ... some university prof's genes theory.

Volume 29 March 1969-February 1970:

> 627 JENSEN, ARTHUR ROBERT--ABOUT
> Jensenism, n. The theory that I.Q. is largely determined by the genes. L. Edson. il N Y T Mag Aug 31 '69 p 10 f Disc p4+ S 21; 38+ S 28 '69
> 385 Edson, Lee
> New York Times Magazine

Is it ever possible to use marijuana as medicine? (Not just someone's opinion--a so-called authoritative answer). Someone says there was such an article published as far back as April 1978, and it had a bibliography.

Volume 38 March 1978-February 1979:

> 830 MARIJUANA--THERAPEUTIC USE
> Marijuana as medicine. S. Cohen. bibl il por Psychol today 11:60-2+ Ap '78
> 316 Cohen, Sidney
> Psychology Today

Former San Francisco mayor Joseph Alioto filed a lawsuit against Look magazine, and you need to know on what the suit was based, so you need to locate and read the Look article, for starters. All you know is that it was written by Brisson Carlson, or a similar sounding name, and published in fall 1969.

Volume 29 March 1969-February 1970:

212   Carlson, Richard [author]
38   ALIOTO, JOSEPH LAWRENCE
      Web that links San Francisco's Mayor Alioto with the Mafia. R. Carlson and L. Brisson. il pors Look 33:17-21 S 23 '69
174   Brisson, Lance

Bartlett's Familiar Quotations (14th edition, 1968) refers to Martin Luther King, Jr.'s comment that "Injustice anywhere is a threat to justice everywhere" in a letter from the Birmingham jail. You want to read the entire letter. There's also a reference to the August 1963 issue of Atlantic Monthly.

Volume 24 March 1963-February 1965:

1108   King, Martin Luther, 1929-
      Letter from Birmingham jail. Christian Cent 80:767-73 Je 12 '63; Excerpts. Ebony 18:23-6+ Ag '63; Time 83:15 Ja 3 '64. Same Negro Hist Bul 27:156 Mr '64.

You could press on back into volume 23 for a possible reference to Atlantic Monthly, or you might go to the June 12, 1963 issue of Christian Century at this point.

You would like to locate some information about the Encyclopaedia Britannica and a comparison of the second and third editions of Webster's unabridged dictionaries in popular magazines.

Volume 23 March 1961-February 1963:

645   ENCYCLOPAEDIA BRITANNICA
      Encyclopaedia Britannica. Chitwood, J. R. Lib J 86:1549-51 Ap 15 '61. Reply H. Ernbinder 86:1706+ My 1 '61
392   Chitwood, Julius R.
      Library Journal
2057   Webster's new international dictionaries. See ENGLISH LANGUAGE--DICTIONARIES
649   ENGLISH LANGUAGE--DICTIONARIES
      Books; differences between Webster's second and third editions. D. Macdonald. New Yorker 38:130-4+ Mr 10 '62; Reply G. Jonas 38:108+ Mr 31 '62
1144   Macdonald, Dwight
      New Yorker

You need to locate a picture of "Olana" an historic New York house, once the home of Frederic E. Church, much in the news in the mid-sixties.

Volume 25 March 1965-February 1966:

    776   OLANA (HISTORIC HOUSE)
          Persia on the Hudson; Olana, home of Frederic E. Church. R. Lynes.
          il Harper 230:30+ F '65.
    638   Lynes, Russell
          Harpers
    755   NEW YORK (STATE)--HISTORIC HOUSES, ETC.

Someone says s/he has just been admitted to the "high IQ fraternity," and is now a Mensa member. Someone else sneers that this is an elitest group. A librarian suggests a Life magazine article back in 1963.

Volume 24 March 1963-February 1965:

    1281 MENSA (SOCIETY)
          High I Q fraternity. S. Alexander. il Life 55: 11+ Ag 16 '63.
    56   Alexander, Shana
          Life

You'd like some contemporary information (written at the time) about the first woman governor: Nellie Ross, around 1925.

Volume 7 1925-1928:

    2181-1 ROSS, NELLIE DAVIS (TAYLOE) (MRS. WILLIAM BRADFORD ROSS)
            First woman governor. L. Donaldson. il pors Woman Cit n s 9:8
            Mr 21 '25
    688   Lee Donaldson
            Woman Citizen (Changed in 1928 to Woman's Journal)

NEW YORK TIMES INDEX

The following problems and exercises relate to use of the New York Times Index, including question 4 of Assignment 4 and "In-Library Practice: Newspaper Indexes."

Assignment 3 (middle of page 3) involved using Readers' Guide in connection with an historical event. The same event should be used in Assignment 4, first part of question 4. These problems are provided with more detail than required in Assignment 4, so that they can also be used with the "In-Library Practice: Newspaper Indexes." Problems relating to the second part of question 4, Assignment 4 follow this section.

IF YOU WERE WRITING A PAPER ON....

the sinking of the Titanic steamship and the TITANIC DISASTER, which took place on April 14-15, 1912....

1912 volume:

> Titanic.   See SHIP BUILDING; SHIPS, TITANIC
> 293   SHIPS--TITANIC DISASTER

the Triangle Shirt Waist Company FIRE disaster of March 1911....

1911 volume:

> 88-9 FIRES--TRIANGLE Shirt Waist Co. (NYC)
> fire kills some 141 workers trapped on upper floors ... owners escape.
> Mr 26, 1:3-7

the execution of Edith Cavell who was accused of being an English spy, which took place in late 1915.

1915 volume, October-December 1915 section:

> 86-7 CAVELL, EDITH
> 86   executed by Germans in Brussels Oct 13, Oct 16, 1:4; details Oct. 18, 1:2....

the sinking of the Lusitania in May 1915....

1915 volume, January-June 1915 section, April-June subsection:

255   Lusitania. See CUNARD LINE; U.S.--GERMANY, RELATIONS WITH

the opposition to the 19th (Suffrage) Amendment <u>after</u> its ratification in August 1920; specifically opposition in Alabama....

1920 volume, July-September

404-406 WOMAN SUFFRAGE--U.S.--NATIONAL--RATIFICATION OF FEDERAL AMENDMENT
404   --ALABAMA
36 members of House affirm opposition to ratification Ag 25 3:3 (Information also accessible under U.S. CONSTITUTION, but not as full.)

Gertrude Ederle's record-breaking swim of the English Channel, August 6, 1926....

1926 volume, July-December section, July-September subsection:

190   EDERLE, GERTRUDE. See also SWIMMING--EDERLE, G.
597   SWIMMING--EDERLE, G.
Swims English Channel in record time of 14 hours, 31 minutes; her career, pictures, Ag 7, 1:8

Hattie Caraway's election as United States Senator in early 1932 from the state of Arkansas....

1932 volume:

439   CARAWAY (MRS.), HATTIE W (US Senator)
... sworn in F 2, 2:4; int, F 14, II, 4:5....

President Franklin D. Roosevelt's appointment of Frances Perkins as Secretary of Labor in March 1933...

1933 volume:

2059-60 PERKINS (SEC), FRANCES (MRS. PAUL WILSON)
2059 Selected by F D Roosevelt for Sec of Labor, Mr 1, 1:5; ed. Mr 2, 16:3....

Abdication of King Edward VIII of Great Britain in 1936....

1936 volume:

877   EDWARD VIII, KING OF GREAT BRITAIN AND IRELAND

The burning of the <u>Hindenburg</u> zeppelin in 1937....

1937 volume:

    1924-5 HINDENBURG (AIRSHIP)

The collision at sea of the <u>Andrea Doria</u> and <u>Stockholm</u> liners in summer 1956....

1956 volume:
   70   ANDREA DORIA (LINER)
          collides with liner Stockholm off Nantucket Lightship, Jl 26, 1:8;
          sinks.

• • •

Assignment 4 (bottom of page 3) question 4 introduces the idea of a periodical index "carrying" information as well as "locating" it.

Using the NEW YORK TIMES INDEX, locate the following information:

Sonia Johnson was the candidate of which political party in the 1984 presidential election? The announcement of her nomination was made in late October 1983.

1983 volume:

   661   JOHNSON, SONIA. See Also PRESIDENTIAL ELECTION 1984
   989   PRESIDENTIAL ELECTION 1984
   994   Mormon feminist Sonia Johnson to seek US Pres nomination of Citizens
           Party (S) O 23 I 41:5 [middle column]

At the time in 1934 that "Public Enemy #1" John Dillinger flourished, automobiles with out-of-state license plates were rarely seen. When a car with Illinois plates was seen outside of Illinois, it so terrified the citizens that there was a panic. Where and when did this take place?

1934 volume:

   710-13 DILLINGER, Jno.
   710   Car with Illinois license plates scares Bronx citizens, as they fear it
          carries Dillinger, Mr 8, 13:7

You need a photo (not just a reference to one) of the world's first baby conceived outside the mother's body. The "test-tube" baby received publicity in 1979 on her first birthday; what is her name?

1979 volume:

   1113 REPRODUCTION (BIOLOGICAL)
          Illus of 'test-tube' baby Louise Brown, age 1, in Chicago TV Studio
          with parents, S 8, 8:2

1114 [photo of] "one-year old Louise Jay Brown, world's first baby conceived outside of the mother's body, is held by her father, John ... her mother, Lesley, is at left."

In 1976 Reggie Jackson's Oakland, California home was destroyed. How?

1976 volume:

762 JACKSON, REGGIE
Oakland, Calif., home destroyed by fire (S), Je 21, 41:4

In November 1974 Karen Silkwood was killed in a car crash while on her way to meeting a New York Times reporter and a union official from Washington, D.C. Where did the accident take place--New York, Washington, or where?

1974 volume:

2186 SILKWOOD, KAREN G. See Also ROADS AND TRAFFIC--OKLAHOMA-- ACCIDENTS, ETC.

Did any member of the Kennedy family provide a "tribute" to former Supreme Court Chief Justice Earl Warren when he died in 1974? If not, who did? When was Warren born?

1974 volume:

1809 Obituaries. See DEATHS, PERSONAL NAMES
2656 WARREN, EARL [Photo with 1891-1974]
References to tributes by President Nixon, Vice President Ford, Senator Edward M. Kennedy, AFL CIO President George Meany, and Chief Justice J. Burger.

In 1972 California State College at San Francisco, as it was then known, voted to give its first honorary degree to Japanese Emperor Hirohito. For what was he honored?

1972 volume:

303 CALIFORNIA STATE COLLEGES
San Francisco campus votes to give shcool's first honorary degree to Japanese Emperor Hirohito for his work in marine biology, O 19, 40:1

The Proud Eagle Tribe was alleged to have been involved in campus rioting in 1970. Identify at least one such "incident."

1970 volume:
1607 PROUD EAGLE TRIBE (ORG) See Also Harvard U, O 15

Resources

    832   HARVARD...
          bombing International Center revolutionary women's group ... someone
          saw "three well dressed women...."

Mod Donna was called "ambi-sexual liberation musical" following its first performance, in the New York Shakespeare Festival Public Theater, April 24, 1970.
Who wrote it?

1970 volume:

    1889   THEATER--REVIEWS AND OTHER DATA ON SPECIFIC PRODUCTIONS--
           MOD DONNA
           M. Lamb and S. Bingham

Rolf Hochhuth's play opened in the mid 1960's in Europe amid much censorship of
the book-of-the-play and picketing of the play; there was also considerable negative publicity in Latin countries. Why was the Vatican disturbed about all this,
what was the playwright's full name and the English-language title of the play itself?

1964 volume:

    428   Hochhuth, Rolf
          ... play Der Stellverter (The Deputy) reviewed, Mr 1, VII, p 1....
    898   ROMAN CATHOLIC CHURCH--POPE (Pius XII)
          R. Hochhuth's play The Deputy stirs Vatican debate over Pope's
          personality and role in history, Mr 8, IV, 4:2,5

The April 9, 1964, issue of the Neshoba [Mississippi] Democrat newspaper included the following editorial statement: "Outsiders who come in here and try
to stir up trouble should be dealt with in a manner they won't forget." This
was also quoted in a book, Witness in Philadelphia [Mississippi], published by
Louisiana State University Press. Approximately how long did it take to deal
with the two outsiders who were in the mind of the writer quoted on April 9,
1964? Their names were Michael H. Schwerner and Andrew Goodman.

1964 volume:

    913   SCHWERNER, MICHAEL H.
          Missing.... Je 23, 1:7
    399   GOODMAN, Andrew (Student) (d 1964)
          Missing.... Je 23, 1:7

When the liners Andrea Dorea and Stockholm collided in July 1956, how many passengers abandoned ship, and were they in the middle of the Atlantic or the
Pacific Ocean, or where?

1956 volume:

    70   ANDREA DORIA (LINER)

collides with liner Stockholm off Nantucket Lighthouse Jl 26, 1:8; sinks.

1125-7 SHIPS AND SHIPPING--ACCIDENTS--ANDREA DORIA AND STOCK-
HOLM (LINERS)
Collide in fog off Nantucket Lighthouse; 1134 Doria passengers aban-
don ship.

Evita Maria Peron made her final appearance in public in 1952. What was the reaction of United States officials at her death? Did any pay tribute?

1952 volume:

836   PERON (PRESIDENT) JUAN DOMINGO
       ... U.S. officials voice shock Jl 27, 1:3.   President Truman's tribute
       Jl 28, 15:5

Following the death of Mahatma Gandhi, as he was referred to by some, what be-came of his body? How did he die in 1948? When was he born?

1948 volume:

407   GANDHI, MOHANDAS KARAMCHAND (1869-1948)
       Shot to death by Hindu, New Delhi
       Ashes strewn upon Ganges F 13, 18:4

You want to read the full text of King Edward VIII's "farewell broadcast" on the occasion of his abdication from the British throne in 1936. At the time, he was accused by whom of copying his notes on constitutional law at Oxford?

1936 volume:

877   EDWARD VIII, KING OF GREAT BRITAIN AND IRELAND
882   C Morley says King copied his notes on constitutional law at Oxford,
       D 10, 20:6
       Farewell broadcast; text.... D 12, 1:4-8

In 1934 Mr. and Mrs. Ernest Dionne made history, when she gave birth to quin-tuplets who survived. What award did they receive for this? In August it was discovered that one of the "quints" had what problem, and what was done about it? Circa August 4th news of the birth of another set of quintuplets, to Señora T de Moscoloni, reached the United States; were they too all girls, and did they survive?

1934 volume:

714   DIONNE (MR & MRS) ERNEST
       Mr & Mrs Ernest Dionne received "... King's bounty for multiple
       births," N 20, 23:2
1929-30 QUINTUPLETS

1929   smallest one gets radium treatment for tumorous growth, Ag 7, 19:1

1930   3 girls and 2 boys born to Señora T de Moscoloni, die within 2 hours, Ag 4, 4:8

In 1934 Frances Howell Marsalis made news for several extraordinary accomplishments and happenings. How many can you glean from the New York Times issues of that year?

1934 volume:

   1488   MARSALIS (MRS), FRANCES HOWELL. See Also AERONAUTICS--
         RECORDS--ENDURANCE
         Killed in plane crash; divorce revealed, Ag 6, 1:5, por, Ag 6, 7:2;
         funeral plans, Ag 7, 7:2; funeral, Ag 8, 17:6
   74   AERONAUTICS--RECORDS--ENDURANCE
         Mrs F H Marsalis and H Richey arrive in N Y in plane in which they
         set record at Miami, Ja 15, 17:5

(This is also an opportunity to introduce the NEW YORK TIMES Personal Name Index, which provides above and other leads to the NEW YORK TIMES INDEX indexing.)

What was the name of The Woman in Red associated with "Public Enemy Number One" John Dillinger in 1934?

1934 volume:

   710-13   DILLINGER, JNO.
   712   Mrs. A Miller (Mrs. A Sage) identified as "Woman in red"

How did Frances Perkins, first woman member of the President's Cabinet, spend her first official day? President Franklin Roosevelt selected her for his Secretary of Labor in March 1933.

1933 volume:

   2059   PERKINS (SEC), FRANCES (MRS. PAUL WILSON)
         First official day filled with conferences, Mr 7, 24:1

When record-breaking swimmer Gertrude Ederle swam the English Channel in August 1926, there were a few associated notable events! Why did the members of the W.C.T.U. (Women's Christian Temperance Union) urge the recall of the American Consul at Boulogne? What happened to Ederle after she reached France in mid-August? How many references to related photographs can you identify?

1926 volume, July-December section, July-September subsection:

   190   EDERLE, GERTRUDE. See Also SWIMMING-EDERLE
         Omaha, Nebraska, W C T U wants W Corcoran, American Consul at
         Boulogne, recalled if he served wine at welcome to her, S 4, 15:3

597 SWIMMING--EDERLE, G
     Kidnapped by villagers from Goetlingen, Ag 15, 22:3
597 pictures, Ag 7, 1:8
597 photos of her channel swim Ag 16, 5:1

The "Monkey Trial" related to teacher John Scopes' teaching evolution in his
biology class. It was in the news circa July 1925. In September that year,
Scopes announced that he was leaving Tennessee; what were his plans? In November that year one of the colleges and schools which burned their books on
evolution made the news; what was its name?

1925 volume; July-December section

    July-September 1925 subsection:
    507 SCOPES, JNO THOS
         To enroll for PhD degree at University of Chicago S 26, 17:3

    October-December 1925 subsection:
    534 Scopes, Jno Thos. See EVOLUTION OF MAN--TENNESSEE
    197 EVOLUTION OF MAN--TENNESSEE
         Southern Junior College burns books on evolution, N 15, II, 1:7

When is the first reference to news of the Kanto Great Earthquake of 1923?
What cities did it affect?

1923 volume: July-December section

153 EARTHQUAKES--JAPAN
     S 2, 1:5; Tokio [Tokyo], Yokohama, Nagoya

Following the execution of nurse Edith Cavell as a British spy during World War I,
there was mass response by the English people. The October 25, 1915 New York
Times reported that ten thousand had done what?

1915 volume; October-December section:

    86-7 CAVELL, EDITH
    86   10,000 enlist in England to avenge her death.... Oct 25, 1:2,3
(This is also an opportunity to introduce the NEW YORK TIMES Personal Name
Index; Cavell is not listed in the NEW YORK TIMES Obit Index.)

Is it true (can you document) that women were barred from the Presidential
Inauguration Parade in 1913?

1913 volume; January-June section:

    101 INAUGURATION--PRESIDENTIAL--PARADE
         Committee bars women from parade, Feb. 12, 8:5

Is it true that English suffragist Sylvia Pankhurst was injured during 1913 forced feeding, and if so, what part of her body was injured?

1913 January-June volume; January-March section:

> 268   WOMAN SUFFRAGE: ENGLAND:--MILITANTS (contd.)
> Sylvia Pankhurst's eyes are injured by forcible feeding.... Mar 25,
> 1:4

The infamous Triangle Shirt Waist Company fire took place in March 1911. However, in 1911, fire victims experienced a real "slow burn"; they were still in the news in April 1911, when the "144th victim dies." Students of what university were involved in the rescue work in March? In December, three hundred women attacked some of the defendants at their trial as they entered court to be tried for the death of which victim (what was her name)? Later that month, what verdict was reached?

1911 volume:

> 88-9   FIRES--TRIANGLE SHIRT WAIST CO (NYC)
> New York University students rescue work described Mr 26, 1:3-7.
> ... tried for death of M. Schwartz D 6, 24:1
> ... not guilty of manslaughter D 28, 1:3

In December 1911, Amundsen reached the South Pole. Where and when did the New York Times publish a diagram of Amundsen's probable route and Scott's planned route?

1911 volume:

> 12   Amundsen. See ANTARCTIC
> Diagram Ap 23, pt 1, p. 3

Lizzie Borden was accused of killing her stepmother and father on August 4, 1892. She was acquitted. The August 5 New York Times reported that a suspect had been identified; what was his name? On August 19th it reported another person had confessed and described that person as a "crank"; what was her/his name? On October 11th it reported that another newspaper's stories had been disproved, and that it had apologized to Lizzie Borden; what was the name of that newspaper?

1890-1893 volume; July 1-December 31, 1892 section:

> 756   MURDERS & HOMICIDES
> Borden, J J, and Wife; J W Morse suspected. Ag 5 (2-2), 6 (1-3)....
> Crank, C H Peckham's confession Aug 19 - 8-4
> Boston Globe stories disproved; apology to Lizzie Borden Oct 11
> (9-1) 12-3-3

Locate information about the Chinese in San Francisco, California in the early part of 1890. You need information describing their living, working and striking methods. Also confirm that they were required by law to locate in special sections of the city.

1890-1893 volume; January 1-June 30, 1890 section:

108   SAN FRANCISCO CAL
      Chinamen's living, working and striking methods described   June 2--
      3-5
      Chinese: ordinance locating in special sections of city   Mar 15--1-2

You need information about someone described as "the new woman of Japan" in a New York Times special article by Miriam Beard. Her name was Raicho Hiratsuka.

NEW YORK TIMES Personal Name Index leads to the NEW YORK TIMES Index for 1924, January-June section, April-June subsection:

244   HIRATSUKA (mme), Raicho
      por in sp art by Miriam Beard on the new woman of Japan   My 18,
      IV, p6

APPLIED SCIENCE & TECHNOLOGY INDEX, HUMANITIES INDEX,
SOCIAL SCIENCES INDEX

The following problem situations are derived from Applied Science & Technology Index, Humanities Index, and Social Sciences Index and their related predecessor titles. They can be used with Assignment 4 as well as in other situations. Some of these provide experience in understanding the historical evolution of periodical publication, and thus indexing, by means of the predecessor titles and their relationships, in this case, Social Sciences and Humanities and International Indexes mainly. (Applied Science & Technology Index and Business Periodicals Index were combined in Industrial Arts Index in the past.) It may be helpful to review "More Library Basics," especially page 6, in connection with use of these indexes.

Assignment 2 introduced use of the LCSH with an interdisciplinary thematic topic. The example which appears in The Course as presented in Chapter 3 is "... information about care of people with chronic diseases in the United States, including information about the Hospice Movement," which is carried through into Assignment 4, where the student 1) decides which of these three semispecialized Indexes--Applied Science & Technology, Humanities, or Social Sciences--is appropriate, and 2) locates a relevant article by efficient use of that Index.

Humanities Index and Social Sciences Index began a new, clearer layout and typography with volume(s) 10, April 1983-March 1984, in the manner of Readers' Guide. Citations to reviews of books segregated in a section at the end of each cumulated volume began with Volume 1, in 1974.

APPLIED SCIENCE & TECHNOLOGY INDEX
(does not provide author entries)

Locate bibliographically an eight-page article published in August 1985 about the FETUS, specifically the results of exposure of pregnant hamsters to arsenate during early gestation.

"1985" volume:

> 874   FETUS
> Constant rate exposure of pregnant hamsters to arsenate during early gestation. V. H. Ferm and D. P. Hanlon. bibl Environ Res 37:425-32 Ag '85
> Environmental Research

Locate bibliographically a four-page article published in April 1981 about COS-METICS IN INDUSTRY. Someone suggests it will be useful for a report about the impact of EPA hazardous waste regulations on cosmetic and toiletry manufacturing.

"1981" volume:

537   COSMETICS IN INDUSTRY
        Impact of EPA hazardous waste regulations on cosmetic and toiletry
        manufacturing. L. T. Flynn. Soap/Cosmet/Chem Spec 57: 30-3+
        Ap '81
        Soap/Cosmetics/Chemical Specialities

Locate bibliographically a two-page journal article published in May 1980 about
ESTROGENS. Someone suggests it will be useful for a report about the plant
estrogen, coumestrol, in animal feeds.

"1980" volume:

806   ESTROGENS
        Analysis of coumestrol, a plant estrogen in animal feeds by high-
        performance liquid chromatography. G. L. Lookhart bib J Agri &
        Food Chem 28: 666-7 My '80
        Journal of Agricultural and Food Chemistry

... one-page article published in November 1978 about HAIR DYEING AND
BLEACHING's relationship to breast cancer. It was written by P. Gwynne.

"1979" volume:

725   HAIR-DYEING AND BLEACHING
        Hair dyes colour breast cancer fears. P Gwynne. N Scientist 80:
        504 N 16 '78
        New Scientist

... a four-page illustrated article published in June 1978 about MINIATURE
COMPUTERS ... useful for a report about Radio Shack's TRS-80 microcomputer.

"1978" volume:

302   COMPUTERS--MINIATURE COMPUTERS
        Radio Shack TRS-80 microcomputer. il QST 62: 36-9 Je '78
        Q S T

... a one-page article claiming that CROCODILES don't indulge in active sleep,
published in late March 1978.

"1978" volume:

358   CROCODILES
        Crocodiles don't indulge in active sleep. N Scientist 77: 848 Mr 30 '78
        New Scientist [Supersedes Atomic Scientists Journal]

... a seven-page illustrated article, accompanied by a bibliography and diagrams, about NUCLEAR PHYSICS EXPERIMENTS, published in January 1977 ... useful for a report on magnets.

"1977" volume:

> 938 NUCLEAR PHYSICS--EXPERIMENTS
> Large diameter thin superconducting solenoid magnets. M Green.
> bibl il diags Cryogenics 17:17-23 Ja '77
> Cryogenics

... a ten-page illustrated article, accompanied by a bibliography, about WOOD AS FUEL, published in May 1973 ... useful for your report about fuel plantations because useful feedback from readers is also indexed (sometimes referred to as "discussion" in indexing.)

"1974" volume:

> 1708 WOOD AS FUEL
> Energy forests and fuel plantations. G. C. Szego and C. C. Kemp.
> bibliog il Chem Tech 3:275-84 My '73; Discussion 3:391-2; Reply
> 392+ Jl '73
> Chem Tech (Chemical Technology)
> (Also in 1973: 566 FUEL--COSTS)

• • •

The following provide considerable challenge:

You need a review of a book titled Developments in Handling and Processing Fish, written around 1965, from the chemical and industrial perspectives of FISH AS FOOD at that time.

"1965" volume:

> 515 FISH AS FOOD
> Developments in handling and processing fish. G. H. O. Burgess.
> Review by C. L. Cutting. Chem & Ind p 1447-8 Ag 14 '65
> Chemistry and Industry

You need information about the preparation of synthetic ESTROGENS in the past, say in 1957. Someone refers you to a three-page journal article published in July that year, which was accompanied by a bibliography.

Volume 45 (1957), Industrial Arts Index:

> 729 ESTROGENS
> Preparations of synthetic estrogens; new syntheses of 1, 1, 2-tri-p-anisyl-ethylene and diethylstilbestrol. K. Sisido and others. bibliog
> Am Chem Soc J 79:3591-3 Jl 5 '57
> Journal of the American Chemical Society (American Chemical Society Journal, Washington, D.C.)

Locate two book reviews of William McCafferty's 1981 <u>Air Pollution And Athletic</u>
<u>Performance</u>.

"1983" volume:

>   2007   McCafferty, W. B.   Air pollution and athletic performance.   1981
>   Atmos Environ 16 no 11:2761-2 '82 J P Lodge, Jr.
>   J Environ Health 45:315 My/Je '83 E Edmundson

Locate two book reviews of Masatoshi Yamaguchi's 1983 <u>World Vegetables;</u>
<u>Principles, Production and Nutritive Values</u>.

"1984" volume:

>   2033   Yamaguchi, M.   World vegetables.   1983
>   Food Technol 38:138 Mr '84 J Augustin
>   Sci Am 250:30-1 My '84 P Morrison

Locate several book reviews of Elizabeth C. Patterson's <u>Mary Somerville</u>, published in 1983.

"1984" volume:

>   2024   Patterson, E. C.   Mary Somerville and the cultivation of science,
>   1815-1840.   1983
>   Am Sci 72:218-20 Mr/Ap '84 T. H. Levere
>   New Sci 99:952-3 S 29 '83 G. Ferry
>   Science 223:580 F 10 '84 S. Sheets-Pyenson

Locate several book reviews of Frederick Sawkins' <u>Metal Deposits in Relation to</u>
<u>Plate Tectonics</u>, published in 1984.   Who wrote the <u>Science</u> review?

"1985" volume:

>   2503   Sawkins, F. J.   Metal deposits in relation to plate tectonics.   1984.
>   Four reviews cited, one of which is:
>   Science 225:708-9 Ag 17 '84. D. F. Strong.

Locate bibliographically a three-page 1979 article by W. G. Bennis about choice
of OCCUPATIONS, which was supposed to describe the future beyond push-
button careers. Locate at least one additional subject-heading source of leads to
such articles at that time.

"1979" volume:

>   1054   OCCUPATIONS, CHOICE OF
>   Future beyond push-button careers. W. G. Bennis. Tech R 81:12-14
>   Mr-Ap '79
>   Technology Review
>   SEE ALSO   JOB SELECTION

Locate bibliographically a three-page 1979 article by G. E. Schauf about OBESITY, which discusses the validity of the caloric theory. Then locate at least one additional subject-heading source of leads to such articles at that time.

"1979" volume:

    1054 OBESITY
          Is the caloric theory valid? G. E. Schauf. Nutr Today 14:29-31
          Ja '79
          Nutrition Today
    SEE ALSO WEIGHT (PHYSIOLOGY)

Locate bibliographically a four-page illustrated article published in 1972, by J. P. Lyon, about MAPPING with airborne spectrometer data. Then locate at least one additional subject-heading source of leads to such articles at that time.

"1972" volume:

    925   MAPPING, AERIAL
          Infrared spectral emittance in geological mapping; airborne spectrom-
          eter data from Pisgah Crater, Calif. R. J. P. Lyon. bibliog il
          Science 175:983-6 Mr 3 '72
          Science
    SEE ALSO SURVEYING, AERIAL

Locate bibliographically a six-page article published in December 1971 about computer models to evaluate alternative methods of HOSPITALS-related industrial engineering; it was written by Kenny and Murray, who provided diagrams and bibliography. Then locate at least one subject-heading source of leads to such articles at that time.

"1972" volume:

    751   HOSPITALS
          Computer models evaluate alternative methods. J. J. Kenny and G.
          R. Murray. bibliog diag Ind Eng 3:20-5 D '71
          Industrial Engineering
    SEE ALSO CLINICS; WATER SUPPLY FOR HOSPITALS

HUMANITIES INDEX

Locate bibliographically a ten-page article published in fall 1978, about LOVE IN LITERATURE. Someone suggests it will be useful for your paper about short fiction and Joyce Carol Oates.

Volume 6 April 1979-March 1980:

    391   LOVE IN LITERATURE
          Joyce Carol Oates's craftsmanship in The wheel of love. J. V.
          Creighton. Stud Short Fict 15:375-84 Fall '78

149   Creighton, Joanne V.
          Studies in Short Fiction

... a fourteen-page journal article published in April 1979, about American LOVE POETRY. Someone suggests it will be useful for your papers about linguistics and Cummings.

Volume 6 April 1979-March 1980:

    391   LOVE POETRY, AMERICAN
           Cummings' love lyrics: some notes by a female linguist. I. R. Fairley. J Mod Lit 7:205-18 Ap '79
    215   Fairley, Irene R.
           Journal of Modern Literature

... a twelve-page article published in October 1978, about french LOVE POETRY. Someone suggests it will be useful for your French literature and philology course paper.

Volume 6 April 1979-March 1980:

    391   LOVE POETRY, FRENCH
           Belleau's descriptions of the female bosom in La bergerie. R. D. Cottrell. Stud Philol 75:391-402 O '78
    145   Cottrell, Robert D
           Studies in Philology

... a fourteen-page article about LOVE IN LITERATURE, published in fall 1979 in a regional review. Someone suggests it will be useful for your American historical fiction paper.

Volume 6 April 1979-March 1980:

    391   LOVE IN LITERATURE
           Romance without women: the sterile fiction of the American West. M. E. Heatherington. Ga R 33:643-56 Fall '79
    283   Heatherington, Madelon E.
           Georgia Review

... an eleven-page article about SHAME IN LITERATURE, published in April 1978. Someone suggests it will be useful for your paper on literature and morals.

Volume 5 April 1978-March 1979:

    588   SHAME IN LITERATURE
           <u>Dike</u> as a moral term in Homer and Hesiod. M. W. Dickie. Class Philol 73:91-101 Ap '78
    158   Dickie, Matthew W.
           Classical Philology

282   HOMER
363   LITERATURE AND MORALS

... a four-page journal article about the Parthenon in ATHENS and the goddess Minerva, published in summer 1977. Someone suggests it will be good for your archaeology course paper, and points out that it has a bibliography following the article itself.

Volume 4   April 1977-March 1978:

    42   ATHENS--PARTHENON
          Parthenon frieze and the sacrifice to Athena. S. I. Rotroff   bibl
          f   Am J Archaeol 81 no 3:379-82   Summ '77
    595   Rotroff, Susan I
          American Journal of Archaeology
    42   ATHENA (MINERVA)

(This is also useful as an example of an article also indexed in <u>Art Index</u> and the <u>Arts and Humanities Citation Index</u>.)

... a twenty-five page article about African FOLK DRAMA, published in fall 1977. Someone suggests it will be useful for your comparative drama course report.

Volume 4   April 1977-March 1978:

    234   FOLK DRAMA, AFRICAN
          African theatre and the West. D. Baker. Comp Drama 11:227-51
          Fall '77
    51   Baker, Donald
          Comparative Drama

... twenty-four page article about William Dean HOWELLS, published in December 1977. Someone suggests it will be useful for your paper on Howells and his magazine readership.

Volume 4   April 1977-March 1978:

    308   HOWELLS, WILLIAM DEAN
          Different view of the iron madonna; William Dean Howells and his
          magazine readers. L. T. Goldman. New Eng Q 50:563-86 D '77
    265   Goldman, Laurel T
          New England Quarterly

... a brief article about CHIMPANZEES from the humanist's perspective, published in November 1975. Someone suggests it will also be useful for your report on humankind's learning from apes.

Volume 3   April 1976-March 1977:

    119   CHIMPANZEES

Learning from apes. E. Doerr. Humanist 35:35 N '75
189 Doerr, Edd
The Humanist

... an illustrated, three-page article about CH'IN Shih-huang-ti, emperor of China (259-210 B.C.), published in October 1975. Someone suggests it will be great for your report on the important archaeological find known as the emperor's "underground army."

Volume 3 April 1976-March 1977:

119 CH'IN SHIH-HUANG-TI, EMPEROR OF CHINA, 259-210 B.C.
First emperor's underground army: an important Chinese find.
R. C. Rudolph. il map Archaeology 28:267-9 O '75
644 Rudolph, Richard C
Archaeology

•   •   •

The following provide considerable challenge:

Locate a review of David Wellbery's 1984 book Laocoon; Semiotics and Aesthetics in the Age of Reason. In fact, locate at least four; who wrote the Times Literary Supplement review?

Volume 12 April 1985-March 1986:

1320 Wellbery, D. E. Lessing's Laocoon. 1984
Four reviews are cited, including:
Times Lit Suppl no 4269-99 Ja 25 '85. J. P. Stern

Locate several reviews (at least four) of Eudora Welty's 1984 book One Writer's Beginnings. Who wrote the review published in the Hudson Review?

Volume 12 April 1985-March 1986:

1320 Welty, E. One writer's beginnings. 1984
Four reviews cited, including
Hudson Rev 38:473-80 Aug '85. D. Flower

Locate several reviews (at least four) of Richard Weisman's 1984 book Witchcraft, Magic, and Religion in 17th-Century Massachusetts. Who wrote the New England Quarterly review?

Volume 12 April 1985-March 1986:

1320 Weisman, R. Witchcraft, magic, and religion in 17th-century Massachusetts. 1984
Four reviews are cited, including
N Engl Q 57:598-602 D '84. B. Rosenthal

Locate several (at least nine) reviews of Roger Anstey's 1975 book <u>Atlantic Slave</u> <u>Trade and British Abolition, 1760-1810</u>. Who wrote the review published in the March 1977 issue of <u>Canadian Historical Review</u>?

Volume 4 April 1977-March 1978:

771 Anstey, R. Atlantic slave trade and British abolition, 1760-1810.
1975.
Nine reviews are cited, including
Can Hist R 58:93-4 Mr '77 R. C. Reinders

Locate several (at least eight) reviews of Sacvan Bercovitch's 1975 book <u>Puritan</u> <u>Origins of the American Self</u>. Who wrote the review published in <u>Cross Currents'</u> Spring 1977 issue?

Volume 4 April 1977-March 1978:

780 Bercovitch, S. Puritan origins of the American self. 1975
Eight reviews are cited, including
Cross Cur 27:115-22 Spr '77 G. Pepper

Locate several (at least three) reviews of David Goldknopf's 1972 book <u>Life of the</u> <u>Novel</u>. Who wrote the review published in the Winter 1974 issue of <u>Books Abroad</u>?

Volume 1 April 1974-March 1975:

553 Goldknopf, D. Life of the novel
Three reviews are cited, including
Books Abroad 48:216 Wint '74. D. L. Maddox

Locate several (at least three) reviews of Harold J. Gordon, Jr.'s <u>Hitler and the</u> <u>Beer Hall Putsch</u>, published around 1972. Who wrote the <u>Journal of Modern</u> <u>History</u> March 1974 issue review?

Volume 1 April 1974-March 1975:

553 Gordon, H. J., Jr. Hitler and the Beer hall putsch
Three reviews are cited, including
J Mod Hist 46:156-8 Mr '74. K. Schonhoven

Locate bibliographically a two-page illustrated article about CHILDREN AS ACTORS, published in Winter 1975-1976. Then identify at least one additional subject-heading source of leads to such articles at that time.

Volume 3 April 1976-March 1977:

119 CHILDREN AS ACTORS
Bad news bears. J. McBride. il Sight & Sound 45:14-15 Wint
'75-76

Sight and Sound
SEE ALSO THEATER, CHILDREN'S

Locate bibliographically a ten-page illustrated article about the Oregon Shakespearean festival, published in spring 1978.

Volume 5   April 1978-March 1979:

460   Oregon Shakespearean festival. See SHAKESPEARE FESTIVALS
588   SHAKESPEARE FESTIVALS
       Oregon Shakespearean festival. A. C. Dessen. il Shakespeare Q
       29:278-85 Spr '78.
       Shakespeare Quarterly, Folger Shakespeare Library, Washington, D.C.

(This also provides opportunity to 1) reinforce "filing rule": SHAKESPEARE
FESTIVALS follows Shakespeare, William in the indexing, and 2) this article is
also locatable by use later of the permuted subject index of the Arts and Humanities Citation Index.)

You understand that there was published in the Winter 1979 issue of an English
literature periodical an "article" which actually consists of references to SOURCES
of information about Richard LOVELACE (1618-1658). This would be very useful
in connection with a term paper in English literature, if you could only track it
down.

Volume 6   April 1979-March 1980:

391   LOVELACE, RICHARD, 1618-1658--SOURCES
       Cavalier country-house poem: mutations on a Jonsonian tradition.
       M. A. C. McGuire. Stud Eng Lit 19:93-108 Wint '79
396   McGuire, Mary Ann C
       Studies in English Literature 1500-1900

You have heard about two articles which sound very useful for your Shakespeare
paper about Hamlet and Measure for Measure. "Desire and the Interpretation of
Desire in Hamlet" (published in 1977) is about his SYMBOLISM AND IMAGERY;
"Head for Maidenhead ... in Measure for Measure (published in 1978) is about
his TECHNIQUE. But, before you bother to get them from the library, you would
like to clear up whether they have been translated into English, and if so, by
whom!

Volume 5   April 1978-March 1979:

588   SHAKESPEARE, WILLIAM--SYMBOLISM AND IMAGERY
       Desire and the interpretation of desire in Hamlet; tr. by J. Hulbert.
       J. Lacan. Yale Fr Stud no 55-56:11-52 '77
339   Lacan, Jacques
       Yale French Studies
588   SHAKESPEARE, WILLIAM--TECHNIQUE
       Head for maidenhead, maidenhead for head: the structure of exchange

504

in Measure for measure; tr. by M. Rosenzweig.
J. Kott. Theatre Q 8:18-24 Aut '78
335   Kott, Jan
      Theatre Quarterly

You've heard about a three-page Russian article titled "In the Manner of the Folkshow," published in 1977, which sounds very useful, <u>but</u> you want to know whether it is translated, and if so, by whom. Also, whether it's illustrated.

Volume 4 April 1977-March 1978:

234   FOLK ART
      In the manner of the folk show; tr. by V. Ivanov. A. Kamensky.
      il Sov Lit no 10:179-81 '77
353   Kamensky, Alexander
      Soviet Literature

SOCIAL SCIENCES INDEX

Locate bibliographically a four-page article published in March 1980 about POR-NOGRAPHY. Someone suggests it will be useful for your paper about liberal ideology in relationship to porn, and also because you're Canadian....

Volume 7 April 1980-March 1981:

768   PORNOGRAPHY
      Pornography's challenge to liberal ideology. L. Clark. Can Forum
      59:9-12 Mr '80
173   Clark, Lorenne
      Canadian Forum

Locate bibliographically a series of articles published starting in June 1978 and followed by discussion into 1980. It is about DECISION MAKING, and the initial article was accompanied by a bibliography about social evolution.

Volume 7 April 1980-March 1981:

245-6 DECISION MAKING
245   Women's status in egalitarian society: implications for social evolu-
      tion. E. Leacock. bibl Cur Anthrop 19:247-75 Je '78; Disc
      19:621-3; 20:184-7, 415-17; 21:406-8 S '78; Mr-Je '79, Je 80.
557   Leacock, Eleanor
      Current Anthropology
1084 WOMEN IN PRIMITIVE SOCIETY
771   POWER (SOCIAL SCIENCES)
Also indexed in Volume 5 April 1978-March 1979 without Discussion.

... a five-page article published in March 1978 about UNMARRIED MOTHERS. Someone suggests this should be useful for your social welfare course.

Volume 5   April 1978-March 1979:

> 1067   UNMARRIED MOTHERS
> Follow-up of unmarried adolescent mothers.   D. F. Clark and R. S.
> Raab.   Soc Work 23:149-53 Mr '78
> 178   Clapp, Douglas F. and Rebecca Staude Raab
> Social Work

... a four-page illustrated article published in January 1978 about environmental aspects of URANIUM MINES AND MINING.   Someone suggests this will be useful for your paper about exporting nuclear fuel.

Volume 5   April 1978-March 1979:

> 1067   URANIUM MINES AND MINING--ENVIRONMENTAL ASPECTS
> Expanding nuclear fuel exports.   R. Paehlke.   il Environment
> 20:2-5 Ja '78
> 734   Paehlke, Robert
> Environment

... an eleven-page journal article about LOVE and attraction; published in June 1977, it may be useful for your social psychology course paper.

Volume 4   April 1977-March 1978:

> 572   LOVE
> Romantic attraction: misattribution versus reinforcement explanations.
> D. T. Kenrick and R. B. Cialdini.   bibl J Pers Soc Psychol 35:381-
> 91 Je '77
> 513   Kenrich, Douglas T. and Cialdini, Robert B.
> Journal of Personality and Social Psychology

... an eight-page report published in June 1977, accompanied by a bibliography, about LOVE; it should be useful for your paper about relationships in successful and unsuccessful marriages.

Volume 4   April 1977-March 1978:

> 572   LOVE
> Analysis of love relationships in functional and dysfunctional mar-
> riages.   A. Fiore and C. H. Swensen.   bibl Psychol Rept 40:707-14
> Je pt 1 '77
> 347   Fiore, Anthony and Swensen, Clifford H.
> Psychological Reports

... a nineteen-page article published in April 1976 in an American review about LOUISIANA SOCIAL HISTORY; it should be very useful for your paper because it is accompanied by a bibliography, and the indexing provides leads to reader reaction ("discussion")! You are concerned with something called repressive justice....

Volume 4   April 1977-March 1978:

    572   LOUISIANA--SOCIAL HISTORY
           Populism and lynching in Louisiana, 1889-1896:   a test of Erikson's
           theory of the relationship between boundary crises and repressive
           justice [mechanical solidarity].   J. M. Inverarity.   bibl Am Sociol
           R 41:262-80 Ap '76; Discussion.   42:355-69, 652-67 Ap, Ag '77
    483   Inverarity, James M.
           American Sociological Review

... a ten-page article published in December 1976 about LOS ANGELES, CALI-
FORNIA, ELECTIONS. It should be useful for your political science course paper
about ethnicity and social class in relationship to municipal elections.

Volume 4   April 1977-March 1978:

    572   LOS ANGELES, CALIFORNIA--ELECTIONS.
           Ethnicity and social class: voting in the 1973 Los Angeles municipal
           elections.   R. M. Halley and others.   W Pol Q 29:521-30 D '76
    406   Halley, Robert M. and others
           Western Political Quarterly

... a fifteen-page journal article, accompanied by a bibliography published in
June 1977, about MENTAL ILLNESS and public opinion. It should be useful for
your paper about social control and mental illness.

Volume 4   April 1977-March 1978:

    609   MENTAL ILLNESS--PUBLIC OPINION
           Effect of sex role differences on the social control of mental illness.
           W. Tudor and others.   bibl J Health & Soc Behav 18: 98-112 Je '77
    992   Tudor, William and others
           Journal of Health and Social Behavior

... a nine-page journal article, accompanied by a bibliography, published in
January 1977, about MENTAL HEALTH SURVEYS; you are particularly interested
in finding information about the effect of interviewer bias on questionnaires for
your psychology course.

Volume 4   April 1977-March 1978

    609   MENTAL HEALTH SURVEYS
           Effect of interviewer bias on mental illness questionnaire responses.
           G. W. McBee and B. Justice.   bibl J Psychol 95:67-75 Ja '77
    575   McBee, George W. and Justice, Blair
           Journal of Psychology

... a ten-page journal article, accompanied by a bibliography, published in
summer 1977, about the behavior of the MENTALLY HANDICAPPED. You are
interested in the "half-way house" concept.

Volume 4   April 1977-March 1978:

    609   MENTALLY HANDICAPPED--BEHAVIOR
          Modification of leisure behavior in a half-way house for retarded
          women. M. S. Johnson and J. S. Bailey. bibl J App Behav Anal
          10:273-82 Summ '77
    501   Johnson, Martha S. and Bailey, Jon S.
          Journal of Applied Behavior Analysis

... a twelve-page international journal article regarding policy related to RURAL
POOR, published in the Fall/Winter 1976-77 issue.

Volume 4   April 1977-March 1978:

    834   RURAL POOR
          Poor rural women: a policy perspective. A. Germain. J Int Aff
          30:161-72 Fall/Wint '76-77
    376   Germain, Adrienne
          Journal of International Affairs

... a six-page illustrated article published in March 1977, about the GIANT
SQUID.

Volume 4   April 1977-March 1978:

    379   GIANT SQUID
          Jumbo squid: dosidicus gigas. K. Straus. il Oceans 10:10-15
          Mr '77
    934   Straus, Karen
          Oceans

... seventeen-page journal article, published in October 1976, about historian
Edward GIBBON's The Decline and Fall of the Roman Empire. You need this for
an economics course.

Volume 4   April 1977-March 1978:

    379   GIBBON, EDWARD
          Gibbon and the publication of The decline and fall of the Roman
          empire, 1776-1976. H. R. Trevor-Roper. J Law & Econ 19:489-505
          O '76
    989   Trevor-Roper, H. R.
          Journal of Law and Economics

... an eleven-page journal article published in Winter 1977 about GESTALT
THERAPY. This should be useful for your psych paper questioning therapies.

Volume 4   April 1977-March 1978:

Is Gestalt therapy a humanistic form of psychotherapy? L. Bergantino.
J Humanistic Psychol 17:51-61 Wint '77
91 Bergantino, Len
Journal of Humanistic Psychology

... a forty-page article about STUDENTS' CIVIL RIGHTS, published in May 1976 and accompanied by a bibliography. Someone says it should be useful in connection with your paper on the role of the federal judiciary.

Volume 3 April 1976-March 1977:

902 STUDENTS--CIVIL RIGHTS
Role of the federal judiciary in directing student-authority interaction.
H. S. Bangser. bibl Educ Urb Soc 8:267-306 My '76
64 Bangser, Henry S.
Education and Urban Society

... a seven-page journal article about SUBLIMINAL PERCEPTION, published in November 1976; someone says it may be useful for your psychology paper.

Volume 3 April 1976-March 1977:

902 SUBLIMINAL PERCEPTION
Effect of embedded words in a brief visual display. D. E. Somekh.
Brit J Psychol 67:529-35 N '76
880 Somekh, David E.
British Journal of Psychology

... an eight-page illustrated article published in Fall 1974, about the social status of the AGED; someone says it is actually about civil rights...

Volume 2 April 1975-March 1976:

15 Compounding impact of age on sex: another dimension of the double standard. T. Sommers. il Civ Rights Digest 7:2-9 Fall '74
826 Sommers, Tish
Civil Rights Digest (Now Perspectives; The Civil Rights Quarterly)
963 WOMEN--SOCIAL STATUS

• • •

The following provide considerable challenge:

Locate several (four) reviews of Peter Worsley's 1984 book, The Three Worlds; Culture and World Development. Who wrote the New Statesman review which appeared in the December 21, 1984 issue?

Volume 12 April 1985-March 1986:

1818 Worsley, P. The three worlds. 1984
      Four reviews, including
      New Statesman 108:50 D 21 '84. A. Foster-Carter

Locate several (four) reviews of Carol T. Schreiber's 1979 book titled <u>Changing Places</u>; who wrote the July 1981 <u>Sociology & Social Research</u> review?

Volume 8 April 1981-March 1982:

    1338 Schreiber, C. T. Changing places; men and women in transitional
          occupations. 1979
          Four reviews, including
          Sociol & Soc Res 65:440-1 Jl '81. T. G. Turk

Locate several (four) reviews of Heribert Adam's 1979 book, <u>Ethnic Power Mobilized</u>; who wrote the review published in the December 1980 issue of <u>American Political Science Review</u>?

Volume 8 April 1981-March 1982:

    1229 Adam, H. and Giliomee, H. Ethnic power mobilized; can South Africa
          change? 1979
          Four reviews, including
          Am Pol Sci R 74:1102 D '80 R. Dale

Your term paper is titled "Contemporary Literature; Women and Nature in Modern Fiction." Someone says there was an article in the fall 1972 issue of <u>Contemporary Literature</u> on exactly that!

Volume 26 April 1972-March 1973 of <u>Social Sciences & Humanities Index</u>:

    560 WOMEN IN LITERATURE
         Women and nature in modern fiction. A. Pratt. Contemp Lit 13:476-
         90 Aut '72
    398 Pratt, Annis

Someone tells you about a poem you <u>must</u> read ... cutesy title is "I'm sick of the nouns in this room; sandstone and dynamite." While you're trying to check it out (all you know is it was published in 1969) in collections of poetry, someone else reminds you that periodical indexes locate such things as book and motion picture reviews, short stories, poems....

Volume 24 April 1970-March 1971 of <u>Social Sciences & Humanities Index</u>:

    364 POEMS--ENGLISH LANGUAGE
         "I'm sick of the nouns in this room." R. Kamenetz. Yale Lit Mag
         138:17-18 Wint '69
    252 Kamenetz, Rodger
         The Yale Literary Magazine

Resources

You are interested in the art of Canadian Eskimos, and would like to get your hands on an illustrated article. Someone thinks there was one published in the Winter 1969-1970 issue of the Hudson Review.

Volume 24 April 1970-March 1971 of Social Sciences & Humanities Index:

    145   ESKIMOS--CANADA
            Art within the Arctic circle. L. R. Lippard. il Hudson R 22:
            665-74 Wint 69-70
    277   Lippard, Lucy R.
            Hudson Review

Someone refers you to an interview by George Stavros of poet Gwendolyn Brooks, published as an article in Winter 1970....

Volume 24 April 1970-March 1971 of Social Sciences & Humanities Index:

    54   BROOKS, Gwendolyn. Interview with Gwendolyn Brooks, by G.
           Stavros. Contemp Lit 11:1-20 Wint '70
    465   STAVROS, George (interviewer). See BROOKS, G. Interview.
           Contemporary Literature

You want to track down Edgar George Kenneth Lopez Escobar's remarks on an infinitary language with constructive formulas, which you understand were published in a 1967 issue of the Journal of Symbolic Logic.

Volume 21 April 1967-March 1968 of Social Sciences & Humanities Index:

    155   Escobar, Edgar George Kenneth Lopez. See Lopez-Escobar, E. G. K.
    305   Lopez-Escobar, Edgar George Kenneth. Remarks on an infinitary
           language with constructive formulas. J Symbol Logic 32:305-18 S '67
           Journal of Symbolic Logic

You need to take over where your instructor left off when s/he referred to a journal article on the influence of religion on career plans and occupational values of college graduates; s/he indicated only that it was in the American Journal of Sociology in mid-1963.

Volume 17 April 1962-March 1964 of International Index:

    719   OCCUPATION, CHOICE OF
           Influences of the religious factor on career plans and occupational
           values on college graduates. A. M. Greeley. il Am J Sociol
           68:658-71 My '63; Reply with rejoinder D. P. Wareirck 69:295-6
           N '63
    420   Greeley, Andrew M
           American Journal of Sociology

Locate an eighteen-page journal article published in August 1981 about MARITAL

VIOLENCE; it should be provided with a bibliography. Then, identify a subject-heading under which additional information will likely be found in the same index at that time.

Volume 8 April 1981-March 1982 of <u>Social Sciences Index</u>:

675 MARITAL VIOLENCE
Status relationships in marriage: risk factors in spouse abuse.
C. A. Hornung & others. bibl J Marr & Fam 43:675-92 Ag '81
491 Hornung, Carlton A. and McCullough, B. Claire
Journal of Marriage and the Family
SEE ALSO WIFE ABUSE
1036 SOCIAL STATUS

You need information about the rights of the unborn. Someone commends to you a two-page journal article published in January 1979 in the United States by psychologists.

Volume 6 April 1979-March 1980 of SOCIAL SCIENCES INDEX:

847 Rights of the unborn. See FETUS--CIVIL RIGHTS
356 FETUS--CIVIL RIGHTS
Civil commitment and the rights of the unborn. P. H. Soloff & others.
Am J Psych 136:114-15 Ja '79
943 Soloff, Paul H.
American Journal of Psychology

Locate a three-page article published in winter 1977 which questioned romantic LOVE. Then, identify a subject-heading under which additional information will likely be found in the same index at that time.

Volume 4 April 1977-March 1978 of <u>Social Sciences Index</u>:

572 LOVE
Whatever happened to romantic love? E. H. Baruch. Dissent 24:
92-4 Wint '77
83 Baruch, Elaine Hoffman
Dissent
SEE ALSO MARRIAGE

Locate a four-page article published in March 1977, accompanied by a bibliography, about children's development and GESTURE. Then, identify a subject-heading under which additional information will likely be found in the same index at that time.

Volume 4 April 1977-March 1978 of <u>Social Sciences Index</u>:

379 GESTURE
Sex-typed mannerisms in normal boys and girls as a function of sex and age. G. A. Rekers and others. bibl Child Develop 48:275-8 Mr '77

812 Rekers, George A. and others
Child Development
SEE ALSO SIGN LANGUAGE

Locate a nine-page article published in April 1977, accompanied by a map, about GHANAn commerce. Then identify a subject-heading under which additional information will likely be found in the same index at that time.

Volume 4 April 1977-March 1978 of <u>Social Sciences Index</u>:

379 GHANA--COMMERCE
Evolution of a port system: the case of Ghana. D. Hilling. map
Geography 62:97-105 Ap '77
421 Hilling, David
Geography
SEE ALSO SHIPPING--GHANA

Locate a four-page article published in January 1976 about foreign STUDENTS; someone says it will be useful in connection with your history of study programs for foreign medical personnel. Then, identify another subject heading under which additional information will likely be found in this index at this time.

Volume 3 April 1976-March 1977 <u>Social Sciences Index</u>:

902 STUDENTS, FOREIGN
Study programs for foreign nurses. R. K. Drury; G. L. Dhillon.
Nurs Outlook 24:41-4 Ja '76
253 Drury, Ruth K.
238 Dhillon, Gita L.
Nursing Outlook
SEE ALSO FULBRIGHT ACT, 1946

You need to locate pictures of the catastrophe at the Indianapolis Speedway in June 1960.

Volume 16 April 1960-March 1962 of <u>International Index</u>:

987 SPEEDWAYS
Collapsing grandstand at Indianapolis [photos] Illus Lond 236:1019
Je 11 '60
Illustrated London News

How would you go about compiling a rather extensive bibliography of contemporary periodical articles on the United States Depression of the 1930's--The Great Depression?

Volumes 6 and 7, July 1931-June 1934 and July 1934-June 1937 of the <u>International Index</u>:

Start in Volume 6 under the subject-heading DEPRESSION, ECONOMIC; see also BUSINESS DEPRESSION and ECONOMIC CONDITIONS.

Practice Using A Periodical Index
Your Name _____

1. These questions relate to using semi-
   specialized periodical indexes
   efficiently; this excerpt appears to
   be from The _____ Index.

   Applied Science & Technology
   Humanities
   Social Sciences

HOSPITALS
Computer models evaluate alternative meth-
ods. J. J. Kenny and G. R. Murray. bib-
liog diag Ind Eng 3:20-5 D '71
Fast-track to quality, speed and economy in
hospital construction M. T. Tengler and
J. W. Smith. diag Bldg Systems Design 68:
19-23 N '71
Health facilities construction, shifting trends.
J. E. Carlson. Archit Rec 151:60 Ja '72
Hospital codes. il DE/J 217:139-40 Je '71
Mount Sinai medical center remodeling. New
York City. il diag Archit Rec 150:100-1 D
'71
   See also
Clinics
Water supply for hospitals

   Air conditioning
Conditioning of biocontainment facilities. M.
Meckler. diags Bldg Systems Design 69:
P27-8 Ap '72
Natural gas cooling/heating brings all-year
comfort to Palm Springs hospital. Bldg
Systems Design 69:7-8 Ap '72
New concept in patient room air condition-
ing. C. Behm. il diag Bldg Systems Design
68:16-19 O '71; Discussion. 69:15 Mr '72

   Cleanliness
Conditioning of biocontainment facilities. M.
Meckler. diags Bldg Systems Design 69:
P27-8 Ap '72
Glass covers walls, cuts costs, adds beauty
durability and fire-resistance. il Glass Ind
53:12-13 My '72

2. These subject headings are all derived from the LCSH.

   TRUE   FALSE

3. Someone interested in journal articles about __HOSPITALS__
   should _____
   also look under the subject heading
   _____ when they use this Index.

4. The excerpt displays #___ articles and #____ cross references.

5. The complete subject heading under which the article by __C. Behm__
   is entered is
   _____

6. You've misplaced your bib cards! Now
   you've got to return to the Index
   volume to get some information.
   Based on the information contained in
   the excerpt, you'll approach first
   which volume of this Index? Put an X
   across it.

   | 1970 | 1971 | 1972 | 1973 |
   | Index | Index | Index | Index |

7. Record on the bib
   card __all__ of the information possible
   for the article
   by __M. Meckler__

   _____
   _____

8. How many of these articles include some bibliographic support? #____

9. The complete title of the __first__ article is "_____
   _____", and it was
   published in volume #____ of the periodical.

10. __Tengler & Smith's__'s article begins and ends on pages _____;
    it appeared in a periodical whose title is abbreviated _____

1. These questions relate to using semi-
   specialized periodical indexes
   efficiently; this excerpt appears to
   be from The _____ Index.

   X   Applied Science & Technology
       Humanities
       Social Sciences

2. These subject headings are all derived from the LCSH.

      TRUE   X   FALSE

3. Someone interested in journal articles about __HOSPITALS_____

   _should_____
    also   look under the subject heading
   CLINICS (&/or WATER SUPPLY FOR HOSPITALS)   when they use this Index.
   _____

```
HOSPITALS
   Computer models evaluate alternative meth-
      ods. J. J. Kenny and G. R. Murray. bib-
      liog diag Ind Eng 3:20-5 D '71
   Fast-track to quality, speed and economy in
      hospital construction M. T. Tengler and
      J. W. Smith. diag Bldg Systems Design 68:
      19-22 N '71
   Health facilities construction, shifting trends.
      J. E. Carlson. Archit Rec 151:60 Ja '72
   Hospital codes. il DE/J 217:139-40 Je '71
   Mount Sinai medical center remodeling, New
      York City. il diag Archit Rec 150:100-1 D
      '71
      See also
   Clinics
   Water supply for hospitals

              Air conditioning
*  Conditioning of biocontainment facilities. M.
      Meckler. diags Bldg Systems .Design 69:
      P27-8 Ap '72
   Natural gas cooling/heating brings all-year
      comfort to Palm Springs hospital. Bldg
      Systems Design 69:7-8 Ap '72
>  New concept in patient room air condition-
      ing. C. Behm. il diag Bldg Systems Design
      68:16-19 O '71; Discussion. 69:15 Mr '72

                 Cleanliness
*  Conditioning of biocontainment facilities. M.
      Meckler. diags Bldg Systems Design 69:
      P27-8 Ap '72
   Glass covers walls, cuts costs, adds beauty
      durability and fire-resistance. il Glass Ind
      53:12-13 My '72
```

4. The excerpt displays # 10 articles and #2 cross references. (Or 11 articles if one "counts" "Discussion" in re Behm article; or 9 if one observes
                                             the Meckler article cited twice.)
5. The complete subject heading under which the article by C. Behm
   is entered is   HOSPITALS-- AIR CONDITIONING

6. You've misplaced your bib cards! Now
   you've got to return to the Index
   volume to get some information.
   Based on the information contained in
   the excerpt, you'll approach first
   which volume of this Index? Put an X
   across it.

   | 1970 | 1971 | X 1972 | 1973 |
   | Index | Index | Index | Index |

7. Record on the bib
   card all of the in-
   formation possible
   for the article
   by M. Meckler
   _____

   _____

   APPLIED SCIENCE & TECH I '72 HOSPITALS-- AIR
   CONDITIONING;HOSPITALS-- CLEANLINESS

   Meckler, M
   "Conditioning of biocontainment facilities".
   Bldg Systems Design 69: P27-8   April 1972

   Has diagrams

8. How many of these articles include some bibliographic support?# 1

9. The complete title of the ___first_____ article is "Computer models
   evaluate alternative methods._____", and it was
   published in volume #_3___ of the periodical.

10. Tengler & Smith's ___'s article begins and ends on pages 19-23 _____;
    it appeared in a periodical whose title is abbreviated Bldg Systems Design

Practice Using A Periodical Index
Your Name _____

1. These questions relate to using semi-
   specialized periodical indexes
   efficiently; this excerpt appears to
   be from The _____ Index.

   Applied Science & Technology
   Humanities
   Social Sciences

OCCUPATIONAL diseases. See Diseases, Indus-
   trial
OCCUPATIONS
   See also
   Negroes—Occupations
   Vocational guidance
   Woman—Occupations
OCCUPATIONS. Choice of
   Future beyond push-button careers. W. G.
   Bennis. Tech R 81:12-14 Mr-Ap '79
   See also
   Job selection
OCEAN
   Application of the parabolic approximation to
   predict acoustical propagation in the ocean.
   S. T. McDaniel. bibl Am J Phys 47:63-8 Ja '79
   Approximate expressions for horizontal electric
   dipole (HED) quasi-static range propagation
   within a conducting slab. P. S. Bannister and
   R. L. Dube. bibl diag Radio Sci 14:27-34 Ja '79
   Attenuation of surface-generated noise received
   deep in the ocean. H. Bradner and A. Par-
   vulescu. Acoust Soc Am J 62:1037-8; 64:322-4
   O '77, Jl '78

2. These subject headings are all derived from the LCSH.

   TRUE   FALSE

3. Someone interested in journal articles about occupational diseases

   should look under the subject heading

   _____ when they use this Index.

4. The excerpt displays #___ articles and #____ cross references.

5. The complete subject heading under which the article by W. G. Bennis
   is entered is

   _____

6. You've misplaced your bib cards! Now
   you've got to return to the Index
   volume to get some information.
   Based on the information contained in
   the excerpt, you'll approach first
   which volume of this Index? Put an X
   across it.

   | 1977 | 1978 | 1979 | 1980 |
   | Index | Index | Index | Index |

7. Record on the bib
   card all of the in-
   formation possible
   for the article
   by Bradner and

   Parvulescu

   _____

8. How many of these articles include some bibliographic support? #____

9. The complete title of the first cited _____ article is " _____
   _____ ", and it was
   published in volume #____ of the periodical.

10. McDaniel's _____'s article begins and ends on pages _____ ;
    it appeared in a periodical whose title is abbreviated _____

1. These questions relate to using semi-specialized periodical indexes efficiently; this excerpt appears to be from The _____ Index.

    X Applied Science & Technology
      Humanities
      Social Sciences

OCCUPATIONAL diseases. See Diseases. Industrial
OCCUPATIONS
    See also
    Negroes—Occupations
    Vocational guidance
    Woman—Occupations
OCCUPATIONS. Choice of
Future beyond push-button careers. W. G. Bennis. Tech R 81:12-14 Mr-Ap '79
    See also
    Job selection
OCEAN
Application of the parabolic approximation to predict acoustical propagation in the ocean. S. T. McDaniel. bibl Am J Phys 47:63-8 Ja '79
Approximate expressions for horizontal electric dipole (HED) quasi-static range propagation within a conducting slab. P. S. Bannister and R. L. Dube. bibl diag Radio Sci 14:27-34 Ja '79
Attenuation of surface-generated noise received deep in the ocean. H. Bradner and A. Parvulescu. Acoust Soc Am J 62:1037-8; 64:322-4 O '77, Jl '78

2. These subject headings are all derived from the LCSH.

    TRUE   X FALSE

3. Someone interested in journal articles about occupational diseases should look under the subject heading DISEASES, INDUSTRIAL when they use this Index.

4. The excerpt displays #4 articles and #5 cross references. (5 articles if one "counts" Bradner and Parvulescu's two issues)

5. The complete subject heading under which the article by W. G. Bennis is entered is OCCUPATIONS, CHOICE OF

6. You've misplaced your bib cards! Now you've got to return to the Index volume to get some information. Based on the information contained in the excerpt, you'll approach first which volume of this Index? Put an X across it.

| 1977 Index | 1978 Index | X 1979 Index | 1980 Index |

7. Record on the bib card all of the information possible for the article by Bradner and Parvulescu

APPLIED SCIENCE & TECH. I 1979   OCEAN

Bradner, H   & A
  Parvulescu
"Attenuation of surface-generated noise received deep in the ocean."
Acoust Soc Am J 62:1037-1038, October 1977; 64:322-324, July 1978.

8. How many of these articles include some bibliographic support? # 2

9. The complete title of the first cited article is "Future beyond push-button careers", and it was published in volume # 81 of the periodical.

10. McDaniel's's article begins and ends on pages 63-68; it appeared in a periodical whose title is abbreviated Am J Phys

1. These questions relate to using semi-specialized periodical indexes efficiently; this excerpt appears to be from The _____ Index.

    Applied Science & Technology
    Humanities
    Social Sciences

2. These subject headings are all derived from the LCSH.

    TRUE   FALSE

3. Someone interested in journal articles about Fiber, Vulcanized
_____
should look under the subject heading
_____ when they use this Index.

4. The excerpt displays #___ articles and #____ cross references.

5. The complete subject heading under which the article by T J Muldoon is entered is
_____

6. You've misplaced your bib cards! Now you've got to return to the Index volume to get some information. Based on the information contained in the excerpt, you'll approach first which volume of this Index? Put an X across it.

    | 1984 | 1985 | 1986 | 1987 |

7. Record on the bib card all of the information possible for the article by H M Staats
_____
_____

8. How many of these articles include some bibliographic support? #_____

9. The complete title of the   last cited   article is "_____
_____", and it was
published in volume #_____ of the periodical.

10. V.C.Setterholm _____'s article begins and ends on pages _____;
it appeared in a periodical whose title is abbreviated_____

Fever
    Response to ethanol reduced by past thiamine deficiency.
    P. R. Martin and others. bibl *Science* 227:1365-8 Mr
    15 '85
Fiber, Vulcanized *See* Vulcanized fiber
Fiber board
    Boxes, corrugated and fibre [Packaging Encyclopedia 1985]
    T. J. Muldoon. diags *Packaging* 30 no4:162-5 '85
    Composite boards require special fasteners. S. Gumbiner.
    Wood Wood Prod 89:196 Ag '84
    Computerizing a panel sizing operation. D. Lenckus. il
    Wood Wood Prod 90:142+ Ag '85
    Continuous laminating line key to German counter-top
    manufacturer's success [TopForm] H. Urban. il *Wood
    Wood Prod* 90:76+ Ap '85
    Cutting tool research and development. H. M. Staats.
    diags *Wood Wood Prod* 89:142+ Ag '84
    Drums, fibre [Packaging Encyclopedia 1985] N. S. Hewitt.
    diags *Packaging* 30 no4:165-6 '85
    Edgebanding cut-to-size panels. *Wood Wood Prod* 90:93
    Je '85
    FPL spaceboard—a new structural sandwich concept. V.
    C. Setterholm. il *Tappi J* 68:40-2 Je '85
    Lumber and particleboard core problems. J. Metz. *Wood
    Wood Prod* 89:22 O '84
    Measure cushioning values of corrugated pads. J. U.
    Liu and J. F. Laundrie. bibl diags *Packaging* 30:58-63
    Ja '85

1. These questions relate to using semi-specialized periodical indexes efficiently; this excerpt appears to be from The _____ Index.

   X Applied Science & Technology
     Humanities
     Social Sciences

> Fever
>   Response to ethanol reduced by past thiamine deficiency.
>   P. R. Martin and others. bibl *Science* 227:1365-8 Mr
>   15 '85
> Fiber, Vulcanized *See* Vulcanized fiber
> Fiber board
>   Boxes, corrugated and fibre [Packaging Encyclopedia 1985]
>   T. J. Muldoon. diags *Packaging* 30 no4:162-5 '85
>   Composite boards require special fasteners. S. Gumbiner.
>   *Wood Wood Prod* 89:196 Ag '84
>   Computerizing a panel sizing operation. D. Lenckus. il
>   *Wood Wood Prod* 90:142+ Ag '85
>   Continuous laminating line key to German counter-top
>   manufacturer's success [TopForm] H. Urban. il *Wood
>   Wood Prod* 90:76+ Ap '85
>   Cutting tool research and development. H. M. Staats.
>   diags *Wood Wood Prod* 89:142+ Ag '84
>   Drums, fibre [Packaging Encyclopedia 1985] N. S. Hewitt.
>   diags *Packaging* 30 no4:165-6 '85
>   Edgebanding cut-to-size panels. *Wood Wood Prod* 90:93
>   Je '85
>   FPL spaceboard—a new structural sandwich concept. V.
>   C. Setterholm. il *Tappi J* 68:40-2 Je '85
>   Lumber and particleboard core problems. J. Metz. *Wood
>   Wood Prod* 89:22 O '84
>   Measure cushioning values of corrugated pads. J. U.
>   Liu and J. F. Laundrie. bibl diags *Packaging* 30:58-63
>   Ja '85

2. These subject headings are all derived from the LCSH.

   TRUE   X FALSE

3. Someone interested in journal articles about <u>Fiber, Vulcanized</u>

   should look under the subject heading <u>VULCANIZED FIBER</u> when they use this Index.

4. The excerpt displays # <u>11</u> articles and # <u>1</u> cross references.

5. The complete subject heading under which the article by <u>T J Muldoon</u> is entered is <u>FIBER BOARD</u>

6. You've misplaced your bib cards! Now you've got to return to the Index volume to get some information. Based on the information contained in the excerpt, you'll approach first which volume of this Index? Put an X across it.

   | 1984 | 1985 (X) | 1986 | 1987 |

7. Record on the bib card <u>all</u> of the information possible for the article by <u>H M Staats</u>

> APPL SCI & TECH I 1985   FIBER BOARD
>
> Staats, H   M
> "Cutting tool research and development"
> Wood Wood Prod 89:142+ Ag '84
>
> (Has diagrams)

8. How many of these articles include some bibliographic support? # <u>2</u>

9. The complete title of the <u>last cited</u> article is "<u>Measure cushioning values of corrugated pads</u>", and it was published in volume # <u>30</u> of the periodical.

10. <u>V. C. Setterholm</u>'s article begins and ends on pages <u>40-42</u>; it appeared in a periodical whose title is abbreviated <u>Tappi J</u>

Course, Date
Instructor

Practice Using A Periodical Index
Your Name _____

1. These questions relate to using semi-specialized periodical indexes efficiently; this excerpt appears to be from The _____ Index.

    Applied Science & Technology
    Humanities
    Social Sciences

2. These subject headings are all derived from the LCSH.

    TRUE   FALSE

3. Someone interested in journal articles about _____ Legionella, should _____ look under the subject heading

_____ when they use this Index.

> Legendre polynomials *See* Polynomials
> Legionella *See* Legionnaires' disease
> **Legionnaires' disease**
> Hospital disease outbreak traced to plumbing links [Britain] *Eng News-Rec* 214:15 Je 27 '85
> Laporte joins battle against legionnaires'. *Chem Ind* no14:452 Jl 15 '85
> Legionnaire's disease causes concern in British industry. *Process Eng* 66:5 Je '85
> Legionnaires' peril from whirlpool baths. D. Mason. *New Sci* 106:5 My 16 '85
> New concern over Legionnaire's disease in cooling towers. *New Sci* 106:8 My 9 '85
> Power stations 'not cause of killer disease'. V. Wyman. il *Engineer* 260:14-15 My 16 '85
> Quickie test for Legionnaires' disease. D. MacKenzie. il *New Sci* 106:20 Je 6 '85
> Scots monitor for Legionnaire bugs. *Chem Ind* no11:348 Je 3 '85
> Wastewater reuse and exposure to legionella organisms. B. Fattal and others. bibl *Water Res* 19 no6:693-6 '85
> **Legislation**
>   *See also*
>   Lobbying
> EAA bogged down [Export Administration Act] W. Schatz. *Datamation* 30:52+ S 1 '84
>   United States
> Budget, other topics keep Congress busy. J. Long. *Chem Eng News* 63:18-19 Ap 15 '85

4. The excerpt displays #___ articles and #____ cross references.

5. The complete subject heading under which the article by J. Long is entered is

_____

6. You've misplaced your bib cards! Now you've got to return to the Index volume to get some information. Based on the information contained in the excerpt, you'll approach first which volume of this Index? Put an X across it.

    1982   1983   1984   1985

7. Record on the bib card <u>all</u> of the information possible for the article by D. MacKenzie

_____
_____

8. How many of these articles include some bibliographic support? #_____

9. The complete title of the <u>third</u> article is "_____", and it was published in volume #_____ of the periodical.

10. V. Wyman's _____'s article begins and ends on pages _____; it appeared in a periodical whose title is abbreviated_____

1. These questions relate to using semi-specialized periodical indexes efficiently; this excerpt appears to be from The _____ Index.

   X   Applied Science & Technology
       Humanities
       Social Sciences

2. These subject headings are all derived from the LCSH.

     TRUE   X FALSE

3. Someone interested in journal articles about _____ Legionella, should _____ look under the subject heading LEGIONNAIRES' DISEASE _____ when they use this Index.

> Legendre polynomials *See* Polynomials
> Legionella *See* Legionnaires' disease
> **Legionnaires' disease**
>   Hospital disease outbreak traced to plumbing links [Britain] *Eng News-Rec* 214:15 Je 27 '85
>   Laporte joins battle against legionnaires'. *Chem Ind* no14:452 Jl 15 '85
>   Legionnaire's disease causes concern in British industry. *Process Eng* 66:5 Je '85
>   Legionnaires' peril from whirlpool baths. D. Mason. *New Sci* 106:5 My 16 '85
>   New concern over Legionnaire's disease in cooling towers. *New Sci* 106:8 My 9 '85
>   Power stations 'not cause of killer disease'. V. Wyman. il *Engineer* 260:14-15 My 16 '85
>   Quickie test for Legionnaires' disease. D. MacKenzie. il *New Sci* 106:20 Je 6 '85
>   Scots monitor for Legionnaire bugs. *Chem Ind* no11:348 Je 3 '85
>   Wastewater reuse and exposure to legionella organisms. B. Fattal and others. bibl *Water Res* 19 no6:693-6 '85
> **Legislation**
>   *See also*
>   Lobbying
>   EAA bogged down [Export Administration Act] W. Schatz. *Datamation* 30:52+ S 1 '84
>   **United States**
>   Budget, other topics keep Congress busy. J. Long. *Chem Eng News* 63:18-19 Ap 15 '85

4. The excerpt displays # 11 articles and # 3 cross references.

5. The complete subject heading under which the article by J. Long is entered is   LEGISLATION-- UNITED STATES

6. You've misplaced your bib cards! Now you've got to return to the Index volume to get some information. Based on the information contained in the excerpt, you'll approach first which volume of this Index? Put an X across it.

     1982   1983   1984   1985
                                       x

7. Record on the bib card all of the information possible for the article by D. MacKenzie

_____

_____

> APPLIED SCIENCE & TECHNOLOGY INDEX 1985
>
> LEGIONNAIRES' DISEASE
>
> MacKenzie, D
> "Quickie test for Legionnaires' disease".
>
> New Sci   106:20 Je 6 '85

8. How many of these articles include some bibliographic support? # 1

9. The complete title of the third article is "Legionnaires' disease causes concern in British industry ", and it was published in volume # 66 of the periodical.

10. V. Wyman's 's article begins and ends on pages 14-15 ; it appeared in a periodical whose title is abbreviated 260

1. These questions relate to using semi-specialized periodical indexes efficiently; this excerpt appears to be from The _____ Index.

   Applied Science & Technology
   Humanities
   Social Sciences

2. These subject headings are all derived from the LCSH.

   TRUE   FALSE

3. Someone interested in journal articles about Chilean poetry in French _____
   should look under the subject heading

   _____ when they use this Index.

CHILEAN literature
   Criticism
   Pablo Neruda's Tentativa del hombre infinito: notes for a reappraisal. R. de Costa. Mod Philol 73:136-47 N '75
CHILEAN literature (French)
   Vicente Huidobro: image as magic. C. Francis. Pa Lang & Lit 12:311-20 Summ '76
CHILEAN poetry (French) See Chilean literature (French)
CHIMMESYAN languages
   See also
   Tsimshian language
CHIMPANZEES
   Learning from apes. E. Doerr. Humanist 35:35 N '75
CH'IN Shih-huang-ti, emperor of China, 253-210 B.C.

4. The excerpt displays # ___ articles and # ____ cross references.

5. The complete subject heading under which the article by R. de Costa is entered is

   _____

6. You've misplaced your bib cards! Now you've got to return to the Index volume to get some information. Based on the information contained in the excerpt, you'll approach first which volume of this Index? Put an X across it.

   | April 1975– March 1976 | April 1976 – March 1977 | April 1977– March 1978 | April 1978 – March 1979 |

7. Record on the bib card all of the information possible for the article by E. Doerr _____

   _____
   _____

8. How many of these articles include some bibliographic support? # _____

9. The complete title of the ___ second cited ___ article is " _____
   _____ ", and it was
   published in volume # _____ of the periodical.

10. C. Francis' _____ 's article begins and ends on pages _____ ;
    it appeared in a periodical whose title is abbreviated _____

1. These questions relate to using semi-specialized periodical indexes efficiently; this excerpt appears to be from The _____ Index.

      Applied Science & Technology
 X Humanities
      Social Sciences

> **CHILEAN literature**
>   Criticism
>   Pablo Neruda's Tentativa del hombre infinito; notes for a reappraisal. R. de Costa. Mod Philol 73:136-47 N '75
> **CHILEAN literature (French)**
>   Vicente Huidobro: image as magic. C. Francis. Pa Lang & Lit 12:311-20 Summ '76
> **CHILEAN poetry (French)** See Chilean literature (French)
> **CHIMMESYAN languages**
>   *See also*
>   Tsimshian language
> **CHIMPANZEES**
>   Learning from apes. E. Doerr. Humanist 35:35 N '75
> **CH'IN Shih-huang-ti, emperor of China, 259-210 B.C.**

2. These subject headings are all derived from the LCSH.

    TRUE   X FALSE

3. Someone interested in journal articles about <u>Chilean poetry in French</u> should look under the subject heading <u>CHILEAN LITERATURE (FRENCH)</u> when they use this Index.

4. The excerpt displays #<u>3</u> articles and #<u>2</u> cross references.

5. The complete subject heading under which the article by <u>R. de Costa</u> is entered is <u>CHILEAN LITERATURE-- CRITICISM</u>

6. You've misplaced your bib cards! Now you've got to return to the Index volume to get some information. Based on the information contained in the excerpt, you'll approach first which volume of this Index? Put an X across it.

April 1975 - March 1976	April 1976 - March 1977 (X)	April 1977 - March 1978	April 1978 - March 1979

7. Record on the bib card <u>all</u> of the information possible for the article by <u>E. Doerr</u> _____ _____

> HUMANITIES INDEX 4/76-3/77 CHIMPANZEES
>
> Doerr, E
>
> "Learning from apes".
>
> Humanist 35:35 November 1975

8. How many of these articles include some bibliographic support? #<u>0</u>

9. The complete title of the <u>second cited</u> article is "<u>Vicente Huidobro: image as Magic</u>", and it was published in volume #<u>12</u> of the periodical.

10. C. Francis' _____'s article begins and ends on pages <u>311-320</u>; it appeared in a periodical whose title is abbreviated <u>Pa. Lang & Lit</u>

Practice Using A Periodical Index
Your Name _____

1. These questions relate to using semi-specialized periodical indexes efficiently; this excerpt appears to be from The _____ Index.

    Applied Science & Technology
    Humanities
    Social Sciences

> children
> **CHILDREN as actors**
> Bad news bears. J. McBride. il Sight & Sound 45:14-15 Wint '75-76
> Kid stuff; Small change; interview by J. McBride and T. McCarthy. F. Truffaut. il Film Comment 12:42-5 S '76
> *See also*
> Theater, Children's
> **CHILDREN as filmmakers**
> Minimoviemakers: child-made films. D. Halleck. il Film Lib Q 9 no3:26-9+ '76
> **CHILDREN in literature**
> Child and the old man in the plays of Edward Bond. J. E. Duncan. Mod Drama 19:1-10 Mr '76
> Houses of fiction in What Maisie knew. C. O. Kaston. Criticism 18:27-42 Wint '76
> I never thought we might want to come back: strategies of transcendence in Tom Sawyer. T. H. Towers. Mod Fict Stud 21:509-20 Wint '75-76
> Joyce's mythic method: structure and unity in An encounter. A. M. Leatherwood. Stud Short Fict 13:71-8 Wint '76
> Nancy Drew, ballbuster. L. Zacharias. J Pop Cult 9:1027-38 Spr '76
> Past and present in That evening sun. J. M. Garrison, jr. Stud Short Fict 13:371-3 Summ '76
> Tom Sawyer, sturdy centenarian. R. L. Coard. Midwest Q 17:329-49 Jl '76
> Warren and Jarrell: the remembered child. B. Quinn. Southern Lit J 8:24-40 Spr '76
> What Maisie knew: the myth of the artist. W. L. Nance. Stud Novel 8:88-102 Spr '76

2. These subject headings are all derived from the LCSH.

    TRUE   FALSE

3. Someone interested in journal articles about CHILDREN AS ACTORS should _____

    also look under the subject heading

    _____ when they use this Index.

4. The excerpt displays #____ articles and #____ cross references.

5. The complete subject heading under which the article by C. O. Kaston is entered is

    _____

6. You've misplaced your bib cards! Now you've got to return to the Index volume to get some information. Based on the information contained in the excerpt, you'll approach first which volume of this Index? Put an X across it.

April 1975 – March 1976	April 1976 – March 1977	April 1977 – March 1978	April 1978 – March 1979

7. Record on the bib card all of the information possible for the article by J. M. Garrison, Jr. _____

    _____

8. How many of these articles include some bibliographic support? #____

9. The complete title of the last cited article is "_____", and it was published in volume #____ of the periodical.

10. T. H. Towers' 's article begins and ends on pages _____; it appeared in a periodical whose title is abbreviated _____

Course, Date
Instructor   KEY

Practice Using A Periodical Index
Your Name _____

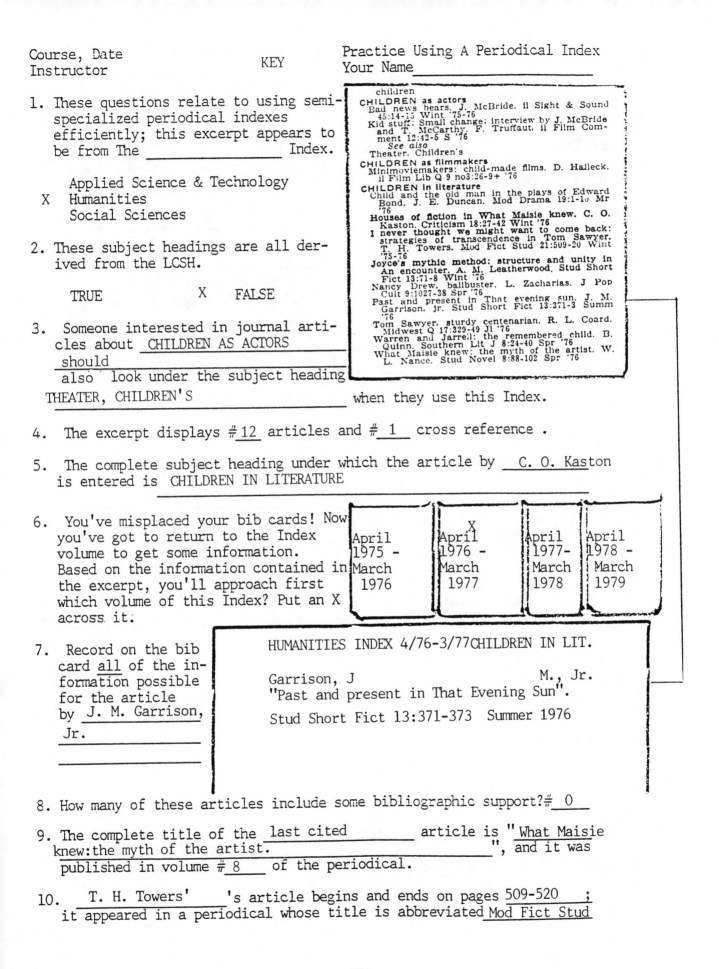

1. These questions relate to using semi-specialized periodical indexes efficiently; this excerpt appears to be from The _____ Index.

    Applied Science & Technology
X Humanities
    Social Sciences

2. These subject headings are all derived from the LCSH.

   TRUE   X   FALSE

3. Someone interested in journal articles about <u>CHILDREN AS ACTORS</u> should also look under the subject heading <u>THEATER, CHILDREN'S</u> _____ when they use this Index.

> children
> **CHILDREN as actors**
>   Bad news bears. J. McBride. il Sight & Sound 45:14-15 Wint '75-76
>   Kid stuff; Small change; interview by J. McBride and T. McCarthy. F. Truffaut. il Film Comment 12:42-5 S '76
>   *See also*
>   Theater, Children's
> **CHILDREN as filmmakers**
>   Minimoviemakers: child-made films. D. Halleck. il Film Lib Q 9 no3:26-9+ '76
> **CHILDREN in literature**
>   Child and the old man in the plays of Edward Bond. J. E. Duncan. Mod Drama 19:1-10 Mr '76
>   **Houses of fiction in What Maisie knew.** C. O. Kaston. Criticism 18:27-42 Wint '76
>   **I never thought we might want to come back:** strategies of transcendence in Tom Sawyer. T. H. Towers. Mod Fict Stud 21:509-20 Wint '75-76
>   Joyce's mythic method: structure and unity in An encounter. A. M. Leatherwood. Stud Short Fict 13:71-8 Wint '76
>   Nancy Drew, ballbuster. L. Zacharias. J Pop Cult 9:1027-38 Spr '76
>   Past and present in That evening sun. J. M. Garrison, jr. Stud Short Fict 13:371-3 Summ '76
>   Tom Sawyer, sturdy centenarian. R. L. Coard. Midwest Q 17:329-49 Jl '76
>   Warren and Jarrell: the remembered child. B. Quinn. Southern Lit J 8:24-40 Spr '76
>   What Maisie knew: the myth of the artist. W. L. Nance. Stud Novel 8:88-102 Spr '76

4. The excerpt displays # <u>12</u> articles and # <u>1</u> cross reference .

5. The complete subject heading under which the article by <u>C. O. Kaston</u> is entered is <u>CHILDREN IN LITERATURE</u>

6. You've misplaced your bib cards! Now you've got to return to the Index volume to get some information. Based on the information contained in the excerpt, you'll approach first which volume of this Index? Put an X across it.

| April 1975 – March 1976 | April 1976 – March 1977 ⟨X⟩ | April 1977– March 1978 | April 1978 – March 1979 |

7. Record on the bib card <u>all</u> of the information possible for the article by J. M. Garrison, Jr.

> HUMANITIES INDEX 4/76-3/77 CHILDREN IN LIT.
>
> Garrison, J   M., Jr.
> "Past and present in That Evening Sun".
> Stud Short Fict 13:371-373 Summer 1976

8. How many of these articles include some bibliographic support? # <u>0</u>

9. The complete title of the <u>last cited</u> article is "<u>What Maisie knew:the myth of the artist.</u>", and it was published in volume # <u>8</u> of the periodical.

10. <u>T. H. Towers'</u>'s article begins and ends on pages <u>509-520</u> ; it appeared in a periodical whose title is abbreviated <u>Mod Fict Stud</u>

525

Practice Using A Periodical Index
Your Name _____

1. These questions relate to using semi-specialized periodical indexes efficiently; this excerpt appears to be from The _____ Index.

   Applied Science & Technology
   Humanities
   Social Sciences

> **HOWELLS. William Dean**
> Different view of the iron madonna: William Dean Howells and his magazine readers. L. T. Goldman. New Eng Q 50:563-86 D '77
> Reality that can't be quite definitely spoken: sexuality in Their wedding journey. G. A. Hunt. Stud Novel 9:17-32 Spr '77
> William Dean Howells and the American Hebrew. G. Monteiro. New Eng Q 50:515-16 S '77
> **HOYT. James L.**
> Courtroom coverage: the effects of being televised. J Broadcasting 21:487-95 Fall '77
> **HOYT. Robert G.**
> Call to reflection. Chr & Crisis 37:253-5, 264-6 O 31-N 14 '77
> Columbia U: the Korean collection. Chr & Crisis 37:210-11 O 3 '77
> **HRAFNKELS saga Freysgoða**
> Discourse of persuasion in Hrafnkatla. K. E. Duhs. Scand Stud 49:464-73 Aut '77
> **HSI-HSIA language. See Tangut language**
> **HSÜN-tzu, 340-245 B.C.**
> Conceptual aspect of Hsün Tzu's philosophy of human nature. A. S. Cua. Philos East & West 27:373-89 O '77
> **HUBERMAN, Elizabeth**
> Mackay Brown's Greenvoe: rediscovering a novel of the Orkneys. Critique 19 no2:33-43 '77

2. These subject headings are all derived from the LCSH.

   TRUE   FALSE

3. Someone interested in journal articles about the Hsi-Hsia language _____

   should look under the subject heading

   _____ when they use this Index.

4. The excerpt displays #___ articles and #____ cross references.

5. The complete subject heading under which the article by K. E. Dubs is entered is

   _____

6. You've misplaced your bib cards! Now you've got to return to the Index volume to get some information. Based on the information contained in the excerpt, you'll approach first which volume of this Index? Put an X across it.

   APRIL 1976-MARCH 1977

   APRIL 1977-MARCH 1978

   APRIL 1978-MARCH 1979

   APRIL 1979-MARCH 1980

7. Record on the bib card all of the information possible for the article by G. A. Hunt

   _____

   _____

8. How many of these articles include some bibliographic support? #____

9. The complete title of the last cited article is "_____", and it was published in volume #____ of the periodical.

10. James L. Hoyt's 's article begins and ends on pages _____; it appeared in a periodical whose title is abbreviated _____

1. These questions relate to using semi-specialized periodical indexes efficiently; this excerpt appears to be from The _____ Index.

   Applied Science & Technology
   X Humanities
   Social Sciences

The excerpt reads:

HOWELLS, William Dean
Different view of the iron madonna: William Dean Howells and his magazine readers. L. T. Goldman. New Eng Q 50:563-86 D '77
Reality that can't be quite definitely spoken: sexuality in Their wedding journey. G. A. Hunt. Stud Novel 9:17-32 Spr '77
William Dean Howells and the American Hebrew. G. Monteiro. New Eng Q 50:515-16 S '77
HOYT, James L.
Courtroom coverage: the effects of being televised. J Broadcasting 21:487-95 Fall '77
HOYT, Robert G.
Call to reflection. Chr & Crisis 37:253-5, 264-6 O 31-N 14 '77
Columbia U: the Korean collection. Chr & Crisis 37:210-11 O 3 '77
HRAFNKELS saga Freysgoða
Discourse of persuasion in Hrafnkatla. K. E. Dubs. Scand Stud 49:464-73 Aut '77
HSI-HSIA language. See Tangut language
HSÜN-tzu, 340-245 B.C.
Conceptual aspect of Hsün Tzu's philosophy of human nature. A. S. Cua. Philos East & West 27:373-89 O '77
HUBERMAN, Elizabeth
Mackay Brown's Greenvoe: rediscovering a novel of the Orkneys. Critique 19 no2:33-43 '77

2. These subject headings are all derived from the LCSH.

   TRUE   X FALSE

3. Someone interested in journal articles about <u>the Hsi-Hsia language</u> should look under the subject heading <u>TANGUT LANGUAGE</u> when they use this Index.

4. The excerpt displays #_9_ articles and #_1_ cross reference .

5. The complete subject heading under which the article by <u>K. E. Dubs</u> is entered is   HRAFNKELS SAGA FREYSGOÐA

6. You've misplaced your bib cards! Now you've got to return to the Index volume to get some information. Based on the information contained in the excerpt, you'll approach first which volume of this Index? Put an X across it.

APRIL 1976-MARCH 1977	X APRIL 1977-MARCH 1978	APRIL 1978-MARCH 1979	APRIL 1979-MARCH 1980

7. Record on the bib card <u>all</u> of the information possible for the article by <u>G. A. Hunt</u>
   _____
   _____

HUMANITIES I 4/77-3/78   HOWELLS, WM. DEAN

Hunt, G   A

"Reality that can't be quite definitely spoken: sexuality in Their Wedding Journey".

Stud Novel 9:17-32 Spr 1977

8. How many of these articles include some bibliographic support? #_0_

9. The complete title of the <u>last cited</u> article is "<u>Mackay Brown's Greenvoe: rediscovering a novel of the Orkneys.</u>", and it was published in volume #_19_ of the periodical.

10. James L. Hoyt's 's article begins and ends on pages <u>487-495</u> ; it appeared in a periodical whose title is abbreviated <u>J Broadcasting</u>

1. These questions relate to using semi-
specialized periodical indexes
efficiently; this excerpt appears to
be from The _____ Index.

    Applied Science & Technology
    Humanities
    Social Sciences

FOLK art
"In the manner of the folk show; tr. by V. Iva-
nov. A. Kamensky. il Sov Lit no 10:179-81 '77
Siras Bowens of Sunbury, Georgia; a Tidewater
artist in the Afro-American visual tradition.
R. F. Thompson. il Mass R 18:490-500 Aut '77
FOLK drama
    See also
    Carnival plays
    Mumming plays
FOLK drama, African
African theatre and the West. D. Baker. Comp
Drama 11:227-51 Fall '77
FOLK drama, German
    See also
    Carnival plays
FOLK drama, Hungarian
Hungarian Christmas mummers' play in Toledo,
Ohio. R. J. Pentzell. il Educ Theatre J 29:179-
98 My '77
FOLK literature, African
      Bibliography
African folklore for African children. N. J.
Schmidt. Res Afric Lit 8:304-26 Wint '77

2. These subject headings are all derived from the LCSH.

    TRUE   FALSE

3. Someone interested in journal articles about ___FOLK DRAMA___
should _____
also look under the subject heading

_____ when they use this Index.

4. The excerpt displays #___ articles and #____ cross references.

5. The complete subject heading under which the article by ___N. J. Schmidt___
is entered is
_____

6. You've misplaced your bib cards! Now
you've got to return to the Index
volume to get some information.
Based on the information contained in
the excerpt, you'll approach first
which volume of this Index? Put an X
across it.

April 1976-March 1977	April 1977-March 1978	April 1978-March 1979	April 1979-March 1980

7. Record on the bib
card all of the in-
formation possible
for the article
by ___R. J. Pentzell___

_____
_____

8. How many of these articles include some bibliographic support?#_____

9. The complete title of the ___second cited___ article is " _____
_____", and it was
published in volume #_____ of the periodical.

10. ___D. Baker___'s article begins and ends on pages _____;
it appeared in a periodical whose title is abbreviated_____

1. These questions relate to using semi-specialized periodical indexes efficiently; this excerpt appears to be from The _____ Index.

    Applied Science & Technology
X   Humanities
    Social Sciences

> **FOLK art**
> In the manner of the folk show; tr. by V. Ivanov. A. Kamensky. il Sov Lit no 10:179-81 '77
> Siras Bowens of Sunbury, Georgia; a Tidewater artist in the Afro-American visual tradition. R. F. Thompson. il Mass R 18:490-500 Aut '77
> **FOLK drama**
>   *See also*
>   Carnival plays
>   Mumming plays
> **FOLK drama, African**
> African theatre and the West. D. Baker. Comp Drama 11:227-51 Fall '77
> **FOLK drama, German**
>   *See also*
>   Carnival plays
> **FOLK drama, Hungarian**
> Hungarian Christmas mummers' play in Toledo. Ohio. R. J. Pentzell. il Educ Theatre J 29:179-98 My '77
> **FOLK literature, African**
>   **Bibliography**
> African folklore for African children. N. J. Schmidt. Res Afric Lit 8:304-26 Wint '77

2. These subject headings are all derived from the LCSH.

    TRUE   X   FALSE

3. Someone interested in journal articles about ___FOLK DRAMA___ should ___also look under the subject heading CARNIVAL PLAYS (&/or MUMMING PLAYS)___ when they use this Index.

4. The excerpt displays #_5_ articles and #_3_ cross references.

5. The complete subject heading under which the article by _N. J. Schmidt_ is entered is ___FOLK LITERATURE, AFRICAN-- BIBLIOGRAPHY___

6. You've misplaced your bib cards! Now you've got to return to the Index volume to get some information. Based on the information contained in the excerpt, you'll approach first which volume of this Index? Put an X across it.

April 1976-March 1977	X April 1977-March 1978	April 1978-March 1979	April 1979-March 1980

7. Record on the bib card **all** of the information possible for the article by _R. J. Pentzell_
_____
_____

> HUMANITIES I 4/77-3/78 FOLK DRAMA, HUNGARIAN
>
> Pentzell, R   J
> "Hungarian Christmas mummers' play in Toledo, Ohio"
>   Educ Theatre J 29:179-198 May 1977
>
> illustrated

8. How many of these articles include some bibliographic support? #_0_

9. The complete title of the _second cited_ article is " _Siras Bowens of Sunbury,Georgia;a Tidewater artist in the Afro-American visual tradition_ ", and it was published in volume #_18_ of the periodical.

10. _D. Baker_'s article begins and ends on pages _227-251_ ; it appeared in a periodical whose title is abbreviated _Comp Drama_

Practice Using A Periodical Index
Your Name _____

1. These questions relate to using semi-specialized periodical indexes efficiently; this excerpt appears to be from The _____ Index.

   Applied Science & Technology
   Humanities
   Social Sciences

SHAKESPEARE. William—

Style
See Shakespeare, W.—Language, style

Symbolism and Imagery
Desire and the interpretation of desire in Hamlet; tr. by J. Hulbert. J. Lacan. Yale Fr Stud no 55-56:11-52 '77
Hamlet: a writing-effect; tr. by J. Hulbert and J. Wilner. D. Sibony. Yale Fr Stud no55-56:53-93 '77
King Lear's good block. W. L. Frazer. Shakespeare Q 28:354-5 Summ '77; Reply. G. W. Williams. 29:421-2 Summ '78
Kings games: stage imagery and political symbolism in Richard III. B. G. Lyons. Criticism 20:17-30 Wint '78
This fell sergeant. Death. R. E. Pitts. Shakespeare Q 20:486-91 Aut '69; Discussion. 26:74-5; 29:94-5 Wint '75, Wint '78

Technique
Contest, riddle, and prophecy: reflexivity through folklore in King Lear. P. Gorfain. Southern Folklore Q 41:239-54 '77
Gross and scope of opinion: Hamlet and the critics. W. Hutchings. Il Crit Q 20:23-32 Aut '78
Head for maidenhead, maidenhead for head: the structure of exchange in Measure for measure; tr. by M. Rosenzweig. J. Kott. Theatre Q 8:18-24 Aut '78
Ironic equation in Shakespeare's Othello: appearances equal reality. E. W. Taylor. CLAJ 21:202-11 D '77

2. These subject headings are all derived from the LCSH.

   TRUE   FALSE

3. Someone interested in journal articles about _Shakespeare's style_ should look under the subject heading _____ when they use this Index.

4. The excerpt displays #___ articles and #___ cross references.

5. The complete subject heading under which the article by _P. Gorfain_ is entered is _____

6. You've misplaced your bib cards! Now you've got to return to the Index volume to get some information. Based on the information contained in the excerpt, you'll approach first which volume of this Index? Put an X across it.

   | APRIL 1977-MARCH 1978 | APRIL 1978-MARCH 1979 | APRIL 1979-MARCH 1980 | APRIL 1980-MARCH 1981 |

7. Record on the bib card _all_ of the information possible for the article by _J. Lacan_

8. How many of these articles include some bibliographic support?#_____

9. The complete title of the _last cited_ article is "_____", and it was published in volume #_____ of the periodical.

10. _B. G. Lyons_'s article begins and ends on pages _____; it appeared in a periodical whose title is abbreviated _____

1. These questions relate to using semi-specialized periodical indexes efficiently; this excerpt appears to be from The _____ Index.

      Applied Science & Technology
 X Humanities
      Social Sciences

2. These subject headings are all derived from the LCSH.

    TRUE   X FALSE

3. Someone interested in journal articles about Shakespeare's style

should look under the subject heading

SHAKESPEARE, WILLIAM-- LANGUAGE, STYLE when they use this Index.

> SHAKESPEARE, William—
>
> **Style**
> *See* Shakespeare, W.—Language, style
>
> **Symbolism and Imagery**
> Desire and the interpretation of desire in Hamlet;
> tr. by J. Hulbert. J. Lacan. Yale Fr Stud no
> 55-56:11-52 '77
> Hamlet: a writing-effect; tr. by J. Hulbert and J.
> Wilner. D. Sibony. Yale Fr Stud no55-56:53-93
> '77
> King Lear's good block. W. L. Frazer. Shakespeare Q 28:354-5 Summ '77; Reply. G. W.
> Williams. 29:421-2 Summ '78
> Kings gulnes: stage imagery and political symbolism in Richard III. B. G. Lyons. Criticism
> 20:17-30 Wint '78
> This fell sergeant. Death. R. E. Pitts. Shakespeare Q 20:456-91 Aut '69; Discussion. 26:74-5;
> 29:84-5 Wint '75. Wint '78
>
> **Technique**
> Contest, riddle, and prophecy: reflexivity through
> folklore in King Lear. P. Gorfain. Southern
> Folklore Q 41:239-54 '77
> Cross and scope of opinion: Hamlet and the
> critics. W. Hutchings. Il Crit Q 20:23-32 Aut '78
> Head for maidenhead, maidenhead for head: the
> structure of exchange in Measure for measure;
> tr. by M. Rosenzweig. J. Kott. Theatre Q
> 8:18-24 Aut '78
> Ironic equation in Shakespeare's Othello: appearances equal reality. E. W. Taylor. CLAJ
> 21:202-11 D '77

4. The excerpt displays # 9 articles and # 1 cross reference . (11 articles if one "counts" the Reply to Frazer and Discussion re Pitts.)

5. The complete subject heading under which the article by P. Gorfain is entered is SHAKESPEARE, WILLIAM-- TECHNIQUE

6. You've misplaced your bib cards! Now you've got to return to the Index volume to get some information. Based on the information contained in the excerpt, you'll approach first which volume of this Index? Put an X across it.

APRIL 1977-MARCH 1978	X APRIL 1978-MARCH 1979	APRIL 1979-MARCH 1980	APRIL 1980-MARCH 1981

7. Record on the bib card all of the information possible for the article by J. Lacan
_____
_____

> HUMANITIES I 4/78-3/79 SHAKESPEARE, WILLIAM--
> SYMBOLISM AND IMAGERY
>
> Lacan, J
> "Desire and the interpretation of desire in Hamlet;
> tr.by J. Hulbert"
> Yale Fr Stud no. 55-56: 11-52 1977

8. How many of these articles include some bibliographic support?# 0

9. The complete title of the last cited article is "Ironic equation in Shakespeare's Othello:appearances equal reality ", and it was published in volume # 21 of the periodical.

10. B. G. Lyons 's article begins and ends on pages 17-30 ; it appeared in a periodical whose title is abbreviated Criticism

Practice Using A Periodical Index
Your Name _____

1. These questions relate to using semi-specialized periodical indexes efficiently; this excerpt appears to be from The _____ Index.

    Applied Science & Technology
    Humanities
    Social Sciences

> Stratford festival Canada. R. Berry. Shakespeare Q 29:222-26 Spr '78
> Theater at Monmouth. H. S. Weil. il Shakespeare Q 29:226-8 Spr '78
> SHAKESPEARE in fiction, drama, poetry, etc.
>   Artist, critic, and performer: Wilde and Joyce on Shakespeare. R. B. Kershner, Jr. Tex Stud Lit & Lang 20:216-29 Summ '78
> SHAKESPEARE memorial, Washington, D.C. See Folger Shakespeare library
> SHALIAPIN, Feodor Ivanovich
>   Irving and Chaliapin. J. Leggio. Theatre Notebk 32 no 1:32-7 '78
> SHAMANISM
>   Meaning of the t'ao-t'ieh. J. Paper. il Hist Relig 18:18-41 Ag '78
>   Research priorities in the study of Ch'u religion. J. S. Major. Hist Relig 17:226-43 F/My '78
> SHAME
>   *See also*
>   Guilt
> SHAME in literature
>   *Dike* as a moral term in Homer and Hesiod. M. W. Dickie. Class Philol 73:91-101 Ap '78
> SHAMMAS, Carole
>   Constructing a wealth distribution from probate records. J Interdiscip Hist 9:297-307 Aut '78

2. These subject headings are all derived from the LCSH.

    TRUE   FALSE

3. Someone interested in journal articles about <u>the Shakespeare Memorial</u> <u>in Washington, D.C.</u> should look under the subject heading

_____ when they use this Index.

4. The excerpt displays #____ articles and #____ cross references.

5. The complete subject heading under which the article by <u>R. B. Kershner</u> is entered is

_____

6. You've misplaced your bib cards! Now you've got to return to the Index volume to get some information. Based on the information contained in the excerpt, you'll approach first which volume of this Index? Put an X across it.

    APRIL 1977-MARCH 1978   APRIL 1978-MARCH 1979   APRIL 1979-MARCH 1980   APRIL 1980-MARCH 1981

7. Record on the bib card <u>all</u> of the information possible for the article by <u>M. W. Dickie</u>

_____

_____

8. How many of these articles include some bibliographic support? #____

9. The complete title of the <u>last cited</u> article is "_____
_____", and it was published in volume #____ of the periodical.

10. <u>J. Paper's</u> _____'s article begins and ends on pages _____; it appeared in a periodical whose title is abbreviated _____

1. These questions relate to using semi-specialized periodical indexes efficiently; this excerpt appears to be from The _____ Index.

      Applied Science & Technology
X Humanities
      Social Sciences

> Stratford festival Canada. R. Berry. Shakespeare Q 29:222-26 Spr '78
> Theater nt Monmouth. H. S. Weil. il Shakespeare Q 29:226-8 Spr '78
> SHAKESPEARE in fiction, drama, poetry, etc.
> Artist, critic, and performer: Wilde and Joyce on Shakespeare. R. B. Kershner, jr. Tex Stud Lit & Lang 20:216-29 Summ '78
> SHAKESPEARE memorial. Washington, D.C. See Folger Shakespeare library
> SHALIAPIN, Feodor Ivanovich
> Irving and Chaliapin. J. Leggio. Theatre Notebk 32 no 1:32-7 '78
> SHAMANISM
> Meaning of the t'ao-t'ieh. J. Paper. il Hist Relig 18:13-41 Ag '78
> Research priorities in the study of Ch'u religion. J. S. Major. Hist Relig 17:226-43 F/My '78
> SHAME
>   See also
>   Guilt
> SHAME in literature
>   Dike as a moral term in Homer and Hesiod. M. W. Dickie. Class Philol 73:91-101 Ap '78
> SHAMMAS, Carole
> Constructing a wealth distribution from probate records. J Interdiscip Hist 9:297-307 Aut '78

2. These subject headings are all derived from the LCSH.

    TRUE   X   FALSE

3. Someone interested in journal articles about the Shakespeare Memorial in Washington, D.C. should look under the subject heading

   FOLGER SHAKESPEARE LIBRARY   when they use this Index.

4. The excerpt displays # 8 articles and # 2 cross references.

5. The complete subject heading under which the article by R. B. Kershner is entered is   SHAKESPEARE IN FICTION, DRAMA, POETRY, ETC.

6. You've misplaced your bib cards! Now you've got to return to the Index volume to get some information. Based on the information contained in the excerpt, you'll approach first which volume of this Index? Put an X across it.

APRIL 1977- MARCH 1978	X APRIL 1978- MARCH 1979	APRIL 1979- MARCH 1980	APRIL 1980- MARCH 1981

7. Record on the bib card all of the information possible for the article by M. W. Dickie

> HUMANITIES I 4/78-3/79 SHAME IN LITERATURE
>
> Dickie, M   W.
> "Dike as a moral term in Homer and Hesiod".
>
> Class philol 73:91-101 April 1978

8. How many of these articles include some bibliographic support? # 0

9. The complete title of the ___last cited___ article is "Constructing a wealth distribution from probate records ", and it was published in volume # 9 of the periodical.

10. J. Paper's ___'s article begins and ends on pages 18-41 ; it appeared in a periodical whose title is abbreviated Hist Relig

1. These questions relate to using semi-
   specialized periodical indexes
   efficiently; this excerpt appears to
   be from The _____ Index.

   Applied Science & Technology
   Humanities
   Social Sciences

2. These subject headings are all derived from the LCSH.

   TRUE   FALSE

3. Someone interested in journal articles about __the wood industry____
   _____
   should look under the subject heading
   _____ when they use this Index.

> **Wood carving, American**
> The American carousel as an immigrant icon. A. Gulliford.
> il *J Am Cult* 7:3-17 Wint '84
> **Wood engraving**
>   *See also*
>   Chiaroscuro
> **Wood engraving, Chinese**
> Chinese woodcuts 1935-49. A. Smedley. il *Mass Rev*
> 25:553-64 Wint '84
> **Wood-Holt, B.**
> Hannah Lightfoot and Isaac Axford. *Notes Queries*
> 31:397-401 S '84
> **Wood in literature**
> Acharnians 181: a jest after all. L. A. Losada. *Am J
> Philol* 105:327-9 Fall '84
> **Wood industry** *See* Lumber industry
> **Woodall, Guy R.**
> Another source for the "misty mid region of Weir
> *Am Notes Queries* 23:8-10 S/O '84
> **Woodbury, Anthony C.**
> Graded syllable weight in Central Alaskan Yupik Eskimo
> (Hooper Bay-Chevak). *Int J Am Linguist* 51:620-3 O
> '85
> **Woodbury, Richard B.**
> Regional archaeological conferences. bibl *Am Antiq*
> 50:434-44 Ap '85; Errata. 51:220 Ja '86
> **Woodcock, George, 1912-**
> Henry Mayhew and the undiscovered country of the
> poor. *Sewanee Rev* 92:556-73 Fall '84

4. The excerpt displays #___ articles and #____ cross references.

5. The complete subject heading under which the article by L. A. Losada
   is entered is
   _____

6. You've misplaced your bib cards! Now
   you've got to return to the Index
   volume to get some information.
   Based on the information contained in
   the excerpt, you'll approach first
   which volume of this Index? Put an X
   across it.

   | APRIL 1984 - MARCH 1985 | APRIL 1985 - MARCH 1986 | APRIL 1986 - MARCH 1987 | APRIL 1987 - MARCH 1988 |

7. Record on the bib
   card __all__ of the information possible
   for the article
   by _A. Smedley____
   _____
   _____

8. How many of these articles include some bibliographic support? #____

9. The complete title of the __last cited___ article is "_____
   _____", and it was
   published in volume #____ of the periodical.

10. Guy Woodall_____'s article begins and ends on pages _____;
    it appeared in a periodical whose title is abbreviated _____

1. These questions relate to using semi-specialized periodical indexes efficiently; this excerpt appears to be from The _____ Index.

   ___ Applied Science & Technology
   X   Humanities
   ___ Social Sciences

> Wood carving, American
>   The American carousel as an immigrant icon. A. Gulliford. il *J Am Cult* 7:3-17 Wint '84
> Wood engraving
>   *See also*
>   Chiaroscuro
> Wood engraving, Chinese
>   Chinese woodcuts 1935-49. A. Smedley. il *Mass Rev* 25:553-64 Wint '84
> Wood-Holt B.
>   Hannah Lightfoot and Isaac Axford. *Notes Queries* 31:397-401 S '84
> Wood in literature
>   Acharnians 181: a jest after all. L. A. Losada. *Am J Philol* 105:327-9 Fall '84
> Wood industry *See* Lumber industry
> Woodall, Guy R.
>   Another source for the "misty mid region of Weir". *Am Notes Queries* 23:8-10 S/O '84
> Woodbury, Anthony C.
>   Graded syllable weight in Central Alaskan Yupik Eskimo (Hooper Bay-Chevak). *Int J Am Linguist* 51:620-3 O '85
> Woodbury, Richard B.
>   Regional archaeological conferences. bibl *Am Antiq* 50:434-44 Ap '85; Errata. 51:220 Ja '86
> Woodcock, George, 1912-
>   Henry Mayhew and the undiscovered country of the poor. *Sewanee Rev* 92:556-73 Fall '84

2. These subject headings are all derived from the LCSH.

   ___ TRUE   X FALSE

3. Someone interested in journal articles about ___the wood industry___

   should look under the subject heading LUMBER INDUSTRY _____ when they use this Index.

4. The excerpt displays #_8_ articles and #_2_ cross references. (Or 9 articles if one "counts" Errata in connection with R. B. Woodbury article)

5. The complete subject heading under which the article by L. A. Losada is entered is WOOD IN LITERATURE _____

6. You've misplaced your bib cards! Now you've got to return to the Index volume to get some information. Based on the information contained in the excerpt, you'll approach first which volume of this Index? Put an X across it.

   | APRIL 1984 - MARCH 1985 | X APRIL 1985 - MARCH 1986 | APRIL 1986 - MARCH 1987 | APRIL 1987 - MARCH 1988 |

7. Record on the bib card __all__ of the information possible for the article by _A. Smedley_
   _____
   _____

   HUMANITIES INDEX Apr 85-March 86   WOOD ENGRAVING, CHINESE

   Smedley, A
   "Chinese woodcuts 1935-49."
   Mass Rev 25:553-564 Winter 1984

   (Illustrated)

8. How many of these articles include some bibliographic support? #_1_

9. The complete title of the __last cited__ article is " Henry Mayhew and the undiscovered country of the poor ", and it was published in volume #_92_ of the periodical.

10. Guy Woodall ____'s article begins and ends on pages _8 - 10_ ; it appeared in a periodical whose title is abbreviated Am Notes Queries

Practice Using A Periodical Index

Your Name _____

1. These questions relate to using semi-specialized periodical indexes efficiently; this excerpt appears to be from The _____ Index.

   Applied Science & Technology
   Humanities
   Social Sciences

2. These subject headings are all derived from the LCSH.

   TRUE   FALSE

3. Someone interested in journal articles about merchandise _____

   _____

   should look under the subject heading

   _____   when they use this Index.

Merchandise *See* Commercial products; Consumer goods
Merchant banks
          Great Britain
   Rhodes and the City of London: another view of imperialism. S. D. Chapman. *Hist J* 28:647-66 S '85
Merchant companies *See* Colonial companies
Merchant marine
          See also
      Merchant seamen
      Shipping
      Steamship lines
Merchant of Venice [Drama] *See* Shakespeare, William, 1564-1616—Plays—Merchant of Venice
Merchant seamen
          See also
      Black seamen
          Recruiting
   Nantucket whalemen in the deep-sea fishery: the changing anatomy of an early American labor force. D. Vickers. map *J Am Hist* 72:277-96 S '85
          Great Britain
   Notes on the antecedents of John Keats: the maritime hypothesis. D. E. Robinson. *Keats-Shelley J* 34:22-52 '85
Merchants, African
   Commerce, Christianity and the origins of the 'Creoles' of Fernando Po. M. Lynn. map *J Afr Hist* 25 no3:257-78 '84

4. The excerpt displays #___ articles and #____ cross references.

5. The complete subject heading under which the article by D. Vickers is entered is

   _____

6. You've misplaced your bib cards! Now you've got to return to the Index volume to get some information. Based on the information contained in the excerpt, you'll approach first which volume of this Index? Put an X across it.

   | APRIL 1984 – MARCH 1985 | APRIL 1985 – MARCH 1986 | APRIL 1986 – MARCH 1987 | APRIL 1987 – MARCH 1988 |

7. Record on the bib card all of the information possible for the article by D. E. Robinson

   _____
   _____

8. How many of these articles include some bibliographic support? #_____

9. The complete title of the last cited article is "_____

   _____", and it was

   published in volume #_____ of the periodical.

10. S. D. Chapman 's article begins and ends on pages _____;
    it appeared in a periodical whose title is abbreviated _____

1. These questions relate to using semi-specialized periodical indexes efficiently; this excerpt appears to be from The _____ Index.

      Applied Science & Technology
  X Humanities
      Social Sciences

> **Merchandise** *See* Commercial products; Consumer goods
> **Merchant banks**
> > **Great Britain**
> > Rhodes and the City of London: another view of imperialism. S. D. Chapman. *Hist J* 28:647-66 S '85
> **Merchant companies** *See* Colonial companies
> **Merchant marine**
> > *See also*
> > Merchant seamen
> > Shipping
> > Steamship lines
> **Merchant of Venice** [Drama] *See* Shakespeare, William, 1564-1616—Plays—Merchant of Venice
> **Merchant seamen**
> > *See also*
> > Black seamen
> > > **Recruiting**
> > Nantucket whalemen in the deep-sea fishery: the changing anatomy of an early American labor force. D. Vickers. map *J Am Hist* 72:277-96 S '85
> > > **Great Britain**
> > Notes on the antecedents of John Keats: the maritime hypothesis. D. E. Robinson. *Keats-Shelley J* 34:22-52 '85
> **Merchants, African**
> > Commerce, Christianity and the origins of the 'Creoles' of Fernando Po. M. Lynn. map *J Afr Hist* 25 no3:257-78 '84

2. These subject headings are all derived from the LCSH.

    TRUE   X FALSE

3. Someone interested in journal articles about __merchandise__ should look under the subject heading __COMMERCIAL PRODUCTS__ &/or __CONSUMER GOODS__ when they use this Index.

4. The excerpt displays #_4_ articles and #_8_ cross references.

5. The complete subject heading under which the article by _D. Vickers_ is entered is __MERCHANT SEAMEN-- RECRUITING__

6. You've misplaced your bib cards! Now you've got to return to the Index volume to get some information. Based on the information contained in the excerpt, you'll approach first which volume of this Index? Put an X across it.

APRIL 1984 - MARCH 1985	X APRIL 1985 - MARCH 1986	APRIL 1986 - MARCH 1987	APRIL 1987 - MARCH 1988

7. Record on the bib card __all__ of the information possible for the article by __D. E. Robinson__

> HUMANITIES INDEX   April 1985-March '86 MERCHANT SEAMEN-- GREAT BRITAIN
>
> Robinson, D   E.
> "Notes on the antecedents of John Keats: the maritime hypothesis."
> Keats-Shelley j 34:22-52 1985

8. How many of these articles include some bibliographic support? #_0_

9. The complete title of the last cited article is "__Commerce, Christianity and the origins of the 'Creoles' of Fernando Po__", and it was published in volume #_25_ of the periodical.

10. __S. D. Chapman__'s article begins and ends on pages _647-666_; it appeared in a periodical whose title is abbreviated __Hist J__

Practice Using A Periodical Index
Your Name _____

1. These questions relate to using semi-specialized periodical indexes efficiently; this excerpt appears to be from The _____ Index.

    Applied Science & Technology
    Humanities
    Social Sciences

2. These subject headings are all derived from the LCSH.

    TRUE   FALSE

3. Someone interested in journal articles about <u>Women's wit and humor</u>

_____ should look under the subject heading

_____ when they use this Index.

Women's studies
False specialization and the purdah of scholarship—a review article. H. Papanek. bibl *J Asian Stud* 44:127-48 N '84
Humanism & humbug; the coming of age of feminism [review article] J. Hughes. *Encounter* 63:50-6 N '84
Tokenism rules OK? R. Foster. *Hist Today* 35:3 O '85
Truth, campaigns & freedom; reflections on a prospectus. D. Holbrook. *Encounter* 65:54-62 D '85
        Bibliography
    See also
    Libraries—Special collections—Women's studies
Women's theater
    See also
    Women in the theater
Aller à la mer; tr. by B. Kerslake. H. Cixous. *Mod Drama* 27:546-8 D '84
French feminism and theatre: an introduction. J. L. Savona. *Mod Drama* 27:540-5 D '84
Heart of the scorpion at the WOW Café. K. Davy. *Drama Rev* 29:52-6 Spr '85
Language and meaning in Megan Terry's 1970s "musicals". K. G. Klein. *Mod Drama* 27:574-83 D '84
Suzanne Lacy's Whisper. the waves. the wind. S. Arnold. il *Drama Rev* 29:126-30 Spr '85
The WOW Café. A. Solomon. il *Drama Rev* 29:92-101 Spr '85
Women's wit and humor *See* Wit and humor, Women's
Wonder
    See also
    Awe

4. The excerpt displays #___ articles and #____ cross references.

5. The complete subject heading under which the article by D. Holbrook is entered is

_____

6. You've misplaced your bib cards! Now you've got to return to the Index volume to get some information. Based on the information contained in the excerpt, you'll approach first which volume of this Index? Put an X across it.

    APRIL 1984 - MARCH 1985   APRIL 1985 - MARCH 1986   APRIL 1986 - MARCH 1987   APRIL 1987 - MARCH 1988

7. Record on the bib card <u>all</u> of the information possible for the article by <u>H. Papanek</u>

_____

_____

8. How many of these articles include some bibliographic support? #____

9. The complete title of the <u>last cited</u> article is "_____

_____", and it was

published in volume #____ of the periodical.

10. K. G. Klein's _____'s article begins and ends on pages _____;
it appeared in a periodical whose title is abbreviated_____

1. These questions relate to using semi-specialized periodical indexes efficiently; this excerpt appears to be from The _____ Index.

     Applied Science & Technology
X   Humanities
     Social Sciences

The excerpt reads:

> **Women's studies**
> False specialization and the purdah of scholarship—a review article. H. Papanek. bibl *J Asian Stud* 44:127-48 N '84
> Humanism & humbug: the coming of age of feminism [review article] J. Hughes. *Encounter* 63:50-6 N '84
> Tokenism rules OK? R. Foster. *Hist Today* 35:3 O '85
> Truth, campaigns & freedom; reflections on a prospectus. D. Holbrook. *Encounter* 65:54-62 D '85
> **Bibliography**
>   *See also*
>   Libraries—Special collections—Women's studies
> **Women's theater**
>   *See also*
>   Women in the theater
> Aller à la mer; tr. by B. Kerslake. H. Cixous. *Mod Drama* 27:546-8 D '84
> French feminism and theatre: an introduction. J. L. Savona. *Mod Drama* 27:540-5 D '84
> Heart of the scorpion at the WOW Café. K. Davy. *Drama Rev* 29:52-6 Spr '85
> Language and meaning in Megan Terry's 1970s "musicals". K. G. Klein. *Mod Drama* 27:574-83 D '84
> Suzanne Lacy's Whisper. the waves. the wind. S. Arnold. il *Drama Rev* 29:126-30 Spr '85
> The WOW Café. A. Solomon. il *Drama Rev* 29:92-101 Spr '85
> **Women's wit and humor** *See* Wit and humor. Women's
> **Wonder**
>   *See also*
>   Awe

2. These subject headings are all derived from the LCSH.

     TRUE   X FALSE

3. Someone interested in journal articles about __Women's wit and humor__ should look under the subject heading __WIT AND HUMOR, WOMEN'S__ when they use this Index.

4. The excerpt displays #_10_ articles and #_4_ cross references.

5. The complete subject heading under which the article by _D. Holbrook_ is entered is __WOMEN'S STUDIES__

6. You've misplaced your bib cards! Now you've got to return to the Index volume to get some information. Based on the information contained in the excerpt, you'll approach first which volume of this Index? Put an X across it.

APRIL 1984 - MARCH 1985	X APRIL 1985 - MARCH 1986	APRIL 1986 - MARCH 1987	APRIL 1987 - MARCH 1988

7. Record on the bib card **all** of the information possible for the article by __H. Papanek__
_____
_____

HUMANITIES INDEX   Apr 85-March 86   WOMEN'S STUDIES

Papanek, H
"False specialization and the purdah of scholarship-- a review article"
J Asian Stud 44:127-148   November 1984

Has bibliography

8. How many of these articles include some bibliographic support? #_1_ (2nd cited article, by J. Hughes, is, however, a review article.)

9. The complete title of the __last cited__ article is "_The WOW Café._", and it was published in volume #_29_ of the periodical.

10. K. G. Klein's _____'s article begins and ends on pages _574-583_ ; it appeared in a periodical whose title is abbreviated _Mod Drama_

Practice Using A Periodical Index
Your Name _____

1. These questions relate to using semi-
    specialized periodical indexes
    efficiently; this excerpt appears to
    be from The _____ Index.

        Applied Science & Technology
        Humanities
        Social Sciences

Gestalt psychology
  Creative individuals: paradoxical personages. W. E. McMul-
    lan. bibl J Creat Behav 10 no4:265-75 '76
  Jungian-Gestalt approach to self-integration: toward a re-
    searchable model. E. Elkin and K. McKell. Simulat &
    Games 8:61-72 Mr '77
  Notes from Pavlov's Wednesdays: gestalt relationships as con-
    ditioned stimuli. H. D. Kimmel. Am J Psychol 89:745-9 D
    '76
      See also
  Field theory (psychology)
Gestalt therapy
  Accept diversity. S. Litt. Am Psychol 32:230 Mr '77; Discus-
    sion. 32:985-7 N '77
  Is Gestalt therapy a humanistic form of psychotherapy? L.
    Bergantino. J Humanistic Psychol 17:51-61 Wint '77
Gesture
  Relation of psychopathology and bilingualism to kinesic as-
    pects of interview behavior in schizophrenia. S. Grand and
    others. bibl J Abn Psychol 86:492-500 O '77
  Sex-typed mannerisms in normal boys and girls as a function
    of sex and age. G. A. Rekers and others. bibl Child Develop
    48:275-8 Mr '77
      See also
  Sign language
Getis, Arthur
  On the use of the term random in spatial analysis. Prof Geog
    29:59-61 F '77

2. These subject headings are all der-
    ived from the LCSH.

        TRUE   FALSE

3. Someone interested in journal arti-
    cles about GESTURE_____
    should _____
    also look under the subject heading

    _____ when they use this Index.

4. The excerpt displays #___ articles and #____ cross references.

5. The complete subject heading under which the article by L. Bergantino
    is entered is
    _____

6. You've misplaced your bib cards! Now
    you've got to return to the Index
    volume to get some information.
    Based on the information contained in
    the excerpt, you'll approach first
    which volume of this Index? Put an X
    across it.

| APRIL 1976-MARCH 1977 | APRIL 1977-MARCH 1978 | APRIL 1978-MARCH 1979 | APRIL 1979-MARCH 1980 |

7. Record on the bib
    card all of the in-
    formation possible
    for the article
    by McMullan_____

    _____

    _____

8. How many of these articles include some bibliographic support? #_____

9. The complete title of the last cited_____ article is "_____
    _____", and it was
    published in volume #_____ of the periodical.

10. Getis_____'s article begins and ends on pages _____;
    it appeared in a periodical whose title is abbreviated _____

1. These questions relate to using semi-specialized periodical indexes efficiently; this excerpt appears to be from The _____ Index.

   Applied Science & Technology
   Humanities
   X Social Sciences

2. These subject headings are all derived from the LCSH.

   TRUE   X FALSE

3. Someone interested in journal articles about <u>GESTURE</u>_____ should _____

   also look under the subject heading <u>SIGN LANGUAGE</u>_____ when they use this Index.

Gestalt psychology
   Creative individuals: paradoxical personages. W. E. McMullan. bibl J Creat Behav 10 no4:265-75 '76
   Jungian-Gestalt approach to self-integration: toward a researchable model. E. Elkin and K. McKell. Simulat & Games 8:61-72 Mr '77
   Notes from Pavlov's Wednesdays: gestalt relationships as conditioned stimuli. H. D. Kimmel. Am J Psychol 89:745-9 D '76
      See also
   Field theory (psychology)
Gestalt therapy
   Accept diversity. S. Litt. Am Psychol 32:230 Mr '77; Discussion. 32:985-7 N '77
   Is Gestalt therapy a humanistic form of psychotherapy? L. Bergantino. J Humanistic Psychol 17:54-61 Wint '77
Gesture
   Relation of psychopathology and bilingualism to kinesic aspects of interview behavior in schizophrenia. S. Grand and others. bibl J Abn Psychol 86:492-500 O '77
   Sex-typed mannerisms in normal boys and girls as a function of sex and age. G. A. Rekers and others. bibl Child Develop 48:275-8 Mr '77
      See also
   Sign language
Getis, Arthur
   On the use of the term random in spatial analysis. Prof Geog 29:59-61 F '77

---

4. The excerpt displays <u>#8</u> articles and <u>#2</u> cross references. (9 articles if one "counts" the Discussion of S. Litt)

5. The complete subject heading under which the article by <u>L. Bergantino</u> is entered is <u>GESTALT THERAPY</u>

6. You've misplaced your bib cards! Now you've got to return to the Index volume to get some information. Based on the information contained in the excerpt, you'll approach first which volume of this Index? Put an X across it.

APRIL 1976-MARCH 1977	APRIL 1977-MARCH 1978	APRIL 1978-MARCH 1979	APRIL 1979-MARCH 1980
	X		

7. Record on the bib card <u>all</u> of the information possible for the article by <u>McMullan</u>
   _____
   _____

   SOCIAL SCIENCES I   4/77-3/78   GESTALT PSYCHOLOGY

   McMullan, W   E
   "Creative individuals; paradoxical personages"

   J Creat Behav 10 no. 4:265-275 1976

   Has bibliog

8. How many of these articles include some bibliographic support? # <u>3</u>

9. The complete title of the <u>last cited</u> article is "<u>On the use of the term random in spatial analysis</u>", and it was published in volume # <u>29</u> of the periodical.

10. <u>Getis</u>'s article begins and ends on pages <u>59-61</u>; it appeared in a periodical whose title is abbreviated <u>Prof Geog</u>

1. These questions relate to using semi-specialized periodical indexes efficiently; this excerpt appears to be from The _____ Index.

   Applied Science & Technology
   Humanities
   Social Sciences

2. These subject headings are all derived from the LCSH.

   TRUE   FALSE

   Students —*See also—cont.*
   Law students
   Married students
   Medical students
   Negro students
   Psychology students
   Science students
   Social work students
   Student aid
   Student nurses
   Student teachers
   Teachers college students
   Vocational-technical students
               Civil rights
   Role of the federal judiciary in directing student-authority
      interaction. H. S. Bangser. bibl Educ Urb Soc 8:267-306 My
      '76
   Student suspensions and the law: some tips for parents. E. A.
      Lincoln. Crisis 83:120-1 Ap '76
   Students' rights. C. S. Pollok and others. Am J Nursing 76:-
      600-3 Ap '76
               Culture
      See Campus culture
               Employment
      See Student employment

3. Someone interested in journal articles about employment of students

   _____

   should look under the subject heading

   _____ when they use this Index.

4. The excerpt displays #___ articles and #____ cross references.

5. The complete subject heading under which the article by H. S. Bangser is entered is

   _____

6. You've misplaced your bib cards! Now you've got to return to the Index volume to get some information. Based on the information contained in the excerpt, you'll approach first which volume of this Index? Put an X across it.

   | APRIL 1975-MARCH 1976 | APRIL 1976-MARCH 1977 | APRIL 1977-MARCH 1978 | APRIL 1978-MARCH 1979 |

7. Record on the bib card all of the information possible for the article by H. S. Bangser

   _____
   _____

8. How many of these articles include some bibliographic support? #____

9. The complete title of the last cited article is " _____ _____ ", and it was published in volume #____ of the periodical.

10. E. A. Lincoln's ____ 's article begins and ends on pages _____ ; it appeared in a periodical whose title is abbreviated _____

542

1. These questions relate to using semi-
   specialized periodical indexes
   efficiently; this excerpt appears to
   be from The _____ Index.

   ___ Applied Science & Technology
   ___ Humanities
   X Social Sciences

2. These subject headings are all derived from the LCSH.

   ___ TRUE   X FALSE

3. Someone interested in journal articles about employment of students

   should look under the subject heading
   STUDENT EMPLOYMENT_____ when they use this Index.

> Students —*See also*—*cont.*
>   Law students
>   Married students
>   Medical students
>   Negro students
>   Psychology students
>   Science students
>   Social work students
>   Student aid
>   Student nurses
>   Student teachers
>   Teachers college students
>   Vocational-technical students
>   **Civil rights**
>   Role of the federal judiciary in directing student-authority
>   interaction. H. S. Bangser. bibl Educ Urb Soc 8:267-306 My
>   '76
>   Student suspensions and the law: some tips for parents. E. A.
>   Lincoln. Crisis 83:120-1 Ap '76
>   Students' rights. C. S. Pollok and others. Am J Nursing 76:-
>   600-3 Ap '76
>   **Culture**
>   *See* Campus culture
>   **Employment**
>   *See* Student employment

4. The excerpt displays # 3 articles and # 14 cross references.

5. The complete subject heading under which the article by H. S. Bangser
   is entered is STUDENTS--CIVIL RIGHTS

6. You've misplaced your bib cards! Now
   you've got to return to the Index
   volume to get some information.
   Based on the information contained in
   the excerpt, you'll approach first
   which volume of this Index? Put an X
   across it.

   | APRIL 1975- MARCH 1976 | X APRIL 1976- MARCH 1977 | APRIL 1977- MARCH 1978 | APRIL 1978- MARCH 1979 |

7. Record on the bib
   card all of the in-
   formation possible
   for the article
   by H. S. Bangser
   _____
   _____

   SOCIAL SCIENCE I 4/76-3/77 STUDENTS-- CIVIL RIGHTS

   Bangser, H   S.
   "Role of the federal judiciary in directing
    student-authority interaction".
   Educ Urb Soc 8:267-306 May 1976

   has bibliog.

8. How many of these articles include some bibliographic support? # 1

9. The complete title of the last cited _____ article is " Students' rights
   _____ ", and it was
   published in volume # 76 of the periodical.

10. E. A. Lincoln's _____'s article begins and ends on pages 120-121 ;
    it appeared in a periodical whose title is abbreviated Crisis

Course, Date
Instructor

Practice Using A Periodical Index
Your Name _____

1. These questions relate to using semi-specialized periodical indexes efficiently; this excerpt appears to be from The _____ Index.

    Applied Science & Technology
    Humanities
    Social Sciences

2. These subject headings are all derived from the LCSH.

    TRUE   FALSE

3. Someone interested in journal articles about diagnosis of mental illness should look under the subject heading

    _____ when they use this Index.

> Mental illness
>   Adult sex roles and mental illness. W. R. Gove and J. F. Tudor. bibl Am J Sociol 78:812-35 Ja '73; Replies with rejoinder. B. P. Dohrenwend and B. S. Dohrenwend. 81:1447-54; 82:1327-45 My '76, My '77
>   Genetic counseling in psychiatric disorders: state of the science and the art [symposium]. bibl Soc Biol 23:108-57 Summ '76
>   Mental health special issue. bibl il Soc Pol 8:2-45 My '77
>   See also
>   Mental health
>   Mentally ill
>   Psychiatry
>   Psychology, Pathological
>   Psychoses
>   Seasonal variations (mental illness)
>   Suicide
>   Diagnosis
>   See Mentally ill—Diagnosis
>   Public opinion
>   Alternative view of the labelling versus psychiatric perspectives on societal reaction to mental illness. M. D. Krohn and R. L. Akers. bibl Soc Forces 56:341-61 D '77
>   Attitudes toward the elderly and toward the mentally ill. J. Drevenstedt and G. Banziger. bibl Psychol Rept 41:347-53 O '77
>   Comparison of the community psychology and medical models: teaching attitudes toward deviance to high school students. C. L. Schultz and others. bibl Com Ment Health J 13:268-76 Fall '77
>   Effect of sex role differences on the social control of mental illness. W. Tudor and others. bibl J Health & Soc Behav 18:98-112 Je '77

4. The excerpt displays #___ articles and #____ cross references.

5. The complete subject heading under which the article by Krohn and Akers is entered is

    _____

6. You've misplaced your bib cards! Now you've got to return to the Index volume to get some information. Based on the information contained in the excerpt, you'll approach first which volume of this Index? Put an X across it.

    | APRIL 1976-MARCH 1977 | APRIL 1977-MARCH 1978 | APRIL 1978-MARCH 1979 | APRIL 1979-MARCH 1980 |

7. Record on the bib card all of the information possible for the article by C. L. Schultz and others

8. How many of these articles include some bibliographic support?#_____

9. The complete title of the last cited article is "_____", and it was published in volume #_____ of the periodical.

10. The mental illnes symposium begins and ends on pages _____; it appeared in a periodical whose title is abbreviated _____

544

1. These questions relate to using semi-specialized periodical indexes efficiently; this excerpt appears to be from The _____ Index.

   _____ Applied Science & Technology
   _____ Humanities
   X Social Sciences

2. These subject headings are all derived from the LCSH.

   _____ TRUE   X FALSE

3. Someone interested in journal articles about <u>diagnosis of mental illness</u> should look under the subject heading <u>MENTALLY ILL-- DIAGNOSIS</u> when they use this Index.

Mental illness
Adult sex roles and mental illness. W. R. Gove and J. F. Tudor. bibl Am J Sociol 78:812-35 Ja '73; Replies with rejoinder. B. P. Dohrenwend and B. S. Dohrenwend. 81:1447-54; 82:1327-45 My '76, My '77
Genetic counseling in psychiatric disorders: state of the science and the art [symposium]. bibl Soc Biol 23:108-57 Summ '76
Mental health special issue. bibl il Soc Pol 8:2-45 My '77
See also
Mental health
Mentally ill
Psychiatry
Psychology, Pathological
Psychoses
Seasonal variations (mental illness)
Suicide
   Diagnosis
See Mentally ill—Diagnosis
   Public opinion
Alternative view of the labelling versus psychiatric perspectives on societal reaction to mental illness. M. D. Krohn and R. L. Akers. bibl Soc Forces 56:341-61 D '77
Attitudes toward the elderly and toward the mentally ill. J. Drevenstedt and G. Banziger. bibl Psychol Rept 41:347-53 O '77
Comparison of the community psychology and medical models: teaching attitudes toward deviance to high school students. C. L. Schultz and others. bibl Com Ment Health J 13:268-76 Fall '77
Effect of sex role differences on the social control of mental illness. W. Tudor and others. bibl J Health & Soc Behav 18:98-112 Je '77

4. The excerpt displays # 7 articles and # 8 cross references. (8 or 9 articles if one "counts" "Replies" to Gove & Tudor)

5. The complete subject heading under which the article by <u>Krohn and Akers</u> is entered is <u>MENTAL ILLNESS-- PUBLIC OPINION</u>

6. You've misplaced your bib cards! Now you've got to return to the Index volume to get some information. Based on the information contained in the excerpt, you'll approach first which volume of this Index? Put an X across it.

| APRIL 1976- MARCH 1977 | X APRIL 1977- MARCH 1978 | APRIL 1978- MARCH 1979 | APRIL 1979- MARCH 1980 |

7. Record on the bib card <u>all</u> of the information possible for the article by <u>C. L. Schultz and others</u>

   SOCIAL SCIENCES I 4/77-3/78 MENTAL ILLNESS-- PUBLIC OPINION

   Schultz, C   L, and others
   "Comparison of the community psychology and medical models: teaching attitudes toward deviance to high school students".
   Com Ment Health J 13:268-276 Fall 1977   Has bibliography

8. How many of these articles include some bibliographic support? # 6

9. The complete title of the <u>last cited</u> article is "<u>Effect of sex role differences on the social control of mental illness</u>", and it was published in volume # 18 of the periodical.

10. The mental illnes symposium begins and ends on pages <u>108-157</u> ; it appeared in a periodical whose title is abbreviated <u>Soc biol</u>

Practice Using A Periodical Index
Your Name _____

1. These questions relate to using semi-
   specialized periodical indexes
   efficiently; this excerpt appears to
   be from The _____ Index.

   Applied Science & Technology
   Humanities
   Social Sciences

> Mental tests. See Intelligence tests
> Mentally handicapped
>   Wordsworth. Hum Ecol Forum 8:19-21 Aut '77
>   *See also*
> Phenylketonuria
> Social work with the mentally handicapped
>   **Behavior**
> Case study: use of differential reinforcement to suppress self-
>   injurious and aggressive behavior. F. Frankel and others. bibl
>   Psychol Rept 39:843-9 D pt 1 '76
> Effects of emotions on altruism and social inference in retard-
>   ed adolescents. R. J. Karpf. Psychol Rept 41:135-8 Ag '77
> Eliminating object-transferring by a profoundly retarded
>   female by overcorrection. J. Martin and others. Psychol
>   Rept 40:779-82 Je pt 1 '77
> Modification of leisure behavior in a half-way house for retard-
>   ed women. M. S. Johnson and J. S. Bailey. bibl J App Behav
>   Anal 10:273-82 Summ '77
> Overcorrection: generalization and maintenance. F. Rusch
>   and others. J App Behav Anal 9:498 Wint '76
> Social disability in chronic psychiatric patients. J. A. Sylph
>   and others. Am J Psych 134:1391-4 D '77
> Some determinants of the reinforcing and punishing effects of
>   timeout. J. V. Solnick and others. bibl J App Behav Anal
>   10:415-24 Fall '77

2. These subject headings are all derived from the LCSH.

   TRUE   FALSE

3. Someone interested in journal articles about mental tests _____
   _____
   should look under the subject heading
   _____ when they use this Index.

4. The excerpt displays #___ articles and #____ cross references.

5. The complete subject heading under which the article by R. J. Karpf
   is entered is
   _____

6. You've misplaced your bib cards! Now
   you've got to return to the Index
   volume to get some information.
   Based on the information contained in
   the excerpt, you'll approach first
   which volume of this Index? Put an X
   across it.

   | APRIL 1976-MARCH 1977 | APRIL 1977-MARCH 1978 | APRIL 1978-MARCH 1979 | APRIL 1979-MARCH 1980 |

7. Record on the bib
   card all of the in-
   formation possible
   for the article
   by F. Frankel and
   others
   _____

8. How many of these articles include some bibliographic support?#_____

9. The complete title of the last cited _____ article is "_____
   _____", and it was
   published in volume #_____ of the periodical.

10. J. A. Sylph _____'s article begins and ends on pages _____;
    it appeared in a periodical whose title is abbreviated _____

1. These questions relate to using semi-
   specialized periodical indexes
   efficiently; this excerpt appears to
   be from The _____ Index.

      Applied Science & Technology
      Humanities
   X Social Sciences

> Mental tests. See Intelligence tests
> Mentally handicapped
>   Wordsworth. Hum Ecol Forum 8:19-21 Aut '77
>   *See also*
> Phenylketonuria
> Social work with the mentally handicapped
>   Behavior
> Case study: use of differential reinforcement to suppress self-
>   injurious and aggressive behavior. F. Frankel and others. bibl
>   Psychol Rept 39:843-9 D pt 1 '76
> Effects of emotions on altruism and social inference in retard-
>   ed adolescents. R. J. Karpf. Psychol Rept 41:135-8 Ag '77
> Eliminating object-transferring by a profoundly retarded
>   female by overcorrection. J. Martin and others. Psychol
>   Rept 40:779-82 Je pt 1 '77
> Modification of leisure behavior in a half-way house for retard-
>   ed women. M. S. Johnson and J. S. Bailey. bibl J App Behav
>   Anal 10:273-82 Summ '77
> Overcorrection: generalization and maintenance. F. Rusch
>   and others. J App Behav Anal 9:498 Wint '76
> Social disability in chronic psychiatric patients. J. A. Sylph
>   and others. Am J Psych 134:1391-4 D '77
> Some determinants of the reinforcing and punishing effects of
>   timeout. J. V. Solnick and others. bibl J App Behav Anal
>   10:415-24 Fall '77

2. These subject headings are all derived from the LCSH.

     TRUE   X FALSE

3. Someone interested in journal articles about <u>mental tests</u>

   should look under the subject heading
   <u>INTELLIGENCE TESTS</u>   when they use this Index.

4. The excerpt displays #<u>8</u> articles and #<u>3</u> cross references.

5. The complete subject heading under which the article by <u>R. J. Karpf</u>
   is entered is <u>MENTALLY HANDICAPPED-- BEHAVIOR</u>

6. You've misplaced your bib cards! Now
   you've got to return to the Index
   volume to get some information.
   Based on the information contained in
   the excerpt, you'll approach first
   which volume of this Index? Put an X
   across it.

APRIL 1976-MARCH 1977	X APRIL 1977-MARCH 1978	APRIL 1978-MARCH 1979	APRIL 1979-MARCH 1980

7. Record on the bib
   card <u>all</u> of the information possible
   for the article
   by F. Frankel and
   others

   > SOCIAL SICENCES I 4/77-3/78 MENTALLY HANDICAPPED--
   > BEHAVIOR
   >
   > Frankel, F   & others
   > "Case study: use of differential reinforcement to
   >   suppress self-injurious and aggressive behavior".
   > Psychol Rept 39:843-849 December part 1 1976
   > Has bibliog.

8. How many of these articles include some bibliographic support?#<u>3</u>

9. The complete title of the <u>last cited</u> article is "<u>Some determinants</u>
   of<u> the reinforcing and punishing effects of timeout</u>", and it was
   published in volume #<u>10</u> of the periodical.

10. J. A. Sylph<u>   </u>'s article begins and ends on pages <u>1391-1394</u>;
    it appeared in a periodical whose title is abbreviated <u>Am J Psych</u>

1. These questions relate to using semi-specialized periodical indexes efficiently; this excerpt appears to be from The _____ Index.

    Applied Science & Technology
    Humanities
    Social Sciences

Midlands (England)

Religion

'Race', religion and ethnicity: religious observance in the West Midlands. M. R. D. Johnson. bibl *Ethn Racial Stud* 8:426-37 Jl '85

Midlarsky, Elizabeth
(jt. auth) See Smith, Patricia A., and Midlarsky, Elizabeth

Midlarsky, Elizabeth, and Hannah, Mary Elizabeth
Competence, reticence, and helping by children and adolescents. bibl *Dev Psychol* 21:534-41 My '85

Midlarsky, Manus I.
Political stability of two-party and multiparty systems: probabilistic bases for the comparison of party systems. bibl *Am Polit Sci Rev* 78:929-51 D '84

Preventing systemic war: crisis decision-making amidst a structure of conflict relationships. bibl *J Confl Resolut* 28:563-84 D '84

Midlarsky, Manus I., and Roberts, Kenneth, 1940-
Class, state, and revolution in Central America: Nicaragua and El Salvador compared. bibl *J Confl Resolut* 29:163-93 Je '85

Midlife *See* Middle age
Midwest *See* Middle Western States
Midwinter, Arthur
Reforming the budgetary process in local government. *Public Adm* 62:473-80 Wint '84

2. These subject headings are all derived from the LCSH.

    TRUE   FALSE

3. Someone interested in journal articles about _midlife_____

    should look under the subject heading

    _____ when they use this Index.

4. The excerpt displays #___ articles and #____ cross references.

5. The complete subject heading under which the article by _M. R. D. Johnson_ is entered is

    _____

6. You've misplaced your bib cards! Now you've got to return to the Index volume to get some information. Based on the information contained in the excerpt, you'll approach first which volume of this Index? Put an X across it.

APRIL 1984 - MARCH 1985	APRIL 1985 - MARCH 1986	APRIL 1986 - MARCH 1987	APRIL 1987 - MARCH 1988

7. Record on the bib card _all_ of the information possible for the article by _M. R. D. Johnson_

    _____
    _____

8. How many of these articles include some bibliographic support? #_____

9. The complete title of the _last cited_____ article is " _____
    _____ ", and it was
    published in volume #_____ of the periodical.

10. _Midlarsky & Roberts____ 's article begins and ends on pages _____ ;
    it appeared in a periodical whose title is abbreviated _____

1. These questions relate to using semi-specialized periodical indexes efficiently; this excerpt appears to be from The _____ Index.

       Applied Science & Technology
       Humanities
   X   Social Sciences

Midlands (England)

Religion

'Race', religion and ethnicity: religious observance in the West Midlands. M. R. D. Johnson. bibl *Ethn Racial Stud* 8:426-37 Jl '85

Midlarsky, Elizabeth
   (jt. auth) See Smith, Patricia A., and Midlarsky, Elizabeth

Midlarsky, Elizabeth, and Hannah, Mary Elizabeth
   Competence, reticence, and helping by children and adolescents. bibl *Dev Psychol* 21:534-41 My '85

Midlarsky, Manus I.
   Political stability of two-party and multiparty systems: probabilistic bases for the comparison of party systems. bibl *Am Polit Sci Rev* 78:929-51 D '84
   Preventing systemic war: crisis decision-making amidst a structure of conflict relationships. bibl *J Confl Resolut* 28:563-84 D '84

Midlarsky, Manus I., and Roberts, Kenneth, 1940-
   Class, state, and revolution in Central America: Nicaragua and El Salvador compared. bibl *J Confl Resolut* 29:163-93 Je '85

Midlife *See* Middle age
Midwest *See* Middle Western States
Midwinter, Arthur
   Reforming the budgetary process in local government. *Public Adm* 62:473-80 Wint '84

2. These subject headings are all derived from the LCSH.

       TRUE   X   FALSE

3. Someone interested in journal articles about _midlife_ _____ should look under the subject heading _MIDDLE AGE_ _____ when they use this Index.

4. The excerpt displays # _6_ articles and # _3_ cross references.

5. The complete subject heading under which the article by _M. R. D. Johnson_ is entered is ___MIDLANDS (ENGLAND)-- RELIGION___

6. You've misplaced your bib cards! Now you've got to return to the Index volume to get some information. Based on the information contained in the excerpt, you'll approach first which volume of this Index? Put an X across it.

APRIL 1984 - MARCH 1985	X APRIL 1985 - MARCH 1986	APRIL 1986 - MARCH 1987	APRIL 1987 - MARCH 1988

7. Record on the bib card _all_ of the information possible for the article by _M. R. D. Johnson_ _____ _____

SOCIAL SCIENCES INDEX Apr 85-March 86   MIDLANDS (ENGLAND)-- RELIGION

Johnson, M   R. D.
"'Race', religion and ethnicity: religious observance in the West Midlands"
Ethn Racial Stud 8:426-437   July 1985

Has bibliography

8. How many of these articles include some bibliographic support? # _5_

9. The complete title of the _last cited_ _____ article is " _Reforming the budgetary process in local government_ _____ ", and it was published in volume # _62_ of the periodical.

10. _Midlarsky & Roberts_ 's article begins and ends on pages _163-193_ _____ ; it appeared in a periodical whose title is abbreviated ___J Confl Resolut___

Practice Using A Periodical Index
Your Name _____

1. These questions relate to using semi-specialized periodical indexes efficiently; this excerpt appears to be from The _____ Index.

   Applied Science & Technology
   Humanities
   Social Sciences

Middle Eastern national characteristics *See* National characteristics, Middle Eastern
Middle Eastern studies
  Russian books on the Arab states of the Middle East. J. M. Landau. *Middle East Stud* 21:362-6 Jl '85
Middle managers
  Cooperativeness and advancement of managers: an international perspective. E. Rosenstein. bibl *Hum Relat* 38:1-22 Ja '85
  Middle managers in contemporary capitalism. V. V. Peschanski. bibl *Acta Sociol* 28 no3:243-55 '85
Middle Western States
  See also subhead Middle Western States under the following subjects
    Cities and towns
        Population
      History—Sources
  Information sources for nineteenth century midwestern migration [gss] G. S. Rose. bibl *Prof Geogr* 37:66-72 F '85
        Regional geography
  The vernacular Middle West. J. R. Shortridge. bibl maps *Ann Assoc Am Geogr* 75:48-57 Mr '85
Middleman minority theory *See* Minorities
Middlemen *See* Marketing
Middlesex County (Ont.)

2. These subject headings are all derived from the LCSH.

   TRUE   FALSE

3. Someone interested in journal articles about Middlemen _____
   _____ should look under the subject heading _____ when they use this Index.

4. The excerpt displays #___ articles and #____ cross references.

5. The complete subject heading under which the article by J. R. Shortridge is entered is _____

6. You've misplaced your bib cards! Now you've got to return to the Index volume to get some information. Based on the information contained in the excerpt, you'll approach first which volume of this Index? Put an X across it.

   | APRIL 1984- - MARCH 1985 | APRIL 1985- - MARCH 1986 | APRIL 1986 - MARCH 1987 | APRIL 1987 - MARCH 1988 |

7. Record on the bib card all of the information possible for the article by G. S. Rose

8. How many of these articles include some bibliographic support? #____

9. The complete title of the ___last cited___ article is " _____ _____ ", and it was published in volume #____ of the periodical.

10. __E. Rosenstein__'s article begins and ends on pages _____ ; it appeared in a periodical whose title is abbreviated_____

Course, Date
Instructor

Practice Using A Periodical Index
Your Name _____

1. These questions relate to using semi-specialized periodical indexes efficiently; this excerpt appears to be from The _____ Index.

    ____ Applied Science & Technology
    ____ Humanities
    X Social Sciences

2. These subject headings are all derived from the LCSH.

    ____ TRUE   X FALSE

3. Someone interested in journal articles about Middlemen _____

should look under the subject heading MARKETING _____ when they use this Index.

> Middle Eastern national characteristics *See* National characteristics. Middle Eastern
> **Middle Eastern studies**
>   Russian books on the Arab states of the Middle East. J. M. Landau. *Middle East Stud* 21:362-6 Jl '85
> **Middle managers**
>   Cooperativeness and advancement of managers: an international perspective. E. Rosenstein. bibl *Hum Relat* 38:1-22 Ja '85
>   Middle managers in contemporary capitalism. V. V. Peschanski. bibl *Acta Sociol* 28 no3:243-55 '85
> **Middle Western States**
>   *See also* subhead Middle Western States under the following subjects
>   Cities and towns
>   **Population**
>   *History—Sources*
>   Information sources for nineteenth century midwestern migration [gss] G. S. Rose. bibl *Prof Geogr* 37:66-72 F '85
>   **Regional geography**
>   The vernacular Middle West. J. R. Shortridge. bibl maps *Ann Assoc Am Geogr* 75:48-57 Mr '85
> **Middleman minority theory** *See* Minorities
> **Middlemen** *See* Marketing
> **Middlesex County (Ont.)**

4. The excerpt displays # 5 articles and # 3 cross references. (Or 4, if one "counts" reference to subhead in middle of excerpt)

5. The complete subject heading under which the article by J. R. Shortridge is entered is MIDDLE WESTERN STATES-- REGIONAL GEOGRAPHY

6. You've misplaced your bib cards! Now you've got to return to the Index volume to get some information. Based on the information contained in the excerpt, you'll approach first which volume of this Index? Put an X across it.

APRIL 1984- - MARCH 1985	X APRIL 1985- - MARCH 1986	APRIL 1986 - MARCH 1987	APRIL 1987 - MARCH 1988

7. Record on the bib card all of the information possible for the article by G. S. Rose _____

_____

SOCIAL SCIENCES INDEX Apr 85-March 86 MIDDLE WESTERN STATES-- POPULATION-- HISTORY-- SOURCES

Rose, G   S.
"Information sources for nineteenth century midwestern migration [gss]".
Prof Geogr 37:66-72 Feb. 1985

Has a bibliography

8. How many of these articles include some bibliographic support? # 4

9. The complete title of the last cited article is "The vernacular Middle West", and it was published in volume # 75 of the periodical.

10. E. Rosenstein 's article begins and ends on pages 1-22 ; it appeared in a periodical whose title is abbreviated Hum Relat

Practice Using A Periodical Index
Your Name _____

1. These questions relate to using semi-specialized periodical indexes efficiently; this excerpt appears to be from The _____ Index.

    Applied Science & Technology
    Humanities
    Social Sciences

> Pacey, Patricia L., and Wickham, Elizabeth D.
>   College football telecasts; where are they going? bibl
>   *Econ Inq* 23:93-113 Ja '85
> Pachella, Robert G.
>   (jt. auth) See Irwin, David E., and Pachella, Robert
>   G.
> Pachter, Henry Maximilian, 1907-1980
>   *about*
>   A search for socialism: an old friend looks back at
>   Henry Pachter's writings [review article] R. Lowenthal.
>   *Dissent* 32:451-5 Fall '85
> Pacific Basin Economic Council
>   The quest for talent. *Far East Econ Rev* 128:91 My
>   23 '85
> Pacific Islands (Trust territory)
>   *See also*
>   Samoa
>   Politics and government
>   Pingelap politics and American-Micronesian relations. D.
>   Damas. bibl *Ethnology* 24:43-55 Ja '85
> Pacific region
>   *See also*
>   Polynesians
>   *See also* subhead Pacific region under the following
>   subjects
>   Marine pollution
>   Commerce
>   *United States*
>   Dangerous dependence. A. Rowley. *Far East Econ Rev*
>   128:52-3 Ap 4 '85

2. These subject headings are all derived from the LCSH.

    TRUE   FALSE

3. Someone interested in journal articles about the Pacific Islands Trust territory should also look under the subject heading

_____ when they use this Index.

4. The excerpt displays #___ articles and #____ cross references.

5. The complete subject heading under which the article by D. Damas is entered is

_____

6. You've misplaced your bib cards! Now you've got to return to the Index volume to get some information. Based on the information contained in the excerpt, you'll approach first which volume of this Index? Put an X across it.

    APRIL 1984 - MARCH 1985   APRIL 1985 - MARCH 1986   APRIL 1986 - MARCH 1987   APRIL 1987 - MARCH 1988

7. Record on the bib card **all** of the information possible for the article by R. Lowenthal

_____
_____

8. How many of these articles include some bibliographic support? #_____

9. The complete title of the last cited article is " _____ _____ ", and it was published in volume #_____ of the periodical.

10. Pacey & Wickham's 's article begins and ends on pages _____ ; it appeared in a periodical whose title is abbreviated_____

The excerpt in the boxed index column reads:

> Pacey, Patricia L., and Wickham, Elizabeth D.
>   College football telecasts: where are they going? bibl
>   *Econ Inq* 23:93-113 Ja '85
> Pachella, Robert G.
>   (jt. auth) See Irwin, David E., and Pachella, Robert
>   G.
> Pachter, Henry Maximilian, 1907-1980
>   *about*
>   A search for socialism: an old friend looks back at
>   Henry Pachter's writings [review article] R. Lowenthal.
>   *Dissent* 32:451-5 Fall '85
> Pacific Basin Economic Council
>   The quest for talent. *Far East Econ Rev* 128:91 My
>   23 '85
> Pacific Islands (Trust territory)
>   *See also*
>   Samoa
>   Politics and government
>   Pingelap politics and American-Micronesian relations. D.
>   Damas. bibl *Ethnology* 24:43-55 Ja '85
> Pacific region
>   *See also*
>   Polynesians
>   *See also* subhead Pacific region under the following
>   subjects
>   Marine pollution
>   Commerce
>   *United States*
>   Dangerous dependence. A. Rowley. *Far East Econ Rev*
>   128:52-3 Ap 4 '85

1. These questions relate to using semi-specialized periodical indexes efficiently; this excerpt appears to be from The _____ Index.

    Applied Science & Technology
    Humanities
 X Social Sciences

2. These subject headings are all derived from the LCSH.

   TRUE   X FALSE

3. Someone interested in journal articles about <u>the Pacific Islands</u> <u>Trust territory should also</u> look under the subject heading <u>SAMOA</u> when they use this Index.

4. The excerpt displays # _5_ articles and #_3_ cross references. (or 4 cross references, depending on how Marine polution reference is interpreted)

5. The complete subject heading under which the article by <u>D. Damas</u> is entered is   PACIFIC ISLANDS (TRUST TERRITORY)-- POLITICS AND GOVERNMENT

6. You've misplaced your bib cards! Now you've got to return to the Index volume to get some information. Based on the information contained in the excerpt, you'll approach first which volume of this Index? Put an X across it.

APRIL 1984 - MARCH 1985	X APRIL 1985 - MARCH 1986	APRIL 1986 - MARCH 1987	APRIL 1987 - MARCH 1988

7. Record on the bib card <u>all</u> of the information possible for the article by <u>R. Lowenthal</u>

> SOCIAL SCIENCES INDEX Apr 85-March 86   PACHTER, HENRY MAXIMILIAN, 1907-1980
>
> Lowenthal, R
> "A search for socialism: an old friend looks back at Henry Pachter's writings."
> Dissent 32:451-455   Fall 1985
>
> A review article

8. How many of these articles include some bibliographic support? #_2_ (Lowenthal article is, however, a review article)

9. The complete title of the <u>last cited</u> article is "Dangerous dependence", and it was published in volume # _128_ of the periodical.

10. Pacey & Wickham's 's article begins and ends on pages <u>93-113</u> ; it appeared in a periodical whose title is abbreviated <u>Econ Inq</u>

Practice Using A Periodical Index
Your Name _____

1. These questions relate to using semi-specialized periodical indexes efficiently; this excerpt appears to be from The _____ Index.

   Applied Science & Technology
   Humanities
   Social Sciences

The excerpt box reads:

Diener, Ed, and others
    Age and sex effects for emotional intensity. bibl *Dev Psychol* 21:542-6 My '85
    Intensity and frequency: dimensions underlying positive and negative affect. bibl *J Pers Soc Psychol* 48:1253-65 My '85
    Persons X situation interactions: choice of situations and congruence response models. bibl *J Pers Soc Psychol* 47:580-92 S '84
Diet
        See also
    Appetite
    Eating
    Food habits
    Nutrition
    Reducing diets
    Vegetarianism
    The government of the body: medical regimens and the rationalization of diet. B. S. Turner. *Br J Sociol* 33:254-69 Je '82; Discussion. 35:62-5 Mr '84; 36:151-4 Je '85
        United States
    Epidemiology of urinary tract infection: diet, clothing and urination habits. B. Foxman and R. R. Frerichs. *Am J Public Health* 75:1314-17 N '85
        Zambia
    Food for thought. *Africa (Lond Engl)* no169:52-3 S '85
Diet, Low-calorie *See* Low-calorie diet

2. These subject headings are all derived from the LCSH.

   TRUE   FALSE

3. Someone interested in journal articles about <u>diet, low-calorie</u> _____ should look under the subject heading _____ when they use this Index.

4. The excerpt displays #___ articles and #____ cross references.

5. The complete subject heading under which the article by Foxman & Frerichs is entered is _____

6. You've misplaced your bib cards! Now you've got to return to the Index volume to get some information. Based on the information contained in the excerpt, you'll approach first which volume of this Index? Put an X across it.

   APRIL 1984 - MARCH 1985   APRIL 1985 - MARCH 1986   APRIL 1986 - MARCH 1987   APRIL 1987 - MARCH 1988

7. Record on the bib card <u>all</u> of the information possible for the article by <u>B. S. Turner</u>

   _____

   _____

8. How many of these articles include some bibliographic support? #____

9. The complete title of the <u>third cited</u> article is "_____", and it was published in volume #_____ of the periodical.

10. Ed Diener's <u>longest</u> article begins and ends on pages _____ ; it appeared in a periodical whose title is abbreviated _____

1. These questions relate to using semi-specialized periodical indexes efficiently; this excerpt appears to be from The _____ Index.

    Applied Science & Technology
    Humanities
X   Social Sciences

> **Diener, Ed, and others**
> Age and sex effects for emotional intensity. bibl *Dev Psychol* 21:542-6 My '85
> Intensity and frequency: dimensions underlying positive and negative affect. bibl *J Pers Soc Psychol* 48:1253-65 My '85
> Persons X situation interactions: choice of situations and congruence response models. bibl *J Pers Soc Psychol* 47:580-92 S '84
> **Diet**
>   *See also*
>   Appetite
>   Eating
>   Food habits
>   Nutrition
>   Reducing diets
>   Vegetarianism
> The government of the body: medical regimens and the rationalization of diet. B. S. Turner. *Br J Sociol* 33:254-69 Je '82; Discussion. 35:62-5 Mr '84; 36:151-4 Je '85
>   **United States**
> Epidemiology of urinary tract infection: diet, clothing and urination habits. B. Foxman and R. R. Frerichs. *Am J Public Health* 75:1314-17 N '85
>   **Zambia**
> Food for thought. *Africa (Lond Engl)* no169:52-3 S '85
> **Diet, Low-calorie** *See* Low-calorie diet

2. These subject headings are all derived from the LCSH.

    TRUE   X FALSE

3. Someone interested in journal articles about <u>diet, low-calorie</u>

should look under the subject heading <u>LOW-CALORIE DIET</u> when they use this Index.

4. The excerpt displays #<u>6</u> articles and #<u>7</u> cross references. (Or 7 articles if one "counts" Discussion of Turner article; or 8 for Discussion's two issues).

5. The complete subject heading under which the article by Foxman & Frerichs is entered is <u>DIET-- UNITED STATES</u>

6. You've misplaced your bib cards! Now you've got to return to the Index volume to get some information. Based on the information contained in the excerpt, you'll approach first which volume of this Index? Put an X across it.

APRIL 1984 – MARCH 1985	X APRIL 1985 – MARCH 1986	APRIL 1986 – MARCH 1987	APRIL 1987 – MARCH 1988

7. Record on the bib card <u>all</u> of the information possible for the article by <u>B. S. Turner</u>

> SOC SCI I Apr '85-March '86 DIET
>
> Turner, B   S.
> "The government of the body: medical regimens and the rationalization of diet"
> Br J Sociol 33:254- 269 June 1982;
> Discussion 35:62- 65 March 1984; 36:151-154 June 1985

8. How many of these articles include some bibliographic support? #<u>3</u>

9. The complete title of the<u>third cited</u> article is "<u>Persons X situation interactions: choice of situations and congruence response models</u>", and it was published in volume #<u>47</u> of the periodical.

10. Ed Diener's <u>longest</u> article begins and ends on pages <u>1253-1265</u> it appeared in a periodical whose title is abbreviated <u>J Pers Soc Psychol</u>

INTER-LIBRARY BORROWING & RELATED TOOLS

The following can be used with both parts of the National Union Catalog Pre-1956 basic set activity. Some are supplemented with other, more challenging uses of the Pre-1956 set. One library is identified in each case.

"Martha Quest," by Doris Lessing, published in 1952 by M. Joseph in London. 328:348. Stanford University; Stanford, California. [CSt]

"The Confession," by Sarah Bernhardt. 49:671. New York Public Library; New York, New York. [NN]

The second edition of Paul Blanshard's "How to Run a Union Meeting." 60:585. Boston Public Library; Boston, Massachusetts. [MB]

"A Comparative Evolution of Preservatives for Use in Eye Solutions," by William Mohn Heller, published in 1955. 239:460. St. John's University; Collegeville, Minnesota. [MnCS]
And when was Heller born? Answer: 1926. Does the U.S. Library of Congress have this book in its collection? Answer: Yes.

"Types of Philosophy" by William Hocking, the revised edition, copyrighted in 1939. 249:69. University of Oregon; Eugene, Oregon. [OrU]
And what is Hocking's full name? Answer: William Ernest Hocking.

"20th Century Typewriting for Colleges, 2nd edition," published in 1936, written by David Daniel Lessenberry, born in 1896. 328:329. University of Washington; Seattle, Washington. [WaU]
And does the U.S. Library of Congress have this book in its collection? Answer: Yes.

"Labor in Southern Cotton Mills," by Paul Blanshard, published by New Republic, Inc., c1927. 60:585. Harvard University; Cambridge, Massachusetts. [MH]

The French-language edition (version) of "Tell Me About Women," by Harry Reasoner. 483:493. New York Public Library; New York, New York. [NN]

"The Subjection of Women," by John Stuart Mill, published in 1895 by the National American Woman Suffrage Association in its Political Science Study Series. 383:671. University of Virginia; Charlottesville, Virginia. [ViU]
And what volume and issue numbers was it in the Political Science Study Series? Answer: Volume 1, Number 2. When did Mill live? Answer: 1806-1873

Eugene O'Neill's one-act play titled "Abortion," published in 1914 in Connecticut. 430:585. University of Pennsylvania; Philadelphia, Pennsylvania. [PU]

"... A Study of Certain Factors Associated with Children's Play Interests...."
by James Daniel Wang, published in 1941. 647:598. University of Missouri;
Columbia, Missouri. [MoU]

The edition of William Shakespeare's "Venus & Adonis" which is illustrated by
Rockwell Kent and was published in 1934. 541:393. University of Texas;
Austin, Texas. [TxU]

"The Young Musician," by Horatio Alger and illustrated by Clyde O. Deland,
published in the United States by the Penn Publishing Company in 1906.
8:532. Brigham Young University; Provo, Utah. [UPB]

"The Man-Made World; Or, Our Andocentric Culture," third edition, by
Charlotte Gilman (1860-1935), published in New York by Charlton Company
in 1914, copyrighted in 1911. 200:291. University of Michigan; Ann Arbor,
Michigan. [MiU]

"The Woman's Bible," by Elizabeth Cady Stanton (1815-1902), published in New
York by the European Company in two volumes, from 1895-98. 564:615.
Princeton University; Princeton, New Jersey. [NjP]

• • •

The following involve using the National Union Catalog Pre-1956 basic set as a
"carrier" of information, in a sense, as a reference book.

"The Humanitarian Movement of the early Nineteenth Century to Remedy Abuses
on Emigrant Vessels to America...." was published some time around 1871.
Kathleen Annette Walpole was its author. While a library might not want to
loan such a book, are there any libraries in Chicago which might let me
examine it?
Answer: 647:17. Newberry Library, Chicago, Illinois. [ICN]

The privately-printed, subscription edition of D. H. Lawrence's "Women In Love"
consisted of only a few hundred, numbered copies. What number copy, if any,
does the United States Library of Congress hold, and how many copies were
printed?
Answer: 319:424. #332 is in the Library of Congress; a total of 1,250 copies
were printed. D. H. Lawrence is David Herbert Lawrence, without a cross
reference.

A brief publication by D. H. Lawrence titled "Taos" was published in 1923.
Suppose it cannot be borrowed.... How can you utilize the information on the
catalog card perhaps to locate it right in our library?
Answer: 319:420 There is a note, "From the Dial volume 74, No. 3
March 1923 p 251-254."

Does any United States library have a copy of the first English edition, bound in
original pictoral light blue cloth, of Jack London's "Before Adam," published
in 1908?
Answer: 339:220 InU is listed, i.e. Indiana University Lilly Library;
Bloomington, Indiana.

"Tank Warfare" was written by J. R. Lester and published some time before 1956. What is Lester's full name?
328:459 John Reginald Lester

On the basis of the descriptive cataloging, can you determine whether there is a Danish-language edition (version) of William Shakespeare's "Venus and Adonis" in an American library, and if so, when was it published?
Answer: 541:393 Harvard University; Cambridge, Massachusetts. [MH]
Published in 1894.

What was the date of the first edition of Izaak Walton's "The Compleat Angler" ... when was it printed? (Walton lived from 1593-1683).
647:407 The University of Wisconsin's content notes for the 1653 edition state "First edition." The date is provided in brackets.

Can you identify a library in New England which has a copy of "Betty Blue and other Mother Goose rhymes with pictures by Blanche Fisher Wright," published and copyrighted in 1914, illustrated, in the By-lo Series?
Answer: 397:611. Brown University; Providence, Rhode Island. [RPB]
Note: The main entry is Mother Goose.

Where would it be possible to view a copy of "The Well-Bred Girl; An Addition to the Hints on Good Manners Contained in the 'Wellbred Boy,'" published in 1844 by T. H. Carter of Boston? How many pages does it have?
655:58. The University of Virginia, Charlottesville; Virginia [ViU] and the University of California--Los Angeles; Los Angeles, California [CLU] are listed as having copies. 124 pages.

ASSIGNMENT 6; "ART INDEX," "BUSINESS PERIODICALS INDEX," "EDUCATION INDEX," AND "PAIS BULLETIN;" AND "BOOK REVIEW DIGEST"

The following problem situations are derived from Art Index, Business Periodicals Index, Education Index, and PAIS Bulletin.   They can be used with "Step #5" of Assignment 6 (pages 4-5), as well as in other ways, some of which are suggested.   The format of the first group of problems for each tool is presented in the Assignment 6 wording:

> You need to track down a #-page article published in [date] about the SUBJECT HEADING. You need it for a _____ course paper; someone says it's [description].

ART INDEX

You need to track down a fifteen-page article published in October 1979 about AVANT GARDE ART. You need it for a humanities course paper; someone says its illustrations are in color.

Volume 28 November 1979-October 1980:

    108   AVANT-GARDE ART
          When MOMA met the avant-garde. I. Sandler. il (pt col) Artnews
          78:114-18 O '79
    886   Sandler, Irving
          Art News

... five-page article published in November 1978 about KYOTO STREETS.
an environmental design course paper; its illustrations are in color.

Volume 27 November 1978-October 1979:

    497   KYOTO--STREETS
          Narrow village streets enliven a crowded Kyoto. M. T. Bring.
          il (pt col) por (p474) Landscape Arch 68:498-502 N '78
    153   Bring, Mitchell I.
          Landscape Architecture

... brief article published in August 1977 about CLOCKS AND WATCHES. an American history course; it's an illustrated description of an exhibition at the Museum of Our National Heritage in Massachusetts.

Volume 26 November 1977-October 1978

273 CLOCKS AND WATCHES--EXHIBITIONS
European and American clocks from the Willis R. Michael collection:
Museum of our national heritage, Lexington, Mass. S. B. Sherrill.
il Antiques 112:184 Ag '77
998 Sherrill, Sarah B.
Antiques

... seven-page illustrated article published in December 1977 about the influence
of SIR ANTHONY VAN DYCK; a fashion drawing course; it's accompanied by a bibliography, includes a drawing by J. Van Aken, and focuses on the influence of
Seventeenth-Century dress on Eighteenth-Century costume.

Volume 26 November 1977-October 1978:

367 DYCK, ANTO VAN (SIR ANTHONY VAN DYCK)--INFLUENCE
Some evidence of the influence of the dress of the seventeenth century on costume in eighteenth-century female portraiture. A. Ribeiro.
bibl f Burl Mag 119:834-40 D '77 il: Mary, Duchess of Lenox
(drwg by J. van Aken)
921 Ribeiro, Aileen
Burlington Magazine
302 COSTUME IN ART

... eight-page article published in April 1974 about LOG CABINS of Kentucky;
an American Studies course; a bibliography follows the article, which is illustrated.

Volume 22 November 1973-October 1974:

456 LOG CABINS
Log houses of Kentucky. J. C. Thomas. bibliog f il (pt col)
Antiques 105:791-8 Ap '74
759 Thomas, James C.
Antiques

... brief article published in 1973 about EMANUEL LOEWY; a humanities course;
it's about the logic of artistic discovery and has a bibliography following the
article.

Volume 22 November 1973-October 1974:

456 LOEWY, EMANUEL
On the logic of artistic discovery: art as mimetic conjecture.
S. Gablik. bibliog f Studio 186:66 S '73
297 Gablik, Suzi
Studio International

... a seventeen-page article published in February 1979 about the conservation
and restoration of BRICK CONSTRUCTION, specifically factors related to the
durability of adobe structures; it's illustrated and accompanied by a bibliography,
tables and diagrams.

Resources

Volume 27   November 1978-October 1979:

  153   BRICK CONSTRUCTION--CONSERVATION AND RESTORATION
        Adobe: factors affecting the durability of adobe structures "with
        appendix." P. W. Brown and others. bibl f il (pt col) tabs
        diags Stud Conserv 24: 23-39 F '79
  159   Brown, Paul Wencil
        Studies in Conservation; the Journal of the International Institute for
        Conservation of Historic and Artistic Works.

... a six-page illustrated article published in June 1978 about the Royal Pavillion
in BRIGHTON, ENGLAND, which is said to include a colored illustration of the
Pavillion.

Volume 27   November 1978-October 1979:

  153   BRIGHTON, ENGLAND--ROYAL PAVILLION
        A C Pugin's drawings of the Royal pavillion at Brighton.   D. Rogers.
        il (pt col) Connoisseur 198:118-23 Je '78.
  759   Rogers, Derek
        Connoisseur, U.K.

... a brief article published in April 1974 about FRANCESCO LOMBARDI; a history
of sculpture course; it has a bibliography following the article.

Volume 22   November 1973-October 1974:

  456   LOMBARDI, FRANCESCO
        Forging of Italian Renaissance Sculpture.   J. Pope-Hennessy.
        bibliog f Apollo ns 99:248 Ap '74
  616   Pope-Hennesy, Sir John Wyndham
        Apollo; the Magazine of the Arts

... two-page article published in March 1970 about FASCISM AND ART; an interdisciplinary humanities course; there's a "Reply" from J. Tagg too.

Volume 19   November 1970-October 1971:

  343   FASCISM AND ART
        Art and civil servants. A Tapies. Studio 179:86-7 Mr '70; Reply.
        J. Tagg 179:246 Je '70
  918   Tapies, Antonio
        Studio International
        (This is indexed in Volume 18, November 1969-October 1970, page 249 under
        FASCISM AND ART, but without reference to the Reply.)

... four-page article published in November 1962 about ANDREW NEWELL WYETH,
who was born in 1917; an American Studies course; it's accompanied by a portrait.

Volume 13   November 1961-October 1963:

   63   WYETH, ANDREW NEWELL, 1917-
         New light on Andrew Wyeth. J. W. Fasburgh por Art news
         61:34-7 N '62
         Art News

●   ●   ●

These offer considerable challenge:

Locate bibliographically a sixteen-page journal article published in 1981 about
LIONS; this illustrated article was followed by a bibliography and focused on the
heraldic lion in Akan art. Then identify another subject-heading under which
you might locate additional articles of interest in this same index at that time.

Volume 32   November 1983-October 1984:

   479   LIONS
         Heraldic lion in Akan art: a study of motif assimilation in southern
         Ghana. D. H. Ross. bibl f il Met Mus J 16:165-80 '81
   698   Ross, Doran H.
         Metropolitan Museum Journal
  SEE ALSO   DANIEL IN THE LIONS' DEN

Locate bibliographically a four-page journal article about the goddess Minerva as
portrayed in frieze architecture, published in summer 1977.

Volume 26   November 1977-October 1978:

   719   Minerva. See ATHENA
   123   ATHENA (MINERVA)
         Parthenon frieze and the sacrifice to Athena. S. I. Rotroff bibl f
         Am J Archaeol 81 no 3:379-82 Summ '77
   942   Rotroff, Susan I
         American Journal of Archaeology
(This article is also indexed in Humanities Index and Arts & Humanities
Citation Index.)

What is contemporary American artist Judy Chicago's real name? She was in the
news in April 1980, for example.

Volume 28   November 1979-October 1980:

   223   CHICAGO, JUDY (JUDY GEROWITZ)
         Chicago's dinner party. L. R. Lippard bib f il por Art in
         America 68:114-26 Ap '80
   595   Lippard, Lucy R.
         Art in America

In May 1974 an illustrated article about a native Mexican potter was published with a portrait of her, in a ceramics periodical. Locate the article bibliographically and the name of the potter.

Volume 22   November 1973-October 1974:

    381   INDIANS OF MEXICO--POTTERY
          Rosa Real de Nieto: Mexican potter. M. Poupeney. il por diag
          Ceramics M 22:24-9 My '74
    624   Poupeney, Mollie
          Ceramics Monthly
    639   REAL DE NIETO, ROSA
    (Also indexed in Readers' Guide 34:872)

Locate a full-color reproduction of artist LUIGI LOIR'S Le Boulevard; it was published in a 1974 issue of an art periodical.

Volume 22   November 1973-October 1974:

    456   LOIR, LUIGI--REPRODUCTIONS
          Le boulevard. Antiques 105:433 Mr '74 (col)
          Antiques

What is graphic artist KURT LONDENBERG's thing ... his bag ... his speciality? Graphis had a big article in 1973-1974 about him, with 28 illustrations and a portrait.

Volume 22   November 1973-October 1974:

    456   LONDENBERG, KURT
          Creativity in paper. A. Allen. 28 il por Graphis 29 no 166:148-55
          '73-74
    12   Allen, Alastair
          Graphis; International Journal of Graphic and Applied Art

The Ford Building at the 1934 World's Fair, held in Chicago and known as "The Century of Progress," boasted a private lounge designed for what type of hospitality? Could you possibly locate a picture of it?

Volume 2   October 1932-September 1935:

    1349 World's fair, Chicago. See CHICAGO--WORLD'S FAIR
    289   CHICAGO--WORLD'S FAIR, 1934--FORD BUILDING
          Background for masculine hospitality; private lounge, Ford building
          Century of Progress. il Arts & Dec 41:2, 34-6, Ag '34
          Arts & Decoration
    275   Century of Progress. See CHICAGO--WORLD'S FAIR

BUSINESS PERIODICALS INDEX

[The Business Periodicals Index does not provide author-access.]

You need to track down a two-page article published on May 28, 1984 about NURSING HOMES AND SECURITIES; for an investments-related course; this "outlook" article focuses on nursing home chains.

Volume 26 August 1983-August 1984:

    1483 NURSING HOMES--SECURITIES
           Excellent prognosis: the outlook for nursing home chains is glowing.
           G. Weiss. Barrons 64:6-7 My 28 '84
           Barrons

... sixteen-page article published in early 1984 about suits and claims in the area of SEX DISCRIMINATION IN EMPLOYMENT; for an international relations course; this relates to the European Economic Community.

Volume 26 August 1983-July 1984:

    1881 SEX DISCRIMINATION IN EMPLOYMENT--SUITS AND CLAIMS
           Recent legislation and case law in the EEC on sex equality in employment [European Economic Community]. C. E. Landau. Int Labour
           Rev 123:53-70 Ja-F '84
           International Labour Review

... six-page journal article published in June 1981 about the NATIONAL FOOTBALL LEAGUE; for a management course; accompanied by a bibliography and tables, it views the NFL as a business organization with objectives for winning.

Volume 24 August 1981-July 1982:

    941 NATIONAL FOOTBALL LEAGUE
           Organizational objectives and winning: an examination of the NFL.
           D. R. Latham and D. W. Stewart. bibl tabs Acad Mgt J 24:403-8
           Je '81
           Academy of Management Journal

... three-page or so article published on October 12, 1981 about the NATIONAL ORGANIZATION FOR WOMEN's advertising; for a mass media course.

Volume 24 August 1981-July 1982:

    941 NATIONAL ORGANIZATION FOR WOMEN
           Last-stand bid for ERA. R. L. Gordon. Adv Age 52:3+ O 12 '81
           Advertising Age

... two-page illustrated article about the WINE INDUSTRY in CALIFORNIA, for a social science course, it was published in August 1981.

Resources

Volume 24 August 1981-July 1982:

    1473 WINE INDUSTRY--CALIFORNIA
    Buyer's guide to California wines. R. Finigan. il Money 10: 103-4
    Ag '81
    Money

... seven-page article published, with tables, in May 1981, about AFFIRMATIVE ACTION PROGRAMS and their enforcement; for an economics course.

Volume 23 August 1980-July 1981:

    34 AFFIRMATIVE ACTION PROGRAMS
    Affirmative action and its enforcement. F. Welch. Tabs Am Econ R
    71:127-33 My '81
    American Economic Review

... a brief article published in August 1980 about CREDIT UNIONS in GREAT BRITAIN; for a consumer-oriented course paper.

Volume 23 August 1980-July 1981:

    400 CREDIT UNIONS--GREAT BRITAIN
    Credit unions--past, present, and future. B. R. Lewis and H. M.
    Smith. Banker 130:33+ Ag '80
    Banker

... a one-page or so article published on July 28, 1980 about PREMIUMS associated with MERCHANDISING; for an advertising course.

Volume 23 August 1980-July 1981:

    1125 PREMIUMS (MERCHANDISING)
    Premiums catch the hot money. C. Galginaitis. Adv Age 51:50+
    Jl 28 '80
    Advertising Age

... six-page article published on July 3, 1978 about advertising in the BOOK INDUSTRY; for a marketing course.

Volume 21 August 1978-July 1979:

    173 BOOK INDUSTRY--ADVERTISING
    Marketing philosophies are as diverse as the people who make the
    decisions. N. Evans. Pub W 214:30-5 Jl 3 '78
    174 BOOK INDUSTRY--MARKETING

... three-page journal article published in September 1977 about the appeal of TELEVISION ADVERTISING to children; for a mass media or psychology paper.

565

Volume 20   August 1977-July 1978:

  1169   TELEVISION ADVERTISING--CHILDREN, APPEAL TO
         Impact of television advertising on children from low income families.
         G. J. Gorn and M. E. Goldberg.   J. Consumer Res 4:86-8 S '77
         Journal of Consumer Research

... six-page article accompanied by tables, published on December 8, 1977, about
TENDER OFFERS of securities; for a paper concerned with debt refunding options.

Volume 20   August 1977-July 1978:

  1180   TENDER OFFERS (SECURITIES)
         Tender offers and other debt refunding options.   S. G. Pollack.
         tabs Pub Util 100:28-33 D 8 '77
         Public Utilities Fortnightly

... three-page illustrated article published in December 1977, about TENNIS; for
a marketing course, and it has a cutesy title.

Volume 20   August 1977-July 1978:

  1180   TENNIS
         How to serve the racquets.   M. Nason.   il Stores 59:17-19 D '77
         Stores

... nine-page article accompanied by a bibliography and published in June 1974,
about DISCRIMINATION IN EMPLOYMENT; for an economics course, this inter-
relates sex, race, and academic discipline factors.

Volume 17   August 1974-July 1975:

  249   DISCRIMINATION IN EMPLOYMENT
         Faculty salaries: Is there discrimination by sex, race, and discipline?
         N. M. Gordon and others.   bibl Am Econ R 64:419-27 Je '74
         American Economic Review

... a brief article, accompanied by a portrait, published in April 1966 and about
banker James DUESENBERRY; for an economics course.

Volume 8   July 1965-June 1966:

  231   DUESENBERRY, JAMES STEBEL
         Banking's spotlight on James S. Duesenberry [Council on economic
         advisers] por Banking 58: 62+ Ap '66
         Banking

... a one-page article about DRUGS' LAWS AND REGULATIONS, published in May
9, 1966; for a chemistry paper.

Volume 8   July 1965-June 1966:

> 230   DRUGS--LAWS AND REGULATIONS
> Belladona label order: Warning about glaucoma. Oil Paint & Drug
> Rep 189:4 My 9 '66
> Oil Paint & Drug Reporter

· · ·

The following provide considerable challenge:

Locate bibliographically a one-page or so illustrated article about NutraSweet,
published on November 7, 1983 describing the marketing techniques used by the
Searle Company.

Volume 26   August 1983-July 1984:

> 1483   NutraSweet. See SWEETENING AGENTS
> 2000   SWEETENING AGENTS--PHYSIOLOGICAL EFFECT
> The brute force approach [aspartame a synthetic sweetener marketed
> by G D Searle] J. A. Pearl. il Forbes 132:256+ N 7 '83
> Forbes
> (Also in Readers' Guide)

Locate bibliographically an eight-page journal article, accompanied by tables and
a bibliography, published in September 1982, about "Comparable worth" from a
management perspective.

Volume 25   August 1982-July 1983:

> 340   Comparable worth. See EQUAL PAY FOR EQUAL WORK
> 549   EQUAL PAY FOR EQUAL WORK
> The salary differential between male and female administrators:
> equal pay for equal work? L. Sigelman and others. bibl tabs
> Acad Manage J 25:664-71 S '82
> Academy of Management Journal

Locate bibliographically a twenty-two page article accompanied by a bibliography
and published in the Spring 1977 issue of a journal, about MARRIAGE, particularly
the transmission and distribution of wealth. Then locate four additional subject
headings which might provide leads to related information.

Volume 20   August 1977-July 1978:

> 740   MARRIAGE
> Effects of marital and fertility patterns on the transmission and dis-
> tribution of wealth. C. K. Clague. tabs J Hum Resources 12:220-41.
> bibl (p. 239-41) Spr '77.
> SEE ALSO DIVORCE; FAMILY; HUSBAND AND WIFE; MARRIAGE COUN-
> SELING

Locate a six-page illustrated article published in February 1975 about remodeling HOUSES as a business.

Volume 17   August 1974-July 1975:

395   Houses--Repair and Construction. See HOUSES, REMODELED
700   Remodeled Houses. See HOUSES, REMODELED
395   HOUSES, REMODELED
      Why would a respectable homebuilder want to go into the remodeling business? [Cor-Lon's Williams]. H. C. Wells. il H & Home 47:62-7 F '75
      House and Home

How old was insurance family head William A. Earls when he died (some time about 1966)?

Volume 8   July 1965-June 1966:

232   EARLS, WILLIAM A.
      William A. Earls was of famous insurance family [death at age 92] ... Nat Underw 70:30 My 13 '66
      National Underwriter

EDUCATION INDEX

You need to track down a ten-page article, accompanied by a bibliography, published in April 1982, about TESTS AND SCALES' SOCIAL ASPECTS. You need it for an education [or psychology] course paper; someone says it's convenient because it summarizes "issues."

Volume 33   July 1982-June 1983:

1259   TESTS AND SCALES
       Non-biased assessment in counseling: issues and guidelines. T. Oakland. bibl Measurement and eval in guid 15:107-16 Apr '82
862   Oakland, Thomas
       Measurement and Evaluation in Guidance

... a brief illustrated article published on May 8, 1981 about educational use of COMPUTERS in Scotland.

Volume 32   July 1981-June 1982:

257   COMPUTERS--EDUCATIONAL USE--SCOTLAND
       Phase two in Scotland; Scottish Microelectronics Development Programme. I. Thorburn. il Times Educ Supp 3385:42 My 8 '81
1203   Thorburn, Iain
       Times (London) Education Supplement

... a three-page illustrated article about the use of COMPUTERS for PRINTING in industry, published in the April 1982 issue of a vocational education periodical.

Volume 32   July 1981-June 1982:

   257   COMPUTERS--PRINTING USE
          Computers transform an industry. J. Simich. il VocEd 57:33-5
          Ap '82
 1044   Simich, Jack
          VocEd

... a twenty-eight page journal article, accompanied by a bibliography, published in April 1981 and about so-called MASCULINITY-FEMININITY TESTS. You need it for a psychology course paper.

Volume 32   July 1981-June 1982:

   698   MASCULINITY-FEMININITY TESTS
          Sex roles, personality, and intellectual abilities in adolescents.
          C. J. Mills. bibl J Youth & Adolescence 10:85-112 Ap '81
  742   Mills, Carol J.
          Journal of Youth and Adolescence

... a seven-page journal article, accompanied by a bibliography, published in July 1979, about WILDERNESS AREAS. You need this for a paper about the effects on children of having environmental experiences.

Volume 30   July 1979-June 1980:

 1158 WILDERNESS AREAS
          Effects of combined advance organizers and field experience on environmental orientations of elementary school children. M. P. Gross and E. L. Pizzini. bibl J Res Sci Teach 16:325-31 Jl '79
  446   Gross, Michael P. and E. L. Pizzini
          Journal of Research in Science Teaching

... a three-page journal article, accompanied by a bibliography, published in December 1979, about research concerning teaching of BUSINESS ENGLISH. You need this for a communications course paper.

Volume 30   July 1979-June 1980:

  142   BUSINESS ENGLISH--TEACHING--RESEARCH
          Needed research in business communication. P. V. Lewis. bibl J Bus Educ 55:127-9 D '79
  601   Lewis, Phillip V.
          Journal of Business Education

... an eleven-page article, accompanied by a bibliography, published in 1979 in a research periodical, about graduate work in BUSINESS MANAGEMENT. You need this for a paper about student evaluations in higher education.

Volume 30   July 1979-June 1980:

142   BUSINESS MANAGEMENT--GRADUATE WORK
      Assessing academic program and department effectiveness using student evaluation data. S. A. Stumpf. bibl Res Higher Educ 11 no 4:353-63 '79
1024 Stumpf, Stephen A.
      Research in Higher Education

... a three-page article published in January 1980, about WIFE BEATING. You need this for a paper about domestic violence in the United States.

Volume 30   July 1979-June 1980:

1158 WIFE BEATING
      Plague of domestic violence in the U.S. M. Miller and J. Miller. USA Today 108:26-8 Ja '80
681   Miller, Mark and Miller, Judith
      USA Today

... a two-page journal article about MEXICAN AMERICANS' alcohol use, published in January 1978, accompanied by a bibliography. You need this for a paper about young people's use of alcohol for a public health [or psychology or Chicano Studies] course.

Volume 28   July 1977-June 1978:

580   MEXICAN AMERICANS
      Alcohol use among Mexican-American youth. R. Guinn. J Sch Health 48:90-1 F '78
391   Guinn, Robert
      Journal of School Health

... a nine-page article published in winter 1977, about OPEN PLAN SCHOOLS.

Volume 28   July 1977-June 1978:

640   OPEN PLAN SCHOOLS
      From the open school room to the open school. C. Samuels. Education 98:188-96 Wint '77
769   Samuels, Curtis
      Education
776   SCHOOL BUILDINGS--DESIGNS AND PLANS

... a ten-page journal article published in fall 1977 about OPINION. You need this for your psychology [or mass media or communications] course paper.

Volume 28   July 1977-June 1978:

   641   OPINION (PSYCHOLOGY)
         Friends, the media, and opinion formation.   J. Beinstein.   J Comm
         27:30-9   Aut '77
    90   Beinstein, Judith
         Journal of Communication

... a six-page journal article published in Winter 1974 about DISCRIMINATION IN
EDUCATION. You need it for a psychology course paper concerned with the 14th
Amendment, and you need a bibliography.

Volume 25   July 1974-June 1975:

   275   DISCRIMINATION IN EDUCATION
         Sex discrimination in student personnel functions [14th amendment and
         Title IX].   E. H. Hammond.   NASPA J   11:27-32   Wint '74
   402   Hammond, Edward H.
         NASPA Journal (NASPA is the National Association of Student Person-
         nel Administrators)

... a four-page article published in January 1975 about SEX ROLE IN LITERATURE,
particularly in the language of elementary school textbooks. You need this for a
psychology course paper.

Volume 25   July 1974-June 1975:

   816   SEX ROLE IN LITERATURE
         Sexism in the language of elementary school textbooks.   L. Harrison
         and R. N. Passero.   Sci & Child 12:22-5   Ja '75
   406   Harrison, Linda
   656   Passero, Richard
         Science and Children

... a four-page illustrated article published in November 1973, accompanied by a
bibliography, about HOMOSEXUALITY's myths. You need this for a religion
course paper.

Volume 24   July 1973-June 1974:

   393   HOMOSEXUALITY
         Myths of homosexuality.   J. Gramick.   bibliog   il   Intellect 102:104-7
         N '73
   356   Gramick, Sister Jeannine
         Intellect
(Notable here is that this is not listed under GAY LIBERATION MOVEMENT,
nor is there a "See" reference to HOMOSEXUALITY from GAY LIBERATION
MOVEMENT. This is also indexed in Readers' Guide volume 33 March 1973-
April 1979, page 507).

... a five-page or so article about the effect of walking in cowboy boots on KNEE action, published in October 1964. You need this for a physical education [or health] course paper.

Volume 15   July 1964-June 1965:

340   KNEE
      Effect of walking in cowboy boots on the knee action. M. Adrian
      and P. V. Karpovich. Am Assn Health Phys Ed Rec Res Q pt 2:398-
      402+ O '64
      American Association for Health, Physical Education and Recreation Research
      Quarterly.

•   •   •

The following provide more challenge:

... an eight-page article published in spring 1984, accompanied by a bibliography, about freedom of INFORMATION. You need it for a paper about the effects on the achievement of adult learners. Then identify an additional subject heading under which potentially useful information can be located in this index at that time.

Volume 34   July 1983-June 1984:

570   INFORMATION, FREEDOM OF
      Disclosure of cognitive style information: effects on achievement of
      adult learners. M. J. Fourier. bibl Adult Educ Q 34:147-54 Spr
      '84
449   Fourier, Mary Jo
      Edult Education Quarterly
SEE ALSO   SCIENTIFIC FREEDOM

... a five-page journal article published in December 1981 about MASCULINITY and men's health. Then identify additional subject headings under which poten-tially useful information can be located in this index at that time.

Volume 32   July 1981-June 1982:

698   MASCULINITY
      Socialized to die younger? hypermasculinity and men's health.
      C. E. Meinecke. Personnel & Guid J 60:241-5 D '81
720   Meinecke, Christine E.
      Personnel & Guidance Journal
SEE ALSO   ANDROGYNY (PSYCHOLOGY); FEMININITY

... a four-page illustrated article published in November 1979 about WILDLIFE CONSERVATION in Alaska. Then identify additional subject headings under which potentially useful information can be located in this index at that time.

Volume 30   July 1979-June 1980:

1158 WILDLIFE CONSERVATION
Protecting our last great frontier; Alaska. C. D. Andrus. il
USA Today 108:27-30 N '79
40 Andrus, Cecil D.
USA Today
SEE ALSO WILDERNESS AREAS; WILDLIFE REFUGES

... a twenty-two page article published in May 1980 accompanied by a bibliography, appraising scholastic aptitude tests.

Volume 31 July 1980-June 1981:

932 Scholastic aptitude tests. See COLLEGE ENTRANCE EXAMINATION BOARD SCHOLASTIC APTITUDE TEST
312 COLLEGE ENTRANCE EXAMINATION BOARD SCHOLASTIC APTITUDE TEST
Scholastic aptitude test; a critical appraisal. W. V. Slack and D. Porter. bibl Harvard Educ R 50:154-75 My '80; Discuss 50:382-401 Ag '80
984 Slack, Warner V. and Porter, Douglas
Harvard Educational Review

You need to locate several reviews (four at least) all in one search of David A. Peterson's 1983 book, Facilitating Education for Older Learners. Who wrote the review for the Journal of Higher Education?

Volume 35 July 1984-June 1985:

1496 BOOK REVIEWS Peterson, D. A. Facilitating education for older learners. 1983
H. R. Moody.

PAIS [Public Affairs Information Service] BULLETIN

The PAIS Bulletin is described as a selective subject list of the latest books, pamphlets, government publications, reports of public and private agencies, periodical articles relating to economic and social conditions, public administration and international relations published in English throughout the world. It functions as an index to the contents of publications--largely periodical in nature--within this scope. It is not a Wilson index (such as Art, Business Periodicals and Education Indexes), but it can be utilized in the same manner. Each subject-entry includes the author's full name; a separate author section in the back of each cumulated volume does not provide the full information provided under the subject-entry.

Volume 68 "1982" October 1981-September 1982:

You need to locate a California Department of Education 1982 publication prepared by Urban Management Consultants on the subject of APPRENTICESHIP. Someone says it's actually an illustrated paperback book about women by a woman; if so, what's her name and where can you get a copy?

    97   APPRENTICESHIP

California Department of Education. The apprenticeship and blue collar system: putting women on the right track. Weston, Kathleen M. '82 vii + 238p il tables charts pa POB 271 Sacramento 95802. Prep by Urban Management Consultants.

You need information about FREEDOM OF SPEECH as it relates to business corporations and stockholders' rights under the First Amendment, i.e. just how far do freedom of speech doctrines protect corporations from interference by stockholders!? Someone says there was a law journal article on this subject in December 1981, although it was around sixty pages in length....

    424   FREEDOM OF SPEECH

Brudney, Victor. Business corporations and stockholders' rights under the First Amendment [degree to which freedom of speech doctrines protect corporate speech from interference by stockholders]. Yale Law J 91:235-91 D '81
Yale Law Journal

You need information about NEWSPRINT PAPER RECYCLING, specifically some of the results from the 1980 supply-and-recovery-of-waste-newspapers survey. Someone says they were published in the fall or winter 1981 Forest Products Review.

    693   NEWSPRINT PAPER--RECYCLING

Post, Howard A. Old news survey completed in four South Atlantic states [supply and recovery of waste newspaper, 1980]. tables Forest Products R 37:12-14 Fall/Winter '81

What were the trends in Americans' DIVORCE style in the early 1980's decade? Someone says there was an illustrated article published in the May 1982 American Demographics about this.

    309-10 310:   DIVORCE

Weed, James A. Divorce: Americans' style [recent trends]. il charts Am Demographics 4:12-17 Ma '82

Volume 67 "1981" October 1980-September 1981:

You need information about industrial MEDIATION AND CONCILIATION, particularly use of grievance mediation. Someone refers you to a conference paper published in the August 1980 issue of a labor law journal.

    628   MEDIATION AND CONCILIATION, INDUSTRIAL

Gregory, Gordon A. and Robert E. Rooney, jr. Grievance mediation: a trend in the cost-conscious eighties (conference paper). table Labor Law J 31:502-8 Ag '80
Labor Law Journal

You need information about the possibility that the personal income tax discriminates against any particular class or group. Someone refers you to a sixteen-page article published in 1981 and accompanied by a bibliography.

    305   DISCRIMINATION AGAINST WOMEN

Andic, Suphan. Does the personal income tax discriminate against

Resources

women? bibl Public Fin(Berlin) 36:1-15 no 1 '81
Public Finance: International Quarterly Journal

Can you track down the results of the 1973 survey regarding the impact of sup-
plemental security income on old welfare recipients? Someone says it was in the
Social Security Bulletin's April 1981 issue.

    704   OLD AGE--HOUSING
        Tissue, Thomas and John L. McCoy. Income and living arrangements
        among poor aged single [impact of the supplemental security income
        program on unmarried older welfare recipients surveyed in 1973].
        bibl tables Social Security Bull 44:3-13 Ap '81

Supreme Court Chief Justice Earl Warren died in 1974. About seven years later,
a prestigious law review published a lengthy article about Warren "as jurist" in
its April issue.

    1029 WARREN, EARL, 1891-1974
        White, G. Edward. Earl Warren as jurist. Va La R 67:461-551
        Ap '81
        Virginia Law Review
    1008 U.S.--SUPREME COURT

What were the answers (conclusions) of California writers in 1981 to the question, "Can a Black (Bradley) Be Elected Governor in 1982?"? An illustrated
three-page article was published in-state in January.

    163   CALIFORNIA--GOVERNMENT AND POLITICS
        Willens, Michele. Can a Black (Bradley) be elected governor in
        1982? [Thomas Bradley, mayor of Los Angeles, Cal.] il Cal J
        12:10-12 Ja '81
        California Journal; The Monthly Analysis ... Sacramento.

Volume 66 "1980" October 1979-September 1980:

You need information about WOMEN ACCOUNTANTS abroad, or, as they're called
in England and Wales, "chartered accountants." Careers information was provided in the Spring 1979 issue of Accounting and Business Research.

    985   WOMEN ACCOUNTANTS
        Silverstone, Rosalie and Allan Williams. Recruitment, training, em-
        ployment and careers of women chartered accountants in England and
        Wales. tables Accounting and Bus Research 9:105-21 Spring '79
    (Also indexed in volume 65 October 1978-September 1979, page 974)

The Review of Radical Political Economics published a ten-page article in Summer
1980 about WOMEN AND WAR in which the author discussed the ideological processes shaping the spheres of the military use of women. What are the uses
identified?

    985   WOMEN AND WAR
        Enloe, Cynthia. Women--the reserve army of army labor [ideological
        processes that shape three spheres of women's military use: as sol-
        diers, as defense industry laborers, as mothers of future soldiers].
        R Radical Pol Econ 12:43:52 Summer '80 this issue $4

Volume 62 "1976" October 1975-September 1976:

An illustrated article published in the June 1976 <u>Washington Monthly</u> described Edward Moore KENNEDY's image in what way?

494   KENNEDY, EDWARD MOORE

Kennedy: the playboy image ["He doesn't belong in the driver's seat, but he can be a great senator."] James Fallows. il Washington Mo 8:11-21 Je '76

Volume 61 "1975" October 1974-September 1975:

Brian M. Jenkins described international TERRORISM as a new kind of what when he appeared before the U.S. House of Representatives' Committee on Foreign Affairs Subcommittee on the Near East and Southern Asia sometime in June 1974? How can you get a copy if the Library doesn't have it?

817   TERRORISM

Brian M. Jenkins' statement on international terrorism [as] a new kind of warfare before the US H of Reps' Committee on foreign affairs Subcmt on the Near East and S Asia. June 1974 approx. $1.00 from Rand Corp. #P5261.

36   Address for Rand Corp., 1700 Main, Santa Monica, CA

Volume 57 "1971" October 1970-September 1971:

You need information about Henry KISSINGER's role at the Harvard international seminar from 1951-1971. Someone suggests an illustrated article published in September 1970....

492   KISSINGER, HENRY ALFRED

A foreign affairs Henry Kissinger at the Harvard international seminar [his role ... since 1951]. Robert Fichter. il Bost 62:52-3+ S '70 Boston Monthly

Volume 56 "1970" October 1969-September 1970:

You're trying to locate a 1969 book about JAPANESE AMERICANS' relocation during World War II. This particular book is illustrated and provided with maps and a bibliography. (You've already consulted the library catalog using LCSH subject-headings.)

480   JAPANESE AMERICANS

Impounded people: Japanese-Americans in the relocation centers. Tucson: University of Arizona Press, 1969. Edward H. Spicer and others.

Volume 50 "1964" October 1963-September 1964:

You're trying to document a contention that Justice Arthur Goldberg questioned "the propriety of imposing the death penalty" on persons <u>convicted</u> of RAPE. Apparently he made a critical comment to this effect sometime prior to April 1964, when it was discussed in a prestigious law review.

696   RAPE

Making the punishment fit the crime [critical comment on Justice Arthur

Goldberg's questioning of the propriety of imposing the death penalty on convicted rapists]. Herbert L. Packer. Harvard Law R 77:1071-82 Ap '64
Harvard Law Review

•   •   •

The following provide considerably more challenge:

"PAIS" can be used as a <u>Wall Street Journal</u> newspaper index. Three articles published in this newspaper need to be tracked down:

(1) the one about ASSAULT AND BATTERY by passengers on airline personnel, which the unions claimed was played down by the FAA ... appeared sometime in February 1980;

(2) the one about MATERNITY LEAVE disrupting firms when it applies to managers ... appeared sometime in July 1981; and

(3) the one about economic conditions in NICARAGUA, focusing on confiscations of business and including a map ... appeared sometime in September 1981.

(1) Volume 66 "1980" October 1979-September 1980:

97   ASSAULT AND BATTERY
Guyon, Janet. Skies aren't friendly for airline people who get assaulted; rising violence by passengers noted by unions, but FAA [Federal aviation administration] and airlines play it down. Wall St J 195:1+ F 27 '80

(2) Volume 67 "1981" October 1980-September 1981:

628   MATERNITY LEAVE
Gottschalk, Earl C., Jr. Maternity leave; firms are disrupted by wave of pregnancy at the manager level. Wall St J 198:1+ Jl 20 '81
(Also indexed in <u>Social Sciences Index</u> October 1980-September 1981)

(3) Volume 68 "1982" October 1981-September 1982:

693   NICARAGUA--ECONOMIC CONDITIONS
Frazier, Steve. After the revolt: Nicaragua is plunged into economic crisis under near anarchy; confiscations of businesses, higher prices and taxes are stirring frustrations. map Wall St J 198:1+ S 15 '81

Locate a reference to a magazine article published in May 1975 about the techniques of saving money on WEDDINGS "without skimping." Then identify another subject heading used by this index at that time which may generate further useful information.

Volume 61 "1975" October 1974-September 1975:

    922   WEDDINGS
            Wedding bills, and how to peel them: here comes the bride--and the bridal consultant, the jeweler....; the idea is to save without skimping. Caroline Donnelly. Money 4:46-8+ My '75
    SEE ALSO MARRIAGE COSTS

"Is there such a thing as an entire book which is all bibliography about WOMEN ATHLETES? What I really want is a guide to information sources. Someone says there was one published in 1980, but I can't find this book in the catalog. And how come I didn't find it?"

Volume 66 "1980" October 1979-September 1980:

    959   WOMEN ATHLETES--BIBLIOGRAPHY
            Remley, Mary L. Women in sport: a guide to information sources. '80 xii + 139p bibl indexes (Sports, games, and pastimes info. guide ser. v. 10) (Gale info. guide lib.) (LC 80-14773) (ISBN O-8103-1461-4) $28--Gale
    Did you try the serials catalog?

"Was there such a thing as the 'displaced homemaker' back in 1975, and if so what was the definition of it then?"

Volume 64 "1978" October 1977-September 1978:

    731   SINGLE PARENT FAMILY
            Chambers, Marjorie Bell. The displaced homemaker: victim of socio-economic change affecting the American family [usually considered to be persons between the ages of 35 and 65 years and divorced, separated or widowed, 65 per cent with children living at home]. charts Inst socioeconomic studies J 3:68-76 Autumn '78
            Journal of the Institute of Socioeconomic Studies

You want to see Executive Order 11752, "Control of environmental pollution at federal facilities ... December 17, 1973." And whose executive order was 11752?

Volume 60 "1974" October 1973-September 1974:

    310   Environmental pollution. See POLLUTION
    659   POLLUTION--U.S.--LEGISLATION
            Control of environmental pollution at federal facilities: Executive order 11752. Dec. 17, 1973. Richard Nixon. W Comp Pres Docs 9:1467-9 D 24 '73
            Weekly Compilation of Presidential Documents.
    606   NIXON, RICHARD--SPEECHES

You're trying to locate information about protection for unmarried fathers.

Someone says there was an article in an issue of a law review published in March 1980.

Volume 66 "1980" October 1979-September 1980:

    955   Unmarried fathers. See FATHERS, UNMARRIED
    367   FATHERS, UNMARRIED--LEGAL STATUS, LAWS, ETC.
        Cohen, Marie Prince. Equal protection for unmarried parents
        [evaluates the U.S. supreme court's response to the issue of dis-
        crimination against the unmarried parent particularly the unmarried
        father]. Iowa Law R 65:679-719 Mr '80
        Iowa Law Review

The June 1980 issue of a law periodical devoted an article to the subject of how violence in college athletics can be controlled, based on "societal concern."

Volume 67 "1981" October 1980-September 1981:

    106   Athletics. See SPORTS; COLLEGE ATHLETICS.
    883   SPORTS
        Rains, Cameron Jay. Sports violence; a matter of societal concern
        [available means by which society can control violence in team contact
        sports]. Notre Dame Lawyer 55:796-813 Je '80
  1018 VIOLENCE
(Also accessible by use of Index to Legal Periodicals)

BOOK REVIEW DIGEST

The following problem situations can be used with Assignment 6, "STEP #6," part C, relating to Book Review Digest. They have been constructed to include other aspects of this tool, so that they can be used in teaching in various ways. The format is:

    Who reviewed the book published around 19__, written by _____, and
    titled _____; the review in question was published in a periodical
    titled "_____."

In each example, the data are presented with the year-volume followed by the page location of the full-display entry, which is under the main entry, generally a personal author; title and date of publication are followed by the periodical and reviewer's name. Frequently an additional query supplements this basic provision, as in the first "problem" below.

"1985" Book Review Digest:

    849-50 Kendrigan, Mary Lou
        Political equality in a democratic society; women in the United States.
        1984
    Political Science Quarterly. Janet K. Boles
    You've checked the library catalog under the author and book-title and

concluded we don't have this book yet; someone else finds it....
Answer: In the serials catalog, under Contributions in women's studies,
a series of which this is number 45, according to the information at the
beginning of the Book Review Digest entry.

850   Kennan, George
           The fateful alliance. 1984
Choice. J. T. Hapak
What is Kennan's full name and when was he born? What is the full title
of The Fateful Alliance?
Answer: George Frost Kennan. 1904. The fateful alliance; France, Russia,
and the coming of the First World War.

968   Lloyd, David Wharton
           The making of English towns. 1984
Times Literary Supplement. Alec Clifton-Taylor
What is the sub-title of this book, what is this book about?
Answer: "a vista of 2000 years."

968   Lloyd, Genevieve
           The man of reason; "male" and "female" in Western philosophy. 1984
Library Journal. Astrid M. O'Brien
This book is accompanied by a particularly useful type of bibliography,
namely?
Answer: An annotated bibliography.

990   MacDonald, Charles Brown
           A time for trumpets. 1984
New York Times Book Review. Linda Charlton
What is the sub-title of this book, what is this book about?
Answer: "the untold story of the Battle of the Bulge."

1125   Moynihan, Daniel P.
           Loyalties. 1984
New Republic. Morton Kondracke
What is Moynihan's full name, and when was he born? In what way does
Moynihan relate to Woodrow Wilson, according to one reviewer?
Answer: Daniel Patrick Moynihan. 1927. "Mr. Moynihan's reaffirmation of
Wilsonian idealism about the supremacy of law in international affairs en-
ables him to occupy the moral high ground" (New York Times Book Review:
William V. Shannon).

"1982" Book Review Digest:

1046-7 Pharr, Susan J.
           Political women in Japan; the search for a place in political life. 1981
Political Science Quarterly. Martha Hoaglund

917   Miller, Roy Andrew
           Origins of the Japanese language; lectures in Japan during the
           academic year 1977-78. 1981
Modern Language Journal. Shigeru Miyagawa

What very useful type of bibliography accompanies the book?
Answer: Annotated bibliography.

1138 Rodriguez, Richard
        Hunger of memory; the education of Richard Rodriguez; an auto-
        biography. 1982
New York Times Book Review. Paul Sweig
Several of the reviewers alude to two controversial issues in contemporary
American life which the author comments upon in relationship to his life;
what are they?
Answer: bilingual education and affirmative action.

1138 Rodrigues, Eusebio L.
        Quest for the human: an exploration of Saul Bellow's fiction.
        1982
Library Journal. Earl Rovit
What type or form of writing did Rodrigues explore in his doctoral work?
Answer: fiction, specifically, the novel.

917 Miller, Ron.
        The grand tour: a traveler's guide to the solar system. 1981
Scientific American. Philip Morrison
What is the name of the other author (the joint author) of this book?
The Library Journal reviewer compared this book to another, related book;
what is the title of that book and in what Book Review Digest annual volume
could you read about it?
Answer: William K. Hartmann. The New Solar System, edited by J. Beatty
and others. Book Review Digest 1981.

917 Miller, Robin Feuer
        Dostoevsky and The Idiot; author, narrator, and reader. 1981
Times Literary Supplement. M. V. Jones

415 Fernandez, John P.
        Racism an sexism in corporate life; changing values in American
        business. 1981
Political Science Quarterly. Jessie Bernard
What was the title of Fernandez's earlier book, published around 1976,
referred to here?
Answer: Black Managers in White Corporations.

402 Fairlie, Alison.
        Imagination and language; collected essays on Constant, Baudelaire,
        Nerval and Flaubert; ed. by Malcolm Bowie. 1981
Times Literary Supplement. Robert Gibson.
The Times Literary Supplement reviewer is most enthusiastic about which
of Fairlie's essays?
Answer: Fairlie's essay on Nerval's Sylvia and Les Chimères.

402 Fairbanks, Jonathan L.
        American furniture, 1620 to the present. 1981
Library Journal. J. P. Brown
Who is the other author (the joint author) of this book? Which of the two

review periodicals excerpted was less enthusiastic about it?
Answer: Elizabeth Bidwell Bates. Library Journal.

402   Fairbank, John King.
         Chinabound; a fifty-year memoir. 1982
New York Review of Books. D. S. Nivison
Of the several reviews excerpted for us by Book Review Digest, who wrote
the one which was the longest in its original form? What was the title of
Fairbank's 1974 book?
Answer: D. S. Nivison. China Perceived.

"1981" Book Review Digest:

1132 Plath, David W.
         Long engagements; maturity in modern Japan. 1980
Annals of the American Academy of Arts and Sciences. Justin Williams.
Which of the review periodicals excerpted was least enthusiastic about this
book?
Answer: Choice, which also is the most specific and least generalized.

"1980" Book Review Digest:

903   Oates, Stephen D.
         Our fiery trial: Abraham Lincoln, John Brown, and the Civil War
         era. 1979
American Historical Review. R. O. Curry
Which reviewer refers to this as "a small book," and how long is it?
Answer: R. O. Curry. The book is 150 pages in length.

794   Malbin, Michael J.
         Unelected representatives; Congressional staff and the future of
         representative government. 1980
Commentary. Elliott Abrams
Is Abrams' review negative, positive, or neutral? Is the book indexed?
Answer: Positive ("... makes a distinct contribution.") Yes, it is in-
dexed.

903   Oates, Joyce Carol
         Bellefleur. 1980
Library Journal. Mary Soete

903   Oates, Joyce Carol
         Unholy loves; a novel. 1979
Christian Science Monitor. Joanne Leedom-Ackerman
Are these two books fiction or nonfiction? Which reviewer refers to Oates'
sentence that was sixty-one lines in length, and how does s/he evaluate
it--successful, unsuccessful? What is the name of Unholy Loves' hero, and
at what college does it take place?
Answer: Fiction, both referred to as novels. Gordon Cheesewright
(Christian Science Monitor) refers to the lengthy successful sentence in his
Bellefleur review; "... 61 lines long, but what a fine sentence it is...."
Alexis Kessler. Woodslee University and Woodslee College are both referred
to (Library Journal, Newsweek).

"1979" <u>Book Review Digest</u>:

    834   Manning, Mary
          The last chronicles of Bollyfungus. 1978
Who or what is Bollyfungus? Was the <u>New York Times Book Review</u> representative of the reviewers' reactions?
Answer: An Irish market town. No--Ryan's review (excellent) is at one extreme; this is a good example of the great span possible in reviewers' perceptions.

"1978" <u>Book Review Digest</u>:

    796   Lewis, Walter H.
          Medical botany; plants affecting man's health. 1977.
<u>Scientific American</u>. Philip Morrison.
How long was Morrison's review? What did it cost at the time it was published?
Answer: Four hundred words. $27.50.

    181   Burnham, Sophy.
          The landed gentry. 1978.
<u>Best Sellers</u>. James Doyle
What is or are gentry? Which of the three reviewers is the most positive?
Answer: "... a group defined as those who derive their principal income from inherited land." James Doyle's excerpt appears the most positive of the three reviews provided.

"1976" <u>Book Review Digest</u>:

   1003 Rich, Adrienne
          Of woman born; motherhood as experience and institution. 1976
<u>New York Review of Books</u>. Helen Vendler.

"1975" <u>Book Review Digest</u>:

    401   Fasteau, Marc Feigen
          The male machine. 1974
<u>Atlantic</u>. Richard Todd

"1974" <u>Book Review Digest</u>:

    727   Little, Kenneth
          African women in towns; an aspect of Africa's social revolution.
          1974.
<u>Library Journal</u>. Carol Holbrook
What are (or were in 1974) walk-about-women? Was Holbrook's review positive?
Answer: Prostitutes. Yes, probably the most positive.

"1971" <u>Book Review Digest</u>:

172 Brown, Martin, ed.
     The social responsibility of the scientist. 1971.
<u>Bulletin of the Atomic Scientists</u>. L. F. Gorr
Martin Brown edited this book; who are some of the contributors (other writers)?
Answer: J. Lederberg, O. Chamberlain, B. Commoner, P. Goodman
(<u>Library Journal</u>)

765 Kolneder, Walter
     Antonio Vivaldi; his life and work; tr. by Bill Hopkins. 1970.
<u>Library Journal</u>. B. D. Henry
What is the publishing history of this book? Sometimes this is referred to as bibliographic history.
Answer: "... revised from the original work published in Germany in 1965."

862 McCullers, Carson (Smith)
     The mortgaged heart; ed. by Margarita G. Smith. 1971.
<u>Best Sellers</u>. Jeanne Kinney
Victor Howes refers to this book as "fugitive pieces." Did you know this term when you started to read his review excerpt? According to Phoebe Adams, how are Margarita G. Smith and Carson Smith McCullers related? Do you understand this term, "fugitive pieces," now?
Answer: Sisters

765 Komisar, Lucy.
     The new feminism. 1971.
<u>Commonweal</u>. E. M. Graves
Is this book suitable for young adults, and how do you know whether it is or not? In what issue of <u>Best Sellers</u> did Cornelia Holbert's review appear?
Answer: It is intended for ages 13-18, and expected to be of special interest to teenagers, etc. However, the "YA" indicates that it was reviewed for this population.

"1967" <u>Book Review Digest</u>:

609 Hinton, William
     Fashen; a documentary of revolution in a Chinese village. 1968.
<u>New York Times Book Review</u>. B. Schwartz

•   •   •

The following provide considerably more challenge. They usually involve recognition of need to use the index or of lag between publication date and appearance of reviews. "See" cross references and title main entries should by now be things which they can apply routinely.

<u>The Women's Health Movement; Feminist Alternatives to Medical Control</u> was published in 1978. Was the review published by <u>Choice</u> journal positive, negative,

or neutral? Would this book be particularly useful towards the beginning of a research project, and if so why? Answer:

"1979" Book Review Digest Subject-Title Index in the back of the volume

1558 Women's Health Movement. Ruzek, Sheryl Burt
1100 Ruzek, Sheryl Burt [full display]
Choice's reviewer was very positive. Because the book has a very long bibliography, is well indexed and provided with [relevant] appendices, it would likely provide good leads at the beginning of a research on this subject.

Vanishing Wildlife was published around 1964. Was J. A. Davis' review in Natural History long or short, positive or negative? Answer: Start in 1962-1966 cumulated subject and title index, which leads to

"1964" Book Review Digest:

934 Pinney, Roy [full display]
Davis' review was the longest and negative.

Mary Daly's 1968 best-selling The Church and the Second Sex was critical of the Catholic Church. What was the Catholic reaction? · Answer:

"1968" Book Review Digest:

304 Daly, Mary [full display]
America contained a review which can be considered positive; they also assigned a woman to provide the review. Ulrich's International Periodicals Directory and other sources indicate that America is a Roman Catholic publication. (Myrtle Passantino's review from the May 11, 1968 issue is excerpted by Book Review Digest; also Don Browning's review in the ecumenical Christian Century.)

Here are titles of four books, reviews of which are excerpted and indexed in three Book Review Digest annuals:
        The burning heart; women poets of Japan...
        Kodansha encyclopedia of Japan.
        Jewish and Christian self-definition; v. 3 Self-definition in the Greco-
            Roman world
        Jewish life in Philadelphia, 1830-1940; edited by Murray Friedman
Why would it be logical to look directly under each of these titles in the main alphabet to find the information about it ... in the B's, K's, and J's? Answer: Because they are main-entried under their titles; each involves the writings of numerous persons.

"1978" Book Review Digest:

181-2 The Burning heart; women poets of Japan; tr. and ed. by Kenneth
      Rexroth and Ikuko Atsumi. 1978.

Library Journal. Val Morehouse

"1984" Book Review Digest:

869   Kodansha Encyclopedia of Japan. 1983.
Library Journal. Kenneth W. Berger

"1985" Book Review Digest:

807   Jewish and Christian Self-Definition; v. 3, Self-definition in the
       Greco-Roman world; edited by Ben F. Meyer and E. P. Sanders.
       1983
Journal of Religion. Robert M. Grant

807   Jewish life in Philadelphia, 1830-1940; edited by Murray Friedman.
       1983.
Journal of American History. Jenna Weissman Joselit

ASSIGNMENT 7; "ESSAY & GENERAL LITERATURE
INDEX," PRACTICE USING ABSTRACTING SERVICES,
AND "COMPREHENSIVE DISSERTATION INDEX/
DISSERTATION ABSTRACTS INTERNATIONAL"

ESSAY & GENERAL LITERATURE INDEX

Volume 9 1975-1979:

You need information about development of Black studies in early 1970's. Someone commends to you an essay published in a 1975 book published by Prentice-
Hall. They can recall only that the essay in the book was approximately five
pages in length.

   Black studies. See AFRO-AMERICAN STUDIES
 20 AFRO-AMERICAN STUDIES
   Brower, A. Black studies and changing times. IN Fairfield, R.P.,
   ed. Humanistic frontiers in American education p 134-38.
 1704 Fairfield, Roy P., ed. Humanistic frontiers in American education,
   2nd edition. Prometheus 1975 c1971. First published in 1971 by
   Prentice-Hall.
 192 Brower, Alston.

You need information about the single parent family in the 1970's decade. Someone commends to you an essay appearing in a 1975 book published by Spectrum.
They can recall only that the essay in the book was approximately eleven pages
long.

   Single parent family. See PATERNAL DEPRIVATION
 1122 PATERNAL DEPRIVATION
   Biller, H. B. & Meredith, D. L. The invisible American father. IN
   Gross, L., ed. Sexual issues in marriage p 277-87.
 1815 Gross, Leonard, ed. Sexual issues in marriage; a contemporary
   perspective.
 152 Biller, Henry B. and Meredith, Dennis
 892 Meredith, Dennis

You need information about the Jesus Freaks and the Jesus Movement from the
1960's. Someone commends to you an essay appearing in a 1977 book published
by Transaction. They can recall only that the essay in the book was about
fourteen pages long.

   Jesus Freaks / Jesus Movement. See JESUS PEOPLE
 777 JESUS PEOPLE
   Adams, R. L. and Fox, R. J. Mainlining Jesus: The new trip. IN
   Henslin, J. M., ed. Deviant life-styles p 87-100.
 1719 Henslin, James M. Deviant lifestyles.
 7 Adams, Robert Lynn and Robert Jon Fox

You need information about pornography in movies, and you're trying to locate a five-page essay ... something about blow-jobs, published in a 1976 book by the University of California Press!

Pornography in moving pictures. See SEX IN MOVING-PICTURES
1338 SEX IN MOVING-PICTURES
      Koch, S. Blow-job and pornography. IN Nichols, B., ed. Movies and methods p 305-09.
1752 Nichols, Bill, ed. Movies and methods; anthology.
829   Koch, Stephen

You need information about Chicanos, and you're trying to locate a thirteen-page essay about Spanish language programs for Hispanics.... Someone commends a 1977 book of essays published by the Modern Language Association of America to you.

Chicanos. See MEXICAN AMERICANS
987   MEXICAN AMERICANS--EDUCATION--SPANISH LANGUAGE
      Fallis, G. V. Spanish language programs for Hispanic minorities: current needs and priorities. IN Minority language and literature p 86-98.
1746 Minority language and literature; retrospective and perspective. Ed. by Dexter Fisher.
500   Fallis, Guadalupe Valdes

You need information about famines in the history of GREAT BRITAIN. Someone commends to you a forty-seven page essay published in a 1976 book published by Cambridge.

611   GREAT BRITAIN--FAMINES
      Kershaw, I. The great famine and agrarian crisis in England, 1315-1322. IN Peasants, knights and heretics p 85-132.
1757 Peasants, knights and heretics; studies in medieval English social history. Edited by R. H. Hilton.
817   Kershaw, Ian

You need information about CARSON McCULLERS. Someone commends to you a forty-five page essay published in a 1977 book by the University of Minnesota Press.

920   MCCULLERS, CARSON (SMITH)--ABOUT
      Graver, L. S. Carson McCullers. IN Howard, M., ed. Seven American women writers of the twentieth century p 265-310.
1722 Howard, Maureen, ed. Seven American women writers of the twentieth century; an introduction.
608   Graver, Lawrence Stanley

You need information about PINBALL MACHINES as American art objects!? Someone commends to you a twelve-page essay published in a 1978 book by Popular Press.

1151 PINBALL MACHINES
      Packard, C. and Browne, R. B. Pinball machine: marble icon. IN Browne, R. B. and Fishwick, M. W., eds. Icons of America p 177-89.
1681 Browne, Ray Broadus and Fishwick, Marshall Williams, eds. Icons of America.
1107 Packard, Cynthia, and Browne, Ray Broadus

You need information about Doris May LESSING's book, <u>The Golden Notebook</u>.
While book reviews are often essays, what you need now is a critique and
literary discussion relating it to her life and views. Someone commends to you
a fifteen-page essay published in a 1977 book by the University of Massachusetts
Press.

    877   LESSING, DORIS MAY--ABOUT--"Individual works] THE GOLDEN
            NOTEBOOK
            Cohen, M. Out of the chaos, a new kind of strength:
            Doris Lessing's The Golden notebook. IN Diamond, A. and Edwards,
            L. R., eds. The authority of experience p 178-93.
   1694 Diamond, Arlyn and Edwards, Lee R., eds. The authority of ex-
            perience: essays in feminist criticism.
    291   Cohen, Mary

You need information about JACK THE RIPPER. Someone suggests a thirteen-page
essay published in a 1977 book by Harper.

    762   JACK THE RIPPER--ABOUT
            Borowitz, A. New gaslight on Jack the Ripper. IN Borowitz, A.
            Innocence and arsenic p 87-99.
   1679 Borowitz, Albert. Innocence and arsenic; studies in crime and
            literature.

You need information about students' rights and teacher's obligations in COLLEGE
TEACHING. Someone suggests a six-page essay published in a 1975 book by the
University of South Carolina Press.

    296   COLLEGE TEACHING
            Strickland, C. G. Students' rights and teachers' obligations in
            the classroom. IN Buxton, T. H. and Prichard, K. W., eds. Ex-
            cellence in university teaching p 80-85.
   1683 Buxton, Thomas H. and Prichard, Keith W. Excellence in university
            teaching; new essays.
   1439 Strickland, Conwell G.

ANDROGYNY as an ideal for human development is the subject of a twenty-four
page essay you're trying to track down. You also recall that it was published in a
1977 book by Rowman & Littlefield.

    56   ANDROGYNY (PSYCHOLOGY)
            Ferguson, A. Androgyny as an ideal for human development. IN
            Feminism and philosophy p 45-69.
   1705 Feminism and philosophy, ed. by Mary Vettereling-Braggin, Frederick
            A. Elliston and Jane English.
    516   Ferguson, Ann

You've read Pharr's book about WOMEN of JAPAN. You'd like to locate any of
her essays which may have been published and eluded you! Someone suggests the
thirty-eight page essay published in a 1977 book about women of eight nations.

   1633 WOMEN--JAPAN
            Pharr, S. J. Japan: historical and contemporary perspectives. IN
            Giele, J. Z. and Smack, A. C., eds. Women: role and status in
            eight countries p 217-55.
   1712 Zollinger, Jane and Chapman, Audrey. Women: role and status in
            eight countries.
   1138 Pharr, Susan J.

You need to locate an eight-page essay published in a 1977 book by Dodd about DECADENCE IN LITERATURE.

    368   DECADENCE IN LITERATURE

            Oberg, A. K. Sylvia Plath and the new decadence. IN Butscher, E., ed. Sylvia Plath p 177-85

  1683   Butscher, Edward, ed. Sylvia Plath and the new decadence; the woman and the work.

  1086   Oberg, Arthur Kenneth

Volume 8 1970-1974:

You need information about FOOD ADDITIVES. Someone suggests a nine-page essay published in a 1971 book by Free Press, which they say has something to do with the scientist's social responsibility.

    528   FOOD ADDITIVES

            Lederberg, J. Food additives. IN Brown, M., ed. The social responsibility of the scientist p 121-30.

  1696   Brown, Martin, ed. The social responsibility of the scientist.

    564   Lederberg, Joshua

You need information about INDIVIDUALISM and personal life of the future. Someone suggests a thirteen-page essay published in a book by the University of Hawaii Press in 1973.

    724   INDIVIDUALISM

            McDermott, J. F. The quality of personal life, 2000. IN Chaplin, G. and Paige, G. D., eds. Hawaii 2000 p 162-75.

  1699   Chaplin, George and Paige, Glenn D., eds. Hawaii 2000; continuing experiment in anticipatory democracy.

    923   McDermott, John F.

You're interested in the subject of involuntary hospitalization--you consider it a crime. Someone suggests part of a 1974 book published by Nelson-Hall should be right up your alley--it's about "this radical Sass fellow!"

    979   MENTALLY ILL

            Szasz, T. S. Involuntary mental hospitalization; a crime against humanity. IN Machan, T. R. The libertarian alternative p 445-57.

  1737   Machan, Tibor R. The libertarian alternative; essays in social and political philosophy.

  1466   Szasz, Thomas Stephen

You need information about MEXICO's FOREIGN RELATIONS with RUSSIA, and the so-called communist tide in South America. Someone suggests a forty-page essay in a 1973 book published by the University of Texas Press.

    985   MEXICO--FOREIGN RELATIONS--RUSSIA

            Oswald, J. G. An introduction to USSR relations with Mexico, Uruguay, and Cuba. IN Herman, D. L., ed. The Communist tide in Latin America p 75-115.

  1722   Herman, Donald L., ed. The Communist tide in Latin America; a selected treatment.

  1115   Oswald, Joseph Gregory

You understand that Dana Densmore has written an essay (about five pages in length) which should be very useful for your paper on new kinds of marriages and proposals for change. A book edited by someone else and published by McKay in 1974 is a collection of related essays.

     360   Densmore, Dana
          On celibacy. IN Perrucci, C. C. and Targ, D. B., eds. Marriage
          and the family p 241-45.
   1748   Perrucci, Carolyn Cummings, and Targ, Dena B., eds. Marriage
          and the family; a critical analysis and proposals for change.
    224   CELIBACY

You understand that Richard L. Block has written an essay (about fifteen pages long) which should be very useful for your report on urban society and civil liberties. The book of which this essay is part was published by Sage in 1971.

    154   Block, Richard L.
          Support for civil liberties and support for the police. IN Hahn, H.,
          ed. Police in urban society p 119-34.
   1719   Hahn, Harlan, ed. Police in urban society.
   1173   POLICE POWER--U.S.--PUBLIC OPINION

Volume 7   1965-1969:

You need information about CERVANTES' characters in Don Quixote. Someone refers you to a six-page essay in a 1968 book published by Columbia University Press.

    206   CERVANTES SAAVEDRA, MIGUEL DE--CHARACTERS--DON QUIXOTE
          Santayana, G. Tom Sawyer and Don Quixote. IN Santayana G. The
          Birth of reason and other essays p 116-22.
   1579   Santayana, George. The birth of reason and other essays; edited
          by Daniel Cory.

You're trying to locate a three-page essay about SINCLAIR LEWIS, published in a 1966 book by Edwards.

    783   LEWIS, SINCLAIR--ABOUT
          Kramer, M. Sinclair Lewis and The hollow center. IN Langford,
          R. E. and Taylor, W. E., eds. The twenties p 67-69.
   1563   Langford, Richard E. and Taylor, William Edwards, eds. The twenties;
          poetry and prose: 20 critical essays.
    736   Kramer, Maurice

Volume 6   1960-1964:

You need information about Graham Greene's The Potting Shed. Someone suggests the essay in Theatre at the Crossroads, published in 1960.

    564   GREENE, GRAHAM--[individual works] THE POTTING SHED
          Gassner, J. Points of return: religion and Graham Greene's The
          potting shed. IN Gassner, J. Theatre at the crossroads p 155-57.
   1551   Gassner, John. Theatre at the crossroads; plays and playwrights of
          the mid-century American stage. Holt.

Volume 4 1948-1954:

You're trying to track down a fourteen-page essay about the San Francisco Bay Area's ancient shellmounds. Someone says it was in a book about California Indians published in 1951.

   1738 SAN FRANCISCO BAY REGION--ANTIQUITIES

        Nelson, N. C. San Francisco Bay shellmounds. IN Heizer, R. F. and Whipple, M. A., eds. California Indians p 130-43.

   2267 Heizer, Robert Flemming and Whipple, Mary Anne, eds. California Indians, a Sourcebook. University of California Press.

   1408 Nelson, Nels Christian

Volume 1 1900-1933:

You want information about the early education of John Stuart Mill. Someone suggests a five-page essay published in a 1926 book by Macmillan.

   1172 MILL, JOHN STUART--ABOUT

        Chubb, E. W. Early education of John Stuart Mill. IN Stories of authors p 162-66.

   1904 Chubb, Edwin Watts. Stories of authors, British and American.

PRACTICE USING ABSTRACTING SERVICES

Most of these problem situations can be used with the Practice Using Abstracting Services exercise in the library and Assignment 7, question II about abstracts. The Assignment 7 question is worded:

> On what page in the INDEX VOLUME do you locate your initial clue, under what subject-heading? [1]   [2]
>
> Abstract # [3]   On what page in the corresponding ABSTRACTS VOLUME do you find the full, author-entry with the abstract following it? [4]   Author[s]' name[s]:   [5]
>
> Title of the journal article "   [6]   "
>
> Title of the serial in which the article was published" [7]   "
>
>   Issue of the serial: Volume # [8] Date of publication [9]
>
>   Inclusive pagination of the article in that issue [10]
>
> Library Call #
>
> Answer to any questions: [11]

Problems have been derived from the following abstracting tools in many libraries; note that most of these are available as data bases:

Abstracts of English Studies

America: History & Life (DIALOG File 38)

Communication Abstracts

Historical Abstracts (DIALOG File 39)

International Political Science Abstracts

Psychological Abstracts (DIALOG File 11)

RILA: Repértoire International de la Littérature de l'Art / International Repertory of the Literature of Art. (DIALOG File 191)

Sociological Abstracts (DIALOG File 37)

United States Political Science Documents (DIALOG File 93)
Women Studies Abstracts

Abstracts of English Studies

You need to read the abstract of a long (98 pages) article published in 1982 about ERIC BERNE. How did the writer-researcher utilize Berne's work in her study of games?

1. Page 421 of the cumulated subject
        index in the back of the 1984
        volume (#27)
2. BERNE, ERIC   3. 84-182
4. Page 31   5. Carr, Carol A.
6. "Play's the Thing: A Study of
        Games in THE ALCHEMIST."
7. Classical and Modern Literature:
        A Quarterly.
8. 18   9. 1982   10. 113-125
11. "The Alchemist has not yet been clearly understood. In looking at it as a
        series of games, and applying methodology from Eric Berne and Johan
        Huizinga, the play can be seen as more clearly play than satire."

America: History & Life

You need to read the abstract of a fourteen-page article published in 1983 about AIR LINES' DEREGULATION. Someone says it will be useful for your report on labor unions' involvement in commercial transportation in the United States. What unions does the author mention?

1. Page 6 of the cumulated subject
        index (Part D) of the 1983
        volumes (#20)
2. AIR LINES. DEREGULATION.
        LABOR UNIONS AND
        ORGANIZATIONS. TRANS-
        PORTATION. COMMERCIAL.
        1978-82.   3. 20A:7515
4. Page 517 in A volume   5. Northrup, Herbert R.
6. "The New Employee-Relations
        Climate in Airlines."
7. Industrial and Labor
        Relations Review
8. 36   9. 1983   10. 167-181
11. The Air Line Pilots Association and the International Association of
        Machinists and Aerospace Workers.

Is it true that United States mail was disinfected during epidemics? Where did this practice originate, and what techniques were used? What were the primary sources used by the authors for their fourteen-page article published in 1980? What additional good effects did DISINFECTION of mail in Europe have at one time?

1. Page 112 of the cumulated subject index (Part D) of the 1981 volumes (#18)
2. DISINFECTION. CONTAGION. EUROPE. MAIL. POSTAL SERVICE.
   1647-1968.   3. 18A:3999
4. Page 269 in A Volume   5. Pearson, Emmet F. and Miles, Wyndham
6. "Disinfection of Mail in the United States."
7. Bulletin of the History of Medicine
8. 54   9. 1980   10. 111-124
11. Yes. Europe; sulphur fumes, formalin and chlorine gas. Reports of state
    and city public health agencies deposited in the National Library of
    Medicine. Helped to eliminate rats, lice, fleas, and mosquitoes.

You need information about FOX HUNTS during the American Revolution, and you
also want to read the abstract of an eight-page article published in 1979. What
was the name of the scout and messenger who, after the war, worked for the
Gloucester Fox Hunting Club? What was the primary source used by the author
for this article? Before you get it out of the library or on interlibrary loan, are
there any illustrations?

1. Page 159 of the cumulated subject index (Part D) of the 1981 volumes (#18)
2. FOX HUNTS. AMERICAN REVO-
   LUTION   3. 18A:5579
4. page 382 in A Volume   5. Cunningham, John T.
6. "Faster Than Foxes"
7. New Jersey History
8. 97   9. 1979   10. 37-44
11. Jonas Cattell. Cattell's pamphlet, Memoirs of the Gloucester Fox Hunting
    Club, 1830. 7 illustrations.

Did mid-19th Century San Francisco prostitutes operate as free agents? In 1850
what was the ratio of men to women in California? What was the name of the
second Chinese female resident of San Francisco (she arrived in 1848)? You want
to find an abstract of a twenty-two page part of a 1979 book published by Houghton
Mifflin; the article is accompanied by a map and tables, and how many notes? Who
prepared the abstract? Was PROSTITUTION practiced by Chinese Americans in
the 1840's and 50's?

1. Page 360 of the cumulated subject index (Part D) of the 1981 volumes (#18)
2. PROSTITUTION. AH-CHOI,
   CALIFORNIA. CHINESE
   AMERICANS. OCCUPATIONS.
   WOMEN. 1840's-50's.   3. 18A:3125
4. Page 204 in A Volume   5. Hirata, Lucie Cheng
6. "Chinese Immigrant Women in Nineteenth-Century California."
7. Women of America: A History, edited by Carol Ruth Berkin and Mary Beth
   Norton.
8. NA   9. 1979   10. 223-244
11. No; 12/1. "Tong members were frequently owners of brothels and there
    were few free agents." Ah-Choi. 18 notes. K. Talley. Yes.

Communication Abstracts

R. L. Clark's article about how women's magazines cover living alone has been suggested to you as possibly providing a statistic on how many there are, but all you know is that it was published sometime in 1982.

1. Since you know the author, look under R. L. Clark in the Author Index for 1982 (Volume #5).   3. 034
6. "How Women's Magazines Cover Living Alone."
7. Journalism Quarterly
8. 58   9. September 1981   10. 291-294
11. 24% of all American women live alone.
(Subject headings under which the article might be located include WOMEN'S REPRESENTATION and WOMEN AND MEDIA)

D. P. Phillips' article about how TV stories of fatal accidents effect the incidence of violence has been suggested to you as possibly providing information comparing male and female suicide-deaths in the United States, but all you know is that it was published in the May 1982 issue of a journal.

1. Since you know the author, look under D. P. Phillips in the Author Index for 1982 (Volume #5).   3. 888
6. "The Impact of Fictional Television Stories on U.S. Adult Fatalities; New Evidence on the Effect of the Mass Media on Violence."
7. American Journal of Sociology
8. 87   9. May 1982   10. 1340-1359
11. "The U.S. female suicides increased proportionately more than male suicides."

Hikaru Kataoka's article about children's TV in Japan has been suggested to you as possibly providing information about regulations of this aspect of the mass media in Japan, particularly since it relates to NHK (government-supported TV, which operates two national networks for the public). You need to confirm something you read in a UN reference book--that almost 100% of Japanese homes have TV; also, does the government exercise no control over program policy? What is the limit on spot advertising time? Are Japanese people satisfied with children's TV programming? Someone suggests Kataoka-san's article, which was, however, published back in 1978! Of what use will that be now?

1. Since you know the author, look under Hikaru Kataoka (and Kataoka Hikaru, too) in the Author Index for 1978 (Volume #1). It would also be possible to look in the subject index on page 565 under JAPAN.
                3. 789
6. "Children's Television in Japan"
7. Phaedrus
8. 5   9. 1978   10. 37-39
11. "... over 99 per cent of Japanese homes have television.... The government has no control over program policy.... Each station must set up its own program content advisory organ. Commercial broadcasters must limit spot advertising to 18 percent or less of total weekly broadcast time. No special criteria govern ads aimed at children ... the consumer's rising

level of awareness has increased the amount of severe criticisms of children's programming...." An article such as this could be useful in a literature search in several ways: 1) You now have the name of a writer in the field, and you can utilize it in other tools; 2) you have identified an abstracting tool which indexes and abstracts information of proven use--COMMUNICATION ABSTRACTS--and furthermore you have (page 440) displayed here two subject-headings to use with this tool: CHILDREN AND TELEVISION and JAPAN; 3) it might be useful to consider Phaedrus too.

Historical Abstracts

You need information about politics in JAPAN during the Meiji period (1868-1912), and information about Kishida Toshiko, in particular. Unfortunately you don't know whether this is a political movement or a ceremony or what. Someone commends to you an article published in 1981; although it is only about fifty pages long, it is accompanied by forty-nine notes! Your perspective is that of a historian who believes in reading the abstracts whenever they're available! You're also looking to define "The Meiji Six." Who abstracted this article?

1. Page 817 of the 1983 (Volume 34) Subject Index, Part A: Modern History portion
2. JAPAN--FEMINISM. KISIHIDA TOSHIKO. 1882-84
   3. 34A:752
4. Page 55   5. Sievers, Sharon L.
6. "Feminist Criticism in Japanese Politics in the 1880's: The Experience of Kishida Toshiko."
7. Signs
8. 6   9. 1981   10. 602-616
11. "Kishida Toshiko, the first woman lecturer...." "The Meiji Six Society initiated the women's movement because of their belief that the backwardness of Japan was a result of low regard for women." S. P. Conner.

You need information about the "October Revolution" (1917), the RUSSIAN REVOLUTION and the establishment of the All-Russian Soviet of Workers' Control to oversee the transfer of control over the means of production from the bourgeoisie to the workers. Someone suggests an historical article published in 1979, and adds that it's accompanied by 48 notes. The abstract should provide information about Georgii Plekhanov and the Mensheviks.

1. Page 739 of the 1982 (Volume 33) Subject Index, Part B: 20th Century portion.
2. RUSSIAN REVOLUTION--DICTATORSHIP OF THE PROLETARIAT. MANAGEMENT 1917-1919.   3. 33B:2096
4. Page 153. USSR & Antecedents section of Abstracts.
                         5. Rucker, R. D.
6. "Workers' Control of Production in the October Revolution and Civil War."
7. Science & Society.
8. 43   9. 1979   10. 158-185
11. "... while Georgii Plekhanov and the Mensheviks thought that only the bourgeoisie was capable of managing Russia's industry.

You need information about SPORTS among the "upper classes" in Great Britain during the late 19th Century. What field sports were introduced--it is said--by wealthy British eccentrics? Someone suggests reading the abstract of an article published in 1979 in a British magazine.

1. Page 284 of the 1980 (Volume 31) Subject Index, Part A portion.
2. SPORTS. GREAT BRITAIN. UPPER CLASSES 19th Century. 1872.
                                       3. 31A:1872
4. Page 128   5. Hastings, Macdonald.
6. "The Tycoons of Sport"
7. Blackwoods Magazine
8. 325   9. 1979   10. 27-31
11. "Describes wealthy British eccentrics who, during the 19th Century, introduced several field sports and promoted others such as horseracing and salmon and trout fishing."

International Political Science Abstracts

You need information you can use to refute the contention that abortion is not a political issue in other English-speaking nations. You need publications from the 1980's, and have been assigned to focus on Australia, while other panelists are concerned with other nations. You would, however, like to learn some of the unique Australian characteristics in the ABORTION issue. Someone suggests a Winter 1982 article.

1. Page 531 of the 1983 (Volume 33) Subject Index, in the back of the volume.
2. ABORTION--AUSTRALIA   3. 4459 (33:4459)
4. Page 419   5. Warhurst, John; Merrill, Vance
6. "The Abortion Issue in Australia; Pressure Politics and Policy."
7. Australian Quarterly
8. 54   9. Winter 1982   10. 119-135
11. "This article describes the role of parties, groups and public opinion in the abortion issue, pointing out its unique Australian characteristics."

John Marshall is widely regarded as an activist judge who molded the Constitution according to his personal political views. You must document your contention that this was not the case, that he was faithful to the Constitution, and his views were rooted in the principle of democratic constitutionalism. Someone suggests a Fall 1982 article.

1. Page 550 of the 1983 (Volume 33) Subject Index, in the back of the volume.
2. MARSHALL, JOHN   3. 4461 (33:4461)
4. Page 419   5. Wolfe, Christopher
6. "John Marshall and Constitutional Law"
7. Polity
8. 15   9. Fall 1982   10. 5-25
11. "His view, rooted in the principle of democratic constitutionalism, confined judicial review to faithful enforcement of a good Constitution...."

Some abstracts are not in English; these are typically associated with publications not in English. Some abstracts of publications not in English are in English, however, which can be very useful. For example, there was a lengthy (almost forty pages) sociological journal article published in its October-December 1980 issue about the WOMEN'S MOVEMENT in Italy. It might identify the social causes underlying this movement as a political actor, and the relationship between it and the Italian political system.

1. Page 731 of the 1982 (Volume 32) Subject Index.
2. WOMEN'S MOVEMENT: ITALY   3. 611
4. Page 88   5. Ergas, Yasmine
6. "Femminismo e crisi de sistema. Il percorso politico delle donne attraverso
        gli anni settanta. / Feminism and the Crisis of the System. Women's
        Political Itinerary in the 1970's / Le féminisme et la crise du système.
        L'itinéraire politique des femmes dans les annés 1970."
7. Rassegna Italiana di Sociologia
8. 21   9. Oct.-Dec. 1980   10. 543-568

Psychological Abstracts

You need information about BIRTH ORDER and family size, spacing and education of siblings, as well as vocational status. Someone suggests a psychology journal article published in November 1979 which covers "all that--if you're interested in an academically elite sample" in the authors' research! Your psych instructor has referred to the "Adlerian position of the uniqueness of the individual within the family, regardless of birth order." Who abstracted the article? Where are (or were) the writers working ("based") at the time they did this research? Are their results in agreement with the Adlerian position? Who else has done work that involved interpretation of Adler in this matter?

1. Page 171 of the January-June 1982 Index (Volume 67).
2. BIRTH ORDER   3. 3444
4. Page 369, Jan.-March Abstracts   5. Hayes, Roslyn F. & Bronzaft, Arline L.
6. "Birth Order and Related Variables in an Academically Elite Sample."
7. Journal of Individual Psychology
8. 35   9. November 1979   10. 214-224
11. J. L. Driscoll. Educational Records Bureau, Wellesley Hills, MA. "Results
        are in agreement with G. J. Manaster (see PA, Vol 61:13291) in his inter-
        pretation of the Adlerian position...."

What are the effects of ELECTROCONVULSIVE SHOCK THERAPY on human learning and memory? This is a controversial big subject! What you need at the start of a report is a review of the literature--even something published as long ago as October 1977 by an international authority, with references, and consideration of the variables involved! Who prepared the abstract? How many references did the authors provide?

1. Page 391 of the January-June 1979 Index (Volume 61).
2. ELECTROCONVULSIVE SHOCK THERAPY
                                          3. 4040
4. Page 406 of the January-March 1979 Abstracts.

5. Robertson, Alwyn D. & Inglis, James
6. "The Effects of Electroconvulsive Therapy on Human Learning and Memory."
7. Canadian Psychological Review
8. 18   9. October 1977   10. 285-307
11. The abstract is signed "Journal abstract," which means it was reproduced in Psychological Abstracts from the journal (Canadian Psychological Review) which published the article. Journals frequently precede the article with an abstract, which is usually prepared by the writer(s) of the article. Five pages of references. Note that the subject indexing indicates that this article includes information about variables and is a literature review.

Are gorillas able to learn sign language? What has been written in the psychology literature about Koko? Does she really have a vocabulary of words? Someone suggests that an article in the January 1978 issue of a journal is devoted to this subject.

1. Page 1089 of the July-December 1978 Index (Volume 60).
2. SIGN LANGUAGE   3. 11025
4. Pages 4-6, Oct.-Dec. 1978 Abstracts.
5. Patterson, Francine G.
6. "The Gesture of a Gorilla; Language Acquisition in Another Pongi."
7. Brain and Language
8. 5   9. January 1978   10. 92-97
11. Koko acquired a vocabulary of 100 words in American Sign Language. Note that the subject indexing indicates that this article includes information about vocabulary, spontaneous utterances, semantic relations and generalization, and sign language acquisition, female gorilla.

Is there any information available about the relationship, if any, between VASECTOMY and marital stability and sexual satisfaction? Was any research being done on this as early as November 1976? Where were the researchers based? Was their research population large enough?
1. Page 1249 of the July-December 1978 Index (Volume 60)
2. VASECTOMY   3. 1549
4. Page 173   5. Maschoff, Thomas A.; Fanshier, Warren E.; and Hansen, Dan J.
6. "Vasectomy: Its Effect Upon Marital Stability."
7. Journal of Sex Research
8. 12   9. November 1976   10. 295-314
11. Tacoma-Pierce County Adolescent Clinic, Tacoma, Washington. They studied fifty couples. Note that the subject indexing indicates that this article includes information relating to marital stability & sexual satisfaction, married couples.

RILA: Répertoire International de la
Littérature de l'Art/International
(Repertory of the Literature of Art)

You need a comparison of the work of painters Münter and Kandinsky. Someone suggests an art journal issue sometime back in 1981, which included four illustrations. But is it in English?!

1. Page 770 of the subject index in the back of the 1982 volume (#8).
2. IMPRESSIONISM AND KANDINSKY 3. 7544
4. Page 587   5. Bachrach, Susan P.
6. "A Comparison of the Early Landscapes of Münter and Kandinsky, 1902-1910."
7. Woman's Art Journal
8. 11   9. Spring-Summer 1981   10. 21-24
11. Yes, it is in English.

Willard Metcalf has been referred to as the peacemaker of Old Lyme. How did his life and work influence a synthesizing of Barbizon and Impressionist traditions? Someone says it's all in the November-December 1981 Art & Antiques. Where and what was Old Lyme, by the way?

1. Page 770 of the subject index in the back of the 1982 volume (#8).
2. IMPRESSIONISM, INFLUENCE ON METCALF
                               3. 7703
4. Page 594   5. DeVeer, Elizabeth
6. "Willard Metcalf: the Peacemaker of Old Lyme."
7. Art & Antiques
8. IV   9. November-December 1981
                               10. 88-97
11. "Discusses Metcalf's work ... synthesizing Barbizon and Impressionist traditions ... the art colony at Old Lyme, Conn. around the turn of the century."

Some people suggest that French pictures are usually constructed to convey narrative, psychological, or allegorical content. Swinging is such a motif, carrying a varied, mostly erotic meaning. This idea has appeared in the literature; for example, the March 1982 Art Bulletin had such an article about EROTIC ART, focusing on works of Watteau and Fragonard. What symbols ("icons") did they use?

1. Page 715 of the subject index in the back of the 1983 volume (#9).
2. EROTIC ART   3. 4815
4. Page 438   5. Posner, Donald
6. "The Swinging Women of Watteau and Fragonard."
7. Art Bulletin
8. LXIV   9. March 1982   10. 75-88
11. hats, shoes, feet.

Sociological Abstracts

Has any sociologist ever investigated the defects in the process of complaining about sex discrimination in academic employment, i.e. whether the system works for or against this particular type of charge? Someone says, yes, only once of which he's aware--in a Fall 1981 thirty-two page article by somebody at California State University, Long Beach. The author concluded that the grievance process itself, undermines collectivist ideals. How? Ultimately, though, didn't these women benefit by their efforts?

1. Page 1800 of the 1982 subject Index volume (volume 30).
2. MERITOCRACY: SEX DISCRIMINATION LAWSUITS, COLLECTIVE PROTEST VS MERITOCRACY PERSPECTIVE....
   3. 82M6914
4. Page 1403 of volume 30:4-5   5. Abel, Emily
6. "Collective Protest and the Meritocracy: Faculty Women and Sex Discrimination Lawsuits."
7. Feminist Studies
8. 7   9. Fall 1981   10. 505-538
11. "The grievance process itself, however, undermined collectivist ideals. The women were forced to couch their cases in individualistic terms, focusing on their own merit and achievements rather than on systemic patterns of discrimination. University grievance committees restricted themselves to procedural matters and ignored larger issues of racism and sexism. Similarly, government agencies often limited their investigations...."

What were the principal reasons given for refusal of termination under the Abortion Act of 1967, which supposedly provides for abortion, in a research reported in the April 1980 issue of a journal concerned with the HEALTH of British women as provided under the National Health Service?

1. Page 1724 of the 1982 subject Index volume (volume 30).
2. HEALTH/HEALTHY: WOMEN REFUSED NATIONAL HEALTH SERVICE ABORTION, EXPERIENCES: INTERVIEWS; WESSEX WOMEN, GB.
   3. 82M6919
4. Page 1403 Feminist Studies selection of volume 30:4-5.
   5. Ashton, John R.
6. "Experiences of Women Refused National Health Service Abortion."
7. Journal of Biosocial Science
8. 12   9. April 1980   10. 201-210
11. "The principal reasons given ... were that the women had insufficient grounds for termination ... or ... were too late."

Can you locate a description of an approach to inner-city health care for elderly high-risk populations of Boston, Massachusetts, published in June 1980 in a prestigious medical journal? What are the components of this particular "continuum of care?"

1. Page 1442 of the October-December 1982 subject Index (Volume 30).
2. HEALTH CARE: INNER-CITY HEALTH CARE: MULTIDISCIPLINARY APPROACH, BENEFITS ASSESSMENT: ELDERLY/HIGH-RISK POPULATIONS. BOSTON, MASS.   3. 82M6696
4. Page 1367-8   5. Master, Robert J.; Feltin, Marie; Jainchill, John; Mark, Roger; Kavesh, William N.; Rabkin, Mitchell T.; Turner, Barbara; Bachrach, Sarah; Lennox, Sara.
6. "A Continuum of Care for the Inner City: Assessment of Its Benefits for Boston's Elderly and High-Risk Populations."
7. New England Journal of Medicine
8. 302   9. June 26, 1980   10. 1434-1440

11. Four neighborhood health centers, three home care programs, and a teaching hospital.

United States Political Science Documents

For a British Commonwealth Areas Studies course, you are trying to track down a journal article published in spring 1984 about SPORTS in late Victorian public schools. Someone tells you not to bother because it's about girls' public schools, but you are nonetheless going to check the abstract. What other "key subjects" were assigned to this article?

1. Part 1 Indexes. 1984 (Volume 10)
2. SPORTS   3. 84001701
4. Part 2 Document Descriptions. Page 230
       5. McCrone, Kathleen E.
6. "Play Up! Play Up! And Play the Game! Sport at the Late Victorian Girls' Public School."
7. Journal of British Studies
8. 23   9. Spring 1984   10. 106-134
11. BRITISH COMMONWEALTH AREA STUDIES; EDUCATION CURRICULUM; ATHLETE; EDUCATION POLICY; CULTURAL HISTORY; FEMININITY; FEMINISM; WOMEN'S EMANCIPATION; WOMEN'S STUDIES

The use of euphemisms and rhetoric (semantic whitewash) to meet political ends is common practice by government. The author of an autumn 1982 journal article focused on the cover-up through euphemistic terminology of the CONCENTRATION CAMPS in which Japanese-Americans were held during World War II. What other parts of American society entered into this? Why is this practice still considered necessary to meet political ends?

1. Part 1 Indexes. 1982 (Volume 8)
2. RHETORIC; ETHNIC STUDIES; CONCENTRATION CAMP; SEMANTICS; LINGUISTICS, etc.   3. 82002697
4. Part 2 Document Descriptions. Page 377.
      5. Okamura, Raymond Y.
6. "The American Concentration Camps: A Cover-Up Through Euphemistic Terminology."
7. Journal of Ethnic Studies
8. 10   9. Fall 1982   10. 95-110
11. "The complicity of the press, the Supreme Court, the civilians employed by the camps, the American public, and even the Japanese detainees themselves, then and now, in the actions of the government and the military and their semantic whitewash.... It has kept the historical record in the government's favor."

Why does leisure require courage? For adults in the modern Western world, what factors are seen by the author of "The Courage to Be Leisured" (published in December 1981) as restricting true leisure?

1. Part 1 Indexes. 1981 (Volume 7)

2. LEISURE TIME ANALYSIS; COURAGE; CREATIVITY; WESTERN SOCIETY; IMAGINATION, etc. 3. 81001228
4. Part 2 Document Descriptions. Page 174
                            5. Wilson, Robert N.
6. "The Courage to Be Leisured."
7. <u>Social Forces</u>
8. <u>60</u>   9. December 1981   10. 282-303
11. "It requires the courage to reject stereotyped, socially sanctioned, ways of seeing, thinking, and living ... true leisure is constained [sic] by the rationally dominated linguistic patterns which limit perception and experience, by the guilt-inducing and self-fragmenting Protestant work ethic, in which play is seen as wasteful or even morally questionable, and by the artificial packaging of life processes in rigid time-slots."

Women Studies Abstracts:

Indian women were asked about their reactions to issues raised during the 1977 elections. This examination was intended to test what assertion? The results were published in the December 1981 issue of a social science research publication. AUTHORITARIANISM was one of the issues focused on.

1. Page 82 cumulated subject index at the end of 1984-85 (Volume 13)
2. AUTHORITARIANISM   3. 2858A
4. Page 21 of Winter 1984-85 Issue #4   5. Khaliq, Zoya
6. "Political Awareness of Lower Class Women in Uttar Pradesh During the 1977 Election."
7. <u>Indian Council for Social Science Research Abstracts Quarterly</u>
8. <u>10</u>   9. July-December 1981   10. 33-40
11. "... that the absence of a serious political and social movement in post-independence India has contributed to the lack of political consciousness among Indian women."

Women's work is nearly done, is the message published in the April 1984 issue of <u>This Magazine</u>, which describes the threat that technological change or automation poses for elimination of jobs throughout the economy. Two-thirds of the female labor force is concentrated in the three occupations most affected. What are they?

1. Page 82 cumulated subject index at the end of 1984-85 (Volume 13).
2. AUTOMATION   3. 1837A
4. Page 13 of Fall 1984, Volume 13, #3
                            5. Menzies, Heather
6. "Women's Work Is Nearly Done."
7. <u>This Magazine</u>
8. <u>18</u>   9. April 1984   10. 32-36
11. Clerical work, sales, and service work.

You need information about the "pioneer of Austrian feminism," Rosa Mayreder. Someone tells you about an article published sometime during the summer of 1984.... What organization did she found and when?

1. Page 82 cumulated subject index at the end of 1984-85 (Volume 13)
2. AUSTRIAN CONFEDERATION OF WOMEN
                                  3. 1355A
4. Page 34 of Summer 1984, Volume 13, #2
                                  5. Reiss, Mary-Ann
6. "Rosa Mayreder: Pioneer of Austrian Feminism."
7. International Journal of Women's Studies
8. 7   9. May-June 1984   10. 207-216
11. Austrian Confederation of Women, in 1893.

DISSERTATIONS & THESES

The following problems can be used with Assignment 7, Part III, Dissertations & Theses, question 2A and B, page 7. The form is:

    2A The locator question-statement: __[1]__

        CDI Author Volume where you start # __[2]__ ; Date(s) of that volume's coverage __[3]__ . Page # in the CDI author volume where you find _____'s dissertation mentioned: __[4]__ . What is the name of the institution which granted _____'s doctoral degree? __[5]__ How many pages in length was the dissertation? __[6]__ What type of doctorate did s/he receive? __[7]__ What is the full title of the dissertation? "__[8]__." What is the ABSTRACT NUMBER which CDI provides? __[9]__

    2B Use the abstract to locate the following information: __[10]__
      Answer: __[11]__

1. Pauline Bart's doctorate was earned in 1967.
2. Volume 33   3. 1861-1972   4. 253
5. University of California--Los Angeles
                               6. 651p
7. PhD   8. Depression in Middle-Aged Women: Some Sociocultural Factors.
                          9. 28/11 B p. 4752
10. Who was her dissertation "chairman"? Describe her research population. What factors are closely associated with depression in middle-aged women according to Bart's findings? What groups have the lowest and the highest rates of depression?
11. Prof. Ralph H. Turner, Chairman. 533 females, ages 40-59. Closely associated with diagnosed depression in hospital first admissions of this group was role loss of various types, e.g. maternal role loss. Low rate: single women; high rate: widows and married women.

1. Leo Buscaglia's appearances on PBS often include his "love classes"; advertisements refer to him as a "noted educator and lecturer at the University of Southern California." His doctorate was completed in 1962.
2. Volume 33   3. 1861-1972   4. 636
5. University of Southern California 6. 84p
7. PhD   8. An Experimental Study of the Sarbin-Hardyck Test As Indexes of Role Perception for Adolescent Stutterers.
                        9. 23/10 A p. 4013

10. With what does Buscaglia appear to equate accurate role perception? Describe his research population. In what field is the abstracted dissertation listed?

11. Sanity. Males. Speech-Theater.

1. William Henry Cosby, Jr.'s doctorate was awarded in 1976.
2. Volume 34   3. 1973-1982   4. 83
5. University of Massachusetts   6. 267p
7. EdD   8. An Integration of the Visual Media Via 'Fat Albert and the Cosby Kids' Into the Elementary School Curriculum ... Increased Learning.   9. 37/09A p.5557
10. Who was his major director? What are the two fundamental issues that Cosby concluded must be addressed?
11. Dr. Norma Jean Anderson. The need to eliminate institutional racism. The second relates to development of a curriculum which transmits the knowledges, skills and attitudes to children so that they may grow to their fullest potential.

1. The brochure advertising Wayne Dyer's audiocassette "game plan" for being a "no limit person" refers to him as "Dr." He received his doctorate in 1970.
2. Volume 34   3. 1861-1972   4. 229
5. Wayne State University   6. 224p
7. EdD   8. Group Counseling Leadership Training in Counselor Education.
          9. 31/07A p.3263
10. Who was his advisor? In what field is the abstracted dissertation listed?
11. Mildred Peters, "Advisor." Education, Guidance & Counseling.

1. Warren Thomas Farrell's doctorate was awarded in 1974.
2. Volume 34   3. 1973-1982   4. 523
5. New York University   6. 560p
7. PhD   8. The Political Potential of the Women's Liberation Movement As Indicated By Its Effectiveness in Changing Men's Attitudes.
          9. 37/06A p.3872
10. In what field is the abstracted dissertation listed? Who was his advisor in this endeavor? How many of the men in his research population scored? Using one of the several possible tools we've considered in this course, now identify the title and publisher of Farrell's trade-book apparently based on this doctoral dissertation work, published in 1974.
11. Political Science, General. James T. Crown, "Adviser." 240. "The Liberated Man; Beyond Masculinity...." published by Random. Optimistically, you could consult the library's catalog first, or Books In Print, or the National Union Catalog....

1. Jeane J. Kirkpatrick's doctorate was earned in 1968.
2. Author volume 35 Hj-Mc   3. 1861-1972   4. 433
5. Columbia University   6. 410p
7. PhD   8. Peronist Politics in Argentina: Composition, Expectations and Demands of the Mass Base.   9. 32/01A p.502
10. What was the principal source material for her study? How many Argentines were interviewed? What is her middle name?
11. Data collected in a national opinion survey, October-December 1965. 2,014. Jorder.

1. David Gardner is President of the University of California system; he received his doctorate in 1966.
2. Volume 34   4. 1861-1972   4. 569
5. University of California--Berkeley 6. 420p
7. PhD   8. The University of California Loyalty Oath Controversy, 1949-
    1952.   9. 28/07A p.2482
10. You're interested in researching the "question" of whether blacklisting, public dismissal, etc. is inevitably damaging to individuals whose names are involved; you've heard of the so-called UC loyalty oath controversy (1949-1952) and want to follow up on some of the persons who were dismissed by the University at that time. Someone says there were only a couple; someone else says (assumes) there weren't any; a librarian suggests the UC president's doctoral dissertation was on loyalty oaths.... How did he conclude in this matter of harmful doing? How many faculty did the Regents vote to dismiss in August 1950? Were they actually dismissed, however?
11. Concludes that the loyalty oath controversy inflicted "no permanent harm." 32 faculty members. Yes.

1. Gerda Lerner's doctorate was earned in 1966.
2. Author volume 35 Hj-Mc   3. 1861-1972   4. 672
5. Columbia University   6. 579p
7. PhD   8. Abolitionists from South Carolina; A Life of Sarah and Angelina Grimké.   9. 30/04A p.1504
10. Lerner considered two documents- one was Sarah's pamphlet. What was its title, and how does Lerner evaluate it? What was the title of Angelina's "unique contribution as a white Southern woman to the antislavery cause?" Lerner also considers several aspects of their courageous lives which are rarely acknowledged in the biographical reference books ... for example?
11. "The Equality of the Sexes and the Condition of Women" represents "the first serious discussion of women's rights by an American woman." "Appeal to the Christian Women of the Southern States." Their ménage à trois with the husband of one of them; "colored" nephews, children of their brother and a slave; the interracial boarding school in New Jersey with which they were involved.

1. Robert (Man From UNCLE) Vaughn's doctorate was awarded in 1971.
2. Author volume 37 Sd-Z   3. 1861-1972   4. 657
5. University of Southern California 6. 597p
7. PhD   8. A Historical Study of the Influence of the House Committee on UnAmerican Activities on the American Theatre, 1938-1958.
                        9. 32/10A p.5819
10. Who were his advisors? What was his methodology, and who were his research population? Using one of the several possible tools we've considered in this course, now identify the title and publishers of Vaughn's trade-book apparently based on his doctoral work, published in 1972.
11. Professors Butler and Dickens. Used detailed questionnaires from forty-eight theatre personalities who had testified before the House Committee on UnAmerican Activities. "Only Victims: A Study of Show Business Blacklisting," published by Putnam.

1. Susan Jane Pharr's doctorate was received in 1975.
2. Volume 37 P-SM   3. 1973-1982   4. 134

5. Columbia University 6. 276p
7. PhD 8. Sex and Politics: Women in Social and Political Movements In Japan. 9. 30/06A p.3993
10. How many persons were in her research population? Where were interviews conducted and when? How did she define "radical egalitarians?" How many (what per cent) of her population met this definition? Using one of the several possible tools we've considered in this course, now identify the title and publisher of a trade book published in 1982 by Pharr which appears to be based on her work for her doctorate.
11. 100 Japanese women ages 18-33. Tokyo, Kyoto and Osaka, 1971-1972. They reject traditional patterns of sex role allocation. 20 per cent. "Political Women In Japan; The Search For A Place in Political Life," published by the University of California Press.

1. Roger E. Wilson's doctorate was awarded in 1968 on a fascinating science topic.
2. Volume 37 3. 1861-1972 4. 928
5. University of Oklahoma 6. 44p
7. PhD 8. Allelopathy As Expressed by Helianthus and Its Role in Oil Field Succession. 9. 29/03B p.903
10. As a result of his research, he concluded that what may help to explain the brief weed stage in this region's [Oklahoma] abandoned oil fields?
11. "... certain associated species do exhibit reduced growth around the sun-flower plants...." in abandoned fields. May help to explain.... (Allelopathy is the reputed baneful influence of one living plant upon another due to the secretion of toxic substances.)

1. Katie P. McLeod's doctorate was awarded in 1980.
2. Another volume 36 L-O 3. 1973-1982 4. 505
5. Florida State University 6. 131p
7. EdD 8. Sex Discrimination Complaints Against Florida Public Institutions of Higher Education: Perceived Effects on the Complainant and the Institution. 9. 41/03A p.962
10. Who was her major professor? How long is her abstract? What "sources" did she use?
11. Dr. Louis W. Bender. Three sentences. Office for Civil Rights Letters of Findings, participants' responses to a questionnaire and interview.

The following two problems are not posed in the Assignment 7 manner. They are examples of approaching CDI/DAI for dissertations on subjects or in fields, rather than associated with the writer.

You need information about SLUDGE. You are in engineering and concerned with the role of the clarifier and clarification process. Were there any dissertations awarded between 1973 and 1982 which would be relevant?

Volume 8: Engineering, SLUDGE, page 232. The 11th entry consists of

A Dynamic model of the completely mixed activated sludge and final clarification processes. Ching, David Laverne. PhD 1980 U Minn 41/12B p.4596

You need information about CHILE. You are in economic history and concerned with the economic development in Chile from 1925 to 1968, which provides a comparison of two growth strategies. Were there any dissertations awarded between 1973 and 1982 which would be relevant?

Volume 25: Economics, History, CHILE, page 182. The 13th entry consists of Economic development in Chile under two growth strategies.
Pitts, Mary Anne, PhD 1975 Syracuse U 36/10A p.6389

PRACTICE WITH BIOGRAPHICAL REFERENCE TOOLS

The following problems can be used with the in-library worksheet, Using Carriers of Information: Biographical Tools, as well as in other ways. Four representative biographical reference tools have been selected because they are in almost all libraries and function in various ways. They also provide opportunity to practice manipulation of other titles in their arrangements. They are:

> Current Biography
> Dictionary of American Biography
> Dictionary of National Biography
> Biography Index

Part of the thought-process involved is recognition of which one of these four, uniquely, is appropriate in the context of what is sought. Next is the identification of the appropriate portion or volume. There is also involved a need to read and think, for these are not directory-type reference tools, e.g. Who's Who in America.

CURRENT BIOGRAPHY, 1940-

It is desirable that the library have the 1940-1985 cumulated index, as well as the complete set.

"1984" Current Biography (with 1981-1984 Index):

Jerome Seymour Breuner is a psychologist and educator well known for the Language Acquisition Support System; his great interest is in the acquisition and use of language by children and the implications for education. Why was he not able to get into the Army during World War II? What type of psychology (e.g. social, child,) does he specialize in? Where was he employed in 1984?

>   47-51 Breuner, Jerome Seymour
>   47   cognitive psychology at Harvard University
>   48-9   blind at birth, two cataract operations were successful at age two
>   although he was not able to get into the Army because of sight.

Canadian author of current best sellers Margaret Atwood dropped out of what university doctoral program? Before dropping out, however, she realized that no critical study of the body of what literature had ever been published? What did she do about it? She contends that Canadian literature reflects the tendency of Canadians to be what?

>   17-20 Atwood, Margaret (Eleanor)
>   18   Harvard University. Of Canadian literature. She prepared a "contro-
>   versial introductory survey" titled "Survival: a Thematic Guide To
>   Canadian Literature" published in 1972 by the House of Anansi.
>   To be willing victims and survivalists.

Rose Elizabeth Bird was the first California woman Supreme Court Chief Justice. As her voter confirmation approached and she campaigned in 1984, of all the persons opposing Governor Brown's appointment of her whose was pointed to as probably the most damaging statements, and why? At what law school has she taught? What was her reason for seeking a job as public defender when she went after her first job after completing law school and serving as a clerk for a year?

26-29 Bird, Rose E(lizabeth)
27-8 Bishop Roger Mahoney stated that she was "emotionally unstable."
27 Stanford University. "To disprove the notion that women were emotionally unsuited for trial work."

"1983" Current Biography (with 1981-1983 Index):

What is the address of the Korean religious leader Sun Myung Moon's national headquarters? Approximately how many businesses in the United States and abroad were owned by the Unification Church as of 1983? What Japanese university did he attend? What did he study? Did he complete his degree work? What is the motion picture title released in 1982, financed by members of the Unification Church? Who starred in it?

253-256 Moon, Sun Myung
253 4 West 43rd St., New York, NY 10036.
255 150
254 Waseda; electrical engineering; unknown.
255 "Inchon"; Sir Laurence Olivier, as General Douglas MacArthur.

"1982" Current Biography (with 1981-1982 Index):

Has Colleen McCullough, author of the best-seller, The Thorn Birds, ever lived in Australia, the novel's setting? What 1977 record did she set? What types of sources did the writer of your source use (e.g. books, magazine articles, newspapers)? Why didn't she follow through on her intention to become a physician?

257-260 McCullough, Colleen
258 Yes; she was born there.
257 Paperback rights were sold to Avon for the highest price ever at that time ($1,900,000).
260 magazines, newspaper, Contemporary Authors reference book
258 Her father was "opposed to medical careers for women," refused to let her continue her studies ... worked as a librarian."

"1981" Current Biography:

Warren Minor Christopher made history as the chief United States negotiator for the release of fifty-two American hostages held in Iran. In May 1980 he asked PBS to do what the New York Times editor considered getting into censorship ... what was it? What is his occupation?

65-68 Christopher, Warren Minor
66-67 "... to consider the offense it would offer a valued American ally by televising the docudrama, Death of a Princess (about the execution of a royal Saudi Arabian young woman for adultery)."
65 Lawyer

"1980" Current Biography (with 1971-1980 Index):

Elisabeth Kubler Ross has identified five main stages that terminally ill patients pass through in reacting to the knowledge of their own death; what are they? What types of resources did the writer of your source use (e.g. periodicals, newspapers, books), and what is the title of one of the books? Is she a psychiatrist or a psychologist, and what is her name exactly?

191-194 Kübler-Ross, Elisabeth

193 denial, anger, bargaining, depression, acceptance. periodicals, a newspaper; Contemporary Authors reference book; Death: The Final Stage of Growth by Kubler-Ross.

191 The article refers to her as a psychiatrist

474 The subject index refers to her as a psychologist.

"1979" Current Biography (with 1971-1979 Index):

Howard Jarvis made the news in the late 1970's with his "Jarvis-Gann Initiative" (Proposition 13). What did it propose to do? Did the League of Women Voters support or oppose "Prop 13"? What was Jarvis' occupation?

185-188 Jarvis, Howard Arnold

186 ... limit the tax allowed on a piece of real estate to one per cent of its full cash value ... the full market value would be reestablished whenever a piece of property was sold. Increased to 2/3 majority the margin needed in the California legislature to enact new state taxes and mandated a 2/3 favorable vote by qualified electors before new local taxes could be imposed. Opposed it. Director of the Apartment Association of Los Angeles County, a lobbying group of landlords.

How is the Ayatollah Khomeini's name pronounced? Is it true that he was brought up by two women? What are the titles of some of the sources the author of your article used? What does his black turban signify, if anything? Does he speak French and English?

207-211 Khomeini, Ayatollah Ruholla (Mussavi)

207 Pronunciation is indicated at the beginning of the article. Yes--

208 his mother and an aunt. That he is a lineal descendant of Mohammed. Speaks only Farsi.

Psychologist B. F. Skinner is one of the most controversial living figures in the field of psychology. Why is he known as the "rat psychologist"? With what unique testing operation did World War II provide him?

361-363 Skinner, Burrhus Frederic

Because of his experimental orientation. He was able to test

363 the practical application of operant conditioning (homing devices).

"1978" Current Biography (with 1971-1978 Index):

In 1977 Rosalyn S. Yalow became the second woman to win the Nobel Prize in medicine. Where did she go to high school, and what did her chemistry teacher urge her to study? At Hunter College, she was encouraged to pursue a career in what? What did she do with her Nobel Prize money? Does she keep a kosher kitchen?

    458-460 Yalow, Rosalyn S(ussman)
    458   Walton High School in New York City; science. Physics.
    460   Banked it. Yes

"1947" Current Biography (with 1971-1978 Index):

How many times was Alice Paul imprisoned for suffrage demonstrating? On what grounds did the League of Women Voters oppose the equal rights amendment at that time?

    499-500 Paul, Alice
    499   Three. Invasion of states' rights, threat to legislation safeguarding women.

DICTIONARY OF AMERICAN BIOGRAPHY

Confirm the "DAB" volume numbers in your library's set to correlate with those provided here, as there are both "consolidated" and "original" editions. The following uses involve the basic set, Volumes 1-20.

It was said that Victoria Claflin Woodhull would do anything to get her name into print and was an advocate of free love. Confirm or disprove using a source which is generally regarded as authoritative. Woodhull and her sister were the first women brokers on Wall Street. She was the publisher of a newspaper which she used, it was said, to shock the delicate senses of society with her radical expositions; its title was the Woodhull and Claflin Weekly. In July 1892, she began to publish the magazine titled what? What is the nearest library having issues of either of these? What is the name of the writer of your source of information?

    20: 493-494 Woodhull, Victoria Claflin
    494   "... free love...." The Humanitarian.
    494   "A.F.H." (In the front of the volume this means Alvin F. Harlow).

Lucy Stone's life-story reads like a movie scenario: as a suffragist, she vowed never to marry, having grown up in a home in which her father believed men divinely ordained to rule women, her mother was docile, and she was denied the vote in her church because she was a woman. Then she met Henry Brown Blackwell.... Did he go along with this suffrage feminist thing? Did they ever have any children? She died in 1893; where are most of her papers?

    18:80-81 Stone, Lucy
        Yes. Yes. (He encouraged her to keep her name; he opposed the word "male" in the 14th Amendment; he helped edit Woman's Journal.)
    81   In her daughter's possession, some in the Library of Congress.

John Swett was born in 1830 in New Hampshire. Why did he "go West?" After he got there, he ultimately settled in what occupation, or, as some would call it, profession? To what office was he elected in 1862? Of what San Francisco grammar school was he principal? Then he was promoted to the principalship of which high school? You are doing research about him and at this point, need a "by and about" bibliography; does the writer of your article provide such a bibliography, or is it simply a list of her/his sources?

    18:244-245 Swett, John

He went West for his health (eyes) and to the gold mines. He is listed as an "educator" at the beginning of this article. He was elected State Supt. of Public Instruction. He was principal of the Denman Grammar School for Girls and of Girls' High School.

245   Yes, there is a bibliography of publications both by and about Swett at the end of the article.

In early 1776 Juan Bautista De Anza explored the site of San Francisco. He marched around the lower end of the Bay and ascended the San Joaquin River for a short distance. He is generally considered the founder of San Francisco. Why was he faulted by his superiors, following his return from this trip and his description of it; what was his fate? Who is the author of your source?

1:322-323   Anza, Juan Bautista de
323   He had reported that the Yuma Indians were very peaceful (pacific), but in 1781 they attacked. This led to his obscurity.
323   "I.B.R." (Irving Berdine Richman as indicated in the front of the volume.)

Artist Mary Cassatt died in 1926. Of what "school" is she generally considered a member? What was the recurring theme in her work? Later in her life she experienced what handicap? Who said "I will not admit a woman can draw like that" as he gazed at her work? Cassatt was chosen among women artists to decorate which building at the Chicago Exposition?

3:567-568   Cassatt, Mary
567   Impressionist. Motherhood. Loss of sight. Degas. The Woman's Building

You've been reading Gerda Lerner's doctoral dissertation, which is titled Abolitionists from South Carolina; A Life of Sarah and Angelina Grimké. (Columbia University, 1966. 30/04A p.1504). These sisters sound rather liberal for their time. Now you want to read something about each of them from a conventional biographical reference book which is regarded as authoritative. Why, according to the authority-author of your source, did they question the institution of slavery ... what specifically caused Angelina and Sarah to question it? Lerner also mentions their brother: Can you find information about him? Who is the author of the article(s)?

7:634-635   Grimké, Sarah Moore
There is no entry for Angelina Grimké. The "Sarah" article appears to be for both of them; there is a cross reference in indexing elsewhere. "... their tender reflective natures made them question the institution of slavery."
7:635-636   Grimké, Thomas Smith
There is an article which refers to their brother, which indicates that he was married, had six children.
Both articles are signed "M.E.C.", which refers to Merle E. Curti, according to the preliminary pages of the volume.

You certainly need an authoritative article to confirm someone's contention that journalist Joseph (Pulitzer Prize) Pulitzer shot a man. (Pulitzer died in 1911.) Who is the writer of your article? When was the article written? Did the World newspaper favor or oppose Prohibition?

15:260-263   Pulitzer, Joseph
260   He shot Edward Augustine.

263 Oswald Garrison Villard wrote this article, which is "signed" "O. G. V.," and identified in the front of the volume.
261 1934
260 Oppose.

President Theodore Roosevelt (1858-1919)'s need for income after leaving the presidency in 1909 led to his doing what? How did he lose the sight of one eye? Roosevelt's interest in conservation focused specifically on what territory? Where can you consult a rather lengthy bibliography of Theodore Roosevelt-related publications which were published for the most part before 1935?

16:135-144 Roosevelt, Theodore
　　　　writing for publication. boxing. concern for the undeveloped lands in United States territories.
143-44 a lengthy bibliography

•　　•　　•

The following uses involve the supplementary volumes of "DAB," and thus, most efficiently, the Dictionary of American Biography Complete Index Guide or Supplement 7, which includes an index to the supplements. See page 2 of the "Using Carriers of Information: Biographical Tools" handout.

You're thinking about law schools. At which law school did Franklin Delano Roosevelt (1882-1945) do his law degree work? How did the catchy term associated with F.D.R.--the "New Deal"--come about? Where can you consult a rather lengthy bibliography of Franklin Roosevelt-related publications which were published for the most part before 1945?

Suppl 3:641-667 Roosevelt, Franklin Delano
664 He did not attend law school--passed the Bar Exams without doing so!
647 In 1932 he pledged a new deal during his nomination-acceptance speech; later, the term was used for his national program.
665-667 a lengthy bibliography

Louise Bryant died in 1959. She was born in Paris, France. What was her occupation according to your authority? What is your authority's name, i.e. who wrote your source material? Bryant was a pioneer in the idea of providing meals for children in school, or "school feeding"; what reason did the Russell Sage Foundation give when it rejected her proposal? Where are The Bryant Papers located?

Suppl 6:80-82 Bryant, Louise Frances Stevens
　　　　Social researcher and medical editor.
82 James Reed
81 it would lead to socialism
82 Sophia Smith College

DICTIONARY OF NATIONAL BIOGRAPHY

Confirm the "DNB" volume and page numbers in your library's set to correlate with those provided here. "DNB" was reissued in twenty-two volumes by Oxford Press, and this set, with its supplements, is in most American libraries. There is a "Corrections & Additions...." covering 1923-1963. Note that these problems do not relate to the Concise Dictionary of National Biography.

Resources

Dictionary of National Biography

The following uses involve the basic A-Z volumes 1-21 set.

Frances Burney is said to have given the first impulse to the modern school of realistic fiction. From which of her publications did Jane Austen take the title of Pride and Prejudice? Who is the author of your source material? Is there a bibliography provided, and if so, is it a "by and about" type bibliography or what?

    Volume 3 Burney, Frances. See Arblay
    1:527-530 Arblay, Frances (Burney), Madam D' (1752-1840)
            from Burney's Cecilia.
    530   "L.S." appears at the end of the article; Leslie Stephen is explained
          in the volume's preliminary pages. A "by and about" bibliography.

Aphra Behn (1640-1689) was an English novelist and pioneer playwright. She has been referred to as the first female writer who had lived by her pen in England. Why did she attempt to write in a style that should be mistaken for that of a man? Can you possibly find an article that provides this information, by an "authority," as well as lists all of her works? What is the name of your authority?

    2:129-131 Behn, Afra, Alphra, Aphara, or Ayfara
    129   so that no one would know that the writer was a woman (meaning she
          wanted it to sell ... "lived by her pen.")
    131   Bibliography of all of her works
    131   "E.G." (Edmund Gosse according to preliminary pages in this volume)

George (Boolean algebra and logic) Boole was a 19th-century English mathematician and logician. What was his most famous work, according to an authority? Who is that authority? Several persons have introduced practical simplifications to his work; who did so in "America"?

    2:831-2 Boole, George, 1815-1864
    832   Laws Of Thought (1854)
    832   "J.V." (John Venn)
    832   C. H. Pierce, E. N. Mitchell, and Miss Ladd.

English artist and caricaturist George Cruikshank was well known as an illustrator of Charles Dickens' novels. What type of abstinence did he advocate? With what did he accuse Charles Dickens?

    5:252-258 Cruikshank, George, 1793-1878
    256   he advocated "teetotalism" (no alcohol)
    255   "... asserted that he suggested the story and incidents of Oliver
          Twist."

What is the difference between Mary Wollstonecraft 1759-1797 and Mary Wollstonecraft 1797-1851? Are they related, in the same family, or what? Wollstonecraft, Mary. See Godwin, Mrs. Mary Wollstonecraft

    8:60-63 Godwin, Mrs. Mary Wollstonecraft (1759-1797)
            She is referred to as a "mis. [miscellaneous] writer." Godwin was her
            second husband, father of her second child, Mary. She died shortly
            after. Her daughter married Percy Shelley.
    18:29-31 Shelley, Mary Wollstonecraft, 1797-1851
            She is referred to as "authoress," second wife of Percy Bysshe
            Shelley. She wrote Frankenstein.

Geoffrey, Count (Duke) of Brittany (1158-1186) appears in Lion in Winter. How did he happen to be called Geoffrey? Whom did he marry and when? Where is he buried?

> 7:1015-1017 Geoffrey 1158-1186 Count (Duke) of Brittany
> 1015 "... was probably called Geoffrey after his uncle, the Count of Nantes, then lately dead, his father ... hoping to provide for him by the acquisition of Brittany."
> 1016 Married Constance, July 1181
> 1017 Notre Dame cathedral.

•   •   •

The following uses involve the supplement volumes of "DNB," starting with Volume 22, which is the first Supplement.

Virginia Woolf was part of the Bloomsbury Circle. (She died in 1941.) What are the names of some of the other Circle members? What type of resources did the writer of your article use? How does he refer to Woolf's A Room of One's Own and Three Guineas ... how does he characterize them? Towards the beginning of the article he refers you to another biographee, Sir Leslie Stephen, when he identifies Woolf as his second daughter; how does he indicate this cross reference?

> 27:975-976 Woolf, Virginia
> 975 Roger Fry, Leonard Woolf, Clive Bell, J. M. Keynes, Lytton Strachey, Edward M. Foster. "personal knowledge." "two feminist pamphlets." "[q.v.]," which is a "see" reference; as used here, it means that there is also an article about Leslie Stephen in "DNB," which you should see.

Isabella Lucy Bird was a 19th-century English woman who travelled throughout the world and wrote about it. She also stood out in several other ways. In 1880 she wrote Unbeaten Tracks in Japan; how could you possibly get hold of it to read without going to the British Museum (which functions like the U.S. Library of Congress in its relationship to British publications)?

> 23:164 Bird, Isabella Lucy. See Bishop
> 166-168 Bishop, Mrs. Isabella Lucy (born Bird) (1831-1904)
> 168 She married a man ten years younger; she was the first woman made a "fellow" of the Royal Geographical Society; she was an expert horse-woman and rower.
> Unbeaten Tracks in Japan is in-print, even available in paperback, from Tuttle Books of Rutland, Vermont. But first check the library catalog.

Anne Cobden and Thomas James Sanderson had mutual interests and a happy marriage. He is known as an English printer and bookbinder, who operated Doves Press from 1900-1916 with Emery Walker. In 1881 he met her and subsequently made several major changes in his life. What were two of them?

> 25:193-194 Cobden-Sanderson, Thomas James
> 193 In 1882 Sanderson changed his name and then his occupation.

George Bernard Shaw (1856-1950) was born in Dublin. What habit of his father influenced his life and affected his childhood especially? Although he was a playwright, towards the very end of his life he returned to political writing and published what three titles? Is it true he asked his wife to marry him in order to save her honor?

27:773-782 Shaw, George Bernard
774 "Tippling" (drinking).
780-81 Intelligent Woman's Guide to Socialism and Capitalism; Adventures of a Black Girl...; and Everybody's Political What's What. Yes.

BIOGRAPHY INDEX

You need to identify the author, title, etc. of a novel about Cleopatra which includes a bibliography. It was published around 1976.
Volume 11 September 1976-August 1979
160 CLEOPATRA, queen of Egypt, 69-30 B.C.--FICTION
"The Alexandrian; a Novel," was written by Martha Rofheart and published by Crowell.

You are trying to track down a book about Rosa Lee Parks which is suitable for children. It would be nice if it had even a short "further reading" bibliography. Someone says something like this was published in 1976.
Volume 11 September 1976-August 1979
607 PARKS, ROSA LEE, 1913- receptionist--JUVENILE LITERATURE
Several references to biographical material are listed, following which, is listed
Kulkin, Mary-Ellen. Her way. Am lib assn '76 p222-4 bibl

Locate a lengthy biography of Queen Emma of Hawaii, published in 1976 and containing a bibliography.
Volume 11 September 1976-August 1979
239 EMMA, Consort of Kamehameha IV, King of Hawaii, 1836-1885
Kaeo, Peter. News from Molokai, letters between Peter Kaeo and Queen Emma, 1873-1876; ed. with introd. and notes by Alfons L. Korn. Univ. of Hawaii press '76 345p bibl

What was the title of J. B. Wiesner's eulogy for John F. Kennedy? In what issue of what periodical did it appear? J.F.K. died in 1963.
Volume 6 September 1961-August 1964
318-319 KENNEDY, JOHN FITZGERALD, 1917-1963, PRESIDENT--EULOGIES
319 Wiesner, J. B. John F. Kennedy: a remembrance. Science 142: 1147-50 N 29 '63

In the spring of 1968 the "Wolf Boy" of India died. Locate the obituary for him.
Volume 8 September 1967-August 1970
892 Index to Professions & Occupations
Wolf boys. See Children, Wild
785 Children, Wild. Ramu
559 RAMU, 1945?-1968, India's "wolf boy"
Obit Newsweek 71:62 Ap 29 '68

In 1978 there was a film about boxer "Cat" Davis. Can you find an illustrated article about Davis?
Volume 11 September 1976-August 1979:
196 DAVIS, CATHY (CAT DAVIS), 1952- .
Kessler, J. Jocks il pors People 9:93-4 My 15 '78

You're trying to locate information about a 17th-century medicine man. Someone tells you about an illustrated section of a book, accompanied by a bibliography, published sometime in the early 1960's about "the chief."

        Volume 6 September 1961-August 1964

    722   Index to Professions & Occupations

        Medicine Men. Pope

    474   POPE, fl 1675-1688, Indian Medicine Man

        Josephy, Alvin M. Patriot chief Vik '61 p65-94 bibliog il map

"Brutal Friendship," a book first published in 1962 about Hitler, was later revised. Who is the author? Did the original version have a bibliography?

        Volume 6 September 1961-August 1964

    266   HITLER, ADOLF, 1889-1945, German Chief of State

        Deakin, Frederick William. Brutal friendship; Mussolini, Hitler, and the fall of Italian fascism. Harper '62 896 p bibliog.

Can you locate an autobiography published in 1956 by a prison chaplain?

        Volume 4 September 1955-August 1958

    1066   Index to Professions & Occupations

        Prison Chaplains--Ball, Baden Powell Herbert

    40   BALL, BADEN POWELL HERBERT, 1900- English prison chaplain

        Ball, Baden Powell Herbert. Prison was my parish. Heinemann. '56 252p

Tools Included in the Course

1. ABSTRACTS AND INDEXES IN SCIENCE AND TECHNOLOGY: A DESCRIPTIVE GUIDE, 2nd EDITION. Owen.

2. ALTERNATIVE PRESS INDEX.

3. AMERICA: HISTORY AND LIFE.

4. AMERICAN STATISTICS INDEX.

5. APPLIED SCIENCE AND TECHNOLOGY INDEX.

6. ART INDEX.

7. ARTS & HUMANITIES CITATION INDEX.

8. BIBLIOGRAPHIC INDEX.

9. BIO-BASE.

10. BIOGRAPHY ALMANAC.

11. BIOGRAPHY INDEX.

12. BIOLOGICAL AND AGRICULTURAL INDEX.

13. BOOK REVIEW DIGEST.

14. BOOK REVIEW INDEX.

15. BOOKS IN PRINT; SUBJECT GUIDE...., P.T.L.A., etc.

16. BUSINESS PERIODICALS INDEX.

17. CHICANO STUDIES PERIODICAL INDEX.

18. COLUMBIA LIPPINCOTT GAZETTEER.

19. COMMUNICATION ABSTRACTS.

20. COMPLETE CONCORDANCE TO SHAKESPEARE.

21. COMPREHENSIVE DISSERTATION INDEX/DISSERTATION ABSTRACTS INTERNATIONAL.

22. CONTEMPORARY AUTHORS.

23. CUMULATIVE BOOK INDEX.

24. CURRENT BIOGRAPHY. 1940-1985 CUMULATED INDEX.

25. CURRENT INDEX TO JOURNALS IN EDUCATION/RESOURCES IN EDUCATION (ERIC).

26. DICTIONARY OF AMERICAN BIOGRAPHY.

27. DICTIONARY OF NATIONAL BIOGRAPHY.

28. DIRECTORY OF AMERICAN SCHOLARS.

29. DIRECTORY OF MEDICAL SPECIALISTS.

30. EDUCATION INDEX.

31. ENCYCLOPEDIA AMERICANA and YEARBOOK(s).

32. ENCYCLOPAEDIA BRITANNICA and BRITANNICA BOOK OF THE YEAR.

33. ENCYCLOPEDIA OF ASSOCIATIONS.

34. ESSAY AND GENERAL LITERATURE INDEX.

35. FACTS ON FILE.

36. FAMILIAR QUOTATIONS. Bartlett.

37. GENERAL SCIENCE INDEX.

38. GUIDE TO REFERENCE BOOKS. Sheehy.

39. Guides to the literature, e.g. INTRODUCTION TO LIBRARY RESEARCH IN WOMEN'S STUDIES. Searing.

40. HISTORICAL ABSTRACTS.

41. HISTORICAL ATLAS. Shepherd.

42. HUMANITIES INDEX. SOCIAL SCIENCES AND HUMANITIES INDEX; INTERNATIONAL INDEX.

43. INDEX.... Congressional Information Service.

44. INDEX TO PERIODICALS BY AND ABOUT BLACKS.

45. INTERNATIONAL ENCYCLOPEDIA OF THE SOCIAL SCIENCES.

46. INTERNATIONAL POLITICAL SCIENCE ABSTRACTS.

47. INTERNATIONAL WHO'S WHO.

48. KODANSHA ENCYCLOPEDIA OF JAPAN.

49. LIBRARY OF CONGRESS SUBJECT HEADINGS.

50. LIBRARY OF CONGRESS SUBJECT CATALOG.

51. M L A INTERNATIONAL BIBLIOGRAPHY...

52. McGRAW HILL ENCYCLOPEDIA OF SCIENCE AND TECHNOLOGY; YEARBOOK; and BASIC BIBLIOGRAPHY.

53. MONTHLY CATALOG; CUMULATIVE INDEX....

54. Your state's government publications access tool, and/or MONTHLY CHECKLIST OF STATE PUBLICATIONS.

55. MUSIC INDEX.

56. NATIONAL UNION CATALOG.

57. NELSON'S COMPLETE CONCORDANCE OF THE ... BIBLE.

58. NEW COLUMBIA ENCYCLOPEDIA.

59. NEW GROVE DICTIONARY OF MUSIC AND MUSICIANS.

60. NEW YORK TIMES INDEX; PERSONAL NAMES INDEX.

61. NOTABLE AMERICAN WOMEN....

62. OXFORD ENGLISH DICTIONARY.

63. PERIODICAL INDEXES IN THE SOCIAL SCIENCES AND HUMANITIES: A SUBJECT GUIDE. Harzfeld.

64. PHYSICAL EDUCATION INDEX.

65. PSYCHOLOGICAL ABSTRACTS.

66. PUBLIC AFFAIRS INFORMATION SERVICE BULLETIN "PAIS."

67. RANDOM HOUSE DICTIONARY OF THE ENGLISH LANGUAGE.

68. READERS' GUIDE TO PERIODICAL LITERATURE.

69. SCIENCE ABSTRACTS.

70. SCIENCE CITATION INDEX.

71. SOCIAL SCIENCES CITATION INDEX.

72. SOCIOLOGICAL ABSTRACTS.

73. STATESMAN'S YEARBOOK.

74. STATISTICAL ABSTRACT OF THE UNITED STATES.

75. Your state's statistical abstract.

76. Style manuals, e.g. A MANUAL FOR WRITERS OF TERM PAPERS, THESES, AND DISSERTATIONS. Turabian.

77. SUBJECT COLLECTIONS. Ash.

78. TECHNICAL BOOK REVIEW INDEX.

79. THESAURUS OF ERIC DESCRIPTORS.

80. TIMES ATLAS OF THE WORLD.

81. ULRICH'S INTERNATIONAL PERIODICALS DIRECTORY.

82. UNION LIST OF SERIALS IN LIBRARIES OF THE UNITED STATES AND CANADA.

83. [UN] STATISTICAL YEARBOOK.

84. U.S. GOVERNMENT MANUAL.

85. U.S. POLITICAL SCIENCE DOCUMENTS.

86. WEBSTER'S BIOGRAPHICAL DICTIONARY.

87. WEBSTER'S NEW GEOGRAPHICAL DICTIONARY.

88. WEBSTER'S NEW INTERNATIONAL DICTIONARY, 2nd EDITION.

89. WEBSTER'S THIRD NEW INTERNATIONAL DICTIONARY OF THE ENGLISH LANGUAGE.

90. WHO'S WHO.

91. WHO'S WHO IN AMERICA.

92. WOMEN STUDIES ABSTRACTS.

93. WORLD ALMANAC AND BOOK OF FACTS.

94. WORLD ARTISTS 1950-1980.

95. WORLD BIBLIOGRAPHY OF BIBLIOGRAPHIES. Besterman.